African Leaders of
the Twentieth Century,
Volume 2

OHIO SHORT HISTORIES OF AFRICA

This series of Ohio Short Histories of Africa is meant for those who are looking for a brief but lively introduction to a wide range of topics in African history, politics, and biography, written by some of the leading experts in their fields.

African Leaders of the Twentieth Century, Volume 2

Cabral, Machel, Mugabe, Sirleaf

OHIO UNIVERSITY PRESS
ATHENS

Ohio University Press, Athens, Ohio 45701
ohioswallow.com
All rights reserved

To obtain permission to quote, reprint, or otherwise reproduce or
distribute material from Ohio University Press publications, please
contact our rights and permissions department at (740) 593-1154.

Printed in the United States of America
Ohio University Press books are printed on acid-free paper ∞ ™

Amílcar Cabral
by Peter Karibe Mendy
© 2019 by Ohio University Press
ISBN: 978-0-8214-2372-1

Mozambique's Samora Machel
by Allen F. Isaacman and Barbara S. Isaacman
© 2020 by Ohio University Press
ISBN: 978-0-8214-2423-0

Robert Mugabe
by Sue Onslow and Martin Plaut
© 2018 by Ohio University Press
ISBN: 978-0-8214-2324-0

Ellen Johnson Sirleaf
by Pamela Scully
© 2016 by Ohio University Press
ISBN: 978-0-8214-2221-2

African Leaders Volume 2 ISBN: 978-0-8214-2474-2

Contents

OHIO SHORT HISTORIES OF AFRICA

AMILCAR CABRAL

A NATIONALIST AND PAN-AFRICANIST REVOLUTIONARY

PETER KARIBE MENDY

Amílcar Cabral (1924–73) was an agronomist who led an armed struggle that ended Portuguese colonialism in Guinea-Bissau and Cabo Verde. The uprising contributed significantly to the collapse of a fascist regime in Lisbon and the dismantlement of Portugal's empire in Africa. Assassinated by a close associate with the deep complicity of the Portuguese colonial authorities, Cabral not only led one of Africa's most successful liberation movements, but was the voice and face of the anticolonial wars against Portugal.

A brilliant military strategist and astute diplomat, Cabral was an original thinker who wrote innovative and inspirational essays that still resonate today. His charismatic and visionary leadership, his active pan-Africanist solidarity and internationalist commitment to "every just cause in the world" remain relevant to contemporary struggles for emancipation and self-determination. Peter Karibe Mendy's compact and accessible biography is an ideal introduction to his life and legacy.

Peter Karibe Mendy is professor of history and Africana studies at Rhode Island College, Providence. His numerous publications include *Colonialismo Português em África: A Tradição da Resistência na Guiné-Bissau, 1879–1959* and (with coauthor Richard A. Lobban) the *Historical Dictionary of the Republic of Guinea-Bissau* (4th ed.).

Amílcar Cabral

*A Nationalist and
Pan-Africanist Revolutionary*

Peter Karibe Mendy

OHIO UNIVERSITY PRESS

ATHENS

Ohio University Press, Athens, Ohio 45701
ohioswallow.com
© 2019 by Ohio University Press

Printed in the United States of America
Ohio University Press books are printed on acid-free paper ⊗ ™

29 28 27 26 25 24 23 22 21 20 19   5 4 3 2 1

Cover design by Joey Hifi

Library of Congress Cataloging-in-Publication Data
Names: Mendy, Peter Michael Karibe, author.
Title: Amílcar Cabral : a nationalist and pan-Africanist revolutionary /
    Peter Karibe Mendy.
Other titles: Ohio short histories of Africa.
Description: Athens : Ohio University Press, 2019. | Series: Ohio short
    histories of Africa | Includes bibliographical references and index.
Identifiers: LCCN 2019004321| ISBN 9780821423721 (pb : alk. paper)
    | ISBN
    9780821446621 (pdf)
Subjects: LCSH: Cabral, Amílcar, 1924-1973. |
    Guinea-Bissau--History--Revolution, 1963-1974. | Cabo Verde--His-
tory--To 1975. | Partido Africano da Independência da Guiné e Cabo
Verde. | National liberation movements--Guinea-Bissau--History--20th
century. | National liberation movements--Cabo Verde--History--20th
century. | Revolutionaries--Guinea-Bissau--Biography.
Classification: LCC DT613.76.C3 M46 2019 | DDC 966.5702092--dc23
LC record available at https://lccn.loc.gov/2019004321

Contents

Illustrations

Maps

Figures

Preface and Acknowledgments

The assassination of Amílcar Cabral, the charismatic leader of the African Party for the Independence of Guinea and Cabo Verde (PAIGC), on 20 January 1973, and the unilateral declaration of the independence of Guinea-Bissau by his liberation movement eight months later, were critical turning points that greatly sharpened my political consciousness. I was born in Gambia, West Africa, during the terminal period of British colonial rule. Both my parents were natives of Guinea-Bissau, then called Portuguese Guinea, located about four hundred miles south. Like thousands of others before them, they left their homeland to escape the harsher colonial order there characterized by forced labor and corporal punishment. While the Portuguese were not the only European colonizers in Africa to maintain the *pax colonica* by brutal repression, they were nevertheless the last to formally end it, in 1961, following the uprisings in Angola that signaled the beginning of armed national liberation struggle there.

Growing up in Gambia before the start of the war of independence in Guinea-Bissau, I heard numerous stories from newly arrived family members of colonial abuse and violence meted out to the majority of the population, contemptuously called *gentios* (heathens). As a student in England during the 1970s, I keenly followed the unfolding brutal war that became known as "Portugal's Vietnam" because of the huge Portuguese troop concentration, the dropping of napalm and white phosphorous bombs, and the removing and resettling of villagers in heavily guarded camps fenced by barbed wire. I also kept abreast of the development of the armed struggle by way of publications obtained from the Mozambique Angola Guiné Information Centre (MAGIC) in London and presentations by Basil Davidson at the Centre of West African Studies at the University of Birmingham, England, where I was a politically active graduate student.

The remarkable achievements of Cabral, who was an accomplished agronomist, an ardent nationalist, an astute diplomat, a brilliant military strategist, a committed Pan-Africanist, and an outspoken internationalist, became an enduring source of inspiration for me. As a revolutionary leader, Cabral remains as significant as his celebrated contemporaries, notably Mao Zedong, Frantz Fanon, Fidel Castro, and Ernesto "Che" Guevara.

A lot has been written about Cabral. Many of the studies are excellent scholarly analyses of him as a revolutionary theoretician and practitioner and of his achievements and legacy. In the English-speaking world, the pioneering work of Basil Davidson, *The Liberation of*

Guiné: Aspects of an African Revolution (1969), inspired or provoked such studies as *Amílcar Cabral: Revolutionary Leadership and People's War* (1983) by Patrick Chabal, *Amílcar Cabral's Revolutionary Theory and Practice: A Critical Guide* (1991) by Ronald H. Chilcote, and *Warriors at Work: How Guinea Was Really Set Free* (1993) by Mustafah Dhada.

However, since most people are not scholars, the findings of scholarship have remained confined to a small group of specialists and general readers. One of Africa's most original thinkers and politically influential figures, Cabral is little known in the Anglophone world. The notable contributions of this creatively pensive and charismatic African leader have yet to be found in high school or college textbooks. In the context of a rapidly globalizing and increasingly unequal world, his insistence that national liberation should not end with "flag independence" but should also empower people to consistently improve their material wellbeing has significance far beyond Africa. The enormous challenges he faced, and the successful approaches and strategies he deployed to find solutions, provide great opportunities to learn important lessons pertinent to the daily struggles of millions of people in the world toiling under the heavy weight of poverty, exploitation, and oppression. A visionary and inspirational leader, his ideas still resonate today. Yet, his life, charismatic leadership qualities, and accomplishments are largely unknown outside the Lusophone world. This short biography is an attempt to address this deficit.

It is singularly appropriate that a book on the life of Amílcar Cabral narrated against the background of his times should be included in the Ohio Short Histories of Africa series. The biographical profile sketched out in the pages that follow will provide some insight into the intensively lived life of a remarkable self-styled "simple African" who became a leading founding father of two independent African nations.

I remain enormously grateful to the Ohio University Press series editor Gillian Berchowitz for providing me the great opportunity to write this book as a contribution. I am also greatly thankful to Gillian for her infinite patience and professional guidance and to Nancy Basmajian, managing editor, for supervising the skillful editing of the manuscript. Further thanks are due to the two anonymous reviewers of the manuscript for their insightful critical comments. This book is based on my own studies on Amílcar Cabral and the colonial and postcolonial periods in Guinea-Bissau, but I am very much indebted to the corpus of research and publications on this important historical figure. I owe a special debt of gratitude to the veterans of the armed liberation struggle in Guinea-Bissau who generously granted me interviews to share their valuable intimate knowledge and memories of Cabral; in particular, I am very grateful to Manuel "Manccas" dos Santos, Lúcio Soares, Samba Lamine Mané, Carmen Pereira (who died on June 4, 2016, six months after granting me an interview), Teodora Inácia Gomes, Douda Bangura, and

Florentino "Flora" Gomes. I am also particularly grateful to Iva Cabral for her prompt response to my request for images of her father, which she generously provided, with kind identification of the photographers and the copyright holders. I remain beholden to my family, including my extended kindred in Guinea-Bissau, for their unfailing support. Ultimately, I take full responsibility for errors of fact and interpretation as well as translation of quoted Portuguese texts.

This book is dedicated to the young generation of committed nationalist and Pan-Africanist *Cabralistas* engaged in life-threatening struggles for social and economic justice, peace, prosperity, and the rights-based unification of the diverse peoples of Africa.

Abbreviations and Acronyms

ANP	Assembleia Nacional Popular (People's National Assembly)
CEA	Centro de Estudos Africanos (Center for African Studies)
CEI	Casa dos Estudantes do Império (House of Students of the Empire)
CEL	Conselho Executívo da Luta (Executive Council of the Struggle)
CFAO	Compagnie Française de l'Afrique Occidentale (French West Africa Company)
CLSTP	Comité de Libertação de São Tomé e Príncipe (Committee for the Liberation of São Tomé and Príncipe)
CONCP	Conferência das Organizações Nacionalistas das Colónias Portuguesas (Conference of the Nationalist Organizations of the Portuguese Colonies)
CSL	Conselho Superior da Luta (Higher Council of the Struggle)
CUF	Companhia União Fabril (Union Manufacturing Company)

DGS	Direção-Geral de Segurança (Directorate-General of Security)
FAP	Força Aérea Portuguesa (Portuguese Air Force)
FARP	Forças Armadas Revolucionárias do Povo (People's Revolutionary Armed Forces)
FLING	Frente de Luta pela Independência Nacional da Guiné (Front for Struggle for the National Independence of Guinea)
FLN	Front de Libération Nationale (National Liberation Front)
FLNG	Front de Libération Nationale de la Guinée (Guinean National Liberation Front)
FNLA	Frente Nacional de Libertação de Angola (National Front for the Liberation of Angola)
FRAIN	Frente Revolucionária Africana para a Independência Nacional das Colónias Portuguesas (African Revolutionary Front for the National Independence of the Portuguese Colonies)
FRELIMO	Frente de Libertação de Moçambique (Liberation Front of Mozambique)
FUL	Front Uni de Libération [de la Guinée et du Cap Vert] (United Liberation Front [of Guinea and Cabo Verde])
ISA	Instituto Superior de Agronomia (Higher Institute of Agronomy)
MAC	Movimento Anti-Colonialista (Anticolonialist Movement)

MDCP	Movimento Democrático das Colónias Portuguesas (Democratic Movement of the Portuguese Colonies)
MFA	Movimento das Forças Armadas (Armed Forces Movement)
MING	Movimento para Independência Nacional da Guiné Portuguesa (Movement for the National Independence of Portuguese Guinea)
MLG	Movimento de Libertação da Guiné (Liberation Movement of Guinea)
MLNCP	Movimento de Libertação Nacional das Colónias Portuguesas (National Liberation Movement of the Portuguese Colonies)
MMCG	Misión Militar Cubana en Guinea y Guinea-Bissau (Cuban Military Mission in Guinea and Guinea-Bissau)
MPLA	Movimento Popular de Libertação de Angola (Popular Movement for the Liberation of Angola)
MUD	Movimento de Unidade Democrática (Movement of Democratic Unity)
MUDJ	Movimento de Unidade Democrática Juvenil (Youth Movement of Democratic Unity)
NATO	North Atlantic Treaty Organization
OAU	Organization of African Unity
PAI	Partido Africano da Independência (African Independence Party)

PAIGC	Partido Africano da Independência da Guiné e Cabo Verde (African Party for the Independence of Guinea and Cabo Verde)
PCP	Partido Comunista Português (Portuguese Communist Party)
PIDE	Polícia Internacional e de Defesa do Estado (International and State Defense Police)
PLUAA	Partido da Luta Unida dos Africanos de Angola (Party of the Unified Struggle of the Africans of Angola)
PRC	People's Republic of China
PS	Partido Socialista (Socialist Party) (Portugal)
PSP	Polícia de Segurança Pública (Public Security Police)
SIDA	Swedish International Development Agency
UDEMU	União Democrática das Mulheres (Women's Democratic Union)
UNGP	União dos Naturais da Guiné Portuguesa (Union of the Natives of Portuguese Guinea)
UPA	União das Populações de Angola (Union of the Peoples of Angola)
UPGP	União das Populações da Guiné dita Portuguesa (Union of the Populations of So-Called Portuguese Guinea)
UPLG	União Popular para Libertação da Guiné (Popular Union for the Liberation of Guinea)
USSR	Union of Soviet Socialist Republics

Introduction

Amílcar Lopes Cabral was among the iconic political leaders of the twentieth century. A consummate nationalist and Pan-Africanist revolutionary, he masterminded the end of Portuguese rule in Guinea-Bissau and Cabo Verde and was also actively engaged in the anticolonial struggles in Angola, Mozambique, and São Tomé and Príncipe. The protracted armed struggle waged by his liberation movement, the African Party for the Independence of Guinea and Cabo Verde (PAIGC), bestowed upon Guinea-Bissau a central role that defined the course and outcome of the decolonization process in the other Portuguese African colonies.

Cabral was born in Guinea-Bissau in 1924 of parents from the island of Santiago in Cabo Verde. The ten-island archipelago was reached and settled by the Portuguese in the fifteenth century. The slave plantation society that was established there was the prototype of what the Americas would later become. When slavery was abolished in 1869 it was replaced by an equally exploitative system that included the use of poor Cabo Verdean *contratados* (indentured laborers) in the cacao plantations of São Tomé and Príncipe. On the other hand, as the main beneficiary of Portugal's educational enterprise in Africa, with a seminary opened on the island of São Nicolau in 1866, Cabo Verde had the lowest illiteracy rate in Portuguese Africa: in 1959, it was 78 percent, compared to 97 percent in Angola, 98 percent in Mozambique, and 99 percent in Portuguese Guinea. The much higher literacy rate in the archipelago largely accounted for the predominance of Cabo Verdeans in the colonial administration of Portuguese Guinea, Cabral's *terra natal* (land of birth), from where, at age eight, he moved to his *terra ancestral* (ancestral land).

In 1945, following the completion of his high school education in Cabo Verde, Cabral left for Portugal and enrolled as an agronomy student at the Technical University of Lisbon, where he graduated in 1950. While in Lisbon he actively engaged in clandestine antistate politics together with other radicalized African students, including Agostinho Neto and Mário Pinto de Andrade from Angola, and Marcelino dos Santos from Mozambique.

Cabral returned to Portuguese Guinea in 1952 to work as an agronomist. For two years he traveled extensively in the colony to conduct its first agricultural census. This gave him the opportunity to learn about the colonial realities experienced by the colonized. His seminal study on land use, crop cultivation, and, among other things, soil conditions, remains a work of reference. But perhaps more important for Cabral was the acquisition of strategic knowledge about the level of discontent among his compatriots, and the likely responses to an anticolonial mobilization drive for independence.

As the leader of the PAIGC he cofounded in 1956, Cabral became a key player in the political, military, and diplomatic battles that had to be won in order to guarantee victory for the armed struggle that was launched in January 1963, following unsuccessful attempts at peaceful decolonization. His true genius was his ability to mobilize and inspire his fellow compatriots to take life-threatening risks. He was also adept at persuading skeptical international opinion of the righteousness of the armed struggle in the context of an intensifying Cold War, and thus able to secure vital political support and material resources without ties and compromises.

A committed Pan-Africanist, Cabral also played a significant role in the establishment of two of the most effective liberation movements in Angola and Mozambique, respectively the Popular Movement for the Liberation of Angola (MPLA) and the Liberation Front of Mozambique (FRELIMO). He was also a cofounder and the spokesperson of the three successive coalitions of liberation movements in Portuguese Africa, namely the Anticolonialist Movement (MAC), the African Revolutionary Front for the National Independence of the Portuguese Colonies (FRAIN), and the Conference of the Nationalist Organizations of the Portuguese Colonies (CONCP).

Cabral consistently expressed his commitment to and solidarity with "every just cause" in the world, from the Vietnam conflict to the Congo crisis, from the civil rights struggles in the United States to the Palestinian movement for statehood. At the same time, he wrote a number of brilliant works on liberation theory and practice, culture, African history, and class formation, for which he received international acclaim and many awards and honors, including honorary doctorates from Lincoln University in the United States and the Soviet Academy of Science in the then Union of Soviet Socialist Republics (USSR).

Notwithstanding his assassination, Cabral's liberation movement was able to proclaim the independence of Guinea-Bissau, on 24 September 1973, which was quickly recognized by over eighty countries around the world. The military and diplomatic victory of the PAIGC contributed significantly to the downfall of the forty-eight-year-old fascist dictatorship in Portugal called the Estado Novo (New State) and the rapid dismantlement of the Portuguese empire in Africa. When viewed against the background of a raging Cold War and the stubbornness of a well-armed NATO member nation bent on maintaining its "overseas provinces" at all costs, Cabral's achievements are indeed remarkable. His ideas, effective charismatic leadership, and achievements are memorialized in many countries in Africa and beyond.

This book aims to demonstrate the importance of leadership by focusing on the political and intellectual challenges and accomplishments of one of Africa's most effective leaders of the twentieth century. Cabral's importance lies in the fact that (i) he competently organized and led one of Africa's most consequential armed liberation struggles, (ii) he skillfully mobilized more than a dozen ethnic groups into a united binationalist cause, (iii) he ably led a successful united front against Portuguese colonialism in Africa, and (iv) he wrote incisive essays and innovative books that still resonate today.

Terra Natal

Early Childhood in Portuguese Guinea, 1924–32

Amílcar Lopes Cabral was born on 12 September 1924 in Bafatá, Portuguese Guinea, the mainland of which was finally conquered by Portugal only nine years earlier. The longstanding "pacification" campaigns that preceded the Berlin Conference of 1884–85 and intensified after 1912 with the arrival of the conquistador Captain João Teixeira Pinto eventually ended with the conquest of the adjacent eighty-eight-island Bijagós archipelago in 1936.

Located in West Africa and wedged between Senegal to the north and east, the Republic of Guinea (also known as Guinea-Conakry) to the south, and the Atlantic Ocean to the west, the area now known as Guinea-Bissau (36,130 square kilometers / 13,948 square miles) was the epicenter of the seven-hundred-year-old Mandinka Kingdom of Kaabu, which emerged after the collapse of the famous Mali Empire founded by the legendary Sundiata Keita in the thirteenth century. From its capital Kansala, near the modern city of Gabu in Guinea-Bissau, the *mansas* (rulers) of Kaabu exercised influence

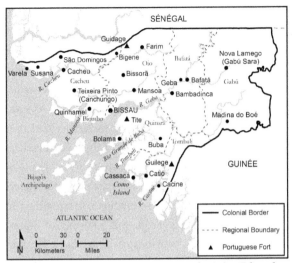

Map 1. Portuguese Guinea, ca. 1960. Map by Brian Edward Balsley, GISP.

northward to the south bank of the Gambia River and southward to parts of northern Guinea-Conakry. During the transatlantic slave trade, Kaabu was engaged in numerous military campaigns that secured captives for the plantations of the Americas. The kingdom collapsed in 1867 as a result of domestic political crisis and increasing external pressure from three ambitious European maritime powers: the British on the Gambia River, the French on the Casamance and Nunez Rivers, and the Portuguese on the network of waterways known as the Rivers of Guinea of Cape Verde.

The Portuguese were the first Europeans to reach Guinea-Bissau, with the landing of the explorer Alvaro

Fernandes in Varela in 1446. Ten years later, some of the islands of the Cabo Verde archipelago were "discovered" by two Genoese sailors in the service of Prince Henry the Navigator, Alvise Cadamosto and Antonio de Noli. Santiago and Fogo island were quickly settled by mainly Portuguese colonists and enslaved Africans from the adjacent coast. Claiming exclusive rights over her "lands of discoveries" in West Africa, Portugal was effectively challenged by her European rivals, resulting in her sphere of influence being reduced to the "Rivers of Guinea of Cape Verde"—roughly corresponding to coastal Guinea-Bissau. From this network of waterways, the voracious activities of illegal Cabo Verdean slave traders called *lançados* facilitated the shipment of millions of African captives to Cabo Verde and the Americas. The *lançados* also became the pioneers of Portugal's centuries-old entrenchment efforts in this area. In 1588, they founded one of the earliest Portuguese settlements on the West African mainland, the fortified town of Cacheu, in northwest Guinea-Bissau. Their attempts to undermine local sovereignties generated bloody conflicts. Nevertheless, over the centuries a constant flow of traders, missionaries, soldiers, colonial officials, and teachers from Cabo Verde continually descended on "Guinea of Cabo Verde," which became "Portuguese Guinea" in 1879.

It was in search of gainful employment that Amílcar Cabral's mother and father, Iva Pinhel Évora and Juvenal António da Costa Cabral, found themselves in Portuguese Guinea during the early decades of the twentieth century. Iva was born on 31 December 1893, the daughter of Maximiana Monteiro da Rocha and António Pinhel Évora, both of modest social backgrounds. She arrived in Portuguese Guinea in 1922 with her nine-month-old son, Ivo Carvalho Silva, and the baby's father, João Carvalho Silva. Shortly afterwards, she and her son separated from João, who had become a minor colonial official in Bolama, the capital of a "possession" hastily proclaimed on 18 March 1879 but yet to be "effectively occupied." Relocating to Bafatá around 1923, Iva met Juvenal Cabral, a primary school teacher in the nearby town of Geba.

The relationship between Iva and Juvenal produced four offspring: Amílcar, the twins Armanda and Arminda, and António. It lasted until 1929, during which time Amílcar lived two years in Bafatá without his father and three years in Geba with both parents.[1] Toward the end of 1929, Iva returned to Santiago, where, on Christmas Eve that year, Amílcar and his twin sisters were baptized at the Catholic Church of Nossa Senhora da Graça (Our Lady of Grace) in Praia, the capital of Cabo Verde.[2] Although she had intended to stay permanently, Iva was obliged to return with her children to Portuguese Guinea less than two years later due to difficulties in securing the basic needs of her family. They lived in Bissau, where Juvenal Cabral, recently married to Adelina Rodrigues Correia de Almeida (future mother of Luís Cabral), also resided. In 1932, Amílcar and his twin sisters returned to Cabo Verde with their father. Iva followed a year or so later and resumed care of her children.

Juvenal Cabral was born on 2 January 1889, the son of Rufina Lopes Cabral, of humble origins, and António Lopes da Costa, a final-year student at the São José Seminary on the island of São Nicolau who was from a notable landowning family in Santiago. Juvenal's paternal grandfather, Pedro Lopes da Costa, was one of the few Cabo Verdeans who "seriously cared about the education of children," such that his family produced "distinguished priests, teachers and civil servants" who "served well and honored well" the *patria* (fatherland) of Portugal.[3] With his father killed when Juvenal was only ten months old, the boy became the ward of his paternal grandfather Pedro and great-aunt Paula Lopes da Costa, and later his godmother, Simoa dos Reis Borges. Simoa inherited property upon the death of her brother in 1894, rented it, and four years later left for Portugal with her husband and eight-year-old godchild.

Juvenal Cabral attended primary school in Santiago de Cassurães, Beira Alta, Portugal, as the only black student "among forty young white boys." Upon graduation he entered the nearby Catholic seminary in Viseu, where one of his contemporaries was António de Oliveira Salazar, later to become the architect and dictator of the Estado Novo established in the aftermath of the 1926 military coup d'état that ended sixteen years of liberal democracy in Portugal. In 1905, due to financial difficulties, Juvenal was forced to abandon the seminary and return to Cabo Verde. Still determined to become a priest, he entered the seminary in São Nicolau, but once again his ecclesiastical studies were short-lived, lasting about a year, due to a disciplinary action against him for fighting with a student from Portuguese Guinea. Rather than endure "shame for being punished, like a child," he quit the seminary and returned to Santiago in July 1907.[4] Four years later, after a brief stay in Praia, he embarked for Portuguese Guinea "in search of employment, through the rewards of which I can decently maintain myself."[5] It was at the end of the first decade of a new century that had been inaugurated in Cabo Verde by a severe drought (1900–1903) that killed sixteen thousand people, a tragedy an angry contemporary Cabo Verdean lawyer, Luiz Loff de Vasconcellos, denounced as "a perfect extermination of a people," blaming Portugal for a "tremendous and horrific catastrophe" that the Lisbon authorities had dismissed with the callous excuse that "the government is not culpable that in Cabo Verde there have not been regular rains."[6]

The "voluntary" emigration of Amílcar's father and mother to Portuguese Guinea, in contrast to the "forced" exodus of Cabo Verdeans as *contratados* (contracted workers) to the notorious cacao plantations of São Tomé and Príncipe, occurred against the background of dire conditions in the archipelago. For more than three centuries, droughts and famines had regularly visited Cabo Verde, often lasting two to three years and causing spectacular death tolls, sometimes amounting to two-thirds of the inhabitants of some islands and up to half the population of the archipelago. These catastrophic natural and man-made disasters, together with brutal colonial exploitation and neglect, underlie the significant movements of the population, particularly during the second half of the nineteenth and first half of the twentieth centuries. Between 1902 and 1922, a total of 24,329 desperate Cabo Verdeans found themselves forced to become contracted migrant laborers, 98.5 percent ending up in São Tomé and Príncipe.[7] On the other hand, during the period 1900–1920 an estimated 27,765 Cabo Verdeans "voluntarily" migrated, mainly to the United States (67 percent), Portuguese Guinea (8 percent), Brazil/Latin America (7 percent), and Senegal/ Gambia (5 percent). The "voluntary" flow to the United States was effectively restricted in 1917, when a new immigration law required, among other things, literacy. Obviously, the prolonged harsh realities in the face of neglect and exploitation render redundant the categorization of migration from Cabo Verde as either forced or voluntary. Both were motivated by the specter of starvation and death.

The relatively high literacy rate in Cabo Verde (22 percent in 1950) provided Portugal with a reservoir of willing collaborators—a collaboration conditioned by the prevalent poverty and limited employment opportunities. With a seminary established in 1866, a secular high school opened in 1917 (the first in Portuguese

Africa), and several primary schools, Cabo Verdeans were indeed the main beneficiaries of Portuguese colonial education. This factor largely accounted for their significant presence in the colonial administration of Portuguese Guinea—about 75 percent of the colonial officials before the beginning of the armed struggle. Such preponderance gave rise to their pseudo-status as "co-colonizers" or "proxy colonizers," notwithstanding the fact that Cabo Verde was a colony and Cabo Verdeans a colonized people with a history of brutal exploitation and callous abandonment to recurrent droughts and famines. With the Cabo Verdeans arbitrarily classified as *civilizados* (civilized), the colonial authorities endeavored to ensure that "to Guiné go only those with literacy skills who are going to fill public and business appointments."[8] For poor Cabo Verdeans, the main attraction to Portuguese Guinea was the territory's reliable agriculture and enhanced food security. As one Cabo Verdean writer and colonial official noted, the colony was the "blessed land of rice and nuts and palm oil, where hunger is unknown and there are no beggars."[9]

Portuguese Guinea was (and remains) a multiethnic and multicultural country inhabited by Balantas and Biafadas, Brames and Bijagós, Fulas and Felupes, Mandinkas and Manjacos, Pepels, Nalus, Susus, and several other minor groups that, altogether, have more in common than the sum total of their differences. Desperate to establish the *pax lusitana*, the Portuguese exploited the differences of language and culture and played off

31

one group against the other, constantly making a distinction between the Islamized "neo-Sudanese" Fulas and Mandinkas of the interior, the "builders of strong states," and the "animist paleo-Sudanese" of the coastal region, the "more backward peoples."[10] Applying a racist anthropology, colonial officials-cum-social scientists considered the neo-Sudanese to be of Hamitic/Semitic racial origins, which supposedly made them superior to all the other groups regarded as paleo-Sudanese. This strategy of divide and conquer would constitute a formidable challenge facing Amílcar Cabral as he and his comrades embarked on mobilizing the people for the armed struggle against Portuguese colonial domination.

Juvenal Cabral first worked as a clerk at the Bolama city hall, followed by two other low-level clerical positions in the colony's treasury department and the office of the secretary-general of the colonial government. In January 1913, he became a primary school teacher in Cacine, in the southern region of Tombali, where he taught half a dozen children in a one-room school. He also taught in Buba, Bambadinca, Bafatá, and Geba. Forming the background to his teaching trajectory were the brutal "pacification" campaigns waged by Captain Teixeira Pinto's mercenary soldiers, led by Senegalese warlord Abdul Injai. Juvenal supported the war against the Pepels of Bissau in 1915 and regarded Captain Pinto as "a great Portuguese" whose "patriotic work" was for "the good of civilization."[11] Such sentiment outraged the members of the Liga Guineense (Guinean League), founded on 25 December 1910 as "an assembly of the natives of Guinea." Reacting to the antiwar position of the Liga, the colonial authorities dissolved the emergent protonationalist organization in 1915.

The wanton brutality meted out to the Pepels of Biombo, one of the petty kingdoms on the island then known as Bissau, resulted in thousands of deaths and the capture of hundreds of fighters, including the ruler, N'Kanande Ká. Defiant in captivity, the king reportedly told Teixeira Pinto that he would never surrender, that as long as he was alive he would always fight to expel the Portuguese from his realm, and that "if he should die, and there in the other world he should meet whites, he would wage war on them."[12] Captain Pinto proudly reported that the Pepel king was promptly condemned to death, then "tied up, mutilated, his eyes plucked out, and buried alive." Luiz Loff de Vasconcellos, the outraged defense lawyer of the victims of the Bissau war, pointed out that after the defeat of the Pepels "the real carnage started," as "men, women, old people, children, and the crippled" were "mercilessly killed," their dwellings sacked and burned and their livestock looted, resulting in their homeland being "in the greatest desolation and misery."[13] That was just nine years before Amílcar Cabral was born. It would take two more brutal pacification campaigns, in 1925 and 1936, to subjugate the last resisters, the people of the Bijagós Islands.

Thus, when Cabral was born, Portuguese Guinea was simultaneously undergoing a brutal war of conquest and the consolidation of colonial domination by a weak imperial power that itself was experiencing tumultuous political upheavals following a bloody revolution that abolished the monarchy in 1910 and established a liberal republic, which was overthrown sixteen years later. In 1932, when eight-year-old Amílcar moved to Cabo Verde, António de Oliveira Salazar became prime minister of Portugal. As the effective dictator of the established New State he would maintain a brutal, repressive regime in the African colonies until his incapacitation by a stroke thirty-six years later. Cabral would devote his life to breaking the stranglehold of this harsh colonial order on the lives of the millions of Africans it subjugated.

Meanwhile, in Bafatá, two years before his son Amílcar was born, Juvenal made a passionate plea to the visiting governor for the provision of more schools for the natives, who were "still wrapped up in the plain cloak of their primitive ignorance."[14] Juvenal was indeed an outspoken advocate of the expansion of education in the territory, pleading strongly in 1915 for "the light of education to be shed on this people so desirous of lights" and insisting that, "as is already proven, the *gentio* is not devoid of intelligence, needing on our part to know only how to encourage him to love education."[15] His son Amílcar would inherit such passion for education, but as a weapon for liberation, "to combat fear and ignorance, to stamp out little by little submissiveness before nature and natural forces."[16]

When Amílcar was born, his father registered his first name as Hamilcar, to honor the great Carthaginian general whose son Hannibal was also a famous general. Bafatá was then a relatively new settlement, elevated to the status of a town in 1917, but would soon after become the second most important trading center (after Bissau) in the territory. Of the population of about 1,500 residents, half were Europeans, Lebanese, Syrians, and numerous *civilizados*—mostly Cabo Verdeans. The local economy was dominated by the production of export crops such as peanuts, cotton, and rubber, which were exported to Portugal and France by Portuguese and French trading companies including the Union Manufacturing Company (CUF), Casa Gouveia, Barbosa e Comandita Limitada, and the French West Africa Company (CFAO).

Notwithstanding his strong emotional and spiritual attachment to Cabo Verde and Portugal, Juvenal nevertheless recognized Portuguese Guinea as "the land where the genealogical tree of my ancestors grew and flourished," and declared that since his youth he had struggled for the "dignification of the black race to which I belong."[17] This firm identification with Portuguese Guinea and his ready recognition of his black African ancestry undoubtedly had an influence on his offspring, particularly Amílcar and his brother Luís Severino de Almeida Cabral (born in Bissau on 10 April 1931), who would later embrace their dualities of birthplace and ancestral home and subsequently adopt binationalism as a strategy for the liberation of their two countries.

35

In November 1932, Juvenal retired to Santiago, taking with him Amílcar and his twin sisters. Iva stayed in Bissau to recover the loss she suffered from a burglary, returning a year later to take custody of her children. Thus, Amílcar Cabral only spent about seven years in Portuguese Guinea before returning, for the second time, to Cabo Verde. Very little is known about his life during those tender years he lived in his *terra natal*. Neither he nor his father—whose autobiography, *Memorias e reflexões* (Memories and reflections), was written when Amílcar was a second-year agronomy student in Portugal—has left any written account of those early formative years.

Amílcar was conscious of the hard life his mother had, of the long hours she had to work to ensure that her four children did not go to bed hungry. The sacrifices, which grew bigger as the children became young adults, and especially in order for Amílcar to complete his high school education in Cabo Verde, would be appreciated by a grateful son. Amílcar would later express his gratitude by describing his mother in a dedicatory poem as "the star of my infancy," with the acknowledgment, "Without you, I am nobody."[18]

Thus, notwithstanding the affirmations of Cabral's notable biographers, particularly Mário de Andrade and Patrick Chabal, that Juvenal played a pivotal role in his son's development of critical political consciousness, it would appear that Iva was the central figure. The radical political consciousness of Amílcar fundamentally

36

challenged his father's core political beliefs. Ironically, although Juvenal was a primary school teacher in Portuguese Guinea, Amílcar was not enrolled in any educational establishment in the territory, in spite of being of school age. It is probable that he was home-schooled, given the importance of education among Cabo Verdeans. Nevertheless, in Cabo Verde, Iva's determination for her children to be educated would be realized. Life in the archipelago would be critical in the molding of Amílcar's character.

2

Terra Ancestral

*Schooling and Adolescence in
Cabo Verde, 1932–45*

Late in November 1932, after an exhausting two-day
boat trip from Portuguese Guinea, Amílcar Cabral and
his five-year-old twin sisters Armanda and Arminda,
accompanied by their father Juvenal Cabral, disembarked in Praia. For about two years the children lived
with their father in the interior of Santiago, in his big
house at Achada Falcão, near Assomada, capital of the
municipality of Santa Catarina and the second-largest
city on the largest island in Cabo Verde. The house
was built on extensive land, shadowed by the Serra da
Malagueta mountain range, that Juvenal inherited from
his godmother, Simoa dos Reis Borges.

Mountainous with relatively fertile valleys, Santiago was also the first island to be settled, initially by
Portuguese migrants from the regions of Alentejo and
Algarve and the Madeira Islands, as well as a sprinkling
of Genoese and Spaniards. The island quickly became
the heartbeat of the archipelago. In 1466, the Portuguese

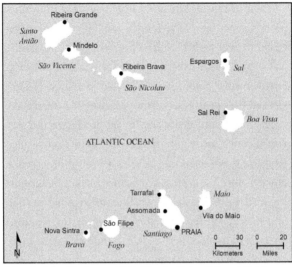

Map 2. Cabo Verde, ca. 1960. Map by Brian Edward Balsley, GISP.

Crown granted the Santiago settlers special privileges to have their own administration and the right to trade on the adjacent West African coast. Six years later, a royal decree gave them the right "to have slaves, males and females, for their services, and to be occasion for their better livelihood and good settlement."[1] But they were prohibited from trading in African captives, and for their defiance they became known as *lançados* (from the Portuguese word *lançar*—"to launch"—meaning those who defiantly "launched" themselves onto the West African mainland), with the Rivers of Guinea of Cabo Verde as their principal area of activity.

The enslaved Africans in Santiago and the other islands constructed the foundations of the new slave-based society with blood, sweat, and great toil. Theirs was a precarious existence that has been described as "hard, brutish and, in times of famine, short."[2] They worked the sugar and cotton plantations, gathered the vegetable dyestuff *urzela* and the oil-producing nut *pur-gueira*, wove the highly esteemed cotton cloths called *panos*, and extracted salt, besides a host of other tasks. Furthermore, the enslaved African women were sexually exploited by their masters, which resulted in the creation of a *mestiço* (mixed-race) racial category that became, through paternal inheritance, a dominant landowning class occupying important positions in the social and political life of the archipelago. The tendency of Portu-guese men in the tropics to "unashamedly" have sexual relations with enslaved and "free women of color" would later be conceptualized by Brazilian sociologist Gilberto Freyre as "lusotropicalism," which theory equates "racial harmony" in the "world created by the Portuguese" with miscegenation. The Lisbon authorities would weapon-ize the concept to maintain the *pax lusitana*. Amílcar Cabral would dismiss Freyre as "confusing realities that are biological and necessary with realities that are socio-economic and historical."[3]

With recurring drought and famine, decline in the transshipment of African captives to the Americas, and the emigration of numerous white settlers, Cabo Verde became a penal colony where Portugal sent her convicts, known as *degredados*. Miscegenation increased substantially during the period 1802–82, when some 2,433 convicts (among them 81 women) were deported to the islands, with Santiago receiving the majority of them.[4] This island would later host a concentration camp built by the Estado Novo in the town of Tarrafal in 1936, where Portugal sent her political dissidents and African nationalist agitators. By 1900, *mestiços* constituted 64 percent of the archipelago's population, among them the rich, the poor, and the marginalized. The "whites" made up 3 percent of the inhabitants, while the "blacks" accounted for the remaining one-third.

Invariably characterized as *brancos* (whites), *mestiços*, and *pretos* (blacks), the population of Cabo Verde had, from the beginning of slavery to the end of the colonial period, also been a race- and color-conscious society. While these socially constructed categories may never have been fiery, contentious issues, the absence of overt racial conflict did not mean the absence of either race/color consciousness or racial prejudice. Historically, race and color have had social, cultural, and psychological significance in the archipelago. From the early days of settlement, the *mestiço* element was differentiated from the black population and generally given favored treatment. The sons and daughters of white men, or their descendants, they generally considered themselves "white, Portuguese, and civilized," naturally superior to the blacks, and thus remained spiritually and psychologically amputated from Africa. Cabral

41

would take issue with such self-perception, admonishing that "some, forgetting or ignoring how the people of Cape Verde were formed, think that Cape Verde is not Africa because it has many *mestiços*," and insisting that "even if in Cabo Verde there was a majority white native population . . . Cape Verdeans would not stop being Africans."[5]

At home in Achada Falcão, Cabral found himself once again among a people with a long tradition of resistance against brutal exploitation and oppression. The municipality of Santa Catarina had been the epicenter of revolts and rebellions by a people referred to as *badius*, the poor black and *mestiço* peasants of the island.[6] Twenty-two years earlier, just a month after the Portuguese monarchy was overthrown and a republic declared (5 October 1910), the tenant farmers of Ribeirão Manuel revolted against the payment of rents, during a time of drought and famine, to the landowners known as *morgados*—a throwback to the latifundia-type system that emerged with the royal land grants of the early settlement period. The brutal response of the colonial authorities to the initial protests ignited a rebellion led by Nha Ana Veiga, popularly known as Nha'Ana Bombolom,[7] who rallied the angry peasants with her legendary call to arms: "homi faca, mudjer matxado, mosinhos tudo ta djunta pedra" (men knives, women machetes, all children gather stones).[8] According to Pedro Martins, a native of Santa Catarina and maternal relative of Cabral who, as a politically active high school student six decades after the Ribeirão Manuel rebellion became the youngest political prisoner in the notorious Tarrafal concentration camp, the defeated leaders were "handcuffed" and "paraded around the island"—much like Gungunhana, the defiant ruler of the Gaza kingdom in southern Mozambique, who was defeated by the Portuguese in 1895, was taken to Portugal and paraded through the streets of Lisbon.

The Ribeirão Manuel revolt was preceded by uprisings in Ribeira de Engenhos in January 1822 and Achada Falcão in January 1841, both motivated by high rents and a highly exploitative land-tenure system dominated by a handful of mostly absentee landlords. The dependence of the majority of Cabo Verdeans on eking out a precarious living from an agriculture conditioned by soil erosion and cyclical droughts would later influence the decision of Cabral to study agronomy.

The struggles of poor peasant farmers in Cabo Verde were paralleled by those of urban workers, especially during the last quarter of the nineteenth and the first two decades of the twentieth centuries when the number of strikes and demonstrations increased in Mindelo, capital of São Vincente Island, where workers at the port, the coaling stations, and the shipping agencies demanded better wages and working conditions.

Resistance in the context of periodic droughts and famines has been a salient feature of the history of Cabo Verde, a history that is also embedded in the various facets of Cabo Verdean culture, including folklore, music, song, and dance. Young Amílcar, like most young Cabo Verdeans, was conscious of this sad trajectory of his ancestral country, but as an adult he would change such static consciousness to active engagement in social transformation, thus reconciling memory and action. As in the case of Portuguese Guinea, Amílcar would later regard the numerous revolts during slavery and the many acts of defiance in the colonial period as sources of inspiration for his anticolonial activism.

Life in Achada Falcão for Amílcar and his sisters was but short-lived, less than two years. Little is known about this brief period when Amílcar intimately lived part of his age of innocence with his father. The family house was big, made of brick with red roof tiles imported from Portugal. The air of opulence it exuded was reinforced by Juvenal's "proverbial generosity" in the face of ubiquitous poverty and misery, a generosity that included "lending money without guarantees."[9] With the severe drought and deadly famine of the early 1940s, having borrowed money against his property as collateral, Juvenal was forced to vacate the house and move with his family to Praia. Amílcar and his sisters had already moved out, when their mother finally reassumed responsibility for them shortly after her return from Portuguese Guinea in late 1933 or early 1934.

In Praia, Amílcar was enrolled at the Escolar Primária Oliveira Salazar, with his mother bearing the full cost of his upkeep and education.[10] During this period the city was under enormous stress due to a slump in agricultural

and commercial activities in Santiago and the other islands, a significant rural urban migration provoked by
cyclical droughts and famines, the perennial neglect of
Portuguese colonial rule, and a world at war. A safety
valve for the accumulating socioeconomic crisis was
the increased recruitment of *contratados* for the cacao
plantations of São Tomé and Príncipe. When two devastating famines (1941–43 and 1947–48) lasting five years
officially killed 45,000 people (25 percent of the population), some 18,513 *contratados*, mostly poor *badius* from
Santiago, "involuntarily" migrated south, mainly to São
Tomé and Príncipe, while 6,898 more fortunate Cabo
Verdeans "voluntarily" emigrated to Portugal (68 percent),
Portuguese Guinea (20 percent), and the United States
of America (5 percent).[11] Young Amílcar lived through
the generalized hardships prevalent in the archipelago,
where he "saw folk die of hunger" and witnessed the
forced migration of "thousands . . . as contracted workers for the Portuguese plantations in other colonies," an
experience that later left him sufficiently revolted and
determined to struggle for the end of Portugal's colonial
rule in Africa.[12]

At primary school, and later in high school, Cabral
followed the same curricula as that of students in
Portugal, since Cabo Verde was officially considered a
"civilized" colony that was sufficiently assimilated to
Portuguese culture, unlike the "uncivilized" mainland
territories of Portuguese Guinea, Angola, and Mozambique. The educational system was broadly Eurocentric

and narrowly Lusocentric, which meant total neglect of African history and culture. The education emphasized the learning of Portuguese language and culture and, besides basic mathematics and science, the celebration of the maritime "discoveries" of the fifteenth and sixteenth centuries, the "genius" of the "Father of Portuguese Literature," Luís de Camões, the miracles of Nossa Senhora de Fatima (Our Lady of Fatima), and the "historical mission" of Portugal. As a graduate of this paternalistic education, Cabral later scathingly commented on its racist content and alienating impact.

> All Portuguese education disparages the African, his culture and civilization. African languages are forbidden in schools. The white man is always presented as a superior being and the African as an inferior. The colonial "conquistadores" are shown as saints and heroes. As soon as African children enter elementary schools, they develop an inferiority complex. They learn to fear the white man and to feel ashamed of being Africans. African geography, history and culture are either ignored or distorted, and children are forced to study Portuguese geography and history.[13]

Thus, in such Eurocentric education, just as the children of the *assimilés* in France d'Outre-mer (Overseas France) were forced to recite "our forefathers the Gauls," so, too, young Amílcar found himself obliged to read "who are we, the Portuguese who for many centuries have lived in this corner of Europe? History says

46

that we are the descendants of many ancient peoples who intermixed and intermingled."[14] He would retrospectively acknowledge the effectiveness of this colonial socialization process: "There was a time in my life when I was convinced that I was Portuguese." But he would also later realize that he was not Portuguese because of his consciousness of "my people, the history of Africa, even the color of my skin."[15] Such awareness was premised on the strong conviction that "the culture of the people of Cabo Verde is quintessentially African."[16]

In July 1937, Cabral graduated from primary school at the top of his class and passed his high school entrance examination with distinction. Together with his mother and siblings, he moved to Mindelo, São Vincente, and became one of the 372 enrolled students at the Liceu Infante Dom Henrique during the academic year that started on 21 October 1937. At age thirteen, he was two years older than the average enrolled first-year high school student. Five days after his enrollment (for courses that included Portuguese and French languages, mathematics, science, art, and physical education), the high school was closed by order of the minister of the colonies, Francisco Vieira Machado, who requested its transformation into a vocational school. The closure provoked strong protests from the enrolled students, who were supported by their families and the general public, resulting in the reopening of the school three months later as the Liceu Gil Eannes. A participant in the demonstrations, the effectiveness of organized

47

protest left an enduring impression on young Amíl-car, a valuable learning experience and useful teachable moment that he would invoke three decades later in a seminar for the cadres of the PAIGC, pointing out, "I waited three months without going to classes at second-ary school, because they [the colonial authorities] had closed it. For them what they had done was enough, no more was needed. From then on only training centres for fishermen and carpenters. The population rose and protested, and the secondary school began operating once more."[17]

The seven years Cabral spent in Mindelo were, as in Praia, extended days and months of hardships and deprivations made bearable by the sacrifices of his mother and older half-brother Ivo, each of whom worked daily many hours for very little pay. Cabral's mother labored in the local fish cannery, earning fifty cents an hour, where she worked eight hours a day when fish was plentiful and only an hour a day when fish was scarce. To supplement her meager income, she also worked as a laundress for Portuguese soldiers stationed on the island, since, despite her old craft as seamstress, "she made nothing from sewing." Amílcar's brother Ivo, who trained as a carpenter, did all kinds of odd jobs to contribute toward the upkeep of the household. Cabral himself helped by tutoring primary school and fellow *liceu* students.

Yet, in spite of the austere conditions he endured with his family in Mindelo, Cabral remained focused on his schoolwork and strove to surpass his classmates in all subjects. He quickly displayed the initiative and determination for which he would become well known. As class president throughout his high school years, his charismatic leadership won him numerous friends and admirers at the same time as it developed and refined his interpersonal skills and negotiating capabilities. The good impression he made on students and faculty lingered for years, as Manuel "Manecas" dos Santos, a later alumnus of the same high school and his comrade-in-arms in Portuguese Guinea, recalls.[18] Cabral was also involved in extracurricular activities in and around Mindelo, including the founding of a high school sports club, the Associação Desportiva do Liceu de Cabo Verde (Sports Association of the High School of Cabo Verde), of which he was not only president but also an active member, being an adept soccer player and a keen sportsman. The honing of his organizing and leadership skills would also include the staging and directing of plays for both high school students and the youth of Mindelo, plays in which he sometimes also performed as actor.

Cabral's extracurricular activities in Mindelo— where the Claridade literary movement, aimed at defining and affirming Cabo Verde's specific Crioulu identity, emerged a year or so before his arrival— also included the writing of poetry and prose. The Cabo Verdean identity that came to be known as Caboverdianidade had, as its organ of expression, the journal *Claridade: Revista de Arte e Letras*, which was first published in 1936 and last appeared (the ninth edition) in 1960. Led by Jorge Barbosa, Manuel Lopes, and Baltasar Lopes da Silva, the proponents of this concept came to be called the Claridosos. They initially set the tone for a nativist literature that focused on the existential crises generated by drought, famine, poverty, isolation, and migration. They did not challenge the colonial order, but instead framed the literary renaissance in a regional setting considered part of Western Europe rather than Western Africa.

Nevertheless, this new literature was a radical departure from the previous Eurocentric focus of the earlier poets and prose writers who were educated at the seminary in São Nicolau. Steeped in the Greco-Roman classics, these pre-Claridade literati were later criticized by Cabral for producing a literature in which "they forget the land and the people."[19] In particular, they composed poetry characterized by the themes of love, personal pain, exalted patriotism, and profound nostalgia. Some of the poems were written and/or translated into Crioulu and song as *morna*, the quintessential Cabo Verdean music and dance genre made famous worldwide by Cesária Évora (1941–2011), a native of Mindelo commemorated by the name of the international airport on São Vincente.

The main factors accounting for the emergence of the Claridosos generation include the archipelago's recurring drama of drought, famine, death, and emigration and the establishment of a secular coeducational high school with largely Cabo Verdean faculty and staff (unprecedented in Portuguese Africa) in Mindelo, the most cosmopolitan city in the archipelago, where the resident educated elite had easier access to foreign literature reflecting the perspectives of realism and impressionism as artistic movements. Significant also was the installation of the fascist Estado Novo and its increasingly suffocating stranglehold on the colonized and the stationing of a large number of Portuguese troops in the archipelago to bolster the defense of the colony. This increased military presence provoked clashes between the local inhabitants and racist white soldiers, which not only insulted the dignity of the Cabo Verdean people but laid bare the falsity of the assimilationist notion of equality between colonizer and colonized. Such developments generated a nativist awakening among the Cabo Verdean intellectuals that coalesced into the concept of Caboverdianidade, whose founders influenced Cabral's early endeavors in poetry and prose writing. He would later commend the Claridosos for having their "feet fixed to the ground" and realistically depicting Cabo Verde as a place "where the trees die of thirst, the men of hunger—and hope never dies."[20]

Thus it was with the outlook of the Claridosos that Cabral wrote his first poems, including "Chuva" (Rain), written in 1943, echoing the "drama of the rain." Cabral's early short stories included "Fidemar" (Son of the sea) and "Hoje e amanha" (Today and tomorrow), respectively written in 1942 and 1944. The first tells the story of a young man who is revolted by the dire conditions in the archipelago and agitates for change but decides to leave the islands and secure the wherewithal needed to make the necessary revolution; however, before he can return, the hero dies at sea during a naval battle. As noted by Chabal, the theme of this "poem of adolescence," as Cabral later characterized it, was not uncommon, being "representative of Cape Verde's sense of isolation from the rest of the world and the need to escape from this insular hell by seeking liberation outside."[21] In the second story, written during his final high school year but published five years later under the pseudonym Arlindo António when he was in the last year of his university studies in Lisbon, Cabral decries the evils of war and injustice, hatred and hardships, yet optimistically embraces a future with better prospects for a son he desires. Mário de Andrade notes that this essay represents "the first philosophical reflection of Amílcar" in which, with his desire for a son, he plans to reshape the future.[22]

While the poets and prose writers of *Claridade* were cultural nativists whose affirmation of Caboverdianidade did not challenge the fundamental premises of Portuguese colonialism, they were nevertheless not totally oblivious to developments in the rest of the African continent. For example, a poem by António da Silva Ramos titled "Abyssinia," which became a *morna* expressing outrage against the invasion of Ethiopia in October 1935 by Italian fascist dictator Benito Mussolini, reveals a rare Pan-African solidarity that urged Negusa Nagast (Amharic for "king of kings"; emperor) Haile Selassie, to defend his kingdom, "which is rightfully yours."[23]

The Claridade movement was later overshadowed by the radical Certeza generation of younger writers and poets who focused on the linkages between the dire conditions of the archipelago and its status as a colony, as well as the historical and cultural links between the islands and the adjacent African mainland. Thus, these literati sowed the seeds for the germination of political consciousness that would lead to nationalist activism. The few issues of the journal *Certeza* that first appeared in 1944 contained poems and prose whose messages were deemed sufficiently subversive by the vigilant International and State Defense Police (PIDE) to ban the publication a year or so later, even though the authors were not yet calling for the overthrow of the colonial status quo.

Although Cabral admired the Claridade and Certeza poets and writers, having recognized their critical role in the emergence of an archipelago-centric literature, he nevertheless criticized them for their limited vision. In a penetrating analysis of Cabo Verdean poetry written in 1952, he pointed out that the messages of the poets and writers had to transcend both "resignation" and "hope" and insisted that "insularity and droughts cannot justify endless stagnation." He further urged that "the escapist dream, the desire to leave, cannot remain the only theme," that a different dream should "no longer be a desire to depart but to create a new land inside our land."[24] It was a clarion call for profound transformational change. His radical political consciousness had crystallized in Portugal during the seven years he spent there as a student and a trained agronomist.

Cabral completed high school at the top of his class in 1944. His journey to Portugal occurred a year later, after he and his family moved back to Praia, where he obtained employment as a clerk in the government printing office. He successfully applied for a scholarship from the House of Students of the Empire (CEI) to study agronomy in Portugal.

Mãe Patria

*Higher Education and Political Militancy in
Portugal, 1945–52*

Early in November 1945, Cabral disembarked in Lisbon,
capital of the *mãe patria* (motherland), about a month
after his classes had begun at the Higher Institute of
Agronomy (ISA) of the Technical University of Lisbon.
The late arrival was due to bureaucratic delays in pro-
cessing his travel documents. The institute had admitted
220 applicants comprising twenty females and two hundred males, including Cabral, the only African student.
The five-year course in agronomy was so rigorous and
intensive that only twenty-five students proceeded to
the third year; among them were Cabral and a female
Portuguese student, Maria Helena de Ataíde Vilhena
Rodrigues, his future wife.

Cabral excelled in his studies at the ISA, earning top
grades in all his subjects and gaining respect and admiration not only from his peers and professors but also
from the rector of the institute, who asked him to tutor
his children. Yet, notwithstanding his demonstrated

intelligence, he remained humble and approachable. His whole university experience enabled him to refine his engaging personality and spirit of tolerance, which enhanced his organizational skills.

Besides his academic and professional training, the historical, political, and sociocultural contexts of Portugal and the dynamic background of the wider world provided the substance for young Cabral's formation of a critical consciousness. This would bring about the fundamental transformations he had to undergo for his self-liberation—profound changes that would serve as a prerequisite for his commitment to struggle for the liberation of his fellow colonized Africans in "Portuguese Africa."

When Cabral started his studies in Portugal, the twelve-year-old Estado Novo regime was still struggling to consolidate its imperial fiat. The fascist dictatorship was established in 1933 to arrest Portugal's decades-old economic decline, a state of affairs aggravated by political upheavals epitomized by the overthrowing of the monarchy, which was preceded by the assassination of King Carlos I and his heir-apparent Prince Luís Filipe on 1 February 1908. This bloody event was followed by the short and ineffectual reign of the assassinated monarch's second son, Manuel II, and the establishment of a precarious liberal republic on 5 October 1910, which was ushered in by a violent coup d'état that claimed over fifty lives. Portugal became the third country in Europe with a republican constitution, after France and

Switzerland. However, during the sixteen years of republican statehood, the country had political instability second to none in Western Europe: scores of political killings, numerous actual and attempted military coups d'état, several civil wars, eight presidents (with only one completing his constitutional term of office), thirty-eight prime ministers, and forty-five governments that lasted, on average, four months.

Having established her present-day borders in 1149 with the final expulsion of the Moslem conquerors who dominated much of the Iberian Peninsula since 711, and having defeated the huge Castilian invading army in the defining battle of Aljubarrota in 1385, Portugal became a powerful unified nation characterized by strong centralized government, political stability, and sociocultural homogeneity. Nationalist pride, bolstered by scientific knowledge and the innovations of the Renaissance, enabled the country to embark on "voyages of discovery" under the visionary leadership of Prince Henry "the Navigator" that had profound impacts around the world. Its vast seaborne empire in Africa, Asia, and South America briefly made the fiercely nationalistic nation the richest country in Europe and the first superpower of modern times. The strong Portuguese nationalism and patriotic fervor demonstrated throughout the centuries were celebrated in literature and folklore and taught in colonial schools as part of the process of "civilizing" the colonized. Yet it did not dawn on the Portuguese colonizers that their unrelenting determination to be free and independent could also be an inspiration to their colonial subjects, like Cabral, to stubbornly seek their own freedom and independence.

Increased fiscal and economic stability under Salazar as minister of finance (1926 and 1928–32) and prime minister (1932–68) enabled the significant improvement of Portugal's physical and social infrastructure, including the establishment of the Technical University of Lisbon in 1930. The science- and technology-based university and its agronomy school were created to address the needs of a predominantly agricultural country and its colonies, endowed with valuable natural resources. It was thus the most unlikely place to produce future political leaders, let alone radical anticolonial activists. Cabral would embrace the vision and mission of the institution but defy the expectation of political conformity.

Already well-steeped in Portuguese history, literature, and culture from his primary and high school education in Cabo Verde, with excellent oral and written command of the "language of Camões,"[1] Cabral arrived with a strong self-esteem that enabled him to withstand the preconceptions and prejudices of his white colleagues and professors, in spite of being legally "Portuguese." Thus, from the onset, Cabral felt at ease with himself and with academic life, unintimidated by the new environment in which he was the only black student among privileged white classmates and professors.

While Cabral was comfortable in his own skin, he still had to deal with racism and its manifold manifestations. In Portugal, as in Europe generally, an upsurge of racism in the nineteenth century was propelled by prominent philosophers, social scientists, and politicians, among others, following Charles Darwin's landmark publications, *On the Origin of Species* (1859) and *The Descent of Man* (1871). The central polemical thesis about the evolution of animal and plant life through natural selection quickly spawned a pseudoscience, Social Darwinism, which expounded the inherent superiority of the white man and his responsibility to the inherently "inferior" races.

Regarding the supposed racial and intellectual inferiority of Africans, the famous Portuguese writer and politician Joaquim Pedro de Oliveira Martins insisted in 1880 that education for Africans was "absurd not only in the light of History, but also in light of the mental capacity of these inferior races." Contemptuous of Portugal's proclaimed double mission of civilizing and evangelizing the "inferior races" and "barbarous peoples" of Africa "placed between man and the anthropoid," Oliveira Martins sneered, "Why not teach the Bible to the gorilla and the orangutan, who have ears even though they cannot speak, and must understand, almost as much as the black, the metaphysics of the incarnation of the Word and the dogma of the Trinity?"[2]

The new generation of passionate *colonialistas* of the late nineteenth century also included António José

Enes (royal commissioner of Mozambique, 1891–95), who considered the African "a big child" and "half savage";[3] Mouzinho de Albuquerque (conquistador of Mozambique, 1895), who insisted that, in order "to educate and civilize the native," it was imperative "to develop in a practical way his aptitude for manual labor";[4] and Eduardo da Costa (governor-general of Angola, 1906–7), who warned about "the gross and dangerous error of considering equal, before the law, the civilized European and the savage inhabitant of the African bush."[5] It was the racist ideas of such staunch imperialists that came to form the cornerstone of Portuguese colonial philosophy and, during the Estado Novo era, became camouflaged with Gilberto Freyre's imaginary tale of "lusotropicalism."

Portuguese imperial triumphalism and hubris were hugely displayed at the three-month Colonial Exposition of Porto inaugurated on 16 June 1934, eleven years before Cabral arrived in Lisbon. Inspired by the London Exposition of the British Empire in 1924 and the International Colonial Exposition of Paris in 1931, this celebration of white supremacy was complete with exhibitions of reconstructed African villages showing the "exotic natives," who supposedly represented, in the words of British poet Rudyard Kipling, the "new-caught, sullen peoples, half-devil and half-child." The exposition was evidence of Portugal taking up Kipling's "White Man's burden." At Porto, the exhibition of sixty-three *pretos da Guiné* (blacks of Guinea) drew huge crowds of spectators who gaped and gawked at the half-naked "savage" women with their exposed breasts, the scantily clad men, and the nude children. The exotic Africans on display also included Angolans and Mozambicans in their replicated "natural habitats" of "primitive" mud-hut villages, in which they were required to live and display their putative lifestyles and cultures for the duration of the exposition. On show in much the same way as the animals in the nearby Porto zoo, the human exhibits were meant to testify to the supposed superiority of the white race. This was also the objective of the many expositions of the other European and American colonial powers during the nineteenth and twentieth centuries.

Thus, when Cabral arrived in Portugal, memories of the human zoo that characterized the Colonial Exposition of Porto were still fresh in the country. Five years earlier, an even bigger celebration of imperial pomposity, the Exposition of the Portuguese World, had been held in Lisbon (June–December 1940), calculated to promote the Estado Novo dictatorship, celebrate the consolidation of Portuguese sovereignty in the overseas provinces, and further reinforce the notion of white superiority.

While Cabral was very much admired by his white colleagues for his intellectual prowess, he nevertheless encountered overt racism within and outside the ISA. But he was psychologically and emotionally prepared. On the eve of his departure from Cabo Verde, his father talked to him about his own experience in Portugal four decades earlier. Juvenal described his stay in the metropole as the happiest years of his adolescence, although "very hard." He accordingly warned his son thus: "It is obvious that in the metropole you will not encounter racism so rooted as, let's say, in the United States. However, even in Lisbon, there can be manifestations of this abominable phenomenon. Do not be astonished nor lose your head, if you note among your future colleagues a certain attitude of reserve in relation to you." Alluding to the possible racial bias of his teachers in Portugal, Juvenal advised his son to always remember that "you must show knowledge more profound than any candidate of Portuguese descent," because, "taking into account your origin, your knowledge will be evaluated with greater rigor."[6] Already a brilliant elementary and high school student, Amílcar would have no problem heeding his father's advice.

Cabral's colleague and girlfriend, Maria Helena Rodrigues, a native of Chaves in northern Portugal, recalled the cold reception he received when she took him home to meet her family. "The adults in the village would not talk to him, only behind his back." But Cabral remained unruffled when the children of the village, who had never seen a black person, ran after him "to see and touch him," a spectacle which he accommodated by "letting them touch his head" and using the occasion as a teaching moment. "He explained to them where he came from, what Africa was and who the Africans were.

He explained to them that despite colour differences all men were equal."[7]

Walking around the ISA campus with Maria Helena, Cabral was "on numerous occasions . . . insulted for being with a white woman."[8] Again Cabral would remain composed and explain away the racist behavior as ignorance and lack of education. Yet he was aware that racism was not entirely due to lack of enlightenment, but rather a phenomenon embedded in Portuguese and European culture that permeated societies and institutions. His self-confidence remained intact and enabled him to teach Portuguese adults in the poor working-class Lisbon neighborhood of Alcântara.

Cabral's arrival in Portugal occurred two months after the formal surrender of Japan on 2 September 1945, which signaled the final end of the Second World War and the dawning of an ideological rivalry between the two emergent superpowers, the United States and the USSR. Against the struggles of the Portuguese people for a democratic Portugal in the aftermath of the defeat of Nazi Germany and Fascist Italy, the Estado Novo dictatorship built a levee of authoritarian rule that effectively blocked the surging second wave of democratization that had begun to wash away entrenched dictatorships, including imperial overlordships, around the world. On the same day that Japan capitulated, the Vietnamese nationalist leader Ho Chi Minh declared the independence of the former French colony of Vietnam, thereby initiating the post-1945 decolonization process.

The fledgling Cold War that divided the world into two powerful blocs with military alliances to counterweigh and outmaneuver each other would be a favorable factor for decolonization.

Cabral's deepening political consciousness and subsequent political activism in Portugal were the result of his engagement in extracurricular self-education and participation in radical politics. At the ISA, he quickly became actively involved in radical student politics. According to Maria Helena, Cabral not only "participated actively in the student antifascist committees," but he also "led the discussions, since he expressed himself very well."[9]

Student opposition to the Estado Novo dictatorship was largely organized by the Movement of Democratic Unity (MUD), which had a youth section, the Youth Movement of Democratic Unity (MUDJ). Established in October 1945, MUD was a coalition of regime opponents that included communists, socialists, liberals, monarchists, labor unionists, and freemasons. The Portuguese Communist Party (PCP), founded in March 1921, was a very active member of MUD, through which it was able to disseminate Marxist-Leninist ideology that would influence Cabral and some of the other African students, including Agostinho Neto from Angola and Vasco Cabral (no relation of Amílcar) from Portuguese Guinea.

As a member of MUDJ, whose leadership included Mário Soares, the future leader of the Portuguese Socialist Party (PS) and president of post–Estado Novo

Portugal, Cabral got involved in electoral mobilization drives and spoke at meetings in which he also led and moderated some of the discussions. With increasing harassment and brutal repression by the International and State Defense Police (PIDE), most of the opposition boycotted the legislative elections, leaving Salazar's National Union party to retain its dominance in the Portuguese National Assembly and over political life in Portugal and her overseas provinces until its demise in 1974. Nevertheless, in spite of the tightening firm grip of the fascist regime, Cabral did not despair. Instead, the unfolding repressive situation strengthened his resolve and energized him to become more actively engaged in life-threatening political activities, as he pointed out in 1949: "I live life intensively and follow from it experiences that have given me a direction, a life I must follow, whatever personal sacrifices it asks of me."[10]

Cabral's intensive life as a politically active student in Lisbon revolved around his engagement in high-risk antiregime activities that were under the close surveillance of the PIDE. He continued to participate in political protests and demonstrations that put some of his African friends in jail, notably Vasco Cabral, Agostinho Neto, Mário de Andrade, and Marcelino dos Santos. Cabral was signatory to a petition to President Francisco Craveiro Lopes protesting Portugal's membership in NATO, which involved expenditure on weapons of war "while the Portuguese people live poorly." Antecedent to his anticolonial struggles, Cabral would gain valuable experience from such political militancy, which included practical experience of organizing clandestine activities in a repressive environment. He would later reference his active involvement in the antifascist struggle of the Portuguese people as his "loyalty" to Portugal "without being Portuguese."[11]

The political activism of Cabral in Lisbon also involved participation in the activities of the Casa dos Estudantes do Império (House of Students of the Empire; CEI), where students from the Portuguese empire congregated and socialized. The Casa was established by the Estado Novo in October 1944, ostensibly as a social center, but fundamentally a means for effective control of potentially subversive student activism. Overseen by the ministry of the colonies, it was considered "indispensable" in the effort to "create among the students a more useful national mentality," in order to count on their "dedication, patriotism and goodwill."[12] Just as the youth of the metropole had to be controlled by creating the Mocidade Portuguesa (Portuguese Youth), a compulsory youth organization established in 1936, so too the potentially restless students from the empire had to be closely managed. Nevertheless, the CEI would fail to abort the birth of anticolonial radicalism, and Cabral would be among the first generation of CEI affiliates to return home and initiate the process of dismantling the Portuguese empire in Africa.

The CEI was a meeting place of two groups of African students: those with scholarships provided by the

Estado Novo and/or colonial authorities, and those whose educational expenses were met by their families—mostly the children of rich white and *mestiço* parents who constituted the economic, bureaucratic, and military elites of the colonies, the overwhelming majority of whom defended the colonial status quo. Cabral belonged to the much smaller group of *bolseiros* (scholarship holders) that also included Vasco Cabral, Agostinho Neto, Mário de Andrade, and Marcelino dos Santos. It was mainly these relatively less privileged African students who began to effectively and sustainably challenge the Portuguese imperial order in their homelands.

The CEI was a house organized along "sections," with Cabral serving as secretary (later vice president and president) of the section representing Cabo Verde, Portuguese Guinea, and São Tomé and Príncipe students. In 1950 he was elected as the secretary-general of the CEI and a year later as its vice president. Cabral was also president of the cultural committee and an active collaborator in the management and publication of the CEI's literary organ, *Mensagem* (Message).

At the CEI, Cabral learned about the realities of colonial rule in Portugal's other African colonies. His acquaintance with fellow African students and the camaraderie that ensued with a handful of them, including Marcelino dos Santos (his roommate), Mário Pinto de Andrade, and Agostinho Neto, facilitated the learning process. Access to radical literature on Marxism,

Negritude, and Pan-Africanism deepened Cabral's knowledge of historical social phenomena and broadened his worldview. Marxist ideology was absorbed from literature provided by the PCP as well as from his militancy in the MUDJ, while the ideas of Negritude and Pan-Africanism were grasped through enthusiastic reading of available published works, beginning with the landmark publication of Léopold Sédar Senghor's critically acclaimed *Anthologie de la nouvelle poésie nègre et malgache de langue française* (1948).

Founded by Léopold Senghor, Aimé Césaire, and Léon Damas, respectively from France's colonies of Senegal, Martinique, and French Guiana, Negritude was a literary movement against French cultural imperialism. It emerged in Paris during the decade before the Second World War, which witnessed the launching of two short-lived literary journals, *La revue du monde noir* (1931–32) and *Légitime défense* (1932), both of which published poems and articles that critically questioned France's policy of assimilation. In 1935, in collaboration with Senghor and Damas, Césaire founded *L'étudiant noir*, the maiden issue of which contained his article "Conscience raciale et révolution sociale" ("Racial Consciousness and Social Revolution"), in which the term "Negritude" was first used. In defiant rejection of assimilation to French and European culture, this equally short-lived journal that launched the Negritude movement broadened the base of attack on French and European imperialism to include the whole world. It thus celebrated African and diaspora African cultures. The cultural resistance was influenced to some extent by the eloquent expressions of the African American ordeal and the celebration of black culture in the United States, as reflected in the works of the Harlem Renaissance poets and writers including Claude McKay, Countee Cullen, Langston Hughes, and Zora Neale Hurston.

The impact of Senghor's *Anthologie* on the evolving cultural and political consciousness of Cabral is reflected in his excitement about the book, which revealed to him "things I had not dreamed of, marvelous poetry written by blacks from all parts of the French world, poetry that speaks of Africa, of slaves, of men, of life, and of the aspirations of men." Cabral further noted that "the book brings me much, including, among many things, the certainty that the black man is in the process of awakening throughout the world."[13]

Consequently, Cabral and the other African students similarly influenced by the central message of Negritude began to focus on addressing the issue of cultural alienation. Cabral would later recall that the quest for cultural identity entailed the "re-Africanization of the spirit," or a "return to the roots" through rediscovery and embracement of African cultural heritages. Accordingly, Cabral and his colleagues organized poetry-reading sessions and talks at the CEI that focused on African cultures and societies. Their Afrocentric writings, including Cabral's poems "Regressa" (Return) and "Rosa Preta" (Black rose) and his short story, "Hoje e Amanhã" (Today and tomorrow), were mostly published in *Mensagem*.

This emergent group of "culturally liberated" African students that Mário de Andrade later called "the generation of Cabral," who read the same books, discussed the same issues and concerns, and closely followed developments in other parts of the world—including "the triumph of the Chinese Revolution, the success of the USSR, [and] what was happening in North America (we all read a book about the blacks of America)"—would later focus their attention and energy on the more dangerous question of the independence of their countries.[14] Hitherto, their political activism had been limited to engagement in the antifascist struggle of the Portuguese people. The shift also reflected a significant divergence between Cabral's group of radical African students and their "comrades" in the PCP and other antifascist organizations on the fundamental question of decolonization. Like their counterparts in France and other European metropoles, the Portuguese progressive forces at the time did not advocate the end of colonialism, nor did they question the racist assumptions of the policy of assimilation. For Cabral and his colleagues who imbibed the ideology of Marxism-Leninism, the anticolonial struggle trumped the proletarian revolution. The imperative was the complete dismantlement of a racist and exploitative colonial structure.

Although Cabral was aware that Negritude was not a political movement, he nevertheless realized that a colonized people could not be truly liberated until they had regained their cultural identity. Seven years into the armed struggle in Portuguese Guinea, he would re-emphasize this awareness during a lecture in the United States in honor of his assassinated comrade in arms, Eduardo Mondlane, which he delivered on 20 February 1970 at Syracuse University: "A people who free themselves from foreign domination will not be culturally free unless . . . they return to the upward path of their own cultures." Therefore, he concluded, "national liberation is necessarily an act of culture."[15]

What Cabral learned from his extracurricular education and political activism in Lisbon would inform his thoughts and actions even before he became an active liberation fighter. On vacation in Cabo Verde in the summer of 1949, when he briefly worked as a substitute broadcaster at the Radio Clube de Cabo Verde, he tried "to awaken Cabo Verdean public opinion against Portuguese colonialism" with his program called *A nossa cultura* (Our culture). In the broadcast, he outlined the links between the archipelago and the West African mainland and characterized Cabo Verdean culture as essentially African, thereby undermining the Portuguese claim that the colonized islanders represented the best example of successful assimilation to the culture of the colonizer. Correctly perceiving the announcement as nuanced criticism, Governor Garcia Alves Roçadas promptly banned the program and fired Cabral.

Nevertheless, Cabral was able to publish five articles on agronomy in the official newsletter *Cabo Verde:*

Boletim de propaganda e informação established by Roçadas. In his critical scientific studies titled "Some Considerations about the Rains" and "In Defense of the Land," Cabral not only diagnosed Cabo Verde's two-hundred-year crippling affliction, but also prescribed remedies that included the storage of rainwater, construction of dikes and dams, and reforestation.

Returning to Portugal, Cabral intensified his quest to "return to the roots" and learn more about Africa. With the CEI under closer surveillance by the PIDE, another venue for the "re-Africanization of the spirit" had to be found. The Center for African Studies (CEA) was housed at the home of a member of the generation of Cabral, Alda do Espírito Santo, a university student from São Tomé and Príncipe who was one of the few females who frequented the CEI. According to Mário de Andrade, the meeting place became "the center of our conversations about Africa: there we studied geography, history, literature, our languages, our political problems." Cabral was actively involved in the organization of the CEA's program of activities, mainly lectures and debates focused on themes including human geography, African society and economy, black identity, Portuguese colonialism, and the African diaspora.

On 21 October 1951, the first of the CEA's series of lectures, organized by Cabral, started with a presentation by Francisco José Tenreiro, a geographer from São Tomé and Príncipe, on the "Geographical Structure of the Continent and Anthropological Structures."

Cabral's lecture on "Cultivation Systems Characteristic of the Black African: Advantages and Disadvantages of the Itinerant System" followed a few weeks later. He had, in the previous year, successfully completed his agronomy coursework at the ISA with a dissertation titled "The Study of Erosion and Land Defense in the region of Cuba (Alentejo)," for which he conducted field studies in that Portuguese region. Other lecturers included Mário de Andrade, Agostinho Neto, and Noémia de Sousa, with presentations largely based on their areas of study.

The CEA thus became the forum where the generation of Cabral learned from each other's research and lived experiences, critically reexamined their own identities and values, and "interpreted the problems of Africa and of the Black world."[16] Collaboration with prominent black intellectuals based in Paris enabled Cabral and some of his CEA colleagues to publish their works in *Présence africaine*, the scholarly journal of the Negritude movement founded in 1947 by the Senegalese writer Alioune Diop. In a special edition of the journal published in 1953 and titled *Les étudiants africains parlent* (African students speak), Cabral contributed an article on "The Role of the African Student" in which he urged educated Africans to strive to serve the laboring masses of the continent who had "no voice to express their most elementary needs."[17]

On 20 December 1951, Cabral married Maria Helena Rodrigues in a simple civil ceremony in Lisbon attended by a few of their close friends. Two months later, having completed an internship at the National Agronomy Station in Santarem, he successfully defended his practicum dissertation titled "About the Concept of Soil Erosion," which earned him the outstanding grade of 18/20.

About a month after qualifying as a professional agronomist, Cabral received a telegram from his brother Luís in Cabo Verde informing him of the death of their father on 20 March 1952. Deeply grief-stricken, he went into self-imposed solitary confinement in his bedroom for several days.

In June 1952, Cabral the trained agronomist signed a three-year contract with the Overseas Ministry to work in the Agriculture and Forestry Services of his *terra natal*. Three months later, he boarded the passenger boat *Ana Mafalda* bound for Bissau, with stopovers in São Vincente and Praia. On 17 September, a day before arriving in São Vincente, he wrote a letter to his wife in Lisbon urging her to "pack up everything quickly and come," because "we have a lot to do and we shall accomplish something, if conditions permit."[18] In Praia, he reunited with his mother and siblings and committed to having them rejoin him in Bissau as soon as possible.

Cabral's sense of mission was reflected in the poem "O adeus à Tapada" (Farewell to Tapada), written at the completion of his studies at the ISA, which was located in the Lisbon neighborhood of Tapada. In it, he bade farewell to his "comrades" and acknowledged "the weapon" with which "to struggle" that he had been provided by the Institute.

Thus, when Amílcar Cabral embarked for Portuguese Guinea, his heavy baggage also contained the weapon of theory and valuable practical experience in clandestine political activism.

4

Return to *Terra Natal*

Colonial Service and
Anticolonial Activities, 1952–56

Cabral disembarked in Bissau on 20 September 1952. Four days later, he wrote another letter to his wife describing his country of birth as one of "the most beautiful lands that I have seen." Imbued with excitement and optimism, he told her that the conditions in the colony were conducive to work and success that hinged on the "vivification of life."[1] Over the course of twenty-one years, Cabral's radical enlivening of spirits would effectively challenge the Portuguese colonial order and culminate in the declaration of the independence of his country, albeit at a high human cost that would include his life.

The year 1952 marked a critical turning point in the life of Cabral. It also witnessed landmark developments in Africa that would favorably facilitate the realization of what Maria Helena described as the great and consuming ambition of her husband: "to go to Guinea and engage in political work . . . to go back 'home' and fight there."[2]

Cabral's return to Portuguese Guinea occurred against the background of a gathering strong "wind of change" in Africa: the end of Italian rule in Libya in December 1951; a coup d'état in Egypt in July 1952 that toppled the British puppet King Farouk and declared the country an independent republic; declaration of a state of emergency in Kenya in October 1952 followed by the arrest and imprisonment of nationalist leaders, including Jomo Kenyatta, which rapidly escalated the armed struggle of the "Mau Mau" rebels (who called themselves the Land Freedom Army) and culminated in independence a decade later; and a series of anticolonial demonstrations and strikes in Morocco resulting in the massacre of several hundred unarmed civilians by the French in December 1952 and the exile of King Mohammed V, intensifying the struggle for independence, which was finally achieved four years later.

Closer to Portuguese Guinea, in the British colony of the Gold Coast, the successful nonviolent "positive action" campaign led by Kwame Nkrumah culminated in a landslide electoral victory in February 1951, his immediate release from a two-year prison sentence, and his appointment as leader of government business, leading to independence in March 1957. Convinced that independence was not only the manifest destiny of his country but also that of all the colonized territories of Africa, Nkrumah would hastily organize the All-African People's Conference in Accra on 8–13 December 1958, described as "a gathering of African Freedom Fighters

... for the purpose of planning the final assault upon imperialism and colonialism."[3] Cabral would be one of the over three hundred delegates who attended the landmark convocation that would resolve to provide "full support to all fighters for freedom in Africa."[4] His liberation movement would be a beneficiary of such Pan-African solidarity.

In the neighboring colony of Guinée Française (French Guinea), the decolonization process gathered momentum in 1952 when the labor union leader Ahmed Sékou Touré became the head of the Democratic Party of Guinea (PDG), the local branch of the African Democratic Rally (RDA)—the interterritorial political party of the French African colonies. The collision course with imperial France would climax six years later, when Sékou Touré and the PDG rejected the neo-colonial project of self-government within a proposed Union Française (French Union). The consequential "No" vote in the referendum of 28 September 1958 would lead to the declared independence of Guinée four days later, and this new nation would greatly facilitate the armed liberation struggle that would be waged by the PAIGC led by Cabral.

A day after his arrival in Bissau, Cabral reported for duty at the Pessubé Agricultural Experimental Station, located on the Granja (farm) in the outskirts of the capital, as *engenheiro agrónomo de segunda classe* (engineer agronomist, second class). He was the first Guinean agronomist. The following day, after lodging in a hotel for three days, he moved to his new home located in the Granja. Thereafter, he busied himself adjusting to his new work environment and the rhythms of colonial life.

The country that Cabral encountered in 1952 was significantly different from the one he left in 1932. In the intervening two decades, Portugal had finally completed her "pacification" of the territory and established "effective occupation." With the obsession of the Estado Novo to maintain the *pax lusitana* at all costs, the colony was inundated with repressive laws aimed at silencing dissent and curbing political activity. A year before Cabral had last left his *terra natal*, strict censorship of the colonial press was imposed, followed two months later by an ominous warning from the first Estado Novo governor that everyone in the colony was expected to "honor the Mother Country by submission to her designs, by respect for her institutions, by love for her venerable traditions."[5]

Prior to Cabral's return, anticolonial activities in Portuguese Guinea were very limited. Before 1950 there were no active political organizations in the territory demanding full independence or autonomy. Significantly, a supposed proto-nationalism had been nipped in the bud decades before, soon after its manifestation in the guise of the Guinean League. Misleadingly describing itself as "an assembly of the natives of Guinea," the League was in fact an assembly of a small group of relatively privileged individuals. The rank-and-file comprised "civilized" petty officials, small traders, and shopkeepers, concentrated mainly in Bissau and Bolama. On the other hand, the League's leadership consisted exclusively of educated Guineans and Cabo Verdeans who were committed to the Portuguese colonial venture. Membership did not extend to the overwhelming majority of "the natives of Guinea." Although it had no political ambitions, the League acquired political relevance through the attempts of colonial authorities to link it to the resistance of the *gentios* against the brutal "pacification" campaigns of the day. As noted earlier, the antiwar criticisms of its members, made from a humanitarian rather than an anticolonial stance, led to its disbandment in 1915.

Thus, dissent in Portuguese Guinea was effectively stifled at a much earlier stage. Unlike Angola and Mozambique, where the protests of the colonial elites were deeply rooted, with numerous forums for reformist/assimilationist politics that lasted through more than three decades of official hostility, the colonial authorities in Portuguese Guinea successfully arrested the growth of incipient nationalism. But opposition to the colonial order continued in the form of passive resistance through which the voiceless masses manifested their discontent and hostility in various ways, from individual defiance against forced labor and the payment of taxes to mass emigration to the neighboring colonies of French Guinea, Senegal, and Gambia. Cabral would characterize this prelude to the armed struggle as a period "of silent repression, of secret recourse to violence, of unsung victims, of disorganized individual reaction, of assaults and crime of all sorts taking place within the four walls of the administrative buildings."[6]

It was in this colonial context that Cabral found himself in Portuguese Guinea. Nationalist agitation was incipient. A year before his return, the Lisbon authorities had tactically changed the nomenclature of their territories from "colonies" to "overseas provinces," in the vain hope of deflecting the growing anticolonial sentiment in such international forums as the United Nations. Aware of the strengthening windstorms gathering over her African colonies, Portugal vowed to withstand the impending wave of decolonization. With the Tarrafal concentration camp in Cabo Verde only a two-day boat trip away, the ruthless International and State Defense Police (PIDE) became active, with four agents in Bissau in the early 1950s. Cabral and his wife, together with other suspected "troublemakers," would be promptly placed under active surveillance. The Cabrals were soon reported to be comporting themselves "in a manner that raises suspicion of activities against our presence."[7] By 1959, the PIDE deployment would increase to thirty-five operatives, and its singular mission would remain the squelching of nationalist upsurge through imprisonment, torture, and assassination.

Nevertheless, to implement his political agenda, Cabral had to acquaint himself with a country and a people he barely knew. He had to start by learning about the realities of the *regime do indigenato*. He was already aware of the country being a divided land of the "civilized" and the "uncivilized," of the "assimilated" and the "heathens"—a color-conscious, compartmentalized universe of *brancos*, *mestiços*, and *pretos*. He understood that the Portuguese strategy of divide and rule had succeeded in creating a category of colonized people that "assimilates the colonizer's mentality, and regards itself as culturally superior to the people to which it belongs and whose cultural values it ignores or despises."[8] He distinguished between a petty bourgeoisie that was "heavily committed and compromised with colonialism" and a potentially revolutionary petty bourgeoisie that was nationalist.[9] Theorizing, he would insist that for the nationalist petty bourgeoisie to identify with and protect the interests of the peasants and wageworkers after the achievement of political independence, it would have to "commit suicide as a class." This would become one of his truly original ideas that still resonates in Africa today.[10]

According to the 1950 population census, the "assimilated" petty bourgeois class to which Cabral belonged numbered 8,320 individuals, or a mere 1.6 percent of the territory's inhabitants. Among them, 27 percent were "whites," 55 percent were "mixed-race" (the overwhelming majority of them Cabo Verdeans), and 18 percent were "blacks." Ironically, in spite of the stated importance of literacy and fluency in Portuguese for "civilized" status, the illiteracy rates among these three racial categories were respectively 24 percent, 51 percent, and 52 percent. Furthermore, among the literates, 27 percent had elementary schooling, 9 percent completed high school, and a miniscule 1.4 percent graduated from postsecondary (including vocational) institutions.[11] Indeed, on the eve of the armed liberation struggle, Portuguese Guinea would have only fourteen university graduates, including Amílcar Cabral.

Cabral's wife arrived in early November 1952 and started working as an agronomist with her husband at the Granja. Their first child, a girl they named Iva Maria, whom Cabral would fondly call "Mariva," was born five months later, in Bissau, on 23 April 1953. The family home in the Granja was an open house where the Cabrals often provided food to their low-level coworkers, besides organizing parties that Cabral would use as a ploy to discuss nationalist politics. Carmen Pereira, who followed her husband (recruited by Cabral) to war and later became the only woman in the twenty-four-member Executive Council of the Struggle (CEL), recalled attending such *festas*, at which Cabral and a small number of male guests would disappear into a locked room while the festivity continued uninterrupted.[12]

Among Cabral's early acquaintances in Bissau were some of the large number of Cabo Verdean colonial functionaries in the territory, including Aristides Pereira, a post office telegrapher, and Abilio Duarte, a bank official: both would become his close comrades in clandestine anticolonial activities. Cabral also knew some of the high-ranking Cabo Verdean officials who, suspecting his political aims, advised him to refrain from "matters" that would jeopardize his prestigious "career as an engineer." And Cabral would be reminded that, like them, he too was "Portuguese." He promptly dismissed these diehard colonialists as a lost cause, noting "there is no cure."[13]

Cabral got to know some of the Guinean nationalists like Rafael Barbosa, Fernando Fortes, and Elisée Turpin, future founding members of the African Independence Party (PAI), which later became the PAIGC. His associates also included some of the metropolitan Portuguese he broadly described as "the human instruments of the state." Among them were a few political exiles, including the pharmacist Sofia Pomba Guerra, the first antifascist woman activist imprisoned in Mozambique, in 1949, for attempting to establish a cell of the Portuguese Communist Party.[14] Released a year later, Sofia ended up in Bissau, where she opened a pharmacy and taught high school English at the same time as she recycled French and Portuguese communist literature to some of the local nationalists. She would introduce Aristides Pereira and other Cabo Verdean and Guinean activists to Cabral. Her pharmacy assistant Osvaldo Vieira would become a famous guerrilla commander in the PAIGC.

Importantly, Cabral needed to familiarize himself with the rural population that bore the brunt of colonial exploitation. His big break came almost a year later, when he was appointed by Governor Diogo Mello e Alvim to conduct an agricultural census, the first of its kind in not only Portuguese Guinea but the entire Portuguese empire in Africa. The survey was commissioned by the Ministry of Overseas Provinces in August 1953, in fulfillment of Portugal's commitment to the United Nations Food and Agriculture Organization six years earlier. For Cabral, it meant extensive travel and the opportunity to learn at first hand the realities of Portuguese colonial rule as experienced by the overwhelming majority of the people, knowledge of which was vital for a successful mobilization for anticolonial struggle.

From the onset, Cabral the agronomist and research director sought to invigorate the Pessubé agricultural station he had found in a state of "lethargy and abandonment" with activities that would address "the need for the existence of an agricultural experimental post whose objective should be the improvement of agriculture."[15] In an undisguised criticism of what had hitherto been the use of the station for the benefit of the Portuguese colonizers and their collaborating colonial elites, he insisted that Pessubé should not serve as the "granja of the State . . . to satisfy the vegetable and fruit needs of some inhabitants of the capital." Consequently, he urged that the research and experimental dimension of the station should be "scientifically oriented, in order to achieve immediate practical results that serve the progress of land and man." To test the seriousness of the colonial authorities, Cabral boldly challenged his superiors "to create the indispensable conditions for a real and useful activity" of the agricultural station—otherwise, he argued, "it is not worth nourishing any longer its fictitious existence." Methodical in approach and praxis, he created a *Boletim informativo* (Information bulletin) "to enunciate the works realized or in progress, as well as the difficulties encountered, the defeats suffered or the victories achieved."[16]

Agriculture was the base of the economy of Portuguese Guinea. The colonial economy was essentially a peasant economy, despite attempts during the early years of the *pax lusitana* to create a plantation economy. The remarkable expansion of commodity production (of peanuts, palm kernels, rubber, and rice) for export was achieved without any fundamental dislocation of indigenous institutions, without any major technological innovations, and without significant expropriation of land or displacement of the peasantry. In particular, the colonized Guineans were spared the brutal enforcement of harsh labor codes notorious in Angola, Mozambique, and São Tome and Príncipe. While the peasants engaged in the cultivation and gathering of export commodities were motivated by the obligation to pay colonial taxes, they were also driven by the need to acquire money to purchase goods and fulfill certain social obligations. Cabral's insistence that the raison d'être of the Pessubé station should be "the improvement and the progress of the Guinean economy" was also recognition of this colonial reality.

The census operations started on 22 September 1953, with Cabral using a sampling method for the survey and applying his scientific methodology of "studying, measuring and inquiring." With his wife Maria Helena (forestry engineer and codirector) and a team of about fifteen census takers trained by him, Cabral spent seven months crisscrossing the mainland and the offshore Bijagós archipelago to gather relevant information about land usage, crop cultivation, and soil conditions, among other tasks. Covering some 60,000 kilometers of travel to visit 356 settlements in 41 districts of the 11 administrative divisions of the territory, the census team surveyed 2,248 peasant family holdings (out of a total of 85,478). Completed in April 1954, the collected data was analyzed and the final report submitted to the governor in December that year. Cabral acknowledged "the understanding and good will manifested by the native farmers, whose civility greatly facilitated the surveys." Acknowledgement of the collaboration of the "uncivilized natives" was most unusual in the publications of colonial officials in Portuguese Guinea. Such gesture reflected Cabral's humanistic values.

Conducting the agricultural census enabled Cabral to gain important knowledge about the essential nature of the colonial economy and the people whose lives and livelihoods depended on it. It was valuable information that showed the exact locus and importance of the various groups in the colonial economy. The landmark study also provided strategic information to the colonial authorities, whose very presence was predicated on the thorough exploitation of the natural and human resources of the territory. Three decades earlier, Governor Velez Caroço blatantly stated that Portugal "should not try to develop Guinea simply to satisfy her own need," but, instead, should "ensure that Guinea . . . will be contributing with her quota to the wellbeing of the metropole."[17]

Cabral's landmark study of the agricultural profile of Portuguese Guinea was published in 1956, two years after its completion, in the *Boletim cultural da Guiné Portuguesa*, the journal of the Portuguese Guinea Studies Center, the executive commission of which he was a member. Besides his key involvement in conducting the census, Cabral also published ten articles on agronomy and related themes in the *Boletim* and the *Ecos da Guiné*. Altogether, within a decade of his first publication on rainfall in Cabo Verde in 1949, his published writings on agronomy and agriculture totaled about sixty works. Meanwhile, five months after completing the agricultural census, Cabral participated in an international conference on the peanut crop in Bambey, Senegal, where he presented two papers on the cultivation of this important West African export commodity.

The 1953 agricultural profile of Portuguese Guinea delineated by Cabral showed that the production of food crops, principally rice, occupied 76 percent of land use, while export crops, mainly peanuts, covered 23 percent of the total of 410,801 hectares, or 12 percent of the surface area of the colony. The coastal Balantas and Manjacos were responsible for 73 percent of the annual production of 100,000 tons of rice, while the Fulas and Mandinkas of the interior accounted for 66 percent of the annual cultivation of 64,000 tons of peanuts. Significantly, Cabral stressed the importance of rice cultivation for the food security and wellbeing of the indigenous population, as opposed to production of peanuts, which caused soil degradation and undermined traditional farming.

Cabral faced formidable challenges to implementing his hidden political agenda in a country where he was generally seen as yet another Cabo Verdean enabler of Portugal's harsh colonial rule. In the first place, the colonial context was such that the colonized "heathens" were naturally suspicious of colonial officials. They had learnt that questions about land use, livelihoods, and livestock could have serious implications—such as the obligation to pay taxes and submit to forced labor. Since the majority of the *chefes de posto*, the middle-level colonial officials in closest contact with the colonized, were Cabo Verdeans, Cabral faced the challenge of overcoming the almost automatic distrust the "uncivilized natives" had of the people they viewed as the colonizers. As the frontline operators of the native-rule system, these officials were often local tyrants. Their almost absolute powers meant direct and regular interference with the daily lives of the subjugated through the use of pliable *regulos* (local chiefs) and zealous *cipaios* (native administrative policemen). Defiance invariably met with summary corporal punishment through whippings and beatings. The *palmatoria*, a wooden paddle with holes to suck in flesh and make the beating more damaging, and the *chicote*, the hippo-hide whip, were favorite tools of correction.

Cabral witnessed several instances of colonial abuse while conducting the agricultural census. For example, in May 1953, while on the Bijagós island of Orango Grande, he found himself forced to stop the beating of an uncooperative elderly woman. Expressing his abhorrence of violence, he later manifested solidarity with the defiant victims who, "wounded in their human dignity, deprived of any legal personality," seized every opportunity "to manifest their non-acceptance of, aversion for and resistance to the Portuguese presence in Guinea."[18] Three months earlier, Cabral had been filled with indignation at the colonial bent for violence that resulted in the Batepá Massacre (3 February 1953) on the island of São Tomé, when hundreds of indigenous inhabitants were killed for refusing to be recruited as cacao plantation contract workers.

While the social dimension of agricultural production in Portuguese Guinea greatly concerned Cabral, the raising of political consciousness and mobilization for emancipatory politics was in fact his major preoccupation. Agronomy fulfilled a professional need, but politics was in fact the stronger passion. As he later pointed out, his return to his *terra natal* was "not by chance"; rather, "everything had been calculated." Acceptance of a position as second-class agronomist was a choice based on a commitment "to follow a calculation, the idea of doing something, to make a contribution to arousing the people for struggle against the Portuguese."[19]

In an attempt to safely navigate the dangerous colonial terrain and initiate the process of "conscientization," Cabral tried to form a sports and recreation club exclusively for the "sons of Guinea," irrespective of their legal status as "civilized" or "uncivilized." As a soccer enthusiast, he knew the game's capacity to bolster self-confidence, nurture collaboration, and foster camaraderie, which he considered critical factors of political mobilization. The PIDE was quick to perceive the fundamental purpose of Cabral's proposed club: "To launch the bases of an organization of natives, binding them in the same faith and the same destinies."[20] Not surprisingly, when the statutes of the club were submitted for approval, the colonial authorities promptly rejected them.

Although Cabral failed to create a soccer club, he would later use the game as a teaching aid to illustrate the importance of "unity and struggle." Using as illustration a soccer team that would comprise significant diversity—"different temperaments, often different education, some cannot read or write . . . different religion"—he underscored the critical cooperation and teamwork needed to "act together to score goals." Without unity of purpose, he insisted, there is no soccer team. The armed struggle was thus analogous to a soccer match between the colonizer and the colonized, and

PAIGC as the "national team" had to win by solid unity and relentless struggle.[21]

Cabral hastily left Portuguese Guinea with his wife and two-year-old daughter on 18 March 1955, in a medical evacuation for a serious bout of malaria. Shortly before his illness, he had a meeting with the discontented Governor Diogo Mello e Alvim, who warned him to "be careful" and "quit subversive activities, because this can cause you many setbacks." The governor knew about the "group with a cultural facade" he had formed, besides seeking "to get mixed up in politics" while conducting agricultural surveys in the rural areas. Cabral was ominously warned to "be careful."[22]

While in Lisbon, Cabral was prescribed a two-month period of convalescence that was later extended for another two months. His expected return to Bissau three days after the expiration of his recovery period did not happen because his contract with the Overseas Ministry was ended by "mutual consent" in July but this only became official on 7 September 1955.[23] Thus, Cabral was never expelled or temporarily exiled from Portuguese Guinea, although the prospects for his return in whatever capacity were not good. A report on his activities during the three years he spent there had been sent to the PIDE in Lisbon, highlighting his anticolonial posture, his "exaltation of the priority of the rights of the natives" and the belief that he "intended and succeeded, together with other natives, in the foundation of the Sports and Recreation Association of Bissau."[24] He was now under closer surveillance.

Now based in Lisbon, Cabral busied himself for the next five years with consultancy work in Portugal and Angola. A close collaborator of Cabral in numerous field studies in Angola was his former ISA professor Ário Lobo de Azevedo, who commended him for his "solid intelligence" and for having been "an applied student, conscientious and honest."[25]

Cabral's first consultancy work in Angola was for the Sociedade Agrícola do Cassequel, a six-month assignment to map the soils of the Catumbelo valley. A day after his arrival in the capital Luanda, on 29 August 1955, he wrote a letter to his wife scathingly criticizing the Portuguese colonial presence. Astonished by "the most miserable things that one can imagine regarding the colonial environment," Cabral described a city where the "poor natives" lived "deplorably" and "the taxi drivers, the servants in the hotels, restaurants, and cafes, etc." were "all Europeans," with very few salaried jobs left for the Africans. He denounced the "misery of all kinds" and "the dirtiest of racism," which he found "nauseating." But he remained sanguine about the prospects for transformative changes, "for the redemption on Earth of these beings who vegetate here."[26]

Between 1955 and 1959, Cabral conducted numerous field studies in Angola for other entities including the Companhia de Açúcar de Angola and the Companhia Angolana de Agricultura. While the consultancy work enriched his professional life, his face-to-face encounter with the abject conditions of the majority of Angolans bolstered his commitment to anticolonial struggle.

In contact with local Angolan nationalists, including Viriato da Cruz, Cabral collaborated in the clandestine founding in Luanda of the Party of the Unified Struggle of the Africans of Angola (PLUAA) in November 1956. The manifesto of the PLUAA declared that "Portuguese colonialism will not fall without struggle" and exhorted Angolan nationalists to form a united front of "all the anti-imperialist forces of Angola, without regard to political colors, the social situation of individuals, religious beliefs, and philosophical tendencies of individuals," behind "the broadest popular movement for the liberation of Angola."[27] This became the origin of the Popular Movement for the Liberation of Angola (MPLA) that emerged as an operational liberation movement in 1960.

Cabral was also in contact with the Guinean and Cabo Verdean nationalists he left in Portuguese Guinea, especially his brother Luís and Aristides Pereira. The official narrative of the PAIGC maintains that, while Cabral was visiting his mother and siblings in Bissau, he cofounded its predecessor, the PAI, together with Aristides Pereira, Fernando Fortes, Rafael Barbosa, Elisée Turpin, and his brother Luís, on 19 September 1956. The Bissau-Guinean historian Julião Soares Sousa, among others, contests the presence of Cabral in Bissau in 1956, and his participation in the creation of the PAI, for lack of corroborating evidence.[28] On the other hand, Mário de Andrade has noted that, since the existence of the PAI was a closely guarded secret, "one would find no *written* trace of the date of its appearance inside or outside the frontiers of Guiné and Cape Verde" (emphasis in original).[29] Since the creation of an anticolonial movement in a colony ruled by a repressive colonial regime can only be done with the strictest secrecy, it is not implausible that Cabral could have been in Portuguese Guinea and clandestinely moved around to evade the surveillance of the PIDE. With the PAI apparently founded exactly a week after Cabral's thirty-second birthday, it is highly probable that he was in Bissau not least to visit and celebrate his birthday with his mother and siblings. Although on the watch list of the PIDE, he was nevertheless free to travel and had the financial means to do so.

Cabral was adept in eluding arrest by the tightening dragnet of the PIDE. Since his student days in Lisbon, he had always been hyperalert and sagacious compared to his closest comrades who ended up in jail. With the menacing words of Governor Mello e Alvin still fresh in his mind, Cabral had to be extremely cautious. Already in 1954, there were five PIDE agents in Bissau building a network of local informants. But even before the arrival of the notorious secret police, the inhabitants of the territory were under the watchful eyes of the brutal Public Security Police (PSP) and the hated *cipaios*. Recalling this period, Aristides Pereira underscored the climate of suspicion and mistrust that hung over Bissau when he was part of a small group of nationalists, some of whom he never met: "I knew that there were more people but never saw them. For example, I knew of Rafael Barbosa, but we never saw each other. It was a special situation, there was a sense of much mistrust in the air that obliged us to be always suspicious."[30]

According to Pereira, it was in the nondescript house he shared with fellow Cabo Verdean Fernando Fortes at 9C Rua Guerra Junqueira, situated on an unpaved street in the center of Bissau, where, on the evening of 19 September 1956, Amílcar and his brother Luís, together with the Guinean nationalists Rafael Barbosa and Júlio Almeida, met with Pereira and Fortes and founded the PAI. For security reasons, no minutes of the meeting were taken. Cabral, the architect of the political project, spoke of the creation of the secret movement as based on the historical and cultural links between Portuguese Guinea and Cabo Verde and "the fact that we continue to be subjected to domination by the same colonial power." As committed nationalists, its members should be "capable of uniting our two peoples." Otherwise, Cabral insisted, "the colonialists would eventually take Guineans to fight against the Cabo Verdean in Cabo Verde," and, likewise, use the islanders to fight the people of his *terra natal*. He emphasized the need for a united front of all the peoples of the Portuguese African colonies. While liberation movements should be created, Cabral entreated, "we must also have a party, with its minimum program and its maximum program." He then moved that "we create an African party of independence and union of the peoples of Guiné and Cabo Verde, whose motto will be unity and struggle."[31]

Cabral was named the PAI's first secretary-general and Barbosa its first president. In 1960, the Partido Africano da Independência (African Independence Party) would become the Partido Africano da Independência da Guiné e Cabo Verde (African Party for the Independence of Guinea and Cabo Verde), in a calculated move to advertise its inherent binationalism.

Binationalism in Action

Passive Resistance and

War Preparations, 1956–63

The founding of the PAI coincided with the opening session of the First International Conference of Negro Writers and Artists (19–22 September 1956), cosponsored by the journal *Présence africaine* and held at the University of Paris–Sorbonne, with participants from the "Negro World" who included the Senegalese Alioune Diop, Léopold Sédar Senghor, and Cheikh Anta Diop, the Martinicans Aimé Césaire and Frantz Fanon, the Haitians Jacques Stephen Alexis and Jean Price-Mars, and the Americans William Fontaine and Richard Wright (W. E. B. Du Bois and Paul Robeson could not attend because they were not issued passports). The deliberations at the four-day landmark event denounced colonialism and urged the formulation of a strategy "to make our culture into a force of liberation and solidarity."[1] Declared by Diop as the "Bandung culturel" ("cultural Bandung," a reference to the previous year's conference of African and Asian states held in Bandung, Indonesia), it was followed three years later by the Second International Conference of Negro Writers and Artists in Rome, which declared that "political independence and economic freedom are the indispensable prerequisites of fecund cultural development . . . in the countries of black Africa in particular."[2] Although Cabral did not attend these two important gatherings, he was nevertheless kept abreast of their developments and outcomes by the point person of the emergent anticolonial front, Mário de Andrade, who had escaped the wide net of the PIDE in 1954 and enrolled as a social science student at the University of Paris–Sorbonne.

In April 1955, a month after Cabral was medically evacuated from Bissau, the Bandung Conference had commenced its weeklong deliberations—yet another favorable external factor in the struggle for decolonization, with its pledges of support to anticolonial forces in the two continents. Four months earlier, the radical British journalist and historian Basil Davidson had published his soon to be influential book, *The African Awakening*, which presented a scathing criticism of Portuguese colonial practices. Cabral would meet Davidson in London five years later and the two would develop an enduring friendship during which the Englishman would travel with the PAIGC guerrillas and report on their war against the Portuguese.

Cabral went to Paris in November 1957 to collaborate with de Andrade, dos Santos, da Cruz, and others in the creation of the National Liberation Movement of the Portuguese Colonies (MLNCP). Significantly, this occurred after the Fifth Congress of the Portuguese Communist Party (PCP) two months earlier, which passed a resolution declaring "unconditional acknowledgement of the right of the peoples of the colonies of Africa dominated by Portugal to immediate and complete independence."[3] Thereafter, "true support" could only be expected from the Portuguese communists, since the rest of "the so-called Portuguese Opposition" was "as colonialist as fascist Salazar."[4] The MLNCP was preceded by the Lisbon-based and PCP-influenced Democratic Movement of the Portuguese Colonies (MDCP), formed mainly by Angolan students led by Neto, de Andrade, and Lúcio Lara in 1954, when Cabral was still in Portuguese Guinea. In early 1958, these two movements merged to form the Anticolonialist Movement (MAC), which had sections in three European cities: Lisbon, headed by Cabral and Neto; Paris, overseen by de Andrade and dos Santos; and Frankfurt, coordinated by Lara and da Cruz. For the next two years, these African nationalists in Western Europe would be busy carrying out the MAC mission of denouncing Portuguese colonialism in Africa.

The leadership of the MAC, through the key position of de Andrade as the secretary of the influential Alioune Diop, had access to the prominent figures of the "Negro World"—in particular, the Negritude founders Senghor and Césaire, the stalwart Pan-Africanists Kwame Nkrumah and Ahmed Sékou Touré, and the revolutionary theorist and practitioner Frantz Fanon. It was Fanon who, in the name of the recently established Provisional Government of the Algerian Republic—the government-in-exile of the Algerian National Liberation Front (FLN) headed by Ahmed Ben Bella—offered to have eleven MPLA militants trained by FLN fighters. Cabral was entrusted with conveying the Algerian offer to the Angolan nationalists in Luanda, but upon his arrival there in September 1959 the leaders he had to contact had already been arrested by the PIDE.

Cabral participated in the All-African People's Conference, in Accra, in December 1958, and together with the other MAC delegates made presentations on the nature of Portuguese colonialism. He appealed for material support of "our brothers in the interior facing the greatest obstacles," who needed "to feel supported." With the favorable outcome of the landmark conference whose host, Kwame Nkrumah, promised political and diplomatic support, Cabral concluded that "in Accra, things went very well."[5] And after pledging "some money, although little," as his personal contribution to the operating expenses of the MAC, Cabral cautioned his comrades to remain alert in the face of the tightening vigilance of the PIDE, confiding, "I don't know up to what point I am being watched."[6] A year later, following the massacre of striking dockworkers at the port of Pindjiguiti in Bissau, his name was high up in the most-wanted list of the PIDE.

The brutal shootings on 3 August 1959 of the Pindjiguiti stevedores and merchant sailors who refused to return to work without a satisfactory resolution of their demands for better salaries and working conditions marked yet another crucial turning point in the life of Cabral. In Bissau, a month after the bloody Pindjiguiti event he called "the most heinous crime," Cabral reported to his MAC comrades in Europe that "the slaughter" carried out by the colonial forces left "24 dead and 35 wounded, some gravely."[7] Later, a PAIGC narrative would indicate "50 dead and over 100 wounded,"[8] while the colonial authorities maintained that it was "nine dead and 14 wounded."[9] Yet, in spite of the discrepancy, the Pindjiguiti Massacre became as decisively shattering for the Guinean nationalists as the Boston Massacre of 1770, with five dead and six wounded, was for the American patriots. Both these incidents were quickly used as effective political propaganda to ignite anticolonial fervor. Amílcar Cabral secretly met with the PAI leadership on 19 September 1959 and together they vowed to take revenge for the massacre: "We swore in silence to avenge our martyrs, the first sacrifices for the liberation of our country."[10]

The Pindjiguiti Massacre led to the jettisoning of the hitherto nonviolent strategy of the PAI. It seemed obvious that the Portuguese colonizers were not only uninterested in a dialogue on decolonization, but manifestly hostile to the very idea of their departure from Africa. Cabral and the PAI leadership thus had no problem reaching the conclusion that liberation from Portuguese colonial domination could only be achieved

The member movements committed to refrain from taking unilateral actions that could significantly compromise "our common struggle against our common enemy, Portuguese colonialism."

Cabral left Tunis for London, and his trip to the capital of the world's largest colonial power was the beginning of a sustained diplomatic offensive to garner international support. Notwithstanding its status as an imperialist power, Great Britain had a long tradition of liberalism that constitutionally enshrined fundamental freedoms which, since the nineteenth century, had attracted exiles of various ideological persuasions from all corners of the world. For more than a decade since the late 1940s, London was abuzz with anticolonial activities, among many other political agitations. With the state visit of Portuguese president Francisco Craveiro Lopes in October 1955, reciprocated by Queen Elizabeth two years later, Cabral was intent on exposing the nature of Portugal's colonial rule in Africa.

Cabral's task was made easier by the contacts established with the Committee of African Organizations run by anticolonial African activists and supported by civil society and political organizations including the Movement for Colonial Freedom, Christian Action, and the Communist Party of Great Britain, besides individual members of the Labor Party, the Liberal Party, and the labor unions. Basil Davidson was among the numerous Britons who formed the critical mass of progressives that actively supported the anti-imperialist and anticolonial struggles, especially in Africa. Thus, when Cabral arrived in London, the prevailing environment was sufficiently enabling for him to publish, under the pseudonym of Abel Djassi, a pamphlet titled *The Facts about Portugal's African Colonies*, with an introduction by Davidson.

Prefaced by the denunciation that there were eleven million Africans under an oppressive fascist colonial system that made them "live on a sub-human standard—little or no better than serfs in their own country," Cabral stated unequivocally the demands of his fellow African nationalists.[18]

> We, the Africans of the Portuguese colonies . . .
> want Portugal to respect and rigidly adhere to the
> obligations set out in the UN Charter. We demand
> that Portugal should follow the example of Britain,
> France, and Belgium in recognizing the right of the
> peoples she dominates to self-determination and
> independence.

Aiming at sensitizing the British government and public to put pressure on the Lisbon regime, however unlikely that might have been, Cabral further pointed out that the nationalist movements of the Portuguese colonies wanted "to re-establish the human dignity of Africans, their freedom, and the right to determine their own future," objectives to be achieved through "peaceful means." However, he and his fellow nationalist leaders were under no illusion, since they were sure that "Portugal intends to use violence to defend her interests," against which they would be ready "to answer with violence." The psychological preparedness of Cabral and his fellow nationalist leaders for armed liberation struggle was thus made explicit, and he would soon head to the Republic of Guinea to prepare for the seemingly inevitable war.

While in Paris en route to Conakry, Cabral wrote to his wife urging her to hasten her definitive departure from Portugal, together with their daughter, to France, where they would wait for their imminent voyage to Conakry. She would improve her French in Paris in preparation for life in Francophone Guinea-Conakry. With the family travel arrangements made, he left for Dakar on 5 May 1960, arriving there on the same day as his brother Luís, who had escaped imminent arrest in Bissau by the PIDE. Married two years earlier to Lucette Andrade, a Senegalese of Cabo Verdean parents, Luís would get a job as a bookkeeper for the Shell Oil Company. He would also become the point person for the PAI in the capital of the newly independent Senegal.

Cabral arrived in Conakry in mid-May to face enormous challenges that would test his personal integrity, intellectual capacity, and leadership qualities. Besides the immediate diplomatic, organizational, and logistical problems he had to deal with in the process of building a solid foundation for the headquarters of the PAI and a base for launching the armed struggle, he quickly found himself embroiled in the "Battle of Conakry."

This was a sustained four-year campaign (1960–63) waged by his political foes from the rival nationalist organizations that were forced to abandon Bissau following the Pindjiguiti Massacre of 3 August 1959. The activists of the short-lived Movement for the National Independence of Portuguese Guinea (MING), founded clandestinely in Bissau in the mid-1950s by Cabral and others, variously went on to create the PAI, the Liberation Movement of Guinea (MLG), and the Liberation Movement of Guinea and Cabo Verde (MLGCV). Factionalism, fueled by personality clashes, ideological differences, and narrow nationalism, was rife within these and other emergent groups. The PAI, predominantly led by nationalists of Cabo Verdean descent, were opportunistically targeted because of the role of the "Portuguese Cabo Verdeans" in the colonial domination of Portuguese Guinea. Cabral, with legitimate birthright claims in both Portuguese Guinea and Cabo Verde, was constantly suspected by the more petty patriots of both countries. The sometimes vicious campaigns of delegitimization questioned not his credentials and capacity but his racial identity.

Parallel to the hostility toward "the Cabo Verdeans" in Conakry was the "Battle of Dakar," wherein the PAIGC's rival organizations launched an equally intense campaign of discrediting and delegitimization. Among the most vocal opponents of Cabral and his party was the Liberation Movement of Guinea–Dakar (MLG-Dakar), founded in Dakar in 1960 by François Kankoila Mendy, which later affiliated with the Front for Struggle for the National Independence of Guinea (FLING), also created in Dakar (3 August 1962). The FLING was an umbrella organization of some seven Bissau-Guinean nationalist groups that included the MLG-Dakar, the Union of the Populations of So-Called Portuguese Guinea (UPGP) headed by Henry Labéry, and the Union of the Natives of Portuguese Guinea (UNGP) led by Benjamin Pinto Bull. Under the leadership of Labéry, the FLING coalition became the most formidable rival of the PAIGC. However, while the MLG-Dakar was the only militarily active member of the FLING, launching attacks against Portuguese posts in the northern border towns of Susana, Varela, São Domingos, and Bigene in 1961 and 1962 with ineffectual outcomes, the anti-PAIGC coalition would be notable for its advocacy of a nonviolent negotiated path to independence. One of its leaders, Benjamin Pinto Bull, would be delegated in July 1963 to meet with Salazar, who refused to discuss the independence of any "overseas province."

Meanwhile, Cabral responded to the concerted campaigns of delegitimization by rising above the personal attacks and striving to undermine the collaborationist activities of his rivals through the formation of anticolonial coalitions like the United Liberation Front (FUL), created in Dakar in July 1961 and comprising several nationalist organizations, including Mendy's MLG-Dakar. The FUL collapsed a year later due to factionalist conflicts and hostility toward Cabo Verdeans. Ironically, the efforts to discredit Cabral's Bissau-Guinean origins were rendered ridiculous by the fact that Mendy and Labéry, his staunchest adversaries, were both born in Senegal, each with one parent who was not of Bissau-Guinean origins. Importantly, within the PAIGC, the anti–Cabo Verdean sentiment was also present and vulnerable to fatal exploitation.

With the collapse of the FUL in 1962, Cabral concentrated his energy on preparations to launch an effective long-term strategy of armed struggle at the political, diplomatic, and military levels. The Angolan uprisings in February 1961 initiated the war against the Portuguese colonial empire in Africa. The Estado Novo regime intuitively viewed the Angolan insurrection as an insult to the sovereignty of the nation, much-lauded as "pluricontinental" and "pluriracial." The MLG-Dakar attacks in northern Portuguese Guinea exacerbated the perceived affront. These "offenses" would turn into humiliations when recently independent Dahomey (present-day Benin) seized the former Portuguese slave-trading port of São João Baptista de Ajudá in August 1961. Four months later, the forceful annexation of the Portuguese enclaves of Goa, Damão, and Diu by India would augment Lisbon's embarrassment. The abrupt ending of over 450 years of Portugal's sovereignty in the territories referred to as the Estado da India (State of India) exploded the myth of a timeless and inviolable empire.

The PAIGC's mobilization campaigns started in earnest following the training of the mobilizers at

Cabral's house in the Minière neighborhood of Conakry soon after his installation in the Guinean capital, where his wife and daughter had joined him shortly after his arrival. The Cabrals stayed together only briefly. Expecting their second child, Maria Helena, who had been employed as a teacher in a local high school, moved with Iva to Rabat, Morocco, for better medical attention during the birth of Ana Luísa, born in 1962. The prolonged separation ended in divorce in 1966. At the end of that year, Cabral married Ana Maria Voss de Sá, a native of Canchungo, Portuguese Guinea, who was a student activist and an affiliate of the House of Students of the Empire (CEI) and the Center for African Studies (CEA) in Lisbon, where they became acquainted. A militant of the PAIGC, Ana Maria underwent university training in Czechoslovakia. In 1969, the couple had a daughter, N'Dira Abel.

Initially, the Cabrals' house in Conakry was transformed into a makeshift school, with Amílcar largely responsible for program content and the few instructors including his wife Maria Helena, his brother Luís, sister-in-law Lucette, and close associate Aristides Pereira. The majority of the students, mostly poor, illiterate young men and women from the countryside, went through an intense literacy program, while the literate urban recruits were trained in persuasive techniques informed by lectures on geography, nationalist history and politics, the principles of the PAIGC, and the aims and objectives of the upcoming armed struggle.

Later, Cabral would secure financial support to acquire a Lar dos Combatentes (Home of the Fighters) situated in the Bonfi neighborhood of Conakry, where the party's young mobilizers were trained and temporarily lodged. This was followed by the establishment of an Escola Piloto (Pilot School), a boarding school opened in 1965 to provide for the education of the children of militants and combatants. The first director of the school was Maria da Luz "Lilica" Boal, a Cabo Verdean from the island of Santiago who, as a politically active history and philosophy student in Lisbon, abandoned her studies in 1961 and left with her Angolan husband, a medical doctor, to join the PAIGC in Conakry. Among the first group of students enrolled in the Pilot School was Florentino "Flora" Gomes, who went on to become a world-renowned filmmaker.

Before his arrest on 13 March 1962, Rafael Barbosa, the president of the PAIGC who stayed in Bissau operating under the pseudonym of Zain Lopes, sent to Conakry some five hundred young city dwellers, most of them belonging to the déclassé category identified by Cabral as recently arrived rural-urban migrants with connections to "petty bourgeois" and wage earners. The usefulness of this group for the mobilization campaigns was its unbroken connection with the rural world. Of the other city dwellers without such close connection with the countryside, who often had at least primary school education, some would go on to hold key positions in the leadership of the PAIGC, including Francisco

"Tchico Te" Mendes, João Bernardo Vieira, Domingos Ramos, Carmen Pereira, and Francisca Pereira. About one thousand party militants were trained at the political school in Conakry.

The political mobilization campaigns launched by Cabral from Conakry were well planned. Profiting from the harsh lived experiences of the rural population, the trained mobilizers initially descended on the southern and northern regions of Portuguese Guinea, covering village by village, asking questions aimed at heightening consciousness, provoking outrage, and invoking rebelliousness. The rehearsed dialogue avoided, as Cabral insisted, giving the peasants the impression that the mobilizers were "strangers who had come to teach them lessons." Instead, they had to behave like they were there to learn. Listening empathetically in order to gain the confidence of the villagers, the questions mobilizers posed were meant to allow the villagers themselves to reach the conclusion "that there is exploitation." Using "a direct language that all can understand," the mobilizers asked questions including the following:

> What is the situation? Did you pay taxes? Did your
> father pay taxes? What have you seen from those taxes?
> How much do you get for your groundnuts? . . . How
> much sweat has it cost your family? Which of you
> have been imprisoned? You are going to work on road
> construction: who gives you the tools? You bring the
> tools. Who provides your meals? You provide your

meals? But who walks on the road? Who has a car?
And your daughter who was raped?—are you happy
about that?[19]

Cabral's political mobilization strategy was largely successful, in spite of the life-threatening dangers that its deployment entailed. The challenges included the noncooperation of some villagers, especially those from the more stratified Fula, Mandinka, and Manjaco societies, where most of the traditional chiefs collaborated with the Portuguese and their loyal followers became informers, resulting in the arrest, torture, and killing of PAIGC mobilizers. On the other hand, the brutal repressions by the colonial authorities obliged some villagers to shun the mobilizers for security reasons: "You come here telling us very beautiful things, but you are not capable of defending us."[20] Nevertheless, the mobilization drive had to run its course. Cabral knew that its success ultimately rested on the internalization by his mobilizers of the imperative to "never confuse what they have in their heads with reality," that the point of departure must always be "from the reality of our land—to be realists." Sophisticated rhetoric about "colonial exploitation" and exhortatory slogans like "land to the landless," while effective in the settler colonies of Angola and Mozambique, had little resonance in Portuguese Guinea. Cabral knew that winning the hearts and minds of an oppressed people and maintaining their active support for armed struggle must be contingent on the recognition and ready acceptance of their fundamental expectations. Thus, he exhorted both mobilizers and combatants:

> Always remember that the people are not fighting for ideas, nor for what is in men's minds. The people fight and accept the sacrifices demanded by the struggle in order to gain material advantages, to live better and in peace, to benefit from progress, and for the better future of their children. National liberation, the struggle against colonialism, the construction of peace, progress and independence are hollow words devoid of any significance unless they can be translated into a real improvement of living conditions.[21]

The war preparations conducted by Cabral from Conakry also entailed military training abroad for the liberation fighters, particularly in the communist countries of the People's Republic of China (PRC), the USSR, and Cuba. The first batch of ten young fighters departed for the PRC in February 1961 to train at the Nanjing Military Academy. They included João Bernardo "Nino" Vieira, Osvaldo Vieira, Domingos Ramos, Francisco "Tchico Te" Mendes, Constantino Teixeira, and Vitorino da Costa. They would return to conduct the armed struggle and become celebrated national heroes. In the context of the intense Sino-Soviet rivalry, this significant achievement was testimony to Cabral's great diplomatic skill and strength of character. He also succeeded in obtaining military assistance from African countries including Ghana, Morocco, and Algeria—the first to supply guns and ammunition to the PAIGC.

The Republic of Guinea, the host country, provided not only a safe haven for Cabral and his comrades to train the party's cadres, mobilizers, and school-age children, but also the use of its military training facilities for its fighters, besides rendering vital political and diplomatic support. Conakry was the propitious place where Cabral was able to forge enduring relations with the Chinese, Soviets, and Cubans, among others, relations that quickly translated into weapons, military training, and technical advisors. The remarkable achievements during this preparatory phase of the armed struggle were largely due to the goodwill and confidence bestowed on Cabral by President Sékou Touré. After skillfully outmaneuvering his most powerful rivals in Conakry, Cabral developed strong relations with Sékou Touré, facilitated by shared ideological outlooks.

Cabral was aware of the strategies and lessons of the successful post-1945 anti-imperialist and anticolonial wars, which he acknowledged "served us as a basis of general experience for our own struggle." But he was against "blindly applying the experience of others." In determining the tactics for the armed struggle, he noted, "we had to take into account the geographical, historical, economic, and social conditions of our own country."[22] Consequently, the war strategy had to be based on rural insurgency and sustained by a politically mobilized peasantry. It would be a "struggle of the people, by the people, for the people."[23] It would aim at not only destroying Portuguese military installations but also dislocating the colonial economy and, within the liberated areas, establishing structures and institutions for political governance, economic sustainability, and social cohesion. Importantly, it would also address the basic needs of the inhabitants to secure their sustained support. Furthermore, he made a distinction between "the struggle against imperialism" and "struggling for national liberation," associating the former with "national independence" and the latter, in which he and his comrades were engaged, with the imperative to go beyond "flag independence" and "struggle against neo-colonialism."[24]

In the context of the Cold War, Cabral envisaged "only two possible paths for an independent nation: to return to imperialist domination (neo-colonialism, capitalism, state capitalism), or to take the way of socialism."[25] The ideological orientation of the PAIGC, as presented by Cabral, was socialist in character, being very much influenced by the Marxist perspective. The program of the PAIGC devised largely by Cabral incorporated both short-term and long-tern goals, with the more urgent objectives including the achievement of political independence and those of a longer timeframe involving economic and social transformations and the unification of his two countries of birth and ancestry.

6

Conducting Armed Struggle

The Liberation of Portuguese Guinea, 1963–73

On 3 August 1961, the second anniversary of the Pindji-guiti Massacre, Cabral announced the PAIGC's passage "from the phase of political struggle to that of national insurrection, to direct action against the colonial forces." Taking stock of the high human cost of passive resistance, he declared that the struggle against the *Tugas* was no longer a question of whether it should be armed or unarmed, since the enemy "is always armed."[1] The critical question, he argued, was whether the Portuguese colonizers should continue to have the monopoly of the gun or "we get arms to shoot them also." Invoking the lesson of the 1959 massacre, he concluded, "This is the truth about the truth . . . as they showed us on the quay of Pindjiguiti."[2]

But Cabral was no bloodthirsty *terrorista* on a mission of vengeful retribution, as he would be portrayed by Portuguese propaganda. He abhorred violence, which he only advocated as a last resort after several appeals to the Estado Novo for a peaceful path to independence.

He insisted on the use of "selective violence" that avoided "collateral damage" and exhorted his fighters to remember that the enemy was "Portuguese colonialism, represented by the colonial-fascist government of Portugal," and not the Portuguese people.[3] Therefore, the "direct action" should be "aimed only at the forces of repression (army, police and colonial agents)."[4]

Cabral continued with the political mobilization of the rural population for another six months. At the same time, he ordered a sabotage campaign involving the downing of telephone and telegraph lines and the destruction of bridges and roads in the southern region of Quinara. But he was still ready to negotiate independence with the Lisbon authorities. Addressing the UN Special Committee on Territories under Portuguese Administration meeting in Conakry held 5–7 June 1962, he declared that "the PAIGC still is and always has been desirous of reaching a peaceful solution of the conflict between them [the people of Guinea] and the government of Portugal."[5] Six months later, he traveled to New York and appeared before the UN Fourth Committee to reiterate his movement's readiness to negotiate: "On our part, we are ready for the contacts and for the negotiations, with or without intermediaries. We declare that we are still ready to negotiate in any place, including Portugal."[6]

But independence was not part of the lexicon of the Estado Novo. Portugal's geographic location and membership in NATO greatly favored the stubbornly intransigent position of the Salazar dictatorship. Situated in the westernmost part of Western Europe, the tiny Iberian country assumed a huge strategic importance in the defense architecture of the United States–led NATO. In particular, on her Atlantic islands of the Azores, the American base at Lajes not only monitored Soviet submarine movements in the Atlantic, but also served as a refueling stop for American military airlift operations to the Middle East and beyond. Washington's strategic priority became an important bargaining chip for the Lisbon authorities to obtain deadly weapons, including napalm and white phosphorous bombs, in order to sustain a brutal war in three African theaters for over a decade. "Everyone knows," Cabral derisively commented, "that Portugal does not make any aircraft, not even as toys for children."[7] Faced with a reality he and his comrades had to come to terms with, Cabral turned to the communist world to secure a steady supply of war material and supplies, particularly from the USSR, the PRC, Czechoslovakia, and Cuba. Thwarted in his numerous initiatives for a peaceful decolonization, Cabral and his comrades concentrated on "answering with violence the violence of the Portuguese colonialist forces and, by all the means possible, eliminating colonial domination from Guiné and Cabo Verde."[8]

Taking full advantage of the Cold War, Portugal dismissed the armed struggle as a communist orchestration emanating from "Moscow, Prague and Peking." A report by the International and State Defense Police

(PIDE) of 17 January 1963, submitted to the colonial authorities in Bissau six days before the launching of full-scale armed struggle by the PAIGC, warned about the danger of nationalist organizations that "receive orders and material support from the outside and are subordinated to international communism." It outlined the "subversive activities" of the PAIGC, whose militants were involved in "the rapid catechization of the masses" through widespread mobilization campaigns and engagements in "acts of terrorism."[9]

About a month before the PAIGC's transition to "direct action," the MLG-Dakar, led by François Kankoila Mendy, had staged a series of attacks on the small Portuguese garrison at São Domingos and the nearby resort towns of Varela and Susana. Governor António Augusto Peixoto Correia dismissed the insurgency as the actions of "armed bandits" who planned "to liberate Portuguese Guinea" but were opposed by the "indomitable will" of the colony's inhabitants, "who do not need this liberation."[10] Besides the five soldiers injured, numerous telephone lines cut, and several dwellings and government facilities set ablaze, the attacks also caused panic among the tiny white population in the colony, which hurriedly flocked to Bissau. The Portuguese were fearful of a rerun of the bloody uprising in northern Angola organized by Holden Roberto's Union of the Peoples of Angola (UPA) just four months earlier, which left a death toll of about a thousand Portuguese settlers indiscriminatingly massacred during the frenzied carnage that a despondent Cabral called "gratuitous violence." The swift and ferocious response of the colonial authorities and armed white civilians was equally gratuitous: "The greatest pleasure of certain whites is to kill blacks. When military trucks full of black prisoners arrive in Luanda, the white civilians shoot them down like dogs."[11]

With only 1,200 mostly native soldiers and no air force or navy in Portuguese Guinea in January 1961, the concerned Lisbon authorities quickly sent reinforcements that included a detachment of F-86 Sabre jet fighter planes provided to Portugal by the United States for NATO deployment in Europe. These were later complemented by American T-6 Texan light attack planes and West German–built Italian Fiat G-91 light attack fighter aircraft. By January 1963, the Portuguese military presence had swollen to 5,500 soldiers, including 311 marines and 354 air force personnel.

Although the attacks by the ill-trained MLG-Dakar fighters inaugurated the armed liberation struggle in Portuguese Guinea, they soon proved ineffective and unsustainable, being poorly armed and ineptly organized. Cabral promptly dismissed the attacks as hasty and adventurous. Nevertheless, Mendy's actions put some pressure on the PAIGC to operationalize its "direct action" program. However, Cabral's war preparations were not only inconclusive but still encountering serious challenges. Already in January 1962, the important task of securing war materiel had hit a serious snag when the Conakry-Guinean customs at the port of Conakry confiscated a concealed consignment of weapons and communications equipment sent from Morocco. Several PAIGC leaders were promptly arrested, including Aristides Pereira, Luís Cabral, Carlos Correia, and Armando Ramos. Cabral, who was attending the Third Afro-Asian Solidarity Conference in Tanzania, hastily returned to Conakry and skillfully negotiated the release of his comrades and the weapons. Most significantly, Cabral obtained official approval for the free importation of war supplies into the host country.

On 23 January 1963, under the banner of "unity and struggle," Cabral ordered his trained fighters to fire the first salvo of the war of national liberation. About twenty guerrillas led by Arafam Mané attacked the Portuguese garrison at Tite, in the Quinara region. The precursors to the "direct action" were the PIDE raids on the PAIGC office in Bissau and the homes of its activists, capturing, on 13 March 1962, the organization's president, Rafael Barbosa, and several of his comrades, together with important documents and a few weapons.[12] A curfew was expeditiously imposed on Bissau. Many of the captured nationalists, including Barbosa, would end up in the Tarrafal concentration camp in Santiago, Cabo Verde. Three months later, the colonial forces launched a brutal wave of repressions, which met with resistance. On 25 June, the PIDE reported that the Balantas in the southern border region of Tombali, "who have long been indoctrinated," had attacked the administrative town of Catió, destroyed a ferry in the town of Bedanda, and

Figure 1. Cabral the revolutionary theoretician: weaponizing theory and conducting war. Copyright, Bruna Polimeni (1971), Fondazione Lelio e Lisli Basso.

cut telephone lines. It was, the PIDE underscored, "the beginning of terrorist activities" in the south. Two days later, in the resistance to repression in the north of the country, a PIDE agent, Augusto Macias, was killed, and two of his colleagues and a police officer were injured. By the end of July, some two thousand nationalists were imprisoned by the PIDE, with two hundred and fifty of them sent to the Tarrafal concentration camp. But the resistance continued unabated.

The southern littoral region bordering northern Guinea-Conakry became the ideal part of the colony to intensify the armed struggle. As an experienced agronomist, Cabral knew very well its geography and topography, characterized by verdant vegetation with thick mangrove forests, abundant palm trees, and a network of waterways that include the rivers Geba, Grande, Corubal, Cacine, and their respective tributaries. The area was well suited for guerrilla insurgency.

As the repression escalated, Cabral ordered the intensification of political mobilization in the south, the impact of which was reflected in the PIDE report that the traditionally "chiefless" Balantas, predominantly rice farmers who had migrated to the area from the central and northern regions and formed the majority of its inhabitants, "continued to be catechized and advised to not work on the *bolhanas* [rice fields], with the justification that there will soon be war." The colonial forces descended heavily on the region and in the ensuing brutal repressions several PAIGC mobilizers were arrested, tortured, and some killed—among them, twenty-five-year-old Vitorino da Costa, recently returned from military training in the PRC. His decapitated head, like those of his comrades, was displayed on a spike to maximize the terrorization of the villagers.[13] But the "catechization of the masses"[14] continued unremittingly. The PIDE was now convinced that it was facing "a properly structured terrorist organization," trained in subversion and guerrilla warfare.[15]

The PAIGC dawn assault on the Tite garrison that formally opened the southern front was quickly followed by a series of actions, including attacks on military installations, ambushes, destruction of transport and communication infrastructure, and the capture, on 25 March 1963, of two commercial vessels at the port of

Cafine. The *Mirandela*, belonging to the Union Manufacturing Company (CUF) subsidiary Casa Gouveia,
and the *Arouca*, owned by Casa Brandão, were respectively captained by company employees José Ocante da
Silva and Joãozinho Lopes, survivors of the Pindjiguiti
Massacre. The captured ships were taken to the nearby
Guinea-Conakry port of Boké, with most of the crew
and numerous dockworkers onboard—recruits for
the armed liberation struggle. The vessels were later
taken to Conakry and used to transport combatants
and war material, thus becoming the first ships of the
PAIGC navy.

The effectiveness of Cabral's military strategy in six
months of full-scale war had, by the admission of the
Portuguese, resulted in the liberation of 15 percent of
the national territory, mostly in the south between the
rivers Geba and Corubal. He had outwitted the colonial
forces with a "centrifugal" war plan that caught them
by surprise, which he explained thus: "We opted for a
strategy we could call centrifugal: from the center to the
periphery."[16] The Portuguese, on the other hand, expecting the MLG-Dakar tactic of cross-border attacks
and withdrawal to safe havens in Senegal, had made
the strategic miscalculation of stationing their troops
in garrisons and fortified camps dotted along the borders. Cabral was now firmly establishing the credibility
of his liberation movement not only internally but also
internationally—especially among the member states
of the recently created Organization of African Unity

(OAU), which aimed "to eradicate all forms of colonialism from Africa," in pursuance of which it established the African Liberation Committee to coordinate political and military support of independence movements in the continent.

The courage and tenacity of the PAIGC fighters was most severely tested when they confronted the enormous Portuguese firepower on the contested strategic onshore island of Como, in Tombali region, in December 1963. Cabral had appointed twenty-four-year-old João Bernardo "Nino" Vieira, a recent graduate of the Nanjing Military Academy, as the military commander of the southern front. Codenamed "Marga," Nino Vieira commanded the PAIGC force that captured Como, prompting the Portuguese to launch Operation Trident on 15 January 1964 to reoccupy the island. Besides its strategic significance for the protection of the commercial hub of Catió, Como had also allowed the Portuguese a location from which to monitor PAIGC activities in the south and the flow of weapons from across the border. Determined to prevent any "rebellion contagion," the colonial authorities organized a massive counteroffensive that was closely watched by some of the Portuguese top brass sent to Bissau from the military high command in Lisbon. Comprising three thousand soldiers, of which two thousand were elite troops hurriedly dispatched from Angola, supported by the Portuguese Air Force (FAP), the task force descended on Como to dislodge a guerrilla force of about three hundred fighters. The local population of mainly Balanta rice farmers supported the guerrillas. Recognizing the importance of victory at this early stage of the armed struggle, Cabral instructed his fighters to defend the island against the tremendous odds they faced.

After seventy-five days of fierce fighting during which the FAP pounded the island with over three hundred and fifty heavy bombs, targeting not only guerrillas and civilians but also rice fields, the reoccupation attempt was abandoned, with contested counts for Portuguese casualties: nine dead and forty-seven injured according to the Portuguese command; "losses of 650 men" according to the PAIGC. The toll for the freedom fighters was calculated at seventy-six dead and fifteen injured. An FAP T-6 Texan plane was downed and six more combat aircraft hit. The Lisbon authorities promptly fired Governor Vasco Martins Rodrigues and the military commander. The new governor, General Arnaldo Schulz—who assumed both of the vacated positions—vowed that "Guinea will never cease to be Portuguese."

The victory at Como, achieved without the cover of the rainy season (ideal for guerrilla warfare) and against an unfavorable balance of firepower, not only demonstrated the military capability of Cabral's liberation movement, but also bolstered its credibility and boosted the confidence of the freedom fighters. The PAIGC had demonstrated its capacity to conquer and defend territory. A jubilant Cabral would underscore that Como and the liberated areas in the south were "from now on *definitely liberated*" (emphasis in the original).[17]

Cabral's fighters were also attacking the Portuguese in the north of the country, where another front was opened in July 1962. The PAIGC forces were under the command of Osvaldo Vieira (cousin of Nino Vieira), with an operational base at Morés in the legendary region of Oio, famous for centuries as a center of resistance against Portuguese imperial ambitions, and only finally "pacified" in 1913.

With initiative and momentum on the side of Cabral's fighters, the colonial forces were fighting a defensive war in which they were steadily losing ground. Absolving himself of responsibility for the ineffectiveness of the colonial forces, the dismissed Portuguese military commander, Colonel Fernando Louro de Sousa, blamed the lack of a strategy of "psychological action and social action" to win the population, "to gain their confidence," as a consequence of which "we now find ourselves in a situation of sending troops and more troops to repress the perhaps irrepressible."[18]

Meanwhile, notwithstanding the favorable developments unfolding in the raging battle of Como, all was not well with the prosecution of the armed struggle. At this early stage, a looming crisis had begun to seriously threaten the achievements of the PAIGC and the prestige of its leadership. Cabral noted that, after only a year of war, "the comrades began not to understand each other, each one on his own, each one abusing, making the abuses he likes in his area, not respecting anyone who goes there as his superior."[19] The chain of command was breaking up and discipline was in disarray. One such "superior" who was "disrespected" when he visited a liberated area (Quitafine) was Luís Cabral, who submitted a scathing report to his brother outlining the terrible behavior of some field commanders, which included "assassinations of men, women, even children, on the accusation of being witches." These acts provoked the "massive exodus of people seeking protection in other areas to escape the abuses and crimes committed."[20] Aristides Pereira, Cabral's deputy, confirmed the "crimes and abuses" committed by the "liberators" against the "liberated," who were increasingly disenchanted with and distrustful of the PAIGC and its leadership.

The successful attacks against the Portuguese colonial forces in the south had emboldened some ethnocentric guerrilla fighters to disobey orders to take the war to the eastern region largely inhabited by the Islamized Fulas. Cabral recounted the defiant cross-questioning by the rebellious guerrillas, mainly Balantas, which seriously undermined the objectives of the armed struggle and years of painstaking preparatory work: "Why should the Balanta go and help to liberate the Fula? Let the Fula do their own work."[21]

Cabral evidently underestimated the depth of ethnic animosity, notwithstanding his political education and mobilization campaigns that emphasized interethnic solidarity. Defiance of the PAIGC's rules of conduct and engagement was facilitated by the autonomy and isolation of field commanders, which is a consequence of the decentralized nature of guerrilla warfare. Ineffective control by the central command in Conakry also encouraged insubordination. During this initial phase of open conflict, Cabral, the multitasking leader, infrequently visited the battlefronts and liberated areas, spending most of his time in Conakry, on diplomatic missions, and at international conferences, to champion the cause of the armed struggle and mobilize vital political, military, and moral support—in addition to coordinating a united anticolonial front representing all the Portuguese African colonies. He would later admit that some of the military commanders "had become too autonomous," resulting in the emergence of "tendencies to self-centered isolation."[22] This unexpected outcome, unanticipated in the various scenarios he had elaborated for the training of guerrilla fighters in Conakry, presented a critical challenge for the PAIGC. In a crucial test of his leadership skills, Cabral had to act promptly and decisively to assert the legitimacy and authority of the liberation movement he led. Thus, the fighters attending the Cassacá Congress would be quickly disarmed and the accused military commanders summoned to appear and respond to charges made against them.

Initially planned as a seminar for the party cadres, Cabral convened what became the first congress of the PAIGC, held on 13–17 March 1964 at Cassacá, a liberated village in the south, as his brother Luís advised, "so that its impact would be greater among our people." Attended by over seventy party cadres, guerrilla fighters, military commanders, political leaders, and village delegates from the liberated areas, the Cassacá Congress addressed the growing political and military crisis, which seriously threatened the very existence of the liberation movement. Cabral astutely recognized that some of the "weaknesses and mistakes" that were "unexpectedly showing up" could become "dangerous for our Party and for our struggle."[23] Besides eroding the support base for the armed struggle, the indiscipline and "criminal behaviors" of the "freedom fighters" also undermined the PAIGC's core principle of civilian control of the military. Outraged by the "abominable crimes being committed in our names" and the resultant "considerable loss of support among the population," Cabral insisted on the precedence and preeminence of politics and accordingly condemned the militarism "which has caused some fighters and even some leaders to forget the fact that we are *armed militants* and not *militarists*" (emphasis in original).[24]

Cabral was dismayed by the cavalier attitude of some of his field commanders who showed up at Cassacá accompanied by several young "wives." One of the commanders even arrived with his *djidiu* (praise singer) extolling his warrior virtues! Among the other alleged crimes were thefts of PAIGC property. Inocêncio Kani, a naval commander and the future assassin of Cabral, was accused of selling a boat engine. The authority of the PAIGC had to be reasserted, discipline restored, and justice seen to be done.

After a lengthy trial, Cabral and the collective leadership moved swiftly to punish the guilty violators: those who were present were immediately apprehended while heavily armed soldiers were sent to arrest those who were absent. Those who resisted arrest, Cabral noted, "were liquidated."[25] Besides executions, the punishments also included demotions and imprisonments. The summary military justice, in the context of a war in its infancy, was deemed imperative. But Cabral would insist on the "rehabilitation" of those fighters found guilty of less serious crimes like theft—including Inocêncio Kani.

The immediate outcome of the Cassacá Congress was the establishment of political control over the military, with the creation of a seven-member War Council, headed by Cabral, as the highest civilian-dominated military organ of the liberation movement. The other members of the War Council included Aristides Pereira, Cabral's brother Luís, Nino Vieira, and Domingos Ramos. In addition to its principal responsibility for conducting the armed struggle, the council also dealt with specialized military training in areas like heavy artillery and antiaircraft weapons. The guerrilla force based on *bi-grupos* (two-group units of twenty to thirty fighters) was reorganized into a more disciplined People's Revolutionary Armed Forces (FARP) comprising three components: a mobile conventional army, the

Popular Army, responsible for the liberation of the entire country; the Popular Guerrillas, to operate in contested areas; and the Popular Militia, to provide local security in the liberated areas. Political commissars with more seniority were paired with military commanders to ensure the primacy of politics over military matters. Also established was a fifteen-member Political Bureau of the PAIGC, an enlarged Central Committee (expanding from thirty to sixty-five members), and seven departments responsible for areas including the armed forces, security, information and propaganda, economy and finance, and foreign affairs.

With these profound structural changes, Cabral felt it urgent to reassert the authority of the civilian-dominated leadership of the PAIGC, in particular his role as the commander-in-chief: "The leadership of the struggle is the leadership of the Party. Inside the Political Bureau there is a War Council of which I am president as Secretary-General of the Party. There is no important military action in our country that does not pass through my hands."[26] Although this may seem an obsessive need to control, Cabral was in fact emphasizing his responsibilities as the civilian leader of a politicized military at war. Nevertheless, the tension between the "militarists" and the "armed militants" would remain a formidable challenge during the prolonged armed struggle, and after independence the militarization of politics would become a defining characteristic of the new nation of Guinea-Bissau.

Administratively, the liberated areas of the south and the north were divided into regions, sectors, and *tabancas* (villages). It was a pyramidal structure that facilitated communication between the Party Secretariat and the subordinate committees at these various levels. Grassroots participation was guaranteed at the lowest and most basic level, where the five members of the *tabanca* committee, two of whom had to be women, were elected. Cabral recognized the important role of women not only in the liberation struggle but also in the new society being created. Even before the launching of the war, a women's wing of the PAIGC, the Women's Democratic Union (UDEMU), was created in 1961. He acknowledged and promoted the active participation of women in the struggle, in their roles as recruiters, porters, nurses, teachers, frontline fighters, and political and military leaders. The new infrastructure in the liberated areas also included the People's Courts, People's Stores, health clinics and hospitals, and schools.

The PAIGC came out of the Cassacá Congress revitalized and more determined to complete the liberation of the country. The historic event was a critical turning point that set the liberation movement on a more secure road to political and military victory. However, the sensitive and thorny questions of ethnic animosity and anti–Cabo Verdean hostility, both being weaponized by the Portuguese, remained inadequately addressed, even though Cabral was well aware of Portuguese exploitation of "tribal contradictions" and practice of "racism

137

on the basis of lighter skin and darker skin." Thus, the threat of factionalism within the ethnically diversified binational liberation movement remained menacingly real.

Nevertheless, battles had to be fought and the war had to be won. Time was of the essence. Cabral focused on equipping his People's Army with 75mm recoilless rifles, rocket-propelled grenades, small cannons, and bazookas, besides the famous Kalashnikovs (AK-47s). He substantially increased the number of men and women sent abroad for military training, mainly to the USSR, the PRC, Czechoslovakia, East Germany, Hungary, Bulgaria, and Cuba, besides African countries like Algeria, Morocco, Ghana, and the host country (Guinea-Conakry). Maintaining the initiative, Cabral's fighters expanded their operations with the opening of the eastern front, such that by 1966 about 50 percent of the colony and half of its population were under the control of the PAIGC.

Determined to recover lost territory and prove that "Guinea will never cease to be Portuguese," Governor Schulz, a veteran of recent repressive military campaigns against Angolan nationalists, ordered sustained air strikes during his four-year tenure, dropping tons of bombs, including napalm and white phosphorous, "to terrorize the terrorists." A military upsurge swelled the Portuguese army to twenty thousand soldiers, with air power that included helicopter gunships. Commenting on the war plan of the Portuguese, Cabral noted that they "follow the tactics and strategies used by the US and other imperialists."[27] Specifically, he had in mind the ongoing American intervention in Vietnam, on which the Portuguese modelled their colonial war. Like the "strategic hamlets program" of the Americans, Schulz established the *aldeamentos em autodefesa* (self-defense villages), strategically located rural settlements, largely in the eastern region, characterized by barbed wire fencing to "protect" the villagers from "communist influence." The *Tugas*, Cabral elaborated, "used every kind of bomb save the nuclear ones," and maintained that "almost every day, they bomb our villages and try to burn the crops. They are trying to terrorise our people."[28]

Cabral admitted that the Portuguese military upsurge was "generally harder for us," because the high-altitude air strikes targeted civilians of the liberated areas as well as the FARP units operating in contested territory. The impact was devastating and demoralizing, causing huge population displacements that swelled the number of refugees in the neighboring countries. As the indiscriminate bombing raged, the liberators "had the unenviable task of having to explain to villagers fleeing bombardment the need to stay put to continue the war effort."[29]

Nevertheless, Cabral and his War Council pressed on and created mobile antiaircraft units to address the deadly menace of Portuguese air power. Cabral got busy procuring the necessary weaponry and securing the needed specialist training. Cuba, which in August 1963 "said yes, but did nothing" about Cabral's request for military and political training for five of his fighters, turned out to be particularly accommodating.[30] Four months after his meeting with Ernesto "Che" Guevara in Conakry on 12 January 1965, Fidel Castro's government delivered 315 crates of arms, medicine, and food. In July that year, about half a dozen Cabo Verdean militants of the PAIGC, including Pedro Pires and Manuel "Manecas" dos Santos, embarked for military training in Cuba in anticipation of initiating the armed liberation of Cabo Verde. However, following Cabral's decision later that guerrilla warfare was infeasible in the archipelago, all the trained Cabo Verdeans joined the war in Portuguese Guinea.

In January 1966, Cabral himself led a PAIGC delegation to Havana to participate in the first Tricontinental Conference of the Peoples of Asia, Africa, and Latin America, where he presented his critically acclaimed thesis "The Weapon of Theory." Greatly impressed, Fidel Castro promptly agreed to Cabral's request for medical doctors, military instructors, and mechanics to provide the PAIGC an effective logistics capability. Six months later, the Cuban Military Mission in Guinea and Guinea-Bissau (MMCG) arrived in Conakry with thirty-one "advisors": eleven artillery specialists, eight drivers, ten doctors (five surgeons, three clinicians, and two orthopedists), an intelligence officer, and the chief of the mission.[31] The first head of the MMCG, Lieutenant Aurelio Ricardo Artemio, was succeeded in 1967 by Major Víctor Dreke Cruz, an African Cuban veteran of the Cuban Revolution and Che Guevara's most trusted commander, then known as Comandante Moja, during the failed Cuban expedition to the Democratic Republic of the Congo in 1965.

Cuban military advisors, particularly Victor Dreke Cruz, who trained and fought alongside the FARP guerrillas inside Portuguese Guinea, worked very closely with Cabral and his War Council, and the collaboration significantly enhanced the FARP's operational capability. It was Cabral who decided where the Cubans would be deployed, dispatching two groups of six instructors and four doctors to the southern and eastern fronts and leaving the rest in Guinea-Conakry. Once in the war zones, the Cubans found themselves facing the "the impossibility of advising and correcting the tactics of the fight without participating directly in the actions."[32] Aware of Cuban participation in the war against them, the Portuguese were elated when Operation Jove (16–19 November 1969) resulted, two days later, in the capture of wounded Cuban infantry captain Pedro Rodriguez Peralta. The captured Cuban was a valuable trophy for Lisbon's propagandistic equation of her colonial wars with "the war against communism." Peralta was flown to Portugal to serve a five-year prison sentence.

With Cuban technical assistance, the PAIGC attacks on all the war fronts increased significantly. According to Mustafah Dhada, the relentless PAIGC offensive increased "from 112 accountable operations in 1967 to 467 traceable attacks in 1968,"[33] Cabral's fighters were hitting and/or downing Portuguese warplanes and intensifying attacks on garrisons, fortified towns, land convoys, and river patrols. The vulnerability of Schulz's military force was dramatically exposed when Cabral ordered one of his antiaircraft units, led by Andre Gomes, to attack on 28 February 1968 the main Portuguese Air Force base at Bissalanca, just seven kilometers from Bissau, destroying "the control tower of the airport, two airplanes, and three hangars."[34] Schulz ended his four-year term with the PAIGC stronger than when he assumed office.

Cabral's new adversary became General António Ribeiro de Spínola, a cavalry officer who visited the German Sixth Army during its unsuccessful attempt to seize Stalingrad in 1942. Spínola was also a veteran of the Portuguese brutal suppression of the Angolan uprisings in 1961. Recognizing the leadership genius of Cabral and the effectiveness of his army, the new governor assumed office in May 1968 with a declaration that "the war in progress in Guinea is eminently psychological," that it could only be won by "persuasion" and not by "coercion."[35] But his "psycho-social" war to win hearts and minds was not in synchrony with the mindset of his superiors in Lisbon.

Although Salazar was incapacitated by a stroke suffered in September 1968, his replacement, Marcello Caetano, a prominent Estado Novo ideologue and former minister of the colonies (1944–47), also had an incorrigible colonialist bent. Caetano's intolerance of

African nationalism and his profound dislike of nationalist leaders in "Portuguese Africa" manifested itself five months later, on 3 February 1969, with the PIDE's assassination in Dar-es-Salaam, Tanzania, of Eduardo Mondlane, founding president of the Liberation Front of Mozambique (FRELIMO). Eulogizing his "companion in struggle" in his famous lecture on "National Liberation and Culture" at Syracuse University in the United States a year later, Cabral delineated the motive behind Mondlane's assassination to be the fact that "he was able to rediscover his own roots, identify with his people and dedicate himself to the cause of national and social liberation."[36] Contemplating a life trajectory not unlike his, Cabral undoubtedly pondered the possibility of a similar fate awaiting him, and the probability of it visiting him at any time.

Spínola devised a two-pronged strategy to defeat Cabral and his movement by launching a *Guiné Melhor* (Better Guinea) program that exploited the colonially generated antagonisms between Guineans and Cabo Verdeans, gave preferential treatment to the former in the colonial administration, and made notable improvements in the colony's social infrastructure. Spínola also released many imprisoned Guinean nationalists, including PAIGC president Rafael Barbosa, who, in a speech prepared by the PIDE, promised "to be as good a Portuguese as His Excellency." Cabral and his comrades promptly declared him a "traitor." That was the carrot.

In this dual strategy, described by Cabral as "smiles and blood," the stick was the implementation of an aggressive counterinsurgency policy entailing the "Africanization" of the war with the creation of the African Commandos and the African Marines, comprised exclusively of "native Guineans." This was complemented by a troop upsurge of forty thousand soldiers, the intensification of air strikes with continued dropping of napalm and white phosphorus bombs, and helicopter-borne assaults.

Although Spínola's Africanization policy was a copy of US president Nixon's "Vietnamization" strategy, the fundamental difference was that the latter was aimed at ending American involvement in an increasingly unpopular conflict, while the former was based in recognition of Portugal's small and overextended armed forces and the imperative to outsource the burden of concurrent fighting in three theaters of war to maintain the *pax lusitana.* The governor's policy reflected a historical trend. The "pacification" of Portuguese Guinea in the early twentieth century was the work of African mercenaries.

Spínola's carrot and stick strategy took almost two years to seriously impact the momentum of Cabral's freedom fighters, who on 5 February 1969 had finally captured the Madina do Boé garrison and who would in 1969 hit twice the number of aircraft (eighteen) than in the previous year. Obeying Cabral's orders to "not let the enemy relax in their barracks . . . not let the colonialist soldier have even one quiet night's sleep in our land,"[37] the FARP conducted some "981 traceable operations in 1970, 300 more than were recorded the year before."[38]

However, Spínola's "psycho-social" war began to produce some of its desired outcomes, including a significant increase in the number of schools, hospitals, and social housing, greater abundance of food in the markets and a wider variety of consumer items in shops, holidays in Portugal for colonial civil servants, and pilgrimages to Mecca and Fatima, respectively, for Muslim and Christian leaders. Together with the intensified air strikes and helicopter-borne attacks, the gains of the liberation struggle came under serious threat. Besides the recently released political prisoners who pledged allegiance to the Portuguese flag, and the increasing

Figure 2. Cabral in pensive mood as the war intensified during the early 1970s. Copyright, Bruna Polimeni (1971), Fondazione Lelio e Lisli Basso.

number of people in the major cities—Bissau, Bolama, Bafatá, Teixeira Pinto (Canchungo), and Nova Lamego (Gabu)—who believed that "independence is unnecessary," Cabral and his comrades also had to deal with the effects of Spínola's counterinsurgency program on the inhabitants of the liberated areas, where the local military commanders "were already losing patience with certain elements of the population they considered traitors, because they gave themselves to the *Tugas* for some trinkets."[39]

To counter the Portuguese propaganda offensive in the "war of the waves," Cabral deployed the PAIGC's new Freedom Radio, broadcasting in Portuguese, French, Crioulu, Fula, Mandinka, and Manjaco, to launch a frontal attack on the belated Portuguese attempts to create a "Better Guinea," underscoring that "*without our struggle, without our Party, the Portuguese colonialists, who have been so long among us without building schools or health centres or housing, would never bother to do these things* (emphasis in original)."[40] Spínola's strategy to win hearts and minds ultimately failed because the overwhelming majority of the beneficiaries of the social dimension of Better Guinea recognized the self-serving nature of the colonial largesse.

Meanwhile, Cabral redoubled his efforts on the diplomatic front, appearing before the Subcommittee on Africa of the US House Committee on Foreign Affairs, chaired by the African American congressman Charles Diggs Jr., where, in spite of the Nixon administration's undisguised support of the Lisbon regime, critical voices echoing American opposition to Portuguese colonialism were still heard. Cabral showed graphic pictures of victims of napalm bombs supplied to the Portuguese by the United States, to the outrage of some committee members, including Diggs. A few months later, on 27–29 June, Cabral participated, together with Agostinho Neto of the MPLA and Marcelino dos Santos of the FRELIMO, in a conference in Rome organized to demonstrate "solidarity with the peoples of the Portuguese colonies" and attended by over 175 organizations from 65 countries. Significantly, at the end of the event he led his comrades to an audience with Pope Paul VI, to whom he gave a dossier on Portugal's violent repression of her colonial subjects. The pontiff told the delegation, "We are on the side of those who suffer. We are for the peace, the freedom, and the national independence of all people, particularly the African peoples."[41]

Pope Paul VI's encounter with the "terrorist leaders" infuriated Prime Minister Caetano, prompting him to declare "the profound regret of the Portuguese Government and Nation" and to recall the Portuguese ambassador to the Holy See. Although he later accepted the Vatican's explanation that there was no political significance to the pope's meeting with Cabral and his comrades, and accordingly restored diplomatic relations with the Holy See, the implicit papal condemnation of Portuguese colonialism was obvious to the world and especially to the people of Catholic Portugal, home of one of the most sacred shrines of Catholicism, the Sanctuary of Fatima. It was a major diplomatic coup for Cabral, who considered the historic audience "a political and moral fact of the greatest importance."

Cabral's "expose and shame" campaign against the Lisbon regime left Portugal increasingly isolated. In Portuguese Guinea, Spínola was becoming increasingly frustrated with the steady gains being made by the *terroristas*. Determined to end the war by "persuasion," the military governor obtained the approval of Caetano to initiate political dialogue with elements of the PAIGC. Exploiting the nativist mantra of *Guiné para os guinéus* (Guinea for the native Guineans), contacts were made and meetings held with some guerrilla field commanders in the northern front. Aware of Spínola's maneuvers and its potentially damaging impact on the cohesion of the liberation movement, the PAIGC leadership abruptly brought an end to the talks when a guerrilla unit ambushed and killed Spínola's negotiating team of three military officers on 20 April 1970. It is not clear whether Cabral knew of or ordered the killing of the Portuguese negotiators, although one historian implicates his brother Luís.[42] The incident left Spínola and the Lisbon authorities furiously vengeful. Considered "Portugal's Vietnam," the "least valuable" of Portuguese colonies had become Caetano's Achilles heel. Given the deteriorating situation, the military governor informed the prime minister of the dire choice they faced: "Either we use all the means at our disposal to eradicate the enemy's sanctuaries or we lose Guinea irrevocably."[43] Caetano accepted the first option.

Spínola took the fight to the PAIGC sanctuary city of Conakry. Operation Green Sea was launched on 22 September 1970, incorporating elements of the Conakry-Guinean opposition movement the Guinean National Liberation Front (FLNG). Closely supervised by Spínola himself and commanded by navy captain Alpoim Calvão, the top-secret seaborne assault by some four hundred mostly black soldiers, half of them FLNG fighters clandestinely trained by the Portuguese on the Bijagós island of Sogá, unexpectedly descended on Conakry but nevertheless met stiff resistance from the Conakry-Guinean forces. The principal objective was to assassinate Cabral and Sékou Touré and install a friendly regime that would expel the PAIGC and the Cubans from the country and effectively end the war.

However, besides rescuing twenty-six Portuguese prisoners of war held by the PAIGC, destroying seven naval boats belonging to the liberation movement and Guinea-Conakry, and killing "over 300 persons," the operation failed to accomplish its primary mission. Cabral and Sékou Touré were still alive, the PAIGC and the Cubans were still operational, and the Conakry regime was still standing. Amid loud condemnations of Portugal around the world, both the Bissau and Lisbon authorities steadfastly denied Portuguese involvement, despite the "smoking gun" evidence of captured soldiers and equipment. The operation's nightmare scenario had become a diplomatic fiasco for Portugal and a boon for the PAIGC and Guinea-Conakry.

Cabral, away in Bulgaria, strongly condemned the invasion. Following the report of a UN fact-finding mission sent to Conakry three days after the aborted invasion, Security Council Resolution 290 (1970), adopted with the abstentions of the United States, the United Kingdom, France, and Spain, reaffirmed "the inalienable right of the people of Angola, Mozambique and Guinea (Bissau) to freedom and independence," condemned Portugal for the aggression, and declared that "the presence of Portuguese colonialism on the African continent is a serious threat to the peace and stability of independent African States." Predictably, the OAU extraordinary meeting in Lagos, Nigeria, on 11 December also condemned the "treacherous aggression," while individual member states, particularly Algeria, Libya, Nigeria, Tanzania, and Zambia, offered military and financial assistance to Sékou Touré's government. The failed invasion temporarily united the radical Casablanca and moderate Monrovia groups of countries that had contrasting visions of Pan-African unification.[44] The USSR, Cuba, the PRC, and other communist countries denounced the "imperialist aggression." Unpredictably, President Nixon sent a "message of sympathy and support" and an aid package worth $4.7 million to the Conakry authorities.[45] The United Kingdom, France, Italy, and West Germany were not at ease with what was effectively Portugal's Bay of Pigs.

Spínola's strategy ended up boosting political and material support for the PAIGC. It was a propaganda bonanza that Cabral skillfully exploited to show "how desperate the Portuguese are in our country" and to rally further international support to ensure that "the advances made by our struggle are irreversible."[46] Moscow, Beijing, Havana, and Prague substantially increased their technical and military assistance to the PAIGC, while Stockholm and the Nordic governments expanded their humanitarian aid.

In the face of their own mounting frustration, the Lisbon authorities accepted the offer by President Senghor of Senegal to mediate a negotiated settlement of the war with Cabral. The Senegalese leader proposed a cease-fire and joint PAIGC-Portuguese administration of the territory for ten years, followed by a referendum on either independence or full autonomy under Portuguese imperial overlordship. However, after the first meeting between Spínola and Senghor in the Casamance resort town of Cap Skirring in May 1972, Caetano ordered the abandonment of the talks. Pressured by pro-empire diehards and fearful of the domino effect that such "concession" could generate, the prime minister rationalized that "it is preferable to leave Guiné through a military defeat with honour than through an agreement negotiated with terrorists which would point the way to other negotiations [in the other colonies]."[47]

Regardless of Caetano's about-face and Senghor's gross miscalculation in assuming that a neocolonial solution would be acceptable to the PAIGC, Cabral already knew that Portugal was being rapidly overtaken by internal and external developments favorable to his liberation movement, that the march of the liberators was unstoppable, and that the protracted armed struggle was on the cusp of victory. Internally, in spite of Spínola's devastating "smiles and blood" strategy, the FARP fighters continued to hold their ground and to administer the liberated areas, which now covered two-thirds of the territory, and where lengthy elections (31 August–14 October 1972) were being held for a People's National Assembly (ANP) that would soon declare independence.

Externally, in his relentless quest for international legitimacy, Cabral invited the UN Decolonization Committee to visit the liberated areas, an offer which was accepted amid strong objections from Portugal. On 2–8 April 1972, a UN observer team entered the liberated areas in the south. In spite of intensified bombings of the region by the Portuguese Air Force, the team successfully completed its mission. Reporting favorably on their visit, the UN observers underscored the popular support enjoyed by the PAIGC and the socioeconomic wellbeing of the inhabitants. On 13 April 1972, the Decolonization Committee meeting in Conakry declared the PAIGC as "the only and authentic representative" of the people of Portuguese Guinea.

The increasingly favorable international environment was also due to Cabral's skillful use of the media to publicize the cause of the armed struggle, particularly in countries that were Portugal's NATO allies. From the early years of the war, he continually invited a number of journalists, writers, and filmmakers to make eyewitness accounts of the armed struggle in progress. The printed and filmed documentation that raised awareness and galvanized support and sympathy for the PAIGC included books by Basil Davidson (*The Liberation of Guiné*, 1969) and Gérard Chaliand (*Armed Struggle in Africa: With the Guerrillas in "Portuguese" Guinea*, 1969) and documentary films by Mario Marret (*Lala Quema*, 1964), Pierro Nelli (*Labanta Negro!*, 1966), and John Sheppard (*A Group of Terrorists Attacked . . .* , 1968). There were also publications and documentaries made by sympathetic authors and filmmakers on the other side of the Cold War divide. For his own part, Cabral created two regular publications for the dissemination of news and information about the armed struggle: the bulletin *Libertação* and the monthly pamphlet *PAIGC Actualités*. Through such efforts, together with his writings, conference presentations, and public lectures, Cabral was able to effectively pull down the wall of silence built around Portuguese Guinea in particular and the Portuguese African empire in general.

Thus, when a confident Cabral once again addressed the UN Decolonization Committee in October 1972, the PAIGC was recognized not just as the only legitimate liberation movement in Portuguese Guinea but also as the party that would form the government of what would soon be an independent country. "The idea of begging for freedom," he told the Committee, "is incompatible with the dignity and sacred right of our people to be free." Therefore, he insisted, "we reaffirm here our steadfast determination, no matter what sacrifices are involved, to eliminate colonial domination from our country and to win for our people the opportunity to build in peace their progress and happiness."[48] Soon after, a General Assembly resolution of 14 November 1972 granted observer status to the PAIGC, which enabled the representatives of the liberation movement to attend its meetings. The "right of self-determination and independence" was also reaffirmed by the General Assembly and the UN Security Council in November 1972, substantially weakening Portugal's position.

Nevertheless, on the ground and especially from the skies of "Portuguese" Guinea, the *Tugas* remained a menace. With total air supremacy, the Portuguese Air Force continued to rain death and destruction with almost total impunity, while helicopter-borne troops wreaked havoc on "terrorist" villages. In 1972, only two Portuguese bombers and two helicopters were hit and/ or downed by PAIGC antiaircraft guns, compared to twenty aircraft in the previous year.[49]

Air attacks were among the most pressing preoccupations for Cabral, who became determined to finally checkmate the Portuguese airpower advantage. In December 1972, while also attending celebrations of the 50th anniversary of the founding of the USSR and being awarded an honorary doctorate in social and political sciences by the Soviet Academy of Sciences, Cabral was able to convince the heretofore reluctant Russians to provide surface-to-air missiles. The PAIGC became the only liberation movement in Africa to possess such hardware. Its deployment three months later was a critical game changer.

Having now outwitted the Portuguese repeatedly, it was a highly confident Cabral who on 31 December 1972, at the stroke of midnight, made the following announcement on the PAIGC's Freedom Radio.

> In the course of this coming year and as soon as it is
> conveniently possible we shall call a meeting of our
> People's National Assembly in Guiné, so that it can
> fulfill the first historic mission incumbent on it: the
> proclamation of the existence of our state, the creation
> of an executive for this state and the promulgation
> of a fundamental law—that of the first constitution
> in our history—which will be the basis of the active
> existence of our African nation.[50]

Behind the remarkable PAIGC accomplishments was Cabral's effectiveness as a charismatic and visionary leader, shrewd politician, ingenious military strategist, and astute diplomat.

Solidarity with "Every Just Cause"

Pan-Africanism and Internationalism
in Action

Driving Cabral's nationalist zeal was an uncompromising Pan-Africanist and internationalist conviction. Although much of his thinking reflects revolutionary nationalism, he nevertheless articulated clear ideas about Pan-African unity and international solidarity. Cabral regarded the armed national liberation struggle in Portuguese Guinea as part of the broader struggle to free Africa from colonialism and neocolonialism, as "one aspect of the general struggle of oppressed peoples against imperialism."[1]

As already seen, Cabral's radical political awakening occurred during his college days in Portugal. He arrived in Lisbon some two weeks after the Fifth Pan-African Congress, held in Manchester, England, in December 1945, had ended with the adoption of two major resolutions addressed to colonized Africans and their European colonizers. Kwame Nkrumah, an organizer of the conference who had recently arrived in England from the United States, prepared the "Declaration to the Colonial Peoples." His mentor, W. E. B. Du Bois, drafted the "Declaration to Colonial Powers." They declared that subjugated Africans had the right to be "free from foreign imperialist control, whether political or economic," and "to elect their own governments, without restrictions from foreign powers"—and advised that, if their European occupiers were "still determined to rule mankind by force, then Africans, as a last resort, may have to appeal to force in the effort to achieve freedom."[2]

Cabral himself first participated in a Pan-African event when he attended the All-African People's Conference in Accra, 8–13 December 1958. At this historic event that was both symbolic and substantive, the host, Prime Minister Kwame Nkrumah, famously declared that his country's newly won independence was "meaningless unless it is linked up with the total liberation of Africa." It is not clear whether Cabral met with Nkrumah during the Accra conference, but he would later develop an enduring personal relationship with the Pan-Africanist champion, who went into exile in Conakry after his overthrow in February 1966. Cabral would regard him as "the head of state in Africa I admired the most." Nkrumah ended his opening speech by assuring delegates of the liberation movements that the independent African nations "stand uncompromisingly behind you in your struggle." When Cabral and his comrades decided to wage armed struggle to end Portuguese colonial domination, the "Spirit of Accra" was stimulative and facilitative.

Cabral went on to attend the 1960 Second All-African People's Conference in Tunis, as a delegate of the Anticolonialist Movement (MAC), and the 1961 Third All-African People's Conference in Cairo, as the leader of the FRAIN delegation. By then, a split had emerged in the Pan-African movement, with the radical Casablanca group of seven countries (Ghana, Guinea-Conakry, Mali, Egypt, Libya, Algeria, and Morocco) favoring accelerated political unification, and the conservative Monrovia group (including Ethiopia, Nigeria, Cameroon, Senegal, Ivory Coast, and Liberia) emphasizing nationalism and interstate cooperation. Cabral, focused on his binationalist imperative of "immediate and total independence," would skilfully manage the tension between the two groups while formulating his own perspective on Pan-Africanism.

As the leader of the FRAIN delegation at the Cairo conference, which was overshadowed by the recent assassinations of African nationalist leaders Félix-Roland Moumié of the Union of the Peoples of Cameroon and Congolese prime minister Patrice Lumumba, Cabral joined the chorus of condemnations denouncing "imperialist machinations." Echoing the opening remarks of host President Gamal Nasser that "many thought imperialism in Africa had ended," Cabral reminded the conference participants to "not forget that not one of our enemies has been really conquered." He urged recognition of the "numerous and great mistakes" in the ongoing liberation struggles, which were not helped by an "African solidarity" characterized by "some hesitation and even improvisation." Cabral further outlined the daunting challenges they faced: the "fascist-colonialist Portuguese" continued to brutally oppress their colonial subjects; the "fascist-racists of South Africa" were daily perfecting "their hateful apparatus of apartheid"; the "Belgians colonialists" had "returned to the Congo"; the "British imperialists" were cleverly manoeuvring to maintain "complete domination" of East Africa and "economic domination" of former West African colonies; the "French imperialists and colonialists" who had recently test-exploded the atomic bomb in the Sahara desert were "killing defenceless people in Algeria" while "increasing their economic domination" over their former territories; and, finally, the "American imperialists," who were "emerging from the shadows and, astonished by the weakness of their partners, are seeking to replace them everywhere."[3]

Determined to broaden the struggle against Portuguese colonialism, Cabral met with his FRAIN comrades in Casablanca on 18 April 1961 and resolved to transform their anticolonial front into the Conference of the Nationalist Organizations of the Portuguese Colonies (CONCP), which now included the Committee for the Liberation of São Tomé and Príncipe (CLSTP). The Liberation Front of Mozambique (FRELIMO) headed by Eduardo Mondlane, which was founded in June 1962 with Cabral's collaboration, also joined the CONCP. While Marcelino dos Santos was the CONCP's first secretary-general, Amílcar Cabral remained its voice and face. He laid the groundwork for the effective mobilization of vital diplomatic and material support for the constituent liberation movements. For example, when in 1970 the Swedish International Development Agency (SIDA) had to decide between the Popular Movement for the Liberation of Angola (MPLA) and the National Front for the Liberation of Angola (FNLA) for its humanitarian support, Cabral's opinion was solicited and he favorably recommended the former. Having developed a close personal relationship with the Swedish Social Democratic Party leader Olof Palme (future two-term prime minister), Cabral was able to leverage the enormous esteem bestowed by Sweden's political class.

Cabral developed a people-centered revolutionary Pan-Africanism that regarded continental unification as a means and not an end. He insisted that African unity was a necessary but insufficient condition for the unification of the continent. "We are," he underscored, "for African unity in favour of African peoples." It was a veiled criticism of state-centric integration as exemplified by the then faltering Ghana-Guinea-Mali Union (1958–63). Declaring the readiness of the PAIGC "to unite with any African people," he stipulated the one condition under which that could happen: "that the gains of our people in the liberation struggle, the economic and social gains, the gains of justice that we pursue and are already achieving little by little, that none of this should be compromised."[4] It was also recognition of the incomplete struggle against colonialism, resulting in "flag independence," that characterized the member states of the recently established Organization of African Unity (OAU).

The magnitude of Cabral's internationalism was reflected in his numerous declarations of commitment to "every just cause in the world," the essence of which was spelt out in a 1968 interview given to *Tricontinental* magazine: "We have as a basic principle the defence of just causes. We are in favour of justice, human progress, the freedom of the people."[5] He expressed strong solidarity with the struggle of the Vietnamese communists against "the most shameful and unjustifiable aggression of the US imperialists." Cabral further elaborated that "the struggle in Vietnam is our own struggle," that at stake in Vietnam was "not only the fate of our own people but also that of all the peoples struggling for their national independence and sovereignty."[6] Perceiving national liberation as essentially a political struggle, Cabral had noted that one of the most important lessons of the French defeat in Vietnam was that politics triumphed over military force: although France still had a large enough army in Vietnam to continue the war in spite of the humiliating defeat at the battle of Dien Bien Phu in 1954, international and domestic pressure nevertheless obliged French withdrawal. Ties between the PAIGC and the Vietnamese were strong enough for Cabral to accept at least two advisors, Tran Hoai-Nam of the Central Committee of the National Liberation

Front of South Vietnam, and Phan Van Tan, a Vietcong military strategist, both of whom Basil Davidson met during his extensive travels in the liberated areas of Portuguese Guinea in the mid-1960s.[7]

To his "brothers" in Cuba, the only country whose offer of fighters he accepted, Cabral emphasized the strong solidarity with "a people that we consider African" because of "the historical, political, and blood ties that unite us."[8] He praised the Cuban people for "defending their fundamental interests" and "deciding their destiny for themselves."[9] At the 1966 Tricontinental Conference in Havana, an international gathering in solidarity with anticolonial and anti-imperial struggles in Africa, Asia, and Latin America, Cabral expressed admiration for "the solidity, strength, maturity and vitality of the Cuban Revolution" and declared that "no power in the world" would be able to destroy it.[10] Fidel Castro, very much impressed by Cabral's "Weapon of Theory" presentation, considered the PAIGC leader as "one of the most lucid and brilliant leaders in Africa," who instilled in him and his comrades "tremendous confidence in the future."[11] The revolutionary solidarity would translate into financial, technical, and military assistance to Cabral's liberation movement, and nine Cubans would die to liberate Portuguese Guinea.

Cabral was also empathetic toward and supportive of the struggles of the peoples of Latin America, who "have suffered enormously," with their independence "a sham" because "governments were created that were

Figure 3. Cabral the consummate freedom advocate: in solidarity "with every just cause." Copyright, Bruna Polimeni (1971), Fondazione Lelio e Lisli Basso.

completely submissive to imperialism, in particular to US imperialism."[12] He was also in solidarity with the Palestinian people, who he believed "have a right to their homeland," and accordingly supported their struggle "to recover their dignity, their independence, their right to live."[13]

Cabral expressed Pan-African solidarity with the struggles of African Americans for civil and political rights, stating in the aftermath of the Watts Rebellion in August 1965, "We are with the blacks of the United States of America, we are with them in the streets of Los Angeles, and when they are deprived of all possibility of life, we suffer with them."[14] Meeting in New York on 20 October 1972 (his last visit to the United States) with some thirty black political organizations, which he described as a "meeting between brothers and sisters trying to reinforce not only our links in blood and in history, but also in aims," he voiced his understanding of "the difficulties you face, the problems you have and your feelings, your revolts, and also your hopes."[15] But he also stated that, more than ties of blood and history, his preferred relationship of solidarity was one of camaraderie, signifying political engagement. Cabral's understanding of the African American situation was also informed by personal interactions with prominent political exiles he met in Africa, including Black Panther leaders Eldridge Cleaver in Algeria and Kwame Ture (formerly Stokely Carmichael) in Guinea-Conakry.

Cabral also expressed Pan-African solidarity with the black people of South Africa where, in the Sharpeville Massacre of March 1960, the apartheid state's police killed 69 people protesting against the requirement to carry a passbook aimed at controlling their freedom of movement, an oppressive system he denounced as a "shameful, vile regime of racial discrimination."[16] To the people of the Democratic Republic of the Congo, where Prime Minister Patrice Lumumba was assassinated on 17 January 1961, Cabral pledged support of their efforts to resist "the aggression of imperialists and the manoeuvres of imperialists."[17]

For Cabral, the flip side of solidarity with "just causes" was the solidarity of people, organizations, and countries with the binational liberation struggle he led and the coalition of anticolonial forces on whose behalf he spoke. The solidarity received in the form of concrete support must be guided by what Cabral called "ethics for aid," emphasizing that it was welcome but it could not be conditional. Such ethics reflected Cabral independence of thought and action, his clarity of purpose, and his stubborn determination to succeed against the odds.

Cabral's frequent absence from Conakry and infrequent visits to the battlefronts and liberated areas of Portuguese Guinea during the early stage of the armed struggle were a significant factor in the indiscipline and crimes committed by some of his commanders and fighters. After the implementation of the structural reforms passed by the inaugural congress of the PAIGC, his numerous essential travels abroad to secure material, diplomatic, and moral support bolstered the confidence and military effectiveness of the liberation fighters. At the same time, Cabral became viewed by the Lisbon authorities as one of Portugal's most dangerous enemies, at the top of the PIDE's list of most wanted *terroristas*.

The "Cancer of Betrayal"

The Assassination of Amílcar Cabral,
20 January 1973

Eulogizing Kwame Nkrumah on 13 May 1972, Cabral emphatically declared, "The African peoples and particularly the freedom fighters cannot be fooled. Let no one come and tell us that Nkrumah died from cancer of the throat or any other sickness, No. Nkrumah was killed by the cancer of betrayal."[1] After surviving five assassination attempts, the preeminent Pan-Africanist leader had reportedly died (aged sixty-two) of prostate cancer in Bucharest, Romania, on 27 April 1972. He had been living in exile in Conakry, as honorary copresident of the Republic of Guinea, following his overthrow by a CIA-supported coup d'état on 21 February 1966 while he was on a trip to North Vietnam and the People's Republic of China. Cabral praised Nkrumah for being "an exemplary revolutionary" and a "strategist of genius in the struggle against classic colonialism." He recognized the former Ghanaian leader as a "personal friend" and a "comrade" who always encouraged the PAIGC's war "against the most retrograde of all colonialisms" and duly acknowledged the "practical support" Nkrumah had provided to the liberation movement. Cabral also warned that so long as imperialism existed, "an independent African state must be a liberation movement in power, or it will not be independent." Concerned about counterrevolutionary activities that tended to become malignant, he advised "reinforced vigilance in all fields of the struggle" as "the best homage we can pay to Kwame Nkrumah."[2] In less than a year, Cabral himself would fall victim to the "cancer of betrayal."

As with Nkrumah, there had been several attempts to assassinate Cabral since the early years of the armed struggle. In November 1966 the PIDE reported that an unknown assassin took a shot at Cabral and his brother Luís in Dakar, but both were unharmed. The Portuguese secret police also reported that the following year, in Ziguinchor, capital of the southern Senegalese region of Casamance, Cabral twice escaped the bullets of aspiring assassins. The frustrated attempts to kill Cabral would broaden to include his host, Sékou Touré.

In 1969, a suspicious Cabral prompted the arrest of a man named Jonjon found at the PAIGC headquarters in Conakry with a hand grenade in his pocket, who "allegedly confessed that it was his intention to liquidate Amílcar Cabral in collusion with the paratroopers of Guinea-Conakry who intended to eliminate Sékou Touré and Kwame Nkrumah."[3] As noted in the previous chapter, the principal objective of Operation Green Sea had been to assassinate Cabral and Sékou Touré. This was later confirmed by the operation's commander, Alpoim Calvão, who boldly asserted that if Cabral had been found in Conakry he would have been "surely eliminated." Further proof lies in the fact that Cabral's house was destroyed by heavy shelling.

The concerted attempts to kill Cabral unfolded against a background of assassinations of outspoken anti-imperialist leaders in Africa, including Félix-Roland Moumié of Cameroon (1961), Patrice Lumumba of the DRC (1961), Mehdi Ben Barka of Morocco (1965), and Eduardo Mondlane of Mozambique (1969). Perceiving radical African nationalism and Pan-Africanism as threatening to their economic and strategic interests, the imperialist nations and former colonial powers became determined to maintain control of their African spheres of influence and possessions by any means necessary, including political assassination and direct military intervention. Cabral was well aware that his political commitment, ideological orientation, and "solidarity with every just cause" made him vulnerable to intricate conspiracies, often exploiting existential racial/ethnic tensions, aimed at eliminating him.

Cabral denounced some of the plots to kill him. Notably, in March 1972 he revealed a three-phase "diabolic plan" to kill him and the rest of the top-level PAIGC leadership that had been hatched by the secret police, now renamed the Directorate-General of Security (DGS), some of whose operatives were trained by the CIA during the previous decade "in the modern practices of the fight against subversion."[4] The first phase involved the recruitment of former and current Bissau-Guinean members of the PAIGC hostile to Cabo Verdeans, to exploit grievances and ethnic resentment among the liberation fighters who, as Cabral noted, "due to errors committed and criticisms made against them, are dissatisfied with the current leadership of the Party." In the second phase, the colonial authorities would launch national and international campaigns of disinformation about the breakup of the PAIGC to discredit and delegitimize Cabral and his leadership team and sap the morale of the freedom fighters. Following up, the recruited disaffected elements of the PAIGC would create a "parallel executive" of Cabral's liberation movement that would seek recognition from political parties in neighboring countries and especially from the government of Sékou Touré. In the third and final phase, with recognition and support secured, Cabral and his closest comrades, as well as the loyal militants, would be "physically liquidated." A new leadership would be created "on the basis of racism and, if necessary, tribalism and religious intolerance," and the war would be ended. With the name of the party changed, the new leaders would negotiate with the Lisbon authorities through the mediation of Spínola for the creation of an autonomous "State of Guinea" with "self-determination under the Portuguese flag." Accordingly, all the recruited agents and the leaders of the new party would be rewarded with "high positions in the political life and armed forces of the future State." Cabral added that these agents and their collaborators would also be "well paid for their betrayal."[5]

Assassination as a weapon against political foes was already a well-established practice in twentieth-century Portugal, evidenced by the killing of King Carlos I and Crown Prince Luís Filipe in 1908, President Sidónio Pais in 1918, Prime Minister António Granja in 1921, renowned painter and sculptor José Dias Coelho in 1961, and presidential candidate Humberto Delgado in 1965. Student activist José Ribeiro dos Santos was also a victim of political assassination in 1972. In the Portuguese African colonies, besides the many summary executions and massacres, there were numerous targeted killings of African nationalists, notably the aforementioned FRELIMO leader Eduardo Mondlane.

On the night of 20 January 1973, at 10:30 p.m., Cabral was killed outside his house in the PAIGC headquarters complex in the Minière neighbourhood of Conakry. Returning from a Polish embassy reception accompanied by his wife Ana Maria, he was about to park his Volkswagen Beetle when a stationary military jeep suddenly turned its headlights full-beam on him and his passenger. He stopped, and as he was getting out of the car a group of armed men jumped out of the jeep, rushed over to him, and ordered him to get into their vehicle. Cabral refused. One of the assailants attempted to tie him up with a rope. Cabral indignantly resisted, reminding the aspiring abductors that one of the main reasons for the armed struggle in progress was to end the colonial practice of tying up subject people before meting out brutal punishment.

According to Ana Maria, the sole witness of her husband's murder, Inocêncio Kani, a dismissed naval commander and ex-member of the Executive Council of the Struggle (CEL) who had been demoted, jailed, and pardoned by Cabral for selling an outboard motor in 1971, fired the first shot at point-blank range. The bullet went through Cabral's right side and pierced his liver. As he dropped on the ground bleeding profusely, Cabral, in Ana Maria's account, "still continues to talk, trying to convince them that the *Tugas* were still in our land, and that if problems exist, they should be discussed openly, as is the custom."[6] The impatient Kani then ordered one of his accomplices wielding a machine gun "to finish Cabral." A hail of bullets left Cabral lifeless on the ground. Kani gave orders for Cabral's widow to be taken to the PAIGC hilltop prison known as the *Montanha* (mountain).

Meanwhile, a second group led by Mamadu N'Djai, interim head of security at PAIGC headquarters, stormed into Aristides Pereira's office, tied him up, and bundled him into a jeep driven by Kani to the port of Conakry, where he was transferred to a PAIGC navy speedboat that headed north toward Bissau. A third group led by João Tomás Cabral, an infiltrated PIDE agent, overpowered the guards at the Montanha prison and freed fellow conspirators, including Mamadu (Momo) Touré and Aristides Barbosa, both party militants jailed for nationalist activities in 1962. These coconspirators had been recruited by the PIDE while in prison and were among the ninety-three prisoners released and pardoned by Spínola in August 1969 and then allowed to "escape" from Bissau to rejoin the PAIGC in Conakry—where, after their cover was blown, they were promptly arrested and incarcerated. Numerous high-ranking members of the PAIGC, almost all Cabo Verdean and Bissau-Guinean *mestiços*, were rounded up and imprisoned, including CEL members José Araújo, Vasco Cabral, and António Buscardini.

As Kani sped toward international waters with his prize captive, his boat was spotted by Conakry-Guinean Air Force MIG fighters and intercepted by a Soviet destroyer. With Aristides Pereira rescued and all the other jailed leaders and militants released following the arrest of the conspirators by the Conakry authorities, President Sékou Touré announced Cabral's assassination by the "poisoned hands of imperialism and Portuguese colonialism" through the use of "Africans belonging to the Portuguese colonialist army who had infiltrated the ranks of the PAIGC by pretending to be deserters."[7]

During his exposition of the plot by the DGS to kill him a year before, Cabral had affirmed that, if he were to be killed, "it will be from within our own ranks," that the liberation movement could only be destroyed from within, and that "it will take one of our own to do it." The murderous betrayal was facilitated by Koda

172

Nabonia, one of Cabral's personal bodyguards, who shared the secretary-general's schedule of activities with his fellow conspirators. Nabonia would commit suicide while in jail awaiting trial. Kani, resentful over his demotion and harboring anti–Cabo Verdean sentiments, was one of Cabral's trusted fighters whom he had sent for training at a naval academy in the Soviet Union and subsequently appointed as the first commander of the PAIGC's burgeoning navy.

A few days after Cabral's death, amid worldwide condemnations of Portugal, the Lisbon authorities responded with predictable denials of involvement, deploying a strategy of deflection with a counter-accusation that President Sékou Touré ordered the assassination as punishment for Cabral's rejection of a proposal for the unification of the two neighboring countries. From Bissau, Spínola also emphatically denied any complicity in the murder, insisting that he needed Cabral as an interlocutor in his quest for a political solution leading to autonomy. Two decades later, the monocled general who tried to kill Cabral in Conakry in November 1970 remained defiant and delusional, maintaining that killing the PAIGC leader was never his plan: "My plan was to integrate him in my government as the secretary-general of Guinea. . . . It would be the glorious end of the war in Guinea."

The condescending racism notwithstanding, Spínola's contention was in fact a total rejection of Cabral's commitment to national liberation. The general was a staunch colonialist who volunteered for a mission to Angola to suppress the 1961 rebellions that initiated the armed struggle there. That the goal of "immediate and total independence" was nonnegotiable for Cabral was never accepted by Spínola, who disingenuously claimed that he "always had in mind a solution that would lead to the self-determination of the people of Guinea," for which "the cooperation of Amílcar Cabral was essential." Cabral's indispensability, Spínola asserted, came from the fact that "there was no substitute in the PAIGC with equal intelligence and *portuguesismo* [Portuguesism, or Portugueseness]."[8]

Yet, while almost all the top colonial administrators and high-ranking military officers in the colony agreed with Spínola's plea of innocence and dismissal of collusion, a few Portuguese officials defiantly spoke out, accusing the DGS of orchestrating the murderous chain of events. Colonel Carlos Fabião, future co-architect of the 25 April 1974 Carnation Revolution (brewed in Bissau) that ended the Estado Novo, affirmed unequivocally, "I have no doubt that it was the PIDE that set up the scheme." Fabião also declared that the Portuguese secret police had previously "tried several times and had failed" to assassinate Cabral and that its motive was "to prevent, or at least delay, the declaration of independence."[9]

Contradicting his initial protestation that he "absolutely [denied] that the death [of Cabral] had been premeditated by the DGS," Deputy-Inspector Fragoso

Allas, head of that secret police organization in Bissau, stated at the end of his mission that "the guys had gone too far, because the mission was to kidnap Amílcar and bring him to Bissau as a hostage. They had not been ordered to liquidate him."[10] Spínola's propaganda officer for the Better Guinea counterinsurgency program, Captain Otelo de Carvalho, another future conspirator of the 25 April revolution, outlined the likely motive for his boss's abduction of Cabral: "the capture of Cabral would give Spínola an enormous shine. It is the typical spirit of the Cavalry: subjugate the adversary, display him as trophy, make him bow, and then negotiate."[11] It was this strategy, the Mozambican-born captain added, that the Portuguese conquistador Mouzinho de Albuquerque used against King Gungunhana of the Gaza Empire (Mozambique) in 1895: capture the enemy, dispatch him to the metropole, and parade him through the streets of the imperial capital. Was this the fate that awaited Cabral had he been abducted?

Cabral's assassination made headlines around the world and provoked a wave of condemnations of the Lisbon regime as well as demonstrations in support of the PAIGC in many countries, including those allied to Portugal. The London *Times* described Cabral as "one of the most extraordinary leaders and thinkers of modern Africa," while the *New York Times* referred to him as "one of the most prominent leaders of the African struggle against white supremacy." In the NATO countries that provided military and technical support to Portugal, as well as in Scandinavia, solidarity groups demonstrated outside Portuguese embassies and consulates.

In the United States, Congressman Charles Diggs, chair of the Subcommittee on Africa of the House Committee on Foreign Affairs, denounced American aid to Portugal and called for an "in-depth investigation under impartial international auspices." Diggs also declared that "the struggle for which Amilcar Cabral dedicated his life—the winning of freedom of the people of Guinea-Bissau and Cape Verde and the throwing out of Portuguese oppression—must go on."[12] The US government condemned the assassination of Cabral but accepted Lisbon's claims of noninvolvement. Yet, a declassified document of the State Department dated 1 February 1973 implicated the Lisbon authorities: "While there is no evidence linking the Portuguese Government directly to the assassination, Lisbon's complicity cannot be ruled out," not least because "the attempted escape of the assassins by sea in the direction of Portuguese Guinea suggests that the Portuguese may have been involved."[13] The US exoneration of Portugal was undoubtedly motivated by Washington's close cooperation with the Lisbon authorities for use of the Azores air base in the context of the Cold War.

In France, the leader of the Socialist Party and future president, François Mitterrand, who met with Cabral in Conakry two months earlier, accused Portugal of complicity by rhetorically asking who the authors of the assassinations of Humberto Delgado and Eduardo

Mondlane were. Among the numerous heads of states and governments worldwide who were outraged by the brutal killing was Prime Minister Olof Palme of Sweden, a close friend of Cabral whose country provided significant humanitarian assistance to the armed struggle he led. Palme echoed the sentiment of hundreds of poignant tributes and eulogies in referring to Cabral as "one of the most impressive personalities I have ever met." At a special session of the UN General Assembly convened on 22 January 1973, where a one-minute silence was observed in memory of Amílcar Cabral, isolated Portugal was strongly condemned for the assassination.

Meanwhile, in Conakry, President Sékou Touré organized and presided over an International Commission of Inquiry, initially comprising leading members of his Democratic Party of Guinea, representatives of the FRELIMO (Samora Machel and Joaquim Chissano were in Conakry on the day Cabral was murdered), and the ambassadors of Algeria and Cuba. Later, the International Commission would comprise seven other Conakry-accredited diplomats, including the envoys of Egypt, Nigeria, Senegal, Tanzania, and Zaire/DRC.

Of the 465 accused persons that appeared before the International Commission, only forty-three were implicated, with nine of them considered active participants in the assassination plot. These suspects were returned to jail and later handed over to the PAIGC following the constitution of its own commission of inquiry. Divided into four groups and tried in the liberated areas, the nine found guilty who included Kani, N'Djai, and Mamadu Touré, were executed by firing squad.[14] The confessions, mostly extracted by torture, directly implicated Spínola, who, exploiting the lingering tension between Cabo Verdeans and Bissau-Guineans, had apparently promised "independence only" following the capture or death of Cabral and the control of the party by *guinéus* (native Guineans of dark skin complexion).

On 2 February 1973, Iva Pinhel Évora attended the funeral service of her assassinated son in Conakry. Before her departure from Bissau, she had a requiem mass said by a priest who was expelled from the colony forthwith, for disobeying the PIDE's order to not mention the name of the deceased "terrorist" during the event. Many guerrilla commanders and fighters also headed to Conakry to attend the funeral ceremony, among them Luís Cabral, Nino Vieira, Pedro Pires, Francisco Mendes, and Carmen Pereira—the only woman member of the CEL, who was in charge of reconstruction in the liberated areas of the south. Also heading to Conakry was Ernestina "Titina" Sila, a member of the Higher Council of the Struggle (CSL) and political commissar in the northern front, who was killed by a Portuguese naval patrol as she crossed the Farim River. Carmen Pereira and Titina Sila were in the first batch of women sent by Cabral to the Soviet Union for training at the beginning of the war. Carmen would later become the vice president of the elected People's National Assembly (ANP) that would convene to proclaim the independence of

Guinea-Bissau eight months after Cabral's death. She would also be the first woman head of state in Africa, albeit for only three days (14–16 May 1984).

According to Carmen, the murder of Cabral "was organized by Spínola" with the complicity of "the comrades": "Cabral died because he had so much trust in his men and did not distrust anyone."[15] In agreement, Cabral's brother Luís affirmed, "My brother's mistake was that he trusted everyone. Without doubt, Amílcar Cabral was not vigilant enough."[16] Not only was trust an important element of Cabral's leadership style, but he also believed in the rehabilitation of sanctioned offenders, hence the amnesties granted to the comrades who fatally betrayed him. Thus, Cabral's humanist ideals facilitated his murder.

Behind the "cancer of betrayal" was the heightened paranoia of the colonial authorities in Lisbon and Bissau with Cabral's announcement of the imminent proclamation of the independence of Guinea-Bissau and its likely domino effect. Notwithstanding Spínola's quest for a negotiated neocolonial solution, his boss, Marcello Caetano, never wavered from his declaration in 1969 that "Portugal cannot cede, cannot compromise, cannot capitulate in the struggle being waged Overseas."[17] And since Cabral was uncompromising on "immediate and total independence," the irreconcilable clash of the logics of domination and liberation made him a disposable enemy, presaged by the assassination of his comrade-in-arms Eduardo Mondlane, and evidenced by the invasion of Conakry in 1970 that failed to "eliminate him."

The funeral ceremony for Cabral, preceded by an international symposium held in the Palace of the People in Conakry the day before, took place at the city's 25,000-seat sports stadium, the Stade du 28 Septembre, where some eighty delegates from around world and the representatives of governments both Western (including the United States, France, West Germany, Italy, and Sweden) and communist (particularly the USSR, Cuba, People's Republic of China, and North Vietnam) joined the thousands of grief-stricken Bissau-Guineans, Cabo Verdeans, and other Africans to pay homage to the man described by the *New York Times* as "the leader of Africa's most successful anticolonialist guerrilla movement." After the two-hour ceremony befitting a head of state, Cabral's remains, in a coffin that had been placed on an artillery carriage drawn by a military truck that circulated the stadium upon its entrance, were deposited in a mausoleum at the Camayenne National Cemetery in Conakry, to be transferred in September 1976 to the Amura Fortress in Bissau.

Portugal steadfastly refused to accept at least moral responsibility for the death of Cabral. Governor Spínola and his close collaborators, especially Fragoso Allas, head of the DGS in Bissau, together with Prime Minister Marcello Caetano and his cabinet, particularly Overseas Minister Joaquim da Silva Cunha, all enjoyed impunity. Spínola returned to a hero's welcome in Portugal and, with the downfall of the Estado Novo, briefly became president of a renascent democracy. He died in 1996 as an "illustrious soldier" promoted to the highest military rank of field marshal, decorated with the highest honor of the Military Order of the Tower and Sword for "valor, loyalty, and merit," and memorialized by the name of an avenue in Lisbon. Overthrown by the 25 April Revolution, Caetano took refuge in Brazil where he died in 1980. Silva Cunha returned to academia as law professor while the whereabouts of Fragoso Allas are unknown.

After more than four decades, postdictatorship Portugal has yet to establish a commission of inquiry to investigate the culpability of Portuguese politicians and colonial officials for the assassination of Cabral, unlike Belgium, which, after four decades of silence, assumed moral responsibility for the murder of Patrice Lumumba. So far it has not been possible to find any archival document in Portugal or Guinea-Bissau showing intention or premeditation by colonial officials or DGS agents to assassinate Cabral. In the turmoil of the 25 April Carnation Revolution, compromising documents disappeared from the archives. It has been observed that "in documentary terms, the assassination of Cabral resembles a shelf filled with . . . lacunas."[18] Yet this is similar to what prevailed in nonrevolutionary Belgium, where no incriminating evidence of the murder of Lumumba has yet to be found, but where a conciliatory gesture has also involved the erection of a statute of the Congolese nationalist on a Brussels public square named after him.

While documentary proof of the involvement of colonialist Portugal cannot be found, Cabral's central role in the most intense anticolonial struggle that seriously threatened the dissolution of the Portuguese empire in Africa provides sufficient motive for his assassination, directly or indirectly. In the context of the Cold War, the elimination of Cabral had the tacit support of her NATO allies, principally the United States, the United Kingdom, and France, the major stakeholders who most feared, as in the case of the DRC, the spread of communist influence in Africa. The significance of Cabral in the downfall of the fascist regime in Lisbon and the dissolution of the Portuguese African empire is evidenced by the dramatic developments that unfolded on the battlefields of Portuguese Guinea in the aftermath of his assassination.

A Luta Continua

The Independence of Guinea-Bissau and Cabo Verde, 1973–75

The death of Amílcar Cabral was a devastating blow to the PAIGC, but the tragic loss did not mean that the liberation movement was now a spent force, as the Portuguese had hoped. "The colonialists thought that the death of Cabral was the end of the war," Carmen Pereira recalled, elaborating that, in the aftermath of the tragedy, the *Tugas* launched a propaganda offensive that exhorted the *terroristas* to surrender "because Cabral has died" and everyone else "could be killed in a 24-hour bombardment."[1]

A week after Cabral was buried, members of the Executive Council of the Struggle (CEL) and the Higher Council of the Struggle (CSL) met for three days in Conakry to discuss the future of the armed struggle. An action plan was approved that included the amplification of political mobilization in both Portuguese Guinea and Cabo Verde, the convening of the first session of the People's National Assembly to declare the independence of Guinea-Bissau as envisaged by the fallen leader, the intensification of the armed struggle on all battlefronts, and the boosting of internal security.[2] Aristides Pereira had been chosen as the interim secretary-general of the PAIGC the day after Cabral's funeral. *A luta continua*, the struggle continues.

The renewed resolve of the PAIGC was facilitated by the groundwork laid by Cabral. Believing that he was not indispensable, that if he "died or disappeared, there would be others in the party capable of continuing the struggle," he had devised a practical framework for the implementation of the strategic objectives of the war. Politically and diplomatically, he had successfully established the PAIGC at the international level, not only as the sole and legitimate representative of the people of Portuguese Guinea and Cabo Verde, but also as the party that would form the governments of the two countries, thus significantly undermining the position of Portugal. His assassination only increased the isolation of the intransigent Lisbon regime and galvanized more support for the PAIGC.

Militarily, Cabral left a restructured fighting force, numbering about 7,000 combatants, well trained, sufficiently disciplined, and enormously courageous in the face of a 42,000-strong NATO-supported colonial army with unchallenged air power. Spínola's strategy of "smiles and blood" that killed and horribly burned victims only hardened the morale of the fighters and gave the able-bodied survivors the irresistible urge to actively support the armed struggle. Cabral's acquisition of heavy artillery, including 75 mm and 120 mm antiaircraft guns, and the appropriate training of his fighters for their efficient deployment was supplemented by his procurement of the more effective shoulder-launched surface-to-air missiles, the Strela-2 (also known as SAM-7), from the USSR and the formation of specialist units to employ them.

Cabral's acquisition of the state-of-the-art weapon was communicated to the Lisbon authorities by British intelligence, but while its arrival in Portuguese Guinea was known to the colonial authorities, its nature and functionality was initially an enigma: both the Directorate-General of Security (DGS) in Bissau and the Portuguese Air Force (FAP) in the colony were apparently ignorant of the existence of such a technological innovation. DGS Sub-Inspector Fernando Gaspar admitted that he "did not know of the existence of this type of weapon," while FAP Lieutenant Colonel Artur Batista Beirão acknowledged that "it was a new weapon that we did not know."[3] Cabral, the brilliant strategist of anticolonial subversion, had yet again outsmarted his "superior" adversaries and in the process rendered baseless the racist dogma of General Kaúlza de Arriaga, ultraconservative professor at the Institute of Higher Military Studies in Lisbon and hawkish commander-in-chief of the Portuguese forces in Mozambique (1969–74). In his *Lessons in Strategy for the High Command Course, 1966–67* he declared, "Subversion is a war above all of intelligence. One must be highly intelligent to carry on subversion, not everyone can do it. Now the black people are not highly intelligent, on the contrary, they are the least intelligent of all the peoples in the world."[4]

The renewed post-Cabral FARP offensive was energetic and furious, but contained by his idea of a "clean war." Prisoners of war were to be treated well and civilian casualties avoided. In 1968, Cabral had released two batches of Portuguese prisoners to the Senegalese Red Cross "to rejoin their families and speak to them about us," since "no contradictions exist between the people of Portugal and our people." He further affirmed that "whatever crimes the colonialists may commit, in the future our people will join hands in fraternal collaboration."[5] But such practice was never reciprocated by the colonial forces, which always viewed the freedom fighters as bloodthirsty *terroristas.* "Most acts of terrorism and atrocities," Captain Otelo de Carvalho recalled, "were committed by our forces, not the PAIGC."[6]

A critical turning point signaling the end of Portuguese air supremacy in the territory was reached on 25 March 1973, when a West German–made Italian Fiat G-91 jet fighter-bomber piloted by Lieutenant Miguel Pessoa was downed near the Portuguese fort at Guiledje, in the south, by a heat-seeking Strela-2 missile fired by Domingos Nsali of the new FARP artillery unit Comando Abel Djassi. Pessoa ejected before his aircraft crashed and was later rescued with a broken leg.[7] Under the command of Manuel "Manecas" dos Santos, who underwent specialist training in the USSR, the Abel Djassi unit had become the real game changer. With the Portuguese still unaware of the type of antiaircraft ordnance being used by the FARP, another Fiat G-91 was blown up in the sky on 28 March 1973, killing its pilot, Colonel José Almeida Brito, the operational group commander at the main air base near Bissau. Brito was on a bombing mission near Madina do Boé, the locale that would soon become the birthplace of independent Guinea-Bissau. Announcing the death of Brito, Spínola declared that the plane was "hit by a ground-to-air rocket launched from the Republic of Guinea, while flying over Portuguese territory on a reconnaissance mission."[8] Two North American Harvard T-6 bombers and a French Alouette III helicopter were also hit by surface-to-air missiles by the end of March, but without loss of life.

The first week of April instilled further fear in the FAP pilots of flying the now dangerous skies of Portuguese Guinea. On 6 April, surface-to-air missiles downed and killed the pilots of three aircraft in the north, near the Guidadje fort: a Harvard T-6 bomber piloted by Major Mantovani Filipe and two West German Dornier Do-27 transport planes (carrying a total of five soldiers who were also killed), respectively flown by Baltazar da Silva and António Ferreira.[9] By the end of the month, another Alouette III helicopter was hit by rocket-propelled grenades and light artillery.

In mid-May, a frustrated Spínola complained to his superiors in Lisbon about the imminence of military collapse. The counterinsurgency strategy that depended on air operations was being frustrated as Cabral's fighters wrested the initiative from their enemies. The FAP, which could reach any point in the territory within forty-five minutes, and upon which the colonial soldiers confined to isolated fortifications depended for supplies and air cover, was virtually grounded. The chilling "new reality" facing the FAP, Lieutenant António Graça de Abreu noted in his diary, was that "the PAIGC already has antiaircraft missiles that are effective. The pilots are afraid of flying, who wants to commit suicide?"[10] With roads mined, forts harassed by heavy artillery, ambushes on land patrols, and intensified attacks on river transport, the Portuguese were in dire straits. Morale was dipping as the number of casualties rose. By year's end they would stand at 2,076 soldiers injured and/or killed, almost two-and-a-half times more than in the previous year and "the second highest since the armed struggle had begun."[11]

Sustaining the pressure on the colonial forces, the FARP launched Operation Amílcar Cabral on 18 May 1973, which simultaneously besieged two of the most important Portuguese forts in the territory, Guidadje in the north near the border with Senegal and Guiledje in the south close to the frontier with Guinea-Conakry. These garrisons were pounded with all kinds of artillery including 120 mm mortars and 130 mm field cannons. Both forts endangered the supply routes of the FARP from the neighboring countries. On 23 May, the six hundred and fifty fighters under the command of Nino Vieira launched a massive attack on the Guiledje fort, forcing the overwhelmed force of thirteen hundred Portuguese troops, deprived of reinforcements, vital supplies, and air cover, to abandon the fort in a full-scale evacuation to the nearby Gadamael garrison. During the hasty retreat, twenty-six soldiers were killed and numerous fleeing trucks destroyed.

The fall of Guiledje was a major victory that further emboldened the FARP to lay siege to the Gadamael fort, situated on the bank of the Cacine River, which also fell during the first week of June. The Guidadje garrison was able to withstand the siege with the arrival of Portuguese reinforcements. The impact of the energized attacks by the FARP and the effectiveness of its antiaircraft weaponry had left the colonial soldiers demoralized, prompting the DGS to inform the Lisbon authorities that "the military situation is worsened by the lack of support from the air force, by the terrorist attacks . . . with many weapons and without restrictions to the use of munitions."[12] Indeed, Cabral had amassed a huge arsenal that included armored vehicles and tanks. He had also formed a new air force and sent the first batch of forty fighters for pilot training in the USSR a few months before his assassination, but the FARP air force had yet to be operational.

Meanwhile, on the home front in the metropole, the Estado Novo regime was also under increasing pressure.

By 1973, the colonial wars in Angola, Portuguese Guinea, and Mozambique were absorbing about 50 percent of the national budget and resistance to compulsory four-year military service was causing hundreds of young Portuguese men and women to flee the country. Opposition to the continuation of the wars and demonstrations of support for the liberation movements were also growing. But Prime Minister Caetano remained as stubbornly inflexible as his predecessor, who died on 27 July 1970. A week before the assassination of Cabral, Caetano told his fellow citizens, "We have only one way, defend the Overseas [Provinces]." He would later feel the depth of anger against the Estado Novo regime outside Portugal when he visited the United Kingdom on 15 July 1973, five days after the London *Times* broke the news of the Wiriyamu Massacre in Mozambique seven months earlier, and was greeted by thousands of demonstrators carrying banners and placards denouncing him as a murderer, expressing solidarity with the FRELIMO, MPLA, and PAIGC, and demanding freedom for the peoples of Portugal and the Portuguese African colonies.

With the military balance of power in their favor, the PAIGC leaders convoked the Second Congress of the PAIGC on 18–22 July 1973, at Madina do Boé in the liberated eastern region of the country. Among the significant outcomes of the Congress were the formal elections of Aristides Pereira as the secretary-general and Luís Cabral as the deputy secretary-general of the

PAIGC. The Congress would prepare the inaugural session of the ANP that would formally proclaim the independence of the country, adopt its first constitution, and approve its first government. Another significant development was the creation of two national bodies of the PAIGC, the National Council of Guinea-Bissau and the National Council of Cabo Verde. The splitting of the party reflected the tension between Bissau-Guineans and Cabo Verdeans, aggravated by the assassination of Cabral—a decision that presaged the death of the binational unification upon which the armed struggle was also predicated.

On 8 August 1973, a frustrated Spínola returned to Portugal and was appointed deputy chief of defense staff. His successor, General Bettencourt Rodrigues, arrived in Bissau on 29 August and was briefed on the much weakened Portuguese position, whereby "almost all of the territory of the province constitutes guerrilla area" and FARP forces could "accomplish spectacular actions of terrorism and sabotage at any point."[13] This fragile Portuguese military situation was also the backdrop of the three meetings held in Bissau on 18, 21, and 25 August 1973 by war-fatigued Portuguese "captains" to vent grievances over recent decrees in Lisbon granting conscripted officers the same pay and privileges as their professional counterparts. The junior officers also discussed the prospects of a costly and unwinnable war. Thus was born the "movement of the captains," led by officers like Otelo de Carvalho, who returned to Portugal and, together with some 135 junior officers at a secret meeting in Alcáçovas on 9 September 1973, founded the Armed Forces Movement (MFA). The Movement accepted the radical idea that the end of Portuguese colonialism in Africa was inevitable—a conviction forced, forged, and concretized on the battlefronts of Portuguese Guinea in particular.

On 24 September 1973, eight months and four days after the assassination of Cabral, the ANP held its inaugural session at Madina do Boé, presided by Nino Vieira, who read the proclamation of the new Republic of Guinea-Bissau. The constitution adopted defined the new nation as "a democratic, anti-colonial and anti-imperialist state." A fifteen-member Council of State (including three women) was elected, to be chaired by Luís Cabral, who would be the president of the new republic. Luís Cabral also headed the seventeen-member Council of Commissioners that constituted the leadership of the working government. Francisco "Tchico Te" Mendes was named principal commissioner (prime minister), while Nino Vieira held two portfolios: president of the ANP and commissioner (minister) of the FARP, with Pedro Pires as his deputy.

Although Portuguese troops still occupied the major towns, including the capital Bissau, the PAIGC's unilateral declaration of independence was immediately recognized by over eighty countries and the new state admitted to the Organization of African Unity forthwith. On 22 October 1973, the UN General Assembly adopted a resolution condemning Portugal's continued occupation of independent Guinea-Bissau, followed by formal recognition of that occupation's illegality on 2 November 1973, with seven countries voting against: Portugal, the United States, the United Kingdom, Brazil, Spain, Greece, and South Africa.

Predictably, the reaction of the Lisbon authorities was one of total dismissal. Caetano contemptuously referred to the new nation as "this delirious phantasmagoria that is the State of Guinea-Bissau, without Bissau and without Guinea," with a presumed capital in Conakry, where it could not receive ambassadors "because it does not have the territory to accommodate them."[14] At the same time, the Portuguese soldiers who faced the fire and fury of Cabral's liberation fighters were becoming increasingly disenchanted and conspiratorial.

On 22 February 1974, Spínola's book *Portugal e o futuro* (Portugal and the Future) was published, becoming an instant bestseller. The central thesis was that the colonial wars should end because they were militarily unwinnable and the colonies should be granted "self-determination" within a "Lusitanian Community"— for which he and his boss, General Francisco da Costa Gomes, were promptly dismissed. A matter of weeks later, in the aftermath of the 25 April 1974 Carnation Revolution, Spínola was invited by the MFA to lead the Junta for National Salvation and become head of state, which office he held from May into September of 1974. His advocacy for an end of the colonial wars was the critical factor for his selection over his rival, General Arriaga, who also published a book, in English—*The Portuguese Answer*—in which he defended Portuguese colonialism in Africa as a response to the "strategic-political upheavals" in the world caused by the "neo-racism of the non-white man against the white man," "banditry organized at the international level," and the "Communist neo-imperialism" that was exploiting the first two causal factors in order to take over Africa. Arriaga urged Portugal to remain in Africa as an answer to the communist threat, a message that pleased not only diehard *colonialistas* but the United States and her NATO allies.

Still, during Spínola's brief presidency, secret negotiations for Portugal's recognition of Guinea-Bissau's independence and Cabo Verde's right to independent statehood were initiated. On 16 May 1974, Mário Soares, a long-time antifascist opposition leader of the Portuguese Socialist Party exiled to São Tomé and Príncipe (after several imprisonments in Portugal) by the Estado Novo regime, now foreign minister under the new dispensation, met with Aristides Pereira in Dakar through the mediation of President Senghor. The talks floundered because of Spínola's refusal to recognize the independence of Guinea-Bissau and his insistence on "self-determination" within the Lusitanian Community he had already proposed. However, although Spínola had the support of the MFA that put him in power, there were ideological allies of the PAIGC among some of that movement's leaders, notably Colonel Vasco Gonçalves,

Major Ernesto Melo Atunes, Major Victor Alves, and Captain Otelo de Carvalho. With pressure from the radical faction of the MFA, the secret negotiations resumed in London on 25 May between Portuguese and PAIGC delegations respectively headed by Mário Soares and Pedro Pires. The PAIGC's insistence that Lisbon also transfer power to it in Cabo Verde led to Spínola suspending the talks once again.

Meanwhile, in Bissau, the newly arrived Portuguese governor, Colonel Carlos Fabião, a veteran of "Portugal's Vietnam" and an ideological sympathizer of the PAIGC, reached an agreement for a *modus vivendi* between the two armies. Conscious of the FARP's advantage, Fabião convened a meeting of all Portuguese military officers in the colony, who urged Portugal to remove "all obstacles placed in her path by reactionary and neocolonial forces" and recognize Guinea-Bissau and the right of the people of Cabo Verde to independence. The message resonated well with the key decision-makers in Lisbon. On 18 July, when Colonel Vasco Gonçalves became prime minister of the second provisional government, he declared his commitment to "a just process of decolonization without ambiguities." On 27 July, an outflanked and dejected Spínola announced that Portugal recognized the right of her African colonies to independence and that negotiations for the transfer of power would begin forthwith. Mário Soares and Pedro Pires resumed negotiations in Algiers and reached an agreement on 26 August that recognized Guinea-Bissau and reaffirmed the right of Cabo Verde to independence.

Spínola's capitulation and Portugal's readiness to decolonize marked the climax of the military, political, and diplomatic victories of the PAIGC engineered by Amílcar Cabral. While the MFA played a crucial role in the general's about-face, the submission was undoubtedly the outcome of Cabral's political astuteness and the military prowess of his fighters. As a direct result of the military successes of the PAIGC under Cabral, a month after Spínola took office the MFA-Guiné section had declared that the Portuguese troops, "who were sent to a war that we did not understand or support," had "a unique opportunity to repair the crimes of fascism and colonialism, to set up the basis for a new fraternal cooperation between the peoples of Portugal and Guinea"—if they were capable of "volunteering" their "disinterested collaboration" with the PAIGC.[15]

Portugal formally recognized the independence of Guinea-Bissau on 10 September 1974 and a week later the country became a member of the United Nations, a membership which the United States had conditioned on Portugal's "granting" of independence, a move aimed at placating the Lisbon authorities in return for continued use of the Azores military base. According to declassified documents, Secretary of State Henry Kissinger—who reacted to the PAIGC's unilateral declaration of independence by cynically remarking, "That's really what the world needed, a country called Guinea Bissau"—had insisted two months before the UN vote that the new nation was "not going to be admitted with our vote until the Portuguese have given it independence." The secretary of state had chosen to ignore the fact that Britain's stubborn seven-year refusal to recognize the unilaterally declared independence of the United States did not delegitimize the hard-won sovereignty of the new nation.

In Bissau, preparations for the withdrawal of the Portuguese colonial officials and troops unfolded peacefully, with former foes fraternizing in informal meetings and events like soccer matches. On 13 October, Fabião departed for Lisbon, followed three days later by the embarkation of the last group of Portuguese soldiers. President Luís Cabral and Secretary-General Aristides Pereira triumphantly entered Bissau on 19 October, symbolizing the complete and effective occupation of the new republic. The eleven-year war, in which less than ten thousand freedom fighters inspired and trained by Cabral defeated an army of over fifty thousand Portuguese and African soldiers, was very costly. With four times the proportionate Portuguese troop concentration in Mozambique and eight times that in Angola, the Guinea-Bissau war also brought the most Portuguese casualties—more than two thousand deaths and about four thousand injured veterans. The number of FARP fighters killed is estimated at between one and two thousand for the entire war, while the casualty count for civilian victims is unknown but undoubtedly much higher.[16]

Meanwhile, Pedro Pires headed the PAIGC team that followed up with the process of Portuguese transfer of power in Cabo Verde, a task complicated by the fact that the liberation movement had not engaged in armed struggle in the archipelago and faced a number of rival nationalist groups that were opposed to any form of unification with Guinea-Bissau. Nevertheless, having concentrated its efforts on clandestine political mobilization that produced a solid base of support, the PAIGC leadership, which included Silvino da Luz, Osvaldo Lopes da Silva, and Carlos Reis, was able, through negotiations and the organization of demonstrations and a general strike, to secure the dominance of Cabral's party. With Spínola toppled by left-wing elements of the MFA on 30 September 1974, the decolonization process accelerated. On 18 December, the PAIGC formed a government of transition with Portugal that organized the elections for the archipelago's own People's National Assembly, which, on 5 July 1975, proclaimed the Republic of Cabo Verde. Aristides Pereira became president of the new republic and Pedro Pires his prime minster, both of them leaders of a party now dominant in two sovereign nations.

Thus, the PAIGC's unilateral declaration of independence on 24 September 1973, the result of its military dominance in the battlefield, and Portugal's reluctant acceptance, the outcome of her military defeat, had started the domino effect feared by the Lisbon authorities. In 1975, the Portuguese empire in Africa collapsed completely. In quick succession, the independence of Mozambique (25 June) was followed by that of Cabo Verde (5 July), São Tomé and Príncipe (12 July), and Angola (11 November).

Amílcar Cabral's pivotal role in the liberation of the peoples of Guinea-Bissau and Cabo Verde is evident, but also discernible is the significant part he played in the dismantling of the Portuguese empire in Africa and the emancipation of the people of Portugal from almost five decades of fascist dictatorship.

Cabral ka Muri

The Legacy of Amílcar Cabral

When Luís Cabal's ex-wife, Lucette Cabral, met Nelson Mandela after his release from twenty-seven years of imprisonment, she admiringly told him, "You are the best." Mandela quickly responded, "No, there is Cabral."[1] The humble remark of the freedom fighter who lived to see the triumph of the long struggle he led was a testimonial to the influence of the liberation fighter who did not survive to witness the victorious end of the protracted resistance and military campaign he commanded. The humility of Mandela, who refused to take credit for the ANC's successful antiapartheid struggle, insisting that "it is not the individuals that matter, but the collective," parallels the modesty of Cabral, who always shunned responsibility for the PAIGC's remarkable achievements, emphasizing instead "collective leadership."

More than four decades after his death, Cabral's ideas continue to resonate in Africa and beyond. For his charismatic personality, inspirational leadership, and remarkable accomplishments, he is memorialized within Africa and outside the continent in the naming of academic institutions, government buildings, public squares, streets and avenues, and, in Cabo Verde, an international airport. Although he did not live to accomplish all that he set out to do, his legacy remains inspirational for generations of Africans and non-Africans challenged by deprivation, exploitation, and oppression.

Cabral's assassination marked a definitive moment in the lives of his friends and admirers around the world, but the tragedy was most momentous for his comrades-in-arms. The men and women he inspired went on to defeat Portugal militarily and politically and establish the independence of Guinea-Bissau and Cabo Verde. But the victory was also consequential beyond the borders of these two countries: its ripple effects contributed significantly to transformative developments in Portugal and the rest of her African colonies.

From humble origins in Guinea-Bissau and Cabo Verde, Cabral suffered hardships, witnessed "folk die from flogging" in his *terra natal* and "folk die of hunger" in his *terra ancestral*, and experienced racism as a student and trained agronomist in Portugal. Developing critical consciousness through lived experience and formal education, driven by moral outrage, a desire for social justice, and an indefatigable quest for freedom from foreign domination, he committed himself to fight against the colonial system that nurtured and sustained the enabling environment of exploitation and oppression. Self-emancipation from cultural alienation preceded engagement in the national liberation struggle—which called for the weaponization of culture, since imperialist domination also entails cultural oppression.

Although a Marxist revolutionary theoretician, Cabral was very reticent to call himself a Marxist or communist. He was never an active member of any such organization, but his political thought was shaped by Marxism and his intellectual work was grounded in materialist theory. Nevertheless, he eschewed dogmatism and avoided abstractions devoid of concrete empirical substantiation. He was adamant about contextual specificity. Unlike most other African leaders of liberation movements, he knew his two countries well. Concerned at an early age about the plight of his colonized people, Marxism became attractive to Cabral because it complemented and validated his humanist ideals. More than Marxist formulations, though, his lived experience convinced him of the need to strive to "end the exploitation of man by man."

Important theoretical contributions of Cabral can be found in "A Brief Analysis of the Social Structure in Guinea" (1964), "The Weapon of Theory" (1966), and "National Liberation and Culture" (1970). Motivated by a quest to understand the objective realities of the context-specific environments in which he was politically engaged, he used a Marxist framework that left him questioning and qualifying Marxism. Critiquing the notion of class and the axiom of class struggle as the determinant of historical development, he emphasized the mode of production as the motive force of history and insisted on "the existence of history before the class struggle," so that the colonized would not be left in "the sad position of being peoples without history."[2]

Cabral was a prolific writer. Besides his voluminous studies on agronomy and agriculture, his political works published in English include *Revolution in Guinea: An African People's Struggle* (1969), *The Struggle in Guinea* (1969), *Our People Are Our Mountains: Amílcar Cabral on the Guinean Revolution* (1971), *Return to the Source: Selected Speeches of Amílcar Cabral* (1973), and, post-humously, *Unity and Struggle: Speeches and Writings of Amílcar Cabral* (1975). Although some of his writings can be dismissed as political propaganda in the context of armed struggle and a raging Cold War, there is no doubt as to his intellectual sophistication, which established him among the most original thinkers of the twentieth century.

Cabral's study of the social structure of his country was significant and revelatory. Contrary to Fanon's emphatic assertion that "in the colonial countries the peasantry alone are revolutionary," Cabral underscored that, in the case of Guinea-Bissau, their mobilization was particularly challenging.[3] He delineated the positions of the colonial *petite bourgeoisie*, urban wage-earners, and the *déclassé* (marginalized) in relation to the colonial order, distinguishing between the "heavily committed," the nationalist, and those receptive to the idea of armed struggle. He further noted that the "really *déclassé*" were totally against the struggle, in contradistinction to the role Fanon ascribed to the lumpenproletariat as the "the most radically revolutionary forces of a colonized people."[4] Acknowledging the leadership role of the nationalist petty bourgeoisie in the armed struggle, Cabral emphasized the need for it to "commit suicide as a class" and "be reborn as revolutionary workers" in order to avoid the "betrayal of the objectives of national liberation" and prevent a transition from colonialism to neocolonialism.[5]

Cabral was committed to the establishment of a socialist state in which "revolutionary democracy" would be practiced. By revolutionary democracy he meant the political accountability of leaders, popular participation in decisions that affect lives and livelihoods, the empowerment of the people to escape the vicious circle of poverty, hunger, disease, and ignorance, and the establishment of an efficient economy to fulfill the fundamental aspirations of the citizenry—which he articulated as the desire "to gain material advantages, to be able to live a better life in peace, to see their lives progress and to ensure their children's future."[6] But these aspirations would be challenged by the dilemma faced by the nationalist *petite bourgeoisie* upon capturing state power: ally with imperialism and neocolonialism or ally with the workers and peasants.[7] They would in fact be incapable of committing "suicide as a class" and the process of state construction initiated in the liberated areas of Guinea-Bissau would be arrested after independence, while revolutionary democracy arrived stillborn. The betrayal of the incipient revolution in Guinea-Bissau by its self-seeking leadership mirrors the duplicity of other self-serving leaders in post-independence Africa.

Although Cabral was not doctrinaire, he nevertheless insisted on a solid ideological base for revolutionary action, noting, "If it is true that a revolution can fail, even though it be nurtured on perfectly conceived theories, nobody has yet successfully practiced Revolution without a revolutionary theory."[8] He considered the paucity or lack of ideology as "one of the greatest weaknesses" of the national liberation movements in the struggle against imperialism. This is pertinent to post-independence Africa, where the "ideological deficiency" of governing parties constitutes a major factor in the failure to deliver the promises of independence.

As a revolutionary practitioner, Cabral was a realist and a pragmatist who was against the wholesale transplantation of revolutionary principles and practices, famously reminding the 1966 Tricontinental gathering of fellow revolutionaries in Havana that "however great the similarity between our cases and however identical our enemies, unfortunately or fortunately, national liberation and social revolution are not exportable commodities."[9] He reiterated this point to a meeting of more than one hundred and twenty African-American activists in New York three months before his assassination, underscoring that "revolution or national liberation struggle is like a dress which must be fit to each individual's body."[10] In this he stood in sharp contrast to Che Guevara, to whom he has been likened, and even referred to as "Africa's Guevara." While Guevara believed in exporting revolution, unsuccessfully leading expeditionary forces in the DRC and Bolivia, Cabral's internationalism was limited to strong expressions of solidarity with "all just causes." Ultimately, Cabral remained skeptical of generic prescriptions for revolution, doubting that Guevara's schematization of guerrilla warfare was "absolutely adaptable to our conditions."

Furthermore, while Cabral accepted active Cuban military intervention in support of his liberation movement, he and his War Council were nevertheless fully in charge of strategy. "I would make suggestions to Amílcar," complained Victor Dreke, chief of the Cuban Military Mission in Guinea and Guinea-Bissau (MMCG), "he would listen without saying yes or no, and eventually he made his own decision. Sometimes he followed my advice, sometimes he didn't."[11] The combination of lengthy political preparation of the peasantry and the permanent embedding of his fighters in the rural communities also contrasts sharply with the strategy deployed by Guevara, whose failure in the DRC and ultimate death in Bolivia can be attributable to his ignorance of contextual realities and the disconnect between his fighters and the local rural populations.

Cabral succeeded in establishing the primacy of politics in the armed struggle, although the principle died with his assassination, leaving the FARP playing a central role in the political life of the new nation. He also succeeded in structurally transforming the liberated areas in tandem with the unfolding war, but the profound changes could not survive the post-independence neoliberal structural adjustment of the economy and the liberalization of politics.

Perhaps Cabral's greatest contributions to the success of the liberation struggle in Guinea-Bissau and Cabo Verde were the defining of its aims and objectives and the ensuring of their sustainability throughout the long years of conflict. His modesty, humility, and approachability played a critical role in the transformation of ethnic loyalties and class solidarities into a multiethnic movement. He pursued the goals of the liberation struggle with integrity, insisting that his comrades "hide nothing from the masses of our people. Tell no lies. Expose lies whenever they are told. Mask no difficulties, mistakes, failures. Claim no easy victories."[12] Unity and struggle were the essential catchwords. The unity was a work in progress, fragile and vulnerable to manipulations that ultimately fatally victimized him, but strong enough to enable the continuation of the armed struggle to a victorious conclusion.

As a Pan-Africanist, Cabral consistently called for the "total liberation of Africa," for the "economic, social and cultural progress of our peoples," and for "the building of African unity." He was committed to a people-centered unification that would empower ordinary Africans and eliminate the politicization of ethnicity and the ethnicization of politics that negatively impact interethnic and interstate cooperation.

Cabral was a humanist and an idealist, but also a realist and a pragmatist. Cabral the humanist and idealist sometimes clashed with Cabral the realist and pragmatist. He was particularly concerned about the plight of his exploited and oppressed people and deeply committed to their emancipation, which he based on objective realities and pragmatic strategies. He was against gratuitous violence and only accepted the death sentences meted out to his fighters at the Cassacá Congress as a political necessity. As leader of a binational and multiethnic liberation movement, he had to constantly perform delicate balancing acts. A Guinean of Cabo Verdean origin, he was mindful of the negative role of Cabo Verdean colonial officials in Portuguese Guinea and was empathetic to the hostile Guinean sentiments toward them. Nevertheless, he underestimated the depth of the colonially engendered anti–Cabo Verdean grievances and the effectiveness of their exploitation by the Portuguese. Furthermore, he downplayed ethnic hostilities as "secondary contradictions" and underappreciated their profundity among his politically mobilized comrades—which turned out to be a fatal miscalculation.

Consistent with Cabral's concept of total liberation was his commitment to fight against patriarchy and empower women to realize their potential and contribute to national development efforts. Yet, while notable progress was made during the war, the only woman in the first post-independence national governance structure, led by Cabral's brother Luís, was Carmen Pereira, the deputy president of the People's National Assembly (ANP). Francisca Pereira, a war veteran, was also mayor of the city of Bolama. Since then, the proportion of elected women legislators has never surpassed 10 percent, while the number of female appointed government ministers has rarely exceeded five out of an average of twenty-five cabinet members.

Cabral's call for the mental decolonization and "suicide as a class" of the Bissau-Guinean and Cabo Verdean nationalist petty bourgeoisie, in order to identify with "the deepest aspirations of the people," remains pertinent to contemporary Africa. In the post–Cold War context of triumphant neoliberalism, the legacy of his visionary leadership lies in the continued relevance of his progressive ideas. In a globalized world where peoples and nations are left impoverished and marginalized, the fundamental challenge facing the current generation of African leaders remains the establishment of people-centric states that derive their legitimacy from performing functions that consistently and incrementally improve the lives of their citizens. The willingness and readiness of this class to have the political will and moral integrity to undergo the kind of self-transformation Cabral deemed imperative will be a decisive factor in the dismantlement of undemocratic and repressive states that often leave citizens frustrated, humiliated, and desperate.

Notes

Chapter 1: *Terra Natal*

1. Julião Soares Sousa, *Amílcar Cabral (1924–1973): Vida e morte de um revolucionàrio africano*, 2nd ed. (Lisbon: Nova Vega, 2012), 56.

2. Ibid., 54.

3. Juvenal Cabral, *Memórias e reflexões* (1947, author's edition; repr., Praia: Instituto da Biblioteca Nacional, 2002), 17.

4. Ibid., 82.

5. Ibid., 145.

6. Cited in Manuel Brito-Semedo, "Do nativismo ao nacionalismo: A construção da identidade nacional," in *Cabral no cruzamento de épocas: Comunicações e discursos produzidos no II Simpósio Internacional Amílcar Cabral*, ed. Fundação Amílcar Cabral (Praia: Alfa Comunicações, 2005), 330.

7. António Carreira, *Migrações nas Ilhas de Cabo Verde* (Lisbon: Universidade Nova de Lisboa, 1977), 299.

8. Eduíno Brito, *A população de Cabo Verde no século XX* (Lisbon: Agência Geral do Ultramar, 1963), 30.

9. João Augusto Silva, *África: Da vida e do amor na selva* (Lisbon: Edições Momento, 1936), 33.

10. Avelino Teixeira da Mota, *Guiné Portuguesa*, vol. 1 (Lisbon: Agência Geral do Ultramar, 1954), 373.

11. Juvenal Cabral, *Memórias e reflexões*, 164.

12. João Teixeira Pinto, *A ocupação militar da Guiné* (Lisbon: Agência Geral das Colónias, 1936), 202.

13. Luiz Loff de Vasconcellos, cited in Peter Karibe Mendy, *Colonialismo português em África: A tradição da resistência na*

Guiné-Bissau, 1879–1959 (Lisbon: Imprensa Nacional–Casa da Moeda, 1994), 249–50.

14. Juvenal Cabral, cited ibid., 340.

15. Juvenal Cabral to Senhor Inspector das Escolas da Provincia da Guiné, cited ibid., 342.

16. Amílcar Cabral, *Unity and Struggle* (New York: Monthly Review Press, 1979), 243.

17. Juvenal Cabral, *Memórias e reflexões*, 196, 164.

18. Cited in Soares Sousa, *Amílcar Cabral*, 93.

Chapter 2: *Terra Ancestral*

1. Cited in António Carreira, *Cabo Verde: Formação e extinção de uma sociedade escravocrata (1460–1878)* (Bissau: Centro de Estudos da Guiné Portuguesa, 1972), 30.

2. T. Duncan Bentley, *Atlantic Islands: Madeira, the Azores, and the Cape Verdes in Seventeenth-Century Commerce and Navigation* (Chicago: University of Chicago Press, 1972), 235.

3. Amílcar Cabral, foreword to *The Liberation of Guiné: Aspects of an African Revolution*, by Basil Davidson (Harmondsworth, UK: Penguin, 1969), 9.

4. Carreira, *Cabo Verde,* 288.

5. Fundação Mário Soares, *Amílcar Cabral: Sou um simples Africano* (Lisbon: Fundação Mário Soares, 2000), 31.

6. A corruption of the Portuguese word *vadio*, meaning "vagrant," "lazybones"—derogatory terms that in reality reflected passive resistance to callous exploitation.

7. The *bombolom* is a slit-log drum used as a musical instrument as well as a message-transmitting device ("talking drum") by the Manjacos, Pepels, and a few ethnic groups in coastal Guinea-Bissau. Its resonance in Cabo Verde is yet another proof of the historical links between the two countries.

8. Pedro Martins, *The Testimony of a Freedom Fighter*, 3rd rev. ed. (São Vicente, Cape Verde: Gráfica de Mindelo, 2009), 100.

9. Mário de Andrade, *Amilcar Cabral: Essai de biographie politique* (Paris: François Maspero, 1980), 15. António Tomás, *O fazedor de utopias: Uma biografia de Amílcar Cabral*, 2nd ed. (Lisbon: Edições Tinta-da-China, 2008), 52.

10. Julião Soares Sousa, *Amílcar Cabral (1924–1973): Vida e morte de um revolucionàrio africano*, 2nd ed. (Lisbon: Nova Vega, 2012), 70.

11. António Carreira, *Migrações nas Ilhas de Cabo Verde* (Lisbon: Universidade Nova de Lisboa, 1977), calculated from Anexo 1—Quadros estatísticos: Quadro 1. Emigração espontânea, segundo os países ou territórios de destino, nos anos de 1900 a 1952; and Quadro 11, Emigração forçada para o Sul, segundo as ilhas de procedência, nos anos de 1941 a 1970.

12. Amílcar Cabral, *Unity and Struggle* (New York: Monthly Review Press, 1979), 41; Amílcar Cabral, *Revolution in Guinea: An African People's Struggle* (London: Stage 1, 1970), 18.

13. Amílcar Cabral, *Unity and Struggle*, 25–26.

14. Cited in Peter Karibe Mendy, *Colonialismo português em África: A tradição da resistência na Guiné-Bissau, 1879–1959* (Lisbon: Imprensa Nacional–Casa da Moeda, 1994), 317.

15. Cited in Soares Sousa, *Amílcar Cabral*, 75.

16. Amílcar Cabral, *Unity and Struggle*, 56.

17. Ibid.

18. Interview with Colonel Manuel "Manecas" dos Santos, Bissau, 5 January 2016.

19. Amílcar Cabral, "Apontamentos sobre poesia caboverdeana," in *Cabo Verde: Boletim de propaganda e informação* (Praia), 3rd year, no. 28 (1 January 1952): 6.

20. Ibid., 7.

21. Patrick Chabal, *Amílcar Cabral: Revolutionary Leadership and People's War* (New York: Cambridge University Press, 1983), 33.

22. Mário de Andrade, *Amilcar Cabral*, 25.

23. Cited in Archibald Lyall, *Black and White Make Brown: An Account of a Journey to the Cape Verde Islands and Portuguese Guinea* (London: Heinemann, 1938), 98.

24. Cited in Chabal, *Amílcar Cabral*, 34.

Chapter 3: *Mãe Patria*

1. Luís Vaz de Camões (c. 1524–1580), author of the long epic poem *Os Luísadas* (published in 1572) that celebrates

Portugal's voyages of discovery, evangelizing mission, and colonial empire, is considered the country's greatest poet and the father of the Portuguese language, much like the status of William Shakespeare in England and the Anglophone world.

2. Oliveira Martins, "A Civilização Africana," in *Origens do colonialismo português moderno (1822–1891)*, ed. Valentim Alexandre (Lisbon: Sá da Costa, 1979), 213.

3. António Enes, *Moçambique: Relatório apresentado ao governo*, 3rd ed. (1893; repr., Lisbon: Agência Geral das Colónias, 1946), 75.

4. Cited in James Duffy, *Portuguese Africa* (Cambridge: Harvard University Press, 1961), 258.

5. Eduardo da Costa, "Princípios de administração colonial," in *Antologia colonial portuguesa*, vol. 1, *Política e administração* (Lisbon: Agência Geral das Colónias, 1946), 88.

6. Cited in Oleg Ignatiev, *Amílcar Cabral* (Moscow: Edições Progresso, 1984), 15.

7. Cited in Patrick Chabal, *Amílcar Cabral: Revolutionary Leadership and People's War* (New York: Cambridge University Press, 1983), 36.

8. Chabal, *Amílcar Cabral*, 36.

9. Cited in Mário de Andrade, *Amilcar Cabral: Essai de biographie politique* (Paris: François Maspero, 1980), 30.

10. Cited in Andrade, *Amílcar Cabral*, 32.

11. Cited in Julião Soares Sousa, *Amílcar Cabral (1924–1973): Vida e morte de um revolucionàrio africano*, 2nd ed. (Lisbon: Nova Vega, 2012), 129.

12. Cited in Daniel dos Santos, *Amílcar Cabral: Um outro olhar* (Lisbon: Chiado Editora, 2014), 79.

13. Cited in Andrade, *Amílcar Cabral*, 33.

14. Mário de Andrade, cited in Tomás Medeiros, *A verdadeira morte de Amílcar Cabral* (Lisbon: Althum, 2012), 43.

15. Amílcar Cabral, *Unity and Struggle* (New York: Monthly Review Press, 1979), 143.

16. Mário de Andrade, cited in Chabal, *Amílcar Cabral*, 45.

17. Cited ibid.

18. Amílcar Cabral to Maria Helena Rodrigues, 17 September 1952, in Iva Cabral, Márcia Souto, and Filinto Elísio,

eds., *Cartas de Amílcar Cabral a Maria Helena: A outra face do homem* (Lisbon: Rosa de Porcelana, 2016), 338.

Chapter 4: Return to *Terra Natal*

1. Amílcar Cabral to Maria Helena Rodrigues, 24 September 1952, in *Cartas de Amílcar Cabral a Maria Helena: A outra face do homem,* ed. Iva Cabral, Márcia Souto, and Filinto Elísio (Lisbon: Rosa de Porcelana, 2016), 348.

2. Cited in Patrick Chabal, *Amílcar Cabral: Revolutionary Leadership and People's War* (New York: Cambridge University Press, 1983), 36.

3. Cited in "Speech by the Prime Minister of Ghana at the opening session of the All-African People's Conference, on Monday, December 8, 1958," http://www.columbia.edu/itc/history/mann/w3005/nkrumba.html.

4. Cited in Modern History Sourcebook, "All-African People's Conference: Resolution on Imperialism and Colonialism, Accra, December 5–13, 1958," https://sourcebooks.fordham.edu/mod/1958-aapc-res1.asp.

5. Cited in Peter Karibe Mendy, *Colonialismo português em África: A tradição da resistência na Guiné-Bissau, 1879–1959* (Lisbon/Bissau: Imprensa Nacional–Casa da Moeda/Instituto Nacional de Estudos e Pesquisa, 1994), 342.

6. Amílcar Cabral, *Revolution in Guinea: An African People's Struggle* (London: Stage 1, 1970), 25.

7. Cited in Daniel dos Santos, *Amílcar Cabral: Um outro olhar* (Lisbon: Chiado Editora, 2014), 124.

8. Amílcar Cabral, *Unity and Struggle* (New York: Monthly Review Press, 1979), 145.

9. Amílcar Cabral, *Revolution in Guinea,* 50–51.

10. Discussed in chapter 10, on the legacy of Amílcar Cabral.

11. Mendy, *Colonialismo português em África,* 311.

12. Interview with Guinea-Bissau War of Independence veteran Carmen Pereira, Bissau, 12 January 2016.

13. Amílcar Cabral, *Unity and Struggle,* 35.

14. Dalila Cabrita Mateus, *A PIDE/DGS na guerra colonial (1961–1974)* (Lisbon: Terramar, 2004), 30.

15. Amílcar Cabral, "Posto Agrícola Experimental dos Serviços Agrícolas e Florestais: Boletim informativo no. 1," *Ecos da Guiné* 3, no. 30 (January 1953): 25.

16. Ibid.

17. Governor Jorge Frederico Velez Caroço, cited in Mendy, *Colonialismo português em África*, 351.

18. Amílcar Cabral, *Revolution in Guinea*, 28.

19. Cited in Mário de Andrade, "Biographical Notes," in Amílcar Cabral, *Unity and Struggle*, xv.

20. Cited in Julião Soares Sousa, *Amílcar Cabral (1924–1973): Vida e morte de um revolucionàrio africano*, 2nd ed. (Lisbon: Nova Vega, 2012), 175.

21. Amílcar Cabral, *Unity and Struggle*, 29.

22. Cited in Soares Sousa, *Amílcar Cabral*, 180–81.

23. Soares Sousa, *Amílcar Cabral*, 181.

24. Cited in Soares Sousa, *Amílcar Cabral*, 181.

25. Ário Lobo de Azevedo, "A propósito da dimensão humana de Amílcar Cabral," in Amílcar Cabral, *Estudos agrários de Amílcar Cabral* (Lisbon/Bissau: Instituto de Investigação Cientifica Tropical/Instituto Nacional de Estudos e Pesquisa, 1988), 11.

26. Amílcar Cabral to Maria Helena Rodrigues, 30 August 1955, in Cabral, Souto, and Elísio, *Cartas de Amílcar Cabral a Maria Helena*, 365.

27. Lúcio Lara, *Um amplo movimento: Itinerário do MPLA através de documentos e anotações*, vol. 1 (Luanda: Edição Lúcio e Ruth Lara, 1998), 26.

28. Soares Sousa, *Amílcar Cabral*, 184–86.

29. Mário de Andrade, "Biographical Notes," in Amílcar Cabral, *Unity and Struggle*, xxvii.

30. Aristides Pereira, *Uma luta, um partido, dois países: Guiné-Bissau e Cabo Verde* (Lisbon: Editorial Notícias, 2002), 85.

31. Amílcar Cabral, cited in Pereira, *Uma luta, um partido, dois países*, 86–87.

Chapter 5: Binationalism in Action

1. Editorial, "Modern Culture and Our Destiny," *Présence africaine*, nos. 8–9–10 (June–November 1956): 6.

2. Quoted in Claude Wauthier, *The Literature and Thought of Modern Africa: A Survey*, 2nd Eng. lang. ed. (London: Heinemann Educational, 1978), 19.

3. Lúcio Lara, *Um amplo movimento: Itinerário do MPLA através de documentos e anotações*, vol. 1 (Luanda: Edição Lúcio e Ruth Lara, 1998), 39.

4. Ibid., 59.

5. Amílcar Cabral, "Relatório de Amílcar Cabral," in Lara, *Um amplo movimento*, 98–99.

6. Ibid., 99.

7. Amílcar Cabral, "Carta de Amilcar Cabral," in Lara, *Um amplo movimento*, 104.

8. Aristides Pereira, *Uma luta, um partido, dois países: Guiné-Bissau e Cabo Verde* (Lisbon: Editorial Notícias, 2002), 86; and Luís Cabral, *Cronica de Libertação* (Lisbon: O Jornal, 1984), 69.

9. Daniel dos Santos, *Amílcar Cabral: Um outro olhar* (Lisbon: Chiado Editora), 167.

10. Amílcar Cabral, "Carta de Amílcar Cabral," in Lara, *Um amplo movimento,* 104.

11. Cited in Basil Davidson, *The Liberation of Guiné: Aspects of an African Revolution* (Harmondsworth, UK: Penguin, 1969), 32.

12. Amílcar Cabral, *Revolution in Guinea*, 31.

13. "Carta de Amílcar Cabral," in Lara, *Um amplo movimento,* 105.

14. Ibid.

15. "Memorandum de Amílcar Cabral e Mário de Andrade," in Lara, *Um amplo movimento,* 234.

16. Cited in "Carta da FRAIN," in Lara, *Um amplo movimento,* 247.

17. "Relatório de Amílcar Cabral," in Lara, *Um amplo movimento,* 98.

18. This and following quotations from Amílcar Cabral, *Unity and Struggle* (New York: Monthly Review Press, 1979), 17, 27, reprinting the pamphlet Amílcar Cabral [Abel Djassi, pseud.], *The Facts about Portugal's African Colonies* (London: Union of Democratic Control, 1961).

19. Amílcar Cabral, *Revolution in Guinea: An African People's Struggle* (London: Stage 1, 1970), 128.

20. Cited in Aristides Pereira, *Uma luta, um partido, dois países,* 145.

21. Amílcar Cabral, cited in Patrick Chabal, *Amílcar Cabral: Revolutionary Leadership and People's War* (New York: Cambridge University Press, 1983), 66.

22. Amílcar Cabral, *Revolution in Guinea,* 111.

23. Amílcar Cabral, *Unity and Struggle,* 75.

24. Amílcar Cabral, *Revolution in Guinea,* 83.

25. Ibid., 87.

Chapter 6: Conducting Armed Struggle

1. "*Tugas*" was a local name for the Portuguese colonialists.

2. Quotations in this paragraph in Aristides Pereira, *Uma luta, um partido, dois países: Guiné-Bissau e Cabo Verde* (Lisbon: Editorial Notícias, 2002), 141.

3. Amílcar Cabral, *Revolution in Guinea: An African People's Struggle* (London: Stage 1, 1970), 63–64.

4. Cited in Basil Davidson, *The Liberation of Guiné: Aspects of an African Revolution* (Harmondsworth, UK: Penguin, 1969), 97.

5. Amílcar Cabral, *Revolution in Guinea,* 36.

6. Cited in Julião Soares Sousa, *Amílcar Cabral (1924–1973): Vida e morte de um revolucionàrio africano,* 2nd ed. (Lisbon: Nova Vega, 2012), 352.

7. Amílcar Cabral, foreword to *The Liberation of Guiné: Aspects of an African Revolution,* by Basil Davidson (Harmondsworth, UK: Penguin, 1969), 14.

8. Amílcar Cabral, *Unity and Struggle* (New York: Monthly Review Press, 1979), 173.

9. A. Costa Pereira, "Apontamentos sobre a política da Guiné Portuguesa e territórios vizinhos," report of the Polícia Internacional e de Defesa do Estado (PIDE), 17 January 1963, available at Casa comum (Fundação Mário Soares), http://casacomum.org/cc/visualizador?pasta=04999.015.

10. António Augusto Peixoto Correia, "Aos propósitos do invasores," *O arauto. Diário da Guiné Portuguesa,* 19th year, no. 4527, 1 August 1961.

11. Cited in Dalila Cabrita Mateus, *A PIDE/DGS na guerra colonial (1961–1974)* (Lisbon: Terramar, 2004), 99.

12. Costa Pereira, "Apontamentos Sobre a Politica."

13. Aristides Pereira, *Uma luta, um partido, dois países,* 145.

14. Costa Pereira, "Apontamentos Sobre a Politica."

15. Ibid.

16. Amílcar Cabral, cited in Daniel dos Santos, *Amílcar Cabral: Um outro olhar* (Lisbon: Chiado Editora, 2014), 324.

17. Amílcar Cabral, *Unity and Struggle* (New York: Monthly Review Press, 1979), 176.

18. Cited in José Matos, "O inicio da guerra na Guiné (1961–1964)," *Revista militar,* no. 2566 (November 2015), https://www.revistamilitar.pt/artigo/1066.

19. Cited in Santos, *Amílcar Cabral,* 362.

20. Luís Cabral, *Crónica da libertação* (Lisbon: O Jornal, 1984), 158.

21. Amílcar Cabral, cited in Basil Davidson, *The Liberation of Guiné: Aspects of an African Revolution* (Harmondsworth, UK: Penguin, 1969), 102.

22. Cited in Patrick Chabal, *Amílcar Cabral: Revolutionary Leadership and People's War* (New York: Cambridge University Press, 1983), 78.

23. Amílcar Cabral, *Unity and Struggle,* 177.

24. Amílcar Cabral, *Revolution in Guinea,* 70.

25. Cited in Chabal, *Amílcar Cabral,* 79.

26. Amílcar Cabral, *Revolution in Guinea,* 131.

27. Ibid., 112.

28. Ibid., 112, 113.

29. Mustafah Dhada, *Warriors at Work: How Guinea Was Really Set Free* (Niwot: University Press of Colorado), 34.

30. "Said yes, but did nothing" is Piero Gleijeses's phrase, in his "The First Ambassadors: Cuba's Contribution to Guinea-Bissau's War of Independence," *Journal of Latin American Studies* 29, no. 1 (February 1997): 47.

31. Ibid., 51.

32. Oscar Oramas, *Amílcar Cabral: Para além do seu tempo* (Lisbon: Hugin Editores, 1998), 82.

33. Dhada, *Warriors at Work,* 35.

34. PAIGC, "Communique of the Political Bureau," cited in Santos, *Amílcar Cabral*, 387.

35. António de Spínola, *Por uma Guiné melhor* (Lisbon: Agência Geral do Ultramar, 1970), 138.

36. Amílcar Cabral, *Unity and Struggle*, 139.

37. Ibid., 231.

38. Dhada, *Warriors at Work*, 43.

39. Pereira, *Uma luta, um partido, dois países*, 192.

40. Amílcar Cabral, *Unity and Struggle*, 191.

41. Cited in R. A. H. Robinson, *Contemporary Portugal: A History* (London: George Allen and Unwin, 1979), 179.

42. Santos, *Amílcar Cabral*, 393–99.

43. Cited in Gleijeses, "First Ambassadors," 57.

44. Following the 1958 All African People's Conference held in Accra, two main groups of independent African nations emerged with opposing visions of Pan-African unification: a small Casablanca group (Ghana, Guinea, Mali, the United Arab Republic, and Morocco, plus the Provisional Government of Algeria), formed in Casablanca in January 1961, which championed immediate continental unification; and a larger Monrovia group (including Nigeria, Liberia, Ivory Coast, Senegal, Cameroon, Ethiopia, Somalia, Tunisia, and the Malagasy Republic), created in Monrovia in May 1961, which advocated a gradualist approach. The establishment of the Organization of African Unity on 25 May 1963 was a compromise between these two groups. See chapter 7 for Cabral's position on Pan-African unity.

45. Keesing's, "Repulse of Raids by 'Mercenaries' and Guinean Exiles," *Keesing's Contemporary Archives* 17 (December 1970): 24353, http://web.stanford.edu/group/tomzgroup/pmwiki/uploads/1385-Keesings-1970-12-a-RRW.pdf.

46. Amílcar Cabral, *Unity and Struggle*, 204

47. Cited in Norrie MacQueen, "Portugal's First Domino: 'Pluricontinentalism' and Colonial War in Guiné-Bissau, 1963–1974," *Contemporary European History* 8, no. 2 (July 1999): 221.

48. Cited by Mário de Andrade, "Biographical Notes," in Amílcar Cabral, *Unity and Struggle*, xxx.

49. Dhada, *Warriors at Work*, 171.

50. Cited in Lars Rudebeck, "Reading Cabral on Democracy," in *Africa's Contemporary Challenges: The Legacy of Amilcar Cabral*, ed. Carlos Lopes (New York: Routledge, 2010), 88–89.

Chapter 7: Solidarity with "Every Just Cause"

1. Amílcar Cabral, *Unity and Struggle* (New York: Monthly Review Press, 1979), 253.

2. Cited in J. Ayodele Langley, *Pan-Africanism and Nationalism in West Africa, 1900–1945: A Study in Ideology and Social Classes* (Oxford: Clarendon, 1973), 354–55.

3. Amílcar Cabral, *Revolution in Guinea: An African People's Struggle* (London: Stage 1, 1970), 14–15.

4. Amílcar Cabral, *Unity and Struggle*, 254.

5. Amílcar Cabral, *Revolution in Guinea*, 120.

6. Ibid., 66, 121.

7. Basil Davidson, *The Liberation of Guiné: Aspects of an African Revolution* (Harmondsworth, UK: Penguin, 1969), 16, 18.

8. Amílcar Cabral, *Revolution in Guinea*, 120.

9. Ibid., 66.

10. Amílcar Cabral, "The Weapon of Theory." Address to the first Tricontinental Conference of the Peoples of Asia, Africa, and Latin America, Havana, 3 January 1966," https://www.marxists.org/subject/africa/cabral/1966/weapon-theory.htm.

11. Fidel Castro, Speech at the Closing Session of the Tricontinental Conference, Havana, 16 January 1966, https://www.marxists.org/history/cuba/archive/castro/1966/01/15.htm.

12. Amílcar Cabral, *Revolution in Guinea*, 121.

13. Ibid., 120.

14. Ibid., 66.

15. Amílcar Cabral, *Return to the Source: Selected Speeches of Amilcar Cabral* (New York: Monthly Review Press, 1973), 75, 92.

16. Amílcar Cabral, *Unity and Struggle*, 255.

17. Ibid.

1. Amílcar Cabral, *Unity and Struggle* (New York: Monthly Review Press, 1979), 117.

2. Ibid., 114–17.

3. Julião Soares Sousa, *Amílcar Cabral (1924–1973): Vida e morte de um revolucionàrio africano*, 2nd ed. (Lisbon: Nova Vega, 2012), 404.

4. Jack Bourderie, "A Tough Little Monkey," in *Dirty Work 2: The CIA in Africa*, ed. Ellen Ray et al. (London: Zed, 1982), 183.

5. Citations from excerpt in Leopoldo Amado, *Guerra colonial e guerra de libertação nacional, 1950–1974: O caso da Guiné-Bissau* (Lisbon: IPAD, 2011), 325.

6. Cited in ibid., 330.

7. Cited in Bruno Crimi, "Les assassins de Cabral," *Jeune Afrique*, 3 February 1973, 8–12, available at *Casa comum* (Fundação Mário Soares, Documentos Amílcar Cabral), http://casacomum.org/cc/visualizador?pasta=07701.005.

8. Antonio de Spínola, interview with José Pedro Castanheiro, first published in two articles in *Expresso* (Lisbon) on 16 January 1993 and 30 April 1994; cited in José Pedro Castanheira, *Quem mandou matar Amílcar Cabral?* (Lisbon: Relógio d'Água, 1995), 232.

9. Cited in Castanheira, *Quem mandou matar Amílcar Cabral?*, 222.

10. Cited in ibid., 225.

11. Cited in ibid., 212.

12. Charles Diggs, text quoted in "Tributes to a Fallen Comrade," *Ufahamu: A Journal of African Studies* 3, no. 3 (Winter 1973): 15, http://escholarship.org/uc/item/4vf0v6ws.

13. Cited in US Department of State, "Portuguese Guinea: The PAIGC after Amilcar Cabral" (Declassified PA/HO Department of State E.O. 12958), https://2001-2009.state.gov/documents/organization/67534.pdf

14. Oleg Ignatiev. *Três tiros da PIDE. Quem, porque e como mataram Amílcar Cabral* (Lisbon: Prelo Editora, 1975), 185.

15. Carmen Maria de Araújo Pereira, *Os meus três amores* (Bissau: Instituto Nacional de Estudos e Pesquisa, 2016), 162.

16. Cited in Castanheira, *Quem mandou matar Amílcar Cabral?*, 81.

17. Marcello Caetano, *Portugal não pode ceder: Discurso pronunciado no Palácio das Necessidades em 6 de Outubro de 1969* (Lisbon: Secretaria de Estado de Informação e Turismo, 1969).

18. Castanheira, *Quem mandou matar Amílcar Cabral?*, 229.

Chapter 9: *A Luta Continua*

1. Carmen Maria de Araújo Pereira, *Os meus três amores* (Bissau: Instituto Nacional de Estudos e Pesquisa, 2016), 162.

2. Partido Africano da Independência da Guiné e Cabo Verde, "*Sobre o cobarde e criminoso assassinato do nosso querido leader, Amílcar Cabral, fundador e secretario geral do PAIGC: Decisões da direcção do partido*" (Conakry: PAIGC, 1973).

3. Cited in José Pedro Castanheira, *Quem mandou matar Amílcar Cabral?* (Lisbon: Relógio d'Água, 1995), 214.

4. Cited in Amílcar Cabral, *Unity and Struggle* (New York: Monthly Review Press, 1979), 214.

5. Amílcar Cabral, *Revolution in Guinea: An African People's Struggle* (London: Stage 1, 1970), 125.

6. Cited in Patrick Chabal, *Amílcar Cabral: Revolutionary Leadership and People's War* (New York: Cambridge University Press, 1983), 148.

7. J. Pinto Ferreira and Miguel Pessoa, "Guiné 63/74–P3859: FAP (6): A Introdução do míssil russo SAM-7 Strela no CTIG," *Luís Graça & camaradas da Guiné* (blog), 9 February 2009, https://blogueforanadaevaotres.blogspot.com/2009/02/guine-6374-p3859-fap-6-introducao-do.html.

8. Ibid.

9. António da Graça Abreu and Luís Graça, "Guiné 63/74–P1668: In memoriam do piloto aviador Baltazar da Silva e de outros portugueses com asas de pássaro (António da Graça Abreu / Luís Graça)," *Luís Graça & Camaradas da Guiné* (blog), 17 April 2007, https://blogueforanadaevaotres.blogspot.com/2007/04/guin-6374-p1669-in-memoriam-do-piloto.html.

10. Ibid.

11. Mustafah Dhada, *Warriors at Work: How Guinea Was Really Set Free* (Niwot: University Press of Colorado, 1993), 52.

12. Cited in Leopoldo Amado, *Guerra colonial e guerra de libertação nacional, 1950–1974: O caso da Guiné-Bissau* (Lisbon: IPAD, 2011), 343.

13. Cited in Castanheira, *Quem mandou matar Amílcar Cabral?*, 215.

14. Marcello Caetano, *Depoimento* (Rio de Janeiro: Distribuidora Record, 1974), 225.

15. Cited in Chabal, *Amílcar Cabral*, 150.

16. Ibid., 102.

Chapter 10: *Cabral ka Muri*

1. Cited in Gérard Chaliand, *La pointe du couteau: Mémoires* (Paris: Robert Laffont, 2011), Kindle edition, "Amilcar Cabral et le marquis de Guinée-Bissau," Location 4246 of 7483.

2. Amílcar Cabral, *Unity and Struggle* (New York: Monthly Review Press, 1979), 125.

3. Frantz Fanon, *The Wretched of the Earth* (Harmondsworth, England: Penguin, 1967), 47.

4. Ibid., 103.

5. Amílcar Cabral, *Revolution in Guinea: An African People's Struggle* (London: Stage 1, 1969), 89.

6. Amílcar Cabral, *Unity and Struggle*, 241.

7. Amílcar Cabral, *Revolution in Guinea*, 57.

8. Amílcar Cabral, *Unity and Struggle*, 123.

9. Ibid.

10. Amílcar Cabral, *Return to the Source: Selected Speeches of Amilcar Cabral* (New York: Monthly Review Press, 1973), 77.

11. Cited in Piero Gleijeses, "The First Ambassadors: Cuba's Contribution to Guinea-Bissau's War of Independence," *Journal of Latin American Studies* 29, no. 1 (February 1997): 63.

12. Amílcar Cabral, *Revolution in Guinea*, 72.

Bibliography

Alexandre, Valentim, ed. *Origens do colonialismo português moderno (1822–1891)*. Lisbon: Sá da Costa, 1979.

Amado, Leopoldo. *Guerra colonial e guerra de libertação nacional, 1950–1974: O caso da Guiné-Bissau*. Lisbon: IPAD, 2011.

Andrade, Mário de. *Amilcar Cabral: Essai de biographie politique*. Paris: François Maspero, 1980.

Barata, Victor. "Guiné 63/74–P1668: In memoriam do piloto aviador Baltazar da Silva e de outros portugueses com asas de pássaro (António da Graça Abreu / Luís Graça)." *Luís Graça & camaradas da Guiné* (blog), 17 April 2007. https://blogueforanadaevaotres.blogspot.com/2007/04/guin-6374-p1669-in-memoriam-do-piloto.html.

Bentley, T. Duncan. *Atlantic Islands: Madeira, the Azores, and the Cape Verdes in Seventeenth-Century Commerce and Navigation*. Chicago: University of Chicago Press, 1972.

Boxer, C. R. *Race Relations in the Portuguese Colonial Empire, 1415–1825*. Oxford: Oxford University Press, 1963.

Brito, Eduíno. *A população de Cabo Verde no século XX*. Lisbon: Agência Geral do Ultramar, 1963.

Brito-Semedo, Manuel. "Do nativismo ao nacionalismo: A construção da identidade nacional." In *Cabral no cruzamento de épocas: Comunicações e discursos produzidos no II Simpósio Internacional Amílcar Cabral*, edited by Fundação Amílcar Cabral, 325–39. Praia: Alfa Comunicações, 2005.

Cabral, Amílcar. "Apontamentos sobre poesia caboverdeana." In *Cabo Verde: Boletim de propaganda e informação* (Praia), 3rd year, no. 28 (1 January 1952): 5–8.

———. *Estudos agrários de Amílcar Cabral*. Lisbon/Bissau: Instituto de Investigação Cientifica Tropical/Instituto Nacional de Estudos e Pesquisa, 1988.

———. Foreword to *The Liberation of Guiné: Aspects of an African Revolution*, by Basil Davidson, 9–15. Harmondsworth, UK: Penguin, 1969.

———. Amílcar Cabral, *Return to the Source: Selected Speeches of Amilcar Cabral*. New York: Monthly Review Press, 1973.

———. *Revolution in Guinea: An African People's Struggle*. London: Stage 1, 1970.

———. *Unity and Struggle*. New York: Monthly Review Press, 1979.

———. "The Weapon of Theory." Address to the first Tricontinental Conference of the Peoples of Asia, Africa, and Latin America, Havana, 3 January 1966. https://www.marxists.org/subject/africa/cabral/1966/weapon-theory.htm.

Cabral, Iva, Márcia Souto, and Filinto Elísio, eds. *Cartas de Amílcar Cabral a Maria Helena: A outra face do homem*. Lisbon: Rosa de Porcelana, 2016.

Cabral, Juvenal. *Memórias e reflexões*. 1947, author's edition. Reprint, Praia: Instituto da Biblioteca Nacional, 2002.

Cabral, Luís. *Crónica da libertação*. Lisbon: O Jornal, 1984.

Cabrita Mateus, Dalila. *A PIDE/DGS na guerra colonial (1961–1974)*. Lisbon: Terramar, 2004.

Caetano, Marcello. *Depoimento*. Rio de Janeiro: Distribuidora Record, 1974.

———. *Portugal não pode ceder: Discurso pronunciado no Palácio das Necessidades em 6 de Outubro de 1969*. Lisbon: Secretaria de Estado de Informação e Turismo, 1969.

Carreira, António. *Cabo Verde: Formação e extinção de uma sociedade escravocrata (1460–1878)*. Bissau: Centro de Estudos da Guiné Portuguesa, 1972.

———. *Migrações nas Ilhas de Cabo Verde*. Lisbon: Universidade Nova de Lisboa, 1977.

Castanheira, José Pedro. *Quem mandou matar Amílcar Cabral?* Lisbon: Relógio d'Água, 1995.

Castro, Fidel. Speech at the Closing Session of the Tricontinental Conference, Havana, 16 January 1966. https://www.marxists.org/history/cuba/archive/castro/1966/01/15.htm.

Chabal, Patrick. *Amílcar Cabral: Revolutionary Leadership and People's War.* New York: Cambridge University Press, 1983.

Chaliand, Gérard. *La pointe du couteau: Mémoires—Tome I.* Paris: Robert Laffont, 2011. Kindle edition.

Chilcote, Ronald H. *Amílcar Cabral's Revolutionary Theory and Practice: A Critical Guide.* Boulder, CO: Lynne Rienner, 1991.

Costa, Eduardo da. "Princípios de administração colonial." In *Antologia colonial portuguesa*, vol. 1, *Política e administração*, 79–96. Lisbon: Agência Geral das Colónias, 1946.

Costa Pereira, A. "Apontamentos sobre a política da Guiné Portuguesa e territórios vizinhos." Report of the Polícia Internacional e de Defesa do Estado (PIDE), 17 January 1963. Available at *Casa comum* (Fundação Mário Soares, Documentos Amílcar Cabral). http://casacomum.org/cc/visualizador?pasta=04999.015.

Crimi, Bruno. "Les assassins de Cabral." *Jeune Afrique*, 3 February 1973, 8–12. Available at *Casa comum* (Fundação Mário Soares, Documentos Amílcar Cabral). http://casacomum.org/cc/visualizador?pasta=07701.005.

Davidson, Basil. *The Fortunate Isles: A Study in African Transformation.* Trenton, NJ: Africa World Press, 1989.

———. *The Liberation of Guiné: Aspects of an African Revolution.* Harmondsworth, UK: Penguin, 1969.

Dhada, Mustafah. *Warriors at Work: How Guinea Was Really Set Free.* Niwot, CO: University Press of Colorado, 1993.

Diggs, Charles. Text quoted in "Tributes to a Fallen Comrade." *Ufahamu: A Journal of African Studies* 3, no. 3 (Winter 1973): 15. http://escholarship.org/uc/item/4vf0v6ws.

Duffy, James. *Portuguese Africa.* Cambridge: Harvard University Press, 1961.

Enes, António. *Moçambique: Relatório apresentado ao governo.* 3rd ed. Lisbon: Agência Geral das Colónias, 1946. First published 1893 by Sociedade de Geographia de Lisboa (Lisbon).

Fanon, Frantz. *The Wretched of the Earth.* Harmondsworth, UK: Penguin, 1967.

Ferreira, J. Pinto, and Miguel Pessoa. "Guiné 63/74–P3859: FAP (6): A Introdução do míssil russo SAM-7 Strela no CTIG." *Luís Graça & camaradas da Guiné* (blog), 9 February 2009. https://blogueforanadaevaotres.blogspot.com /2009/02/guine-6374-p3859-fap-6-introducao-do.html.

Fordham University Modern History Sourcebook. "All-African People's Conference: Resolution on Imperialism and Colonialism, Accra, December 5–13, 1958." https://sourcebooks .fordham.edu/mod/1958-aapc-res1.asp.

Fundação Mário Soares. *Amílcar Cabral: Sou um simples Africano.* Lisbon: Fundação Mário Soares, 2000. Exhibition catalog.

Gleijeses, Piero. "The First Ambassadors: Cuba's Contribution to Guinea-Bissau's War of Independence." *Journal of Latin American Studies* 29, no. 1 (February 1997): 45–88.

Ignatiev, Oleg. *Amílcar Cabral.* Moscow: Edições Progresso, 1984.

———. *Três tiros da PIDE. Quem, porque e como mataram Amílcar Cabral.* Lisbon: Prelo Editora, 1975.

Keesing's. "Repulse of Raids by 'Mercenaries' and Guinean Exiles." *Keesing's Contemporary Archives* 17 (December 1970): 24353. http://web.stanford.edu/group/tomzgroup /pmwiki/uploads/1385-Keesings-1970-12-a-RRW.pdf.

Langley, J. Ayodele. *Pan-Africanism and Nationalism in West Africa, 1900–1945: A Study in Ideology and Social Classes.* Oxford: Clarendon, 1973.

Lara, Lúcio. *Um amplo movimento: Itinerário do MPLA através de documentos e anotações.* Vol. 1. Luanda: Edição Lúcio e Ruth Lara, 1998.

Lopes, Carlos. *Guinea Bissau: From Liberation Struggle to Independent Statehood.* Boulder, CO: Westview Press, 1987.

Lyall, Archibald. *Black and White Make Brown: An Account of a Journey to the Cape Verde Islands and Portuguese Guinea.* London: Heinemann, 1938.

MacQueen, Norrie. "Portugal's First Domino: 'Pluricontinentalism' and Colonial War in Guiné-Bissau, 1963–1974."

Contemporary European History 8, no. 2 (July 1999): 209–30.

Martins, Pedro. The Testimony of a Freedom Fighter. 3rd rev. ed. São Vicente, Cape Verde: Gráfica do Mindelo, 2009.

Matos, José. "O Inicio da guerra na Guiné (1961–1964)." Revista militar, no. 2566 (November 2015). https://www.revistamilitar.pt/artigo/1066.

Medeiros, Tomás. A verdadeira morte de Amílcar Cabral. Lisbon: Althum, 2012.

Mendy, Peter Karibe. Colonialismo português em África: A tradição da resistência na Guiné-Bissau, 1879–1959. Lisbon/Bissau: Imprensa Nacional–Casa da Moeda/Instituto Nacional de Estudos e Pesquisa, 1994.

Nkrumah, Kwame. "Speech by the Prime Minister of Ghana at the opening session of the All-African People's Conference, on Monday, December 8, 1958." http://www.columbia.edu/itc/history/mann/w3005/nkrumba.html.

Oramas, Oscar. Amílcar Cabral: Para além do seu tempo. Lisbon: Hugin Editores, 1998.

Partido Africano da Independência da Guiné e Cabo Verde. Sobre o cobarde e criminoso assassinato do nosso querido leader, Amílcar Cabral, fundador e secretario geral do PAIGC: Decisões da direcção do partido. Conakry: PAIGC, 1973.

Pereira, Aristides. Uma luta, um partido, dois países: Guiné-Bissau e Cabo Verde. Lisbon: Editorial Notícias, 2002.

Pereira, Carmen Maria de Araújo. Os meus três amores. Bissau: Instituto Nacional de Estudos e Pesquisa, 2016.

Pinto, João Teixeira. A ocupação militar da Guiné. Lisbon: Agência Geral das Colónias, 1936.

Ray, Ellen, William Schaap, Karl Van Meter, and Louis Wolf, eds. Dirty Work 2: The CIA in Africa. London: Zed Press, 1982.

Robinson, R. A. H. Contemporary Portugal: A History. London: George Allen and Unwin, 1979.

Rudebeck, Lars. Guinea-Bissau: A Study of Political Mobilization. Uppsala: The Scandinavian Institute of African Studies, 1974.

———. "Reading Cabral on Democracy." In *Africa's Contemporary Challenges: The Legacy of Amilcar Cabral*, edited by Carlos Lopes, 87–96. New York: Routledge, 2010.

Santos, Daniel dos. *Amílcar Cabral: Um outro olhar*. Lisbon: Chiado Editora, 2014.

Silva, João Augusto. *África: Da vida e do amor na selva*. Lisbon: Edições Momento, 1936.

Soares Sousa, Julião. *Amílcar Cabral (1924–1973): Vida e morte de um revolucionàrio africano*. 2nd ed. Lisbon: Nova Vega, 2012.

Sousa Ferreira, Eduardo de. *Portuguese Colonialism in Africa: The End of an Era*. Paris: UNESCO Press, 1974.

Spínola, António de. *Por uma Guiné melhor*. Lisbon: Agência Geral do Ultramar, 1970.

Teixeira da Mota, Avelino. *Guiné Portuguesa*, Volume I: Lisbon: Agência Geral do Ultramar, 1954.

Tomás, António. *O fazedor de utopias: Uma biografia de Amílcar Cabral*. 2nd ed. Lisbon: Edições Tinta-da-China, 2008.

United States Department of State. "Portuguese Guinea: The PAIGC after Amilcar Cabral" (Declassified PA/HO Department of State E.O. 12958). https://2001-2009.state.gov/documents/organization/67534.pdf.

Wauthier, Claude. *The Literature and Thought of Modern Africa: A Survey*. 2nd Eng. lang. ed. London: Heinemann Educational, 1978.

Index

232

235

OHIO SHORT HISTORIES OF AFRICA

MOZAMBIQUE'S SAMORA MACHEL

A LIFE CUT SHORT

ALLEN F. ISAACMAN AND BARBARA S. ISAACMAN

WITH A FOREWORD BY ALBIE SACHS

Samora Machel (1933–86), the son of small-town farmers, led his people through a war against their Portuguese colonizers and became the first president of the People's Republic of Mozambique.

Machel's military successes against a colonial regime backed by South Africa, Rhodesia, the United States, and its NATO allies enhanced his reputation as a revolutionary hero to the oppressed people of southern Africa. In 1986, during the country's civil war, Machel died in a plane crash under circumstances that remain uncertain.

Allen and Barbara Isaacman lived through many of these changes in Mozambique and bring personal recollections together with archival research and interviews with others who knew Machel or participated in events of the revolutionary or postrevolutionary years.

Allen F. Isaacman, Regents Professor of History at the University of Minnesota and Extraordinary Professor at the University of the Western Cape, is the author of seven books, including the coauthored (with Barbara Isaacman) *Dams, Displacement, and the Delusion of Development*, winner of the ASA Book Prize (formerly Herskovits Award) and the AHA Klein Prize in African History. He is a fellow of the American Academy of Arts and Sciences and has won fellowships from the Guggenheim and MacArthur Foundations, among others.

Barbara S. Isaacman, a retired criminal defense attorney, worked with the Mozambican Women's Movement (OMM) and taught at the law faculty of the Universidade Eduardo Mondlane while living in Mozambique in the late 1970s. She wrote *Mozambique—Women, the Law, and Agrarian Reform* and coauthored with Allen Isaacman several books, including the award-winning *Dams, Displacement, and the Delusion of Development*.

Mozambique's Samora Machel

A Life Cut Short

Allen F. Isaacman

Barbara S. Isaacman

Foreword by Albie Sachs

OHIO UNIVERSITY PRESS

ATHENS

Ohio University Press, Athens, Ohio 45701
ohioswallow.com
© 2020 by Ohio University Press
All rights reserved

Printed in the United States of America
Ohio University Press books are printed on acid-free paper ⊚ ™

30 29 28 27 26 25 24 23 22 21 20   5 4 3 2 1

Library of Congress Cataloging-in-Publication Data
Names: Isaacman, Allen F., author. | Isaacman, Barbara, author. | Sachs,
  Albie, 1935- writer of foreword.
Title: Mozambique's Samora Machel : a life cut short / Allen F. Isaacman,
  Barbara S. Isaacman ; foreword by Albie Sachs.
Other titles: Ohio short histories of Africa.
Description: Athens : Ohio University Press, [2020] | Series: Ohio short
  histories of Africa | Includes bibliographical references and index.
Identifiers: LCCN 2020016049 | ISBN 9780821424230 (paperback) | ISBN
  9780821446942 (pdf)
Subjects: LCSH: Machel, Samora, 1933-1986. | Presidents--Mozambique--20th
  century--Biography. | Nationalists--Mozambique Biography. |
  Mozambique--Politics and government--To 1975. | Mozambique--Politics and
  government--1975-1994.
Classification: LCC DT3393.M33 I73 2020 | DDC 967.9051092--dc23
LC record available at https://lccn.loc.gov/2020016049

To the Mozambican people

Contents

Illustrations

Foreword

The words "*A luta continua*" appear in an artwork next to the doors of South Africa's Constitutional Court, which stands in the heart of the Old Fort Prison. They remind us of leaders like M. K. Gandhi, Albert Luthuli, Nelson and Winnie Mandela, Helen Joseph, Fatima Meer, Oliver Tambo, and Robert Sobukwe who were locked up there for their pursuit of justice and freedom. To this day, when people in South Africa challenge corruption and abuse of office in high places, they say, "*A luta continua!*" The struggle continues! The phrase reminds us of our connection with Mozambique and with Samora Machel. It brings back to me the inspiration I received from Samora during the eleven years I lived and worked in that country and nearly died there.

How we loved to hear Samora speak to vast crowds in Independence Square. He was funny, melodious, entrancing, conveying big political ideas with clarity and simplicity. You always learned something. You felt connected with him and with tens of thousands of others listening avidly to every word.

And how he delighted us with his invocations of internationalism. He constantly reminded the thousands filling the square that Mozambique had gained its independence with enormous international support and that people from all over the world were welcome to cooperate in building a new society. In the crowd I would see scores of people from a multitude of countries. Among them would be Cubans sent by Fidel, Chileans who had escaped from Pinochet, and Brazilians and Argentinians who had evaded the military dictatorships in their countries. There were South Africans—Ruth First, before she was assassinated, Alpheus Manghezi and Rob Davies from the Centre for African Studies, me from the newly created law school at Eduardo Mondlane University, and students like Ben Mokoena and Tom Moyane. And there would be Allen Isaacman, preeminent historian of contemporary Mozambique, and his wife Barbara Isaacman, my colleague at the law school (the "Isaacpeople," as we jokingly called them), the authors of this magnificently researched and most compelling book.

We all felt proud to be there. Samora would lead us in singing freedom songs, and then in the "vivas": "Long live the just struggle of the oppressed people of South Africa!"—"Viva!" "Long live the emancipation of women!"—"Viva!" "Down with racism, tribalism, and regionalism!"—"*Abaixo*!" "*A luta. . .*," Samora would declaim and pause, and we would respond, "*continua*!"

We especially loved Samora's humor and sense of humanity. Referring to Africa's homegrown exploiters, he would tell us there were people who would fiercely resist being eaten by a foreign tiger but not mind at all being devoured by a local lion. Discussing relations with countries like Zambia and Tanzania, he would observe that there were people in neighboring countries who

12

thought they were superior because they had been colonized by the British and not the Portuguese. Or he might ask, Why was it that in colonial times our waiters would serve the Portuguese soldiers with courtesy and respect, but now would be rude to their own people? The answer was that the enemy was camping in our heads—we still had the mentality of underdevelopment.

Stories about Samora became legend. I remember how inspired I was by the tale of an exchange between Samora and his father. In the colonial period, Samora's father was expelled from a fertile piece of land along the Limpopo River to make way for Portuguese peasants to grow rice there. When independence came and the colonists returned to Portugal, Papa Machel asked his son when he could go back and start planting there again. To his dismay and to our delight, Samora replied that Frelimo had not fought for the president's father to get land, but for the nation to get food. Our joy was unmitigated.

We believed that the beneficiaries of the revolution should be those in greatest need, rather than those close to the president, and that private ownership of land should give way to more collectivized, socialist forms of land use. With Bulgarian help, the Frelimo government created a huge state farm on the banks of the Limpopo. Tractors came to till the soil, which was good, but they put in too much fertilizer, which was bad. The rice grew too quickly and volunteers from the towns were needed to harvest the premature crop. Now, if anybody asks me to come and cut rice, even when it was before the bomb and I still had two arms, I know they are in desperate straits. Even if for me it was fantastic to be out in the fields with the workers cutting rice with a sickle, for the country it was a disaster. Our delight turned to dismay. The objective was noble and, given the absence of an indigenous managerial class, the temptation to place everything in state hands was understandable. But the result was calamitous. Today, not even the most radical thinkers would deny that Samora's father should have gotten back his land, not because he was the president's father, but because he had been forced off it in the first place.

This happy story turned sad reminds me of one of Samora's favorite sayings: to know the taste of an avocado pear, you must cut it in half. By this he meant that instead of attempting to suppress political contradictions, you should bring them out into the open, deal with them decisively, and emerge stronger as a result. This book is packed with carefully sourced and compactly presented information dealing with many of the contradictions with which Frelimo had to grapple.

I had long known about the struggle between two lines inside Frelimo in its early days, how Samora had ardently supported nonracialism in the ranks, refused to kill captured Portuguese soldiers, assisted Josina Machel in her determination to bear arms, and insisted that the enemy was not a race but a system of exploitation. I was also familiar with the way Frelimo artfully navigated the difficult waters of the Cold War. But in page after page of this book, I discovered new information. I learned about the fragmented state of Frelimo at the time its founder Eduardo Mondlane was assassinated, of intense later debates in the Frelimo leadership, about details of the Matola Raid by Pretoria's commandos, of how the Nkomati Accord with Botha came to be signed, about the killing of Simango and others who had been expelled from Frelimo, and, finally, fascinating details about Samora as a caring, loving, but stern father of five children.

I was, of course, familiar with the fierce contradiction between newly independent Mozambique, constructed on notions of people's power, and its neighbor, racist South Africa, built on the premise of white supremacy. I knew much about South Africa's determination to destabilize all the Frontline States, Mozambique and Angola in particular. But I was surprised to discover the immensity of the price that Mozambique paid for supporting our liberation struggle.

When Pretoria mouthed military threats, claiming Mozambique had secret weapons from the Soviet Union, Samora responded that his country's secret weapons were people like Ruth First, who, for her belief in human dignity and justice for all, had been killed by a letter bomb from South Africa sent to her at the Centre for African Studies. Yet Pretoria's aggression against Mozambique went well beyond Ruth First's assassination and the killing of other ANC members in the country.

It involved provoking and fanning the flames of civil war. South African commandos regularly sabotaged electricity lines. When South African musician Abdullah Ibrahim gave a memorial piano recital for Ruth on the night of her death, all the lights in the city went out, and Abdullah's musical homage continued memorably with a single candle burning. A bridge over the Zambezi River was blown up. Ships from abroad and trains from the interior of Africa would be rerouted away from Maputo Harbor. There were millions of refugees. The economy was never able to achieve liftoff. Scores of children were recruited by Renamo as soldiers in the fight against Frelimo. Hundreds of thousands of people died. Thousands more lost limbs to land mines. Though I survived the bomb placed in my car by agents of South African security, losing my right arm and the sight of one eye, two Mozambicans died from shrapnel injuries.

Some of the most powerful passages in this book deal with the way the plane carrying Samora, his assistant Fernando Honwana, director of the Centre for African Studies Aquino de Braganca, and more than twenty others was lured to destruction on South African soil. It was bringing them back from a meeting of some of the Frontline States in Zambia, undertaken to reinforce the opposition to Pretoria. We were stunned in Mozambique. We wept openly. A week before the crash, Rob Davies, who listened to the SABC *Current Affairs* propaganda broadcast every morning, had prepared a report to be sent to Oliver Tambo in Lusaka indicating that he had noted a profound shift in Pretoria's stance with regard to Samora Machel. Until that week, he pointed out, the line from Pretoria had been that Samora must be rescued from the claws of his communist controllers. Now the broadcaster said that Samora had shown himself to be the enemy of good neighborliness in the region and the back of his power had to be broken. Days later, Samora died.

Samora often spoke about the People—*o Povo*. "The People never die," he would tell us. "Leaders come and leaders go, but the People never die." And now

16

Samora was dead. The people were to endure several more years of bitter civil war, thousands more were to die, and hundreds more would lose their legs to land mines. The energy and optimism that marked the revolution and the nation's founding had been destroyed. New problems of corruption and authoritarianism were to emerge.

And then, in the strange way in which history works, as beautifully captured here, the indomitable spirit of Samora began to emerge once more. This time it was not through his songs and speeches as head of state in Independence Square, but through cassettes and rap music listened to by people on the ground. And so it came to pass that it was the memory of Samora in the minds of the people that never died.

Our thanks must go to Allen and Barbara for capturing so much of this remarkable story. Allen the idealist and Barbara the sceptic joined forces to provide us with a portrait of a great African leader that is rich, loving, and incisive. The book reminds us how interdependent the peoples of Africa have been and must continue to be. It reveals the terrible price in blood and treasure that Mozambique was forced to pay before we in South Africa were able to bring apartheid down. It shows how Mozambique became a crucible for political development in our part of the world, teaching us the importance of having good leadership and leaders rather than a single great leader. Above all, it calls upon us to continue Samora's quest to transform our society and economy in favor of the poor and the marginalized, but to do so through the complex and constitutionally defined mechanisms of an open and democratic society.

This was a lesson those of us living and working in Mozambique learned not from books or ideology, but from experience.

Samora was a proud African, a proud liberator, a proud internationalist, and a proud and humane human being with great cultural sensibility. He had his faults, and the system in which he grew and that he helped to grow had its deficiencies. But flaws and all, *o Povo*, the People, are right to revere his memory. My generation honors and loves him for the way he transformed the nature of what an African revolutionary leader could be. He indigenized revolutionary theory, fought against racism and tribalism, and spoke passionately about the emancipation of women. He is loved by ordinary people in Mozambique today for epitomizing qualities they fail to see in most current leaders: his integrity, his warm, engaging, and culturally rich humanity, his independence of mind and spirit, and, above all, his profound and resolute determination to enable the poor to transform their lives.

Viva Samora Machel, viva! May the struggle for which he gave his life continue! *A luta continua*!

Albie Sachs
Cape Town

Acknowledgments

We owe a special debt of gratitude to numerous Mozambican friends and colleagues who, over the years, have taught us so much about their country's history. Special thanks to Yusuf Adam Azagáia, Isabel María Casimiro, Arlindo Chilundo, João Paulo Borges Coelho, Frances Christie, Flávia Gemio, Eulésio Viegas Felipe, Carlos Fernandes, Raul Honwana, Suzette Honwana, Benedito Machava, Denise Malauene, Ricardo Rangel, Daniel Ribeiro, Alda Saute, Teresa Cruz e Silva, António Sopa, Amélia Neves de Souto, Joel Tembe, Carmen Zucula, and Paulo Zucula. Luís Bernardo Honwana, our close friend, over the years shared with us much of his family's past, but, as head of the Office of the President during much of Samora's presidency, he chose not to divulge information about either its inner workings or his relationship with Samora and the Frelimo leadership.

Without the first-hand knowledge of Aquino de Bragança, José Luís Cabaço, Iain Christie, Teodato Hunguana, António Alves Gomes, Oscar Monteiro, João Velemo Nunguanbe, Jacob Jeremias Nyambir, Prakash Ratilal, Honorata Simão Tschussa, and António Hama, we would not have been able to write this book. Their recollections provided invaluable insights on Samora the man and political leader, and they filled in gaps in our knowledge about the significant forces shaping the trajectory of Mozambican history.

We were fortunate to have the opportunity to speak with members of Samora's immediate family on several occasions. Our conversations were frank and far-reaching, sometimes lasting several hours. Through their story-telling, dating back to Samora's youth, we were able to piece together a better understanding of this complex leader. We especially thank Graça, Olívia, Ornila, Jucelina, and Samito, as well as Samora's nieces and nephews, who made these encounters so informative and enjoyable.

Several prominent scholars of Mozambique read this manuscript carefully and critically. We are particularly indebted to Edward Alpers, Heidi Gengenbach, Paolo Israel, William Minter, David Morton, and Jeanne Penvenne. Their comments made this a far better book, as did the valuable suggestions offered by Paul Fauvet and Elizabeth Schmidt.

We have benefited from the smart and sensitive suggestions from close friends who have accompanied us over the years on our Mozambican journey. To Jim Johnson, Roberta Washington, Sara Evans, Ray Arsenault, and Gillian Berchowitz we owe profound thanks.

We are especially grateful to Daniel Douek, who shared his personal copies of Truth and Reconciliation Commission testimony, to Paolo Israel, who provided songs about Samora he had collected in Cabo Delgado, to the archivists at the Centro de Documentaçao Samora Machel for the time and energy they devoted to assisting us and the photographs of Samora they shared. The book is also graced with photographs from the Centro de Documentação e Formação Fotográfica.

The University of Minnesota Foundation provided research funds through Allen's Regents Professorship, and the Graduate School helped to fund our overseas research.

We dedicate this book to the people of Mozambique, who, for fifty years, have welcomed us, opened their homes to us, and shared with us recollections of their history.

Mozambique. *Courtesy United Nations.*

Prologue

The Challenge of Representation

Samora Machel is remembered as Mozambique's first president and one of a number of assassinated prominent African leaders, such as Patrice Lumumba (Congo), Amílcar Cabral (Guinea-Bissau), and Thomas Sankara (Burkina Faso). For Mozambicans, he was the head of FRELIMO (Frente de Libertação de Moçambique), the guerrilla army that, against great odds, brought freedom to their homeland, but on the international scene he was much more.

Throughout southern Africa, Samora was a hero to the oppressed. His military successes against a colonial regime buttressed by South Africa, Rhodesia, the United States, and its NATO allies enhanced his revolutionary reputation. His support for Zimbabwean liberation forces and the African National Congress, which came at great cost to his nation, further elevated his stature. To the settler government ruling Rhodesia and South Africa's apartheid regime, he was the embodiment of evil—a powerful black man committed to building a nonracialist socialist society on their borders.

Samora also enjoyed international prominence far beyond Mozambique's significance. In 1975, when Mozambique became independent, the world looked appreciably different than it does today. Revolutionary movements with radical socialist agendas were on the rise. Cuba had withstood American efforts to destroy its revolution, the United States had been defeated in Vietnam, the Sandinistas had come to power in Nicaragua, and the winds of change were threatening to sweep away settler governments in southern Africa. Samora was part of a new generation of revolutionary leaders—Fidel Castro, Daniel Ortega, Michael Manley, and Yasser Arafat—with whom he shared a common vision and warm friendships.

For China and Russia, which supported FRELIMO during the armed struggle, Samora was an important ally helping to counter the West's influence in Africa. After independence, however, the Soviets never completely trusted him—he was too independent, refusing to follow the dogmatic Marxist-Leninist line or support Moscow in its battles with Beijing. By contrast, the NATO countries tracked Samora's rise to power with concern. The United States viewed Mozambique through the same Cold War prism as the Soviets, but for Washington he posed a threat to America's growing interest in Africa. Samora also played an important role in the Non-Aligned Movement, where he took a militantly anti-imperialist stance and fervently opposed both Eastern and Western attempts at global hegemony.

By the 1980s, however, Samora's standing, both domestically and internationally, had suffered. Nevertheless, he still posed such a significant threat to the apartheid regime and its allies that South African officials plotted to eliminate him. On October 19, 1986, he died in a mysterious plane crash.

His passing was a terrible loss to the country and the region, as well as for those throughout the world who shared his ideals. We were among them.

We learned of Samora's death the following night, well after midnight in Minneapolis, by a telephone call from Roberta Washington, a dear friend and fellow *cooperante* with whom we had worked closely in Mozambique. In a subdued voice, she told us that Samora Moises Machel and many of his closest advisers had died when the plane carrying them back from Zambia smashed into a mountainside in Mbuzini, South Africa.

During the two years (1978–79) that we lived in Mozambique with our two young sons, we had gotten to know Samora, whom we admired greatly, both from afar and through various personal interactions. Among those who lost their lives that night were many close Mozambican friends who were like family to us, including Aquino de Bragança and Fernando Honwana. We mourn their loss to this day.

Our relationship with Mozambique and its people had begun decades earlier. In 1968, we traveled to the then-Portuguese colony so Allen could conduct research for his doctoral dissertation. He had selected Mozambique partly because of his desire to help liberate its past from the cultural arrogance and racist assumptions that framed the colonial representation of the Mozambican people. For too long, their experiences had resided in the shadow of historical scholarship that focused almost exclusively on the Portuguese.

As activists at the University of Wisconsin in the early 1960s committed to social justice, the civil rights movement, the antiwar campaign, and the efforts to

25

dismantle the apartheid regime, the armed struggle being waged by FRELIMO to end centuries of Portuguese oppression intensified our interest in the colony. (In this study, "FRELIMO" refers to the liberation movement and "Frelimo" to the postindependence political party.) Happily, Portuguese authorities were unaware of our politics. We only received clearance because a high-ranking Portuguese official believed we would discover there that Lisbon was pursuing a benign multiracial social experiment known as "lusotropicalism." Since colonial authorities were convinced that illiterate Africans had no real history and we would only be studying "myths and legends," Allen's research appeared to pose no threat to the status quo.

Once in the interior, however, a sympathetic colonial administrator alerted us that the notorious secret police known as PIDE (Polícia Internacional e de Defesa do Estado) were following us. His warning came after we created a ruckus in the small interior town of Sena, where we were renting a room in the rear of the local bar. In violation of social conventions, we had encouraged our translator to use our bathroom, which we shared with the owner's family, rather than relieving himself outdoors. The owner's wife was furious, publicly berating us about the dangers of allowing uncivilized *pretos* (blacks) to use European bathrooms. The next day, PIDE agents questioned those who had witnessed this exchange. After independence, we discovered that this interrogation was not an isolated incident. In the archives was a lengthy PIDE report describing how PIDE agents had shown up to question the Africans with whom we spoke in every village we visited.

Such an incident, although largely insignificant, revealed the inherently exploitative and degrading nature of Portuguese colonialism. When colonial officials, loyalist chiefs, and known informers were not present, elders across the Zambezi Valley described in detail the abuses experienced on a regular basis.[1] We learned how, under Portugal's forced labor regime (*chibalo*), which the elders characterized as a modern-day form of slavery, colonial administrators compelled Africans to work for six-month periods for little or no pay on public works projects and European plantations, farms, and mines. Those trying to run away were beaten and jailed. Even compliance, however, did not protect them from the overseers' physical abuses. The tattered rags many villagers wore and the malnourished and uneducated children we encountered daily stood in sharp contrast to the luxuries enjoyed by the settler community.

For most Africans living in Lourenço Marques, the colonial capital, or Beira, the colony's second-largest city, life was only marginally better. We regularly witnessed Africans being slapped, humiliated, even arrested for behavior considered inappropriate. We walked through teeming *subúrbios* (shantytowns) crowded with reed huts (*caniços*) that lacked running water, a sewage system, proper drainage, and other basic infrastructure. The cities where Europeans lived were off-limits to almost all Africans except during working hours.[2] The informal but vigorously enforced color bar limited educational and job opportunities for the majority of the African population. Racial intermarriage was frowned upon, although many Europeans frequented the red-light district. All these indignities revealed the true nature of "lusotropicalism."

Of course, a small number of Africans escaped the most dehumanizing colonial practices. We encountered *assimilados* and African bureaucrats with European *padrinhos* (patrons) who had acquired cement houses on the edges of the European cities and were able to provide their children with more than a rudimentary education.[3] Samora's family members were assimilados, as was his widow, Graça Machel, who had been the only African student in her high school class.[4]

The modest economic and social reforms promulgated in the 1960s did not protect Africans from the whims of settlers, although not all Portuguese were abusive. In the privacy of their homes or in quiet cafes, a handful of Portuguese felt comfortable enough to openly criticize the fascist dictatorship of the late António Salazar. Some even acknowledged a certain sympathy for FRELIMO.

We could not remain silent, given the exploitative nature of what we observed during our year in Mozambique. Upon our return to the United States in 1970, Allen met with Sharfudin Khan, FRELIMO representative to the United Nations, to offer support and joined the fledgling Committee for a Free Mozambique. When the book based on his dissertation won the 1974 African Studies Association's Herskovits Prize, he donated a portion of the prize money to FRELIMO and, more importantly, pushed the ASA to condemn Portuguese colonial rule in Mozambique, Angola, Guinea-Bissau, Cabo Verde, and São Tomé. In June 1975, Allen appeared before the US Congress to condemn American support for the Lisbon government, and he subsequently testified at congressional

subcommittee hearings on the situation in postindependence Mozambique.

On June 25, 1975, Mozambique, under Frelimo's
leadership, gained independence and Samora Machel
became its first president. Two years later, we were invited to teach at Eduardo Mondlane University (UEM),
named for FRELIMO's first president, who had been assassinated by the Portuguese. The seventeen months we
lived there were heady times, despite food shortages and
long lines for bread and meat. The children on our block
quickly befriended our two sons—partly because they
had the only soccer ball in the neighborhood—and we,
as well as other cooperantes, were treated as comrades
and *progressistas*. Barbara worked for the Mozambican
Women's Organization (OMM), wrote a book about the
legal position of women in Mozambique as part of the
United Nations Decade for Women, and taught labor
law at the UEM's law faculty. Allen helped train the first
generation of postindependence Mozambican histori-
ans. We were energized and committed to participating
in the revolution. We believed anything was possible,
even if it required us at times to suspend our critical
faculties.

Under the auspices of the Office of the President
we undertook several projects, including surveying the
living and working conditions of Western cooperantes
and serving as liaisons with Business International, a
Western-based organization promoting investments
across the world. Allen and his colleague Iain Christie
conducted a five-hour interview with Samora that appeared in several Western newspapers and journals. We
also met periodically with President Machel and came

29

away impressed with his energy, intellect, and deep commitment to ending social injustice.

Samora had a wry sense of humor, a big ego, and loved to hold court. On one occasion, the American cooperantes living in Maputo made a donation to help rebuild a village attacked by US mercenaries working for the white settler regime in neighboring Rhodesia. We stood in a receiving line and, as Samora walked by with his entourage, he introduced Barbara as "Allen Isaacman's wife," to which Barbara replied, "No, he is my husband." Samora laughed and nodded approvingly to the entourage accompanying him.

Upon our return home in 1979, we continued to support Mozambique and its socialist project. We organized the Mozambican Education Fund—which to our surprise was granted tax-exempt status by the Internal Revenue Service—through which we sent several thousand badly need books to rural schools established after independence. We also worked closely with Valeriano Ferrão, Mozambique's ambassador to the United States, to mobilize opposition to the increasing aggression of South Africa and its surrogates inside Mozambique.[5]

Barbara returned to Mozambique periodically and was a guest at the 1982 OMM conference. At the Frelimo-organized reception, President Machel greeted her and asked where Allen was. When she told him that her husband was, of course, at home caring for their children, he laughed and responded, "You see, we have something to learn from you Americans." Around the same time, Barbara's book *Women, the Law and Agrarian Change*, co-written with June Stephens, was translated into Portuguese and read widely throughout the country.

For the next several years Allen spent most summers in Mozambique collecting oral histories. At the end of every visit he met with President Machel and other government officials to discuss conditions in the countryside and politics in the United States. While his critique of Frelimo's disregard for rural culture and history sometimes fell on deaf ears—on one occasion a party ideologue dismissed his criticisms as the idealistic views of an "*Africanista*"—Samora always gave his full attention to Allen's accounts of the abuses of power, incompetence, and corruption he had witnessed. Samora made many errors and was quick to anger, but he also demonstrated the capacity to listen, challenge inherited orthodoxies, and engage in self-criticism.

We have sketched our connection with Mozambique and FRELIMO to underscore that we were both students of and witnesses to an important period in Mozambican history. We also hope to show how our interpretation of this history is informed by our personal experiences, politics, and somewhat different temperaments (Barbara was always somewhat more skeptical about FRELIMO's policies than Allen). In some ways, we are telling a life story where the relationship between authors and subjects is inseparable from the story told.[6]

Although we were partisans, we are also scholars who prize intellectual rigor and careful analysis. As engaged scholars, we are committed to challenging social hierarchies and oppressive institutions and the racist assumptions supporting them. Not content to critique the status quo, in our own small way we have sought to change it. We are driven by a mutually reinforcing intellectual and political commitment, and we reject the

31

notion that there is a singular authentic history. Our allegiance to scholarship and activism, however, poses a serious challenge. We recognize the problematic relationships between biographer and subject. Passionate commitments to worldly causes must not undermine the capacity to question or the willingness to criticize the causes and movements we support and the men and women we admire. Edward Said put it bluntly when he cautioned, "never solidarity before criticism."[7]

In this social biography of Samora Machel we have tried to maintain that critical stance and avoid the tendency to romanticize a man we held in high regard. It has not been easy; some may conclude that we have not been successful. While we do not apologize for our stance, readers must recognize that our interpretations of this critical period in Mozambique's history necessarily differ from those of people who criticized FRELIMO's revolutionary agenda or actively opposed it.

In writing this biography, we have consulted both academic publications and a substantial body of unpublished primary material. The Centro de Documentação Samora Machel in Maputo houses a rich collection of Samora's papers and other documents related to his family. The secret police (PIDE) files in the Arquivo Nacional de Torre de Tombo, while generally depicting Samora as a Marxist pawn of China or the Soviet Union, contain voluminous material on the FRELIMO leadership and its strategy. We were not able to review thousands of FRELIMO wartime documents that fell overboard into the Indian Ocean when FRELIMO transferred its office from Dar es Salaam to Maputo, nor the very substantial collection of documents from the armed struggle housed in the FRELIMO archives, which are still not open to the public and would have supported a more comprehensive analysis of Samora's role.[8]

This study also relies on over twenty interviews with figures who had close relationships with Samora, collected by FRELIMO-sanctioned researchers in the wake of Samora's death and now deposited in the archives of the Centro de Documentação. We have also drawn on our interviews of members of his immediate family and several close advisers. To try to avoid the "bias of proximity," we spoke to former guerrilla fighters, peasants, Portuguese settlers, a rap singer, and a Portuguese priest; referenced material we collected in Mozambique over the past half-century; and consulted John Marcum's recently published *Conceiving Mozambique*, which contains detailed oral accounts from disenchanted former members of FRELIMO who studied in the United States. We intended to supplement this information with interviews of prominent Beira residents who were outspoken opponents of Samora, but two days before our scheduled flight to Beira in March 2019, Typhoon Ida devastated the city and surrounding areas, making that impossible.

The oral and written documents we consulted are all social texts that often contain multiple or contradictory meanings. Nostalgia, limits of memory, and the politics of forgetting complicate their construction. We are reminded of the often-cited admonition of the French anthropologist Marc Augé: "tell me what you forget and I will tell you who you are."[9] Understanding these complexities informs how we analyzed the texts themselves, the different perspectives of the authors, and their interpretations of events.

Two examples illustrate memory dissonance. When Samora and the platoon he led began training in Algeria, there were intense disagreements among the recruits on whether whites and South Asians born in Mozambique should be allowed to participate. On occasion, the debate precipitated conflict between Samora and another guerrilla who vehemently disagreed with Samora's insistence that one did not have to be either black or Mozambican to fight with FRELIMO. Raimundo Pachinuapa, Samora's political ally, described Samora physically subduing his rival. Jacob Jeremias Nyambir, who was also there, insisted that an older guerrilla, Lindoklindolo, intervened to prevent the fight. They not only told different stories, but disagreed about when and where the altercation occurred. Nyambir claimed this was in Algiers, shortly after the FRELIMO recruits arrived from Dar es Salaam. Pachinuapa recalled it taking place somewhat later at Marniah, a remote region near the Algerian-Moroccan border. Pachinuapa's account, collected after the president's death, emphasized Samora's masculinity and physical prowess—an image both Samora and FRELIMO promoted—and thus might have been affected by nostalgia. Nyambir shared his account with us in 2019. While respectful of Samora, he had no reason to embellish the story—but his memory, so many years later, might have been faulty.

The second example is common in contemporary Mozambique. After years of pervasive corruption and rapidly increasing inequality, many citizens longingly look back to the time of Samora's presidency, when social and economic justice were the stated goals of the revolution and corruption was severely punished. In doing so, they often romanticize Samora's leadership, forgetting the difficulties of daily life.

While most writing about Samora focuses on him as a political actor and his public persona, we have expanded our perspective, whenever possible, to include neglected aspects of his personal life. We do so not only to humanize Samora, with all his foibles, flaws, and passions, but also to challenge constructions of his life that separate public from private and political from personal. Too often biographers pay little attention to the personal lives of prominent male political leaders.[10] Historical agents cannot be fully understood, however, without reference to the personal.

Throughout his life Samora struggled to balance his personal and political commitments. His correspondence with his first wife, Josina, whom he lovingly referred to as Jozy, is filled with anguish and a sense of remorse that military responsibilities kept him away from her and their baby Samito for long periods of time. He was particularly concerned about her frail health—with good reason. On August 7, 1971, less than two years after they married, Josina died. Although Samora was devastated, he returned to the battlefield almost immediately after the funeral, leaving his son in the care of his surrogate FRELIMO "family."

Similarly, he was reluctant to remove from their high-ranking positions "old comrades" who had become ineffective or corrupt, because of deep personal bonds or his appreciation of their previous sacrifices. This tendency complicated and contradicted his public persona as a leader who did not tolerate incompetence or corruption.

As researchers, we have the responsibility to reflect, analyze, and access contemporary representations of the past and to raise new questions about Samora's legacy. Hopefully, we will continue to join other scholars in delving into the issues raised here. Samora Machel, and the many other less visible women and men who died in struggles for freedom, left an indelible mark on the continent. Their stories, told from various perspectives, must not be lost to posterity.

Living Colonialism

The Making of an Insurgent

Samora Moises Machel was born on September 29, 1933, in the village of Chilembene in Gaza Province, located in the southern part of Mozambique. The son of Mandande Moisés Machel and Guguiye Thema Dzimba, he entered the world as a colonial subject defined by a great number of legal and social restrictions. In Mozambique's racial geography, there were schools he could not attend, hospitals where he could not be admitted, places he could not live, and occupations he could not pursue. Indeed, forces beyond his control regulated much of his early life.

Racism, economic exploitation, and limited possibilities helped shape the formative years of Samora and his age-mates. Most Africans suffered silently, trying to find ways of coping with a harsh world in which survival was a challenge. A handful, like Samora, defied the colonial order. This youthful defiance earned him a reputation as a rebel. As he matured, Samora began to dream of an entirely different world, finding ways to express his opposition to colonial policies and colonialism itself.

Southern Mozambique: The Colonial Context

Although Portugal established a nominal presence along the coast of Mozambique in the late fifteenth century, Lisbon was only able to impose a semblance of control over the southern hinterland in 1895 when its army defeated the Gaza ruler Ngungunyane. Samora's grandfather, Malengani, was a well-known warrior who was seriously wounded fighting alongside Ngungunyane. Tales of Malengani's battle-scarred body and heroism circulated throughout southern Mozambique, and the personal accounts passed down to Samora made him proud of his family's anticolonial past and became part of his political education.

During the early twentieth century the colonial army, consisting largely of African recruits, was with its superior firepower able to overrun other resisting African polities, allowing Lisbon to impose a highly structured authoritarian regime throughout most of the country. Ranked below the colony's governor general were the provincial or district governors (usually military officers), district administrators, and their local counterparts, *chefes de posto*. Each district was divided into European areas, enjoying limited self-government, and non-European ones where residents had few basic human rights. Poorly educated and poorly trained, colonial administrators often ruled as petty tyrants with absolute power to accuse, apprehend, try, and punish their subjects.

The colonial regime similarly depended on African subordinates. Local chiefs (*regulos*), exempt from taxation and forced labor (*chibalo*), became state functionaries empowered to enforce colonial policies, settle minor disputes, and maintain public order. African police (*sipaios*), often recruited from the ranks of colonial soldiers and families of loyalist chiefs, were stationed at every administrative post, where they collected taxes, recruited labor, transmitted the orders of the administrator, and intimidated the local population. Separate legal systems governed "civilized" Europeans and "uncivilized" Africans (*indigenas*), whose lives were profoundly shaped by harsh labor and tax codes and the particular personality and practices of the local administrator.

A miniscule number of educated Africans who adopted a veneer of Portuguese culture were granted *assimilado* status by the state. These were a small number of men and even fewer women of African descent who were gainfully employed, Christian, spoke and wrote Portuguese, and no longer practiced "native customs." Under the authoritarian Salazar regime (1932–68), however, the rights of citizenship meant very little, even for whites. As Raul Honwana emphasizes, noted assimilados were exempted from the forced labor system and offered "a way of seeking a less degrading life for our children," but little else.[1] In 1950, the 4,380 assimilados comprised less than one tenth of 1 percent of the estimated 5.65 million Africans.[2] Although the assimilado community expanded with the colonial reforms around 1960, its numbers remained extremely small.

Because Portugal's own economy was underdeveloped and effectively bankrupt, it lacked the capital to make Mozambique profitable.[3] The only resource readily available for exploitation was the colony's African population. Lisbon turned them into commodities through implementation of the Native Labor Code, which subjected all unemployed African males to forced labor.[4] Whenever the state needed workers to construct roads, lay railroad tracks, install telegraph lines, or dig irrigation ditches, local administrators rounded up peasants. On occasion, administrators provided chibalo laborers to private Portuguese enterprises. The minimal compensation received by workers was rarely enough even to pay local taxes, and their withdrawal from household labor led to food shortages and other suffering. Although women were legally exempt from chibalo, many were not only forced to work but also made to submit sexually to Portuguese and African overseers.[5]

Lisbon also made the colony profitable by renting African workers to labor-starved South African gold mines and, to a much lesser extent, to white farmers and industrialists in neighboring Southern Rhodesia. Beginning in 1897, the Rand National Labour Association, subsequently renamed the Witwatersrand National Labour Association, paid the government a fee for each Mozambican worker. It also set up a deferred payment system under which workers received half their wages when they returned home and Lisbon was paid an equivalent amount in gold.[6] By 1910, approximately eighty thousand Mozambicans—representing from 30 to 50 percent of the able-bodied male population in some districts of Southern Mozambique—were working in the gold mines.[7]

Samora's father, Mandande, and another uncle, Toqouisso Gabriel Machel, like the vast majority of Mozambicans who labored in the South African gold mines, came from Gaza Province.[8] To earn money for his taxes, plows, and other commodities, Mandande spent most of the years between 1912 and 1926 apart from his family.

In 1926, a military coup brought down the Lisbon government. Four years later, António Salazar came to power, ruling Portugal and its colonies for over forty years.[9] Salazar premised his colonial strategy on two broad propositions—that the colonies must remain a permanent part of Portugal to advance its international standing and strengthen its economy, and that Portugal's role was to "civilize" the Africans. To bolster the metropolitan economy, Mozambique was expected "to produce the raw material and sell it to the Mother Country in exchange for manufactured goods," which necessarily required the continued exploitation of cheap African labor.[10] The Salazar regime paid only lip service to its civilizing mission: in 1941 it made the Catholic Church responsible for educating Africans up to the third-grade level, which clearly was insufficient to lead the African from "a savage to a civilized life."[11] The only exceptions were the small number of assimilado children who were allowed to attend European schools.

Medical treatment was also primarily reserved for the settler community in the urban centers. Health facilities in rural areas remained virtually nonexistent. Only a handful of doctors worked in the countryside and the state allocated limited funds for rural health services. Africans' poor diets and the lack of medical facilities and sanitation systems made them highly susceptible to infections and parasitic diseases, such as cholera and smallpox, and diseases caused by malnutrition, such as kwashiorkor.

Life under Colonial Rule

It was into this harsh, uncertain, and often violent world that Samora was born. His first name came from a maternal uncle, Samora Mukhavele, who fought in the Portuguese army during World War I, battling German forces in northern Mozambique, and came back with tales of far-off insurrections there. Samora also reveled in the exploits of his grandfather Malengani and listened intently as his father, mother, and especially his aunt Malungwanya Machel—who was remembered as a "living library"—described in detail the exploits of family members dating back nine generations.[12] Elders also recall that as a boy Samora often rested under a large tree that was a symbol of Gaza resistance, musing on the past.[13] History was clearly one of his early passions.

Singing was another. Samora was brought up in a culture in which music was an integral part of daily life. People sang when they were happy and when they were sad. They sang at births and deaths and other critical moments in the life cycle. They sang while working in the fields and herding cattle. Samora was no exception.

Thanks to the labors and sacrifices of his parents, Samora was born into a relatively prosperous family. Beginning in 1912, his father, like thousands of other young Mozambicans, avoided chibalo by trekking long distances to the South African mines. Dangerous conditions meant that many Mozambicans suffered from rockslides, industrial accidents, contagious diseases, and even death—conditions that adversely impacted the Machel family in many ways. When Samora's eldest brother died in the mines, the mining company sent forty pounds as compensation. Other relatives came home without limbs, blind, or deathly sick from tuberculosis or pleurisy—for which they rarely received even token compensation.[14] Nevertheless, men kept going back and some rural families, including Samora's, whose father worked there for nine eighteen-month periods, became relatively affluent as a result.[15]

Samora never forgot their suffering. Half a century later he spoke of his pain and anger with Allen and António Alves Gomes as they walked along the white sands of Wimbe Beach in Pemba, taking umbrage with those who criticized him for signing the unpopular Nkomati Accord with the apartheid regime. "I have spent my life fighting apartheid and there is not one day that I do not remember the suffering [the South Africans] caused my family and the people of the region."

Samora's mother and thousands of other women were left not only to perform the household labor necessary to sustain the family, but also to chop down trees and clear brush to create the maize and sorghum fields and small vegetable gardens they spent long hours cultivating. Some of these more strenuous tasks had been performed by women even before colonialism because men were often absent for long periods of time, hunting or visiting relatives. After the opening of the mines, Guguiye had to learn how to plow with the draft animals purchased with her husband's wages, despite local taboos that barred women from such tasks.

By 1926, Mandande and his family no longer lived off his wages from the mines. They had become successful farmers, using his four plows and animal traction to cultivate upwards of sixty acres in the rich alluvial soils adjacent to the Limpopo River and selling their agricultural surplus at local and regional markets. By the time Samora was ten, he was working in the family cotton fields and learning how to use a plow. Forty years later, Samora's father proudly told Allen that Samora "worked very hard and was very respectful."[16]

Nevertheless, the family's relative prosperity was precarious. African farmers were forced to sell their produce at artificially depressed prices because colonial administrators fixed prices in ways that privileged European producers. In a 1974 interview, Samora complained that "we would produce and sell one kilo of beans at three and a half escudos while the European farmers produced and sold at five escudos a kilo."[17] European merchants would then resell the beans to Africans for almost double the buying price.

Despite their lack of control over the markets, Mandande and other farmers worked hard and were able to save some of their income, which they reinvested in cattle and agricultural equipment. A handful of prosperous farmers who, like Samora's father, had been schooled at Protestant missions were even recognized as assimilados. Although his family benefited from this relatively privileged status, it never blinded Samora to the suffering of those around him, and he was very critical of those who internalized the colonial civilizing myth and tried to emulate the Portuguese.

Samora was raised in a stern, but loving, home. His deeply religious Protestant parents bestowed upon him the middle name Moises to honor both his father and the biblical figure who led his people out of captivity. A half-century later at the time of his father's death, Samora described him as a "soldier, successful cattle-keeper, innovative farmer, and a moral giant who fought against paganism, against witchcraft and alcohol. But above all else he was like a giant tree whose resolve against colonialism never wavered."[18] Although there is no evidence that Mandande was involved in early nationalist activities, like many of his generation he instilled in Samora a sense of pride in his African past and encouraged his son to think critically about Portuguese rule.

Samora's mother, according to family friends, was a powerful woman in her own right from whom he inherited his self-confidence, defiant attitude, and great pride in his African past.[19] She devoted herself to organizing and maintaining the Compound Mission, a Free Methodist church. When in 1937 Roman Catholic priests, aided by colonial authorities, pressured members of her community to convert to Catholicism, she mobilized fellow church members in opposition.[20] Under her watchful eyes, Samora went to church weekly and listened to pastors preach the virtues of hard work, discipline, education, and righteousness. He continued to espouse these values throughout his life.

We know precious little about Samora's early childhood. Like most prepubescent boys, he spent much of his time herding. While the cattle grazed, he and his agemates engaged in stick boxing (*mugayiso*), wrestling, and fist fighting. To avoid powerful blows to the head, stick boxers had to be dexterous and fast. From these activities Samora developed a passion for martial arts and boxing.[21] His children recalled that he continued to take pride in being a champion stick fighter and insisted that this skill had helped him to think strategically in battle.[22]

Those who knew Samora in his youth remember him in different ways, but all agreed about his strong personality. His classmate and lifetime friend Aurélio Manave described him as "competitive and prone to argue if things were not going in the right direction."[23] His cousin Paulo remembered his early bravery, describing the time a calf was caught by a crocodile after wandering to the river's edge. Alerted by another herder, Samora impulsively jumped in the water and threatened the crocodile by screaming and waving a stick. When the frightened beast released the calf, Samora pulled it out of the water by its tail and treated its wounds. Although this story may be apocryphal, it is still told widely in the region.[24]

Over time, Samora increasingly encountered the harsh colonial world beyond his home. Lisbon's grant to the Catholic Church of a monopoly over the education of virtually all African children meant that, if Samora wanted to be educated, he had to attend the Catholic native school at Uamexinga, five miles from his home. This was a windowless cement structure divided into a handful of classrooms where students spent the mornings receiving rudimentary training, with an emphasis on religious education and physical labor, and the afternoons cultivating cash crops and foodstuffs for the church. Because African students were considered inferior, their teachers regularly failed them. Samora's classmate Aurélio Manave remembered that "on average black students had to attend six years of primary education to complete a three-year course."[25]

It took Samora two years to complete the first grade, after which he was expelled—possibly because of his defiance. Indeed, it was during this period that his classmates began referring to him as "the rebel." Others suggested that the expulsion was due to his Protestant affiliation. Whatever the case, he returned to his family kraal and herded cattle for two years before his father insisted he return to the school. Despite numerous conflicts with his teacher, Samora managed to complete third grade in 1948 at the age of 14.

By the time he enrolled in fourth grade, Samora had become a voracious reader with a passion for learning. He was preparing for his fourth-grade examination when church officials informed him he could only take it if he converted to Catholicism.

> When there were just 15 days to go before the 4th grade exam, they told me: either you are baptized, or you leave the mission. It was Father Romano who said so. The Sisters of Charity came to talk to me and they said: either you are baptized or you leave the mission. . . . It was blackmail. I agreed, and I was baptized and christened. They gave me a lot of gifts. Bags with pictures of St. Francis Xavier etc. They were pleased because they had won, they had converted a Protestant. That was in 1950.[26]

Samora was one of only a handful who passed the exam. Two years earlier, only two African students out of more than seven thousand in the region had done so.[27] By then, Samora was dreaming of becoming a doctor, which both the priests and local Portuguese officials deemed outlandish, suggesting instead that he enter a seminary.

As a teenager, Samora defied prevailing social hierarchies and blurred ethnic and racial categories by having a serious romantic relationship with a young *mestiça* (mixed-race) girl from a wealthy trading family. When he informed his parents of his intention to marry her, they strenuously objected—not because of her race but because they had bigger dreams for Samora and feared that her father, who owned several rural shops, would pressure Samora to work in one or serve as his chauffeur instead.[28]

Frustrated by his inability to pursue his dream, in 1951 Samora left Gaza for Lourenço Marques, the capital. Because he lacked proper travel documents, the police detained him and sent him back to Gaza, where he worked briefly as an orderly in Xai-Xai. Upon securing the appropriate documents he returned the next year to Lourenço Marques, where he entered the nursing program at Miguel Bombarda Hospital. Nursing was one of the few relatively high-paying jobs open to Africans.

Although Samora was now living in an urban area, he never forgot the suffering and exploitation of rural Mozambicans that he had previously regularly witnessed. Three types of exploitation stood out. First, in the late 1930s the state imposed a forced cotton regime in southern Mozambique. Women and children were required to spend most of their days from September through May felling trees, cleaning fields, planting, weeding, harvesting, and carrying the cotton to market. For a year's labor many households received less than five dollars, which was insufficient to buy the grain they did not have the time to grow. Those who tried to sneak off to their gardens were beaten and sometimes sexually abused by African police and European overseers.[29]

The hardships associated with the cotton regime left an indelible mark on Samora. Decades later, Herb Shore, an antiapartheid activist, asked Samora what had led him to join FRELIMO. Samora smiled and replied, "Perhaps you might expect me to say I read Lenin and all the other books, but that is not the way it happened. As a boy I went with my father. He was forced to raise cotton, I learned from the way he was cheated when he brought his crop to sell. From my own life I was led to FRELIMO."[30]

The second occurred when the Salazar regime required Africans living in the wetlands adjacent to the Limpopo River to cultivate one to two acres of rice for export. Many of Samora's friends and neighbors were forced into this work and others were compelled to construct and maintain the canals and irrigation systems that sustained rice production on European farms. As with the cotton regime, conscription made it extremely difficult for families to produce sufficient food to meet household needs.[31]

The third—displacement of African farmers from their lands in the Limpopo Valley—began in the early 1950s when the colonial state started recruiting hundreds of farmers in Portugal to resettle there. Under the *colonato* scheme, the colonial administration expropriated sixty thousand acres of fertile land, transferring it to settlers who used dispossessed African conscript labor to work the marshes. Within a decade, virtually all of the lower Limpopo valley had been given to colonatos. The results were as far-reaching as they were disastrous. According to Samora, "All those who were farmers, today their ploughs and tractors are useless. All those who had good houses built of stone were expelled to make way for the settlers and forced to live in one room. Our land was expropriated and designated for settlers. . . . The Africans were put on arid lands that don't produce anything, and the regions handed over to the settlers are irrigated by the River Limpopo."[32]

Samora's initial radicalization was shaped not only by the suffering caused by this exploitation but also by other abuses inflicted by the colonial regime, white settlers, cotton company employees, rural merchants, and missionary teachers. Aurélio Manave, who met Samora shortly after he came to Lourenço Marques, remembered his sense of indignation. "[Samora] complained a lot. He always complained a lot. He complained about real issues and of injustices."[33] Samora, however, was not satisfied only to privately find fault with the colonial system. He was openly critical of colonialism and, although he was forced to register for the colonial army in 1958, he vowed that he would never serve.[34]

Samora's critique of colonialism started long before he arrived in the capital. It grew out of the many hours he sat near a sacred tree in Chilembene, where the famous rebel leader Maguiguane, with whom he closely identified, had organized the 1897 insurgency. Samora brought his mother's spirit of defiance, his father's pride in his African past, and his own understanding of oppression with him to Lourenço Marques where he would meet militant nurses, striking dock workers, and radical students, all struggling to end colonial oppression. It was here that he first encountered Eduardo Mondlane, the Mozambican nationalist who would become the founding President of FRELIMO. It is to this story that we turn next.

2

The Early Political Education of Samora Machel

The Making of a Freedom Fighter, ca. 1950–63

Samora's political education followed a distinctly different path from that of Kwame Nkrumah, Julius Nyerere,
Amilcar Cabral, and his compatriots Eduardo Mondlane and Marcelino dos Santos. Unlike these prominent
nationalist leaders who studied at universities abroad
and lived in major cosmopolitan centers, Samora had
only a limited formal education and spent much of his
formative years in rural Gaza.

While his radicalization began in the countryside,
in the capital he experienced the full weight of colonialism and was exposed to broader anti-imperialist
thinking. As a nursing student he encountered abysmal
conditions in the African wards and observed the poor
treatment non-whites received. In both the city and his
workplace he suffered numerous racial indignities and
became keenly aware of the power of the secret police
and its informants, who seemed to be everywhere. At
the same time, he met young African men and women
who also longed to be free and became acquainted with
a handful of sympathetic Portuguese, *mestiços*, and

Mozambicans of Goan descent who were organizing clandestine opposition to the Salazar regime. Through these encounters, he became aware of the anticolonial and anti-imperialist struggles going on in Africa and many other Third World countries. Then, in 1962, he met Eduardo Mondlane, who later become the first president of FRELIMO and would remain a source of inspiration throughout Samora's life.[1]

Samora's Career as a Nurse

Nursing was one of the few professions open to Africans, predominantly men, that paid reasonably well—making competition for admission to the nursing programs very intense.[2] This was especially true at Miguel Bombarda Hospital, the colony's largest health center. Most African applicants were children of peasants. All had excelled in school, but, unlike Samora, some—such as António Mondlane and Aurélio Manave—had actually been encouraged by sympathetic missionaries and other Portuguese to pursue careers in medicine. António recalled that, because there were few jobs in Chibuto, he had cautiously raised the subject of becoming a nurse with a local doctor. To his surprise, the physician "not only did not oppose it, but thought it was a good idea and urged me to apply."[3] Aurélio similarly benefited from the support of João Filipe, an engineer who allowed him to work part-time so he could prepare the necessary paperwork the Health Service required.[4] Both men became Samora's colleagues and close friends at the hospital.

The hospital was a highly racialized and regimented institution. Male African students and poorer mestiços were housed in a crowded segregated dormitory adjacent to the psychiatric wards. Disquieting shrieks from this wing often punctuated the students' night-time studies. The dormitory was divided into rooms, each housing several dozen students who slept on narrow beds arranged in tight rows. They lacked proper ventilation, were hot in summer and cold in winter, and had poor sanitary conditions. Female students resided on the other side of the hospital. European and more prosperous mestiço trainees lived off-campus with their families or in nearby residences.[5] While all students spent upwards of sixty hours a week taking classes and assisting doctors and nurses, there was one program for the more privileged and another for *pretos* (blacks).[6]

Samora quickly earned a reputation as a troublemaker because he refused to be subservient in the classroom. According to one colleague, "he complained a lot and wanted to be respected and did not allow himself to be looked down upon by the European teachers and professors."[7] João Ferreira, a Portuguese drug salesman who frequented the hospital, shared this recollection: "Samora was a person with a strong personality. I believe that Samora was born without any sense of racial inferiority or fear. Samora looked at people as equal and treated them accordingly. On racial matters, anyone who thought that he or she was racially superior to Samora got a rude awakening. Samora confronted anyone who was disrespectful or treated him without dignity."[8]

Samora was no less defiant when responding to the callous indifference of many Portuguese nurses and doctors when they ignored or mistreated patients—which earned him the wrath of some of his professors. "There were several occasions after he criticized the doctors,"

Aurélio Manave recounted, "when they wanted to hit him with an X-ray plate, but he blocked them. He did not hesitate a second. This behavior made some people afraid of him."[9] Years later, Samora reflected on the Europeans' lack of concern for African lives.

> In the hospital were various categories or classes reflecting the social and racial structure of colonial-capitalism, ranging from the white settlers to the "assimilated black" and even to the "native." Here was a total lack of concern for the poor patient, which was manifested in the way the doctor or nurses looked at him, in the absence of hygiene in the wards, in license and indiscipline among the workers. Our people were used in the hospital as guinea pigs for new drugs and certain operations, which if successful could later be applied to the bourgeoisie in the private clinics and consultancies.[10]

Predictably, Samora's behavior angered many of the teachers and nurses who evaluated him. Finding him "stubborn and disrespectful," they punished him by ordering, despite his academic record, that he repeat the second year—during which he graduated at the top of his class.[11]

The nursing program, although similarly hierarchical and racist, was also filled with contradictions. African and European students studied together, worked in close proximity, performed similar tasks, and sometimes socialized outside the hospital. As Manave recalled, "we developed very good relationships . . . even though [white students] never stayed in the dorms."[12]

For Samora and his cohort, the segregated dorms became a free space beyond the gaze of European supervisors and state officials, although they always worried about infiltration by PIDE informants. In hushed voices, students from different parts of the colony shared stories of oppression and humiliation. They pored over South African newspaper accounts of African and Asian leaders agitating for independence, and bolder students even smuggled in political tracts by revolutionaries such as Frantz Fanon and Mao Zedong. They read about the National Liberation Front guerrilla campaigns in Algeria, Gamal Nasser's efforts against the British during the 1956 Suez Crisis, and Ho Chi Minh's military campaign to end French rule in Vietnam. In their beds at night, Samora and his colleagues listened to Voice of America and Radio Moscow. They were particularly excited about Ghana's impending independence under the leadership of Kwame Nkrumah and the growing prospect of freedom in neighboring Tanzania and Zambia.

Samora was often at the center of these conversations. Fellow students remember both his militancy and his insistence that "we only live once, and we cannot continue to accept things as they are."[13] Occasionally, these discussions spilled over into whispering in corners of the cafeteria or in stairwells, beyond the gaze of PIDE informers.

His passion for boxing almost matched his fervor for politics. In his youth he had been taken with stick boxing, wrestling, and other martial arts, but with little time in the hospital for such activities he instead began each day with a rigorous round of exercise punctuated by long intervals of rope skipping. Samora was proud of his trim physique and the discipline required to maintain it. Unlike Nelson Mandela, Samora never fought in the ring—although contemporaries recalled one fight with a fellow student to determine who would be leader of the nursing dormitory.[14] He was, however, a fanatical fan of professional boxing. He read the Brazilian magazine *O cruzeiro* religiously, and on the wall above his bed were photos of famous black pugilists—Joe Louis, Ezzard Charles, Archie Moore, and Jersey Joe Walcott—whose legendary accomplishments he would enumerate to anyone willing to listen. While most of his colleagues preferred soccer, Samora regularly attended bouts or listened to international fights, usually involving South African boxers. His obsession with boxing earned him the nickname "the Manassa Mauler" after his hero, the white prizefighter Jack Dempsey.

Since Samora had no responsibilities on Sundays, he partied most Saturday evenings at African dance halls with either female nursing students or girls from the local secondary schools. He especially loved the Djambo Orchestra, considered the finest African band in Lourenço Marques. A dapper dresser with an infectious smile, Samora had a well-deserved reputation as a lady's man. Graça Simbine, who years later became his wife, remembered him as "a person who took pride in his looks, always very well dressed, always well groomed, and . . . eager to impress."[15]

After graduating, Samora's first assignment was at a small hospital on Inhaca, an island across the bay from Lourenço Marques, where he worked from 1956 to 1959.[16] He quickly improved his knowledge of Ronga, the local language closely related to Shangaan, his mother tongue, so he could communicate more effectively with his patients, primarily fishermen and their families. They suffered mostly from outbreaks of malaria, cholera, and dysentery caused by polluted water and lack of proper sanitation, and from tuberculosis and polio brought back by men from the South African mines. According to his neighbor, David Chiankomo, Samora was very popular because he made after-hours house calls. He studiously avoided discussing sensitive political subjects and tried to stay clear of the local Portuguese administrator. "When he was with us," Chiankomo remembered, "he only spoke about fishing, how the construction of our homes was going, but never politics."[17]

During this period Samora began a serious relationship with Sorita Chiankomo, with whom he had two children—Jucelina and Edelson.[18] Although they never married, he brought his family back to the mainland in 1959, when he returned to attend high school in the evenings while working as a nurse at Miguel Bombarda Hospital during the day.

Racism at the hospital was still rampant. As Samora related, "we discovered the very different treatment [of European and African nurses], the different attitudes toward them and to us. And then, of course, we discovered the different level of wages."[19] For the cash-strapped night student, paying tuition was difficult, especially with the birth of his next two children, Olívia and Ntewane.[20] Nevertheless, Samora saved enough to rent a small wood-framed zinc-paneled house with a corrugated roof in the African neighborhood of Mafalala, where he also treated patients.[21] Compared to many of his neighbors who lived in reed dwellings, his family was relatively privileged.

In 1961, Samora transferred to a night school program run by the Methodists, who reputedly were more sympathetic to Africans than their Catholic counterparts. After completing the program, he applied for an advanced nursing course from which blacks had previously been excluded. While excelling in the written exam, he failed both the practical and the oral ones, even though he was conducting research on malaria at the nation's largest hospital.[22] It is likely that his reputation as a troublemaker prevented him from breaking the color bar.

The long hours Samora spent working, studying, and on his increasing political activity did not diminish his passion for reading, boxing, or music. He also undertook to improve his Portuguese by studying classical Lusophonic literature with Adalberto de Azevedo, a respected Portuguese scholar.[23] Meanwhile, he continued holding court about the world's great boxers and listening to rock and roll, jazz, and local *marrebenta* music.

While living with Sorita and their children, Samora became romantically involved with Irene Buque, a young nurse working at the hospital who shared his anticolonial sentiments.[24] They would soon have a daughter, Ornila. Although a critical political thinker, Samora not only failed to question conventional patriarchal norms but actively and selfishly took advantage of them—as did many other revolutionaries of his time.

The Changing Political Landscape in Mozambique

In the early 1960s, three interconnected developments dramatically transformed the political landscapes of both Mozambique and Africa. First, winds of change were sweeping across the continent. Ghana, Guinea, Algeria, the Congo, and Kenya had gained independence, change was imminent in Malawi and Zambia, and in neighboring Tanzania, Julius Nyerere, its first president, was implementing sweeping economic and social reforms.

Even in the most recalcitrant settler states of southern Africa, Africans were openly contesting injustice. In Southern Rhodesia, nationalists organized the Zimbabwe African Peoples Union, led by Joshua Nkomo, to struggle against Ian Smith's white settler regime. In South Africa, Africans, people of mixed race and Asian descent, and progressive whites were intensifying their nonviolent antiapartheid campaign in the face of harsh and swift state reprisals. After the 1960 Sharpeville massacre, both the Pan-African Congress and African National Congress (ANC) announced plans to use military force to bring down the apartheid regime. The Portuguese colonies were not immune. That same year, nationalists in both Angola and Guinea-Bissau launched military attacks against Portuguese installations.

Second, nationalist activities in neighboring states inspired Mozambicans to step up clandestine anti-Portuguese activity in Lourenço Marques and Beira. The Núcleo dos Estudantes Africanos Secundários de Moçambique (NESAM), founded by Eduardo Mondlane and other educated Africans in the late 1940s, gradually emerged as a significant voice of opposition. With branches across the country, its members celebrated Mozambique's rich and diverse history and spoke out against Lisbon's racial policies. In 1947, after Mondlane was deported from South Africa for protesting against racial discrimination, he had returned to Lourenço Marques, where he became a leading force in NESAM. In the 1950s, NESAM was further radicalized when it attracted younger, more militant adherents, most notably Joaquim Chissano,[25] Armando Guebuza,[26] Filipe Samuel Magaia,[27] Mariano Matsinhe,[28] and Luís Bernardo Honwana,[29] who would all become prominent figures in FRELIMO and close allies of Samora.

Despite being under constant surveillance, NESAM engaged in a variety of subversive activities. In 1961, Magaia and other student activists in Lourenço Marques and Beira, aided by their Portuguese friend João Ferreira, left anti-colonial publications in post offices, public bathrooms, bus stations, and other frequented locations.[30] Members supported striking stevedores at the port of Lourenço Marques, met with teachers opposed to the colonial regime, and held covert political meetings in the shantytowns.[31] They organized clandestine outings to the countryside in order to, as Joaquim Chissano later wrote, "help urban students understand the realities in the countryside and, if possible, be in contact with peasants."[32] NESAM even launched a magazine, *Alvor*, which, although severely censored, subtly addressed many critical issues of the day.

NESAM was not the only critic of Portuguese rule. Around 1960, the leadership of the Associação dos Naturais de Moçambique, a club for Mozambique-born whites, was taken over by antifascist Portuguese, many from families who had fled to Mozambique to escape the tyranny of the Salazar regime. The Associação opened its doors to all races and began to organize night-school classes in African townships, which led to its banning in 1961.[33] There were also a handful of radical whites, including João Ferreira,[34] Jacinto Veloso,[35] Rui Nogar,[36] José Luís Cabaço,[37] and Rui Balthazar,[38] who covertly supported the early nationalist movements and, later, the armed struggle.

NESAM and other internal opponents of colonialism received a big boost when Eduardo Mondlane, by then a United Nations employee based in New York, visited Mozambique in February 1961. Protected by diplomatic immunity, Mondlane, antiapartheid activist and recent PhD, was greeted as a hero. In urban churches and shantytowns and his rural Gaza homeland, he met publicly and on occasion privately with dissidents of all persuasions. Mondlane avoided language that PIDE could use as a pretext to deport him or arrest those with whom he met, but when he returned to New York he wrote a widely circulated condemnation of Portuguese rule aimed at mobilizing international public opinion.

Simultaneously, opposition was intensifying in the Mozambican countryside. In early 1960, Mozambican exiles in Tanzania, members of Tanganyika Mozambique Makonde Union (TMMU), sent militants into northern Mozambique to mobilize rural communities.[39] The result was the first large-scale rural protest, which occurred that June in the northern highlands of Mueda. Thousands of peasants rallied peacefully to complain about the abuses of the forced cotton regime, *chibalo*, and price-gouging at rural shops. Colonial retribution was swift, turning into a bloodbath.[40] In a widely reproduced account, Alberto Chipande, who witnessed the killing, described the events leading up to the massacre.

> The governor invited our leaders into the
> administrator's office. . . . The governor asked the
> crowd who wanted to speak. Many wanted to speak,
> and the governor told them all to stand on one side.
>
> Then without another word he ordered the
> police to bind the hands of those who had stood on

one side, and the police began beating them. . . . At that moment the troops were still hidden, and the people went up close to the police to stop the arrested persons from being taken away. So the governor called the troops, and when they appeared he told them to open fire. They killed about 600 people.[41]

Although this number, which became part of FRELIMO's revolutionary narrative, was no doubt exaggerated, Honorata Simão Tschussa, a nine-year-old girl at the time, shared with us a similar account: "People surrounded the car transporting prisoners. The Portuguese troops opened fire and massacred them."[42] Cornélio Mandande was even more graphic: "People fell as if they were mangoes during a cyclone."[43]

Third, the role of exiled opponents of Mozambique's colonial regime was changing dramatically. That TMMU members crossed the border from Tanzania to organize protests in Mueda on such a scale was an early indication that the struggle had entered a new phase. Meanwhile, facing the threat of incarceration, hundreds of young men and women from all over the colony, and even some elders, fled to neighboring countries where they joined others already in exile to create organizations committed to overthrowing the colonial regime.

Three distinct opposition groups in exile appeared around 1960. The Mozambican African National Union (MANU), which grew out of TMMU, brought together a cluster of self-help and cultural associations whose members were primarily Makonde.[44] Most were sisal plantation workers in Tanzania and dockworkers in Kenya. In its founding documents, MANU embraced the language of Mozambican nationalism and Pan-

Africanism.[45] Based in Dar es Salaam, it was the largest of the three opposition movements.

The National Democratic Union of Mozambique (UDENAMO) was composed of young dissidents and migrant laborers who came primarily from central and southern Mozambique.[46] Most fled to Southern Rhodesia, which became the center for its activities.[47] Nevertheless, UDENAMO was able to organize secret cells in Lourenço Marques. It later moved headquarters to Dar es Salaam. In 1962, influential opposition figures from the Beira region, most notably Reverend Uria Simango, joined UDENAMO.[48] So did Marcelino dos Santos,[49] a mestiço intellectual who had studied in France, and Helder Martins, a Portuguese doctor.[50]

The National African Union of Independent Mozambique (UNAMI) was the smallest of the three. Headquartered in Blantyre, Malawi, its members came primarily from parts of Tete and Zambézia districts bordering the neighboring British colony. Many had lived there for a long time before joining UNAMI, and its official communiques were primarily in English.

This brief overview reveals the narrow bases of these organizations and the importance of migrant laborers in their membership. Their regionalism and ethnic parochialism posed obvious organizing problems. So did the colony's geographical expanse, which stretched over twelve hundred miles from the Tanzanian to the South African borders. Both factors made forging a broad-based anticolonial coalition a daunting task.

This task fell to Eduardo Mondlane, who was already well-known in anticolonial circles. Shortly after his 1961 visit to Mozambique, he resigned from his

United Nations position and relocated to Dar es Salaam. There, with the help of Tanzanian president Julius Nyerere and the backing of President Kwame Nkrumah of Ghana, Mondlane forged a fragile alliance of these three organizations under the banner of the Frente de Libertação de Moçambique (Front for the Liberation of Mozambique; FRELIMO). The process proved difficult and was never fully realized. After three months of discussion during which the parties tried to hammer out the goals of the movement, some prominent exiles stopped participating. "There was always opposition," recalled Alberto Chipande, who was later selected to lead the initial FRELIMO attack inside Mozambique.[51]

At FRELIMO's First Party Congress in September 1962, Mondlane was elected president, Uria Simango, whom Mondlane defeated, was selected as deputy president, Marcelino dos Santos took charge of external relations, and Joaquim Chissano was appointed Mondlane's personal secretary. Many of the other leaders were either mission-educated Mozambicans from the south whom Mondlane knew personally, or northern Mozambican militants who were primarily Makonde—precipitating charges of favoritism from guerrillas born in the central part of the country. That FRELIMO was a "front" comprised of groups with competing views and agendas underlay its fragility. Looking back, participants agreed that "the early days of FRELIMO were marred by mutual recriminations, expulsion and withdrawal."[52]

Samora's Anticolonial Activity

Samora gradually became involved in nationalist activities. After returning to Lourenço Marques from Inhaca in 1959, he helped organize clandestine meetings of nurses, orderlies, and other workers at the hospital, where he distributed anticolonial material. Because he was a nurse he did not participate in NESAM, but he was in contact with Joaquim Chissano and other militant students. Two years later, he and a fellow nurse, Albino Maheche, met with Mondlane at the home of Mozambican poet João Craveirinha. When PIDE arrested Maheche soon afterward, he refused to implicate Samora in any subversive activities.[53]

From then on, however, Samora was under constant PIDE surveillance, which merely accelerated his flight from Mozambique. For some time, he and two other activists, Thomas Kumalo and Simeão Massango, had been planning to flee to Dar es Salaam so they could join FRELIMO. Samora's long-term goal, however, was to continue his education abroad, and he hoped that FRELIMO would send him to Moscow's Patrice Lumumba University. Father Matias Chicogo of the Anglican Church in Maciene, who had close personal connections with King Sobhuza II of Swaziland, was helping to organize their escape.

Despite being brought up by Christian parents, Samora had not totally rejected the elders' beliefs that ancestor spirits would protect travelers on long and dangerous journeys. Thus, it was not surprising that he and Kumalo consulted a well-known Ronga healer before fleeing abroad. A close confidante of Samora's described the encounter.

> The launch of *tihlolo* [when the healer pulls out
> a basket filled with numerous bones, stones, and
> divining shells] is a moment that fills with anticipation

and anxiety for all those who consult a healer. . . . After he had muttered some imperceptible words, the healer raised his eyes and stared at the two men. "I see you fleeing from this land. But you did not commit any crime. You are scared you will suffer a lot during the journey. But you will arrive. You will not be arrested and this one—pointing the index finger to Samora—I see you coming back again as a great Chief."[54]

In March 1963, while escape plans were crystallizing, João Ferreira, a white anticolonialist activist who had befriended Samora and Irene, learned from his friend Vitório Hugo, an officer in the colonial army, that Samora would soon be detained by PIDE. Ferreira slipped into the infirmary where Samora was working and urged him to escape immediately.[55] Alarmed, Samora and Kumalo took his advice, planning to join up with Massango, who had already left Mozambique.

After securing a holiday leave at the hospital and meeting with underground FRELIMO members who had planned the journeys of other dissidents, Samora informed his family "that he was going abroad to fight [for] Mozambican freedom"—a concept many of them did not fully comprehend.[56] His wife Irene, who only three weeks earlier had given birth to a baby girl, tearfully begged him to stay. Samora, for whom politics trumped family obligations, was unmoved.[57] He quickly arranged for Lomba Viana, a sympathetic Portuguese doctor, to watch over his family and bid Irene farewell.

For the next decade Samora had no contact with his relatives, who paid a heavy price for his commitments. Because of their relationship, his brother Josefate was imprisoned for more than a decade. In 1968, Portuguese security forces burned down his parents' brick home in Chilembene, forcing them to relocate to a crowded thatch-roof hut.[58]

On March 4, Samora and Kumalo took a ferry to Catembe and trekked through Matuituine district, crossing into Swaziland four days later. For Samora, March 8th would always be a day of celebration "marking his freedom from colonialism."[59] By the time PIDE learned of their flight, they were safely in Swaziland. With the help of Reverend Chicogo's son and Swazi officials, they were whisked through the kingdom. After crossing through South Africa, they were arrested at the Southern Rhodesian border. While many compatriots were either incarcerated or died mysteriously after similar detentions, Prince Macucu of the Swazi royal family convinced the Southern Rhodesian police to let the two return to Swaziland, from which they crossed into South Africa and made their way to Botswana, as had other militants before them.[60] In Francistown, Samora and Kumalo contacted members of the Botswana Peoples Party and the exiled ANC. According to Joe Slovo, commander of its military wing, the ANC guerrillas were so impressed by Samora's resolve that they bumped one of their recruits from the flight to Dar es Salaam to make room for him.[61] To Samora's delight, his old friend João Ferreira followed shortly thereafter on a military plane commandeered by Jacinto Veloso, a renegade Portuguese Air Force captain.

The Struggle within the Struggle, 1962–70

When Samora arrived in Dar es Salaam in May 1963, FRELIMO was embroiled in an intense internal conflict. FRELIMO's official story, that there were two factions, one "reactionary" and the other "revolutionary," obscures more than it reveals. In reality, the cleavages were multiple, reflecting deep-seated disagreements over race, regionalism, and tribalism and different visions of the appropriate political, economic, and social structure of an independent Mozambique. Personal rivalries and jealousy exacerbated these tensions. In fact, members of the Front agreed about very little other than their desire for independence.[1]

Samora and other new recruits were questioned by Raimundo Pachinuapa, a senior FRELIMO figure and close supporter of Mondlane whose job was to determine if they were spies for the colonial regime. Asked why he had fled Mozambique, Samora did not hesitate in rejecting Pachinuapa's assumption that he had run away, since for him that would have been a cowardly act: "We did not flee, we came here to join FRELIMO."

Pachinuapa also asked each recruit whether he preferred to study or begin military training. This was a sensitive subject, given that many came to Tanzania believing they would receive scholarships to study abroad. Despite Samora's dream of advancing his education by studying in Moscow, he responded without hesitation that he would prefer to get military training first.[2]

When the new recruits met with President Mondlane, he posed the same question. This time, Samora's response was more tentative. Speaking for his compatriots, he said it would be difficult for many to give up their dreams of advanced education and asked Mondlane to give them time to consider their options. That night, he and his roommate decided to commit to the struggle because they worried that a request to be sent abroad "would reinforce the notion that President Mondlane sends young people from the center and the north to military training, while those of us from the south receive schooling."[3] Mondlane, told of Samora's decision, appointed him chief of a seventy-two-man contingent going to Algeria for guerrilla training.[4]

Before the recruits departed, Mondlane met with them to emphasize "Mozambique's rich history and that they were fighting against Portuguese colonial rule, not against whites."[5] Later in the meeting, he elaborated: "There will be a place on our shores for those Portuguese originally from Mozambique who wish to live there. As citizens they will have equal rights in a free Mozambique."[6]

Training in Algeria

The first platoon of FRELIMO recruits, led by Filipe Samuel Magaia, former NESAM activist and FRELIMO military chief of staff, was sent to Algeria for training in 1962. Algeria was a logical place. The Front de

Libération Nationale had substantial guerrilla experience fighting the French a decade earlier and Algeria's president, Ahmed Ben Bella, was an ardent supporter of liberation struggles. Algeria's geographic position also protected it from Portuguese military incursions, and its Mediterranean ports allowed FRELIMO to receive military support from the Socialist Bloc and economic assistance from supporters in Western Europe. Samora's platoon arrived at the end of the following year. That Mondlane and Pachinuapa accompanied the group suggests the importance FRELIMO's leadership was placing on preparation for the struggle.

The training did not start smoothly. After Mondlane gave a pep talk at the staging area and said Algerians would arrive shortly with provisions, he left to meet with local authorities. Not fluent in Arabic, French, or any of the local languages, the recruits could do nothing but wait, which they were forced to do for some days. "We did not leave, no one appeared, no military authorities, we slept there without even having tea. The next morning Mondlane appeared and expressed surprise that we were still there," recalled Pachinuapa. It turned out the wait was due to the Mozambicans' failure to contact appropriate Algerian authorities. From this fiasco Samora learned two important lessons—that you could not go into an area without preparation and that you needed to establish direct links with local communities.[7]

The recruits eventually were taken by truck to the FRELIMO base at Marniah, a desolate site near the Moroccan border lacking even minimal sleeping accommodations. After constructing makeshift barracks and receiving boots and uniforms, the platoon was divided into three sections, each with a group leader. As part of building a common sense of nation, Samora included guerrillas from different regions in each group. For some, this was initially shocking. Jacob Jeremias Nyambir, who was from the south, admitted that his encounter with northern Makonde recruits was jarring. "This was the first time I lived with someone who had facial scarring and lip plates and I was scared. But after a short while we became good friends."[8]

While awaiting their Algerian instructors and supplies, they kept busy performing makeshift tasks—rising early for exercises, working on the barracks, sweeping and cooking. Conversation invariably turned to politics, during which they shared their views and dreams for the future. As instructors and weapons still failed to arrive, these exchanges quickly degenerated into gripe sessions about having to perform domestic chores most considered women's work. Samora responded by example: "He took a rag and began to wipe the floors and tables. Others followed."[9]

Meanwhile, fault lines began to surface. There were complaints about the presence of *assimilados* and *monhé* (a derogatory term for Mozambicans primarily of Goan descent). Some recruits insisted that, because these people were not Africans, neither they nor Mondlane, who considered them Mozambicans, could be trusted. Some, on the other hand, worried they would not be loyal to Mondlane.[10] Others simply objected to the fact that many of these "non-Africans" held positions as nurses, teachers, and group leaders thanks to their greater access to education under the Portuguese colonial regime.

Samora organized mandatory study groups to tackle the divisive issues of race and national identity.

Initial results were mixed. "We scheduled political meetings, and some did not attend. They would say, 'we are not going to those classes, they are tricksters' classes and they are planning how to get rid of Mondlane.' When we were all together as a group, the discussions were heated and sometimes caused indiscipline." During one particularly intense debate, Samora abruptly interrupted, as he was often prone to do. "We are here to train for the armed struggle against Portuguese colonialism. . . . We are not against whites, not against mulattoes. . . . We are not assassins, we want to liberate our country. That is our objective, that and nothing else."[11] Tino Armando, another recruit, vehemently disagreed, insisting that mulattoes and whites were evildoers. Samora became livid, an altercation ensued, and Samora was victorious.[12]

Once the Algerian instructors arrived, there was little time for study groups or political debate. Samora's platoon was sent inland for training. The Algerians, working through translators, pushed its members and the small group of African National Congress fighters training with them day and night.

> It was crazy. It was really crazy. . . . From the moment
> we awoke we were always on the move. We had fifteen
> minutes for breakfast. We would carry food to eat
> while we were training. We would take everything:
> ammunitions, grenades, and everything. Our bodies
> would feel heavy. Sometimes we would even put a
> whole watermelon in our backpacks, but we often did
> not have [time] to eat it and had to carry it back to
> camp. Sometimes we would fill canteens with water,

but not have the time to drink it. The instructors would walk while giving lessons and they would arrive at a place and stop there and offer a class. They would run, climb a mountain, and stop at the top of the mountain, they would provide more instruction while running down the mountains. The instructors would come behind us. They would open fire not with fake bullets but with real bullets. The bullets landed around us and the instructors would say, "if you die it is not my fault, I am here to train you." It was very tough training and it was every day. Samora was always there disciplining everybody.[13]

After more than six months of training, Samora and his contingent returned to Tanzania.[14]

Divisions within FRELIMO

Samora was subsequently placed in charge of the military training camp at Kongwa. By 1965, he was commanding FRELIMO's major base at Nachingwea—less than seventy miles from the Mozambican border—which became the staging area for FRELIMO attacks inside Mozambique.

As a senior military leader and one of Mondlane's trusted allies, Samora became embroiled in FRELIMO's internal debates. The leadership's disagreements were ferocious, generating distrust, intrigues, defections, even assassinations. The united front FRELIMO presented to the outside world actually masked two sets of alliances, which themselves disagreed on many issues.

The first centered around President Mondlane and others, including Samora, who embraced the radical and

Figure 3.1. Samora's parents, Moises Mandande Machel and Guguiye Thema Machel. Courtesy of Centro de Documentação Samora Machel (CDSM)

Figure 3.2. Samora exercising. (CDSM)

Figure 3.3. Samora as a nurse. (CDSM)

nonracial platform adopted at the First Party Congress in 1962.[15] The West's support of Portuguese colonialism had driven Mondlane and many of those around him to adopt a more radical anti-imperialist stance, to the consternation of some of his more nationalist followers. This first group was backed by their host President Nyerere of Tanzania, who facilitated Mondlane's meetings with the Organization of African Unity and the socialist countries.[16]

The second faction consisted of discontented nationalists who rejected FRELIMO's new direction.[17] The two most prominent figures were Vice President Uria Simango and Lazaro Nkavandame, a respected Makonde elder who had organized a cotton cooperative in northern Mozambique and helped FRELIMO organize Makonde migrant workers in Tanzania.[18] Mateus Gwenjere, a priest from Sofala who joined FRELIMO in the mid-1960s with a number of his students, also criticized Mondlane's group. Although all three opposed FRELIMO's radical turn and the leadership's punishment of dissidents, they did not speak in one voice. While Simango and Gwenjere adopted an antiwhite stance, Nkavandame did not. Similarly, neither Nkavandame nor Gwenjere flirted with Maoism, which Simango found appealing. Gwenjere was also critical of the leadership for failing to send recruits abroad to study.

FRELIMO's internal conflicts centered around multiple but interrelated questions: What role did race play, if any, in determining who should be considered Mozambican? Who was the enemy? What role should educated Mozambicans have in FRELIMO? What tactics would be most effective in carrying out the armed struggle? What type of postcolonial society did FRE-LIMO envision?

These cleavages further exacerbated preexisting regional and religious animosities. They were also fueled by personal ambition and Lisbon's sustained propaganda campaign focusing on historic tensions between Makua and Makonde and the influence of Marxists within FRELIMO.[19]

Even with this mix of factors, the racial question and the related issue of who was an "authentic Mozambican" was at the center of the conflict. Simango, Nkavandame, and their supporters defined the enemy exclusively in racial terms. For them, all settlers living in Mozambique, including mulattoes and Asians, were either collaborators or simply benefited from Portuguese rule, making them the enemy.[20] They rejected the First Party Congress's antiracialist policy and were livid that Mondlane and his allies welcomed progressive whites, mulattoes, and Asians into FRELIMO. Their vocal opposition violated a cardinal principle of FRELIMO's political culture, that militants had to speak in one voice once consensus had been reached.

The issue of race was brought to a head by the arrival in Dar es Salaam of João Ferreira and Jacinto Veloso, two white Portuguese who came to join FRELIMO.[21] Simango and his supporters were irate, insisting that only black Africans were authentically Mozambican. For both Mondlane, married to a white North American, and dos Santos, pigmentation was subordinate to politics. Matters only worsened with the appearance of Helder Martins, a dissident doctor of Portuguese descent whose services were badly needed by the undertrained FRELIMO medical staff, and Fernando Ganhão, a prominent educator, both of whom had fled Lisbon. Under pressure from Tanzanian security officials, FRELIMO leaders agreed to send the four to Algeria and elsewhere to work with other political exiles.[22] Although there is no indication that Samora opposed this decision, he must have been disappointed, given his position on the issue of race.

The divide over race also influenced FRELIMO's military strategy. Those who viewed all Portuguese as the enemy advocated random attacks on European settlers and urban violence—similar to what had occurred in Algeria. On August 24, 1964, a month before FRELIMO's war announcement and six months before the celebrated attack at Chai in Mueda, a small band led by Lucas Fernandes, a FRELIMO member who had publicly expressed his hatred for whites, killed a Dutch clergyman at the Catholic missionary station in Nangolo, in Cabo Delgado.[23] FRELIMO condemned the murder. Both Mondlane and Samora rejected rash urban violence, which would necessarily kill defenseless men, women, and children and put their supporters at risk.[24]

Mondlane, Samora, and other senior military officers envisioned an alternate strategy focusing on political and military mobilization of exploited peasants. It required FRELIMO guerrillas to forge bonds with local villagers based on shared political goals and peasant involvement in all aspects of the struggle. This position was heavily influenced by the successful anticolonial struggles of the Chinese and North Vietnamese.

Regional cleavages also figured prominently in the bitter dispute over FRELIMO's role in furthering the education of its recruits. Many students who fled to Dar es Salaam in the early years came from rural areas in central and northern Mozambique, where there were limited opportunities to study, and had joined FRELIMO hoping they would be sent overseas to advance their education.[25] Few wished to follow Samora's example by going first to the front lines. In 1966, however, FRELIMO's Executive Committee abandoned its policy of sending recruits overseas, fearing the program was creating two tiers of militants—those educated abroad and those forced to fight. The new directive, pushed by Armando Guebuza, FRELIMO's education secretary, also required that those studying abroad or attending the Mozambican Institute in Dar es Salaam undergo months of military and political training at Nachingwea, under Samora's command. Thereafter, they would be assigned duties on the front line, such as working with illiterate peasants in bush schools or constructing makeshift medical facilities.

This did not go over well with many students.[26] By the beginning of 1968, students at the Mozambican Institute were in open rebellion. After Samora helped quell the protest, the institute was closed. William Minter, a teacher there, wrote that some who protested were motivated by "the idea that their own personal success and future education [took] priority over the needs of the revolution."[27] Some frustrated students fled to Kenya or the United States and other Western nations, where they helped to form the União Nacional dos Estudantes Moçambicanos to oppose FRELIMO policies. Although not terribly successful, UNEMO did publish a bitter attack on Mondlane, claiming that he forced them to interrupt their educations to maintain his position as the only FRELIMO member with a PhD.[28]

The two factions also held very different visions of an independent Mozambique. Simango and Nkavandame adopted a nationalist position under which an educated black elite would rule, as Malawi and Kenya were governed. Samora sided with Mondlane and the FRELIMO Executive Committee in condemning this elitist approach, which, they argued, would lead Mozambique toward a neocolonial arrangement common in other African countries. Instead, they imagined a society free of racial, social, and economic inequality, responsive to the needs of peasants and workers, that would attack poverty and underdevelopment through the transforming capacity of education, science, and technology.[29]

In 1968, Mondlane acknowledged that FRELIMO was moving in a socialist direction, the first time any FRELIMO leader had made a public reference to Marxism. Several years earlier, however, Samora was already contemplating a more radical trajectory. Among his personal papers, we discovered a tattered field notebook written either in late 1966 or early 1967. After asking himself whether FRELIMO should be a united front or a single party, he listed twenty-two social and political objectives, all of which were later incorporated into FRELIMO's revolutionary ideology. Among the most significant were:

- Support the masses
- Armed struggle within the country
- Unity of all comrades
- Establishment of liberated zones based on people's power

- Down with racism and tribalism
- Avoid revolutionary slogans
- Social justice[30]

Samora's Ascension to Power

As Samora became an increasingly influential advocate of the socialist line, opponents argued that he had been brainwashed by Marxist intellectuals who had hijacked FRELIMO. They pointed to his close relationship with Marcelino dos Santos, Jorge Rebelo, Oscar Monteiro, and Sérgio Vieira, who they insisted were not authentic Mozambicans because of their Goan descent. Implicit in their claims was the elitist assumption that Samora's peasant background and limited education made him incapable of comprehending the complexities of Marxism.[31]

Samora's rivals, however, completely misread the roots of his radicalism, which stretched as far back as his youth. Later, in Lourenço Marques, he experienced discrimination in his workplace, was denied access to segregated theaters, was prevented from moving freely through the city at night, and could be arrested and beaten on the slightest pretext.[32] During this period he also began to question the limited success of African nationalist movements, to recognize the broader achievements of the revolutions in Vietnam and Cuba, and to become aware of how international entities were responding to FRELIMO's anticolonial struggle. In Dar es Salaam, he observed first-hand how China, Vietnam, and Eastern Bloc nations provided FRELIMO military and diplomatic support, while the West turned a deaf ear to its requests for assistance and continued to support Portugal. Samora later described his political development this way: "During the liberation struggle somebody gave me a copy of a book by Marx. I read it, and I realized I was 'reading' Marx for the second time."[33] As one FRELIMO leader explained, "Samora's Marxism came from his gut."[34]

Under Mondlane's tutelage, Samora quickly rose through the ranks. In 1966, FRELIMO's Central Committee appointed him defense secretary to replace Filipe Samuel Magaia, who had been killed on patrol by a dissident FRELIMO member.[35] The decision to select Samora over Casal Ribeiro, Magaia's second-in-command from central Mozambique, fueled suspicions that a southern clique was consolidating power. Samora embraced his new responsibility for planning and coordinating FRELIMO's military campaigns and building a military force and command structure committed to the leadership's radical vision. During the 1968 Second Party Congress, Mondlane would single out Samora for his extraordinary accomplishments.

Meanwhile, PIDE, which had infiltrated FRELIMO, fanned the flames of discord. Its operatives spread rumors ranging from claims of a Marxist takeover to allegations that Mondlane and his wife Janet were CIA agents. PIDE surreptitiously bought off key militants and unleashed a formidable propaganda campaign aimed at exacerbating ethnic and regional tensions by telling members from the center and north that southerners, including Mondlane and Machel, had captured FRELIMO and were promoting friends and family.

The biggest challenge to Mondlane and Samora, however, came from within the FRELIMO leadership.

As the power and influence of the dissidents slipped, they became more outspoken. Simango insisted whites and Asians were corrupting FRELIMO's leaders and that he would not hand over power to "Marxists from the South." Nkavandame opposed the radical turn and, through his ties to senior figures in the Tanzanian government, tried to drive a wedge between Nyerere and the FRELIMO leadership.[36] Gwenjere encouraged alienated students to ransack the FRELIMO office in Dar es Salaam, during which event Central Committee member Matheus Sansão Muthemba was murdered.

On the morning of February 3, 1969, Mondlane was assassinated. As recounted in *Mozambique Revolution*, "on that day, early in the morning, our President went to the office and worked with several comrades. At about 10 a.m. he collected all his mail from the office and went to the home of a friend [an American, Betty King], a quiet place to work undisturbed. Among the mail he took with him was a book, wrapped and addressed to him. Once at the house he started opening his mail. When he opened the book, there was a great explosion, killing our President."[37]

The Portuguese police, probably with the help of a hit man named Cassimo Monteiro, had orchestrated the killing. Although no Mozambicans were charged, PIDE appears to have had accomplices inside FRELIMO who arranged to have the package delivered directly to Mondlane. The two primary suspects were Silveiro Nungu, administrative secretary at the FRELIMO office in Dar es Salaam, and Lazaro Nkavandame.[38]

Mondlane's death precipitated an intense power struggle. In a preemptive move, immediately after the funeral Simango declared himself president. However, his public differences with Mondlane, narrow race-based perspective, and lack of battlefield experience caused many in the leadership to object. At an emergency meeting of the Central Committee weeks later, Simango failed to win a majority, but in an unsuccessful effort to paper over the conflict the Central Committee approved a troika of three coequal presidents: Samora, the military commander; dos Santos, secretary for foreign affairs; and Vice President Simango.

In response, Simango wrote "The Gloomy Situation in FRELIMO," a blistering attack on the other two leaders, in which he claimed that his opponents had usurped power, eliminated political rivals, and planned to kill him. He also condemned Mondlane, arguing that he had fostered the growth of a new form of colonialism in FRELIMO by allowing Portuguese to dominate the institute, brainwash students, and infiltrate the Central Committee. Simango denied that he and his supporters were racists and insisted they were defending the people's interests by vigilantly preventing imperialists from infiltrating FRELIMO.[39] He also decried the leadership's political violence within FRELIMO and claimed that Samora had personally masterminded the killing of his predecessor, Felipe Samuel Magaia.

Two months later, the Central Committee expelled Simango from FRELIMO and selected Samora to fill the leadership vacuum.[40] He was chosen because of his ties to Mondlane, skills as a military commander, popularity among the guerrillas, and ability to win over rural communities in northern Mozambique. Simango escaped to Cairo and subsequently joined the Comite

Revolucionário de Moçambique, a nationalist organization based in Zambia.[41] Some suspected he was involved in Mondlane's assassination, an accusation that has never been proven.

At roughly the same time, Nkavandame, who had been charged with corruption and exploiting peasants in northern Mozambique, deserted to the Portuguese along with his supporters and urged other Makonde to put down their arms. The colonial regime used his defection to try to win over Makonde communities, but unsuccessfully. This failure was significant because Cabo Delgado had by then become a principal terrain of struggle and an important route used by FRELIMO guerrillas to extend their campaign into Niassa and more southern provinces.

Samora and the Armed Struggle, 1964–75

While the FRELIMO leadership was embroiled in conflict, it was also preparing its guerrillas to confront Mozambique's colonial army and facing the difficult task of winning support in rural communities that knew little about the liberation movement. Samora played a decisive role in dealing with both these challenges.

Preparing for Armed Struggle

When Samora's platoon returned from Algeria, it was initially stationed at the FRELIMO camp in Bagamoyo, Tanzania. Worried the camp would be an easy target for Portuguese spies, given its proximity to Dar es Salaam, and that family members living in Dar might distract guerrillas, FRELIMO moved it to Kongwa in central Tanzania and appointed Samora its commander.

Conditions at Kongwa, site of an abandoned groundnut scheme with only three shacks, were even worse than those in Algeria. The soldiers had only what they brought with them—blankets, some provisions, and personal belongings, but no weapons. As Pachinuapa recalled, "[on the] very first day we needed to eat. So, the question arose who would actually do the cooking. We considered ourselves well-trained soldiers because we had completed the military course [in Algeria]. Nobody was interested in working in the kitchen. We were fighters not cooks. Samora volunteered. He set the example."[1]

Samora insisted the camp become self-sufficient as quickly as possible. He divided his hundred soldiers into two groups, each spending part of the day working in the fields and building barracks and latrines while the rest engaged in training. Lacking weapons, they simulated combat with sticks until the first cache of light arms arrived from Algeria. Later, they received training with weapons provided by China and Eastern Bloc countries. They learned first aid, how to organize ambushes, and where to plant land mines. During the evenings they engaged in political education and attended literacy classes. According to Chipande, officers and foot soldiers were expected to train side-by-side, work together in the fields, and prepare meals together. This regimen was introduced by Samora to foster recognition that, no matter where in the colony they were born, their survival now depended on supporting each other.[2]

In 1965, FRELIMO moved its major training base closer to the border. It was now at Nachingwea, on an abandoned plantation located less than seventy miles from Cabo Delgado, where FRELIMO had launched its first military actions the year before. Aided by a contingent of Chinese instructors, Samora oversaw the training of more than two thousand male and female guerrillas. With its schools, clinic, collective fields, and women's brigade, Nachingwea was a microcosm of FRELIMO's imagined new Mozambican society. Years later, Samora described it as the "laboratory and forge" of the new nation.[3]

As part of the militants' political education, Samora and the leadership stressed FRELIMO's revolutionary values, demanding the guerrillas shed decadent habits inherited from colonialism and the "obscurantist" beliefs they had learned as children. Helder Martins, who trained nurses at Nachingwea, described the profound influence of the Chinese advisers on Samora's thinking: "They were not only military instructors; they were also political instructors. They suggested readings for Samora, including *The Complete Works of Mao Zedong*, which stressed collectivism, self-discipline, and solidarity with the peasantry."[4]

Samora also sought to create a sense of national identity by instituting cultural activities—dance, song, and theater—from various parts of the colony. On most Saturday nights militants could be found engaging in these activities, which were a welcome break from military and political training. According to Oscar Monteiro, who taught at Nachingwea, these social nights helped to reinforce bonding among the comrades.[5]

Life at Nachingwea was demanding. Work in the fields, military training, and political education consumed all day and much of the evenings. Living conditions were harsh and supplies scarce. Some trainees became dispirited; others abandoned the movement.[6] Another vexing problem was the large number of female recruits who became pregnant during training—and the challenge of supporting these young unwed mothers and their children.[7] Given the leadership's gender biases, it isn't surprising that childcare was left to the mothers and members of the Women's Detachment, who took on the role of "aunties." This sexist behavior notwithstanding, the "lessons of Nachingwea" were an important part of FRELIMO's idealized revolutionary discourse.[8]

Samora could be a severe taskmaster, but he was also sensitive to the difficulties recruits had in adjusting to the demands of life at Nachingwea. On one occasion, he met with a rebellious student from the Mozambican Institute who had been sent to Nachingwea. The student expected to be severely punished. Instead, Samora listened to his grievances, complaints of homesickness, and frustration at not being allowed to train as an artilleryman, which had always been his dream. The following day he was transferred to an artillery unit being trained by the Chinese and became part of the first artillery brigade to fight inside Mozambique.[9]

Guerrilla penetration into northern Mozambique began in 1964. The first front was opened in Cabo Delgado with a sustained incursion into the Makonde highlands led by Alberto Chipande. In November 1965, FRELIMO opened a second front in eastern Niassa. After marching for eleven days and avoiding at least one Portuguese ambush, the small expeditionary force led by Samora arrived at the village of the senior Yao chief, Mataka V. According to some accounts, Samora's group, dressed in Muslim garb to avoid suspicion, met surreptitiously with Mataka and convinced him and his subjects to relocate by following the guerrillas to an area beyond the control of colonial authorities.[10] Years later, António Eanes, president of Portugal, who had been a captain in the colonial army, presented a fuller account of this maneuver at a state dinner—explaining that Mataka was under arrest at a Portuguese administrative center when Samora, dressed as a Muslim holy man, entered the post and whisked him away. Samora, not known for his modesty, grinned and willingly added details. With Mataka free, some of his followers joined FRELIMO in Tanzania. Others who had relocated provided food and logistical support to insurgents passing southward through the Niassa corridor.[11]

This episode clearly demonstrates that Samora understood the important role traditional African leaders could play in the liberation struggle. Mataka's ancestors, like Samora's, had fought against the Portuguese occupation. These living memories nurtured a tradition of resistance, which helps explain why Mataka's Yao followers supported the guerrillas, while other African polities in Niassa that had not resisted were more ambivalent. Years later, Samora appealed to a similar tradition of resistance to mobilize rural supporters in the Zambezi Valley, where anticolonial opposition had persisted until 1921.[12]

By the end of 1965, FRELIMO, having made important inroads in Cabo Delgado and Niassa, opened a front in Tete. While Samora was involved in planning the strategy, he did not personally direct the military campaign. This effort was abandoned months later when it became clear that FRELIMO forces were overextended elsewhere. It was not until 1969 that FRELIMO again challenged Portuguese forces in the Tete region.

Implementing Strategies to Carry Out the Armed Struggle

In pursuing the armed struggle inside Mozambique, FRELIMO had to develop strategies to deal with the challenges that arose. While much has been written on this subject, we will focus on the four most significant challenges Samora faced as military commander.

The first was the guerrillas' relative weakness. FRE-LIMO had barely 250 men under arms, whose weapons were limited to handguns, outdated rifles, light machine guns, and land mines. In his reports from the front lines, Samora complained that lack of arms and ammunition was impeding guerrilla advances both in Cabo Delgado and Niassa.[13] The colonial force numbered more than thirty thousand and had modern weapons, communications equipment, helicopters, jets, and napalm, all provided by Lisbon's NATO allies. Given this imbalance of power, Samora and his comrades calculated it would take twenty years or more to liberate Mozambique.[14]

The second challenge was that, in order to compensate for this enormous imbalance, Samora had to recruit large numbers of sympathizers. FRELIMO's leadership had become convinced that Mao's model of protracted guerrilla warfare, with its emphasis on political mobilization of the peasantry and socioeconomic transformation of the countryside, was the best strategy for liberating Mozambique. Borrowing from the Maoist maxim, Samora and his commanders stressed that "the people are to the guerrillas as water is to fish. Out of the water a fish cannot live. Without the people, that is to say, without the support of the people, the guerrillas cannot survive."[15] To gain this needed support, FRELIMO militants organized meetings in rural communities to explain the objectives of the struggle and grapple with the immediate problems the peasants faced.[16] Samora also used these occasions to establish personal bonds with members of these communities, some of which lasted a lifetime.

In the war zones of Cabo Delgado and Niassa, sympathetic rural communities surreptitiously provided critical foodstuffs and carried war materiel to the front lines from FRELIMO's bases. Maintaining the supply lines was an arduous process and extremely dangerous for the carriers.[17] FRELIMO also deployed younger children to carry messages, since they were less likely to be noticed by Portuguese troops.

Recruiting supporters was challenging. Fear of retribution deterred many peasants from assisting the guerrillas or joining their ranks. Sometimes, FRELIMO forces attacked communities loyal to the Portuguese and coerced members into becoming part of the armed struggle.[18] According to Thomas Henriksen, a historian often critical of FRELIMO, evidence suggests that "the colonial forces were more guilty of indiscriminate killing and mass murder," while FRELIMO engaged "in selective violence and abductions."[19]

The third challenge was effectively incorporating women in all aspects of the struggle. FRELIMO's thin ranks and urgent need to continue expanding its support in the countryside required more cadres. Women were the obvious choice. The Liga Feminina Moçambicana (Mozambican Women's League) was founded in 1966. Its function was to recruit women to transport supplies, provide information about Portuguese military activity, and even carry out small acts of sabotage. They were not, however, seen as potential guerrilla fighters.

Some women, dissatisfied with such constraints, requested military training. The following year, FRELIMO established the Destacamento Feminino (Women's Detachment) under female commanders who had trained at Nachingwea. After training, brigades were dispatched to Mozambique to mobilize peasant women and carry out limited guerrilla activities. The participation of Mozambican women in military campaigns stimulated the gradual restructuring of gender roles within FRELIMO.

One of the first women to be trained was Josina Muthemba, who was born in Inhambane to a rural family with deep nationalist roots. An active member of NESAM and clandestine member of a FRELIMO cell in the capital, she tried in 1964 to flee to Tanzania to join the liberation movement. Rhodesian security forces arrested her and, as was standard practice, handed her over to PIDE. Despite then being under state surveillance, she managed to escape with several other FRELIMO supporters, arriving in Dar es Salaam the following year. For a time, Josina assisted Janet Mondlane, wife of the FRELIMO leader, at the Mozambican Institute. She was later sent to Mozambique to work with orphans and young mothers, organizing day-care centers and securing food, blankets, clothing, and medical supplies. In 1967, she and twenty-four other women were the first to volunteer for military training at Nachingwea, after which she became a leader of the Destacamento Feminino.[20]

Josina's dedication to FRELIMO attracted the attention of Eduardo Mondlane and other senior leaders, including Samora. He was drawn to the energetic and beautiful young militant who had turned down a scholarship to study in Sweden in favor of participating in the struggle. Above all else, he admired Josina's independence of mind and commitment to the revolution. In a letter dated October 22, 1970, he wrote to her that it "brings me joy to know your great capabilities, and how effective you are in the struggle for liberation and particularly in the struggle for Mozambican women."[21]

Despite having a wife and family in Lourenço Marques, Samora openly courted Josina. Shortly thereafter, with FRELIMO's approval, they were married at the FRELIMO Education Center in Tunduru on May 4, 1969—three months after Mondlane's assassination. In a gesture of solidarity, the Reverend Uria Simango, FRELIMO vice president and Samora's principal rival, officiated at the wedding, with many senior FRELIMO and Tanzanian officials attending, including President Nyerere. That November, Josina gave birth to a chubby baby boy they named Samora Jr. but called Samito—"little Samora."

Josina and other female militants pushed FRELIMO leaders to confront a number of issues adversely affecting young women. They lobbied to abolish female circumcision rites and to increase support for pregnant militants. In both regards they were successful. A 1972 FRELIMO commission conducted a study in the liberated zones of the effects of circumcision rites on Makua and Makonde girls and boys. The following year, despite opposition from traditionalists, they recommended eradicating the practice.[22]

His war experiences, pragmatic considerations, and relationship with Josina altered Samora's thinking on gender equality. On several occasions he apologized for his irresponsible and inappropriate behavior toward women, and, despite opposition from more conservative members of FRELIMO, celebrated their importance in the armed struggle. In his much-cited keynote address to the first conference of the Organization of Mozambican Women in 1973, Samora proclaimed:

> The emancipation of women is not an
> act of charity, the result of a humanitarian or
> compassionate attitude. The liberation of women
> is a fundamental necessity for the Revolution, the
> guarantee of its continuity and the precondition for
> its victory. The main objective of the Revolution is
> to destroy the system of exploitation and build a new
> society which releases the potentialities of human
> beings, reconciling them with labour and with
> nature. This is the context within which the question
> of women's emancipation arises. . . .
>
> If it is to be victorious, the Revolution
> must eliminate the whole system of exploitation
> and oppression, liberating *all* the exploited and
> oppressed.[23]

Note, however, that his thinking had not sufficiently evolved to include gender oppression in the household and the community.

The last challenge was to move beyond the racialized notion held by many of the militants that all Portuguese were necessarily the enemy. Samora refused to accept this and did not allow his forces to commit random acts of violence against European settlers and their descendants.[24] In some areas, commanders even courted European missionaries and sympathetic Portuguese settlers. Samora developed a close personal relationship with Manuel Braz da Costa, a Portuguese farmer in Niassa who provided supplies and information about the movement of colonial forces.[25]

It was also forbidden to abuse Portuguese prisoners of war.[26] This stood in sharp contrast to the well-documented and widespread torture of FRELIMO captives and sympathizers carried out by the Portuguese. In FRELIMO publications, speeches, discussions, and meetings with foreign journalists, Samora regularly highlighted FRELIMO's humane treatment of captured Portuguese soldiers—which proved to be excellent propaganda, challenging Lisbon's claim that the insurgents were little more than "black terrorists." FRELIMO won praise from Western European and North American activists who organized anticolonial protests in African American communities, progressive churches, universities, and labor halls.[27]

Overcoming these four challenges enabled FRELIMO to slowly advance into northern Mozambique. Once it eliminated the Portuguese presence from these areas, dismantling the colonial administration, it had to establish new revolutionary structures, which became the basis for the liberated zones.

The Liberated Zones and *Aldeamentos*: A Terrain of Struggle

The vast, sparsely populated regions of northern Mozambique were the principal terrains of struggle between the guerrillas and the Portuguese regime. Both sides prioritized reorganizing rural society and "protecting" communities under their control, although their strategies were very different. For the FRELIMO leadership, liberated zones brought opportunity to begin to transform social and economic relationships in the countryside. For colonial planners, the goal was to relocate hundreds of thousands of peasants into strategic hamlets to isolate FRELIMO guerrillas from their peasant base of support, depriving them of foodstuff, intelligence and new recruits.

Samora's dual challenge was to create new structural relationships with peasant communities in liberated areas, and to relocate peasants who fled either as individuals or as communities from areas still under Portuguese oppression. Where the guerrillas had replaced the colonial regime, primarily in the northern parts of Cabo Delgado, Niassa, and Tete, FRELIMO established liberated zones. As Teresa Raica, who came from Maua district in Niassa, understood it, FRELIMO's goal was to win hearts and minds and recruit younger people for the struggle by any means possible.

> At first, I was sent to the Gungunhana base and worked as a cook. Then I reached a certain age when I trained at the Mswisisi base. I was with men and other women. We were all together regardless of our ethnic backgrounds. Each spoke her own language. There were no old people. Most were in their 20's. We grew cassava, sorghum and vegetables in the field belonging to the cooperative. I was happy with my life because I chose it. Those who were forcibly recruited did not try to escape because many of them began to warm towards FRELIMO's political views after attending meetings and training. I always said to the people who were captured and brought to the base: "This is for your own good. This is for us to be free. We have to kick out the whites. Let's fight together so that we can

97

live wherever we want." People at the base always said that unity meant to free ourselves. Socialism? I don't know about that.[28]

This persistent belief that the goal was to "kick out the whites" suggests that, like Raica, many peasants in the liberated zones, even after attending political education sessions, had only a superficial understanding of the FRELIMO ideology.

FRELIMO used regularly scheduled meetings to engage the peasantry, giving voice to villagers' concerns and raising their political consciousness. There was nothing Samora valued more than feeling connected to the people, even if these encounters stretched well into the night or early morning. At the end of every meeting, he would urge his listeners to replace loyalist chiefs with popularly elected leaders who would preside over local meetings, establish guidelines for behavior, and organize collective production.

Education as a means to combat illiteracy and superstition was central to Samora's vision of how best to develop popular democracy, and he vigorously promoted educational programs in the liberated zones.[29] Working with the local population, FRELIMO teachers created an embryonic educational infrastructure where few, if any, schools had previously existed. By 1966, more than ten thousand students were said to be attending primary school—a number that tripled over the next four years. Even more adults attended literacy classes, which were seriously overcrowded and lacked enough of both primers and teachers.[30] This was many Mozambicans' first opportunity to learn to read and write—and to be exposed to FRELIMO's revolutionary ideology.

On several occasions, Samora told the story of a captured Portuguese soldier who, to the amazement of FRELIMO guerrillas, could neither write his name nor read. When the prisoner was given a pen and paper he "simply drew lines and stripes, there were no letters, no alphabets. We were trying to figure out if it was Arabic, Asian, Indian, or Chinese. . . . So we asked him to read for us and he responded that he did not know how."[31] The story was instructive both because it underscored the limited educational opportunities available to poor rural Portuguese, and because it challenged the commonly held belief among his own illiterate soldiers and peasants in the Europeans' superiority.

Despite the acute shortage of African doctors, nurses, and other health workers, Samora and his comrades were able to introduce a rudimentary health-care system in the liberated zones.[32] It necessarily emphasized preventative medicine. FRELIMO reported that in 1966 it vaccinated more than a hundred thousand peasants in Cabo Delgado against smallpox.[33]

The colonial agricultural system privileged cotton production for the metropole over family farming and caused recurring food shortages and famines.[34] FRELIMO instead emphasized collective production of basic staples for families and FRELIMO militants. In parts of Cabo Delgado, peasants worked the land jointly and shared produce and profits equally. In other areas they retained control over their own plots but worked collectively several days each month in a communal field growing food for the military. Because Samora believed collective labor helped cement the unity between fighters and local populations, guerrillas on occasion joined peasants in cultivating the communal fields.[35]

For all the benefits of being in liberated zones, conditions were harsh and precarious. There were threats of Portuguese attacks, shortages, intense political education sessions, long working days, and FRELIMO's military discipline, which was very different from how the peasants had previously lived their lives. Some peasants fled, alone or with disillusioned chiefs, while others were seduced by Portuguese promises of food, clothing, and amnesty.[36]

Nevertheless, life in the liberated zones was appreciably better than what most Mozambicans experienced when compelled to relocate to Portuguese strategic hamlets (*aldeamentos*), euphemistically known as "protected villages."[37] The forced relocation of dispersed communities and the colonial state's designation of the vast emptied areas as "free-fire zones" where the military could shoot moving targets on sight intensified resentment of the Portuguese.[38] Government officials estimated that by 1973, fully 67 percent of the African population of Niassa and almost half that of Cabo Delgado had been moved from their historic homelands into aldeamentos.[39] As the war heated up, forced evictions became hastier and more chaotic as entire communities were shoved off their land at a moment's notice, in some cases before any housing was in place.[40] During an unusually frank conversation with Australian journalists, a Portuguese military commander boasted that coercion had no limits: "We give the blacks two weeks to come into fortified villages. If they don't, we shoot them."[41]

Figure 4.1. Samora and Eduardo Mondlane. Courtesy of Centro de Documentção e Formação Fotográfica (CDFF)

Figure 4.2. FRELIMO's first president, Eduardo Mondlane. (CDFF)

Figure 4.3. Samora instructing members of FRELIMO's Women's Detachment. Courtesy of Centro de Documentação Samora Machel. (CDSM)

Figure 4.4. FRELIMO guerrillas training. (CDSM)

Figure 4.5. Samora addresses soldiers during the armed struggle. Courtesy of António Alves Gomes

Figure 4.6. Josina Machel. (CDSM)

Figure 4.7. Samora and Joaquim Chissano with FRELIMO guerrillas. (CDSM)

Figure 4.8. A woman from the liberated zones offering a papaya to Samora. (CDSM)

The Cost of the War

The conflict was shifting in FRELIMO's favor.[42] In 1970, its forces had withstood a major Portuguese air and ground counteroffensive known as Gordian's Knot. By 1973, several thousand guerrillas were fighting inside Mozambique. In 1974, FRELIMO forces were able for the first time to cross the Zambezi River and open new fronts in Manica and Sofala in the colony's strategic heartland. Lisbon's position was further undermined by increasing international pressure, sparked by the 1972 massacre of four hundred villagers at Wiriyamu in Manica Province.[43] With no end in sight, the Portuguese officers who had overthrown the fascist Portuguese government on April 15, 1974, began negotiating with FRELIMO to end the war.

Nevertheless, it would be a mistake to assume that FRELIMO had won the war or even that victory was near. Claims of the inevitability of such an outcome—which became part of the patriotic narrative after independence—obscure the difficulties on the ground. The guerrillas had suffered heavy losses of both men and materiel.[44] The war had taken the lives of prominent leaders, including Eduardo Mondlane, Filipe Samuel Magaia, and Samuel Kankhomba, and others like Uria Simango and Lazaro Nkavandame had defected.

Samora suffered the loss of many comrades, but most notably Eduardo Mondlane, his mentor and hero. Alberto Chipande, who broke the news to Samora at Nachingwea, remembers him "[falling] to the ground when I told him. I had never seen him crying. He bawled."[45]

The struggle was also difficult for Samora and Josina. Shortly after their marriage, Samora returned to the battlefield. He wrote regularly, describing his pride in all Josina had accomplished, bemoaning the fact that he was gone from her and their child for such long periods, and acknowledging that his absence had complicated her life.[46] His letters expressed deep love for her, as did the parting salutation—"I kiss you passionately Joze"—with which he always ended. Samora was especially concerned about Josina's poor health and urged her not to let the burdens of the struggle wear her down. She persisted in working with war orphans and single mothers, however, even after contracting leukemia.

On April 7, 1971, Josina, his bride of only two years, died at the age of twenty-six. The depth of Samora's pain is expressed in the poem he wrote as a eulogy to his wife and lover, which also reveals how revolutionary discourse permeated personal expressions of grief:

> Josina you are not dead because we have assumed
> your responsibilities and they live with us.
> You have not died, for the causes you championed
> were inherited by us in their entirety.
> You have gone from us, but the weapon and rucksack
> that you left, your tools of war, are part of my
> burden.
>
> . . . .
>
> The Revolution renews itself from its best and most
> beloved children.
> This is the meaning of your sacrifice: it will be a
> living example to be followed.
> My joy is that as patriot and woman you died doubly
> free in this time when new power and the new
> woman are emerging.[47]

Samora also faced long periods of separation from his son. Almost immediately after Josina's funeral, Samora returned to the battlefield, leaving Samito at

Nachingwea in the custody of FRELIMO "aunties."[48] The care they provided offers a glimpse into the political kinship of the FRELIMO "family" and the female social networks that enabled men to go to war. A few times a year, Samora would return to Nachingwea to spend time with Samito. Despite having only vague memories of his father, Samito fondly recalled how they frolicked on the beaches near Dar es Salaam, swam in the Indian Ocean, visited the game reserve at Arusha, and even flew to Zanzibar.[49] For Samora, who had no contact with his five children in southern Mozambique, Samito was a precious reminder of everything for which he was fighting.

In the bush without his family and immediate friends, Samora spent most of his time devising military strategies and putting them into practice. When not engaged in battle, he read, wrote poetry, doodled, and followed a daily exercise regimen to maintain his physical fitness. He was also an inveterate list-maker, which was hardly surprising given his very structured and disciplined personality.

The Lusaka Accord and Its Aftermath

The Portuguese coup by the Armed Forces Movement was led by dissident junior officers opposed to continuing the colonial wars. After overthrowing Salazar's handpicked successor, Marcelo Caetano, they installed General António Spinola as the new head of state. Spinola wished to end the African wars but had no intention of granting independence to the colonies. Instead, he envisioned a Lusophonic commonwealth in which Mozambique, Angola, Guinea-Bissau, and Cabo

Verde would remain under Lisbon's control with some measure of local autonomy.

Samora and his comrades were caught off guard. Even as word of the coup arrived, they were mapping out the next phase in the guerrilla war, which they assumed would last another decade. As Oscar Monteiro remembered,

> We were in Nachingwea and it was around nine thirty in the morning. We were taking a break between the classes. Gideon Ndobe rushed in to announce that he just heard on shortwave radio that there might have been a military takeover in Lisbon.... By one p.m., Samora had gathered the FRELIMO Executive Committee and officers from the general staff to formulate our response. Within a few hours we had prepared a statement in which we affirmed our support for the democratic forces in Portugal, but we insisted that we did not take up arms to become black Portuguese in a liberal democracy. Until Lisbon agreed to Mozambican independence, we would continue the armed struggle.[50]

Two months later, the Armed Forces Movement proposed an immediate cease-fire. At a meeting in Lusaka organized by President Kaunda of Zambia, Mario Soares, Portugal's new socialist foreign minister, reiterated his call for an end to the fighting and a national referendum to determine Mozambique's future. Although Kaunda endorsed this proposal, FRELIMO rejected it because it failed to recognize either that the Mozambican people had the right to be independent or that power should immediately be transferred to

FRELIMO. Unable to resolve their differences, the parties agreed to meet again in the coming months.

In the interim, Samora instituted a three-pronged military, diplomatic, and psychological campaign. He ordered the general command to intensify the war effort by opening a new front in Zambézia, the colony's most populous province. Approximately a thousand Portuguese troops deserted there in the face of FRELIMO attacks. In August, FRELIMO scored a major victory in Cabo Delgado. Employing the most sophisticated weapons in its arsenal, including Russian artillery and rocket launchers, guerrillas bombarded the Portuguese stronghold at Milele, capturing 126 colonial troops. While Portuguese negotiators insisted that storming the base was a violation of the spirit of Lusaka, Samora maintained that the cease-fire was predicated on Lisbon's willingness to accept a transfer of power.[51] The Portuguese chief of staff, for his part, admitted the armed forces no longer had the will to fight.[52]

At the same time, Samora traveled to the Organization of African Unity's meeting in Mogadishu to garner support. His position was that, given the shift in power, the time for a referendum had long passed: "One does not ask a slave if he wants to be free, especially after he has rebelled, and still less if one is a slave owner."[53]

Samora also reached out to Mozambique's Portuguese community with a plea for reconciliation without recrimination. In a radio broadcast beamed into Mozambique from Tanzania, Samora affirmed that "FRELIMO belongs to the Mozambican people," and that "in our ranks, there is room and work for every Mozambican woman and man, for all those who wish to be Mozambicans, including those who, although not born here, want to experience and build the new Mozambique."[54]

After a secret meeting in Holland initiated by the Portuguese, negotiations reconvened in Lusaka.[55] FRELIMO demanded independence and rejected any role for anti-FRELIMO African organizations, maintaining that they lacked popular support and their presence would ultimately lead to a neocolonial arrangement.[56] In the end, Portuguese negotiators acquiesced, but FRELIMO had to accept important economic concessions, including Lisbon's right to retain ownership and control over the giant dam at Cahora Bassa until Mozambique repaid the $500 million debt Portugal had incurred by building it.[57] Thus, FRELIMO was unable to break the colonial chains of dependency—leading Aquino de Bragança, one of Samora's advisers, to warn that Mozambique could end up like many other African nations, with "independence but not decolonization."[58]

Reconvening in Lusaka on September 7, 1974, the Armed Forces Movement agreed to a transfer of power to FRELIMO within the year. Thirteen days later a transitional government, led by Joaquim Chissano and composed of six representatives of FRELIMO and four Portuguese officials, was installed in Lourenço Marques.

Despite Samora's guarantees, news of the Lusaka Accord unleashed immediate fears in Mozambique's Portuguese community. On the day of the signing, right-wing settlers calling themselves Fico (I am staying) and Dragões da Morte (Dragons of Death) launched an abortive coup in the capital. Supported by some Portuguese commandos and PIDE officials, they captured the radio station and newspaper and blew up an arsenal on the outskirts of the city. Shantytown residents rose up against this putsch and an estimated sixty civilians were killed and more than 450 wounded before a joint force of Portuguese and FRELIMO troops crushed the rebellion three days later.

On the eve of independence, with rumors circulating of an impending South African or Rhodesian invasion, Samora went on the radio and warned that such aggression would evoke a response by FRELIMO's allies. While no attack materialized, the Ian Smith regime in Rhodesia began recruiting Africans who had worked for PIDE or served in its elite commando force, Flechas (Arrows). This was the origin of the Mozambican National Resistance, predecessor of RENAMO, which would create havoc in the new nation during the next decade.

FRELIMO continued to face internal opposition. Separatist movements such as the União Nacional Africana de Rombézia sought to detach northern Mozambique from the rest of the country, and the Fico white settler movement remained active. These groups received support from Malawi, Rhodesia, and elements in the Portuguese military. It was even rumored the CIA was trying to resurrect the Comite Revolucionário de Moçambique, an allegation the American embassy denied.[59] The militantly anticommunist archbishop of Lourenço Marques, Custódio Alvim Pereira, urged from his pulpit that Africans must "love your land which is Mozambique integrated with Portugal" and warned that "the present African liberation movements are against the church."[60] Nationalists such as Uria Simango also continued to insist that political and economic power be in the hands of the African majority, and that FRELIMO represented the interests of whites, mulattoes, and *assimilados*.

Samora acknowledged that these explosive issues were not just a remnant of the past. On the eve of independence he wrote, "In the course of the struggle our great victory has been in transforming the armed struggle for national liberation into a revolution. In other words, our final aim in the struggle is not to hoist a flag different from the Portuguese, or . . . to put a Black president into the Ponto Vermelha Palace in Lourenço Marques instead of a White governor. We say our aim is to win complete independence, establish people's power, build a new society without exploitation, for the benefit of all those who identify as Mozambicans."[61]

He then embarked on a month-long journey in an old prop airplane from the Rovuma River in the far north to the Maputo River in the south. Traveling with his son Samito and Nyeleti Mondlane, the daughter of his assassinated predecessor, he landed in every province, visiting cities and towns to win over skeptics. Samora knew how to read his audience. At the site of the Mueda massacre he spoke reassuringly, addressing the apparent diffidence of his audience: "It seems as if everybody's afraid, but the administrators aren't here anymore, right? Yesterday it was the bomb that made a noise, but now it is our victory."[62]

For most Mozambicans, the unimaginable was happening. A black man was taking the reins of power. Not any black man, but one dressed in guerrilla garb who understood their suffering and their dreams for the future, who not only spoke from the podium but enthusiastically waded into crowds to embrace the elders and dance with all, young and old.

His speech on June 14th in the strategic city of Beira, a colonial stronghold and home to a loose coalition of anti-FRELIMO forces and white settler groups, revealed Samora's oratorical skills. Thousands, many from surrounding shantytowns, came to hear him. He addressed the audience in what Colin Darch and David Hedges have called "Mozambican Portuguese—a liberating language spoken in short and repetitive phrases, simplified grammar fused with words, images and rhythm from African languages." [63] At various points he connected with the audience by asking, after each statement, if he was accurately describing the oppression they had experienced under colonialism.

On the evening of June 24, 1975, thousands of Mozambicans poured into Machava Stadium in the capital to watch the lowering of the Portuguese flag and the transfer of power to FRELIMO. Samora led the crowd in the national anthem while Alberto Chipande, who had fired the first shot at Chai, raised the Mozambican flag. With family members, friends, and militants cheering wildly, Samora declared "the total and complete independence of Mozambique." Pandemonium broke out, people wept, and celebrations erupted throughout the country among those who had been listening by radio. Raul Honwana, father of four FRELIMO militants, summed up the collective euphoria within the stadium: "At zero hour on the 25th of June, at seventy years of age, I witnessed with incredible emotions the moment of the independence proclamation of the sovereign nation of Mozambique."[64]

This must have been a bittersweet moment for Samora. His dream of a free Mozambique had been realized. He had become the embodiment of the revolution: in South Africa, black students who considered him their champion as well yelled out his name while rejoicing in the streets of Durban and at the University of the North.[65]

Samora, however, had paid a heavy personal price. He had suffered the loss of many comrades, including Mondlane and Josina. He had not seen his four older children for many years. Two months earlier, his mother had passed away,[66] and his dream of sharing this moment with her died as well. Above all else, Samora was acutely aware of the pressing problems his government would need to address the following day.

Politics, Performance, and People's Power, 1975–ca. 1977

On the eve of independence, the FRELIMO Central Committee had ratified Mozambique's first constitution, which affirmed that its president would be the president of the nation. To distinguish the liberation movement from the political party into which it morphed, it became common practice to refer to the party as "Frelimo."

At forty-two, President Samora was entering uncharted waters as he and his newly appointed government faced both inherited problems and new challenges. The next morning, as the first order of business, Samora and senior military officials met with a Chinese delegation over breakfast, during which he tried unsuccessfully to obtain sophisticated weapons to protect the new nation from attacks by Rhodesia and South Africa.

Like other newly independent countries in Africa, Mozambique faced illiteracy, poverty, ethnic and regional cleavages, underdevelopment, and the challenge of organizing a state capable of remedying these ills. Other problems, including a number with which FRELIMO had already grappled, arose specifically from the Mozambican experience. How would Frelimo create a sense of national unity and overcome a history of ethnic and regional particularism that had been heightened by colonial propaganda? How should it deal with emotionally charged issues of race and national identity? How could it translate the popular support it already enjoyed in liberated regions and among clandestine supporters, particularly in Lourenço Marques, to other parts of the country, when there was no longer a common oppressor?

Samora's promise to avoid the pitfalls of "tribalism" and neocolonialism also posed serious ideological and practical questions. How would a front whose members were sometimes at odds over their vision of an independent Mozambique build a nation out of disparate populations, many of which had limited contact with each other? How would Frelimo give meaning to the somewhat vague notion of People's Power? What were the most effective ways of transforming Mozambique's colonial economy, established to serve the metropole, into one that served the Mozambican people—especially given the flight of Portuguese settlers who had enjoyed a near monopoly on education and filled all the managerial positions?

Ongoing threats from Rhodesia and South Africa made finding solutions for these issues appreciably more difficult. Both white regimes saw independent black African states on their borders as existential threats. During the armed struggle, Rhodesia had sent troops into Mozambique to fight alongside the Portuguese and had created the Mozambique National Resistance—composed primarily of disgruntled FRELIMO members, former colonial soldiers, and other collaborators with the Portuguese—which engaged in terrorist acts even before the ink on the Lusaka Accord was dry. Shortly after independence, Magnus Malan, chief of the South African Defense Force, warned President Machel that, "if threatened," his troops could occupy the capital in less than a day. The apartheid regime's fears about Frelimo were well founded. During the 1976 Soweto uprising, high school students took to the streets chanting the Frelimo slogan, *A luta continua*, a graphic reminder that Mozambique's liberation had captured the imagination of South Africa's young militants.

Now, in speeches, writings, and interviews, Samora focused on the challenges of nation- and state-building and transforming Mozambican society. Both the power of his ideas and the style of his public performance captivated his followers and advanced Frelimo's program. This far-reaching agenda, however, was not Samora's alone. While he was the face of the nation and first among equals, the Frelimo leadership included other critical thinkers and strong personalities—Marcelino dos Santos, Joaquim Chissano, Armando Guebuza, Jorge Rebelo, and Oscar Monteiro, to name a few—who had their own ideas about the revolution's path. All were members of the Frelimo Political Bureau, which gave direction to the party, shaped state policy, and directed ministries.

Samora vigorously promoted social reforms in education, health, and housing, and was a proponent of gender equality. He looked to support from socialist allies to enable the newly independent nation to overcome the crushing realities of an overwhelmingly poor and underdeveloped country surrounded by hostile neighbors. Additionally, he sought to construct a modern society in which the voices, interests, and aspirations of peasants and workers would shape his new government's policies. These principles embodied Samora's notion of People's Power.

Instituting People's Power was a tall order, however, and Samora was an impatient leader. He was unwilling to tamp down his expectations or tolerate corruption. He fought to achieve these objectives, but in his haste to transform society Samora often underestimated social complexities on the ground. The lessons of the liberated zone, the socialist vision expressed through speeches and posters, his personal popularity, and the euphoria of the moment were insufficient to ensure radical transformation. Thus, his administration rarely fulfilled his most ambitious goals.

Nevertheless, during the first years after independence, life for most Mozambicans improved. Gone were the colonial political structures that had instilled fear in their daily lives—although state abuses of power persisted on a smaller scale in the name of enforcing Frelimo's revolutionary and moralistic dictates. In independent Mozambique, Africans were no longer beaten in the fields, humiliated at work, or denied entrance to restaurants, sports clubs, or theaters. They rarely suffered racial indignities and were not forced to live in segregated shantytowns or strategic hamlets enclosed in barbed wire. Millions of Mozambicans now had access to the education and health care previously available to only an elite few. For Mozambicans of Asian descent, there was no fear of expulsion, as was occurring in Uganda and Kenya.

The political, social, and economic transformations Samora's government initiated were organically connected, and policies pursued in one domain had profound and sometimes unintended or contradictory effects on other aspects of Mozambican life. While people were encouraged to vote in local elections, Frelimo outlawed all rival parties. Campaigns to abolish polygamy and bride-wealth, which had an emancipatory impact on millions of women, alienated many men, traditionalists, and some older women. Meanwhile, the commitment to neighboring liberation struggles—supported by most Mozambicans—triggered a reign of terror through much of the countryside, backed by Rhodesia and South Africa, that devastated many Frelimo initiatives.

Samora also faced the personal challenge of reconstituting his family, most of whom he had not seen for more than a decade. His five children lived in three different households, and most were only informed of their father's identity on the eve of independence, making this more difficult. Olívia Machel, his third-oldest child, first heard about Samora when he was being vilified by the Portuguese in state-controlled media as a "notorious terrorist leader." As she later recalled, "I was born in 1961 and my father left when I was less than two. I had no memory of him. We had no communication. My maternal uncle changed my last name and that of my sibling to Tchikomo to protect us from PIDE. In 1973, our mother explained that Samora and FRELIMO were not terrorists but fighting for Mozambican independence. A year later, my paternal grandmother came to Lourenço Marques for health treatment and told me that Samora was my father."[1]

119

Building a Nation

Like many other African countries, Mozambique's boundaries had been arbitrarily delineated during colonial-era negotiations between Portugal, Britain, and Germany. Their agreements completely disregarded the histories and cultures of the multiple ethnic groups residing in Mozambique, whose members maintained their social identities into the postindependence period.

The challenge of nation-building was further complicated by Frelimo's weak presence in much of the central and southern half of the country—especially in Beira and Maputo, Mozambique's two major cities, where colonial values and practices were most deeply entrenched and a variety of opposition groups were still trying to subvert its legitimacy. Millions of Mozambicans had only the vaguest idea of Frelimo's message and ideology, requiring Samora's government to rapidly create a new social cohesion that would bind individuals of diverse communities, religions, and ethnic groups to the emerging nation. Samora recognized that this new "imagined community" was both a political and cultural artifact—difficult to construct and even harder to sustain.[2]

In his speech on Independence Day, transmitted by radio across the country, Samora had passionately addressed the meaning of national identity and citizenship. "We do not recognize tribes, region, race or religious beliefs. We only recognize Mozambicans who are equally exploited and equally desirous of freedom and revolution." Underscoring the dangers that these prior loyalties posed to the new nation, he warned, "to be united, it is not enough to state that one is united. It is necessary to wage a constant battle against all divisive situations and tendencies."[3]

The principle that citizenship was not contingent on origin or skin color was enshrined in Mozambique's new constitution, which outlawed all acts creating divisions or privileged positions based on race, gender, ethnic origin, or class position. Immediately after independence Frelimo initiated campaigns against ethnic regionalism, racism, and sexism. Broadcasts, newspaper articles, comic strips, bulletin boards, murals, and graffiti stressed the message that "from the Rovuma to the Maputo, we are all Mozambicans."

Deeds, more than slogans, however, demonstrated this commitment. One example illustrates Samora's commitment to spreading the benefits of independence. Shortly after independence, Fidel Castro offered to train nine hundred Mozambicans as doctors, engineers, and scientists. After convincing Castro to raise that number to twelve thousand over the course of a decade, Samora announced that 120 young men and women of all races and religions would be selected annually in each of Mozambique's ten provinces to train in Cuba and then return to their provinces to work.[4] This was a first step in closing the educational gap between northern and southern Mozambicans, the latter of whom had historically had more access to education. He also arranged for other students to advance their education in Eastern Europe.

Nonracialism was another central component of Frelimo's vision. When we arrived in Maputo in 1977, one of the first things we noticed was an enormous poster depicting black and white arms embracing. Its caption read "Abaixo com racismo" ("Down with racism").

Samora selected prominent guerrillas and clandestine supporters of FRELIMO regardless of race to fill senior positions in his administration, including the cabinet and senior provincial appointees. The twenty-person cabinet included fifteen Africans and *mestiços*, three white Mozambicans, and two of Goan descent. The faces of the ministers figured prominently in the national media, reinforcing the message that Mozambique was becoming a nonracial society.

In stark contrast, women were conspicuously absent from state and party leadership. Rhetoric about gender equality and the need to include women in all aspects of the revolutionary struggle did not translate into access to the inner circles of power. There was only one woman in the first cabinet—Samora's fiancé, Graça Simbine, who was named minister of education.[5]

Building a nation was a cultural as well as a political process. Societal transformation required popularizing the cultural dimensions of the nation's diverse ethnic groups, making them part of the national consciousness, while internalizing revolutionary values. Samora promoted the view that this synthesis was the key to creating a distinct Mozambican identity. As he put it in one speech, "Let art seek to combine old forms with new content, then giving rise to new forms. Let painting, written literature, theater and the artistic handicraft be added to the traditional culture, dance, sculpture and singing. Let the creativity of some become that of all, men, women, young and old, from the north to the south, so that the all new revolutionary Mozambican culture may be born to all."[6]

Such public exhortations were an essential feature of Samora's effort to "perform the nation"—a task he relished.[7] A charismatic leader and natural orator, he was at his best in large outdoor meetings. On stage, dressed in guerrilla fatigues, with his swagger, infectious smile, and biting sarcasm on full display, he left his audiences entranced. Samora understood the power of imagery and the appeal to national pride his performances evoked. According to Luís Bernardo Honwana, Samora's chief of staff, he relished the fact that he was the embodiment of the revolution, inspiring hope for the future of the nation.[8] His characteristic use of singing to engage his listeners led Fidel Castro to exclaim that Samora was "the first leader I've seen who can bring order to the masses through revolutionary songs."[9]

A careful reading of Samora's speeches and writings reveals an emancipatory project laced with puritanical undertones reflecting his missionary education. In speech after speech, he stressed moral rectitude, appropriate comportment, and self-discipline. One historian has said Samora's speeches "read like evangelical sermons . . . a moral crusade as well as a political revolution."[10]

Simply reading Samora's speeches fails to capture the complexity of his performances. His repertoire included the intentional use of repetition, incorrect grammar, body language, and engagement with the audience through song, humor, and sarcasm. He intuitively understood that songs evoke powerful emotions and memories, instill a sense of purpose, self-confidence, and power in the listeners, and create a deep personal bond with them.

On several occasions, we attended rallies in which Samora silenced the crowd's murmuring by breaking into "Kanimambo, FRELIMO" (Thank you, FRELIMO), singing each stanza in a different African language. This would be followed by one or two other songs, most commonly "Não vamos esquecer" (We will never forget) or "O povo organizado" (The people organized), with crowds singing along or humming the melody. Then Samora would raise his voice and shout a revolutionary slogan: "*Abaixo com Apartheid*" (Down with apartheid) or "*Abaixo com Xiconhoca*" (Down with Xiconhoca—a cartoon character embodying all that was corrupt or immoral about colonialism that continued to exist in the new Mozambique). The crowd shouted back, "*Abaixo!*" So convincing were his performances that Kok Nam, Mozambique's leading photographer who regularly accompanied Samora, was heard to brag that "Samora could even convince a cadaver."[11]

As the Mozambican journalist Carlos Cardoso recalled, "When the people talk of our president, they don't say 'Samora Moisés Machel, president of Frelimo, president of the People's Republic of Mozambique.' The people say 'Samora,' or 'Comrade President' . . . with joy, because they feel, they know, that he is their comrade."[12] Perhaps Beira resident Pinto de Abreu summed up best how Samora touched the lives of ordinary Mozambicans. Forty years after meeting Samora while on his way to study in Cuba, he still remembered and cherished their brief encounter: "This day was great for me, not only because I had come so close to Samora . . . but especially because I was touched by his loving greeting. Samora naturally affects with his character, with his magnetic presence. It was not a gesture of political fabrication or charm that had been rehearsed the day before, it was something that came spontaneously from within him, from the heart."[13]

Samora periodically stepped out of his role as father of the nation and moral guardian to work alongside ordinary Mozambicans. In 1977, he was featured on the cover of *Tempo*, the country's leading weekly magazine, harvesting rice at a state farm in Gaza along with thousands of volunteers from Maputo. Newspapers and billboards regularly showed him laboring side-by-side with peasants and workers.[14] Such images projected to the nation Samora's belief that work and human dignity were inextricably intertwined. Photographs like these were important building blocks in Frelimo's nationalist and socialist iconography.[15]

Building a State: Postcolonial Politics

To build a nation required a strong and effective state serving the common good. The skills needed to engage in guerrilla struggle and those required to construct a state were very different. In a moment of self-reflection during his Beira speech immediately before independence, Samora acknowledged the enormity of this task, while maintaining his confidence in the ultimate success of the revolution: "The truth is that we fully understand what we do not want—oppression, exploitation, humiliation—but, as to what we want and how to get it, our ideas are necessarily still vague. They are born out of practice, corrected by practice. We undoubtedly will run into setbacks. But it is from these setbacks that we will learn."[16]

Frelimo had little governing experience and only a minimal presence in many parts of the country. Samora was acutely aware of the country's small number of economists, medical personnel, jurists, and diplomats. He recognized that many of the most qualified cadres were in their late twenties and thirties, with little practical knowledge of how to organize the ministries to which they were appointed or to govern in the provinces.[17] For all of these reasons, he admonished against romanticizing the armed struggle and exhorted militants not to succumb to triumphalism. Complacency, he warned, would undermine the revolution.[18]

To mobilize Mozambicans in their rural communities, urban neighborhoods, and workplaces was a task beyond the capacity of the relatively small number of Frelimo cadres. The critical job of mobilizing the masses fell to grassroots organizations known as *grupos dinamizadores* (dynamizing groups), which were first implemented in Nachingwea during the war. Dynamizing groups generally consisted of approximately a dozen elected Frelimo sympathizers. For Samora, this was the essence of People's Power.

We attended several meetings in our Maputo neighborhood organized by our local dynamizing group. To us, the meetings seemed freewheeling, unruly, and time-consuming. Nevertheless, they did provide an opportunity for frank, sometimes heated, discussions on a wide array of issues affecting the community. Participants raised concerns ranging from family disputes and conflicts with their neighbors to larger social problems such as poor sanitary conditions, price gouging, crime, and prostitution. Dynamizing groups also organized neighborhood work parties and cultural events and encouraged community members to attend plays, marches, and rallies celebrating the new Mozambique.

Two of their most important functions were transmitting Frelimo ideology and serving as Frelimo's eyes and ears. They explained and led discussions of state policies, promoted patriotism, and denounced suspected enemies of the revolution. Roberta Washington, an American architect working in the Ministry of Housing, described what transpired during dynamizing group meetings there, held every Saturday from 8:00 a.m. to noon: "Cooperantes [like Washington] did not need to attend, but I was curious about what took place, so I regularly attended. Sometimes, it was Marxist theory made boring by people not that good at explaining it. But mostly, it was a time to talk and get to hang out with colleagues and friends. Except during that period when Mozambicans who were suspected to have worked with PIDE were being made to 'confess' before everyone; then, it was just downright eerie."[19] Despite the tendency of men to dominate these meetings, the inefficiencies, and the occasional misuses of power, the dynamizing groups were widely accepted.

Before Frelimo could construct a strong and effective state, it had to dismantle colonial institutions. One of the first targets was the colonial police force. To replace it, Samora's administration encouraged the creation of militias in neighborhoods and workplaces. The mandate of these People's Vigilance Groups was "to neutralize enemy action, defend vital points of the economic productive sector, and detect infiltrators aiming to undermine the economy and state apparatus." Many joined for patriotic reasons—to defend against traitors and guard strategic sites—while others volunteered to protect their communities from criminals, alcoholics, and drug abusers. Members also derived very real benefits, including preferred access to ration cards.[20] The militia members' poor training, relative autonomy, and revolutionary fervor sometimes led to abuses of power. Overzealous members arrested citizens for minor infractions like noise-making and public displays of affection. Women wearing miniskirts and high heels were presumed to be sex workers and were frequent targets.[21]

Another colonial institution that was an early target was the judicial system. Under postindependence legal reforms, Africans for the first time had their cases tried in a court of their peers. This was a radical departure from their past experiences, in which capricious colonial authorities and state-appointed chiefs applied some combination of "customary law" and the colonial penal code.

Samora's government also rejected widescale use of incarceration to punish those who violated societal norms, Instead, reeducation centers were established shortly after independence. Samora's faith in revolutionary pedagogy and restorative justice shaped his thinking about the reeducation process, which dated back to the armed struggle.[22] Moral and political education and the development of a work ethic would serve as the basis for rehabilitation. Samora articulated this vision in the following terms: "The reeducation center should be a school where professional knowledge should be passed on and made use of. It is the fundamental task of officials in charge of reeducation centers to know the history of each one of the people being re-educated—his life history and his origin—in order to understand why he committed his crimes."[23]

Although reeducation camps dated back to the armed struggle, the actual organization and functioning of these centers in the postindependence period bore little relationship to Samora's vision. He appointed Armando Guebuza, Frelimo's political commissar and a very harsh disciplinarian, to oversee them. Under his direction, more than fifteen thousand Mozambican citizens were detained in the first years of independence for minor offenses or inappropriate behavior, including beer brewing, prostitution, and petty crimes. Many were arbitrarily incarcerated. To this group were added old and new Frelimo dissidents and opponents of the regime. Thus, even as the legal system was being restructured to allow Africans to have their day in court, many "enemies of the revolution" were being severely punished without trial.

Although the state outlawed political parties other than Frelimo, voting was an important component of People's Power because it engaged citizens in the political process. All Mozambicans except those who had worked for the secret police or other repressive colonial institutions had the right to vote. Between September and December 1977, more than twenty-two thousand men and women—all professed supporters of Frelimo—were elected to serve as deputies in 894 local elections.[24] A *New York Times* reporter observing the election process noted, "If enthusiasm has waned in other places [in Africa], it is palpable here. . . . There is evidence that the degree of mobilization and national purpose attained here is great and may be more durable than anything black Africa has known."[25]

Nevertheless, the levers of power were pressed behind closed doors. Critical meetings of the National Council of Ministers and the Central Committee of the Political Bureau were closed to the public and press, making it impossible to determine the scope and intensity of debate and the extent of ideological faultlines, competing factions and court intrigues. Thus, until the last years of Samora's rule Frelimo presented a united front. Meanwhile, within this tightly knit circle, Samora could instill fear as well as admiration. One confidante noted that, on occasion, we "were all fearful of a quiet, non-talkative Samora with his cutting gaze."[26]

The memoir of Helder Martins, Mozambique's first minister of health, provides a glimpse of Samora's dominant role in his brief description of the Council of Ministers' debate about nationalizing the health system. Martins had been instructed by Samora to develop a long-term strategy. After studying the problem for over a year, he proposed delaying implementation because of logistical challenges and shortages of trained personnel. Samora asked each member of the council to comment, listening carefully and asking many questions. After they had all agreed with Martins, Samora opined that, if the government did not act immediately, "in two years' time everyone would have arguments to seek a new postponement." In the end, Samora prevailed.[27]

Samora was clearly first among equals. Nevertheless, there are several documented instances of ministers speaking out against his favored positions. In 1978, Joaquim Carvalho, minister of agriculture, opposed

Samora's plan to support the private family sector as well as large state farms.[28] On another occasion, Teodato Hunguana, minister of justice, wrote a confidential memo to Samora disagreeing with his decision to reinstate corporal punishment, including the colonial practice of whipping.[29] Both ministers were sacked, although they were later appointed to different senior positions.

At times, however, Samora was a good listener. He often invited individuals or small groups to the presidential palace where, over after-dinner drinks, he encouraged them to air their concerns or sought their advice. On several occasions he even reconsidered policies already in place, when convinced they were misguided or ineffective. Several years after Carvalho's dismissal, João Ferreira, then the minister of agriculture, lobbied successfully for scarce resources to be redistributed from the failing communal village system to family agriculture.[30] Aquino de Bragança, a free-thinking Frelimo intellectual, was notorious for disagreeing with the president on a range of issues in closed-door meetings. And despite Samora's tendency to view the press with suspicion, the maverick reporter Carlos Cardoso could pose challenging questions in public, confident that he would not be denied future access. According to Graça Machel, Samora appreciated Cardoso's intellect and willingness to spar with the president.[31]

One of the hallmarks of political life under Samora was the absence of corruption or accumulation of personal wealth by the country's leaders. Samora dressed well, but he had neither Swiss bank accounts nor palaces, yachts, or overseas properties. High-level government and party officials maintained an equally

unpretentious lifestyle, although they did live appreciably better than the average Mozambican citizen. They
resided in state-owned homes abandoned by wealthy
Portuguese and had access to special state stores where
they could purchase commodities not generally available.[32] The "children of the revolution" also had access
to the best education and health facilities in Mozambique and abroad.

In the same vein, members of official delegations
traveling abroad received only three dollars per day for
discretionary expenses, while the head of the mission
received two dollars more. In the words of one former
minister, the "amount was hardly enough to purchase
trinkets for my children."[33] Before visiting Swaziland,
we once asked a friend who happened to be the wife of
a senior minister if she wanted us to buy anything for
her. She replied sheepishly that she would love some bil-
tong (beef jerky) but had no hard currency to pay for it.
José Luís Cabaço remembered that during his tenure as
minister of information he was forced to ask an Italian
acquaintance to purchase microphone batteries that his
ministry badly needed, because he lacked the foreign
currency to do so himself.[34]

Transforming Society

As a young man, Samora was heavily influenced by
Frantz Fanon's contention that "colonizing the mind"
was the most insidious legacy of colonialism. In his 1977
acceptance speech upon receiving an honorary doctor
of law degree from Nigeria's Ahmadu Bello University, Samora emphasized that "the ultimate effort [of
colonialism was] to make out of each Mozambican an

Figure 5.1. Samora speaking at independence celebration.
Courtesy of Centro de Documentção e Formação Fotográfica
(CDFF)

Figure 5.2. Samora and father. Courtesy of Centro
de Documentação Samora Machel (CDSM)

Figure 5.3. Samora speaking at a rally. (CDFF)

Figure 5.4. Samora with students. Courtesy of António Alves
Gomes

Figure 5.5. Samora with Presidents Julius Nyerere, Kenneth Kaunda, and Seretse Khama. Courtesy of António Alves Gomes

Figure 5.6. Wedding of Samora and Graça Machel. (CDSM)

Figure 5.7. Samora dancing up a storm. (CDSM)

Figure 5.8. Samora meeting with Portuguese president António Eanes. (CDFF)

assimilado, a little Portuguese with a black skin" and defined colonialism as a cultural act of rape.[35] He believed the democratization of knowledge would free Mozambicans from the shackles of illiteracy, the tyranny of superstition, and the cultural arrogance of missionary education. Learning was a social act reinforced through daily practice in the household, community, and workplace, and the family was the most significant institution of instruction: "All of us have responsibilities. We educate our children, we educate our youth in various ways. The behavior of parents, the way they live at home is more significant than the five hours [a day] that students are in contact with their teachers."[36]

Samora's ideological position and pragmatism made him a strong proponent of liberating girls and women through education. In public meetings across the country, he joined representatives of the Mozambican Women's Organization to chastise parents who kept their daughters at home to work on the family's fields and prepare for marriage, thus keeping them ignorant and dependent and depriving the nation of a well-trained labor force.

Under the direction of Graça Machel, Samora's administration embarked on a program to expand access to education and reorganize the curriculum. In an interview with Allen and Iain Christie, Samora proudly cited statistics demonstrating that "today education is for everyone . . . [and] free. In 1973 there were 588,868 attending schools. Five years later it had increased by more than 100 percent."[37] The new curriculum eliminated discussion of the heroic exploits of Henry the Navigator and the civilizing mission of the Catholic Church.

Instead, it emphasized Mozambique's rich heritage, its long tradition of resistance, and the church's collaboration with the colonial state to obliterate its past.[38]

The unholy alliance of the Catholic Church and the colonial state, which had deleteriously shaped Samora's own development, convinced him to nationalize church property in 1976 and eliminate its stranglehold on African education. The policy pained many Christian supporters of Frelimo and alienated others.[39]

Samora also stressed the strategic importance of adult literacy. That more than 90 percent of Mozambicans could neither read nor write, he argued, deprived both them and the nation of the results of their creative potential. Colonial values and "irrational and unscientific ideas from the past" froze Mozambicans in a permanent state of backwardness.[40]

Universal education and widespread literacy campaigns were critical elements of Frelimo's cultural politics, embodied in the twin notions of *Moçambicanidade* (Mozambican-ness) and *o Homen Novo* (the New Man)—ideas the liberation movement first developed in Nachingwea.

Moçambicanidade was a synthesis of indigenous cultural practices with a new revolutionary content.[41] In 1977, high school students and researchers from Eduardo Mondlane University traveled the countryside collecting local traditions, histories, songs, and dances and identifying important archeological sites. The government organized cultural festivals that brought together representatives from all parts of the country. Although forging a unified culture remained largely aspirational, these initiatives did have an impact on the ground, particularly in Maputo. The director of the National Song and Dance Company (CNCD) wrote about the significance of culture in the nation-building process.

> The encouragement of dance in a country engulfed
> by war and famine might seem like sacrilege. Yet
> in Mozambique, dance is life. The nation has long
> discovered and expressed itself in terms of dance—
> dance by villagers for the victorious guerrilla fighters
> in the long war for independence against Portuguese
> colonialism, dance by triumphant soldiers themselves
> to celebrate independence in 1975, and then a vast
> postindependence dance festival ("the people in
> motion").... Today every factory, school, hospital,
> and farming enterprise has its dance groups. In the
> community, the people drum and dance—dance
> is communication, dance is affirmation, dance is
> criticism, and dance is simply dance.[42]

Believing that from this cultural synthesis would emerge the New Man—guardian of the revolution and guarantor against future backsliding—Samora stressed that "even when the systems of exploitation have been destroyed, if we do not fight the mentality underlying them, then sooner or later, slowly or rapidly, the system will spring up again, nourished by the negative values preserved within us." The New Man would be militant, hardworking, proud of his identity, history, and culture, educated in modern science, and reject the obscurantist and exploitative practices of the past. He would be respectful to women and opposed to bride-price and polygamy.[43] Still, this formulation nowhere addressed the enduring privilege of patriarchy.

The New Man was the antithesis of the cartoon character Xiconhoca. The name was a combination of "Chico," a notorious PIDE official, and *nhoca* (snake), and the character represented the enemy within, preying upon unknowing, defenseless individuals. In comics, posters, and bulletin boards set up in every administrative center, Xiconhoca was variously portrayed as an insensitive bureaucrat complicating the lives of the people, a citizen who refused to work, a pimp, drug dealer, or prostitute, a woman who wore miniskirts and high-heeled shoes, a young person who partied at nightclubs, a polygamist, a parent who failed to send children to school, or a traitor spying for South Africa or Rhodesia.

There were also radical changes to the health-care system. Less than a month after independence Samora announced the nationalization of medicine, making medical care a right of citizenship rather than a commercial venture fraught with racism. Implementing such a far-reaching program with only eighty-seven doctors in the country was a major challenge. By 1977, the Ministry of Health had recruited more than five hundred foreign medical workers from over twenty nations. In subsequent years, drawing on the examples of China and Vietnam, the government continued to bring hundreds of "barefoot doctors" and infirmaries to the countryside. This enabled it to launch a vaccination campaign against measles, smallpox, and tetanus that reached 90 percent of the country during the next two years. The World Health Organization declared it one of the most successful initiatives in Africa.[44] Another preventative initiative was the latrine campaign to reduce cholera and other waterborne diseases. Samora proclaimed two successive Sundays in 1977 as National Latrine Days and, with pickaxe and spade, joined other citizens digging and building latrines. Thanks to these and other measures, the estimated 20 percent decline in infant mortality during the first five years of independence suggests the degree to which Mozambique's new health system was making inroads.[45]

Frelimo also nationalized rental properties to prevent urban landlords from profiting from apartment blocks left vacant by Portuguese who had fled Mozambique. The new legislation also targeted black slumlords in the shantytowns. In Maputo alone, more than fifty thousand units were nationalized.[46] Within the next two years, more than 160,000 Mozambicans living in substandard housing had been relocated to urban residences taken over by the state.[47]

Although initial accomplishments in the social sphere were substantial, these ambitious policies were never fully implemented. Even with the budget sharply increased, dramatic rises in the number of students meant there were never enough schools, trained teachers, books, and supplies.[48] The nationalized health-care delivery system similarly strained the state's capacity. Newly built rural infirmaries were inadequately staffed and supplied and the widely hailed "barefoot doctors" were often not up to the task. Nationalizing housing without sufficient oversight enabled corrupt bureaucrats to allocate the best housing to their friends, families, and those willing to offer bribes. The loss of their rental income had the unintended consequence of increasing the flight of skilled Portuguese who, Samora had hoped, would continue to keep the economy going.

The cultural politics Samora promoted were also problematic. Cultures are not divisible, and traditions are not frozen artifacts of the past. Samora's efforts to preserve many aspects of the past while abolishing traditional chiefs and attacking polygamy ignored the complexities of local culture and generated antipathy toward the new government, especially in the countryside. His attack on the church also alienated many devout Christians who were also fervent nationalists.

Economic Transformations

Few newly independent nations inherited as many deeply embedded economic problems as Mozambique, with its already low level of food production, high unemployment rate, embryonic industrial sector, negative balance of payments, and extremely low gross national product.[49] These factors were all negatively affected by the mass exodus of Portuguese, whose number dropped from 250,000 to 20,000 between 1974 and 1976. Gone were the vast majority of the country's engineers, accountants, mechanics, and agronomists. Departing settlers frequently destroyed what they could not take with them, sabotaging everything from trucks to factory equipment, from tractors to trains.

Between 1975 and 1977 the government took numerous steps to reverse the economic hemorrhaging. By nationalizing abandoned farms and plantations and reorganizing them into large state farms, jobs were preserved for thousands of rural workers. To prevent their total collapse, the government nationalized strategic industries and took control of mismanaged firms. It established *lojas do povo* (people's shops) to ensure that poor people had access to basic commodities at sub-sidized prices. These interventions were more tactical than ideological—a response to economic breakdown and fear of paralysis.[50]

Under pressure from the Mozambican Women's Organization and feminist critics, Samora introduced policies to combat the institutional oppression of women and create new opportunities in the workplace. Urban women made small but significant breakthroughs, for the first time finding employment as tractor drivers, construction workers, police officers, and administrators. Women also constituted nearly half of the students selected to study in Cuba to be trained as engineers, doctors, dentists, teachers, and other professionals.[51]

Nonetheless, women who entered the workforce still encountered gender discrimination in their house-holds and communities. For many, the opportunity to gain employment in the cash economy simply meant more work, since few men were prepared to perform domestic labor.

Reconstituting His Family

On September 7, 1975, following a short but discreet romance, Samora married Graça Simbine. They had moved in similar circles in the colonial capital but had never socialized. They reconnected in 1974 when Graça came to Dar and joined the liberation movement.

After Graça's appointment as minister of education, they worked hard to keep their personal and govern-mental relationships separate, although Graça told us with a gleam in her eye that "pillow talk" went in many different directions. While Samora rarely discussed their relationship, in her personal correspondence she often addressed him as "Cheri" and ended with such heartfelt salutations as "I live for your love and our family."[52]

Forging a blended family was a challenge. The children, born from three different mothers, were unfamiliar with each other. For more than a decade, only Samito had had contact with their father. Given Samora's patriarchal tendencies, the emotional cost of his lengthy separation from his children, and his emphasis on the importance of family, it's not surprising that he acted decisively, if insensitively, to bring them all to Maputo. Graça remembered that "he was insistent that all the children live together under one roof," despite her reservations about separating them from their mothers. They both rejected a Frelimo proposal that the children live nearby and only eat with them.[53] The transition did not go smoothly. While Irene Buque consented, Sorita Chiankomo and her relatives refused to be separated from her children. Samora ignored their wishes, ordering that the children be brought immediately to the presidential palace.[54]

Despite the demands on him as head of state, Samora devoted time and emotional energy to his children, although it was Graça who oversaw their daily lives while serving as minister of education. In interviews we conducted with four of his children, Olívia, Jucelina, Ornila, and Samito, they described Samora as both a tough disciplinarian and a loving parent who, whenever in Maputo, carved out time to spend with them.[55] During one of these discussions Olívia recalled:

> Our father insisted that we all have dinner at seven o'clock. Nothing could get in the way. Around the

table he and Graça would question us about how our day went and if we had any problems. We often discussed the current situation not only in Mozambique but around the world. He also loved to discuss our family history and could recite events going back nine generations. If one of us did not get a chance to talk, our sibling would insist on having a turn.[56]

Samora also addressed specific problems each of the children faced. Olívia remembered that "he had a lot of patience with me, because, when I arrived at the presidential residence, I could only speak Ronga. He encouraged me when I struggled with Portuguese in special classes that Graça had arranged for me."[57] This concern and compassion extended to all the children. "Although they came from different mothers, he treated them all the same—regardless of parentage and gender."[58]

Samora's insistence that dinner be served promptly was part of the discipline he tried to instill. Both Graça and Olívia described having to rise by 5:30 a.m. to exercise for an hour before breakfast. After school they were expected to complete their homework and exercise at the nearby gym before dinner. Weekends were somewhat less regimented and, when time permitted, Samora would spend part of them playing with the children. Given his competitive nature, he enjoyed challenging them in swimming or running—most often winning until Jucelina and Edelson, another of Samora's sons, became accomplished athletes.[59]

For all his warmth and patience, Samora reacted sternly when his children behaved inappropriately or abused their family position. When Ornila became pregnant as a teenager, he was furious. Apart from the family difficulties it created, she had violated Samora's pronouncements against birth out of wedlock. After a long conversation with her and a family meeting, he publicly announced that she and the father had been sent to a reeducation camp in Niassa. Similarly, when Edelson was sixteen he went to an international trade show and was given a motorcycle he had admired there. After his return he initially lied, claiming it was an unsolicited gift, but ultimately admitted the truth. Samora ordered Edelson to return the motorcycle and warned him that next time he would be severely punished. When Edelson next acted inappropriately, Samora sent him into the army—under a false name, so he would not receive special treatment.[60]

Samora's notion of family extended beyond blood relatives to include many of his closest comrades and their offspring. Nyeleti Mondlane, Eduardo Mondlane's daughter, visited the presidential residence for substantial periods of time. In many of her letters to Graça and Samora, she addressed them as "Dear Parents" and shared intimate details of her life and thoughts.[61] Samora and Graça watched over Nyeleti and her siblings as if they were their own children. Ilundi dos Santos, daughter of Marcelino, along with the offspring of Aquino de Bragança and Joaquim Chissano, had a special place in the hearts of Graça and Samora and spent many hours in the Machel household. On weekends the family often lunched with Jorge and Pamela Rebelo or other old comrades. They celebrated the birthdays and weddings of militants and their children, and Armando Guebuza and Alberto Chipande were asked to "give away" two of Samora's daughters at their weddings.

Being part of Samora's familial network had obvious advantages, but also came with a cost. When Allen asked longtime freedom fighter General Hama Thay to describe Samora's principal shortcoming, he replied without hesitation that "Samora regularly intervened in the private lives of those around him. He was quick to give unsolicited advice and ordered subordinates to cease being womanizers and either act more responsibly or marry their partners."[62] Teodato Hunguana, who had been removed as justice minister, noted that "as a person, Samora cared a great deal about these relationships, but as a president he could be very harsh."[63]

6

Samora Machel's Marxism and the Defense of the Revolution, 1977–82

The year 1977 marked a turning point. At the Third Party Congress, Frelimo transformed itself from a mass organization committed to People's Power to a Marxist-Leninist party serving the class interests of workers and peasants. For the educational sector, this ideological shift meant little, since the state had already assumed responsibility for primary and secondary education. In the economic sector, by contrast, the new policies generated far-reaching structural changes. Formal recognition of socialist countries as the new nation's "natural allies" also followed.

Mozambique's embrace of Marxism provided justification for Rhodesia and South Africa to intensify their attacks since a Marxist state governed by a revolutionary tied to the Socialist Bloc posed a much greater threat than a merely independent African country. For the West, Frelimo's decision was a major setback in the Cold War.

Moving toward Socialism

The first Mozambican leader to utter the term "socialism" publicly was Samora's mentor, Eduardo Mondlane.

Given the practice of collective self-education in which the leadership typically engaged, it is hardly surprising that Samora's thinking evolved in similar ways. Long before the Third Party Congress, he had begun to embrace the Marxist critique of colonial capitalism. At the time, though, he was more concerned with figuring out how best to prosecute the war than with whether Frelimo should remain a front or become a vanguard revolutionary party. On the eve of independence, Samora had still not decided whether such a transformation made sense in Mozambique. In a 1974 paper presented to policymakers and academics in Moscow, he explained that "the absence of a vanguard party . . . is the result of a web of historical circumstances we face, with characteristics including basically the non-existence of an organized working class and tradition, the lack of struggle experience by the broad masses . . . [and] the isolation of communities, particularly in the countryside."[1]

Nor had Frelimo itself made this determination. Some militants held that Frelimo should continue as a front for the foreseeable future, pointing to the Sandinistas in Nicaragua who had maintained space in their revolutionary party for different progressive tendencies. Aquino de Bragança, an adviser to Samora, warned that becoming a vanguard party would stifle dissent and create an unnecessary link to unpopular and inhumane regimes, such as that of Kim Il-Sung in North Korea. He proposed instead that Frelimo adopt a more generalized socialist project he called "Samorismo," rooted in the new Mozambican reality.[2]

Most senior figures around Samora, however, including Marcelino dos Santos, Sérgio Vieira, Jorge Rebelo,

Oscar Monteiro, and cadres trained in the Soviet Union and China, disagreed. They rejected both Aquino's critique and that of their longtime ally Julius Nyerere. They maintained that Nyerere's notion that precolonial African societies were organized around socialistic principles was an overly romantic reading of the past, one that could neither support radical transformation nor protect Mozambique from counterrevolutionary threats.[3] Support from the socialist camp during the armed struggle and a belief that the defeat of the United States in Vietnam had shifted the global balance of power strengthened their argument. It had also become clear that continued military and economic aid from the Soviet Bloc was predicated on adopting a Marxist line.

By 1976, Samora had concluded that Marxism offered the best path forward. The West's continued antipathy, his romantic view of life in the Soviet Bloc, and the high regard he held for Fidel Castro reinforced his leanings.[4] That said, he was neither pro-Soviet nor pro-Chinese, but committed instead to forging a socialist society born out of Mozambique's experiences. As his old friend José Cabaço recalled, "Samora's socialism came from his visceral reaction to the abuses of colonial capitalism."[5]

Frelimo's debate about the best way forward occurred behind closed doors, making it impossible to discern how the actual process unfolded. Oscar Monteiro, then minister of state apparatus, provides a summary.

> In February 1976, at the end of the 8th Central
> Committee meeting, Samora made a speech calling
> for Frelimo to create a vanguard party. To everyone's
> surprise, I, rather than Armanda Guebuza [the

national political commissar], was assigned the task of preparing the planning documents for the Third Party Congress. There were several others with whom I worked, including [Fernando] Ganhão and Luís [Bernardo Honwana]. We presented two options to the Political Military Committee, whose members included Samora, Marcelino, Chissano, Chipande, and Guebuza. The first option was to create a highly disciplined Marxist-Leninist party based on a Soviet model, capable of mobilizing the people against internal class enemies and external threats. The other alternative rested on the proposition that classes were not yet clearly defined and that Frelimo lacked strong support throughout the country, making it necessary to think of *democracia nova*—something like the Chinese used to mobilize the peasantry.[6]

The leadership unanimously voted for the former.[7] A year later, at the Third Party Congress Samora chaired, the delegates affirmed this position.[8]

While adhering to an orthodox Marxian formulation that the industrial working class is the leading force in forging a socialist society, the congress also departed from it and elevated the role of the peasantry because, during the armed struggle, it "had already presented great proof of its engagement in the revolutionary transformation of our society." In this language one can hear Samora's long-standing appreciation of peasants' political agency. The congress agreed that Frelimo would become a vanguard party whose "historic mission is to lead, organize and educate the masses, thus transforming the popular class movements into a powerful instrument for the destruction of capitalism and the construction of socialism."[9]

During a long interview with Allen Isaacman and Iain Christie two years later, Samora insisted on Marxism's relevance for Mozambique.

> I am going to prove to you, Isaacman, so that you can tell your colleagues [how] peasants and workers, who cannot read or write, come to understand Marxism-Leninism. . . . Illiterate peasants learned the essence of the system of exploitation of men by men from a new group of exploiters, represented by [Uria] Simango and Lazaro [Nkavandame], who wanted to introduce exploitation into the liberated zones. It was not a Marxist who went to tell them what exploitation was, they did not read it in any book. But they felt the exploitation and knew their exploiters. . . . They were the ones who fought and made the exploited succeed against the exploitative merchants and landowners. . . . Marxism-Leninism does not come to our country as an imported product. Hear this very well, this is the idea we want to fight against. . . . Our party is not a group of intellectuals reading and interpreting Marx, Engels, and Lenin.[10]

While Samora's claim that exploited peasants would necessarily gravitate to Marxism is problematic, his deep respect for many aspects of rural life was clear during this interview.

The Third Party Congress adopted plans to revitalize agriculture and industry along socialist lines. In this report to the congress, Samora sketched out the broad outlines of the new master plan: "Our strategy for development rests on agricultural production. The communal villages are the fundamental lever for liberating the people in the rural areas. Industry is the dynamizing factor for economic development. The building of Socialism demands that the economy be centrally planned and directed by the State."[11]

At the center of rural transformation was the dramatic expansion of communal villages. Samora confidently predicted communal villages would stimulate the agricultural sector and create the opportunity for "a new style of life."[12] Communal village life would be the crucible for the creation of the rural version of the New Man.

Communal villages with their associated agricultural cooperatives appeared to have much to offer. Their location near roads and markets would give them access to services—schools, clinics, storage facilities for crops, and consumer and craft cooperatives—absent in much of the countryside. Ideally, communal villages would be located in fertile zones on carefully laid-out grids with proper housing and sanitation. Collective life and collective production would also enhance the revolutionary consciousness of the peasantry.[13]

It was Frelimo's task to convince peasants, through collective discussions in every locality, to leave their scattered homesteads and move into these large communities. At the end of 1977, there were around a hundred communal villages, including those established during the armed struggle or right after independence, ranging in size from the fifty families at Makonde in Niassa Province to more than eleven thousand families at Julius Nyerere in Gaza. Two years later, over a million peasants were living in communal villages; by

153

1981, there were 1.2 million—almost 15 percent of the population. In Cabo Delgado more than 90 percent of peasants and refugees returning from Tanzania were resettled in communal villages. In Gaza, with the second-largest number of communal villages, 30 percent were living communally. In no other province did the number exceed 20 percent.[14] One of the most successful was Communal Village 24 de Julio near Xai-Xai in Gaza, close to Samora's home, which was established by local officials working with peasants displaced by floods.[15]

Problems surfaced almost immediately. Planners in the Ministry of Agriculture underestimated the effects of relocation on displaced communities, which lost control over where and how to live as well as access to critical economic and cultural resources. For many, the move also disconnected them from the spirits of ancestors who protected their communities and guaranteed the fertility of women, land, and cattle. Despite their alleged expertise, state planners were often ignorant of the most suitable locations for agriculture and cattle grazing. The government failed to provide peasants with the technical support, seeds, equipment, and consumer goods necessary to make their villages self-sustaining.[16] When productivity declined, officials blamed it on the peasants' inefficient practices, unwillingness to innovate, and lack of motivation, rather than on the government's own failures—all echoes from the colonial past.

Specific local and regional factors also eroded peasant support for communal life. In Nampula Province, party officials aligned with unpopular local chiefs to promote this experiment.[17] Peasants relocating from coastal areas of Cabo Delgado, Inhambane, and Gaza lost their profitable cashew trees without compensation. Moreover, as the war with RENAMO intensified, some provincial governors herded peasants into villages to separate them from the insurgents, leading critics to liken them to the colonial *aldeamentos*.[18]

Peasants increasingly defied state planners, much as they had colonial ones. In Zambézia and Nampula, the two most populous provinces, only 6 percent of the peasant population agreed to join communal villages.[19] Those living in communal villages would work their own fields rather than the collective ones. By 1982, only one-sixth of the communal villages had functioning agricultural cooperatives, and even their most politically motivated members spent only a few hours working in the collective fields.[20] Many men chose to work on state farms rather than in unprofitable communal fields because that was the only way to support their families. Other dissatisfied communal village members simply disappeared.

The government's allocation of most of its limited resources to state farms further undermined the viability of communal villages. Immediately after the Third Party Congress, the Ministry of Agriculture allocated state farms $40 million for heavy equipment, such as tractors, combines, and irrigation pumps, rather than providing peasants with necessary technical inputs. The following year, two-thirds of the agricultural budget went to heavy equipment for state farms.[21]

By allocating scarce resources in this manner, Samora and his advisers were succumbing to the logic of high socialist modernism. Without economies of scale, without agroecological knowledge, even without providing for trained mechanics and spare parts, they believed that simply introducing advanced agricultural technology would by itself increase Mozambique's food security, expand agricultural exports, and provide raw material for its nascent industries. Samora also anticipated that state farms would employ the 150,000 to 200,000 rural workers idled when settlers and foreign companies abandoned their holdings, and that these workers would forge a new class consciousness by laboring together free from colonial exploitation.[22] His conclusions were based on optimistic projections from the Ministry of Planning, directed by Marcelino dos Santos and filled with East German technocrats with no knowledge of the complex and varied agroeconomic and social conditions on the ground.

Although this policy cut rural unemployment and generated modest gains in agricultural production, the state farms failed dismally. Despite receiving the lion's share of the agricultural budget, by 1982 they only accounted for 20 percent of output and none turned a profit. Poor planning, lack of management skills, the limited and largely unhelpful expertise of foreign advisers, failure to maintain equipment, inability to mobilize workers, and low wages that forced farms to rely on seasonal labor doomed the experiment. Nowhere was this clearer than in the fertile Limpopo Valley, where peasants were not prepared to work for low wages as agricultural laborers when they could earn more in the South African mines.[23]

The scale and pace of state control of the industrial sector meanwhile increased dramatically after the Third Party Congress. Planners emphasized heavy industry and large development projects requiring trained workers and substantial investment. Initially, Samora sought assistance from the Socialist Bloc. Ten thousand Mozambicans were sent to East Germany for training beginning in 1979.[24] Samora believed that having Mozambican workers from different regions and social backgrounds living and working side by side in socialist countries would cement their sense of identity as Mozambicans, national pride, and working-class consciousness.[25]

Efforts to revitalize and restructure the industrial sector brought mixed results. Between 1977 and 1981 the economy experienced a modest recovery.[26] By 1979 more than 150,000 industrial workers were again employed fulltime, and absenteeism had dropped by 20 percent.[27] Several industrial projects were completed, including two textile mills, a fish-processing complex, and a joint-venture tire factory funded by American capital. Salaries and working conditions improved in some existing and new factories.[28] Samora felt so confident that he declared Mozambique would solve underdevelopment in the 1980s.[29]

His optimism was misplaced. Despite massive state intervention, by 1980 the economy was in a downward spiral. According to Prakash Ratilal, governor of the central bank during most of this period, a combination of international and domestic factors precipitated the decline, and promised assistance from Western countries was too limiterd to have any significant impact.[30] In the international arena, Mozambique's decision in 1976 to enforce United Nations sanctions against Rhodesia by closing its port at Beira to the settler regime cost the young nation dearly. The following year, South Africa abrogated its agreement to continue the colonial practice of paying the government's wage remittances for migrant laborers in gold at prices well below the world market. Pretoria also reduced its use of the port of Maputo from six million tons before independence to half that figure in 1981. Two years later it capped the number of migrant Mozambican miners at 41,000 rather than 110,000. The steep jump in oil prices with the 1979 Iran-Iraq War also had a devastating effect. Recurring floods, droughts, and cyclones disrupted agricultural production, as did crippling attacks by South African–backed RENAMO terrorists.[31]

As early as 1979, Samora expressed concerns to his economic advisors about the viability of a state-planned economy. After Moscow rebuffed Mozambique's effort to join the Council for Mutual Economic Assistance, the Socialist Bloc's economic union, in 1981 Samora dispatched senior officials to Washington to begin exploratory conversations with the World Bank and the International Monetary Fund. The Soviet Union and East Germany were furious.[32]

By the early 1980s industrial production was still well below preindependence levels. Basic commodities remained in short supply. Almost all factories were still limited to the Maputo-Matola corridor. The socialist countries remained reluctant to provide the necessary capital for large-scale projects. Almost all their aid was tied to disadvantageous barter agreements, in which they exchanged outdated equipment for Mozambique's agricultural exports. In an attempt to jump-start the economy, Samora announced his willingness to seek investment from Western businesses as long as they were "interested in mutually beneficial projects that would ensure an appropriate transfer of technology and guarantee the training of local workers."[33]

Figure 6.1. Lancaster House negotiations: Samora with other Frontline presidents and Zimbabwe leaders Robert Mugabe and Joshua Nkomo. Courtesy of Centro de Documentação Samora Machel (CDSM)

Figure 6.2. Samora greeting African National Congress president Oliver Tambo. Courtesy of Centro de Documentção e Formação Fotográfica (CDFF)

Figure 6.3. Samora and Leonid Brezhnev. (CDFF)

Defending the Revolution:
Combating the Internal Enemy

From the moment Samora assumed the presidency, he feared collaborators and class enemies might subvert the revolution. In a 1977 speech he warned of ominous consequences if Frelimo let down its guard: "Instead of maintaining the offensive, instead of destroying the head of the snake in the egg, if we go back on the defensive, we will discover the snake only when it is fully grown and lifting its venomous head to kill us."[34] These perceived enemies included settlers who longed for a return to white rule, former PIDE officials, Africans who had fought in the colonial army, and covert supporters of rival nationalist organizations. Merchants large and small and religious leaders and churchgoers—especially Jehovah's Witnesses, who refused to recognize the authority of the new government—were also suspect.

Samora also expressed concern about the small but influential urban bourgeoisie, whose lifestyle and values threatened to undermine those the government was trying to instill. The principal culprits were price-gouging merchants and officials who abused their positions to accumulate wealth.

Even more troubling were abuses of power by members of the military or Frelimo cadres. In a 1979 interview with Allen and Iain Christie, Samora described why such abuses of power occurred: "[FRELIMO was] met by godsons of the administrators, godmothers of the [right-wing] national women's movements, members of ANP and of PIDE. They offered cars, houses . . . set up parties and [arranged nice girls] for the FRELIMO commanders."[35] He warned in his Beira speech that corrupt police, security officials (in the Serviço Nacional de Segurança Popular), and party members posed a threat to Mozambique and its citizens and urged the audience to identify and speak out against such traitors.[36]

So obsessed were Samora and his closest colleagues about "covert class enemies" that even clandestine members of the liberation movement who had spent years in colonial jails were not above suspicion. In July 1978, these ex-prisoners were publicly interrogated to determine if any had betrayed the revolution while incarcerated. Samora himself chaired the proceedings. Most were exonerated.[37]

There was particular concern about the more than ninety thousand Africans who had served in the colonial army or secret police, which itself made them "compromised" (*comprometidos*) in Frelimo's eyes.[38] After independence they were disarmed and most were allowed to return home—but in November 1978 Samora ordered that they come forward and acknowledge their collaboration with the colonial regime, after which their pictures were displayed at their workplaces. Samora attended the public meetings, where he ridiculed the comprometidos, called some out by name, and demanded that others perform acts of contrition. Many who denied their complicity were incarcerated without trial. Others were sent to the army.[39] For four years, the comprometidos remained social outcasts. Only in 1982 were those who had acknowledged their misdeeds exonerated and their pictures removed from public display.

As economic and military conditions worsened, calls to punish enemies of the revolution grew even louder. The reintroduction of the unpopular death penalty in 1980 was an indication of how far Samora was willing to go to suppress internal opposition.[40] Three years later the death penalty was allowed for those convicted of serious economic crimes such as smuggling. At roughly the same time the parliament passed the "*lei de chicotada*," which reinstituted corporal punishment, including the colonial practice of whipping, for a wide variety of crimes. Many of Frelimo's most loyal supporters were appalled, but only one member of the government, Justice Minister Teodato Hunguana, opposed the policy.

Defending Mozambique's Sovereignty: Regional Alliances, Nonalignment, and Natural Allies

The final communiqué of the Third Party Congress stressed "Mozambique's commitment to strengthening . . . the struggle against colonialism, racism, neo-colonialism and imperialism." Despite its radical tone, the communiqué also expressed a willingness to establish "mutually beneficial relations with all states, regardless of their social and economic systems."[41]

In order to defend Mozambique's territorial integrity and protect the revolution, the highest priorities were to strengthen relations with the other Frontline States (then comprising Tanzania, Zambia, Angola, and Botswana), challenge South African and Rhodesian military and economic hegemony, and provide support to the African National Congress and Zimbabwe African National Union. Mozambique joined the Organization of African Unity and the Non-Aligned

Movement, promoting the struggles for liberation not only in southern Africa, but also in the western Sahara and Portugal's Asian colony of East Timor.

Samora and Foreign Minister Joaquim Chissano insisted that nonalignment not be equated with neutrality. Addressing the Summit Conference of Non-Aligned States in Havana in 1979, Samora was unequivocal on this point: "Non-alignment is a specific strategy of our peoples to guarantee independence and peace in the face of the cold war imposed by imperialism. . . . Non-alignment is an anti-imperialist strategy for the total liberation of our people." He went on to stress that "it is precisely with the appearance of socialist countries that the correlation of force changed in our favor. . . . The socialist countries are natural allies of our peoples."[42] He rejected efforts by more moderate members to make the Non-Aligned Movement an autonomous third bloc, independent of the superpowers.

Western analysts portrayed Mozambique as a Soviet satellite, ignoring contrary evidence. The staunchly pro-Moscow Marcelino dos Santos insisted to Allen in 1977 that Frelimo had not fought for freedom for fifteen years "to become the pawn of yet another foreign power."[43] His position was similar to what Samora had maintained at the 1976 meeting of nonaligned nations in Sri Lanka, where he strenuously opposed the presence of foreign warships in the Indian Ocean and the circulation or storage of nuclear weapons there. Chissano was even more adamant on this point: "If the United States and the Soviet Union want to fight, they can fight in their own house."[44] To the dismay of Moscow, Samora refused to provide a strategic naval base at one of its ports. He rejected stationing Cuban forces in Mozambique to protect it from Rhodesian and South African aggression, fearing that a Cuban military presence would embroil Mozambique in the Cold War.

Tensions also surfaced around Moscow's "socialist paternalism." Samora privately acknowledged his anger when the Soviets rejected a request to build a steel mill in Mozambique, insisting that such a project was inappropriate given its level of development. The reluctance of Eastern European ideologues to recognize Mozambique as a legitimate socialist country inspired Samora's acerbic comment that "some people seem to think that the development of Marxism ended in October 1917."[45]

Even American diplomats came to realize the paramountcy of Samora's commitment to maintaining Mozambique's sovereignty. Frank Wisner, a senior State Department official who more than once butted heads with the Mozambican leader, acknowledged after his death that "I always knew that he embodied the hopes and aspirations of the Mozambican people for independence, peace and prosperity."[46]

Samora saw no inconsistency between defining the Socialist Bloc as "natural allies" and maintaining a warm relationship with the Scandinavian countries. Norway and Sweden, in particular, had aided FRELIMO during the armed struggle and continued to provide significant material and diplomatic support after independence.

When it was in Mozambique's interest, Samora even reached out to Western countries that had supported Portuguese colonialism. The clearest example was Mozambique's critical role in the 1979 Lancaster House negotiations that led to the independence of Zimbabwe.

Through these deliberations Mozambique scored a double victory. Rhodesia and the military threat it posed to Mozambique were gone forever, and the negotiations raised Samora's stature as a statesman, with the United Kingdom's influential leader Margaret Thatcher hailing him as a man of peace. She subsequently facilitated Mozambique's opening to the West.

Defending the Nation against South African Destabilization

The Rhodesian and South African–backed Mozambique National Resistance was originally composed of remnants of the colonial opposition to FRELIMO and disaffected or expelled FRELIMO guerrillas. Shortly after independence, it adopted a Portuguese name, Resistência Nacional Moçambicana (RENAMO), and Rhodesian security appointed former FRELIMO members André Matsangaissa and Afónso Dhlakama to senior leadership positions in order to create the appearance of legitimacy.[47]

RENAMO unleashed a campaign of fear and terror, torturing and maiming unarmed peasants, press-ganging women and children, burning down rural communities, plundering communal villages, destroying schools and clinics, and sabotaging railroad lines and electrical pylons.[48] Vernácio Leone, who lived in a colonial aldeamento, recounts that "when RENAMO would enter a village, they would call all the people together. Then, they would go into our huts and steal all that was inside. They forced the people back into their homes, which they set on fire."[49] Such violence, including forcing children to cut off the ears or breasts of their mothers to make the children pariahs with no alternative but to join the terrorists, was a central feature of RENAMO strategy—as several interviewees who fled RENAMO as young boys and later asked to remain anonymous described to Allen.[50] According to Stephen A. Emerson, a military historian and former civilian analyst for the US Department of Defense, the "use of terror to intimidate their enemies and ensure support among wavering peasant populations is well-documented in anecdotal accounts, refugee interviews, and multiple postwar studies on the use of violence during the conflict."[51]

Samora and his advisers underestimated the destructive capacity of RENAMO, which they dismissed as a group of "armed bandits," and misjudged the critical role it would play in Pretoria's destabilization campaign. Mozambique's military leadership believed instead that a full-scale invasion from Rhodesia and South Africa was more likely. According to their thinking, a conventional army backed by Soviet-supplied jets, helicopters, tanks, and artillery would best defend against this likelihood. As a result, Mozambique's relatively effective guerrilla force was transformed into an inexperienced, ill-equipped, and poorly led army unable to contain mobile RENAMO bands operating in the countryside.

The assumption that RENAMO would collapse with the fall of the Rhodesian government was another strategic error. Instead, it found a new patron when the South African army transferred RENAMO headquarters and bases to Phalaborwa in the Transvaal. The South African Special Forces Brigade reorganized RENAMO's command structure, trained recruits, planned major operations, and resupplied RENAMO through airdrops and naval landings.[52]

In private, Samora acknowledged that his military was unprepared for RENAMO's resurrection. He sent several elite platoons to the Soviet Union for antiguerrilla training and even recruited African former soldiers who had been part of the Portuguese army's elite counterinsurgency force.[53] It was, however, too little, too late.

By 1982, RENAMO was causing havoc in the countryside. Destruction for destruction's sake was taking its toll. The size of its force had increased from several hundred to several thousand, mostly through coerced recruitment, according to State Department findings.[54] At the same time, Frelimo's tendency to denigrate many aspects of traditional culture as reactionary or obscurantist, its removal of local chiefs, disdain for all religions, and unpopular communal village campaign were alienating many peasants. Savvy RENAMO commanders used this to garner local support in parts of Manica, Sofala, Zambézia, and Nampula by calling for a return to "authentic" African society.[55] Mozambique's experiment was in serious trouble.

The Unraveling of Mozambique's Socialist Revolution, 1983–86

By Samora's eighth year as president, many Mozambicans had become exhausted and disillusioned. The military could not protect citizens, declining economic production was exacerbated by RENAMO attacks, and there were food shortages everywhere. The common refrain, "before, we had colonialism and potatoes, now we have independence and no potatoes," captured the growing sense of despair.

Because Frelimo's Marxist strategy no longer seemed able to solve the growing crises, Samora pushed the leadership to critically assess the assumptions underlying its plans for Mozambique's future. Three seemingly unrelated but inextricably interconnected policies emerged:

- the retreat from socialism announced at the 1983 Fourth Party Congress;

- Operação Produção, a massive relocation to the countryside of the urban unemployed and participants in the informal economy; and

- the Nkomati Accord with South Africa's apartheid regime.

Coming within a year of each other, they shook the revolution to its core.

The Retreat from Socialism

In the last months of 1982, Samora and his comrades took steps they hoped would reverse the party's declining popularity. After high-profile meetings with religious leaders, the government returned some previously nationalized Catholic Church property, created a Department of Religious Affairs inside the Ministry of Justice, and recognized Christmas Day as a national holiday—euphemistically named "Family Day." Samora ordered the pardoning of more than a thousand reputed collaborators and jettisoned the most strident Marxist rhetoric, including such terms as "class enemy" and "vanguardism," in favor of language that instead emphasized patriotism and nationalism.[1] He even rehabilitated several precolonial African rulers—most notably the Shangaan king Ngungunyane, whose bones Samora personally brought back from Lisbon—all of whom had previously been labelled "feudal lords."

None of these gestures addressed the severe economic effects of a mismanaged state economy. Despite heavy investments in sugar, cotton, and other cash crops, output had plummeted, depriving Mozambique of millions of dollars in hard currency. Many state-run farms and industries collapsed, putting thousands of employees out of work. At the same time, the need to import more food and consumer goods intensified the country's severe balance of payment crisis and forced the government to negotiate food aid from whatever sources it could find. The fact that the minister of finance and the governor of the central bank met weekly to determine such questions as whether to import food or medication indicates the severity of the crisis.[2]

Frelimo publicly blamed Mozambique's economic plight on South Africa's destabilization campaign, whose damage was estimated to be as high as $55 billion. In private, however, Samora and some of his closest advisers came to the conclusion that the command economy was also part of the problem.[3] As early as 1980, he announced that the state would no longer be in the business of selling matches and beer, which was better left to private merchants. He also began meeting with Western investors to promote joint economic ventures.

It was not until the Fourth Party Congress in April 1983 that far-reaching economic reforms were proposed and ratified. A report from the Commission for Economic and Social Directives reaffirmed Frelimo's commitment to develop "the bases of a socialist economy," but suggested "radical changes in the structure of the economy." For the first time, the commission recognized the critical role of family-based production and the need for increased state aid, calling for investment in agricultural equipment for the private peasant sector and technical support for organizing a "restructured rural marketing system" to stimulate exchanges.[4] Samora's selection of João Ferreira, an advocate of state funding for peasant initiatives, as minister of agriculture was the clearest indication that practical considerations now overrode ideological concerns.[5]

The report's other radical proposals included calls to achieve greater coordination between private and state companies, "integrate private companies into the planning system," and "encourage foreign capital investments." Until then, the most significant deviation from Marxism-Leninism had been Samora's 1981 authorization of exploratory talks with the World Bank and the International Monetary Fund, which broke down when they demanded that Mozambique end food subsidies and radically reduce social expenditures. To carry out these policies, Mozambique needed to adopt technology appropriately, "ensuring that our tractor driver is able to understand the machine and keep it in operation."[6] At a rally shortly after the congress, Samora acknowledged that Frelimo had "erroneously developed a hostile attitude to private enterprise that must be changed."[7]

The mandates of the Fourth Party Congress and resulting government policies were somewhat contradictory. While continuing to follow a socialist master plan, Samora's administration "responded to pressure from below by relaxing restrictions on trade, working together with private companies, or allocating land to smallholders."[8] It discarded fixed salaries in state-owned industries, allowing managers to set wages based on productivity. It contracted with foreign firms to restore the country's transportation network and Cahora Bassa's power lines, both severely damaged by RENAMO. Long-term loans from France and Italy totaling more than $300 million and an economic accord with Brazil were the first major commercial agreements with Western countries outside Scandinavia.

Several of the most dogmatic ideologues vehemently opposed this retreat from Marxism. Samora countered that he was not abandoning socialist ideals, but seeking "a socialism that would work in Mozambique." He reaffirmed this position in a *60 Minutes* interview on American television. When asked whether he was a communist, he responded, "I want to feed my people, I want to dress my people, I want wealth to go to my people. If that means that I am a communist, then I am a communist."[9]

Operação Produção

Unlike responses to pressures from below, Operação Produção—"Operation Production," a project to make urban citizens "economically productive"—was an example of Samora's and Frelimo's slide toward authoritarianism. Even as the state loosened its control over the economy, it tightened the regulation of city dwellers. These two seemingly contradictory policies were, in fact, connected.

Mozambique's economic decline had precipitated the migration of thousands to the major urban centers in search of employment and a better life. The additional influx of refugees fleeing RENAMO and recently fired mineworkers returning from South Africa compounded economic and social problems in Maputo and elsewhere. Between 1973 and 1978, Maputo's population almost doubled, and it continued increasing at a rapid rate. This infusion strained housing, food supplies, and health care.[10]

Much has been written about abuses associated with the "cleansing" of the cities, which Frelimo had unsuccessfully attempted several times. Its leaders, many of whom had spent more than a decade in the bush, never fully comprehended the complexities of urban life or the vibrancy of its informal economy, particularly in the shantytowns. At independence, the Frelimo leadership was surprised that Maputo and Beira suffered from rampant crime, widespread violence, extensive drug networks, and gangs of robbers and racketeers. Samora insisted that there were "tens of thousands of prostitutes in the big cities at the time of our independence."[11] He attributed this moral decay to the bourgeoisie—both black and white—who continued to hold a grip on urban life.[12] In response, he became the moral guardian of the nation, specifying appropriate comportment for the "masses" and defining the enemy "according to a taxonomy of moral failings—laziness, corruption and self-indulgence."[13]

Seven years of Frelimo rule had not eliminated these activities. Arresting prostitutes, drug dealers, smugglers, black marketeers, petty criminals, and malingerers had no significant impact.[14] The continued homelessness, hunger, unemployment, and crime was an affront to Samora's dream of creating the New Man. To tackle these problems and more effectively control the urban population, a radical moral and political intervention was needed. To Samora and the Frelimo leadership, the issuance of residence cards was the appropriate solution.

In 1982, the government began distributing residence cards to every worker with a recognized job as proof of urban citizenship. These cards had to be shown to access basic social services ranging from housing and health care to food rations and transport. According to Teodato Hunguana, "most urban residents approved of the cards, seeing them as an effective form of population control that would reduce vagrancy."[15]

Their introduction, however, did not solve the problems facing urban areas. The continued influx of migrants and increasing unemployment convinced Samora that the only alternative to urban decay was a radical purge of "unproductive" citizens from the cities. The plan under Operation Production was to relocate them to faraway, underpopulated Niassa Province, whose fertile land would easily support them.

At the Fourth Party Congress there was general consensus that "the cities were overcrowded with idle rural migrants who made it difficult for the working people to have enough food, housing and all the other benefits of citizenship."[16] Addressing a rally on May 21, 1983, Samora declared that "only those who have work, who have waged work, are entitled to residence [in the city]. . . . The marginals, the unemployed, the vagrants should be sent to the countryside, to production."[17]

Samora selected Minister of the Interior Armando Guebuza to oversee this urban cleansing. Guebuza had played a similar role in a previous unsuccessful attempt by Frelimo to rid Maputo of undesirables and "wicked women." So began the much-hated Operation Production, which was initially voluntary. The unemployed were asked to register and encouraged to relocate outside the cities. When few actually did, expulsion quickly became compulsory.

The most basic problem with Operation Production was the complete lack of knowledge about informal-sector employment. The absence of agreed definitions of "vagabonds" and "socially marginal" persons was a related obstacle. For the Frelimo leadership, those working in the informal sector, such as petty traders, handymen, artisans, barbers and beauticians, reed-house builders, and others who were self-employed, did not count as "real" workers and were lumped together as potential Xiconhocas.

The campaign began in June 1983 and ended in May 1984. In less than a year, approximately one hundred thousand citizens were arbitrarily rounded up and sent to Niassa, the most remote and least developed province in the country. Almost half came from Maputo, but thousands were also expelled from Beira, Nampula, and other urban centers. Single women, already suspect, were particularly vulnerable, since they were less likely to have registration papers. Most of the displaced were sent directly to reeducation camps, although several hundred more fortunate souls went to the state farm at Unango to work as paid laborers.[18]

The entire process suffered from "unruliness and gross violations of the most basic civil rights."[19] Overworked judges, under pressure from local party officials, rarely investigated whether those detained were actually in the cities illegally. State officials and even ordinary citizens sometimes used Operation Production as a way to settle old scores.

The rural reeducation centers bore little relationship to those established by FRELIMO during the armed struggle, which had been designed to wipe out corrupt tendencies and instill revolutionary values.[20] There were few classes and the camp commanders themselves, many of whom had fought in the armed struggle, rarely had more than rudimentary educations. Detainees spent their time working in the gardens, building and repairing thatch huts, or merely sitting. To escape boredom, many smoked *dagga* (marijuana), which was easily accessible. Thus, the "socially marginal" detainees, discarded and forgotten by all but their families and close friends, derived nothing beneficial from being sent there.

The reeducation camps did not resemble Soviet Gulags, as Samora's critics claimed.[21] Benedito Machava, in a scathing indictment of Frelimo's reeducation camps, is clear on this point: "The iconic elements of internment camps—barbed wires, watch towers, and armies of well-equipped security forces—were absent from Mozambique's camps. Reeducation camps had no fence, no watch tower, and few armed guards. Authorities assumed that the remote location of the camps . . . was enough to curb escapes."[22] Our brief 1984 visit to a reeducation center in Niassa supports Machava's contention.

Concerns about conditions in the camps, raised by Mozambican visitors living in Niassa, fell on deaf ears. Niassa's governor, Sérgio Vieira, acknowledged the problems in public meetings but insisted that only Guebuza had the authority to make changes.[23] A delegation of concerned citizens actually flew to Maputo to present Guebuza with accounts of the deplorable conditions and even brought photos of dead babies dismembered by lions. After they waited all day to meet with him, he responded coldly, "Don't you think I know this? Go home."[24]

Operation Production was an unmitigated disaster. It failed to alleviate economic and social problems in Mozambican cities, permitted gross abuses, erased important gains in revamping the judicial system, and violated the rule of law. It put a terrible strain on local resources in Niassa and disrupted airline service throughout the country during the four months it took to transport all the "undesirables." There were no plans to return the displaced to their urban homes, and, according to Arlindo Chilundo, Niassa's former governor, thousands of the displaced and their descendants still reside in Niassa today.[25]

Operation Production also seriously damaged Samora's reputation as a man of the people. Teodato Hunguana, minister of justice, had warned him that forced expulsion trampled on the constitutional rights of citizens.[26] Many journalists expressed their outrage and victims and their families wrote directly to Samora about the suffering. In response, Samora effectively ended the program eleven months after it began—although it was not officially abolished until four years later in May 1988.[27]

According to those close to him, Samora was furious when he learned of the abuses. In 1985, a year after ending Operation Production, he expelled Guebuza from the Political Bureau and stripped him of his position as minister of the interior, demoting him to minister without portfolio. Samora also raged that the abuses Guebuza had committed had created additional internal enemies.[28] Only Guebuza's support within the military and state security apparatus and his membership on Frelimo's Political Bureau prevented Samora from removing him entirely from the government.[29]

In addition to the reeducation camps established during Operation Production, Frelimo had been detaining political prisoners since the time of the armed struggle. Among the most significant were Frelimo dissidents Uria Simango and Lazaro Nkavandame, as well as Joanna Simião, who had been a leader of an anti-FRELIMO separatist organization based in Beira.

At independence, all three were being held in a re-education center in northern Mozambique. It was Samora's intention to periodically showcase them to teach future generations about the threats posed by internal enemies.

In areas where Frelimo's policies were most unpopular, particularly Nampula and Zambézia, insurgent commanders were able to rally local communities and chiefs to create a base of supporters. In 1983, after significant RENAMO advances in northern Mozambique, Samora and his military and intelligence advisers feared that, to enhance its claim of being a legitimate nationalist movement, RENAMO soldiers would try to free the three political prisoners. Samora ordered Aurélio Manave, governor of Niassa, to ensure that RENAMO was unsuccessful. Manave, together with senior officials from internal security (Serviço Nacional de Segurança Popular) and military intelligence, executed the "traitors" to make sure they would never fall into RENAMO's hands.[30]

The degree of Samora's involvement remains in dispute. Simango's biographer claims that Samora personally ordered him killed. Fernando Ganhão, Frelimo's official historian, and others close to the Mozambican leaders maintain that Samora had no knowledge of the execution.[31] Ganhão's assertion seems fanciful, since it is highly unlikely that such a significant decision could have been taken without at least Samora's tacit approval.

On the other hand, José Luís Cabaço, minister of information at that time, recently told Allen that when Samora found out, he angrily called the killing of Simango "the height of stupidity."[32] A former journalist who had regular access to the leadership insisted that

Samora only learned of the execution from the Portuguese ambassador, who objected to Manave's proposed appointment as Mozambique's ambassador to Lisbon based on a report by Portuguese intelligence that Manave was involved in Simango's murder.[33] After receiving this information, Samora removed Manave from his position as governor of Niassa.

No matter who actually planned and carried out the killings, Samora, as president, bore ultimate responsibility and his reputation suffered accordingly. Relations with his longtime allies Presidents Nyerere and Kaunda were damaged when they learned Samora had failed to keep the promise he made to them at the time of independence, to protect the three prisoners from harm.

The Nkomati Accord

Despite assistance from Zimbabwe and Tanzania, the military situation continued to deteriorate. Eventually, RENAMO's advance's convinced Samora and his advisers that the war could not be won. They were forced to acknowledge that protecting Mozambique's sovereignty would require both a negotiated settlement with South Africa and elimination of the perception that Mozambique was a pawn of the Soviet Union.

By 1982, Samora had come to realize that the Soviets and their allies were either unwilling or unable to provide the military hardware Mozambique needed. Apart from a handful of MiG-21 jet fighters and Mil Mi-24 helicopter gunships, the heavy weaponry they had received from the Soviets was out of date, costly, and useless against guerrillas. Samora was also rebuffed when he requested assistance in training the larger numbers of counter-insurgency soldiers needed to effectively contain RENAMO. Soviet military officials eventually agreed to take only a small number of officers, who were trained in Siberia, of all places. Moscow's reluctance led Samora to conclude that its principal objective was not to deter RENAMO but to use Mozambique as a pawn in its Cold War struggle against the West. Samora turned to the British and Portuguese, but while they provided counter-insurgency training for Mozambican soldiers, the numbers trained were inadequate.

Samora's plans also met resistance from some senior military commanders who prized their access to heavy weaponry and were committed to conventional warfare. Ignoring his orders, they dispersed members of the newly trained units rather than following Samora's instructions to deploy them together on strategic fronts. It was the first time any generals had disobeyed Samora. It would not be the last.

Samora's unenthusiastic reception in Moscow the following year, while heading a military delegation, solidified his belief that Mozambique was no longer a high priority. Upon his return, disappointed and disillusioned, he confessed to one minister that "we can no longer accept the notion that the Soviet Union is our certain natural ally."[34]

To blunt South African aggression, therefore, Mozambique needed to strengthen its ties to the West. Samora first reached out to British prime minister Margaret Thatcher. She arranged a meeting the following year with her close ally President Ronald Reagan, who Samora endearingly addressed as "Ronnie."[35] Neither provided tangible assistance.

At this point, the only way to end the war was to initiate negotiations with South Africa. Samora brought this plan first to Frelimo's Political Bureau and then to the Council of Ministers. No one appears to have disagreed.

Three of Samora's closest advisors took the lead in negotiating the broad contours of the "Agreement on Non-Aggression and Good-Neighborliness," which came to be known as the Nkomati Accord. Jacinto Veloso, minister of security, was the senior member of the negotiating team. Oscar Monteiro, an attorney and member of the Political Bureau, also played a pivotal role. Fernando Honwana, a rising star in Frelimo who had been Samora's personal representative during the Lancaster House negotiations, was the third key member.

Serious discussions only began in December 1983, although the year before Honwana had held exploratory conversations in Switzerland with RENAMO representatives. Negotiations were long and arduous. The parties recognized, however, that an accord was in both their interests. After difficult discussions punctuated by a South African walkout following Monteiro's denunciation of Pretoria's history of racist aggression, they hammered out the final terms, which included a nonaggression pact and establishment of a joint commission to implement the accord.[36] The final document was signed in a public ceremony in Nkomati, a South African town on the Mozambican border, on March 16, 1984.

Many of Frelimo's allies were infuriated with Samora. They had seen him in military garb speaking civilly with his and their arch-enemy, South African Prime Minister P. W. Botha. They had heard Samora declare that the signing of the agreement was "a high point in the history of relations between our two states and a high point in the history of our region."[37] And they realized that, with this treaty, Frelimo was abandoning its historic commitment to the African National Congress (ANC). President Julius Nyerere of Tanzania, who had been informed of the general terms of the accord before its signing and who privately agreed that Mozambique had no alternative, was publicly furious.[38] The Soviet Union and its allies, the South African Communist Party, and antiapartheid activists across the world condemned the decision as a betrayal of massive proportions. Senior ANC militants, while initially hostile, reluctantly concluded that Mozambique had no other options.

Within some circles in Mozambique there was confusion and anger, especially after Samora claimed Mozambique had forced Pretoria to the bargaining table and that the accord was a great victory for the revolution. Carlos Cardoso, many of his colleagues at the state-run Mozambican Information Agency, and some Eduardo Mondlane University faculty members challenged this representation of the agreement. For them, the Nkomati Accord was an shameful retreat.[39] Rumors began circulating in Maputo that dissatisfied security forces linked to Guebuza were planning a coup.[40]

Under the treaty, South Africa and Mozambique pledged that neither would permit its country to be used by third parties to commit acts of violence against either the territorial integrity or political independence of the other. For South Africa, the accord ensured that Mozambique stopped supporting the ANC and precluded possible attacks by Soviet forces stationed in Mozambique—about which Pretoria was paranoid. In exchange, Mozambique received South Africa's guarantee that it would cease its military assistance to RENAMO.[41] Although South Africa also sought diplomatic recognition and other concessions, Samora refused to budge.

Samora's belief that the Nkomati Accord would provide opportunity for Mozambique to rebuild turned out to be illusory, since Pretoria never ended its military assistance to RENAMO. The South African Defense Force continued to air-drop arms and ammunition, use submarines operating off Mozambique's coast to resupply guerrilla units, and allow large numbers of RENAMO insurgents to cross into Mozambique from their camps in the Transvaal.[42] Documents captured in 1985 at RENAMO headquarters in Gorongoza revealed the extent of the charade.

South African security forces also kept resupplying RENAMO forces based in Malawi, adjacent to the Mozambican border.[43] Anxious to stem this flow of men and arms, Samora flew to Malawi in 1985 in a failed attempt to convince President Hastings Banda to stop supporting RENAMO. Over the next year, several thousand RENAMO terrorists launched major attacks in central Mozambique from their Malawian bases, capturing district capitals and threatening to cut Mozambique in half.[44] RENAMO scored a propaganda victory by claiming that it was now fighting in all ten Mozambican provinces.

It wasn't long before Mozambique was forced to allow inclusion of a RENAMO representative on the accord's monitoring commission, which both legitimated

RENAMO and allowed South Africa to claim the role of peacemaker between two warring Mozambican factions. In October 1985, Mozambique withdrew from the monitoring commission, marking the effective end of the Nkomati Accord.

Still, the accord benefited Mozambique in a number of ways. Although South Africa secretly continued to support RENAMO, the amount of assistance decreased. More importantly, without the accord, covert aid from the United States to South Africa and RENAMO would likely have risen as the Reagan administration intensified its efforts to blunt Soviet influence.

Supporters of the accord also maintained that it paved the way for the 1986 Pretoria meetings, in which RENAMO representatives met with the same Mozambican officials who had negotiated at Nkomati. Several senior Frelimo leaders criticized this meeting because it gave additional credibility to RENAMO.[45] Nonetheless, the discussions were an important first step in the long process toward peace, culminating in the Rome Agreement in 1992.

By 1986, most of Samora's dreams had evaporated. He was becoming increasingly ill-tempered and isolated. Early in the year, the Council of Ministers and the Political Bureau of Frelimo decided to offset Samora's power by creating the new positions of prime minister and president of the Popular Assembly. Although this was presented as an opportunity for Samora to focus on the war against RENAMO, the backstory is more complicated. A group of young Turks, frustrated that their generation had been frozen out of positions of power, allied with at least one senior official to introduce the changes at a meeting of the Central Committee. Samora was startled, but he ultimately agreed and, in a face-saving gesture, publicly announced the changes.[46]

There were additional challenges to his authority. In parliament, Guebuza and supporters criticized Samora's rehabilitation of the Gaza king Ngungunyane, questioning why he had ignored other important rulers with whom he had no ethnic affiliation.[47] Senior military officials disregarded or disobeyed his orders, there were rumors of imminent military coups, and at least of one of his closest comrades privately accused him of acting like a dictator.[48] By negotiating with the apartheid regime, he had irreversibly damaged his position as a revolutionary hero, domestically and internationally.

Samora's personal life suffered as well. His children remember that their fun-loving father became more distant and short-tempered.[49] Life became tense after there was at least one attempt on his life and rumors surfaced about an impending coup.[50] Samora's relationship with Graça, who worked hard to keep the family together, suffered as well. She confided to a friend that "Samora was in a very bad way."[51]

Worst of all, Samora would never live to see his dream of peace in Mozambique realized.

Who Killed Samora?

At approximately nine o'clock on the night of October 19, 1986, the presidential jet carrying Samora and his advisers from Lusaka to Maputo mysteriously smashed into the Lebombo Mountains in South Africa, less than one kilometer from the Mozambican border. Of the thirty-five passengers, all but nine perished—Samora among them.

The next afternoon, after hours of public uncertainty and rumor, Marcelino dos Santos announced, his voice breaking, that Samora was dead. The official declaration from the Popular Assembly, Council of Ministers, and Frelimo Central Committee described his death as an "irreparable loss for the Mozambican people, for Africa, and for humanity."[1]

Mozambicans were in shock. *Tempo*, the nation's leading weekly, was flooded with letters expressing disbelief and sorrow. Many condemned the apartheid regime. One headline read "the Boers killed the best son of the people of Mozambique" while another predicted that "the blood of those who fell will burn apartheid."[2] Typical was the letter from Estêvão Passangeze, who referred to Samora as "our father," a term that many Mozambicans used to describe his special place in their hearts. Estêvão wrote of his fury at the apartheid regime and assured Samora that "you will always be in our souls and together we will continue the Revolution you inspired." Eduardo Mussegula, a high school student in Nampula, echoed this sentiment, predicting that Samora's memory and all he had accomplished "would live on for eternity."[3]

Messages from dignitaries around the world ranging from Fidel Castro to Maureen Reagan, as well as from ordinary foreigners, mourned Samora's loss.[4] Coretta Scott King, in her letter of condolence to Graça Machel, drew parallels between the tragic loss of Samora and her husband's murder: "President Machel possessed exceptional grace and sensitivity. He seemed to perceive things in a fresh light. . . . When I was in his presence, I saw a man who exhibited unsuspected possibilities of purpose and action. Your dear husband lived to see a free and independent People's Republic of Mozambique. Like Martin, he may have not lived long enough to fulfill his own possibilities, but his dream remains for you, your family and his people, who he loved dearly."[5]

Two key South African figures on opposite sides did not attend Samora's funeral. President P. W. Botha's request to participate was vehemently rejected. In disbelief, a high-level official declared, "it is simply unimaginable that Botha come here."[6] From his jail cell on Robben Island, Nelson Mandela pleaded to be allowed to personally honor his fallen comrade. In more than twenty years of incarceration, this was the only time he had asked to be temporarily released. His request fell on deaf ears. In a personal letter to Graça, Winnie Mandela wrote:

> Never before have we made application to leave South Africa. Today we believed that our place was to be with you physically.

> Each one of us is imprisoned in different jails. We were prevented from being present with you today to share your sorrow, to weep with you, to lighten your grief, to hold you very close. Our grief for Comrade Samora is so deep that it tears away at the heart. Throughout the night we have kept vigil with you. Throughout today we shall mourn with you for a mighty soldier, a courageous son, and a noble statesman.[7]

In Zimbabwe on the morning of October 20th, an estimated crowd of five thousand stoned the offices of South African Airlines, Malawi Airways, and the American embassy.[8] Citizens throughout South Africa mourned his death in other ways. A young South African film producer said of Samora, "In his military fatigues and AK-47 he was our guerrilla in the bush."[9] From Guinea to Portugal and Mali to Egypt, there were days, even weeks, of national mourning for the "beloved son of Africa who fought against racial discrimination and was a source of inspiration for those in this continent and across the world."[10]

The Prelude to the Crash

After Zimbabwe's independence in 1980, the Malawian government allowed South African military officers to enter the country and provide arms and training to RENAMO forces based there. This assistance continued even after the signing of the Nkomati Accord. On September 11, 1986, Samora flew to Blantyre to meet with President Banda. He provided Banda with documentation of the Malawi–South Africa connection and warned there would be harsh consequences if Malawi's aid to RENAMO continued. The meeting failed to yield any tangible results.

Samora was livid. During an impromptu news conference at the Maputo airport upon his return, he accused the South African military of using Malawian territory to destabilize and destroy Mozambique. When asked what Mozambique would do, he laid out a plan of action: "First, put missiles all along the Malawian border. We've got plenty of missiles, they just don't have a target. Secondly, close Malawi's route through Mozambique to Zimbabwe and South Africa."[11] He then took a highly publicized trip to Tete to assess the preparedness of troops stationed along the Malawian border.[12] Further stoking public outrage, the Mozambican Youth Organization demonstrated outside the Malawian embassy in Maputo. There were protests near the Malawian border in Tete Province, where the participants expressed "rage . . . and frustration with the fact that Malawi was supporting RENAMO's effort to divide Mozambique along the Zambezi."[13] Samora then made another publicized visit to Mozambique's principal air base in Nacala, from which MiGs could easily attack Malawi.

Whether Samora's threats were bluster or not, they clearly concerned Pretoria, which over the next month undertook an intense saber-rattling campaign. Defense Minister Magnus Malan threatened reprisals after a land mine exploded in South Africa, for which it held Mozambique responsible.[14] South African military jets regularly violated Mozambican airspace. Pretoria announced it would no longer allow Mozambican workers in South African mines, costing Mozambique $50 million in hard currency. The state-aligned media began circulating rumors that Samora had lost the confidence of his people and was facing strong opposition within his government.

One account even falsely claimed that Samora had been forced to flee Maputo to nearby Inhaca Island.[15]

Pretoria had many reasons to want Samora dead. He had long been a symbol of opposition to apartheid, capturing the imagination of South Africa's militant youth who adopted the Frelimo slogan, *A luta continua*, as their own. Protestors regularly carried signs celebrating the Mozambican revolution, teenagers sauntered through shantytowns playing rap songs that lionized Samora, and photographs and drawings of him were plastered surreptitiously in public spaces and on abandoned buildings.

On October 11, 1986, the Mozambican government announced that Pretoria was planning to attack Maputo in order to replace Samora with a leader more to its liking. Later that day, Samora met privately with a small group of Mozambican journalists. When Carlos Cardoso expressed his fear that the South African regime was planning to assassinate him, Samora interrupted, declaring, "They've already tried. In November 1985, they infiltrated bazookas into Mozambique that were to have been used to assassinate me." He paused and then declared, "I am in their way, I have not sold out to anyone."[16] Although no independent verification of such an attempt exists, South African hit squads had previously killed African National Congress members in Maputo and there is evidence they were still operating there.[17]

Eight days later, Samora and senior advisors flew to Zambia to meet with President Kaunda and Angola's president José Eduardo dos Santos to explore ways of containing South Africa's regional destabilization efforts.[18] The meeting ended at dusk. Although standing policy prohibited the president from flying at night,

Samora insisted on returning to Maputo that evening so he could attend a meeting the following morning at which he planned to announce sweeping changes to the military leadership. He intended to replace ineffective or compromised senior officials with better-trained younger officers in whom he had greater confidence.

It was not until ten hours after the crash that South African foreign minister Roelof "Pik" Botha informed Sérgio Vieira, Mozambique's interior minister, of the deaths of Samora and most of the others on the plane. In the interim, security forces combed through the wreckage, removing personal belongings and confidential documents. The delegation from Maputo arrived early that afternoon. They found the bodies of the victims covered with sheets and blankets and Samora's remains in a sealed plastic bag inside a coffin. Carlos Cardoso described the moment he saw Samora's corpse: "The bag was opened from the head downwards, but my first strong feeling that I really was looking at the body of Samora Machel came when I saw his right hand, resting on his abdomen. Those hands in life never stopped moving. They are engraved on the memories of many Mozambicans through personal contact with the President, through photographs and films, through the many meetings and rallies he addressed. Only later did I notice a small portion of the beard that become famous across the world."[19]

The Death of Samora: Pointing toward Murder

More than thirty years later, only incomplete evidence has been released about the cause of the crash. Those who planned and carried out the plot to kill Samora remain unidentified despite investigations by the Margo

Commission, established by white-ruled South Africa in 1987; postapartheid South Africa's Truth and Reconciliation Commission, which heard testimony on the crash in 1998; and a joint Mozambican–South African commission established in 2010.

Predictably, South Africa immediately denied any involvement, blaming the "accident" on pilot error. Foreign Minister Botha announced that traces of alcohol had been found in the blood of the Soviet pilots.[20] Rumors circulated that the pilot lacked experience, despite the fact that Captain Yuri Novodran had flown in and out of Maputo more than seventy times, mostly at night.[21] The 1987 Margo Commission also blamed pilot error, but materials that might shed light on its investigation remain under lock and key in South Africa's military and national archives. Eleven years later, Colonel João Honwana, a Mozambican Air Force commander who was an expert witness at the Truth and Reconciliation Commission (TRC) investigation, challenged Pretoria's mischaracterization of the pilot and crew's experience and skill, noting, "I had flown in the very aeroplane with them many times."[22]

The TRC heard other evidence, including from South African military officials, that casts serious doubt on the Margo Commission's findings. Much of the testimony, which has only recently been released, points directly to involvement by the apartheid regime.[23] Certainly, Pretoria had a motive, and it had attempted to assassinate Samora before.[24]

The most probable explanation is that the South Africans had placed a powerful portable navigation beacon near the crash site.[25] Since it transmitted on the same frequency as the VOR beacon at the Maputo airport and used the same code sign, it would have been able to override Mozambique's, which may have been turned off. The pilots were relying on signals they thought were coming from Maputo when, eighty miles from the capital, they were lured off course. Testifying before the TRC, Colonel João Honwana confirmed that, based on the limited evidence Mozambique had "through the flight data and the cockpit voice records, it was clear to us that the crew was convinced that they were following the VOR. The Maputo VOR."[26]

The first inkling of electronic sabotage surfaced the morning after the crash. Sérgio Vieira, who was leading the Mozambican delegation, was inexplicably told by Johan Coetzee, the local South African police commissioner, that "my [helicopter] crew is saying you have to look for a beacon over there [near the crash site]." The following day, a United Press International correspondent reported receiving an anonymous tip from a man claiming to be a South African Air Force officer that the military had placed a decoy beacon near the site.[27] Subsequent review of the transcript from the cockpit's voice recorders revealed the pilot's surprise that the VOR was directing the automatic pilot to fly southwest, rather than remaining on course. He could be heard reporting to the Maputo tower that he could not see the lights of the city.

Pretoria refused to share information with the Mozambican technical and security teams that might have clarified the cause of the crash. Nevertheless, Armando Guebuza, then minister of transportation, who oversaw the Mozambican side of the investigation, expressed confidence that the fragmentary evidence was sufficient to support the conclusion that "the plane was following signals from a VOR which was not the one in Maputo. It was this VOR that caused the plane's fatal turn away from its normal route."[28]

According to Willem Oosthuizen, a member of the South African Security Branch testifying at the TRC, this was not the first time Pretoria had used such a ruse, having deployed portable beacons in Namibia as early as 1979. Even more damaging was his testimony that two weeks after the crash, at a small military intelligence base near the crash site, he observed a cylindrical "movable beacon" about four feet in height with an aerial on top. "When I saw it . . . I realized that it was no accident."[29] Oosthuizen also testified that while subsequently on patrol along the Indian Ocean coast he noticed people on a trawler throwing things overboard, including a cylinder that "looked specifically like the one I had seen a few days earlier at the Security Police" base.[30] Afraid for his life, he had remained silent for more than a decade, until he was threatened with prosecution if he refused to testify.

The TRC also heard from three other South African Defense Force members, all of whom described a beacon they had seen prior to the crash and opined that it could easily have been transported by jeep. Colonel Mossie Basson, an electronics warfare expert, reported that members of the ultra-secret Signals Intelligence Division had been in Mbuzini the night of the crash.[31] Local residents also recalled a temporary military camp at Busoni that was dismantled around that time.[32] Additionally, TRC investigators learned that South African military forces were on full alert the night of the crash and that an elite commando reconnaissance unit had been dispatched to the area where the plane went down.[33] Finally, senior military officials, including Special Forces general Jeep Joubert and Chief of Military Intelligence Kat Liebenberg, reportedly flew into the area and spent the night of the crash at the nearby Spitskop Special Forces base.[34]

There is additional evidence that implicates the apartheid regime. Several days before the crash, South Africa's defense minister Magnus Malan flew secretly to Malawi, where he and his Malawian counterparts discussed the best way to eliminate Samora.[35] A night or two before the crash, Paulo de Oliveira, the RENAMO chief in Lisbon, received urgent instructions from South African security that the insurgents should "claim responsibility for shooting down Samora's plane."[36]

Much of the most damning information was uncovered by TRC researcher Debra Patta. She received anonymous death threats, including one from a caller warning her that if she did not cease her investigation he "would put a gun to her head." On another occasion, she was confronted by individuals who told her that she would "be burned up altogether" if she continued to play with fire.[37]

Within Mozambique, many still believe that disgruntled Mozambican officials played a part in Samora's death. Although they are reluctant to speak on the record for fear of retribution, some insist the crash could not have happened without some Mozambican involvement, pointing to the malfunctioning Maputo airport beacon and erratic radio communications between the tower and the presidential plane.[38] Others stress that Samora had many enemies and that his erratic behavior and declining popularity emboldened his opponents.

Under domestic and international pressure to determine who actually planned Samora's death, Mozambique and the government of postapartheid South Africa formed a bilateral commission in 2010 to do just that. After conducting extensive interviews in Mozambique, South Africa, and neighboring countries, in 2014 the investigators requested a meeting with President Guebuza. It apparently never occurred. The status and substance of whatever report was produced remains unknown, and there is no indication that further investigation was ever undertaken.[39]

8.1 Female soldiers responding to the death of Samora Machel.

The Political Afterlife of Samora and the Politics of Memory

In the last years of his life Samora and the entire Frelimo leadership had been forced to compromise their radical agenda. Mozambique's next president, Joaquim Chissano, who served from 1986 to 2005, went even further, totally abandoning the socialist project in favor of neoliberalism and market capitalism.

As part of the process of repudiating Frelimo's radical past, Mozambique's leaders sought to diminish Samora's significance. Yet this campaign, which M. Ann Pitcher has aptly described as "organized forgetting," did not eradicate the memories of the late president from the hearts and minds of millions of Mozambicans. For many, in death Samora became a romanticized symbol. So powerful was the nostalgia surrounding him that Chissano's successor, Armando Guebuza, who served from 2005 to 2015, reversed course and resurrected Samora's image. He did so to promote his own narrow nationalist agenda, despite the tension that had existed between the two during Samora's life.

Erasing Socialism, Erasing Samora

When Chissano took office, the country was in the throes of multiple crises. The most pressing were the continued economic collapse and the enormous national debt, estimated at over $3 billion. With limited options, Chissano sought relief from the International Monetary Fund and the World Bank. These institutions demanded, as a precondition for extending loans, that the Chissano government adopt a policy of structural adjustment requiring two major concessions: eliminating state subsidies for food, housing, health care, and education and reducing support for other social services; and removing barriers to private foreign investment.

After a brief attempt to commingle socialist ideals with free-market policies, both Chissano's government and Frelimo succumbed to the pressure. At the Fifth Party Congress in 1989, Frelimo formally abandoned Marxist-Leninism, dropping its claim to be a "party of the worker-peasant alliance." Instead, it became a conventionally nationalist "party of all the people" with a free-market agenda.

The 1987 IMF agreement was the death knell of Mozambican socialism. The preamble of the new constitution enacted in 1990, while celebrating the struggle that led to independence, omitted any reference to free health care and education as rights of citizenship. May Day parades became tepid events at which officials simply called for higher wages and limits on inflation. The capitalist entrepreneur replaced the socialist New Man in government publications and investment journals.[1]

Mozambique's relationship with RENAMO was similarly whitewashed. No longer was RENAMO referred to as a group of armed bandits, or even as insurgents. Instead, during peace negotiations that extended from 1990 to 1992, President Chissano embraced them as "our brothers in the bush." The June 1992 treaty signed in Rome under the auspices of the Catholic Church recognized RENAMO as a legitimate party with the right to participate in the political process.

The long, highly contested process of rewriting the national anthem was emblematic of the general struggle to rewrite the past. The original composition, written by militants on the eve of independence, celebrated "the overthrow of colonialism," "the struggle against imperialism," and expressed confidence that "our country will be the graveyard of capitalism and exploitation." Its final stanza stressed that the labor "of workers and peasants will always produce wealth."[2] A 1983 revision had retained its celebration of socialism.[3]

The 1994 parliament, which included a number of RENAMO delegates, mandated a new national anthem that would reflect Mozambique's achievements without embodying any specific ideology. Chissano's administration launched a competition with a jury of both Frelimo and RENAMO representatives, the winner to receive a hefty prize of 25 million meticals. It took four years to reach an acceptable version, as writers and jury grappled with whether the text should break with the past or continue to celebrate past accomplishments. The final version referenced neither capitalist exploitation nor the struggles of workers and peasants, in favor of a nationalist message celebrating the people of Mozambique.[4]

Effacing Mozambique's socialist past necessarily meant diminishing the historical significance of Samora. After the newspaper accounts of Samora's death and long lines of people waiting for hours to pay their respects, after the moving photos of his burial and the family's grief, stories about the deceased president became increasingly rare. Coverage of Samora in *Tempo*, *Notícias*, and *Diário de Moçambique* dwindled. To be sure, his name was still invoked at Independence Day celebrations, there was some coverage on his birthday and the anniversary of his passing, and reporters periodically raised questions about his suspicious death.[5] Frelimo also organized nationwide events on the tenth, twentieth, and thirtieth anniversaries of the plane crash.[6] Samora had been reduced to an artifact of history. Looking back at Chissano's desire to establish his own identity free of "Samorismo," José Luís Cabaço, former minister of information, found this erasure inevitable: "The Chissano administration had to silence the past to guarantee the successful implementation of its new neoliberal policies."[7]

Twenty years after Samora's death and two years after Armando Guebuza came to power, Samora's image was resurrected and he was again honored in official circles. Ironically, this was part of a cynical ploy by Samora's former rival to increase his own popularity and reinforce his legitimacy as a nationalist leader. He linked himself and his administration to Samora in emphasizing their shared nationalist commitment, but at the same time ignored Samora's socialist policies.

Guebuza's maneuvers to exploit Samora's stature as the father of the country came in rapid succession. He ordered that Samora's face be placed on all new Mozambican currency and that monuments of him be built in every province as symbols of a resurgent Mozambican nationalism. In 2008 he orchestrated a national celebration of Samora's seventy-fifth birthday. Samora's image began to appear again on Frelimo posters and in Frelimo publications. Guebuza helped to establish the Samora Machel Documentation Center. Pro-government newspapers published retrospectives celebrating the deceased president, and his exploits figured prominently in the spate of memoirs written by both Samora's allies and ordinary citizens.[8]

Remembering from Below

Despite efforts to obliterate Samora's memory, it never truly died. In the decades after his death, his leadership was heralded in memoirs written by those who had fought alongside him. The Association of Ex-Combatants collected and archived oral accounts from its members of the armed struggle under Samora's leadership.

For their part, trade unionists were unprepared to have eviscerated all they had achieved during the socialist moment. They lamented the new pro-market policies that intensified economic hardship for their members as well as the short shrift given by Chissano's government to May Day celebrations, which Samora had made one of the cornerstones of popular culture. A 1997 letter to the editor published in *Notícias* under the title "Once upon a Time It Was the First of May" captured this sentiment. The writer said of May Day that "those were golden moments, and it is with great nostalgia that many workers like me remember those moments. There were parades all over the country, and especially in Maputo, where the demonstrations were of great importance."[9]

Samora and other fallen comrades were also remembered through public art. In 1996 a team of

Mozambicans led by architect José Forjaz constructed a memorial at Mbuzini to Samora and the thirty-four other Mozambicans who died with him. Spare in design, the thirty-five rusted steel poles rising from the crash site mark the brutality of the event, the suffering of family and friends, and the trauma of lost social and political accomplishments.[10]

Remembering from below was not limited to those who knew Samora personally or who had benefited from his socialist commitments. Nor was it felt only in southern Mozambique, where he was born and held in particularly high regard, but throughout the country. Many peasants and workers celebrated Samora's commitment to a just society—even as RENAMO supporters, sympathizers, and some Mozambican intellectuals railed against his harsh rule and failed socialist policies.[11]

During a visit to Mozambique in 2019, we encountered men and women wearing T-shirts, caps, headdresses, and loincloths emblazoned with Samora's portrait. "*Samora Vive*" (Samora Lives) was stamped on much of this apparel. Graffiti and drawings of the late president are common sights, and his image is preserved at historic sites. The most famous is in the panorama of Mozambican history located near the memorial in Maputo to Mozambique's fallen heroes. At the center of this massive mural are the faces of Samora and Eduardo Mondlane. Thousands pass it daily on their way to work or the airport.

Samora has also been memorialized through song, dance, theater, poetry, and pirated recordings of his speeches. Nowhere is the invocation of his name more prominent than in contemporary Mozambican rap music, particularly in Maputo.[12] Rap might seem an unlikely genre in which to salute Samora's legacy, since throughout the time he governed rap music was considered bourgeois decadence. His administration closed nightclubs where rap was performed, criticized artists who did not use revolutionary themes, attacked long hair and hip clothing, and associated rap with prostitution and drugs. Nevertheless, for many musicians Samora, in death, became a culture hero. In the late 1990s a new generation of artists disillusioned with postrevolutionary Mozambique began to lament Samora's passing and reminisce about his socialist ideology. "Samora Machel" by Xitiku ni Mbawula captures this sentiment.

> I hold a piece of paper to write freestyle
> I am invoking the great name of Samora Moíses Machel
> You died and left us freedom
> You died and left us with what you did
> You died fighting to eradicate the suffering of your
>   people
> Your name stays in my heart
> Everywhere I go your words keep me alive
> During your time children were like roses which would
>   never fade away
> but today it has all changed
> The roses now just fade away for lack of water.[13]

Mozambique's most popular artist, Azagaia, goes even further. In his video "Combatentes da fortuna" (Soldiers of fortune), in which he intersperses Samora's voice and image with his own singing, the fallen leader can be heard asking those accused of collaborating with the Portuguese to confess their errors. Paraphrasing

Samora's 1982 exhortation against corruption, the video lacerates the Guebuza administration: "It is impossible to develop welfare and happiness among thieves / they have to be chased away / and nobody chases them away except you [the people]."[14] As the video concludes, Azagaia passes in front of the image of Samora, marking his identification with the fallen leader. In live performances, Azagaia often dresses in military garb similar to Samora's to remind his audience of their ideological connections.

In our interview, Azagaia did acknowledge that Samora could be harsh and act like a dictator. When we asked him why Samora has become so popular among Mozambique's youth, he responded that Samora's legacy lives on because "he is a reference point, a symbol of the Mozambican nation; so we can be poor but still have our pride."[15] According to musicologist Janne Rantala, Samora's "speeches now belong to public memory and often return to the streets through voice recordings. He has been given a new political afterlife as a voice of criticism against current politics."[16]

Samora's speeches and singing are readily available on inexpensive pirated discs and cassettes. His speeches are often played on buses as a form of entertainment. Even in Beira, a RENAMO stronghold, two decades after his death six hundred people crowded into the São Jorge Theater for a film and discussion about Samora's life.[17]

A story shared by a former government minister captures the power of Samora's voice. Before the second swearing-in of President Chissano in 2002, technicians were testing the loudspeakers at Independence Square. To their surprise, the disc they were using contained one of Samora's speeches. When his voice was heard across much of downtown Maputo, throngs of Mozambicans rushed to the square in disbelief.[18]

In the countryside, traditional songs and poetry celebrate Samora, not only praising his bravery and commitment to the poor but offering commentary on contemporary Mozambican society. Years after his death, market women in southern Mozambique still sing about their profound sense of despair and sorrow.

Leader: Look at Botha
Chorus: Ya ya, yayayee
Leader: Look at Botha of South Africa.
Chorus: Ya oyoa, yaoyaoyee

Leader: He killed our President
Chorus: Ya, yayayee
Leader: Samora Moises Machel
Chorus: Ya ya, ya, ya, yee
Leader: Wi, wi, wiwee
Chorus: Wi, wi, wiwee

Leader: Botha, Botha, you have destroyed Mozam-
          bique, you have killed the great hero
          We are this day mourning this hero
          Our development has suffered a big setback
          Mozambique is full of ninjas [criminals]
          When Samora was alive there were no ninjas
          in this country
          Machel, we mourn you!
          We want you to enter our hearts so that your
          [teachings] will continue to bear fruit in
          the country
          The country has now turned upside down, as
          it has no owner [ruler]

Chorus: Look at Botha
          Yo, yo, yoyoyo!
          Look at Botha in South Africa
          Yo, yo, yoyoyo!

```
Leader:   Who sabotaged our aeroplane?
Chorus:   Yo, yo, yoyo!
Leader:   Look at Botha
Chorus:   Yo, yo, yoyoyo!
Leader:   He killed our hero
Chorus:   Yo, yo, yoyoyo![19]
```

More than a thousand miles away in Cabo Delgado, rural residents continue to mark Samora's passing with a similar refrain, stressing that his death was part of a long line of sacrifices that Frelimo leaders made so the country would be free.

> Kulila wetu kulila Moshambiki
> > *We cry, in Mozambique we cry*
> Elo tunkulila kwetu
> > *Yes, we cry*
> Samora pakupela tutenda dashi
> > *When Samora died, how could we do?*
> Wetu vanang'olo tutenda dashi?
> > *Us elders, how should we do?*
>
> Wetu tundishanga shilambo shetu
> > *We are desperate in our country,*
> sha-Moshambiki
> > *Mozambique*
> Mwanashiva amalilike
> > *Orphanhood must end*
> Atunduvenge baba Mondlane kupela
> > *Papa Mondlane died first*
> Josina kupela
> > *Then Josina died*
> Tundishanga tunama dashi?
> > *We are desperate, how to live?*
>
> Akapele baba Mondlane
> > *When papa Mondlane died*
> Wapela mama Josina
> > *And mama Josina died*
> Tundishukulu
> > *We were grateful*

207

Tundipata junji Samora Machele
to get Samora Machel
Andidiva pamwe Mondlane
He substituted for Mondlane
Wetu tundishukuru
We were grateful
Continua yashimadengo
We carried on with the work

Nelo tunkumbukila mwamboli wetu
Today we remember our liberator
Tunkumbukila Samora
We remember Samora
Angola na Tanzania
In Angola and Tanzania
Ku-Zimbabwe
And in Zimbabwe[20]

Their songs also affirm their adoration of the late president. In 2005, Paolo Israel recorded this Makonde celebration of "papa Machel's" life.

Kwaendile
Where he went
Kwaendile baba Machele kwaendile
Where papa Machel went, where he went
Ata kukalepa dashi
Even if it's far, then what?
Wetu mwanda
We go
Tummwoda baba Machel kwaendile kula
We follow papa Machel there, where he went
Ata pakadingadinga dashi
It may be tortuous, so what?
Tundapaleta pele
We will slip in
Tummwoda baba Machel kwaendile akó
We follow papa Machel, where he went
Mukaigwa kwaendile kushu kwanungu akulepa
And if you hear: he went far, at God's place, that's far

Tuvene tupaleta vila pele
Us, we'll just slip in
Kwannungu akulepa
God's place, that's far away.[21]

In 2004, *mapiko* performers beseeched President Chissano not to forget them, but to come and visit their communities as Samora had on so many occasions.

Baba Chissano kukunagwela vyakutumidya
Papa Chissano, you like to dispatch envoys
Shaida umwene
You should come yourself
Utulole mwatunamila
To see how we live
Mujo Samora ashindaida awenawena mudialudeya
*Your friend Samora used to come and
roam the villages*
Atulole mwatunamila
To see how we live

Kanji wako:
But you:
"Wena Chipande wena
"Go, Chipande, go
Wena Raimundo wena
Go, Raimundo go
'Kavalole mwavanamila"
Have a look at how they live"[22]

In the aftermath of Samora's death, South Africans and Zimbabweans also paid homage to the fallen leader's memory through songs and poetry. Zimbabwean writer Musaemura Zimunya expresses his grief at Samora's death and celebrates his continued significance.

See now how they cry on the streets and tears fill
the country
while they drink from your head and toast to the
god of blood

as your children weep for your land and our destiny
they exult with song and braai and tumult in this loss.

In this end that is no end you will whisper com-
    rade, today, and tomorrow and tomorrow still
    you will whisper
beyond
the silence of the tomb and the crash
till your voice fills stadia of this land and many lands
and leaders to come
will proclaim in many voices of hope and wrath
    that's louder
than even the storm that thunders ever louder.
A luta! A luta! A luta continua![23]

These sentiments persist today. In June 2018, Allen engaged in numerous conversations with taxi drivers, street vendors, shoe shiners, and market women. Some described Samora as harsh or bemoaned his attacks on the Christian churches. All, however, emphasized his concern for the poor, his attempts to end the abusive practices of the colonial past, the power of his personality, and his infectious laughter. Perhaps a taxi driver put it best: "Samora could be harsh, but he was not corrupt. He would not have permitted all the corruption that exists today. He cared for us."[24]

Social media provides a new platform for the discussion and reshaping of Samora's memory. Posts on Facebook and Instagram about present-day corruption in Mozambique often include Samora's 1982 admonition regarding Guebuza's early accumulation of wealth: "If a leader builds a house, the people must demand to know where he got the money." Samora's thoughts on social justice, the public good, immorality, and racism are also summoned up on social media as commentary on Mozambique's present ills.[25]

Most of these positive representations of Samora come from Maputo, which has always been a Frelimo stronghold. Additional research is necessary to determine the depth of his popularity in other parts of the country.[26] In Beira, some rappers have criticized Samora. The well-known Beira rapper Y-Not, in "Tempo que passou" (Times past), a critique of the popular Frelimo song "Não vamos esquecer" (We will never forget), chastised Samora for his authoritarian practices that perpetuated colonial abuses.[27]

Conclusion

Samora's Life Revisited

Samora was a tragically flawed hero who brought independence and hope to millions of Mozambicans. Through personal experience and the writings of Mao Zedong, Frantz Fanon, Kwame Nkrumah, and Amilcar Cabral, he came to believe that colonialism and capitalism were inextricably interconnected. In different ways, each of these authors presented a powerful critique of imperialism and the colonial order and offered a blueprint for attacking class injustices and the colonizing of the mind. Nevertheless, Samora's socialism was always rooted in Mozambican reality. For him, the Mozambican revolution faced its own specific challenges, making it inappropriate to simply mimic other socialist nations.

Samora left an indelible mark on the young nation as a charismatic leader inspiring loyalty and a spirit of sacrifice. He used state power and the bully pulpit to attack illiteracy, disease, exploitation of women, and other forms of oppression. He introduced anti-corruption policies, reminding Frelimo's leaders and cadres that they would be held accountable if they used their positions to accumulate wealth or influence. He also championed Frelimo's nonracial ideology and encouraged residents of Portuguese and Asian descent to become citizens of the new Mozambique.

It is equally clear that Samora relied both on heavy-handed tactics and the power of his personality to carry out Frelimo's policies. When Frelimo's socialist project lost credibility and the armed forces were unable to contain RENAMO, his administration became increasingly authoritarian. Its use of force to expand the communal village system and cleanse the cities of the "socially marginal" are examples. The reintroduction of corporal punishment, including whipping, remains a significant blemish on his record. History will not and should not forget the murders of Simango, Nkavandame, and Simião. Samora's refusal to permanently remove Guebuza and others from leadership positions after they had committed serious abuses of power also tarnished his presidency and created problems that continue until today.

Samora's tendency to dismiss African religious beliefs as obscurantist revealed his misunderstanding of their significance in many Mozambican communities. His assumption that persuasion and scientific rationalism would easily undermine indigenous and Christian beliefs was naïve, as was his confidence that Frelimo could construct a new moral order.

In his quest for economic and social justice, Samora was often myopic, convinced Mozambique could jump over history. Despite the dearth of financial experts, agronomists, and technical personnel, he believed that a state-run command economy could transform Mozambique's underdeveloped and distorted economic system. However laudable his attempts to restructure the health and educational sectors, the same lack of resources impeded their successful implementation.

But, Samora was also a realist. When socialist planning failed to meet the needs of the Mozambican people, Samora, rather than admitting defeat, searched for alternatives. Mozambique's move toward a mixed economy, which Samora oversaw, flowed directly from these setbacks—as did the recalibration of its relations with the wider world.

Samora's foreign policy aimed to protect both Mozambican sovereignty and its nonaligned status. This was not always possible. Because most Western governments supported Portugal during the armed struggle, FRELIMO had no choice but to seek military assistance from the Soviet Union and its allies. When Samora realized his young nation had become excessively dependent on Moscow, he resisted Soviet entreaties for a naval base in Mozambique, refused to become embroiled in the Sino-Soviet split, deepened Mozambique's involvement in the Non-Aligned Movement, strengthened ties with the Nordic countries, and used the Lancaster House negotiations resulting in Zimbabwe's independence to improve relations with the West. Nevertheless, he was unsuccessful in convincing the NATO allies to end their support for the apartheid regime that was seriously threatening Mozambique's sovereignty.

Perhaps his most significant foreign policy blunder was the bellicose rhetoric directed at South Africa, which provided it an excuse to intensify its destabilization campaign. While Samora's goal of dismantling apartheid was courageous and principled, it was highly unrealistic, given the imbalance in military power. Samora also miscalculated Pretoria's long-term commitment to RENAMO and RENAMO's destructive capacity. Both he and Mozambique paid a heavy price.

Two years before Samora's death, he reaffirmed that he would never forget for whom he was fighting: "I remain a 'guerrilla,' a combatant for the interests of my country, and of my people."[1] Today, Mozambican intellectuals, activists, and politicians of all stripes continue to debate how Samora should be remembered. He also figures prominently in the conversations, gossip, debates, and popular culture of many ordinary citizens. Although the memories that Mozambicans hold of their deceased leader are neither fixed nor uniform, more than thirty years after his death many still share his vision of a just society.

It remains to be seen whether Samora's vision of a society based on social and economic equality will ever be realized.

Notes

Prologue: The Challenge of Representation

1. When villagers began to discuss these abuses or any other sensitive political matters, we always turned off our tape recorder. We feared that, if the tapes or their transcriptions were confiscated, the elders would suffer harsh retributions.

2. For a pioneering study on life in the subúrbios, see David Morton, *Age of Concrete: Housing and the Shape of Aspiration in the Capital of Mozambique* (Athens: Ohio University Press, 2019).

3. An *assimilado* (assimilated person) was one who, by virtue of having adopted Portuguese cultural norms, enjoyed full rights of citizenship under the law. The term *padrinho* refers to a godfather or personal patron.

4. Graça Machel, interview, Maputo, n.d., Centro de Documentação Samora Machel (CDSM), folder 58.

5. During this period, Allen, Roberta Washington, William Minter, and Prexy Nesbitt organized the Mozambique Support Network to coordinate these efforts.

6. This is very similar to what feminist scholars define as "intersubjective knowledge." We are indebted to Heidi Gengenbach for this observation (personal communication, August 8, 2019).

7. Edward Said, *Representations of the Intellectual* (New York: Pantheon, 1994), 32.

8. The FRELIMO archives are housed at the Arquivo Histórico de Moçambique.

9. Marc Augé, *Oblivion*, trans. Marjolijn de Jager (Minneapolis: University of Minnesota Press, 2004), 18, quoted in Olga Shevchenko and Oksana Sarkisova, "Remembering Life in the Soviet Union, One Family Photo at a Time," *New York Times,*

217

December 27, 2017, https://www.nytimes.com/2017/12/27/opinion-soviet-union-one-photos.html.

10. See Mary Jo Maynes, "U.S. Labor History in Recent Biography," *Radical History Review* 72 (1998): 183.

Chapter 1: Living Colonialism

1. Raul Honwana, *The Life History of Raul Honwana* (Boulder, CO: Lynne Reiner, 1988), 105.

2. Thomas Henriksen, *Revolution and Counterrevolution: Mozambique's War of Independence* (Westport, CT: Greenwood, 1983), 219.

3. Eric Allina, *Slavery by Any Other Name: African Life under Company Rule in Colonial Mozambique* (Charlottesville: University of Virginia Press, 2012), 25.

4. Ibid., 151.

5. Allen Isaacman, *The Tradition of Resistance in Mozambique: The Zambesi Valley, 1850–1921*, in collaboration with Barbara Isaacman (Berkeley: University of California Press, 1976), 157–58.

6. Because the international banking community had established a relatively low fixed price for gold bullion, in sharp contrast to its mounting free-market price, Lisbon was able to sell gold on the open market in South Africa at several times its bullion value for three decades—earning an additional windfall from this arrangement. The funds generated were a major source of income for Portugal.

7. Toward this end, Portugal developed the port of Lourenço Marques as a gateway to the Transvaal and other South African markets. The port at Beira served a similar function for landlocked Southern Rhodesia.

8. C. M. Braun, May 1, 1946, CDSM, folder 64.

9. See A. H. Oliveira Marques, *History of Portugal*, vol. 2 (New York: Columbia University Press, 1972); António Figueiredo, *Portugal: Fifty Years of Dictatorship* (Harmondsworth, UK: Penguin, 1975); Hugh Kay, *Salazar and Modern Portugal* (London: Eyre and Spottiswoode, 1970).

10. See Leroy Vail and Landeg White, *Capitalism and Colonialism in Mozambique: A Study of Quelimane District* (Minneapolis: University of Minnesota Press, 1981), 247. The Portuguese state had implemented neo-mercantile policies even before Salazar. In 1929, Lisbon canceled the charter of the Niassa Company and the following year abolished the *prazo* system, under which large estates were leased to colonists. Neither added much to the national economy. Five years later, state authorities nationalized the holdings of the Mozambique Company and shortly thereafter introduced the Circular of 1942, which envisioned a more systematic use of "African labor for the public good." Malyn Newitt, *A History of Mozambique* (Bloomington: Indiana University Press, 1995), 445–62; Vail and White, *Capitalism*, 296.

11. *O brado africano* (Lourenço Marques), February 27, 1931.

12. Olívia Machel, interview, Maputo, March 7, 2019; Julius Nyerere to Samora Machel, February 25, 1984, CDSM, folder 24.

13. Iain Christie, *Samora Machel: A Biography* (London: Zed Press, 1987), 5.

14. Samora Machel, interview, Pemba, October 15, 1984.

15. Gerhard Liesegang, "Samora Moisés Machel: The Formative Years (1933–1963)," in *Samora: Man of the People,* ed. António Sopa (Maputo: Maguezo Editores, 2001), 19–29.

16. Mandande Moisés Machel, interview, Chilembene, February 20, 1979.

17. Christie, *Samora Machel*, 3.

18. Samora Machel to Oliver Tambo, June 5, 1984, CDSM, folder 8.

19. José Luís Cabaço, interview, Maputo, June 11, 2018.

20. Aurélio Chambale, interview, n.d., CDSM, folder 58.

21. Aurélio Manave, interview, n.d., CDSM, folder 58.

22. Samito Machel, interview, Maputo, March 23, 2019.

23. Aurélio Manave, interview.

24. Summarized in Christie, *Samora Machel*, 3.

25. Aurélio Manave, interview.

26. Liesegang, "Samora Moisés Machel," 23.

27. Ibid.

28. Samora Machel to Oliver Tambo, June 5, 1984, CDSM, folder 8.

29. See Allen Isaacman, *Cotton Is the Mother of Poverty* (Portsmouth, NH: Heineman, 1996).

30. Herb Shore, "Mondlane, Machel and Mozambique: From Rebellion to Revolution," *Africa Today* 21, no. 1 (Winter 1974): 7.

31. Otto Roesch, "Migrant Labour and Forced Rice Production in Southern Mozambique: The Colonial Peasantry of the Lower Limpopo Valley," *Journal of Southern African Studies* 17, no. 2 (June 1991): 239–70.

32. Christie, *Samora Machel*, 7.

33. Aurélio Manave, interview.

34. A copy of his draft registration card can be found in CDSM, folder 31.

Chapter 2: The Early Political Education of Samora Machel

1. For the story of his life, see Eduardo Mondlane, *The Struggle for Mozambique* (London: Zed Press, 1983); Janet Rae Mondlane, ed., *O eco da tua voz: Cartas editadas de Eduardo Mondlane*, vol. 1 (Maputo: Imprensa Universitária UEM, 2007).

2. For important studies of the gendered division of labor in the urban centers of colonial Mozambique, see Kathleen Sheldon, *Pounders of Grain: A History of Women, Work, and Politics in Mozambique* (Portsmouth, NH: Heinemann, 2002); and Jeanne Marie Penvenne, *Women, Migration and the Cashew Economy in Southern Mozambique, 1945–1975* (Oxford: James Currey, 2015).

3. António Mondlane, interview, n.d., CDSM, folder 58.

4. Aurélio Manave, interview.

5. Ibid.

6. Ibid.; António Mondlane, interview.

7. Aurélio Manave, interview.

8. João Ferreira, interview, n.d., CDSM, folder 58.

9. Aurélio Manave, interview.

10. Christie, *Samora Machel*, 11.

11. Aurélio Manave, interview.

12. Ibid.

13. Derived from interviews with António Mondlane, Aurélio Manave, and João Ferreira; see also Matias Mboa, *Memórias da luta clandestina* (Maputo: Marimbique, 2009).

14. Liesegang, "Samora Moisés Machel," 13.

15. Graça Machel, interview.

16. For a detailed account of his experiences on Inhaca, see Ana Piedade Monteiro et al., *Samora Machel na ilha de Inhaca (1955—1959)* (Maputo: Imprensa Universitária UEM, 2012).

17. David Chainkomo, interview, n.d., CDSM, folder 58.

18. Ibid.; Olívia Machel, interview.

19. Barry Munslow, ed., *Samora Machel, an African Revolutionary: Selected Speeches and Writings* (London: Zed Press, 1995), xii.

20. Magarida Buque, interview, n.d., CDSM, folder 58.

21. Graça Machel, interview, Maputo, March 24, 2019.

22. This material is derived from Liesegang, "Samora Moisés Machel," 24–25.

23. António Alves Gomes, interview, Maputo, June 11, 2018.

24. Margarida Buque, interview.

25. Chissano was born in Chibuto in Gaza Province and attended high school at Liceu Salazar, where he became active in NESAM. He briefly studied medicine in Lisbon, where he met other anti-colonial nationalists from Angola and Guinea-Bissau. Under surveillance by the secret police, he fled to France and then joined FRELIMO. Joaquim Alberto Chissano, *Vidas, lugares e tempos* (Maputo: Texto Editores, 2010).

26. Guebuza was born in Nampula. His father was a nurse. At eight, his family moved to Lourenço Marques. He became president of NESAM in 1963 and on his second attempt successfully fled to Dar es Salaam via Swaziland, South Africa, Bechuanaland, and Zambia. When he arrived in Dar es Salaam he joined FRELIMO. Colin Darch, *Historical Dictionary of Mozambique* (Lanham, MD: Rowman and Littlefield, 2019), 180–81.

27. Magaia was born in Mocuba in Zambézia Province. His father was a nurse who moved around the country. While attending high school in Lourenço Marques, he joined NESAM

and became a leading militant within the organization. Darch, *Historical Dictionary*, 238–39.

28. Matsinhe was born in Casula in Tete Province where his father taught at a missionary school. In 1950, he moved to Lourenço Marques, attended high school there, and became actively involved in NESAM. Ibid., 400.

29. Born in Lourenço Marques, Honwana was active in NESAM and was a leading voice of cultural nationalism, as well as Mozambique's most prominent writer. In 1964, he published *Nós matámos o cão-tinhoso*, subsequently translated as *We Killed Mangy-Dog*. He was arrested in 1967 for subversive activities "in support of FRELIMO and against Portuguese sovereignty in Mozambique" and was imprisoned for several years. After his release, he went to Lisbon and subsequently fled to Tanzania, where he began his military training at Nachingwea. Raul Honwana, *The Life History of Raul Honwana* (Boulder, CO: Lynne Reiner, 1988), 165.

30. João Ferreira, interview.

31. Luís Bernardo Honwana, interview, Maputo, March 11, 1979; Esperança Abatar Muethemba, interview, April 15, 1979; Albino Magaia, interview, June 7,1979. The latter two interviews were conducted by Isabel María Casimiro as part of a senior seminar on popular resistance Allen Isaacman taught at the Universidade Eduardo Mondlane.

32. Chissano, *Vidas, lugares e tempos*, 178.

33. Christie, *Samora Machel*, 13.

34. Of Portuguese descent, Ferreira served in the colonial army and then became a salesman for a pharmaceutical company. He befriended Samora when Samora worked as a nurse at Miguel Bombarda Hospital and warned Samora of his impending arrest by PIDE (João Ferreira, interview).

35. Veloso was born to a Portuguese family in Lourenço Marques. He went to Portugal in 1955 to train as an air force pilot and then returned to Mozambique. While in the Portuguese air force there, he hijacked a plane and flew it to Tanzania, where he joined FRELIMO. Jacinto Veloso, *Memories at Low Altitude* (Cape Town: Zebra Press, 2012).

36. Born in Lourenço Marques to an immigrant family from Goa, Nogar was a poet and early proponent of Mozambican cultural nationalism. Darch, *Historical Dictionary*, 294.

37. Born in Lourenço Marques, Cabaço attended law school in Lisbon and studied sociology in Italy, where in 1966 he made contact with FRELIMO. José Luís Cabaço, *Moçambique: Identidade, colonialismo e libertação* (São Paulo: Editora Unesp, 2009).

38. Born in the Mozambican capital, Balthazar was a highly respected lawyer who defended several prominent political prisoners. Darch, *Historical Dictionary*, 257.

39. Honorata Simão Tchussa, João Velemo Nunguanbe, and Jacob Jeremias Nyambir, interviews, Maputo, March 27, 2019.

40. Cornélio João Mandande, interview, Mueda, July 30, 1979; Zacarias Vanomoba, interview, Mueda, August 2, 1979; João Bonifácio, interview, Mueda, August 2, 1979.

41. Mondlane, *Struggle for Mozambique*, 118. Other estimates of the number of deaths ranged from seventeen to five hundred (Yussuf Adam and H. A. Dyutie, eds., "Entrevista: O massacre de Mueda: Falam testemunhas," *Arquivo: Boletim do Arquivo Histórico de Moçambique* 14 [October 1993]: 117–28). For an important reinterpretation of the events surrounding the Mueda massacre, see Paolo Israel, "The Matter of Return: The Mueda Massacre in Colonial Intelligence" (forthcoming).

42. Honorata Simão Tchussa, interview.

43. Cornélio João Mandande, interview.

44. Many of the older militants had lived abroad for more than a decade. Matthew Michinis and Mamole Lawrence Malinga initially led the militant group, which also enjoyed the support of the powerful Makonde chief Lazaro Nkavandame.

45. Paolo Israel, personal communication, August 12, 2019.

46. Lopes Tembe Ndelana, *From UDENAMO to FRELIMO and Mozambican Diplomacy* (Terra Alta, WV: Headline Books, 2016), *passim*; João Velemo Nunguanbe, interview.

47. Ndelana, *From UDENAMO*, 40.

48. Simango was the son of a Protestant minister who had been an outspoken critic of colonial abuses. Following in his father's footsteps, he was arrested in 1953 and three years later

was ordained in the Church of Christ. Simango rejected a scholarship to study in Lisbon because he thought it would deflect from his political agenda. Instead, he fled to Salisbury, Southern Rhodesia, joined UDENAMO, and reached out to Joshua Nkomo, leader of the Zimbabwe African Peoples Union, and Kwame Nkrumah, president of Ghana. Barnabé Lucas Ncomo, *Uria Simango: Um homem, uma causa* (Maputo: Edições Nováfrica, 2003).

49. Santos was born in 1929 in Lumbo, near the Island of Mozambique, to an Afro-Goan family. His father was an activist in the Associação Africana. He spent much of his youth in Lourenço Marques and in 1947 went to Portugal to study at the Instituto Superior Téchnico, where he met Africans and Asians from the Portuguese colonies who were members of the Casa dos Estudantes do Império. In 1951 Marcelino escaped to France. In Paris he played a pivotal role in the Federation of African Students, which was closely aligned with the French Communist Party. In 1955 he helped organize the Movimento Anti-Colonialista and in 1961 he was elected secretary-general of the Conference of Nationalist Organizations of the Portuguese Colonies, which superseded MAC. Based in Algeria, CONCP was an umbrella organization coordinating diplomatic and military support for the principal liberation movements seeking independence from Lisbon. Marcelino Dos Santos, interview, Maputo, March 2003.

50. See Helder Martins, *Porquê Sakrani? Memórias dum médico duma guerrilha esquecida* (Maputo: Editorial Terceiro Milénia, 2001).

51. Alberto Joaquim Chipande, interview, n.d., CDSM, folder 58.

52. FRELIMO, Dept. of Information, "Editorial: 25th of June, the Starting Point," *Mozambique Revolution*, no. 51 (June 1972): 1.

53. Liesegang, "Samora Moisés Machel," 25.

54. Mboa, *Memórias*, 85.

55. João Ferreira, interview.

56. Margarida Buque, interview.

57. This was true not only of young men but also of the small number of young women who fled. Among them was Josina Muthemba, whom Samora married in 1969.

58. Olívia Machel, interview.

59. Graça Machel, interview.

60. Mboa, *Memórias*, 86–87.

61. Christie, *Samora Machel*, 23.

Chapter 3: The Struggle within the Struggle, 1962–70

1. FRELIMO, Dept. of Information, "Editorial: 25th of June, the Starting Point," *Mozambique Revolution*, no. 51 (June 1972): 1.

2. Raimundo Pachinuapa, interview, n.d., CDSM, folder 58.

3. Mboa, *Memórias*, 87–88.

4. Alberto Joaquim Chipande, interview.

5. Jacob Jeremias Nyambir, interview, Maputo, March 27, 2019.

6. José Manuel Duarte de Jesus, *Eduardo Mondlane: Hope Destroyed* (self-pub., CreateSpace, 2016), 291.

7. Raimundo Pachinuapa, interview.

8. Jacob Jeremias Nyambir, interview.

9. Ibid.

10. Ibid.

11. Ibid.

12. Raimundo Pachinuapa, interview; Jacob Jeremias Nyambir, interview.

13. Alberto Chipande, interview.

14. Jacob Jeremias Nyambir, interview.

15. This group, representing a majority of the FRELIMO leadership, included Marcelino dos Santos, Joaquim Chissano, Armando Guebuza, and the senior military commanders Filipe Samuel Magaia, Alberto Chipande, Raimundo Pachinuapa, Jorge Rebelo, and Samora.

16. Oscar Monteiro, interview, Matola, March 26, 2019; Duarte de Jesus, *Eduardo Mondlane*, 24–26, 636–37.

17. For a detailed discussion of the opposition within FRE-LIMO, drawing on reports from Portuguese, Soviet Union,

Chinese, and East German intelligence operatives based in Tanzania, see Duarte de Jesus, *Eduardo Mondlane*, 263–344.

18. Born in 1904, Nkavandame founded the Liguilanilu cooperative. He contacted MANU soon after its formation and later fled to Tanzania with many of his followers. In June 1963 he was appointed to the FRELIMO Central Committee with a mandate to promote trade in the liberated zones and between the liberated zones and Tanzania. Darch, *Historical Dictionary*, 292.

19. Edward Alpers, "Islam in the Service of Colonialism? Portuguese Strategy during the Armed Liberation Struggle in Mozambique," *Lusotopie*, no. 6 (1999): 165–84.

20. Duarte de Jesus, *Eduardo Mondlane*, 270–77.

21. Alberto Chipande, interview.

22. Helder Martins returned to Tanzania to work as a FRELIMO doctor. Martins, *Porquê Sakrani?*, 265–99.

23. Fernandes's racial hatred may have been the reason for his later expulsion from FRELIMO. Thomas Henriksen, *Revolution and Counterrevolution: Mozambique's War of Independence* (Westport, CT: Greenwood, 1983), 24–25. Although Chai is considered the beginning of the armed struggle in FRELIMO lore, Paolo Israel, a researcher working in northern Mozambique, has collected evidence indicating that MANU guerrillas had attacked a Portuguese location inside Mozambique in 1960 (personal communication, August 13, 2019).

24. Barbara Cornwell, *The Bush Rebels* (London: André Deutsch, 1973), 53–54.

25. Jacob Jeremias Nyambir, interview.

26. For a history of the Mozambican Institute and the racial, cultural, and linguistic divisions within it, see Felipe B. C. C. Bastos, "Políticas de língua e movimentos nacionalistas: Campos de interação histórica entre Tanzânia e Moçambique (1961–1969)" (master's thesis, Universidade Estadual de Campinas, 2018), 191–241.

27. William Minter, "Report on meeting with Forms l and Forms ll, an analysis of reasons for discontent among the students" (unpublished document in authors' possession, January 19, 1968).

28. Douglas L. Wheeler, "A Document for the History of African Nationalism: The UNEMO 'White Paper' of 1968, a

Student Reply to Eduardo Mondlane's 1967 Paper," *African Historical Studies* 3, no. 1 (1970): 169–80.

29. Hama Thay, interview, Maputo, June 20, 2018.

30. Field Notebook of Samora Machel, 1965–67, CDSM, folder 66.

31. Simango's biographer, Barnabé Lucas Ncomo, describes the contempt in which Samora's opponents held him. Ncomo, *Uria Simango*, 141–42.

32. Samora Machel, interview, Maputo, May 7, 1979.

33. Christie, *Samora Machel*, 123.

34. José Luís Cabaço, interview, Maputo, June 13, 2018.

35. According to Jacob Jeremias Nyambir, who was walking in front of Magaia in a dry riverbed when shots rang out, Magaia thought he had been wounded by a grenade. Efforts to revive him failed. When the platoon's weapons were examined, a guerrilla whose gun barrel was still hot and smelled of gunpowder was arrested (Jacob Jeremias Nyambir, interview). Lourenço Matola spent five years in prison before escaping and fleeing to Kenya. The findings of a FRELIMO inquiry into the murder have never been made public, leading to an array of rumors about who was responsible for his death (personal communication, Paolo Israel, August 12, 2019).

36. Oscar Monteiro, interview, Matola, March 6, 2019.

37. Christie, *Samora Machel*, 57.

38. For an analysis of events surrounding Mondlane's murder, see George Roberts, "The Assassination of Eduardo Mondlane: FRELIMO, Tanzania, and the Politics of Exile in Dar es Salaam," *Cold War Histories* 17 (2017): 1–19.

39. Ncomo, *Uria Simango*, 400.

40. According to Ncomo, Simango's downfall can be traced to the greed for power of the south-regionalist wing, allied with the Goan, *mestiço*, and white Marxists. Ibid.

41. Ibid., 193–97.

Chapter 4: Samora and the Armed Struggle, 1964–75

1. Raimundo Pachinuapa, interview.

2. Ibid.; Alberto Joaquim Chipande, interview.

3. Darch, *Historical Dictionary*, 283.

4. Helder Martins, "Samora na Luta Armada (1965–68)," in António Sopa, *Samora: Homen do Povo*, 111.

5. Oscar Monteiro, interview, March 6, 2019.

6. Field Notebook of Samora Machel, 1965–67, CDSM, folder 66.

7. For a discussion of these issues, see CDSM, folder 1.

8. See Samora Machel, "Nota de estudos para os instructores: Comprender a nossa tarefa," December 6, 1970, CDSM, folder 2: Documentos a FRELIMO; and Aquino de Bragança and Immanuel Wallerstein, *Quem é o inimigo?* (Lisbon: Iniciativas Editoriais, 1978), 201–25.

9. Interview with anonymous insubordinate student, n.d., collected by Paolo Israel.

10. Samora Machel to Josina Machel, October 22, 1970, CDSM, folder 4.

11. Christie, *Samora Machel*, 38–41; Sayaka Funada-Classen, *The Origins of War in Mozambique: A History of Unity and Division* (Oxford: African Minds, 2013), 298–301.

12. See Isaacman, *Tradition of Resistance*, 199.

13. Field Notebook of Samora Machel.

14. Martins, *Porque Sakani?*, 265–98.

15. FRELIMO, Dept. of Information, "Shaping the Political Line," *Mozambique Revolution*, no. 51 (June 1972): 18.

16. Cornwell, *Bush Rebels*, 93.

17. Ibid., 65.

18. Funada-Classen, *Origins of War in Mozambique*, 319.

19. Henriksen, *Revolution and Counterrevolution*, 118.

20. See *Biografia oficial de Josina Machel*, n.d., CDSM, folder 31; and Renato Matussa and Josina Malique, *Josina Machel* (Maputo: ARPAC, 2007).

21. Samora Machel to Josina Machel, October 22, 1970, CDSM, folder 4.

22. "Resolucões sobre ritos de iniciação," Segunda Conferência de Departamento da Defesa, February 20, 1971, CDSM, folder 2.

23. Samora Machel, *Mozambique: Sowing the Seeds of Revolution* (London: Committee for Freedom in Mozambique,

Angola and Guiné, 1975), 24; emphasis in original. For a history of the Organização da Mulher Moçambicana, see Helena Hansen, Ragnar Hansen, Ole Gjerstad, and Chantal Sarazin, "The Organization of Mozambican Women," *Journal of Eastern African Research and Development* 15 (1985): 230–44.

24. Civilians were inadvertently killed by land mines, which were one of the most effective tactical tools at the guerrillas' disposal (Alberto Chipande, interview).

25. Manuel Braz da Costa, interview, Lichinga, August 15, 1980.

26. Ibid.; Henriksen, *Revolution and Counterrevolution*, 123. Henriksen notes that when FRELIMO forces entered the settler zones of Manica and Sofala, they killed a white settler and his wife and there were also some attacks on European farms. While FRELIMO leaders publicly denied them, they privately acknowledged the attacks, claiming they were mistakes (127).

27. Allen Isaacman and Barbara Isaacman, *Dams, Displacement and the Delusion of Development* (Athens: Ohio University Press, 2013), 89.

28. Funada-Classen, *Origins of War in Mozambique*, 319.

29. Mondlane, *The Struggle for Mozambique*, 178.

30. Maria Teresa Veloso, interview, Maputo, August 24, 1977.

31. Samora Machel, interview, May 7, 1979.

32. Interview with Helder Martins, *World Medicine* 12 (January 26, 1977): 22.

33. FRELIMO, Dept. of Information, "Shaping the Political Line," *Mozambique Revolution*, no. 51 (June 1972): 25.

34. On the devastating effects of the forced cotton regime, see Allen Isaacman, *Cotton Is the Mother of Poverty* (Portsmouth, NH: Heinemann, 1996).

35. Samora Machel, *Mozambique: Sowing the Seeds*, 72–73.

36. Funada-Classen, *Origins of War in Mozambique*, 326–27.

37. The only exceptions were those few aldeamentos that were turned into model villages for propaganda purposes.

38. João Paulo Borges Coelho, "Protected Villages and Communal Villages in the Mozambican Province of Tete (1968–1982): A History of State Resettlement Policies, Development and War" (PhD thesis, University of Bradford, 1993), 160–69.

39. Ibid., 205. See also Arquivo Histórico de Moçambique, FMA, Cx. 107, Secretário Provincial de Terras e Povoamento, "Criação de um grupo de trabalho coordenador dos aldeamentos," December 22, 1971.

40. Peter Size and Fedi Alfante, joint interview, Chinyanda Nova, May 25, 1998.

41. *Australian*, no. 2359, February 3, 1972, in Arquivo Nacional de Torre do Tombo (ANTT), PIDE/DGSSC, Proc. 8743, CI (2), folder 2.

42. W. Nusey, "The War in Tete: A Threat to All in Southern Africa," *Johannesburg Star*, July 1, 1972.

43. Mustafa Dhada, *The Portuguese Massacre of Wiriyamu in Colonial Mozambique, 1964–2013* (New York: Bloomsbury Academic, 2016).

44. The Portuguese also paid a price, with over 130 soldiers killed and double that number seriously wounded.

45. Alberto Chipande, interview, CDSM.

46. Samora Machel to Josina Machel, October 20, 1970, CDSM, folder 4.

47. Barry Munslow, ed., *Samora Machel, an African Revolutionary: Selected Speeches and Writings* (London: Zed Press, 1995), xvii.

48. Samito Machel, interview, Maputo, March 25, 2019.

49. Ibid.

50. Oscar Monteiro, interview, March 26, 2019.

51. Ibid.

52. Christie, *Samora Machel*, 82.

53. Ibid., 83.

54. Ibid., 84.

55. FRELIMO was represented by Oscar Monteiro, the only lawyer involved in the armed struggle. The Portuguese delegation included Melo Atunes from the Armed Forces Movement and Almeida dos Santos, a member of the anti-Salazar opposition now minister of overseas coordination.

56. Oscar Monteiro, interview, March 26, 2019.

57. Isaacman and Isaacman, *Dams, Displacement*, 150–87.

58. A decade later, he articulated his concerns more fully in Aquino de Bragança, "Independência sem descolonizacão: A

transferência do poder em Moçambique, notas sobre os seus antecedentes" (paper presented at the conference "African Independence: Origins and Consequences of the Transfer of Power, 1956–1980," University of Zimbabwe, Harare, January 1985).

59. Henriksen, *Revolution and Counterrevolution.*

60. Munslow, *Samora Machel*, 5.

61. Ibid., 3.

62. Colin Darch and David Hedges, "Political Rhetoric in the Transition to Mozambican Independence: Samora Machel in Beira, June 1975," *Kronos* 39, no. 1 (2013): 41.

63. Ibid., 57.

64. Honwana, *Life History*, 171.

65. Paul Fauvet and Marcelo Mosse, *Carlos Cardoso: Telling the Truth in Mozambique* (Cape Town: Double Storey, 2003), 24.

66. Olívia Machel, interview, March 7, 2019.

Chapter 5: Politics, Performance, and People's Power, 1975–ca. 1977

1. Olívia Machel, interview, March 7, 2019.

2. Benedict Anderson, *Imagined Communities: Reflections on the Origin and Spread of Nationalism* (London: Verso, 1988).

3. *Review of African Political Economy* 2 (1975): 3.

4. António Alves Gomes, interview, Maputo, June 13, 2018.

5. Graça Simbine was born in Gaza in 1945. She went to a missionary school for primary education and was the only African in her class in Liceu António Enes, her high school, gaining the highest score in Mozambique in the national French examination. She studied at the Universidade de Lisboa and joined FRELIMO in 1973. Two years later, at the age of thirty, she became Mozambique's first minister of education and culture. She married Samora later that year. Graça Machel, interview.

6. Samora Machel, *The Tasks Ahead: Selected Speeches of Samora Machel* (New York: Afro American Information Service, 1975), 4.

7. This term is derived from Kelly Askew, *Performing the Nation: Swahili Music and Cultural Politics in Tanzania* (Chicago: University of Chicago Press, 2002).

8. Luís Bernardo Honwana, interview, Maputo, March 7, 2019.

9. Christie, *Samora Machel*, 170.

10. Malyn Newitt, *A Short History of Mozambique* (London: Oxford University Press, 2017), 156.

11. Rui Assubuji, "Samora's Legacy in Kok Nam's Photography" (paper presented at the conference "The Living Legacies of Samora Machel," Centre for Humanities Research, University of Western Cape, February 12, 2019).

12. Quoted in Paul Fauvet and Marcelo Mosse, *Carlos Cardoso: Telling the Truth in Mozambique* (Cape Town: Double Storey, 2003), 50.

13. António Pinto de Abreu, *Algumas das memórias que eu ainda retenho* (Maputo: Madeira e Madeira, 2017), 76.

14. Sarah Lefanu, *S Is for Samora: A Lexical Biography of Samora Machel and the Mozambican Dream* (New York: Columbia University Press, 2012), 107–8.

15. Rui Assubuji and Patricia Hayes, "The Political Sublime: Reading Kok Nam, Mozambican Photographer (1939–2012)," *Kronos* 39, no. 1 (2013): 66–111. This performance was not unique to Samora. Leaders on the left and right from Castro to Mussolini have been depicted tilling the land and engaged in other critical labor for the nation.

16. Samora Machel, "A Nossa Luta," *Notícias de Beira*, June 7, 1975.

17. Oscar Monteiro, the senior legal advisor in the Lusaka Accord negotiations, was only thirty-three. Prakash Ratilal was four years younger when he was appointed the principal monetary official and vice governor of the Central Bank. Oscar Monteiro, interview, Matola, March 21, 2019; Prakash Ratilal, interview, Maputo, March 16, 2019.

18. Samora Machel, *Establishing People's Power to Serve the Masses* (Dar es Salaam: Tanzania Publishing House, 1977), 7.

19. Roberta Washington, personal communication, New York, August 26, 2019.

20. Benedito Luís Machava, "The Morality of Revolution: Urban Cleanup Campaigns, Reeducation Camps, and Citizenship in Socialist Mozambique (1974–1988)" (PhD diss., University of Michigan, 2018), 202.

21. On how colonial and postcolonial states defined "wicked women," see Dorothy L. Hodgson and Sheryl A. McCurdy, "*Wicked" Women and the Reconfiguration of Gender in Africa* (Portsmouth, NH: Heinemann, 2001).

22. Machava, "Morality of Revolution," 18.

23. Ibid., 15.

24. *Tempo* (Maputo), January 1, 1978, 53–54.

25. Michael T. Kaufman, "Mozambique Is Viewed as Africa's Best Hope for the Flowering of Socialism's 'New Man,'" *New York Times*, November 14, 1977.

26. Fernando Ganhão, "Samora," in *Samora: Man of the People,* ed. António Sopa (Maputo: Maguezo Editores, 2001), 17.

27. Helder Martins, *Porquê Sakrani? Memórias dum médico duma guerrilha esquecida* (Maputo: Editorial Terceiro Milénia, 2001), 91.

28. Darch, *Historical Dictionary*, 80.

29. Teodato Hunguana, interview, Maputo, June 21, 2018.

30. João Ferreira, interview.

31. Samora also engaged in serious private discussions with Cardoso. For an excellent study of his life and career, see Fauvet and Mosse, *Carlos Cardoso*. According to Graça Machel, "they had a strong intellectual relationship—even when they disagreed" (63).

32. In 1981, the government established a commission to impose guidelines limiting who had access to the stores, how much each family could purchase, and what products would be available.

33. José Luís Cabaço, interview.

34. Ibid.

35. Samora Machel, "Knowledge and Science Should Be for the Total Liberation of Man," *Race & Class* 19, no. 4 (1978): 400.

36. Samora Machel, *Fazer de escola uma base para o povo tomar o poder* (Maputo: Instituto Naçional dos Livros e Discos, 1979), 11–12.

37. Samora Machel, interview, May 7, 1979.

38. Judith Marshall, *Literacy, Power, and Democracy in Mozambique: The Governance of Learning from Colonization to the Present* (Boulder, CO: Westview, 1993), 91–103.

39. Judite Frederico de Almeida e Faria to Samora Machel, June 25, 1975, CDSM, folder 17.

40. José Luís Cabaço, "The New Man," in Sopa, *Samora: Man of the People*, 106.

41. Ibid., 103–11.

42. "Song for Samora," n.d., CDSM, folder 29.

43. Samora Machel, "Knowledge and Science," 400.

44. UNICEF/WHO Joint Committee on Health Policy, *National Decision-Making for Primary Health Care* (Geneva: WHO, 1981).

45. Alexandre Gonçalves, "Priorité à la médicine préventive," *Afrique-Asie* 217 (July 1980): 47.

46. David Morton, *Age of Concrete: Housing and the Shape of Aspiration in the Capital of Mozambique* (Athens: Ohio University Press, 2019), 220.

47. Allen Isaacman and Barbara Isaacman, *Mozambique: From Colonialism to Revolution* (Boulder, CO: Westview, 1983), 139.

48. Similar problems plagued the literacy campaign. As one Canadian teacher noted, "the path proved to be both jagged and uneven, marked by advances and retreats and holds." (Marshall, *Literacy, Power, and Democracy*, 267).

49. By 1975, Mozambique was importing twice what it exported, the trade deficit had ballooned to $50 million, and the gross national product had dropped by 17 percent. Jens Erik Torp, *Industrial Planning and Development in Mozambique* (Uppsala: Scandinavian Institute of African Studies, 1979), 31.

50. Prakash Ratilal, "O processo de adesão de Moçambique às instituições de Bretton Woods" (unpublished paper, Maputo, April 30, 2010), 5.

51. See Isabel Casimiro, *"Paz na terra, guerra em casa": Feminismo e organizaçãoes de mulheres em Moçambique* (Recife: Editora UFPE, 2014).

52. Graça Machel, interview, March 24, 2019.

53. Ibid.

54. Ibid.

55. Olívia, Jucelina, and Ornila Machel, joint interview, Maputo, March 15, 2019; Samito Machel, interview, Maputo, March 23, 2019.

56. Olívia, Jucelina, and Ornila Machel, joint interview.

57. Olívia Machel, interview, March 7, 2019.

58. Samora Machel, interview, May 7, 1979.

59. Olívia Machel, interview, Maputo, March 8, 2019. Juce-lina, an outstanding runner, represented Mozambique in the 1980 Olympics. Edelson was considered one of the country's best swimmers.

60. Graça Machel, interview, March 24, 2019.

61. Nyeleti to Graça and Samora, September 23, 1981, CDSM, folder 8.

62. Hama Thay, interview.

63. Teodato Hunguana, interview.

Chapter 6: Samora Machel's Marxism and the Defense of the Revolution, 1977–82

1. Samora Machel, "The People's Democratic Revolutionary Process," in *Samora Machel, an African Revolutionary: Selected Speeches and Writings,* ed. Barry Munslow (London: Zed Press, 1995), 42.

2. Sílvia Bragança, *Aquino de Bragança: Batalhas ganhas, sonhos a continuar* (Maputo: Ndjira, 2009), 277–78.

3. See Julius Nyerere, *Freedom and Unity: Uhuru na Umoja* (Oxford: Oxford University Press, 1966).

4. In a conversation with Allen Isaacman and Iain Christie, Samora insisted that "the main characteristic of a socialist society is the establishment of cooperation and fraternity among men." Samora Machel, interview, May 7, 1979.

5. José Luis Cabaço, interview, June 11, 2018.

6. Oscar Monteiro, interview, March 5, 2019. See also Jorge Rebelo to Graça Machel, n.d., Centro de Documentação Samora Machel (CDSM), folder 27.

7. After Samora's death, Chissano and Guebuza dropped any pretense of being Marxists. Both returned to the church and became wealthy property owners, as did many of their former comrades.

8. Agência de Informação de Moçambique, *Information Bulletin* 9–10 (1977): 6.

9. Ibid., 11.

10. Samora Machel, interview, May 7, 1979.

11. Frelimo, *Central Committee Report to the Third Congress of Frelimo* (London: Mozambique, Angola, Guinea-Bissau Information Centre, 1978), 43–44.

12. Samora Machel, interview, May 7, 1979.

13. Frelimo, *Central Committee Report*, 216.

14. *Notícias* (Maputo), August 28, 1982.

15. Otto Roesch, "Socialism and Rural Development in Mozambique: The Case of Aldeia Communal 24 de Julho" (PhD diss., University of Toronto, 1986), *passim*.

16. M. Anne Pitcher, *Transforming Mozambique: The Politics of Privatization, 1975–2000* (Cambridge: Cambridge University Press, 2002), 95.

17. Alice Dinerman, *Revolution, Counter-revolution and Revisionism in Post-colonial Africa: The Case of Mozambique, 1975–1994* (London: Routledge, 2015), 68.

18. Paul Fauvet, personal communication, Maputo, July 13, 2019.

19. *Notícias* (Maputo), August 20, 1982.

20. In Gaza's Communal Village Eduardo Mondlane, 35 percent of the cooperative members worked collectively fifty days or less in a year (*Notícias* [Maputo], June 25, 1982).

21. David Ottaway and Marina Ottaway, *Afrocommunism* (New York: Africana, 1981), 87.

22. Samora Machel, interview, May 7, 1979.

23. Merle L. Bowen, "Peasant Agriculture in Mozambique: The Case of Chokwe, Gaza Province," *Canadian Journal of African Studies* 23, no. 3 (1989): 355–79.

24. Marcia Catherine Schenck, "Socialist Solidarities and Their Afterlives: Histories and Memories of Angolan and Mozambican Migrants in the German Democratic Republic, 1975–2015" (PhD diss., Princeton University, 2019), 44.

25. These ideas were stressed in a speech by Graça Machel, minister of education, to students leaving for Cuba in 1977 (*Notícias* [Maputo], September 3, 1977).

26. Ratilal, "O processo de adesão," 7.

27. Business International, *Mozambique: On the Road to Reconstruction and Development* (Geneva: Business International, 1980), 50–51.

28. Pitcher, *Transforming Mozambique*, 82.

29. Joseph Hanlon, *Mozambique: Who Calls the Shots?* (Bloomington: Indiana University Press, 1991), 12.

30. Ratilal, "O processo de adesão," 5.

31. Hanlon, *Mozambique*, 7–11.

32. Prakash Ratilal, interview, Maputo, March 23, 2019. These talks broke down when Samora rejected demands that Mozambique end food subsidies and reduce expenditures on health, education, and housing. The parties did reach agreement in 1985.

33. Samora Machel, interview, May 7, 1979.

34. Samora Machel, *Establishing People's Power to Serve the Masses* (Dar es Salaam: Tanzania Publishing House, 1977), 7.

35. Samora Machel, interview, May 7, 1979.

36. Samora Machel, "Make Beira the Starting-Point for an Organizational Offensive," in Munslow, *Samora Machel*, 73.

37. António Alves Gomes, interview, Maputo, March 3, 2019.

38. Included among the "compromised" were a small number of FRELIMO supporters who had been imprisoned by the Portuguese. Because they had not participated in political education during the armed struggle, some were initially considered suspect. See Benedito Luís Machava, "State Discourse on Internal Security and the Politics of Punishment in Post-Independence Mozambique (1975–1983)," *Journal of Southern African Studies* 37, no. 3 (2011): 60.

39. António Alves Gomes, interview, March 3, 2019.

40. "Para compreender as crimas contra o povo e do estado," *Tempo* (Maputo), March 18, 1979, 18–22.

41. Frelimo, *Central Committee Report*, supp. 6.

42. Samora Machel, speech at the Sixth Conference of Heads of State and Government of the Non-Aligned Countries, Havana, Cuba, September 4, 1979, Agência de Informação de Moçambique, *Information Bulletin* 39 (1979), supp. 6.

43. Marcelino dos Santos, interview, Maputo, August 2, 1977.

44. Allen and Barbara Isaacman, "Mozambique Tells Big Powers: 'Stay on Your Own Blocs,'" *Christian Science Monitor*, November 18, 1980.

45. Quoted in John S. Saul, *The State and Revolution in Eastern Africa* (New York: Monthly Review Press, 1979), 443.

46. Frank Wisner to Graça Machel, October 22, 1986, CDSM, folder 4.

47. See Stephen A. Emerson, *The Battle for Mozambique: The Frelimo-Renamo Struggle, 1977–1992* (Solihull, UK: Helion, 2014).

48. For documentation of these abuses, see Robert Gersony, *Summary of Mozambican Refugee Accounts of Principally Conflict-Related Experience in Mozambique* (Washington, DC: Department of State, Bureau for Refugee Programs, 1988).

49. Vernácio Leone, interview, Estima, May 19, 1998.

50. Their accounts are confirmed in Gersony, *Summary of Mozambican Refugee Accounts*, and William Minter, *Apartheid's Contras: An Inquiry into the Roots of War in Angola and Mozambique* (London: Zed Press, 1994), which also documents coercive mechanisms used by RENAMO to prevent desertions and intimidate the population under its control.

51. Emerson, *Battle for Mozambique,* 165.

52. RENAMO's leader, Afónso Dhlakama, boasted to Portuguese journalists that South African defense minister Magnus Malan had made him a colonel and assured him that his army was now part of the South African Defense Force. Colin Legum, "The Counter Revolutionaries in Southern Africa: The Challenge of the Mozambique National Resistance," *Third World Reports* (March 1983): 13.

53. José Luís Cabaço, interview, June 11, 2018.

54. Gersony, *Summary of Mozambique Refugee Accounts.*

55. Sérgio Chichava, "'They Can Kill Us but We Won't Go to the Communal Villages!': Peasants and the Policy of 'Socialisation of the Countryside' in Zambezia," *Kronos* 39, no. 1 (January 2013): 112–30; Dinerman, *Revolution, Counter-revolution,* 122–26; Christian Geffray, *A causa das armas: Antropologia da guerra contemporânea em Moçambique* (Porto: Afrontamento, 1991).

1. Margaret Hall and Tom Young, *Confronting Leviathan: Mozambique since Independence* (Athens: Ohio University Press, 1997), 156–57.

2. Prakash Ratilal, interview, March 23, 2019.

3. M. Anne Pitcher, *Transforming Mozambique: The Politics of Privatization, 1975–2000* (Cambridge: Cambridge University Press, 2002), 103–6.

4. "Report from the Commission for Economic and Social Directives: Frelimo Fourth Party Congress, 1983," reproduced in Allen Isaacman and Barbara Isaacman, *Mozambique: From Colonialism to Revolution* (Boulder, CO: Westview, 1983), 157.

5. Allen Isaacman, "Mozambique Rethinks Marxism, Encourages Private Enterprise," *Christian Science Monitor*, June 15, 1983.

6. "Report from the Commission," 198, 200.

7. Isaacman, "Mozambique Rethinks Marxism."

8. Pitcher, *Transforming Mozambique*, 106.

9. José Luis Cabaço, interview, June 13, 2018.

10. Pitcher, *Transforming Mozambique*, 117.

11. Samora Machel, *Establishing People's Power to Serve the Masses* (Dar es Salaam: Tanzania Publishing House, 1977), 7.

12. Samora Machel, interview, May 7, 1979.

13. Hall and Young, *Confronting Leviathan*, 75.

14. Samora Machel, "Make Beira the Starting-Point for an Organizational Offensive," in Munslow, *Samora Machel*, 73.

15. Teodato Hunguana, interview, June 21, 2018.

16. Quoted in Benedito Luís Machava, "The Morality of Revolution: Urban Cleanup Campaigns, Reeducation Camps, and Citizenship in Socialist Mozambique (1974–1988)" (PhD diss., University of Michigan, 2018), 107.

17. Ibid., 112.

18. Paulo Zucula, interview, Maputo, March 13, 2019.

19. Machava, "Morality of Revolution," 113.

20. Ibid., 15.

21. See, for example, João M. Cabrita, *Mozambique: The Tortuous Road to Democracy* (New York: Palgrave, 2000), 96.

22. Machava, "Morality of Revolution," 15.

23. Carmen Zucula, interview, Maputo, March 16, 2019.

24. Anonymous interview, Maputo, March 28, 2019.

25. Arlindo Chilundo, interview, Maputo, March 9, 2019.

26. Teodato Hunguana, interview, June 21, 2018.

27. Machava, "Morality of Revolution," 154.

28. António Alves Gomes, interview, June 21, 2018.

29. Personal communication from Paul Fauvet, Maputo, July 10, 2019.

30. António Alves Gomes, interview, June 21, 2018.

31. Ibid.

32. José Luís Cabaço, interview, June 13, 2018.

33. António Alves Gomes, interview, June 21, 2018

34. José Luís Cabaço, interview, June 11, 2018.

35. Ibid.; António Alves Gomes, interview, June 21, 2018

36. Oscar Monteiro, interview, Matola, March 15, 2019.

37. Samora Machel's closing statement at the signing of the Nkomati Accord, March 16, 1984, authors' collection.

38. Nyerere had previously told Monteiro that he understood Frelimo had few options and that it was not in the interest of independent Africa for Mozambique to be destroyed just so the ANC could engage in symbolic hit-and-run attacks (Oscar Monteiro, interview, March 15, 2019).

39. Paul Fauvet and Marcelo Mosse, *Carlos Cardoso: Telling the Truth in Mozambique* (Cape Town: Double Storey, 2003), 127.

40. Testimony of João Honwana to Truth and Reconciliation Commission, n.d., South African Historical Archives, file AL2878_BO1.75.01.29.01.

41. Oscar Monteiro, interview, March 15, 2019.

42. On South Africa's military support, see Hall and Young, *Confronting Leviathan*, 115–57.

43. Alice Dinerman, *Revolution, Counter-revolution and Revisionism in Post-colonial Africa: The Case of Mozambique, 1975–1994* (London: Routledge, 2015), 59.

44. William Finnegan, *A Complicated War: The Harrowing of Mozambique* (Berkeley: University of California Press, 1992), 142.

45. Jacinto Veloso, *Memórias em voo rasante* (Maputo: JV Editores, 2011), 159–94.

46. Anonymous interview.

47. Oscar Monteiro, interview, March 26, 2019.

48. José Luís Cabaço, interview, June 13, 2019.

49. Olívia Machel, interview, March 7, 2019.

50. Olívia, Jucelina, and Ornila Machel, joint interview.

51. Anonymous interview.

Chapter 8: Who Killed Samora?

1. *Diário de Moçambique,* October 22, 1986.

2. Jeremy Gavron, "Emotional Funeral for President Machel," *Daily Telegraph* (London), October 29, 1986.

3. *Tempo* (Maputo), November 23, 1986.

4. These are contained in "Telex, Cartas dos Paises Socialistas Sobre o Morte de Samora Machel," 1986, CDSM, folder 4.

5. Letter of condolence from Coretta Scott King to Graça Machel, October 27, 1987, CDSM, folder 4.

6. Godwin Matatu, "Machel's Mourners Snub Botha's Funeral Plea," *Observer* (London), October 26, 1986.

7. Christie, *Samora Machel: A Biography. (*London: Zed Press, 1988), xvii.

8. *Independent* (Lusaka), 22 October, 1986.

9. Lawrence Hamburger, interview, Cape Town, February 29, 2019.

10. *Diário de Moçambique,* 22 October 1982, 22.

11. Paul Fauvet and Marcelo Mosse, *Carlos Cardoso: Telling the Truth in Mozambique* (Cape Town: Double Storey, 2003), 156.

12. Daniel L. Douek, "New Light on the Samora Machel Assassination: 'I Realized That It Was No Accident,'" *Third World Quarterly* 38, no. 9 (2017): 2050–51.

13. Testimony of João Honwana, n.d., 14, SAHA, file AL2878_B01.5.75.01.29.01.

14. Fauvet and Mosse, *Carlos Cardoso,* 156.

15. Testimony of João Honwana, n.d., 10, SAHA, file AL2878_B01.5.75.01.29.01.

16. Fauvet and Mosse, *Carlos Cardoso*, 159.

17. Douek, "New Light," 2056.

18. Another objective for the meeting was to pressure Zaire's president Mobutu Sese Seko to stop supporting UNITA, an Angolan opposition group linked to both Pretoria and the United States.

19. Fauvet and Mosse, *Carlos Cardoso*, 162.

20. Douek, "New Light," 2055.

21. Fauvet and Mosse, *Carlos Cardoso*, 164.

22. Testimony of João Honwana, n.d., 6–7, SAHA, file AL2878_B01.5.75.01.29.01.

23. This material is located in the South Africa History Archives (SAHA), file AL2878_B01.5.75.01.29.01–29.09. For an informative exploration of these documents, see Douek, "New Light."

24. Fauvet and Mosse, *Carlos Cardoso*, 156.

25. Pretoria dismissed the claims regarding a beacon, which it labeled "communist propaganda," in an hour-long TV documentary produced by military intelligence and psychological officers and aired by the South African Broadcasting Company in 1987 (Douek, "New Light," 2056–58).

26. Testimony of João Honwana, n.d., 5, SAHA, file AL2878_B01.5.75.01.29.01.

27. Fauvet and Mosse, *Carlos Cardoso*, 166–67.

28. Ibid., 170.

29. Douek, "New Light," 2055.

30. Ibid., 2056. See testimony of Willem Oostuizen, n.d., 300–305, SAHA, file AL2878_B01.5.75.01.29.09.

31. Testimony of J. H. Basson, n.d., 166–67, SAHA, file AL2878_B01.5.75.01.29.09.

32. Testimony of João Honwana, n.d., 7, SAHA, file AL2878_B01.5.75.01.29.01.

33. Douek, "New Light," 2058.

34. Ibid., 2050.

35. Testimony of Debra Patta, n.d., 146, SAHA, file AL2878_B01.5.75.01.29.04.

36. Ibid., 45, 142.

37. Ibid., 116.

38. According to a radio-monitoring expert who was based in Swaziland at the time, it is possible that the Maputo VOR was functioning properly but was simply overridden by a more powerful signal (personal communication with William Minter, Washington, D.C., January 14, 2019).

39. António Alves Gomes, interview, Maputo, March 12, 2019.

Chapter 9: The Political Afterlife of Samora and the Politics of Memory

1. M. Anne Pitcher, "Forgetting from Above and Memory from Below: Strategies of Legitimation and Struggle in Post-socialist Mozambique," *Africa: Journal of the International African Institute* 76, no. 1 (2006): 96–98.

2. Maria-Benedita Basto, "The Writings of the National Anthem in Independent Mozambique: Fictions of the Subject-People," *Kronos* 39, no. 1 (2013): 193.

3. Perhaps the most memorable line in this version was "we are soldiers of the people fighting the bourgeoisie" (personal communication from Paul Fauvet, Maputo, July 13, 2019).

4. Amélia Neves de Souto, "Memory and Identity in the History of Frelimo: Some Research Themes," *Kronos* 39, no. 1 (2013): 289.

5. *Domingos* (Maputo), October 29, 1986; *Njigniritane*, November 2, 1986; *Domingos* (Maputo), October 20, 1997; *Demos* (Maputo), October 15, 1997; *Zambeze* (Beira), June 26, 2003.

6. *Savana* (Maputo), April 18, 2004; *Domingos* (Maputo), October 22, 2006; *Notícias* (Maputo), October 17, 2006; *Notícias* (Maputo), October 8, 2016.

7. José Luís Cabaço, interview, June 21, 2018.

8. Souto, "Memory and Identity," 292–95.

9. Quoted in Pitcher, "Forgetting from Above," 104.

10. Khalid Shamis, "The Mbuzini Memorial: A Film Project" (paper presented at the conference" The Living Legacies of Samora Machel," Center for Humanities Research, University of Western Cape, February 12, 2019).

11. David Hoile, *Mozambique: Propaganda, Myth and Reality* (London: Mozambique Institute, 1991); Victor Igreja, "Frelimo's Political Ruling through Violence and Memory in Postcolonial Mozambique," *Journal of Southern African Studies* 36, no. 4 (December 2010): 781–99; Sérgio Chichava, "'They Can Kill Us but We Won't Go to the Communal Villages!': Peasants and the Policy of 'Socialisation of the Countryside' in Zambezia," *Kronos* 39, no. 1 (January 2013): 112–30.

12. Janne Rantala, "'Hidrunisa Samora': Invocations of a Dead Political Leader in Maputo Rap," *Journal of Southern African Studies* 42, no. 6 (November 2016): 1162.

13. Ibid., 1174.

14. Ibid., 1172.

15. Azagaia, interview, Maputo, March 30, 2019.

16. Rantala, "'Hidrunisa Samora,'" 1162.

17. António Alves Gomes, interview, June 21, 2018.

18. José Luís Cabaço, interview, June 21, 2018.

19. Alpheus Manghezi, "Samora Machel: Man of the People," in *Samora: Man of the People,* ed. Antonio Sopa (Maputo: Maguezo Editores, 2001), 135.

20. This *mapiko* song from Shitunda was composed by songmaster Bernardino Juakali Namba, who had been arrested in 1960 for singing a song on the Mueda massacre. Recorded in Cabo Delgado, 2008, by Paolo Israel; Israel's translation.

21. Mang'anyamu Matambalale was an animal masquerade group. Recorded in Cabo Delgado, 2005, by Paolo Israel. In Paolo Israel, *In Step with the Times: Mapiko Masquerades of Mozambique* (Athens: Ohio University Press, 2014), 229.

22. Lingundumbwe Mbwidi (Nangade) was one of the last women's groups to perform historical dances. Recorded in Cabo Delgado, 2004, by Paolo Israel.

23. Musaemura Zimunya, "In Memory of Machel," in *Samora! Tribute to a Revolutionary,* ed. Chenjerai Hove, Gibson Mandishona, and Musaemura Zimunya (Harare: Zimbabwe Writers Union and Zimbabwe Newspapers Ltd., 1986), 14. *Braai* is Afrikaans for barbecue.

24. This was part of a conversation Allen had with a taxi driver who was transporting him around Maputo in May 2018.

25. Mantchiyani Samora Machel, *My love: A nossa forma de estar e a cegueira deliberada* (Maputo: Kapicua Livros e Multimédia Maputo, 2017).

26. Two days before our scheduled departure for Beira to speak to critics of Samora, Cyclone Ida devastated the city and much of the surrounding region, making our trip impossible.

27. Janna Rantala, "'*Chambocadas todos ali*': Ambivalence of Samora and His Time in Mozambican Rap" (paper presented at the conference "The Living Legacies of Samora Machel," Center for Humanities Research, University of Western Cape, February 12, 2019).

Conclusion: Samora's Life Revisited

1. *Nóticias*, April 9, 1984, 1.

Recommended Reading

Reference Books

Christie, Iain. *Samora Machel: A Biography.* London: Zed Press, 1988.

Darch, Colin. *Historical Dictionary of Mozambique.* Lanham, MD: Rowman and Littlefield, 2019.

Gomes, António Alves, and Albie Sachs, eds. *Samora Machel.* Cape Town: African Lives, 2018.

Le Fanu, Sarah. *S is for Samora: A Lexical Biography of Samora Machel and the Mozambican Dream.* Durban: University of Kwa-Zulu Natal Press, 2012.

Mondlane, Eduardo. *The Struggle for Mozambique.* London: Zed Press, 1983.

Newitt, Malyn. *A History of Mozambique.* Bloomington: Indiana University Press, 1995.

Sopa, António, ed. *Samora: Man of the People.* Maputo: Maguezo Editores, 2001.

Souto, Amélia Neves de, and António Sopa, eds. *Samora Machel: Bibliografia (1970–1986).* Maputo: Centro de Estudos Africanos, Universidade Eduardo Mondlane, 1996.

Memoirs

Bragança, Sílvia. *Aquino de Bragança: Batalhas ganhas, sonhos a continuar.* Maputo: Ndjira, 2009.

Caliate, Zeca. *A odisseia de um guerrilheiro.* Self-published, CreateSpace, 2014.

Chipande, Alberto Joaquim. *Como eu vivo a minha história.* Maputo: Kadimah, 2018.

Ferrão, Valeriano. *Embaixador nos USA.* Maputo: Ndjira, 2007.

Chissano, Joaquim Alberto. *Vidas, lugares e tempos*. Maputo: Texto Editores, 2010.

Honwana, Luís Bernardo. *A velha casa de madeira e zinco*. Maputo: Alcance, 2017.

Manghezi, Nadja. *The Maputo Connection: ANC Life in the World of Frelimo*. Cape Town: Jacana, 2009.

Martins, Helder. *Porquê Sakrani? Memórias dum médico duma guerrilha esquecida*. Maputo: Editorial Terceiro Milénio, 2001.

Mondlane, Janet Rae, ed. *O eco da tua voz: Cartas editadas de Eduardo Mondlane*. Vol. 1. Maputo: Imprensa Universitária UEM, 2007.

Monteiro, Óscar. *De todos se faz um país*. Maputo: Associação dos Escritores Moçambicanos, 2012.

Nihia, Eduardo Silva. *M'toto: Combatente pela liberdade*. Maputo: Imprensa Universitária UEM, 2016.

Pachinuapa, Raimundo, ed. *Memórias da revolução, 1962–1974: Colectânea de entrevistas de combatentes da luta de libertação nacional*. Vol. 1. Maputo: Centro de Pesquisa da História da Luta de Libertação Nacional, 2011.

Pelembe, Joao Facitela. *Lutei pela pátria: Memórias de um combatente da luta pela libertação nacional*. Maputo: self-published, 2012.

Veloso, Jacinto. *Memories at Low Altitude: The Autobiography of a Mozambican Security Chief*. Cape Town: Zebra Press, 2012.

Websites

JSTOR, Struggles for Freedom Southern Africa. https://www.aluka.org/struggles.

Mozambique History Net. Colin Darch, ed. http://www.mozambiquehistory.net.

Academic Studies

Adam, Yussuf. *Escapar aos dentes do crocodilo e cair na boca do leopardo: Trajectoria de Moçambique pós-colonial (1975–1990)*. Maputo: Promédia, 2005.

Alpers, Edward A. "Islam in the Service of Colonialism? Portuguese Strategy during the Armed Liberation Struggle in Mozambique." *Lusotopie*, no. 6 (1999): 165–84.

Bowen, Merle L. *The State against the Peasantry: Rural Struggles in Colonial and Postcolonial Mozambique.* Charlottesville: University Press of Virginia, 2000.

Cruz e Silva, Teresa. *Protestant Churches and the Formation of Political Consciousness in Southern Mozambique (1930–1974).* Basel: P. Schlettwein, 2001.

Darch, Colin. "Are There Warlords in Provincial Mozambique? Questions of the Social Base of MNR Banditry." *Review of African Political Economy*, no. 45/46 (1989): 34–49.

Darch, Colin, and David Hedges. "Political Rhetoric in the Transition to Mozambican Independence: Samora Machel in Beira, June 1975." *Kronos* 39, no. 1 (2013): 32–65.

Dhada, Mustafah. *The Portuguese Massacre of Wiriyamu in Colonial Mozambique, 1964–2013.* New York: Bloomsbury Academic, 2016.

Dinerman, Alice. *Revolution, Counter-revolution and Revisionism in Post-colonial Africa: The Case of Mozambique, 1975–1994.* London: Routledge, 2015.

Douek, Daniel L. "New Light on the Samora Machel Assassination: 'I Realized That It Was No Accident,'" *Third World Quarterly* 38, no. 9 (2017): 2045–65.

Emerson, Stephen A. *The Battle for Mozambique: The Frelimo-Renamo Struggle, 1977–1992.* Solihull, UK: Helion, 2014.

Finnegan, William. *A Complicated War: The Harrowing of Mozambique.* Berkeley: University of California Press, 1996.

Funada-Classen, Sayaka. *The Origins of War in Mozambique: A History of Unity and Division.* Oxford: African Minds, 2013.

Geffray, Christian. *A causa das armas: Antropologia da guerra contemporânea em Moçambique.* Translated by Adelaide Odete Ferreira. Porto: Afrontamento, 1991. Originally published as *La cause des armes au Mozambique: Anthropologie d'une guerre civile* (Paris: Karthala, 1990).

Hall, Margaret, and Tom Young. *Confronting Leviathan: Mozambique since Independence.* Athens: Ohio University Press, 1997.

Hanlon, Joseph. *Mozambique: The Revolution under Fire.* London: Zed Books, 1984.

Isaacman, Allen. *Cotton Is the Mother of Poverty: Peasants, Work, and Rural Struggle in Colonial Mozambique, 1938–1961.* Portsmouth, NH: Heinemann, 2004.

Isaacman, Allen, and Barbara Isaacman. *Dams, Displacement, and the Delusion of Development: Cahora Bassa and Its Legacies in Mozambique, 1965–2007.* Athens: Ohio University Press, 2013.

———. *Mozambique: From Colonialism to Revolution.* Boulder, CO: Westview, 1983.

———. *The Tradition of Resistance in Mozambique: Anti-colonial Activity in the Zambesi Valley, 1850–1921.* Berkeley: University of California Press, 1976.

Manning, Carrie. *The Politics of Peace in Mozambique: Postconflict Democratization, 1992–2000.* Westport: Greenwood, 2002.

Marcum, John A. *Conceiving Mozambique.* Cham, Switzerland: Palgrave Macmillan, 2018.

Marshall, Judith. *Literacy, Power, and Democracy in Mozambique: The Governance of Learning from Colonization to the Present.* Boulder, CO: Westview, 1993.

Matusse, Renato. *Coronel-General Fernando Matavele: De cidadão vulgar a patriota invulgar.* Maputo: Texto Editores, 2012.

Mboa, Matias. *Memórias da luta clandestina.* Maputo: Marimbique, 2009.

Minter, William. *Apartheid's Contras: An Inquiry into the Roots of War in Angola and Mozambique.* London, Zed Press, 1994.

Munslow, Barry. *Mozambique: The Revolution and Its Origins.* London: Longman, 1983.

———, ed. *Samora Machel, an African Revolutionary: Selected Speeches and Writings.* London: Zed Press, 1995.

Newitt, Malyn. *A Short History of Mozambique.* London: Oxford, 2017.

Roesch, Otto. "Renamo and the Peasantry in Southern Mozambique: A View from Gaza Province." *Canadian Journal of African Studies* 26, no. 3 (1992): 462–84.

Saul, John S., ed. *A Difficult Road: The Transition to Socialism in Mozambique.* New York: Monthly Review Press, 1985.

———. *The State and Revolution in Eastern Africa.* New York: Monthly Review Press, 1979.

Sheldon, Kathleen. *Pounders of Grain: A History of Women, Work, and Politics in Mozambique.* Portsmouth, NH: Heinemann, 2002.

Tembe, Joel das Neves, ed. *História da luta de libertação nacional.* Vol. 1. Maputo: Ministério dos Combatentes, Direcção Nacional da História, 2014.

———, ed. "Uhuru ni Kazi: Recapturing MANU Nationalism through the Archive." *Kronos* 39, no. 1 (November 2013): 257–79.

Vines, Alex. *RENAMO: From Terrorism to Democracy in Mozambique?* 2nd rev. ed. London: James Currey, 1996.

Wilson, K. B. "Cults of Violence and Counter-violence in Mozambique." *Journal of Southern African Studies* 18, no. 3 (September 1992): 527–82.

Young, Tom. "The MNR/RENAMO: External and Internal Dynamics." *African Affairs* 89, no. 357 (October 1990): 491–509.

Index

256

OHIO SHORT HISTORIES OF AFRICA

ROBERT MUGABE

SUE ONSLOW AND MARTIN PLAUT

Zimbabwean President **Robert Mugabe** (1924–2019) sharply divided opinion and embodied the contradictions of his country's history and political culture. As a symbol of African liberation and a stalwart opponent of white rule, he was respected and revered by many. This heroic status contrasted sharply, in the eyes of his rivals and victims, with repeated cycles of gross human rights violations. Mugabe presided over the destruction of a vibrant society, capital flight, and mass emigration precipitated by the policies of his government, resulting in his demonic image in Western media.

This timely biography addresses the coup, led by some of Mugabe's closest associates, that forced his resignation after thirty-seven years in power. Sue Onslow and Martin Plaut explain Mugabe's formative experiences as a child and young man; his role as an admired Afro-nationalist leader in the struggle against white settler rule; and his evolution into a political manipulator and survivalist. They also address the emergence of political opposition to his leadership and the uneasy period of coalition government. Ultimately, they reveal the complexity of the man who stamped his personality on Zimbabwe's first four decades of independence.

Sue Onslow is deputy director of the Institute of Commonwealth Studies, School of Advanced Study at the University of London. She has written widely on British foreign policy and decolonization, and southern Africa in the Cold War era.

Martin Plaut is senior research fellow at the Institute of Commonwealth Studies, School of Advanced Study at the University of London. He was Africa editor, BBC World Service News, until 2013. He has since published three books on South Africa and Eritrea, including *Promise and Despair: The First Struggle for a Non-Racial South Africa.* He has advised the UK Foreign Office and the US State Department on African affairs.

Robert Mugabe

Sue Onslow and Martin Plaut

OHIO UNIVERSITY PRESS

ATHENS

Ohio University Press, Athens, Ohio 45701
ohioswallow.com
© 2018 by Ohio University Press
All rights reserved

Printed in the United States of America
Ohio University Press books are printed on acid-free paper ⊗ ™

Cover illustration and design by Joey Hi-Fi

28 27 26 25 24 23 22 21 20 19 18   5 4 3 2 1

Library of Congress Cataloging-in-Publication Data
Names: Onslow, Sue, 1958- author. | Plaut, Martin, author.
Title: Robert Mugabe / Sue Onslow and Martin Plaut.
Other titles: Ohio short histories of Africa.
Description: Athens, Ohio : Ohio University Press, 2018. | Series:
Ohio short
   histories of Africa | Includes bibliographical references and index.
Identifiers: LCCN 2018000073| ISBN 9780821423240 (pb : alk.
paper) | ISBN
  9780821446386 (pdf)
Subjects: LCSH: Mugabe, Robert Gabriel, 1924- |
   Presidents--Zimbabwe--Biography. | Zimbabwe--Politics and
government--1980-
Classification: LCC DT3000 .O57 2018 | DDC 968.91051092--dc23
LC record available at https://lccn.loc.gov/2018000073

Contents

Illustrations

Maps

Plates

Following page 172

Tables

Abbreviations

Abbreviation	Full Name	Significance
ANC	African National Congress	South African liberation movement
AU	African Union	Successor of OAU since 2001 as the continental body uniting African states
CAF	Central African Federation	A short-lived British creation, uniting Northern and Southern Rhodesia [today Zambia and Zimbabwe] with Nyasaland [present day Malawi], 1953–63
CIO	Central Intelligence Organisation	Security Service founded by whites in 1964, but retained by Mugabe
FRELIMO	Frente de Libertação de Moçambique	Mozambican liberation movement
GPA	Global Political Agreement	Agreement to establish a coalition government of ZANU-PF and MDC, 2008
MDC	Movement for Democratic Change	Opposition party born out of trade unions and civil society organizations in 1999

OAU	Organisation of African Unity	Predecessor of the African Union as the continental body uniting African states in one organization, 1963–2002
SADC	Southern African Development Community	Founded April 1, 1980, the organization designed to unite independent African states in confronting the white government of South Africa; today mainly a regional developmental grouping
UDI	Unilateral Declaration of Independence	Independence from Britain by white Rhodesians, November 1965
ZANLA	Zimbabwe African National Liberation Army	ZANU's armed wing
ZANU	Zimbabwe African National Union	Mugabe's party, founded in 1963
ZANU-PF	Zimbabwe African National Union (Patriotic Front)	Mugabe's party after it united with Joshua Nkomo's ZAPU in 1987
ZAPU	Zimbabwe African People's Union	Led by Joshua Nkomo, founded in 1961
ZIPA	Zimbabwe People's Army	Short-lived attempt to unite the military wings of Zimbabwe's rival liberation movements, 1975
ZIPRA	Zimbabwe People's Revolutionary Army	ZAPU's armed wing

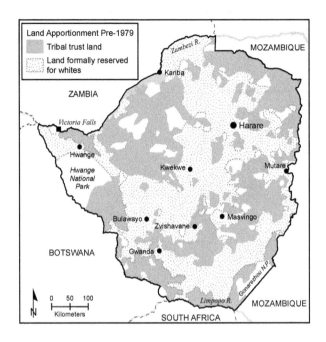

Map 1. Land apportionment pre-1979. Map by Brian Edward Balsley, GISP.

Map 2. June 2000 parliamentary elections. Map by Brian
Edward Balsley, GISP.

Introduction

On November 21, 2017, the Zimbabwean military forced President Robert Gabriel Mugabe to resign from office. At the age of ninety-three, he had been in power for thirty-seven years. He was worn down by the decades in office, falling asleep during official functions, and surrounded by sycophants. By the time he was overthrown, Mugabe appeared to be little more than an African despot, ruling via his security services and dominated by a much younger, rapacious wife who dreamed of succeeding him.

Yet Mugabe was, in reality, more than this caricature. His tragedy was that he stayed in office as leader of the country and head of his party, ZANU-PF,[1] for far too long. His real achievements had long since faded from public consciousness. When he finally resigned, there was a dominant public narrative of Zimbabwe as a tyrannical "basket case." Responsibility for this tragedy was laid squarely at his door. The truth is more complicated. Certainly, leadership in young African democracies has been a key factor in determining their postindependence trajectories. However, Zimbabwe's

13

fortunes since independence cannot be distilled down to the attitude and actions of just one man. Mugabe, both as a dedicated leader within a liberation movement and as a political personality, was intricately linked to the outcome of the original struggle for independence and the end of white domination in 1980. He shaped the course of his country since independence, but Western misunderstanding of the importance of political cultures and structures of power in Zimbabwe has oversimplified the picture.

Robert Mugabe emerged as head of the political wing of one of the two main liberation movements—the Zimbabwe African National Union (ZANU)—through a combination of luck, guile, ideological focus, and persuasion. As prime minister, and later as president of Zimbabwe, Mugabe proved to be a master of "divide and rule." He had perfected these political skills while maneuvering between rival factions within his own movement then operating from external bases in neighboring Mozambique in the mid-1970s. Mugabe won the initially reluctant endorsement of the guerrilla fighters as they took on the army of the white regime. In 1979 Britain finally persuaded all the factions involved in the conflict to come to London for talks at Lancaster House. Mugabe still believed he could win the guerrilla war, and was reluctantly persuaded by African heads of state to accept British-supervised multiparty elections. The war-weary population, influenced by the infiltration of ZANU guerrillas, was persuaded of the attractions—as well as the necessity—of a victory for Mugabe's party in the 1980 independence elections. From then on, Mugabe worked to ensure the unquestioned dominance of his party and policies. In the mid-1980s he unleashed a violent campaign against the rival liberation movement, Zimbabwe African People's Union (ZAPU), and its leader, Joshua Nkomo. Thousands died in southwestern Zimbabwe, and Mugabe progressively arrogated more and more power to himself.

Mugabe's political and international reputation achieved its high point between 1987 and 1995. At the outset of Zimbabwe's independence, the country attracted remarkable international goodwill and a substantial injection of foreign funds, including British and Canadian financial support for a land reform program. There were dramatic improvements in education and primary health care. By the early 1990s, Mugabe had established an international political image and reputation as one of the senior successful national liberation leaders turned politicians, a pillar of the modern Commonwealth, and a key regional advocate for transition in neighboring South Africa. Mugabe's rhetoric of reconciliation and nation building, which was so striking to both the suspicious white population and the international community, faded as the years went on. He renewed calls for a continuation of the liberation struggle's goals. By the end of the 1990s, his star was in relative eclipse. His thwarted attempts to accelerate land reform and domestic austerity, along with mounting social and political challenges at home, caused Mugabe's popularity to decline, while his reputation was damaged on the international stage by the flawed decision to intervene in the war in the Democratic Republic of Congo.

As he had done before, and would do time and again in future under pressure from multiple quarters, Mugabe presented himself as the only solution to his movement, ZANU-PF's problems. At the same time, he buckled in the face of war veterans' demands for larger pensions—with disastrous financial results for the Zimbabwean public purse. Then Mugabe decided to answer calls for land redistribution by encouraging the initially haphazard invasion of mainly white-owned farms. From 2000 the country experienced a progressive economic meltdown and the growing militarization of government administration. Long accustomed to using violence as a political language, his party's leadership and security chiefs unleashed a program of abduction, beatings, and intimidation against the opposition and civil society activists.

By this point, the country was effectively being run by the security apparatus's Joint Operations Command. At the apex of these structures of state security sat Robert Mugabe with key elites who had a direct interest in sustaining his rule. These members of the military and security services refused to let Mugabe stand down following the 2008 election. Mugabe proved to be the ultimate political survivor, repeatedly outsmarting political rivals. When participating in a Government of National Unity from 2009 to 2013, Morgan Tsvangirai, the most serious political opponent to emerge since independence, found himself outmaneuvered by the veteran leader. Mugabe served the interests of the military, political, and business elites who kept him in power for nearly four decades, until they finally turned on him, fearful that he would install his wife, Grace, in the presidency.

As a man and a leader, Mugabe proved a deeply complex and contradictory individual. His character mixed qualities and vices in equal measure. Like Nelson Mandela, he was a "prison graduate," having spent ten years in a Rhodesian jail. The experience taught him remarkable self-possession. He could contain his anger at personal tragedy, but was deeply embittered by racial and social injustice in Rhodesia and its delayed transition to black majority rule. A highly intelligent and learned man—as Lord Carrington (the key British negotiator at the Lancaster House talks) once observed—he could be magnanimous when things were going his way, but vicious in adversity. His cabinet colleagues realized that resigning from office was not an option, as he could turn on them as potential political rivals. Instead, they should wait to be dismissed.

An intellectual shaped by his Jesuit education and his Marxist beliefs, there was a remarkable consistency to his thinking. Despite the fact that the rest of the world and the international political economy had moved on, he resolutely refused to do so. A bibliophile—even as Zimbabwe's leader—Mugabe would fly incognito to

London to browse the shelves of Dillon's bookshop. An eloquent and charismatic speaker, he tailored his message according to his audience, and ensured that his words resonated directly with the hopes and aspirations of his listeners. His particular outlook, his political skills, his dominance of his party, and his extraordinary longevity in office meant Robert Mugabe's personal history is woven through that of his country. The two cannot be separated.

Controversial and Divisive Leader

Robert Mugabe was head of the Zimbabwean liberation movement, the Zimbabwean African National Union (ZANU), then his country's first prime minister in April 1980. Zimbabwe had experienced a particularly tumultuous path to internationally recognized independence from formal British rule: from quasi-autonomous colonial status in 1923 as Southern Rhodesia; then as part of the decade-long experiment of the Central African Federation; and subsequently as Southern Rhodesia and the defiant attempt at white settler independence from London between 1965 and 1979. From the outset in 1980, his role as head of government, then executive head of state was an especially important variable in Zimbabwe's postindependence history. Addressing the challenges of colonial legacies and meeting expectations for development and progress placed particular demands on his vision, personal qualities, intellectual attributes, and ability to sustain necessary political alliances. None of this could be separated from the wider international environment. Western governments hoped Zimbabwe under Mugabe's leadership would represent a successful transition to multiracial, modified capitalism which could be held up as a model for neighboring apartheid South Africa. The Zimbabwean economy was the second-most-diversified economy in sub-Saharan Africa. At the independence celebrations, President Julius Nyerere of Tanzania advised Mugabe, "You have inherited a jewel. Keep it that way."[1] However, under Mugabe's leadership, the country advanced in some areas, only to lurch into cycles of crisis and decline, disappointing these early hopes.

Mugabe embodied the complexity and contradictions of Zimbabwe's history and political culture. At independence, his emphasis on racial and political reconciliation antedated President Nelson Mandela's call for national solidarity in South Africa in the 1990s. To the puzzlement of Western observers, Mugabe remained respected and revered by admirers across the African continent as a symbol of African liberation. "To many he is the embodiment of black pride, of achieving true psychological independence, of sticking two fingers up to the arrogant West."[2] This heroic status contrasted sharply—in the eyes of his many detractors—with repeated cycles of social and economic disruption, capital flight, mass unemployment, and emigration, precipitated by the policies of his government.

Since 2000, Zimbabwe's political economy has endured a roller-coaster ride, directly associated with the Fast Track Land Reform Programme (FTLRP). Following the short-lived stabilization of the economy between 2009 and 2014, there have been renewed socioeconomic problems, an acceleration of political protest via social media, and bitter factional infighting within the ruling party, ZANU-PF, over the presidential succession. Furthermore, Mugabe's leadership is rightly associated with the brutal repression of political opposition in the early years of independence. There have been repeated patterns of state-engineered violence and intimidation around election campaigns, and against individual political opponents, together with massive corruption and theft of Zimbabwean state assets. There is bitter historical irony in the fact that, just as in the period of Rhodesia's unilateral declaration of independence, Zimbabwe's fractured political and social landscapes since the 1990s have contributed to regional instability. For many, it is now difficult to remember Mugabe was once widely admired as a progressive leader, a respected chairman of the Non-Aligned Movement (1986–89), a leading Front Line States[3] president in the international struggle against apartheid, and a pillar of the Commonwealth in the 1980s and 1990s. There is also the bitter irony that Mugabe hosted the Commonwealth summit in 1991 which produced one of the key declarations of this international association, supporting democracy, good governance, human rights, and the rule of law.[4]

Although journalists and commentators remarked over the years that Mugabe "changed," the highly respected analyst Stephen Chan has pointed out that he was remarkably consistent in his outlook and ideological beliefs. Instead, it is the rest of the world which has moved on.

What of Mugabe's own ideological thinking and thought processes? Political commentators have debated whether Mugabe was an African nationalist, a determined socialist, a Marxist, or a Maoist in his ideological thinking.[5] "'Marxist'—The term is relative. . . . Mugabe made it clear in our discussions that his greatest mentor was Marshal Tito of Yugoslavia, the founder of the Non-Aligned Movement, from whom he had learned that adherence to communism does not necessarily mean subservience to Russia."[6] Mugabe was brought up in the Roman Catholic faith, but British intelligence realized he was not a practicing Catholic by the late 1970s, although his first wife, Sally Mugabe, herself a convert, regularly went to Mass. Arguably, there are elements of all these ideological and values-based influences in his outlook, which have endured to the present day. As leader of the revolutionary movement, the Zimbabwe African National Union (ZANU), he certainly impressed journalists that he was persuaded by the egalitarian and redistributive qualities of socialism. Mugabe found Marxism to be a useful theoretical critique of white settler capitalism, as well as offering appropriate structures of linkages between party organization and the wider population. However, despite acute international concern over what were deemed to be his extreme Marxist views, at independence he did not seem to have been as committed to

22

Marxism as the radical nationalist leadership in neighboring Mozambique or Angola.[7]

Mugabe's earlier ideas and advocacy of "developmental nationalism" hardened through the years of crisis and decline in the 1990s and 2000s into a narrower version of Afro-radicalism and nativism, with its reliance on cultural nationalism. This was not a rejection of his earlier ideological outlook, but rather a reinvigoration, which drew increasingly upon "an exclusionary and more adversarial imagery of the nation."[8] The Fast Track Land Reform Programme (see chapter 5) encapsulated his view of state prescriptions combining with popular mobilization to reinforce a particular version of Zimbabwean national identity. This then was a question of "changing deployment and articulation of nationalism."[9]

Mugabe's Afro-radicalism was purposive—as a state ideology, and also as a self-serving political imagination for a specific elite. This was not a fixed construct, but susceptible and available for manipulation and control. (It must be said Mugabe himself was remarkably consistent in his arguments.) In Mugabe's case, this articulation of Zimbabwean nationalism—referred to as "patriotic blackness" by some commentators[10]—enabled him to reenergize his links and support among the people (the *"povo"*). It also provided an alternative legitimacy and countermanding narrative to multiracial liberalism and cosmopolitanism, typified by the challenge of the Movement for Democratic Change (MDC) and its supporters. In this mind-set, the MDC represents a regressive, counterrevolutionary, "neocolonial" force, and one that must be resisted at all cost. This mirrors the paradox at the heart of other postcolonial transformations by national liberation movements elsewhere in Southern Africa. In Mugabe's case, his thinking typified a vision which combines radicalization and embourgeoisement, satisfying the Zimbabwean dispossessed and their demands for social justice, and the vested interests of ZANU-PF party elite and its allies in their search for resource accumulation. In this version of the African national project, Zimbabwe will achieve national unity and solidarity. It demands the merger of party and state to wield control of the economy according to a narrative which privileges indigenous advancement, expressly to resist rollback by external, malign, "neocolonial" forces.

Under Mugabe's leadership, therefore, ZANU-PF's decolonization project was not simply a need; it was an entitlement. Thus, those who point out Mugabe did not understand the influences and importance of the forces of globalization on Zimbabwe—only one of his many degrees is in economics—miss the point. Other critics of his ideological thinking focused on his great age and outdated ideas—that by the age of ninety-three, his ideas of monopoly capitalism (formed in the 1950s and 1960s) and conviction of the autonomy of the party-state as paramount socioeconomic actor and driver of development did not correspond to the current international political economy. This outlook was

24

also fundamentally out of step with the predominant thinking of international financial institutions and international money markets.

Mugabe's Afro-radicalism remained undaunted and undimmed. He remained intent on socioeconomic transformation and its intimately associated racial dimensions through redistributive justice and indigenization of the economy, forging unity and solidarity before moving then to the (increasingly distant) phase of social equity. While to his critics this way of thinking proved to be the ultimate disruptive "denial politics," and hypocritical in the extreme, to Mugabe, these ideological practices and tenets were entirely rational. His criteria had long been national assertion and identity, agency and status, and a rejection of Western "imperialist" knowledge cultures and neoliberal prescriptions. Everything should be focused on expunging the "colonial personality" of Zimbabwean state and society. This also was bound up in Mugabe's view of what now defines the nation, who is a citizen—and correspondingly, who is not—and ultimately, what comprises a "good Zimbabwean." This definition was intimately connected to belonging to a particular political community, participating in and endorsing the ZANU-PF project, with Mugabe as its leader and keeper of the flame of patriotic memory.[11]

Mugabe's Afro-radicalism should also be seen in a broader context beyond the domestic sphere, as it had direct implications for Zimbabwe's foreign policy during his time in power. Responsibility for foreign policy was concentrated in his office, and in his position as first prime minister then president. Mugabe's advocacy and standing in the Non-Aligned Movement in the 1980s was a deliberate attempt to chart a more independent course in Southern Africa in the Cold War era—a "rough neighborhood," given apartheid South Africa's counter-insurgency activities—which was equidistant between the superpower blocs. This was a concerted effort to give Zimbabwe greater room for maneuver and more influence on the international stage. Until 2003, he also used the postcolonial modern Commonwealth as a platform to promote Zimbabwe's national interests, and to criticize both the United States and the United Kingdom (particularly over the crisis of the American invasion of Grenada in 1983.) His Afro-radicalism was also bound up with his view of revitalized Pan-Africanism, manifest through the Southern African Development Community and the Organisation of African Unity (OAU) and its successor organization since 2001, the African Union (AU). (This determined assertion of African identity and entitlement in opposition to what he deemed to be Western imperialism, and Zimbabwe's own progressive diplomatic isolation, led him to collaborate actively with the maverick Libyan leader, Muammar Qaddafi, in the late 1990s and 2000s, with sinister consequences.[12]) Mugabe long regarded the AU's economic agenda, and its evolving peace and security architecture, through the lens of African postcolonial autonomy in the international community. This was an extension of expunging the "colonial personality" of international interference, aid, and assistance to the continent, involving "weaning" the AU from foreign donor support. Despite being Africa's oldest head of state, Mugabe was appointed chairman of the AU in 2015. His acceptance speech encapsulated his determination to ensure African control over its natural resources and to reduce foreign exploitation of its mineral wealth: "African resources should belong to Africa and to no one else, except to those we invite as friends. Friends we shall have, yes, but imperialists and colonialists no more."[13] (To Mugabe's chagrin, 60 percent of the AU's funding has come from international donors such as the World Bank, the European Union, and other individual Western governments.[14]) Mugabe's one-year appointment exasperated his many critics at home and in Western capitals, who felt it reflected poorly on the AU's agenda of good governance and human rights. However, after 1980 Mugabe refused to be deflected from his version of good government and African states' rights. He was indeed remarkably consistent in his arguments and approach.

As for his personal characteristics, Mugabe was supremely disciplined, and well into late middle age, would wake early, around 4:30 a.m., exercise, meditate, and then return to his books. This was a regime he established in his thirties in Ghana and maintained throughout his incarceration by the Rhodesian government, exile in Mozambique, and even after his election as prime minister and then president of Zimbabwe. This denotes determined self-control—using routine to instil order at the core of his daily life, even when surrounded by political turmoil, violent disorder, and upheaval. Unlike Nelson Mandela, Mugabe emerged from prison in the mid-1970s into an extraordinary degree of factional infighting within his movement, tumultuous liberation politics, and regional criticism and dissent. He therefore faced intense challenges which required remarkable personal resilience, inner conviction, the ability to marshal a disciplined team, and a ruthless determination to exploit weakness and opportunity.

Over the years his political opponents repeatedly described Mugabe as intellectual but withdrawn, emotionally cold but with extraordinary personal energy. On first meeting him in Lusaka in December 1974, his domestic opponent Bishop Abel Muzorewa characterized him as slender and intense: "He was quite the opposite of the imagined big-shouldered militant."[15] British foreign secretary David Owen, his political antagonist in the 1970s, likened him to "a coiled spring, tense and very prickly and also somewhat withdrawn."[16] "Reserved, almost shy in manner, Mugabe at first impression seemed more cut out for the priesthood than for leadership of a political party. This was soon belied by his formidable intelligence and steely determination."[17] Another British foreign secretary, Lord Carrington, was struck by his poise and lack of bitterness at his long imprisonment. "I am not bitter against people personally. . . . But I am bitter against the system, the regime."[18] He impressed

Swedish officials in 1977 (whom he was approaching for substantial financial support) as a humble, soft-spoken, and intelligent man—the very opposite of the expected popular stereotype of a guerrilla leader as "fierce, rugged, pugnacious, bombastic and permeated through and through with megalomania."[19]

In contrast to this moderate picture, as a leader post-1980, he came across as "very opinionated." President Ronald Reagan found their encounter in 1983 rather trying: "He talked a monologue for 20 mins. Got round to our—as he put it—intervening in Angolan affairs because of our effort to get Cuba out of Angola. Then moved to El Salvador and Nicaragua. I caught him taking a breath and interrupted." Reagan noted tartly that Zimbabwe had by that point voted against the USA in the UN even more than the Soviets.[20]

However, great liberation fighters are not necessarily great nation builders,[21] and Mugabe was not even a proven combatant in the liberation war. This placed him at a disadvantage in the eyes of the proven guerrilla commanders, and those who were more radical in their outlook within the ZANU-PF Central Committee. Once in power, did Mugabe display "transformative leadership," showing courage, integrity, and intellectual honesty? The following chapters will argue that at times, the answer is "yes," although Mugabe lacked emotional intelligence and capacity for empathy. Over his long political career he demonstrated a remarkable ability to keep certain constituencies on side, to mobilize and inspire them. To his chagrin, he was regarded as a lesser leader than Nelson Mandela—he certainly did not provide responsible and enlightened leadership in the Western sense. It is fair to describe his as an amoral style of leadership, but also a curiously hybrid one, with its emphasis on anti-imperialism, constitutional forms, and electoral legitimacy. There is a long-lasting cult of respect for his leadership among some Zimbabweans, although he was ultimately responsible for unleashing periods of ruthless violence to solidify and perpetuate ZANU-PF's rule. His love of Savile Row suits, admiration for the British monarch,[22] and cultivated British accent when speaking English sat oddly with his vehement denunciation of British imperialism and interference in Zimbabwe's sovereign affairs.

Over the course of his long political career, Mugabe fell out with all of his former radical nationalist allies and colleagues. His relationship with his rival as a nationalist leader, Joshua Nkomo, was also fraught with difficulty throughout the liberation struggle period. Their mutual antagonism degenerated into bitter recrimination in the 1980s, before Nkomo's party ZAPU was subsumed into ZANU-PF in 1987. Unlike the less charismatic Mugabe, Nkomo had the "quality of the common touch" and approachability.[23] Within the ZANU-PF hierarchy, Mugabe progressively fought with his former comrades, who became his most vocal critics (see chapter 8). As his former ZANU colleague Ibbo Mandaza has pointed out, plotters within ZANU-PF tried to unseat their leader since at least the 1980s,[24] yet his version of electoral autocracy continues to triumph. Contemporary observers felt the death of his first wife, Sally, in early 1992, removed a crucial restraining influence on his political outlook.[25] In recent years Mugabe's relationship with a core coterie within the ZANU-PF Politburo was underpinned by his connections with his own ethnic subgroup, the Zezuru. This "trust" network became increasingly important with the passage of time and his advancing age. His grip on power went beyond personalized control, as these connections provided mutually reinforcing patrimonial networks. These informal networks also fed into the formal institutions of the state, as the judiciary, the executive, the administration, and business have been progressively co-opted by party control and patronage. This matrix of relationships is compounded by the militarization of state administration since 2000.[26] Mugabe sat at the apex of this pattern of power and privilege, which represents the "ZANU-fication" of the Zimbabwean state.

To his neoliberal detractors, then, Mugabe poses an object lesson in the dangers of political elites trying to pursue economic policies or developmental models in isolation from the international political economy. At home, Mugabe's attachment to election processes to legitimate his party's continued political preeminence was paralleled by his willingness to license violence to achieve political goals. A conviction politician dedicated to the decolonization of Zimbabwean society, he remained constant to his belief in redistribution in the name of the *povo* and in the likelihood of malign agency of hostile Western imperialist and neocolonial forces. His example and message still have considerable contemporary resonance in South Africa, while even his African critics privately admire his successful defiance of Western lecturing. As a political persona, he represented a complex amalgam of European ideological thinking of revolutionary transformation and Zimbabwean ethnic and cultural particularism. His stress on nationalist ideology and its particular version of Zimbabwean black nationalism combined with a vast network of corruption and patronage. This represents a fusion of a nationalist transformation agenda, an enduring authoritarian political culture inherited from the "white settler" colonial period, "spoils politics" of greed and corruption, and the expedient use of the security apparatus. Mugabe was part of the "complex picture of how individuals and groups became bound up in the project of state- and nation-building, despite contesting or even rejecting aspects of it."[27] In sum, he embodied the dictum: l'Etat, c'est moi.

2

Birth of the Revolutionary

Mugabe's formative years in colonial Southern Rhodesia had a lasting influence on his political beliefs. He was born on February 21, 1924, at the small Roman Catholic Kutama Mission in the impoverished Zvimba Communal area, about fifty miles outside the colonial capital, Salisbury. He was the third surviving child of Bona and Gabriel Mugabe. His maternal grandparents were farmers from the Zezuru community, which forms part of the wider Shona people.[1] Biographers have emphasized the modest circumstances of his childhood and his father's abandonment of the family in search of work in Bulawayo following the death of his older brother in 1934. At the age of nine, Robert Mugabe became the nominal man of the household. The departure of his father cemented his devotion to his mother. Bona Mugabe imbued her son with the sense that he was destined for great things, and consistently stressed the importance of education and learning—much respected in Zimbabwean culture as the means of personal and familial advancement. The importance of learning was matched by her emphasis on the importance of faith.

The Catholic fathers, too, exerted a particular influence on the young Mugabe, not least according to the tenets of a Jesuit education: "Give me the boy and I will show you the man." His education instilled in Mugabe a strong sense of personal discipline, an extraordinary fluency and ability to articulate his ideas in English, a remarkable cultivated British accent, and a forensic ability to deconstruct arguments, find flaws, and pose counterarguments. As a child, Mugabe was bookish and a "loner." Commentators stress his lifelong love of study, the importance he always attached to education and learning. Indeed, Mugabe is still described by his ZANU-PF colleagues as "the headmaster"—which suggests a stern disciplinarian and austere authority figure. The habits of instruction, together with a conviction that ultimately he has all the right answers, clearly never left him. Others have emphasized his remarkably trained mind, harnessed to his ability to listen.[2] While he might not be intellectually brilliant,[3] he was certainly clever, with a Jesuitical feel for politics and maneuver.

As a young man, Mugabe was also shaped by the environment of racial discrimination in Southern Rhodesia, with its evident white minority privilege. The Southern Rhodesian state's particular brand of white settler capitalism and extensive white land ownership contrasted with the Cartesian logic of his Catholic education. (The Catholic fathers in Southern Rhodesia later became widely known for their criticism of white minority rule and the violence associated with the state's counterinsurgency campaign in the Rhodesia UDI period. This led the Catholic fathers toward active support for Zimbabwean nationalism.) Therefore Mugabe was educated within an inspirational, rather than an institutional, church.[4] His mentor, Father Jerome O'Hea, also imbued him with a particular historical perspective of Irish nationalism and its long and ultimately victorious struggle against British imperial rule, partially achieved with the creation of the Irish state in 1922. During the Lancaster House conference in the autumn of 1979, Mugabe told a British delegate that he would like to pay his respects at Father O'Hea's grave.[5]

Mugabe's formative political experiences were also infused with the diverse political traditions of Zimbabwe's contested history and the development of the nationalist movement. Violence has long been embedded in the political landscape of the country. The Ndebele migration from South Africa led to the establishment of their hegemony over the existing peoples in the 1840s, continuing a pattern of "raiding, conquest, incorporation and assimilation of other communities, groups, and individuals as they migrated to the north."[6] Another surge of violence accompanied the arrival of the Pioneer Column, funded by the South African–based mining magnate, Cecil Rhodes. This led to the crushing of the Ndebele state. The subsequent Chimurenga wars of the 1890s, which united large sections of the Shona and Ndebele in revolt against white seizure of their land, were similarly victories for white colonial violence. In

1900, the defeat of the revolt by the Shona chief, Mapondera, meant that African resentment and attempts to dislodge colonial rule thereafter adopted a less confrontational approach.

A period of attempted accommodation followed, through "a proto-nationalist" period between the two world wars. During Mugabe's childhood and adolescence in the 1920s and 1930s, African political mobilization built upon self-help structures and activities of church groups and solidarity organizations. This political mobilization then moved into more formal structures of trade union organization (particularly within the Rhodesian railways and other state-run bodies) and voters' associations. These African organizations were relatively small-scale and focused on their own group interests, aiming their activities at securing concessions from the colonial administration rather than acting as a political voice for the black Zimbabwean masses. As protest organizations, they sought better government and the inclusion of their members in the colonial elite project. The most effective association in mobilizing mass support was the Rhodesian Industrial Commercial Workers Union, which agitated for better pay and conditions as well as against police harassment and the restrictive pass laws. However, in the 1930s "majority rule was a concept that neither the Africans nor the settlers entertained as a remote possibility. [White rule] seemed so entrenched at that point that few could doubt it as a fixed element of the natural order of creation."[7]

The failure of the Rhodesian colonial government to respond to emerging African political mobilization and these demands for accommodation radicalized African political consciousness. Change came in the post-1945 period. The Second World War acted as a catalyst, transforming the milder form of prewar "petition politics" for reform into more militant nationalism and mass mobilization. The 1950s saw demands for greater political representation and the removal of economic and residential discrimination. Politicized African soldiers in Southern Rhodesia were incensed that white soldiers were rewarded with land grants and generous financial support, whereas they had to return to the increasingly crowded African reserves and continued marginalization. African grievances were further aggravated by government displacement of rural communities to more arid and malarial areas to make way for white immigrants under the government-sponsored resettlement campaign.

This was also an era in which Southern Rhodesian society experienced dramatic change, with a rapidly expanding white population (from 30,000 in 1945 to 255,000 by 1965).[8] Class identity also played into the Southern Rhodesian social picture: the overwhelming majority of British migrants to Southern Rhodesia were ex-servicemen or economic migrants seeking an improved standard of living away from the grim austerity of postwar Britain. The country legalized job discrimination on the basis of color and limited African access to education. Furthermore, accelerated land alienation saw the additional eviction of over 100,000 Africans from their land. African grievances around land alienation were exacerbated by the appalling long-term conditions of African farmworkers on white-owned land. In addition, the expansion of the African urban workforce, a direct product of the country's industrialization and economic diversification, compounded problems of poor housing in the African urban settlement areas. These pressures were matched by rising demands for official recognition of workers' rights and trade union organization. There were also the daily humiliations of a racially divided and segregated society: separate queues in the post office, on buses and park benches, and at public amenities; and instances of racially motivated street harassment by white youth. As a youth, Mugabe had to endure the racial slurs and humiliations of colonial Rhodesia. Eddison Zvobgo, a childhood friend, described them both seeing the vicar's wife disinfecting the seat on which the young Mugabe and Zvobgo had been sitting, when invited to tea in form 4.[9]

Mugabe's world as a child and young man was therefore bound by racial and class hierarchies. His access to tertiary education and his employment prospects were consequently limited. He qualified as an elementary school teacher in 1941 and began teaching at Kutama in 1942, when he was eighteen. Coming from a relatively impoverished family, Mugabe did not have the means to apply to the University of Rhodesia. He worked briefly as a teacher at Garfield Todd's Dadaya New Zealand Churches of Christ Mission School in Midlands (where Ndabaningi Sithole was a fellow young teacher), earning the princely sum of £3.00 a month. Sponsored by his grandfather and Father O'Hea, Mugabe then spent two years at Fort Hare, the only black South African university, where he completed his teacher training education. There he met a number of South African black activists and was exposed to an extraordinary range of ideas of nationalist transformation and socialist modernity. These ideas emphasized black majority rule and the importance of state-directed development and centralized control of the economy. He was greatly influenced by ANC Youth Leaguers and the Africanist ideology of Anton Lembede. This was also his first encounter with Marxism, via contacts with the Communist Party of South Africa.

This was the era of the Central African Federation (CAF)—a decade-long British creation which fused the quasi-autonomous colony of Southern Rhodesia with the colonies of Northern Rhodesia and Nyasaland in 1953. This postcolonial federal experiment was short lived. As the 1950s progressed, the Conservative government in London was confronted by growing nationalist resentment within the CAF's composite parts. However, the CAF as an expanded economic area meant wider job opportunities for its inhabitants. Mugabe went to work in Northern Rhodesia, at a time of increasingly militant nationalism in Nyasaland and Northern Rhodesia against British colonial rule.

The catalyst of Mugabe's growing militancy was his move in 1958 to Ghana, where he worked at a teacher training college. As Mugabe later explained, "I went as an adventure. I wanted to see what it would be like in an independent African state."[10] He remained there for nearly three years, moving into the heady political climate of newly independent Ghanaian nationalism and of its charismatic leader, Kwame Nkrumah. It was also an era of considerable hope for African rapid "take-off" postindependence. In 1958, Mugabe attended the All African People's Conference in Accra, hosted by Nkrumah. The conference "openly declared independent Africa's support for the liberation struggles of colonised peoples of Africa."[11] Mugabe listened to Nkrumah speak in person on many occasions, and was inspired by his eloquent emphasis on "Pan-Africanism" as the means to "decolonise the African mind." Sally Hayfron, his colleague at Takoradi Teacher Training college and later his wife, remarked that their personal bond was grounded in their lengthy animated political discussions, shared outlook, and activism.

Mugabe's decision to return to Southern Rhodesia from Ghana in 1960 coincided with growing African nationalist dissent across the CAF, which heralded its dissolution in 1963. Spurred on by the success of African nationalist movements across the continent, Zimbabwean urban youth organization and trade union militancy, based in Bulawayo, fused to form the Southern Rhodesian African National Congress (SRANC) in

1958—soon known simply as the ANC. It was the first African/Zimbabwean political mass organization to demand black majority rule. Parallel attempts at accommodation by the African educated elite with the claimed "multiracial partnership" project and collaboration with white liberals, such as in the Inter-Racial Association and Capricorn Africa Society, were increasingly sidelined by this growing confrontational politics which fused urban youth resentment and trade union militancy with rural discontent.

Politics in Southern Rhodesia was becoming increasingly polarized. White resistance to accelerated black political and economic rights had already emerged in the late 1950s, in opposition to Prime Minister Garfield Todd, who was thought to be excessively sympathetic to African advancement. This white opposition was fueled by British prime minister Harold Macmillan's "wind of change" speech in Cape Town in February 1960 and its call for decolonization across sub-Saharan Africa. There was also the eruption of violence and descent into civil war in the Congo following Belgium's abrupt departure. The spectacle of lawlessness, attacks on remaining colonists, and white Congolese refugees camped on Salisbury showground entrenched white Rhodesian determination to ensure "responsible government" under white minority direction. Meanwhile, rising African nationalism combined with violent street demonstrations in Salisbury and Bulawayo resulted in a government crackdown, with the introduction of the Law and Order (Maintenance) Act which gave the Rhodesian authorities far-reaching powers of arrest and detention. Prime Minister Edgar Whitehead sought to bridge this divide with a drive for African advancement through a limited expansion of the franchise. The 1961 Constitution allowed for a modest advance of African voting rights through the creation of a complicated two-tier electoral roll. This constitution also proposed the election of fifteen African MPs to Parliament, but this was rejected by African nationalists. Whitehead also introduced a concerted drive to desegregate Rhodesian daily life, which proved deeply unpopular with the white electorate. A strong white backlash led to the victory of the reactionary Rhodesian Front in the December 1962 election. Ian Smith, a former fighter pilot with the Royal Air Force, emerged as a leading proponent of these right-wing policies.

This then was the febrile world of nationalist politics to which Mugabe returned from Ghana, on what was originally intended to be a short visit to his family. He was rapidly drawn into urban political activism. By now most members of the Zimbabwean nationalist elite rejected multiculturalism.[12] At this point Mugabe was very much in the mainstream of African nationalism, and was increasingly attracted to Marxist rhetoric of class antagonism. He was committed to the achievement of full black political rights, far-reaching economic redistribution, and Pan-Africanism. He threw himself into the Zimbabwean nationalist cause with the same single-minded fervor he had devoted to teaching. He was one of the first nationalists to advocate the shift to armed struggle, convinced that only this would overcome white resistance to the accelerated transfer of black political and economic rights. In 1961 he married Sally Hayfron, who matched her husband in her passion for politics and African advancement; she also shared his sense of injustice at colonial oppression and imperialist interference and control. By all accounts, theirs was a remarkable political marriage and a deeply affectionate personal relationship. Sally herself was intelligent, highly articulate, politically combative, and committed to the nationalist struggle. She also combined astute and instinctive judgment of character with shrewd political judgment and pragmatism, and was one of the very few people who could make Mugabe pause and reflect.

These were turbulent and fractious times in Zimbabwean urban politics. Within the next two years Zimbabwean nationalism went through three organizational name changes, culminating in the banning of the Zimbabwe African People's Union (ZAPU), then headed by trade union leader Joshua Nkomo. By this point the nationalist movement had made two important decisions: the shift to the acquisition of arms, sabotage, and ultimate armed confrontation to colonial rule; and the recruitment and military training of cadres overseas in Algeria, China, Czechoslovakia, Egypt, and Ghana. However, Zimbabwean nationalism was now also fatally fractured by personal rivalries and political difficulties, and the realities of an oppressive colonial state with greater force at its disposal. Mugabe had been one of those who criticized Nkomo's initial acceptance of the 1961 constitutional proposals in London as unlikely to accelerate African political rights. In 1963 ZAPU split into two parties with the creation of a new nationalist party, the Zimbabwe African National Union (ZANU). Unhappy with Joshua Nkomo's leadership, a group led by the Reverend Ndabaningi Sithole broke away and formed this rival political movement. Mugabe was appointed secretary general on the ZANU Central Committee.[13]

As the Central African Federation was breaking into its constituent parts and moving to independence as Zambia and Malawi, Zimbabwean nationalism's drive for black majority rule fractured into two deeply hostile and embittered political movements with limited appeal beyond the urban environment. The rival movements confronted each other on the streets. They also faced a repressive colonial state and its powerful security apparatus (the majority of whom were black). The white minority government in Salisbury collaborated with tribal chiefs in the rural areas who were determined not to see any erosion of their authority and control by their wayward "children." The political imagination of Rhodesia/Zimbabwe was thus a fractured and conflicted map of class, ethnic, linguistic, and racial divides. However, each African nationalist movement was focused on "a cult of unity"—"the obsession of African nationalist politicians with what they see as the vital need to present a united front," which led directly to hostility to opposition.[14] At this stage ZAPU remained the larger nationalist force, and Joshua Nkomo was by now well known internationally. Small groups of ZANU fighters were sent abroad for training (to Egypt, Ghana, the People's Republic of China, and Tanzania), but their political campaign had little actual impact inside Zimbabwe, as there was no base from which they could operate inside the country.

The political tide was moving against Mugabe and his fellow nationalists. The election of the Rhodesian Front, followed by Ian Smith's appointment as Rhodesian prime minister in April 1964, and then the advent of the Labour government in the United Kingdom in October 1964, set London and Salisbury on a collision course. This led directly to Rhodesia's unilateral declaration of independence (UDI) in November 1965. Smith and his Rhodesian Front colleagues were "white ostriches" who infuriated Prime Minister Harold Wilson and his civil servants. In the meantime, Mugabe and his colleagues in ZANU looked to London to stop Smith, if necessary by force. Ironically, at this point the UK high commissioner identified ZANU as the party more likely to reach some sort of negotiated settlement with the Rhodesian government, and even contemplated sending covert British funds to support the organization.[15] Nothing came of this idea, as London concluded African nationalism inside Rhodesia "remains divided, frustrated, proscribed and without a single national leader of real stature."[16]

International African solidarity was to be an important component in Zimbabwean radical nationalism's eventual victory in 1980. In 1963, the Organisation of African Unity set up the Liberation Committee, based in Dar-es-Salaam, to provide diplomatic and logistical support, as well as funding and publicity for all the liberation movements recognized by the OAU. However, the African heads were bitterly divided on the best method and strategy. Crucially, it was ZAPU which was recognized as one of the "Authentic Ones." In the run-up to UDI, the OAU offered diplomatic solidarity and support: the first OAU meeting of African heads of state denounced an impending declaration of independence by the Southern Rhodesian government, and also called for the immediate release of African nationalist detainees. Africa's leaders looked to Britain to stop the slide toward UDI, and to use force if necessary, but were sorely disappointed.

In August 1964 both ZANU and ZAPU were banned, and along with other Zimbabwean radicals, Mugabe was arrested "for subversive speech" and imprisoned. (Sally Mugabe was briefly detained for political protest in 1964.) He remained in prison for the next decade. When Wilson visited Salisbury in October 1965, in a last throw of the dice to prevent a unilateral declaration of independence, he insisted on meeting the jailed African nationalist leaders. As the third-ranking ZANU member,

46

Mugabe was included in the ZANU group which met the British prime minister. Wilson argued that the threat of economic sanctions was an appropriate alternative political lever to prevent the Rhodesian government's defiance of London and the international community.[17] To the African nationalists, sanctions were a farce and would not succeed.[18] The director of the Rhodesian Central Intelligence Agency, Ken Flowers, later recalled that Wilson's statement gave the Rhodesian cabinet their opportunity; there was a meeting within hours of Wilson's press conference, on November 1, 1965, which confirmed the decision to go for UDI.

The Labour government resolutely refused to launch a military strike against the white settler rebel government. London felt it was simply incapable of asserting its authority over the Smith government.[19] This was the product of a combination of geopolitical, military, and domestic factors: logistical difficulties; the relative strength of the Rhodesian armed forces, which had inherited the CAF's modern air capability; profound concern over the reliability of British pilots and troops being asked to fight the white settler government, which had supported Britain in World War II and included many ex-service men; and concern over the possibility of wider racial war. Rhodesian UDI was also a fraught domestic political issue, and the Labour government only enjoyed a parliamentary majority of four. Furthermore, the Labour government had considerable doubts about the divided Zimbabwe nationalist movements.

In all, Wilson's government did not believe that it possessed the "dispassionate constitutional power to hold the ring . . . to prevent the ambitions of the two communities reaching their present state of uncompromising mutual hostility."[20] Sanctions instead were regarded as the least bad option and—as Wilson argued—would bring the Rhodesian Front to heel "in a matter of weeks, if not months." This was a grave miscalculation. In 1966, with the backing of the UN Security Council, Britain did send ships of the Royal Navy to enforce a blockade off the Mozambican coast. The "Beira Patrol" (1966–75) had only a limited effect on Rhodesia, since oil and other key commodities continued to be imported via Lourenço Marques (Maputo) and South Africa.[21]

For the next decade Rhodesia seemed a defiant success story. Prior preparation by the Rhodesian government, South African financial and commercial collaboration and communications, and trading links through neighboring Portuguese-controlled Mozambique ensured that the rebel regime successfully defied international sanctions. Import substitution policies also boosted the Rhodesian economy, which enjoyed 7 percent growth until the mid-1970s. Sitting in Gonakudzingwa detention camp, close to the railway line to Portuguese Mozambique, detained nationalists could see sanctions-busting oil shipments from Lourenço Marques rolling toward Salisbury (now Harare). In 1966 and 1968 the small incursions of guerrillas from Zambia into the arid and sparsely populated Zambezi

48

valley were rapidly crushed by the well-equipped and better-trained Rhodesian security forces. Following the failure of further negotiations with the British government on HMS *Tiger* and HMS *Fearless* in 1966–68, the Rhodesian Front government seemed to be riding high.

The years from 1964 to 1974 were therefore bleak ones for Mugabe and his fellow detainees. He had no hope of being released, but regarded his imprisonment as a necessary sacrifice for the liberation struggle and generations coming after him. For much of this time, he was held in prison in Salisbury with fellow ZANU dissidents Maurice Nyagumbo and Edgar Tekere; the three adjacent cells opened out onto a confined, covered concrete exercise area approximately 20ft x 40ft. The prisoners whiled away time by a rigorous routine of exercise, academic study, and impassioned discussions on politics. Mugabe completed two university degrees at the University of London (by correspondence course) while he was in jail. These were also years of personal tragedy. His young son died of cerebral malaria in Ghana in 1966, and he was refused permission to travel to the funeral. He was allowed personal letters, although these were always vetted by the prison authorities. Sometimes it proved possible to smuggle messages.

In the meantime, the liberation struggle was moving on without him. Under Herbert Chitepo, a military alliance was gradually established with FRELIMO from 1968, and in 1970 a front was opened in Tete Province, Mozambique. The ZANU leadership in exile undertook a detailed review of the movement's political and military activities, in conjunction with Chinese military instructors. This emphasized the importance of political preparation of guerrillas and the rural population in target areas before launching a guerrilla campaign, as the keys to success. Consequently, conventional incursions were rejected in favor of a phased and gradual build-up of revolutionary activity, using the countryside to encircle the towns. The attack on Altena Farm in December 1972 marked a new phase in ZANU's armed struggle as its guerrillas began infiltrating northeastern Rhodesia. Sixteen months later, the Portuguese "Carnation Revolution" in Lisbon in April 1974, the associated collapse of Portuguese colonial rule in southern Africa and acceleration of Mozambique's independence under the FRELIMO liberation movement was to prove a regional geopolitical earthquake. Now the Salisbury government was confronted by a porous border 1,500 kilometers long and by growing guerrilla attacks and infiltration into tribal trust lands and rural areas. Prodded by the South African government, the Rhodesian government embarked on talks with African nationalists.

Mugabe's contribution to the liberation struggle over the next five years (1974–79) should be seen as one particular piece of the jigsaw of radical Zimbabwean nationalism, rather than "the answer" to this complex picture. He emerged only gradually as the principal political spokesperson for ZANU, arguably more because of the flaws and failings of his rivals than for his own dynamic, charismatic leadership. Mugabe also won only reluctant endorsement from African presidents. His appointment as political leader of ZANU in August 1974 was the product of prison politics and profound disillusionment with the party leadership. The willingness of the Reverend Ndabaningi Sithole to enter into talks with the Smith government was greeted with disgust by the ZANU detainees and culminated in Mugabe's nomination as leader. But no one outside Que Que prison knew him.[22]

Ironically, Mugabe owed his "break" to Ian Smith. Mugabe was "temporarily" released from prison in late 1974 to attend the "unity" talks in Lusaka. This international summit between African nationalist leaders and Ian Smith was backed by the leaders of the Front Line States, with the involvement of the South African prime minister, B. J. Vorster, in the hope that an international settlement could accelerate the transfer to black majority rule. However, Mugabe was clearly determined not to compromise with the Rhodesian Front government, as his loathing of colonialism was undiminished. Talks were "too early," and he bitterly resented what he regarded as African heads of state "selling us out." He agreed only under duress to go to Zambia for a preliminary meeting.

The Lusaka summit in December 1974 was a heated and divisive affair. Mugabe was not a popular choice to lead his political movement. President Nyerere of Tanzania was particularly trenchant in his criticism of

Mugabe's unsuitability. Nyerere was furious at the idea of a ZANU leader sent to Lusaka with the Rhodesian government's connivance. He refused to talk to Mugabe, and demanded he return to Rhodesia and only come back with Sithole. Sithole himself rapidly agreed to a unity pact with ZAPU. Fractures continued within the party leadership: while appearing to yield to concerted Front Line States' pressure for a united front and to enter into negotiations with the Smith government, Mugabe and a narrow circle of trusted friends made clandestine plans for a recruitment drive for ZANU's military wing—ZANLA—now based inside Mozambique. These activities soon aroused the attention of the Rhodesian security forces, who had only reluctantly released Zimbabwean political prisoners as part of a South African–Zambian backed amnesty. In April 1975 Edgar Tekere and Mugabe used their sympathetic Catholic networks to make a hurried escape into Mozambique.[23]

Mugabe's ten-year incarceration had stiffened his determination to establish an egalitarian people's state. But the signs were far from auspicious. As a political liberation movement, ZANU had been experiencing profound internal conflicts, exacerbated by personality, ideology, and ethnicity. These culminated in the assassination of the ZANU national chairman and leader of ZANU's external supreme council, Herbert Chitepo in Lusaka in March 1975. Convinced that Chitepo had been the victim of internal party conflicts, the Zambian authorities rounded up leading ZANU figures they believed were implicated in his death. (In fact, the Rhodesian security forces were responsible.) This political crisis and Ndabaningi Sithole's "de facto non-leadership" of the ZANU rump in Zambia had repercussions for the movement's military wing, ZANLA, now based in Mozambique, where Mugabe was now trying to assert his political authority. There was a short-lived attempt to unite the military wings of the rival liberation movements (ZANU and ZAPU) into ZIPA (the Zimbabwe People's Army). African leaders hoped that under veteran military commander Rex Nhongo (the *nom de guerre* of Solomon Mujuru) ZIPA would gradually lead to the withering away of the competing factions led by Mugabe, Sithole, and Nkomo. However, within twelve months ZIPA had itself unraveled. The collapse of this joint military effort meant that for the rest of the liberation war, the two rival liberation movements fought parallel campaigns, ZANU based in Mozambique and ZAPU based in Zambia. Although nominally politically collaborating under a Patriotic Front umbrella, the movements were in reality bitter opponents. Mugabe was particularly critical of Nkomo's decision to keep most of his forces in Zambia, while ZANU fighters attacking from bases in Mozambique were dying in clashes with better-armed and better-trained white-led soldiers inside Rhodesia.

Mugabe was not responsible for the shift of the liberation struggle to guerrilla war based on rural mobilization. This had taken place under Chitepo's leadership, and as a tactic, it was to prove decisive in the outcome of the nationalists' conflict with the Rhodesian State.[24] Mugabe's initial plan upon arriving in Mozambique had been to build up a following for his position as leader of ZANU in the refugee camps. However, the Mozambique nationalist leader Samora Machel—who was initially very suspicious of Mugabe, whom he first regarded as a possible Smith agent—put him under house arrest in Quelimane (a port city over 1,500 kilometers north of the capital Maputo) "to keep him out of trouble."[25] In Machel's view, leaders of an armed struggle should emerge from the guerrilla ranks. Machel's distrust of Mugabe only dissipated slowly—the youthful ZIPA fighters named him as a possible alternative leader to Sithole, since they regarded Sithole as "completely hopeless and ineffectual"; but they didn't really know him.[26] Ironically, just as Machel was very reluctantly shifting to support Mugabe as the ZANU political representative, the youthful guerrilla fighters who had contributed to his rise were poised to reject him. Mugabe's leadership style and ideological orientation had profoundly alarmed the fighters. Their leader (himself the former leading ZANLA political commissar) Wilfred Mhanda later reflected, "It became obvious very quickly that we'd made a terrible mistake . . . that he was arrogant, paranoid, authoritarian and ruthless, a man believing only in power."[27] A group of several hundred party cadres— some of whom were in Tanzania—were detained and some were murdered. Outspoken criticism of Mugabe following the massive loss of life in the Rhodesian raid at Chimoio in November 1977 was ruthlessly suppressed by ZANLA military leaders Tongogara and Nhongo. In this way, Mugabe succeeded in incarcerating and containing his youthful critics.

Equally important to fighting this protracted and increasingly brutal liberation struggle was the responsibility for carrying the struggle to the outside world. It was a slow process. Having been in jail since 1964, Mugabe had little domestic or international visibility. In terms of reaching an audience inside Rhodesia, the *Voice of Zimbabwe* was broadcast over Radio Mozambique every evening. Together with guerrilla infiltration and indoctrination, this was a key means of rural mobilization and the Rhodesians regularly sought to jam these transmissions.[28] (The increasingly brutal behavior of the Rhodesian counterinsurgency forces, and forced displacements under the Protected Villages Scheme, also served to alienate many in the rural areas.) The *Zimbabwean News*—ZANU's official publication— had a regular, if small, circulation. Unlike his later fellow "jail graduate," Nelson Mandela, Mugabe did not benefit from a sustained campaign by the international Anti-Apartheid Movement identifying him as the iconic figure of Zimbabwean nationalism. He owed his rise in international awareness to information networks and personal sympathy for national liberation movements among radical Commonwealth leaders. Thanks to Jamaican prime minister Michael Manley's personal invitation, it was Nkomo who was able to speak to Commonwealth leaders in closed session at the Kingston Commonwealth Heads of Government meeting in Jamaica in April 1975. The creation of the Patriotic Front (a nominal political alliance of his movement with Joshua Nkomo's ZAPU) in October 1976 was only thanks to pressure from Tanzanian president Julius Nyerere, who was determined that Zimbabwean nationalism should present a united opposition during the constitutional talks in Geneva.

By the autumn of 1976 Mugabe was gradually gaining international recognition as the political leader of ZANU, even if he remained a relative unknown quantity. He was chosen to lead the ZANU delegation to the Geneva conference and insisted his colleagues be released from Zambian jails. As a liberation leader, Mugabe had no experience of diplomatic negotiations—skills which the Commonwealth secretary general, Shridath ("Sonny") Ramphal, realized were notably lacking. Consequently, the Commonwealth Secretariat provided constant administrative support for the Zimbabwe liberation delegations throughout the three-month-long fractious meeting in Geneva. Puzzled CIA and M16 surveillance reports compared notes on whether Mugabe was a Soviet "client" and concluded that the Soviet legation in Geneva was as much in the dark as diplomatic intelligence in London and Washington. His austere style and demeanor contrasted sharply with the established figure of Zimbabwean nationalism, *bon viveur*

Joshua Nkomo, who was known to rely on the financial largesse of the chairman of the Lonrho mining group, Tiny Rowland, and on his willingness to provide air transport. Gradually developing international contacts, Mugabe managed to persuade his international listeners that ZIPA was under ZANU's control—rather than the other way around.[29] However, the Geneva conference broke up in acrimony in late 1976, and Mugabe was obliged to return to exile in Mozambique.

From Freedom Fighter to President of a One-Party State

Mugabe spent the next three years based in Maputo. His wife, Sally, who had been in London from 1970, lobbying for the ZANU nationalist cause, had already joined him in Mozambique in 1975. An immensely loyal and practical person who understood the symbolism of politics, she threw herself into providing practical support for the liberation struggle—such as securing cloth and sewing machines from donors, and even making clothes herself for combatants and refugees. Gestures such as these ensured she was seen "as a caring and concerned person who was doing her best to alleviate the suffering of the freedom fighters and refugees."[1] This was an important boost to her husband's political popularity.

These were difficult times for ZANU. Gaining President Machel's support was only one of Mugabe's problems. ZANU's fighters remained short of funds for weaponry, food, and supplies in the field. The Chinese remained the main source of support for Mugabe's political and military movement throughout the liberation struggle.[2] Although Beijing did not supply vast quantities of sophisticated heavy weaponry, it did provide substantial shipments of small arms, mines, and explosives. However, these were inadequate, and by the late 1970s Mugabe was obliged to look for additional support from socialist countries. He was repeatedly rebuffed by the Soviet Union and the East Germans (the GDR), who regarded ZANU as a "splitist organization" unworthy of aid, but did get arms from North Korea, Romania, and Yugoslavia. Similarly, Mugabe bitterly resented continued Soviet pressure for a merger with ZAPU (led by his rival, Joshua Nkomo) after 1976, as well as Moscow's criticism for describing Mugabe as a "Marxist-Leninist of Maoist thought."[3] He developed an antagonism toward the Soviet Union for its insensitivity and insulting refusal to accord him recognition. While ZANU was doing most of the fighting, Moscow further alienated Mugabe by denying ZANU sophisticated weaponry, while channeling weapons to ZAPU forces (which were largely sitting idle in Zambia). Mugabe's ideological and military indebtedness to Beijing and his enduring suspicion of Moscow considerably influenced Zimbabwe's foreign relations postindependence.[4]

Meanwhile, ZANU's rival liberation movement, ZAPU, based in Zambia, received the lion's share of international support through the OAU, the Soviet bloc, and the Anti-Apartheid Movement's international network. Mugabe remained determined to ensure that ZANU was not absorbed into Nkomo's organization, while quashing all attempts to challenge his leadership.

Having gained international exposure at the abortive Geneva conference, Mugabe ordered the arrest of 600 fighters in ZANU's military wing, ZANLA, to prevent a possible military rebellion. The 64 top commanders were detained, in appalling conditions, until February 1980, when they were released on Lord Carrington's insistence under the Lancaster House settlement.

By March 1977, Mugabe was formally declared president of ZANU and leader of the guerrilla movement at a ZANU Central Committee meeting. This endorsement by his colleagues (and crucially the top military commanders) marked the beginning of the "Mugabe era," and the cult of the leader, "Comrade Robert Mugabe." It also saw his short-lived domination of the guerrilla war phase. Tekere later characterized Mugabe's behavior as "very insecure" and described his "need to be surrounded by admirers" because "this make him feel stronger and more assured"[5]—combined with aptitude for domination and control, using divide-and-rule tactics.[6] It was an environment in which Mugabe was surrounded by people vying for power and seeking favors. Tekere commented that Mugabe "didn't expect his word to be final at the beginning. But he began to like the idea." It was the start of the Mugabe personality cult.[7]

Under his leadership, ZANU was restructured and reorganized, with the establishment of a new Central Committee. Mugabe brought in a new cohort of university graduates from the Zimbabwean diaspora in Europe and proposed a two-phase revolutionary struggle: first, a nationalist revolution with the overthrow of the white state, then a socialist revolution.[8] Internal and external discipline was vital—and was seen as requiring unalloyed loyalty. Dissension was regarded as rebellion.[9] Using the Leninist concept of "democratic centralism," Mugabe insisted that power had to be focused and concentrated. In practice, this resulted in a narrow leadership group where the leader had the final say. He won FRELIMO's support, as Samora Machel was also preaching centralized control.[10]

Mugabe continued to face tensions with the ZANLA military leadership,[11] but he succeeded in winning the support of ZANLA "old guard" guerrilla commanders Nhongo and Josiah Tongogara, who shared his profound and enduring hostility toward ZAPU. ZANU made Mugabe commander in chief of the military wing, ZANLA.[12] The formal links between the two were through ZANU's "war council," itself dominated by civilians, not guerrilla fighters. The military wing's penetration of Rhodesia was organized by geographic sector and broken down into detachments and section commanders. This meant that ZANLA, despite the poor quality of its armaments and often lamentable training of its guerrillas, possessed far greater organization and infiltration into Rhodesia than Nkomo's ZAPU, with its vastly superior weaponry. ZAPU's political decision to hold back the bulk of its forces reinforced the image of ZANLA as the movement truly fighting for the liberation of Zimbabwe.

How was ZANU's nationalism constructed? It fused anticolonialism and twentieth-century ideological thinking and organization with traditional national forces and beliefs, combining ideas of the progressive nation-state with populist African faith systems, social discontent, and national grievances. It drew directly on the role of Shona spirit mediums in the first Chimurenga struggle of the 1890s. This was a tactical maneuver aimed at winning the hearts and minds of the people in eastern Zimbabwe along the Mozambican border. Mugabe himself was later skeptical about spirit mediums. As he told Father Traber in April 1979, "There are just too many *midzimu* . . . far beyond the traditional Shona belief. It is all too much for my liking."[13] This comment reflects Mugabe's Westernized and elitist Zezuru sense of superiority over other Shona-speaking communities. However, with the help of the spirit mediums, ZANLA guerrillas were able to infiltrate areas and politicize the rural population, establish arms caches, and recruit aspiring fighters.

ZANLA recruited from particular Shona-speaking areas in eastern Zimbabwe, and then reentered and dominated the rural population—but crucially, both Zimbabwean radical nationalist movements appealed to and operated in both language groups inside the country. This was a complicated and often ugly picture of peasant mobilization. ZANU used protest literature and particularly music to denounce colonial rule. Popular African protest songs (known as Chimurenga music, with traditional instruments and rhythms) were used by guerrilla fighters in the camps and to mobilize support for the liberation struggle. However, there were also substantial levels of violence to co-opt rural support. Although the use of intimidation, mutilation, mass killings, and rape was officially against party instructions, in the field these tactics were often deployed to brutal effect. Caught between the Rhodesian security forces' increasingly ferocious counterinsurgency campaign and the guerrillas' deliberate use of violence as a political tool, it was the hapless rural population in eastern and southeastern Zimbabwe which bore the brunt.

At the same time there remained a sharp division between the leadership of the political and military wings of the struggle. Conflict arose when Mugabe was thought to be interfering in military matters, and vice versa.[14] Mugabe was relatively overshadowed by ZANLA's veteran military commanders, Nhongo and Tongogara, and only belatedly emerged as the symbol of the movement.[15] Mugabe did not possess a physically commanding presence and relied on his creativity and imagination to instill confidence. His willingness to fight for as long and as hard as was necessary to triumph was another important factor, although Mugabe was patently not a warrior. Instead he presented himself as the eloquent orator, whereas Tongogara was the charismatic, brilliant, but brutal military leader.[16] Mugabe's emergence as ZANU leader was controversial. Some detractors felt that this was a personal "power grab" that betrayed the political principles of their movement.[17]

Faced with internal tensions and factional machinations, Mugabe's heavy-handedness further complicated and exacerbated these strains. "What should have been an exercise in discipline turned into centralization of power" and the brutalization of young fighters.[18] The rebel fighters' grievances mounted against the corruption and elitism of the ZANLA commanders. Ethnic rivalries between the Karanga and Manica further complicated the struggle.

After Geneva, Mugabe lost what little faith he had had in diplomacy and a negotiated settlement. He was quite convinced the conflict could be settled only by "a bitter and bloody war," which could be resolved "only on the battlefield." It proved impossible to persuade him to talk to Ian Smith, and he was implacably insistent on the need for retribution. British foreign secretary David Owen picked up on Mugabe speaking to "a collective brief." However, he impressed Owen with his honesty.[19] Mugabe remained acutely skeptical of continued Anglo-American attempts to broker a settlement, unlike the pragmatist Joshua Nkomo, who was far readier to agree to a solution. Ultimately, though, it was Nkomo who miscalculated in thinking that by not splitting the Patriotic Front he would emerge as its eventual leader.

Between 1977–79 the civil war inside Rhodesia intensified dramatically, as ZANU forces increasingly infiltrated Rhodesia from neighboring Mozambique and the Rhodesian security forces retaliated. Against the escalating violence in the countryside, the Rhodesian Front government embarked on internal negotiations with the moderate nationalists, Bishop Abel Muzorewa, Sithole, and prominent Rhodesian traditional chiefs, leading to an Internal Settlement in March 1978. Owen then began months of clandestine diplomacy to see if the settlement could be widened to include Joshua Nkomo. Both the British and the Rhodesians were determined to exclude Mugabe from any power-sharing agreement. Owen's plans were wrecked by President Nyerere, who denounced Zambia's involvement and deeply embarrassed the Nigerian government, which had tried to help broker a deal.

Against this backdrop of public discord among Africa's leading statesmen, Mugabe remained intent on prosecuting the struggle. His New Year message to the ZANU faithful in 1979, code-named "*Gore reGukurahundi*" (The Year of the People's Storm), was accompanied by a massive recruitment drive and a stepping up of attacks all over the country, with the aim of establishing local committees under the direction of the party. (Groups of ZANLA troops 100 strong infiltrated Rhodesia, and by June there were at least 13,000 ZANLA guerrillas in the country.) The Muzorewa government offered an amnesty in the vain hope that Mugabe's and Nkomo's movements would lay down their arms. As the United Kingdom foresaw, it was only when the Internal Settlement failed to bring peace and stability to the country, with a resulting deadlock in the power struggle, that there would be a greater chance of an internationally negotiated settlement.

The arrival of Mrs. Thatcher in Downing Street in May 1979 proved to be a game changer in the history of the liberation war. Despite a vocal Conservative right wing which regarded Robert Mugabe as the demonic leader of the "pro-Soviet, totalitarian, terrorist Patriotic Front,"[20] Foreign Secretary Lord Carrington (with Thatcher's initially reluctant backing) embarked on one last diplomatic drive to resolve the long-running crisis. The Patriotic Front leaders were deeply angered at their exclusion from the Commonwealth Heads of Government conference in Lusaka in August and the summit's decision to convene an all-party conference in London in September. Having persuaded the head of the Zimbabwe/Rhodesian Government of National Unity, Bishop Muzorewa, to attend, the pressure was now on the liberation leaders to come to the table. Mugabe saw no need to negotiate, convinced that the tide of events was flowing his way: the longer the war lasted, the greater the chances of achieving his ultimate objectives and dictating his terms.[21] Aware of this, the Rhodesian security forces tried to assassinate him twice in Maputo in June 1979.[22] Mugabe only agreed to attend the London talks under intense pressure from southern African leaders at the Non-Aligned Movement meeting in Havana in early September 1979.

Throughout the Lancaster House talks it was deliberate British government policy "to run fast" and to drive the Zimbabwean nationalist negotiators hard.[23] The British were well aware that the unity of the Patriotic Front was largely a fiction.[24] With the painful lesson of the Geneva conference at the forefront of British thinking, a great deal of time and care was devoted to the framing of the all-party talks and the order in which issues where addressed.[25] Carrington's team exploited the "home turf" advantage and excluded the Americans and the Commonwealth as much as possible. Charles Powell was designated as the Foreign Office liaison official with ZANU and tasked with regular private meetings with Mugabe and his colleagues. Powell recalled meeting Mugabe, describing a cold, aloof, and isolated figure, sitting in his coat in a bleak hotel room near Marylebone. Carrington had astutely realized that Mugabe was "the one party who was not particularly enthusiastic about a conference or impatiently in favour of a settlement . . . reckon[ing] the tide of events was anyway flowing his way; that his people would, given time, outlast their enemies . . . that he was comparatively young; that he need assent to nothing unless it provided certainty that he would emerge on top."[26]

These were tense and bitterly controversial negotiations, fraught with brinkmanship and repeated threats of walkouts. In recognition of the political disaster which would ensue if Mugabe were to come to harm in London, Mugabe was protected by a Scotland Yard detail throughout the fifteen-week talks—a wise decision, as the Rhodesian secret service tried to assassinate him during the negotiations.[27] The accommodation of each of the Zimbabwean nationalist delegations was bugged by their British hosts, and summaries of their discussions were relayed to Carrington's team every morning when it would convene to discuss how to handle the day's negotiations. This ensured that the small British team was fully briefed on the thinking of the three Zimbabwean delegations and could tailor British handling of the conference discussions accordingly. Carrington's technique was to hold a series of bilateral meetings with each delegation, to present British proposals for the delegations to consider. Within a short space of time, Carrington would decree that there had been enough opportunity for discussion, and ask for their decision. There was a brutal logic to Carrington's approach, given the backdrop of the ongoing war in Rhodesia and massively destructive Rhodesian army raids in neighboring Zambia and Mozambique.

Mugabe viewed the conference proceedings with enormous distrust, betrayed by his nervous and agitated demeanor on meeting Carrington at the formal opening of the conference. By contrast, Joshua Nkomo made the greater impression as a negotiator and lead spokesperson for the Patriotic Front.[28] Mugabe was consistently quieter, listening carefully and only interjecting after others had declared their position. During each of the three great crises of the conference—over the constitutional proposals for land, the transition arrangements, and the ceasefire proposals the conference came perilously close to breaking up—it was Mugabe who was the most obdurate. It required the diplomatic input of multiple actors to achieve success.

Given the subsequent importance of land in Zimbabwean politics, it is worth considering Mugabe's part in the settlement that emerged at Lancaster House. "Stolen land" had been one of the key "national grievances" behind the liberation struggle, and the rhetoric of liberation fighters had stimulated popular expectations of far-reaching land restitution. Furthermore, since 1977, an international development fund of US$1.2 billion had formed an integral part of the Anglo-American proposals for an internationally recognized settlement. Therefore, although the British negotiators at Lancaster House were at pains to declare that this sum was no longer on the table, it had become embedded in popular nationalist expectations of land transformation and substantial British largesse. The available evidence points to a deliberate policy by Britain to manage a potentially explosive question, rather than an abnegation of responsibility, given the political and regional context of 1979.[29] This contrasted sharply with Mugabe's understandable declaratory stress on British moral responsibility as the formal colonial power. To Mugabe, land was important in terms of redressing the theft by a colonial regime and an element in the future transformation of the country's economy. Land therefore formed part of an agenda of power, as a key element of political mobilization, rather than the driving force to address land hunger.[30]

Mugabe was infuriated by the Muzorewa delegation's refusal to discuss points of difference with the Patriotic Front delegations. Speaking to a British journalist in

1990, he recalled: "At one time I said, 'Oh look here, why even on a fundamental issue like land don't you say something? You see, that was the main grievance throughout the war, land, land, land . . .' [Y]ou are Africans, how dare you accept that the proposition on land shall be governed by the Bill of Rights? We can't get anywhere with the Bill of Rights. Don't you remember your history? The land was never bought from us. Support our position on this one!' They said no, they could not."[31]

The southern African observer group of Botswana, Mozambique, Tanzania, and Zambia held regular sessions with Mugabe and Nkomo. These comprised informal evening meetings at the Commonwealth secretary general's private residence, as well as regular discussions between Commonwealth African high commissioners at Marlborough House, the headquarters of the Commonwealth Secretariat. The message from these meetings was that there was a well-established precedent in how land would be addressed in the constitutional discussions: either by prompt payment of adequate compensation for land or compulsory property purchase by the state. Mugabe was incensed that Zimbabwe was not being treated differently from "any normal country without a land distribution problem." "It must be accepted that full and unfettered political, military and economic power must (be vested) in the people as a whole and that . . . the constitution must contain no racist or other abridgement on the power of the people

70

acting either directly or through their representatives in Parliament to freely alter or abolish it."[32]

As the conference appeared to be breaking down, Mugabe got in touch with Mark Chona, Zambian president Kenneth Kaunda's special political adviser. "[He] called me to his flat and told me the negotiations were going to collapse over land. 'Could you please call your American friends and ask them if Kissinger's pledge [for a development fund] is still on the table?' So I picked up the phone . . . and I called [US diplomat] Gib Lanpher, who was . . . an observer [at Lancaster House]. I asked him a straight question, if that offer was still available, and Gib said, 'Well, Mark, I can't say it is still viable, but we'd be prepared to consider the possibility of funding that kind of programme.'"[33] This, combined with a separate request to the Americans from Ramphal and hurried high-level consultation with the White House, produced an American commitment to help underwrite substantial land restitution.

Throughout the Lancaster House negotiations, the British had signaled "with winks and nods" to General Peter Walls, head of the Rhodesian security forces and a formidable member of Muzorewa's delegation, that Mugabe would be excluded from the final settlement.[34] Mugabe similarly found himself increasingly isolated on the transition arrangements when the proposal was made for a British governor. He described the proposals for the ceasefire at a press conference as "just rubbish. Absolute rubbish."[35] It required President Machel's personal intervention to persuade a bitter Mugabe to sign the Lancaster House settlement.[36] A back-channel appeal from the Foreign Office to President Machel outmaneuvered Mugabe. The message came back from Maputo that there were no issues at stake which would justify the breakup of the conference, and Mozambique was not prepared to accept responsibility for this. The ZANU delegation was informed that they could remain in Mozambique, but "they would be on the beach" writing their memoirs, as no training camps or rear bases would be permitted.

On the face of it Mugabe was the major loser at Lancaster House. He had little to show for his revolutionary rhetoric and repeated attempts to take an independent stand from Nkomo. One-man-one-vote had been watered down to a 20 percent blocking vote for the whites (3 percent of the population); the land deal meant not even uncultivated land could be expropriated without compensation; the new government would inherit both public debt and pensions; and the Rhodesian army would form the core of a new Zimbabwe army, rather than being disbanded. Furthermore, the charismatic army commander Josiah Tongogara appeared to have stolen the diplomatic limelight by being surprisingly conciliatory.[37] Machel's message reached Mugabe as he was on the point of leaving London, following the inconclusive final plenary session at Lancaster House, to take his case to the United Nations in New York. A contemporary photograph of the Patriotic Front leaders shows a furious Mugabe, whose twisted facial features radiate his anger and humiliation that his arguments for escalating to all-out war had been publicly overruled. Mugabe's body language in the surviving news footage betrays his enduring sense of having been cheated: the Lancaster House "deal" had robbed him of victory.[38]

The truth was that by the time of the ceasefire in early January 1980 his military forces had been weakened by Rhodesian attacks.[39] However, now the struggle for Zimbabwe shifted to the ballot box. Mugabe left London without consulting Nkomo on a common approach, and announced at the meeting of southern African leaders in Mozambique that ZANU would be fighting the election as a separate party.[40] Mugabe and his wife returned to Zimbabwe in February 1980 to rapturous crowds. His political manifesto was unexpectedly moderate, singularly lacking Marxist rhetoric or calls for revolutionary transformation. (Machel had strongly advised this approach, but this was largely overlooked by commentators.) The subsequent election campaign was bitter and divisive, with violence and intimidation, and dirty tricks by all three sides. ZANU-PF was the greatest culprit. Over 17,000 fighters arrived at assembly camps, but another 7,000–10,000 political commissars remained in the rural areas to "deliver" the election. Mugabe himself survived two further assassination attempts by Rhodesian security forces.

His relationship with the British governor, Christopher Soames, remained fraught throughout the election campaign.[41] Given proven reports of intimidation, there was considerable pressure on Soames to proscribe Mugabe and his party—from the Rhodesian military, as well as from Muzorewa and Nkomo. Soames realized this would spell disaster: "to disallow Mugabe's involvement would make nonsense of all (the UK) had been trying to achieve, and would place at probably fatal risk the international endorsement . . . so tenuously procured."[42] At the end of February 1980, the election result became clear: ZANU-PF had won 57 seats, Nkomo's party 20, Bishop Abel Muzorewa's party had secured only 3, with the Rhodesian Front sweeping the designated block of 20 white seats. It was the first time an apparently avowed Marxist had been voted into power in Africa. Before the result was announced, the threat of a coup by Rhodesian middle-ranking officers loomed. This was averted only by intense British pressure. Another coup, planned to coincide with Independence Day and backed by the South African military intelligence, was thwarted by the Rhodesian Special Branch.[43]

Despite his sweeping victory, Mugabe's position appeared vulnerable to potential threats—from the South African apartheid government, appalled that the ballot box had delivered victory to a radical black nationalist; and from a deeply angered and resentful Nkomo, who was shattered by the election result and still regarded himself as the rightful father of Zimbabwean nationalism. Mugabe initially tried to persuade Nkomo to accept the ceremonial presidency, but with access to cabinet papers and the brief to advise Mugabe. Nkomo rejected this offer, and when Mugabe's proposal was then leaked, the idea was unanimously vetoed by his ZANU colleagues.[44] It took considerable pressure from President Kaunda and all the persuasive powers of his highly experienced emissary, Mark Chona, to induce Nkomo to join in a government of national unity as minister of home affairs. Nkomo remained profoundly disgruntled, as he did not believe he had been given a suitably important portfolio by Mugabe, whom he regarded as his former junior.

Mugabe came to recognize the enormity of the task he faced in transforming Zimbabwe's war economy, reintegrating the returning fighters and refugees in a hostile regional environment, and facing implacable internal critics and their disgruntled and heavily armed fighters.[45] He came to value Soames and tried to persuade the governor to stay on for eighteen months. Soames's presence would have represented the imprimatur of British support and continued investment in Mugabe's new position. Although Soames refused to stay for more than six weeks, he used his considerable political influence in Whitehall to secure more funds to support Zimbabwe's reconstruction. At Soames's encouragement, Prime Minister Thatcher also wrote to President Carter, who promised to increase dramatically America's support for reconstruction and development. Soames also actively encouraged Mugabe's apparent moderation. In fact, Mugabe surprised everybody.[46]

Ten years before Nelson Mandela's similar gesture of goodwill and policy of reconciliation, Mugabe went on television to declare:

> If yesterday I fought you as an enemy, today you have become a friend and ally in the same national interests, loyalty, rights and duties as myself. If yesterday you hated me, today you cannot avoid the love that binds you to me and me to you. If ever we look to the past, let us do so for the lesson the past has taught us, namely that oppression and racism are iniquities that must never again find scope in our political and social system. It could never be a correct justification that because the whites oppressed us yesterday when they had the power, the blacks must oppress them today because they have the power. An evil remains an evil whether practiced by white against blacks or by black against white.[47]

To the remaining 170,000 Zimbabwean whites, Mugabe's determination "to draw a line through the past" made a remarkable impression.[48] It was also an appeal to Africans who might be contemplating reprisals. How to square this image of a benevolent and forgiving Mugabe with his later antagonism? Carrington summed it up as Mugabe's responding directly to the environment around him: faced with a tense and threatening situation, as in Geneva, he proved vindictive and resentful, swift to condone violence against his opponents. However, flushed with triumph in 1980, he could be generous and magnanimous. Ken Flower, the long-standing director of the Central Intelligence Organisation who served as the first intelligence/security adviser and head of CIO to Mugabe, felt in 1980 the president emerged "as someone with a greater capacity and determination to shape the country's destiny for the benefit of all its people than any of his four predecessors."[49] He was "conciliation personified," his "own man," "careful in his considerations, a fine judge of a man's worth," someone who attached great weight to personal loyalty and felt a corresponding sense of betrayal if this was not publicly and privately consistent.[50]

President Machel, too, had urged him to encourage the whites to stay, and to include Smith in government. At this, Mugabe laughed and murmured, "We will have to think about that." Nyerere did not support this idea of including Ian Smith, but felt that the government should include some whites.[51] As further insurance against Rhodesian military disaffection, Soames also encouraged Mugabe to keep the Rhodesian army commander, General Walls, who was mystified to be told by Mugabe, "The teachings of Karl Marx are identical to those of Jesus Christ." Walls agreed to stay out of a sense of patriotism, only to resign the following year.

It is clear that Mugabe initially made a profound impression on those around him. "It was a time when he really cared about the country. When he really cared about the people."[52] There was considerable relief among remaining white Rhodesians, especially white farmers.

On the advice of Machel and Nyerere, Mugabe accepted the principle of keeping Rhodesian civil servants, with appointed African deputies who would replace them as they retired. There were intense hopes for the future of a prosperous multiracial Zimbabwe, as a showcase for transition for the greater problem of apartheid South Africa. However, to the observant, there were early signs of trouble soon after the 1980 election campaign in the roadblocks manned by white troops between Victoria Falls and Bulawayo.[53] The Zimbabwean security forces feared that returning disaffected ZIPRA fighters, trained by the Cubans in neighboring Angola and armed by the Soviet Union, would be mobilized against their political opponents.

The honeymoon was short lived. To Mugabe, reconciliation meant starting afresh, and forgetting the past. Those who didn't agree would find themselves "in trouble."[54] Mugabe's emphasis on reconciliation was not shared by others within ZANU-PF. The militants wanted to press ahead with the revolutionary transformation of Zimbabwe, even if this offended the whites. More serious was the situation in Matabeleland where ex-ZAPU fighters had buried Soviet-made arms caches.[55] Sporadic fighting and attacks on farmers and civilians broke out in Bulawayo in early 1981. Mugabe was also under pressure from Nkomo to allow the opening of a Soviet embassy in Harare. Given the substantial level of Soviet military support for ZAPU during the liberation struggle, there was a continued fear of the ZAPU/Soviet relationship within the

ZANU-PF leadership.[56] Nkomo's repeated demands for the opening of a Soviet embassy[57] encouraged Mugabe's contact with North Korea in August 1981, and the subsequent military training of the ex-ZANLA Shona-speaking Fifth Brigade, accountable to the prime minister.

Together with the flawed land settlement, this failure to address the issue of rival nationalist armies has later been judged as one of the most serious failures of peacemaking at Lancaster House.[58] In 1979 the Patriotic Front delegations "had hardly any plans about the future of the guerrillas who decided not to join the army."[59] Carrington had only raised this once—that many guerrillas would want to return to civilian life, and this would be the responsibility of the government post independence. However, it was comprehensively overlooked by the Patriotic Front.[60] White Zimbabwean officers were acutely aware of the problems and dangers of fusing two separate guerrilla armies. The British military training team tasked with creating a national army from disciplined troops and poorly trained guerrilla fighters was equally aware of the challenges. As heavily armed ZIPRA fighters established themselves at a strategic redoubt in Matabeleland, local observers and journalists warned that war was looming. Mugabe's argument to camera was calm but uncompromising—as he told Thames *TV Eye* in 1981, "in any event, we will have to disarm them, whether they like it or not."[61]

Mugabe's speech to the Zimbabwe Parliament in April 1981 clearly indicated that ZANU-PF was the only party which should represent Zimbabweans. "The concept of setting up a party merely to oppose ... and not to assist a government in being, to govern on a national basis, is repugnant to me. Not that I have anti democratic principles, but rather that I cherish the principle of national unity ... where their main concern is achieving peace, getting people to work together nationally ... embarking on programmes of development where everybody's effort is required. To my mind, it is a luxury to indulge in the politics of opposition."[62] "We were not fighting [the war] for the two major tribes ... we were fighting it for one people who are now constituted into one nation, and it is this one-ness that we would want to see urged and facilitated."[63]

This was a clear call for a one-party state. As the North Korean–trained Fifth Brigade moved into Matabeleland to crush the dissidents, British media reports appeared on the atrocities, which were steadfastly denied by Zimbabwe government spokesmen. Political commentators were slow to realize Mugabe's degree of ultimate responsibility. "He was such an articulate person, he was such an intelligent person. To imagine him as a thug? I really could not get that into my head."[64] Western leaders and diplomats were in an acute quandary: the British had 100 officers retraining the new Zimbabwe national army. If this failed, would the country slide into all-out civil war? Mugabe adeptly deflected British journalists' suggestions at press conferences that Amnesty International should be allowed into southern

Zimbabwe to investigate the violence and killings, with a robust countercharge that Britain would never dream of doing this in Northern Ireland during the Troubles. Prime Minister Thatcher had a long and uncomfortable meeting with Mugabe in May 1983 discussing "his increasingly tyrannical imposition of a one-party state, rigged trials for RAF officers (who were Zimbabwe citizens) and rumours of political murders."[65] For the Commonwealth, which had presented itself as the proud midwife of Zimbabwe's independence, it appeared a very confused picture, but the Commonwealth secretary general, Sonny Ramphal, accepted African states' determined attachment to sovereignty and non-interference and failed to act. It was a shameful silence. Nkomo fled from Zimbabwe and appealed to external backers of the Lancaster House settlement, but nothing was done. By 1987, the Fifth Brigade's violence against the Ndebele and Kalanga people had resulted in at least 20,000 deaths and a deeply traumatized community.[66] ZAPU had run out of friends and options. In 1987, ZAPU signed a Unity Pact with ZANU-PF, and Zimbabwe became an effective one-party state under its new president, Robert Mugabe.

Refashioning the State, and the Hope of Multiracial Zimbabwe

Mugabe's grip on power after signing the Unity Accord with Nkomo on December 27, 1987, was stronger than ever. In a ceremony just three days later, Parliament declared him executive president, to the refrain of "You Are the Only One."[1] Mugabe now combined the roles of head of state, head of government, and commander in chief of the defense forces. He had powers to dissolve Parliament and declare martial law. His office controlled all the major levers of power, including the civil service, defense force, police, and parastatal organizations. Mugabe's hand was further strengthened by the expiry of the agreement reached at Lancaster House reserving whites 20 seats in the 100-seat lower house of parliament.

As if these powers were insufficient, the state of emergency that Ian Smith had introduced was retained. It was finally lifted in 1990, but even then the president held many arbitrary powers of detention. State radio and television were also tightly controlled by the government, with only a handful of independent newspapers attempting to provide an alternative to the official sycophantic coverage of Mugabe and his government. The leading independent newspapers were the *Daily News* and three weekly publications: the *Financial Gazette, Zimbabwe Independent,* and *Sunday Standard.* Newspaper editors and journalists were routinely put under pressure, with arrests and attacks on their offices. Press restrictions tightened just as middle-class urban opposition grew. The *Daily News* was critically important, with a readership of around 900,000, and came under intense pressure.[2] Its printing press was bombed in 2002 and it was shut down the following year after it refused to register under the government's draconian legislation.

Mugabe was also leader of ZANU-PF. Although on the face of it Joshua Nkomo and ZAPU were brought into the fold, they had little say in the direction of the party. Mugabe had subordinated his main political rival as nationalist leader. The ZANU-PF Politburo and Central Committee became the main focus of political debate, usurping the policy-making roles of the cabinet and of Parliament itself. This included the establishment of a Politburo committee to supervise the work of civil servants, leading to a public dispute with the minister responsible for the civil service, Eddison Zvobgo.[3] Soon the civil service was populated with party loyalists, whose chief remit was to satisfy their political masters.

Senior politicians began using their newfound resources to purchase property. By 1990 senior party leaders, including the two vice presidents and the president's sister, had all acquired farms.[4] At a local level, ZANU-PF mayors and town councilors followed suit. The *Economist* concluded that looting of the parastatals and corruption in the public sector had reached "epidemic" proportions.[5]

As has been indicated earlier, land was the key issue in the newly liberated country. Dispossession had been a critical problem since the 1830s, when the Ndebele invaded from South Africa, fleeing from the Zulu revolution, known as the *mfecane.* The Ndebele had lost many of their own people during this migration and engaged in what Professor Sabelo Ndlovo-Gatsheni describes as "limited wars of conquest of the south-west since the people of this area did not readily accept their rule."[6] Seizing territory in what is today Zimbabwe from tribes that became known as the Shona, the Ndebele made their home in the west of the country, around Bulawayo.[7] The Pioneer Column sent by Cecil Rhodes in 1890 marked the beginning of an even more extensive dispossession.[8] Vast tracts of land were taken and distributed by Rhodes's British South Africa Company to the white "pioneers" who had served its aim of securing mineral rights. Rhodes had promised each of the 200 pioneers free farms of 3,175 acres. But men like Major Sir John Willoughby, formerly of the Royal Horse Guards and chief of staff of the Pioneer Column, were given far larger land holdings.[9] He alone was granted a staggering 600,000 acres. Willoughby went on to buy further stretches of land as whites moved off farms to seek their fortunes on the mines, eventually accumulating no less than 1.3 million acres. Missionaries too were granted large tracts of land. Within ten years of the arrival of the pioneers the whites had taken nearly sixteen million acres—or one-sixth of the entire land mass of the country. This deprivation of their land (predominantly in the more fertile and less disease-prone areas of the country, with higher rainfall) was fiercely resisted by the black population, who rose twice in the period 1896–97. First the Ndebele and then the Shona fought back in what became known as the Chimurenga.

Over the next century this annexation continued, and by independence in 1980 just 6,000 large-scale, mostly white, farmers owned 42 percent of all the land.[10] These commercial farmers, well capitalized and using modern farming techniques, dominated the agricultural sector. They were successful, producing three-quarters of all output and 95 percent of all sales. By contrast, approximately 4 million black Africans were making a living in the overcrowded communal lands, comprising 41 percent of the country. There they grew crops for consumption rather than for export.[11] A government commission established after independence recommended that nearly half of the black farmers should be resettled. The commission concluded that the communal areas could only sustain 325,000 of the 780,000 families who lived on them; the remainder would have to be found new farms.[12] Somehow this land would have

85

to be acquired, if the war against white rule was to have any meaning.

During the first ten years of independence the land redistribution program had to operate under the terms of the Lancaster House agreement.[13] As has been seen, when the issue was being debated in London, Mugabe had denounced other African leaders for not taking a harder stand on this issue.[14] In the end a compromise was arrived at. Compulsory land acquisition had to take place on a "willing seller, willing buyer" basis and in 1981 the British government provided £20 million to fund the program.[15] There was also a very substantial multilateral aid agreement, which included development of the rural economy, although the Canadians were the only other foreign government expressly to earmark aid for land reform. The land was purchased from the mainly white farmers represented by the Commercial Farmers Union, who had produced the majority of the agricultural output that fed the towns and went for export. The process was slow and cumbersome, exacerbated by the fact that the injection of demand inflated land prices. The government also had too few civil servants competent to implement the program.[16] By 1990 only modest progress had been made in achieving a real transfer of land to the majority population.

One of the issues that brought matters to a head was the growing realization that many choice farms were being acquired by the elite who surrounded Mugabe. "By 1990 a new class of landowners was firmly established:

ministers, MPs, senior civil servants, police and defence officials, and parastatal managers. In all, they had managed to acquire 8 percent of commercial farmland since independence, although little of it was put to productive use."[17] Not all the money Britain had provided to help purchase farms had been taken up by the Zimbabwean authorities. The British overseas development minister pointed this out to the Mugabe government in 1988, but received no reply.[18] Tensions with Britain rose and were exacerbated when the Labour aid minister, Clare Short, wrote to Mugabe in November 1997 suggesting that her Irish ancestry meant that she too was a victim of British history and therefore could not be held responsible for previous British imperialism.[19] "I should make it clear that we do not accept that Britain has a special responsibility to meet the costs of land purchase in Zimbabwe. We are a new government from diverse backgrounds without links to former colonial interests. My own origins are Irish and as you know we were colonised and not colonisers." Mugabe saw the remarks as incendiary. Furious, he described Prime Minister Tony Blair as "worse than the Tories."[20]

While relations with Britain were deteriorating, Zimbabwe was forging new ties with its neighbors. Mugabe's relationship with South Africa's ruling party after 1994—and Nelson Mandela's presidency—was particularly important. Liberation movements led both nations after 1994. On the face of it they should have had much in common. In reality the relations were fraught—dating back to the struggles against white rule. Mugabe's party ZANU had been aligned with the Chinese and at least nominally in alliance with South Africa's second-largest liberation movement, the Pan Africanist Congress. It was Joshua Nkomo's ZAPU that had strong ties with the ANC leadership and their supporters in the Soviet Union.[21]

The ANC established a military alliance with Nkomo on August 15, 1967.[22] The deal was signed as ANC cadres were deployed alongside ZAPU guerrillas who fought a series of bloody but not particularly successful battles against the Rhodesian armed forces, in what became known as the Wankie campaign of August and September of that year. As a result, South African paramilitary police units were sent into the Zambezi valley, while South African communication engineers established a permanent listening post next to Lake Kariba. The action was sharply criticized by Mugabe's South African allies—the Pan Africanist Congress. They argued that it was a mistake to take on a regular army in a conventional battle; what was needed was guerrilla warfare. ZANU's official newspaper *Zimbabwe News* took a similar line. If the ANC wished to help Zimbabweans, they should fight in South Africa, not in Rhodesia.[23]

When the results of Zimbabwe's first election were announced at the London headquarters of the Anti-Apartheid Movement (which took its lead from the ANC) there were very long faces indeed when Robert Mugabe emerged as the victor. The South African Communist Party (allies of the ANC) at first regarded

ZANU's victory as the result of a "conspiracy with international capital"[24]—which was ironic, since Mugabe was a self-proclaimed Marxist. Cold War allegiances in Southern Africa were notoriously complicated. Reestablishing trust between the ANC and ZANU took a long time. The Mandela presidency had relatively little to do with Mugabe. It was left to Thabo Mbeki (who had played a key role in ANC foreign policy for years and took over the reins of power in June 1999) to attempt to deal with Zimbabwe's growing malaise. Thabo Mbeki went out of his way to accommodate Mugabe. As Mbeki's biographer Mark Gevisser described, their relationship was built on a shared belief that they faced a white enemy, both in South Africa and in the West. As black Africans they were "kith and kin," and Mbeki would not allow them to be divided.[25] Rather, using the mandate given him by regional leaders in the Southern African Development Community (SADC), he attempted to achieve a mediated resolution to Zimbabwe's political crises.

The Mbeki government did everything in its power not to put pressure on its northern neighbor, despite intense demands from the international community. Quite why this was the case has been a matter of speculation for some time. The academic Merle Lipton explained this (at least in part) by South Africa's reluctance to abrogate the principle of sovereignty and noninterference in the affairs of another state—especially one led by another national liberation movement.[26] But she acknowledged that Pretoria's position was "perplexing." While she provides some possible explanations, they are tentative at best.

Mbeki himself has recently offered his own interpretation of why he was so determined to stand by Robert Mugabe. It was—he says—an attempt to head off regime change.[27] "In the period preceding the 2002 Zimbabwe Elections, the UK and the US in particular were very keen to effect this regime change and failing which to impose various conditions to shorten the period of any Mugabe Presidency. Our then Minister of Intelligence, Lindiwe Sisulu, had to make a number of trips to London and Washington to engage the UK and US governments on their plans for Zimbabwe, with strict instructions from our Government to resist all plans to impose anything on the people of Zimbabwe, including by military means." Mbeki went on to cite Lord Guthrie, former chief of defense staff of the UK armed forces, as saying, "Astonishingly, the subjects discussed" with Prime Minister Tony Blair included invading Zimbabwe, "which people were always trying to get me [Guthrie] to look at. My advice was, 'Hold hard, you'll make it worse.'"

It is difficult to know what to make of this story. A spokesman for the former British prime minister denied the allegations: "Tony Blair has long believed that Zimbabwe would be much better off without Robert Mugabe and always argued for a tougher stance against him, but he never asked anyone to plan or take part in any such military intervention."[28] In reality it need never have come to this. One of Mbeki's white predecessors, John Vorster, had merely turned the screws on the Rhodesian regime: slowing imports and leaving the country short of oil and other vital supplies for the government to cave in; but this was a path Mbeki was not prepared to contemplate.[29]

Certainly, South Africa would have never accepted that an outside power (especially a former imperial power like Britain) should oust a neighbor. But the relationship is more complex than that. There was also an element of indebtedness: Zimbabwe had put its land reform program on hold in 1990–93 because of negotiations on South Africa's transition, and to reassure white South Africans.[30] Stephen Chan, a longtime Zimbabwe analyst, puts it down to a range of reasons.[31] These include a shared intellectual position, an unwillingness to go out on a limb, and Mbeki's assessment that there was really no other suitable leader in Zimbabwe. Perhaps Chan comes closest to explaining the phenomenon when he says: "Mugabe genuinely holds Mbeki, and many other African presidents, in thrall. His personal charisma and position as the grand old man of liberation gives him both seniority and pedigree that no one else can match. What is taken as senseless rhetoric in the West is a rhetoric of great meaning in a continent where the welts and scars of racism and colonialism will take another generation to heal."

There was also an enduring conviction that regime change would be "counterrevolutionary" and regressive, allowing "neoimperialist forces" and their stooges back into southern Africa. This perception played an important part in the mind-set of Marxists and African nationalists. Mbeki was also in an invidious position. He was expected to be the regional "fixer" by the Western powers, yet was looked to by other African governments and leaders to be their champion beyond the African continent. Mbeki adopted a practice of "quiet diplomacy," which put minimum public pressure on Zimbabwe and eschewed the practice of the apartheid government of interfering in its neighbor's affairs. When the Commonwealth moved to suspend Zimbabwe following the contested elections of 2002, Mbeki was a key member of the three-leader "troika" which tried to bring Mugabe back into line on Commonwealth democratic values. This failed miserably at the Abuja meeting in 2003. Mugabe was so furious at what he saw as unacceptable interference in Zimbabwe's sovereignty that he declared Zimbabwe was immediately leaving the Commonwealth without even consulting his ZANU-PF colleagues.[32]

Mbeki was prepared to go to extraordinary lengths to conceal the extent of human rights abuses in Zimbabwe. The South African presidency, from Mbeki to Zuma, spent years fighting court cases to prevent an official report on Zimbabwe's violent 2002 election from being made public.[33] The report had been commissioned by Mbeki from two highly respected South African judges. When it was finally published in 2014, the report was damning. The judges found that the 107 politically motivated murders were what they called the "hallmark" of the election campaign, and that ZANU-PF militia deployed during the process were the "primary perpetrators of the violence." As Justices Dikgang Moseneke and Sisi Khampepe concluded: "Having regard to all the circumstances, and in particular the cumulative substantial departures from international standards of free and fair elections found in Zimbabwe during the pre-election period, these elections, in our view, cannot be considered free and fair."[34] Revealed twelve years after the results were announced, this judgment had only a limited impact.

While South African leaders deferred to Mugabe, another foreign question was making itself felt: the war in the Congo. The Democratic Republic of Congo had been unstable since independence in 1960 when the first prime minister, Patrice Lumumba, was overthrown and then assassinated with the assistance of the Belgians, the CIA, and the British.[35] Having overthrown Lumumba, his successor, Joseph Mobutu, was then ousted by rebels led by Laurent-Désiré Kabila in 1997. But Kabila then fell out with his own former allies, Uganda and Rwanda, which sent forces to attack President Kabila in the capital, Kinshasa.[36] This attack outraged other regional powers. In 1998 Angola, Zimbabwe, and Namibia entered the conflict on the side of the government, in what became known as the Great War of Africa. The fighting was to last for nearly five years, causing the death of over two million people and massive internal displacement. The war ended only in July 2003. Nations as remote as Sudan, Chad, and Eritrea became entangled in the war, but it is Zimbabwe's role that is significant here.

Mugabe's reasons for entering the war were complex, but he was influenced by the fact that he had a substantial military at his disposal and was responding to a request from the Congolese government for forces to ward off "imperialism."[37] The initial deployment of just 600 Zimbabwean troops grew inexorably to 16,000 within thirty months. Whatever the rights or wrongs of this venture, it took an extraordinarily high toll on Zimbabwe. The cost (estimated at US$30 million a month) was admitted by the government to be Z$10 billion in August 2000, and rising.[38] The burden on the Zimbabwean economy was unsustainable, Dr. Simba Makoni, Zimbabwe's finance minister, admitted, but this was not an argument Mugabe was willing to tolerate. "Don't talk of resources as if resources are more important than the security of the people and the sovereignty of the country. . . . The only way to bring peace to the country is to confront the rebels."[39]

Economist John Robertson put the total cost of the Congo war to Zimbabwe at US$1 billion. The exact number of Zimbabwean lives lost has remained a state secret.[40] There was also a heavy loss of military equipment, which the country could not afford to replace. "On balance," concluded Martin Rupiya, "the country appears to have made a huge sacrifice for its involvement in the war, which has left it scarred, impoverished, and politically divided."[41] The only winners appeared to be the senior officers and businessmen, who were reported to have made vast sums of money out of Congolese diamonds and timber, as well as air cargo and road haulage contracts.[42]

While this foreign engagement was under way, relations between the government and civil society were declining. Three parallel trends developed. The first was the emergence of discontent among the urban working class and the trade union movement; this was a direct product of the failed structural adjustment program of the early 1990s, originally designed to kick-start the Zimbabwean economy. However, state retrenchment directly affected the most vocal section of the population. This found expression in the formation in 1999 of the Movement for Democratic Change (MDC) led by the secretary-general of the Zimbabwe Congress of Trade Unions, Morgan Tsvangirai. The second trend was the gradual erosion of support for the state among the churches. Finally, there was the growing resistance by civil society groups to the attempts by the Mugabe government to reduce their room for maneuver and centralize all power in the hands of the ruling party.

Declining living standards, increases in taxation, and falling health and educational provision led the unions to call a successful "stay-away" in December 1997.[43] In January and February the following year there were food riots in the townships or "high-density areas" around Harare. The protests were first banned, and then the army was sent in to quell the unrest. Tsvangirai was attacked, and the union offices in Bulawayo were burnt down. Despite this the protests continued, both against rising prices and the army's role in the Congo.

The churches, some of which had played key roles in supporting the resistance to white rule, were initially cautious about their relationship with the Mugabe government. While they engaged in criticism of proposals to establish a one-party state in the late 1980s, they were keen not to break their links with the new government.[44] For example, the Catholic Church refused to make public a highly critical report on the atrocities in Matabeleland, leading to the resignation of the respected head of the Catholic Commission for Justice and Peace, Mike Auret. But as time went by the churches' attitude changed. In the late 1990s these concerns crystallized around the constitution. In May 1997 members of the Zimbabwe Council of Churches brought together unions, NGOs, and church members to consider the excessive powers invested in the president and how the constitution might be revised. A National Constitutional Assembly was launched, chaired by Morgan Tsvangirai.

The government's response was perhaps predictable. They launched a rival Constitutional Commission and traveled the country collecting views from ordinary people. Some church leaders were persuaded to participate in this official review, which asked questions such as: "How many terms can the head of state serve?"[45] In the end the Commission's findings were referred to the ruling party, which overruled a number of its recommendations. Some church leaders, including Bishop Ambrose Moyo of the Evangelical Lutheran Church, resigned. A referendum on the proposals from the Commission was scheduled to be put to the people in February 2000. Opponents of the Commission's draft constitution argued that the proposal for an executive presidency would leave too much power in Mugabe's hands, and suggested that executive authority should be replaced with a prime minister accountable to Parliament. Government propaganda accused unnamed and interfering foreign governments and meddling overseas donors of calling for a vote against the new constitution. It was against this background that the Movement for Democratic Change was launched in September 1999, headed by Tsvangirai. With union support, it appeared to be a viable alternative to ZANU-PF. It also had the backing of academics, business leaders, and NGO activists. As such it was—in the view of Sarah Rich Dorman—the "first nationally grounded opposition party to challenge ZANU (PF)."[46]

Mugabe's response was to label his critics "Western stooges." The president and his party declared that rejecting the draft constitution would be tantamount to voting for colonialism. A full-page advertisement in the *Herald,* the main government-run newspaper, showed a white couple wearing Vote No T-shirts above the words: "Don't follow them back to the dark days of the past, when they were kings and queens."[47]

It was against this background that the referendum was held on February 12–13, 2000. To the astonishment of Mugabe and the ruling party, the people voted overwhelmingly against the constitutional proposals, rejecting them by 57.7 percent to 45.3 percent. Crowds celebrated in Harare, waving posters saying "Yellow card Mugabe" and "Tanaura Jongwe," literally "we've plucked the feathers of the cockerel"—the cockerel being the symbol of ZANU-PF, and therefore of Robert Mugabe.[48] Although the president went on television accepting the outcome, he was shaken to the core. Never had he faced a rejection by the people of Zimbabwe. It rocked the legitimacy of his party's rule, and the model of governance he had constructed as leader. In his view, it appeared to threaten letting in "counterrevolutionary" forces; Mugabe was determined it never be repeated.

5

Revolution Redux, or "Why It All Turned Sour"

The result of the referendum was a devastating blow for Mugabe and taught him a lesson he would never forget. From that moment on he was determined never again to put his trust in his own people: to allow a free and fair vote whose outcome he could not control. Mugabe, who had spent so many years in jail as a national liberation activist, believed it was illegitimate to question the direction that he, their leader, was taking them in. The explanation that presented itself was that national liberation had faltered, and that it risked going into reverse under the pressure of malign external forces. He declared openly that the referendum result had only been brought about by the forces of imperialism.[1] Britain and America, he declared, were working through white farmers and their black surrogates (the farmworkers), who had misled the people of Zimbabwe. Those who supported his opponents were divisive, and "sell-outs."

There were other pressures on the president: there was growing unrest. "By the end of the first structural adjustment programme in 1996, national politics had come to a boil, and the legitimacy of the ruling party as the 'guardian' of the nation was under severe challenge."[2] Beset by rising militancy across the public sector and wildcat strikes by farmworkers, Mugabe's government was also challenged internally by the re-emergence of the war veterans in national politics. Precipitated by a financial scandal and the collapse of the state-sponsored War Veterans Compensation Fund, the war veterans demanded that the state compensate them from the national budget. This opened up the split within the ZANU-PF movement between the elites and their proclaimed policy of "indigenization" and the lower echelons who had missed out on the benefits of independence, many of whom were living in acute poverty. This reignited discontent over the fate of national liberation. Mugabe caved in to the veterans' demands for a substantial compensation package, even though it had not been included in the national budget. In addition, the ZANU-PF government gazetted 1,470 white commercial farms for compulsory acquisition, and promised 20 percent of the farms to the war veterans. Mugabe's policy decisions immediately put enormous pressure on the economy, and the Zimbabwe dollar plummeted. To outsiders they appeared to be entirely self-serving actions by the president. However, "the war veteran challenge was of a different magnitude, for the war vets were also firmly embedded in the state apparatus and, indeed, were in charge of security, including the President's office."[3]

As the Zimbabwe economy spiraled downward, these events galvanized another round of negotiations with international donors leading to a nominal settlement in 1998. However, no progress was made within the country on the land question, and by 2000 national politics was boiling over.

Once Mugabe recovered from the humiliation of the referendum he set about systematically attacking the sources of opposition. He began with the white farmers and their farm workers. Mugabe believed that many of these employees had voted "no" on the instructions of their employers, although there is no evidence for this. The attacks on the farms were followed by an assault on the urban areas that had also rejected ZANU-PF's advice to support the constitutional changes. The next targets were the churches and nongovernmental organizations that backed the opposition. Finally, Mugabe's wrath fell on the opposition parties themselves and the men who led them. This was a lengthy, vicious and well-coordinated campaign to ensure that there would be no chance of removing Mugabe or his party from power, as long as he lived.

Mugabe decided to ride the tiger of land hunger and farm invasions, thereby rekindling ZANU-PF's alliance with peasants and war veterans. In one sense, it could be seen as resistance to "exhausted neo-liberalism" of the 1990s.[4] National grievances over the slow pace of reform and failure to deliver the benefits of liberation were very real across rural Zimbabwe. There had been sporadic farm invasions by nominal "war veterans" (some of whom had never fought in the war of independence) and landless peasants since the mid-1990s. By the late 1990s the government had developed a policy strategy for managed accelerated transition. Thanks to Mugabe, this went by the board, as he unleashed an onslaught on the commercial farmers. Going on television on February 12 as the referendum ended, Mugabe had singled out the white community, declaring that whites had "sloughed off apathy and participated vigorously in the poll." Michael Auret, of the Catholic Church, pointed out that few whites understood just how chilling these words really were.[5] Less than two weeks later, gangs of "war veterans" armed with axes and machetes invaded farms across the country.[6] Transported by government trucks and given rations, they were paid a daily allowance to stake claims to the land. Most were urban unemployed youths who were too young to have fought for their country's independence, but they were described as "war vets" nonetheless. Some of the white farmers whose land was seized had purchased their farms after independence and had certificates to prove that the government had no interest in their property. Despite this, they were taken, often with considerable violence. In July 2000 the dispossession was given a name: the Fast Track Land Reform and Resettlement Programme.

Over the next two years 6 million hectares were confiscated from farmers, most of whom were white. They were redistributed to 127,000 families as small farms and to 7,200 black commercial farmers. But the best land—often close to the major urban areas—went to Mugabe's cronies.[7] This was, argued the South African journalist Alistair Sparks, a pattern that had been established early in the Mugabe presidency. "Eighteen months after independence the Mugabe government had bought up 435,000 acres of white farmland, but re-settled fewer than 3,000 black peasants. In a pattern that was to become even more apparent in the years that followed, scores of government-owned farms were being handed out on leases to cabinet ministers, MPs, top civil servants and other senior members of the ruling party—few of which were put to productive use."[8] Some have challenged this view, pointing out that only around 10 percent of the land went to the political elite.[9]

While the experience of black dispossessed farmers failed to make the international headlines, the plight of the white farmers was shown on television across the world. Armed gangs were seen arriving at farmsteads, confronting the owners and then brutally assaulting them if they resisted before looting the home and then putting it to the torch. Dramatic as these images were, they failed to capture the fate of those worst affected by the program: the 1.3–1.9 million farm workers and their families.[10] This radically changed the Zimbabwean rural economy in terms of housing, access to health clinics and education, as well as the farmworkers' future livelihoods. Few understood why they were so badly treated. One farmworker described how her house was burnt down and she was assaulted because she had allegedly supported the opposition: "We were just accused of voting for MDC, quite a number of us were beaten up at the farm, the five of us. I do not even know where the MDC meetings were held."[11] Often their children were forced to watch the beatings, while the victims had to sing liberation songs, or join the ruling party.

Agricultural output plunged. Production of maize, the country's staple crop, was severely reduced, as small-scale farmers struggled with shortages of farm machinery, access to fertilizer and seed, capital to support irrigation infrastructure, and market access. During the years following the 2000 land redistribution, output fell by between a tenth and three-quarters.[12]

Table 1: Zimbabwean annual maize production

Time span 1990s average	2002/3	2005/6	2006/7	2007/8	2009/10	2010/11
Production (000 tonnes)						
1,685.6	1,058.8	1,484.8	952.6	575.0	1,322.66	1,451.6
% change						
	−37.2	−11.9	−43.5	−74.2	−21.5	−13.9

In recent years this trend has continued, exacerbated by severe drought. The UN's Food and Agricultural Organisation (FAO) reported that the 2015 maize harvest was 742 thousand tonnes and that the prospect for 2016 (given the severe drought across the whole of the region) was even worse.[13]

This is an intensely political issue, and others paint a rather different picture. The Zimbabwe government statistical office questioned the totals reported by the FAO and scholars. In 2015, according to the Zimbabwe National Statistics Agency, more than a million tonnes of maize were produced (1.081 million tonnes).[14] Of this total the majority (663,000 tonnes) came from the communal areas—the traditional "African Reserves," as they used to be known. Much of this harvest would traditionally have been consumed by the farmers and their families, not sold on the open market. It is unlikely to have been available to feed the urban population or for export.

A considerable body of literature has emerged calling for a reexamination of the question of land and agriculture.[15] Ian Scoones and his colleagues have produced an alternative interpretation of the program, and they are certainly right in concluding that it is a complex question.[16] They show that the land reform program was not a complete failure and argue that the revolutionary transformation of land access, production, and management would take time to work through; that the beneficiaries were not largely Mugabe's political "cronies"; and that the new settlers did indeed invest in the land that they received. They point out that the rural economy has not collapsed and agriculture is not "in complete ruins creating chronic food insecurity." The authors are correct to indicate that the terrible droughts that have hit the country in recent years were the fault of neither the government nor the new farmers. At the same time, Scoones and his coauthors cannot deny two key points. First, that Zimbabwe has ceased to be a net food exporter and is now almost always a large food-importing nation, one that cannot feed its urban population. Second, that although about 1 million people received farms,[17] approximately as many farmworkers were driven off the land and ended up impoverished in the communal areas, scraping an existence in marginal, highly insecure environments; moving to towns; or going into exile in South Africa.

The results of President Mugabe's land policies are mixed, to say the least. Even those who received farms complain that they have seen few benefits. "We thought when we were placed there that we'd be helped, but no, we were just left," said Alec Kaitano, a twenty-three-year-old who abandoned his smallholding outside the northeastern town of Bindura a year ago and survives by selling blemished fruit he finds in garbage cans in Harare.[18] "Those white farmers we displaced had money to farm, but we didn't, so we failed." There are reports that farms that once grew some of the best tobacco in the world now stand idle and abandoned as farmers head for the urban areas.

While the land was being redistributed there were equally dramatic events in the cities. Mugabe understood the threat that the MDC represented, and he ensured that the party came under sustained attack. As has been seen, particularly in the run-up to the 2000 and 2002 elections, opposition supporters were beaten and MDC rallies broken up. Young ZANU-PF activists, known as the "Green Bombers" and trained in National Service camps, manned roadblocks and attacked MDC members. Polling agents and candidates were kidnapped and "disappeared." Despite these tactics, the MDC did manage to win council elections in the capital in 2002. An MDC mayor and council were elected in the capital in a landslide—with the party taking 44 of the 45 wards in Harare. The mayor, Elias Mudzuri, took over 80 percent of the vote, but the party's victory was not to last. Within a year the mayor had been forced out of office to be replaced by a government-appointed commission.[19]

Aware that the urban populations were no longer reliable, Mugabe moved against them. In October 2004—amid suggestions in the papers that Harare needed "tidying up"—Operation Murambatsvina was launched. It meant, literally, "Drive out rubbish." Systematic urban clearances were undertaken, with shanties demolished, informal markets and workshops shut down, and goods confiscated. The United Nations sent a team to report on what had taken place, led by a Tanzanian, Anna Tibaijuka, executive director of the United Nations Human Settlements Programme.[20] She reported that there had been a systematic destruction of property and livelihoods, carried out by the police and army. "It is estimated that some 700,000 people in cities across the country have lost either their homes, their source of livelihood or both. Indirectly, a further 2.4 million people have been affected in varying degrees," she concluded. "Hundreds of thousands of women, men and children were made homeless, without access to food, water and sanitation, or health care." With their urban base disrupted, the prospects for the opposition were poor. Then they suffered another, self-inflicted, blow. In 2005 the MDC split.[21] One faction was led by Tsvangirai, the other by his former allies, Welshman Ncube and Arthur Mutambara.

The battle to control Zimbabwe's urban population took place as hundreds of thousands of impoverished men and women left for South Africa, believing there was little hope of making a living on the land or in the cities. Working in South Africa was a tradition going back to the nineteenth century, with Zimbabweans traveling to the mines. The liberation war of the 1970s and '80s led to a flight to safety. But it was really only in the 1990s that this trend intensified, with clashes between Mugabe and Nkomo and the wider political unrest. By 1995 over 700,000 Zimbabweans had gone south in search of sanctuary and employment.[22]

As the repression intensified, they were joined by tens of thousands of others. Some were farmworkers who had been displaced by land reform, others came from towns and cities. Most were black, but they were joined by a substantial proportion of Zimbabwe's white population. There was a huge "brain drain," which soon included half of all doctors. By 2009 nearly 150,000 had been granted asylum, but this was a tiny fraction of the Zimbabweans who went to live in South Africa, estimated at between 1.5 million and 3 million.[23] More than half said they still wanted to return to their own country. In the meantime, they were saving the wages and salaries they earned to send goods and money home. As Zimbabwe's economic situation deteriorated, these remittances became increasingly vital for the survival of their families.

By 2008 Zimbabwe was in a sorry state. The formal economy was in sharp decline, harvests had fallen, the opposition supporters in the urban areas had been attacked, and civil society was struggling to survive. Radio stations critical of the government had been closed and opponents physically attacked and intimidated. The chronic instability of the late 1990s, compounded by the chaos and disruption of the revolutionary land program, capital flight and skills emigration, and fiscal mismanagement by the Central Bank, all pulverized the value of the Zimbabwe dollar. In 2008, hyperinflation hit 79.6 billion percent. At that point, the government gave up trying to produce official statistics. Yet worse was to follow.

"Look East" for Foreign Friends

The political crisis came to a head in 2008. General elections were held in March and June of that year, and for a moment it appeared as if the opposition had made a breakthrough. In March the MDC-T won more seats than ZANU-PF (99 to 97). More worrying for Mugabe, he received a lower share of the vote than Tsvangirai (48 percent to 43 percent).[1] The two men had to stand against each other in a runoff election, scheduled for June 27, 2008. The president's response was to unleash a brutal campaign of intimidation, code-named Operation Mavhotera Papi, or "How did you vote?" This was particularly targeted at key opposition strongholds in Mashonaland-East and Midlands. A ZANU-PF Politburo member left the public in no doubt about what was expected of them. "We're giving the people of Zimbabwe another chance to mend their ways, to vote properly . . . this is their last chance." Grace Mugabe, the president's wife, underlined the message. "Even if people vote for MDC, Morgan Tsvangirai will never step foot in State House."[2] Faced with this regime-sanctioned onslaught, which saw murders and kidnapping, vicious beatings, and fire-bombings, Morgan Tsvangirai declared he could not in all conscience ask the Zimbabwean people to vote, and pulled out of the election five days before the poll. In the June election 85 percent backed Mugabe. This terrible period in Zimbabwe's recent history now has a label: "the Fear."

Robert Mugabe had, once again, asserted his authority, but the question of who would rule the country was not resolved. Even if the political crisis had ebbed, the economic crisis had not. Despite his nominal triumph at home, Mugabe found himself under sustained pressure. At an African Union summit he discovered that former allies, including Nigeria, Botswana, Kenya, Liberia, and Senegal gave him a hostile reception.[3] Led by Thabo Mbeki, the region's leaders in the South African Development Community twisted the arms of the main players. Mbeki himself had little time for Morgan Tsvangirai: he did not regard Tsvangirai as a capable leader-in-waiting and he had scant respect for Tsvangirai's limited educational achievements. Furthermore, he came from the trade union movement and was not a liberation leader.[4] Mbeki also had a considerably more powerful union movement of his own—COSATU—and he did not want South African trade unionists to think they could found a party to rival the ANC.

So it was, on July 21, 2008, that the three party leaders—Mugabe and the two leaders of the MDC factions, Tsvangirai and Mutambara—signed a Memorandum of Understanding establishing an inclusive government in which all had a role. The deal, which became known as the Global Political Agreement, overseen by Mbeki, was designed to share power. Yet despite the handshakes, there was little love lost between the political leaders.

If Mugabe was having difficulty making African leaders see things his way and facing opposition from Western capitals, he did not appear particularly disturbed. At home the security forces and the military were clearly supportive of their president, as were key sections of the intelligence services. Abroad Mugabe knew he could rely on other friends: the president turned to the East.

This was, of course, not the first time he had done this. Mugabe's ties with the Chinese went back to the earliest days of his fight with the white rulers of Rhodesia.[5] In 1966 Josiah Tongogara and Emmerson Mnangagwa had been among a group of fighters who were trained at the Nanking Academy. They were taught everything from military intelligence to guerrilla warfare.[6] ZANU's ties were with Beijing, rather than Moscow, which saw ZAPU as its candidate for liberation movement. After independence in 1980, relations between China and Zimbabwe developed gradually, with the construction of hospitals and the National Sports Stadium. Ties were cemented when Mugabe traveled to Beijing in 1985 and returned with loans worth $55 million.[7] When Mugabe decided to eliminate ZAPU as a serious rival, it was to North Korea that he looked, signing a deal with Kim Il Sung in October 1980—an agreement that later led to the formation of the notorious Fifth Brigade, whose murderous activities left thousands dead in Matabeleland.[8] While Western nations might raise troublesome human rights issues, friends in the East did not. As relations with the West deteriorated, Zimbabwe adopted a formal "Look East" policy in 2003, which developed into a "special relationship" with China.[9] "We have turned East, where the sun rises, and given our backs to the West, where the sun sets," Mugabe memorably declared.

The policy soon paid dividends. Not only were there several bilateral meetings, but Beijing was willing to deploy its diplomatic muscle on Zimbabwe's behalf. The Chinese used their veto in the UN Security Council to block sanctions and attempted to intervene directly in the controversial 2008 elections. Beijing's stand contrasted with the European Union's approach. Since 2002 the former president and his wife have faced an EU travel ban and an asset freeze, while the country has been placed under an arms embargo.[10] Beijing stepped in once again. A shipment of Chinese weapons, destined for Zimbabwe, was held up in the South African port of Durban only because trade unionists refused to unload it, following fears that the weapons would be used to repress Mugabe's political rivals.[11] It was a rare example of an international intervention by a nonstate actor to prevent an abuse of human rights, and helped prevent a brutal election from becoming even more violent.

As it happened, by 2008 economic interests and political interests coincided with this new development in

Zimbabwe's geopolitics: diamonds were the key. Two years earlier a rich alluvial diamond field had been discovered by villagers in the Marange district in the southeast of the country.[12] Initially local people regarded this as a windfall. At first the government allowed the area to be developed privately and by local prospectors. A subsidiary of the De Beers Company had been working in the area, but was replaced by a British-based company, African Consolidated Resources (ACR). Soon, however, ARC was forced to abandon its claim by the Zimbabwean police, who denied the company access to the area. A free-for-all developed, with informal mines springing up across the diamond fields. The government stepped in to grant the state-owned Zimbabwe Mining Development Corporation (ZMDC) exclusive rights to the area, and the local miners were elbowed out. The diamond fields—reputed to be among the richest in the world—were sealed off from November 2006, with not even members of Parliament or diplomats allowed to visit the area.[13]

In February 2007 Mugabe went one step further, declaring that only the government would mine the diamonds.[14] In reality, a range of operators had become involved in a proliferating smuggling operation with the gems being taken out to Lebanon, the United Arab Emirates, India, Pakistan, and Europe. Local agents (mostly Zimbabweans) bought up the gems locally, with the big money made by the main buyers (known as "barons") who lived in Harare, Mozambique, or South Africa and enjoyed political, military, or police protection.[15] Some five hundred syndicates were said to be in operation in November 2008.[16] According to Human Rights Watch, the process was accompanied by extreme violence. This included the establishment of torture camps, gross abuse, and killings. In one government-organized operation in 2008, 1,500 troops encircled freelance miners and massacred over 88. In 2009 the Kimberley Process banned the formal trade of Zimbabwean diamonds, which simply moved to illegal networks. Since there were vast sums of money to be made and Zimbabwe was in the throes of an economic crisis, this was probably unsurprising. Initially the main beneficiaries were police, about six hundred of whom were deployed in the area. One policeman claimed he made as much as $10,000 in bribes and backhanders in just three months.[17]

Mugabe decided that these riches should come under his control, rather than allowing them to be distributed in an arbitrary way among the security services. The president later revealed that he had been briefed on who would be allowed to participate in the exploitation of these reserves. "We had a list of companies applying," Mugabe is quoted as saying. "Finally two of them, Mbada and Canadile, were chosen. They were recommended and I was shown the papers and the proposals."[18] There is no suggestion that the money raised from the mining went to the state. Although there were promises by the Ministry of Mining that the diamond mines would generate $600 million, the Ministry of Finance complained that it had not received the revenue. The finance minister noted, "We are beginning to sound like a broken record in emphasising the need for transparency in the handling of our diamond revenues and, indeed general revenue from the rest of the mining sector."[19] Based on externally available figures, Zimbabwe received more than $1.7 billion from diamond exports from 2010 to 2014, but less than $200 million in taxes, royalties, and dividends were remitted to government.[20]

With the control of the mines allocated by Mugabe to the companies he favored, the Chinese became involved. Before 2003 only three Chinese companies had invested in Zimbabwe. In the next decade the figure rose to sixty-three.[21] An investigation by Global Witness indicated that the Chinese took considerable stakes in the companies involved in the exploitation of the diamonds.[22] There was said to be a complex system of company holdings in a variety of geographical locations, but these companies were, in reality, designed to benefit two groups of people: senior Zimbabweans military officers and Chinese businessmen.[23] The beneficiaries were said to have included (on the Zimbabwean side) Martin Rushwaya, the permanent secretary in the Ministry of Defence; Oliver Chibage, a commissioner of police; and former air vice marshal Robert Mhlanga. The links between the Chinese and Zimbabwe's military were underlined by claims that revenue from one of the companies was used to finance the construction of the country's National Defence College.[24]

It was not long before the relationship with the Chinese deepened. Early in 2010 the *Daily Telegraph*'s veteran Zimbabwe correspondent, Peta Thornycroft, broke the news that a giant runway was being constructed in the diamond fields.[25] The newspaper carried photographs of the airfield, complete with control tower: "Diplomats and analysts believe that the mile-long runway is intended for arms shipments, probably from China, for which troops loyal to President Robert Mugabe would pay on the spot with gemstones from the Chiadzwa diamond mines." Although the airfield allegedly was only designed to allow light aircraft to land, to fly the gems to Harare, it soon became clear that long-range aircraft (an Antonov An-12 cargo plane, with a range of 5,700 km) were landing twice a week.[26] The Antonov brought in members of the Chinese army as well as mining equipment. The plane is also said to have delivered weaponry. Chinese soldiers were reported to have taken control of security of the mining concerns.[27] From Zimbabwe's point of view, it would appear that most of the diamonds were smuggled out of the country, with little benefit accruing to Zimbabwe. As an academic put it: "One can conclude that the security agencies remained the primary, if not the sole, beneficiaries of China's mining of the Marange diamonds."[28]

There is another aspect of Zimbabwe's relationship with the East that must be mentioned, and that is the personal. President Mugabe and his second wife, Grace, found in the East an escape from the worries of everyday life and a playground for their personal plea-sures. Zimbabwe's media were full of stories of Grace's extravagance. She has presided over the construction of two ostentatious presidential residences since their marriage in 1996, one of which is known colloquially as "Gracelands." (Such is the extent of her purchase of a particular type of blue ceramic tile, from China, it is now known as "Grace Blue.") She selected a farm north-west of Harare, ordering the elderly couple who owned it off the land.[29] Since then she and her husband have built up a substantial property portfolio abroad.

So extensive did her properties become that since 2002 Commonwealth, European Union, and United States agencies were reportedly investigating Mugabe's wealth around the world.[30] This included a property in the Malaysian capital, Kuala Lumpur, where the fam-ily was assured of a safe haven should the situation in Zimbabwe deteriorate.[31] This dates back to the personal and political friendship between the Malaysian prime minister, Dr. Mahathir bin Mohamed, and Mugabe from the 1980s and 1990s. There is another £4 million villa in Hong Kong's New Territories, where their daugh-ter, Bona Mugabe, studied. In recent years ownership of the property has been disputed, with a Taiwanese-born South African citizen claiming that it is only leased to the Mugabes.[32] The Mugabe family also reputedly owns prop-erties in Cape Town, Dubai, and two in Manchester.[33]

During his final years as president, Mugabe spent increasing periods of time outside Zimbabwe, much of which is speculated to have been for medical treatment. Tendai Biti, former finance minister, alleged that in the first six months of 2016 the president clocked up 200,000 kilometers of travel, at a cost of $80 million.[34] This is said to have included no fewer than ten visits to Singapore. With an entourage of up to forty people, he is said to have taken $6 million from the Treasury on his trips.[35] This means that he and his family treated the Zimbabwe central bank as their personal ATM. It is impossible to verify the accuracy of these reports. All that can be said is that they have been repeated widely down the years, and there is little to contradict what was said.

7

Mugabe and the People

Robert Mugabe's performance as a political leader was often challenged. There was no shortage of criticism of his authoritarianism, with plenty of evidence of his ruthless determination to acquire, and then hang on to, power. This could be traced back to his earliest days in the liberation movement fighting white Rhodesian rule. No one who witnessed the crushing of his opponents, inside his own party or outside it, could doubt this. Whether it was confronting Joshua Nkomo and the Matabele challenge or the MDC in later years, who could dispute the lengths to which Mugabe would go to eliminate his rivals? Urban Zimbabweans who questioned his authority and farm laborers who supported his political enemies felt the retribution of the security forces. The president's political history is littered with bodies.

At the same time it is important to consider how many political leaders can match his record. Here is a man who took the oath of office on April 17, 1980; he led Zimbabwe for over thirty-seven years. There were plenty of opportunities to oust him through the ballot box. On several occasions (as tables 2 and 3 indicate) the ruling party came close to losing elections, despite evidence of vote rigging. It would also have been possible to resume the armed struggle to confront Mugabe's authoritarian rule. Yet no one succeeded in ousting him before November 2017, nor were there any serious attempts to begin an armed resistance. Only Botswana came close to supporting the MDC as a military force, and even though deeply critical of the Zimbabwean government, Botswana backed away from this option.[1] Mugabe was certainly not a leader who remained at home, for fear of a coup in his absence: quite the opposite. He was reported to have made no fewer than twenty-two foreign visits in the first half of 2015 alone.[2] He sometimes remained no longer than forty-eight hours in Zimbabwe before flying out again. No wonder he was dubbed the "visiting leader"! During the president's time out of the country, all major decisions were put on hold. "When Mugabe goes on holiday, he goes on holiday with the state," said Pedzisai Ruhanya, a political analyst and the director of the research group Zimbabwe Democracy Institute. "Mugabe's behaviour is inconsistent with practices in other countries, with general state practices. This is kind of strange."[3]

This display of self-confidence was not simply the result of an authoritarian state; it is important to consider the sources of his power, which were wider than the elite that clustered around him within the ruling party and the military. Perhaps Mugabe's hold over his

Table 2: Zimbabwe elections for House of Assembly since independence

Date	ZANU-PF vote %	ZANU-PF seats	Next largest party % vote	Next largest party seats	Total seats elected
Feb 1980[a]	63.0	57	ZAPU 24.1	ZAPU 20	100
June/July 1985	77.2	64	ZAPU 19.3	ZAPU 15	100
March 1990	30.5	117	Zimbabwe Unity Movement 17.6	Zimbabwe Unity Movement 2	102
April 1995	31.4	118	Zimbabwe African National Union-Ndonga 6.9	Zimbabwe African National Union-Ndonga 2	120
June 2000	48.6	62	Movement for Democratic Change 47.0	Movement for Democratic Change 57	120
March 2005	59.6	78	Movement for Democratic Change 40.0	Movement for Democratic Change 41	120
2008	46.8	99	Movement for Democratic Change 45.2	Movement for Democratic Change 100	210
July 2013	62.4	159	Movement for Democratic Change 30.3	Movement for Democratic Change 49	210

Source: African Election Database.

Note: Only two largest parties shown, http://africanelections.tripod.com/zw.html#1980_House_of_Assembly_Election.

[a] In the February 1980 election the Rhodesian Front took the 20 seats reserved for whites in Parliament. These reserved seats were abolished in 1987. There are additional seats that are appointed by the president and ex officio members from among the traditional rulers.

Table 3: Presidential elections Zimbabwe

Date	Name	Party	Votes	Percentage of votes
March 23, 1990	Robert Mugabe	ZANU-PF	2,026,976	83.05%
	Edgar Tekere	ZUM	413,840	16.95%
March 17, 1996	Robert Mugabe	ZANU-PF	1,404,501	92.76%
	Abel Muzorewa	UP	72,600	4.80%
	Ndabaningi Sithole	ZANU-Ndonga	36,960	2.44%
March 9–11, 2002	Robert Mugabe	ZANU-PF	1,685,212	56.2%
	Morgan Tsvangirai	MDC	1,258,401	42.0%
	Three other candidates			1% or less
March 29, 2008 (first round)	Morgan Tsvangirai	MDC	1,195,562	47.87%
	Robert Mugabe	ZANU-PF	1,079,730	43.24%
	Simba Makoni		207,470	8.31%
June 27, 2008 (second round)	Robert Mugabe	ZANU-PF	2,150,269	90.22%
	Morgan Tsvangirai	MDC	233,000	9.78%
July 31, 2013	Robert Mugabe	ZANU-PF	2,110,434	61.09%
	Morgan Tsvangirai	MDC-T	1,172,349	33.94%
	Welshman Ncube	MDC-N	92,637	2.68%

own party is partly explained by the veteran opposition politician David Coltart concerning the manner in which the president was treated by cabinet ministers from his own party. Coltart described his own swearing in as a minister in the Government of National Unity and says: "I was struck by how short and frail he seemed. However, from the very first day it was clear that ZANU PF ministers were in awe of him. Aside from reverently referring to him as 'H.E.' (His Excellency), they were painfully obsequious." [4] This went well beyond the traditional respect that is accorded African leaders and elders. It is important to acknowledge that Mugabe retained the affection, respect, and support of a good number of his countrymen and countrywomen. Those who benefited from the land reforms feel they owe him a great deal. He remains, in their eyes, the liberator of their country and the source of the land that they now hold. Mugabe had particularly strong support in Shona areas that benefited from state patronage and remained loyal to ZANU-PF.

Some academics see land reform as a success. "In the biggest land reform in Africa, 6,000 white farmers have been replaced by 245,000 Zimbabwean farmers," argue commentators who support the policy, implicitly denying the nationality of white farmers. The same authors go on to state: "These are primarily ordinary people who have become more productive farmers. The change was inevitably disruptive at first but production is increasing rapidly." [5] The productivity of the new farmers might be questioned; what cannot be disputed is that they owe their new farms and status to the Mugabe government, and the majority of them are duly appreciative.

The same cannot be said of the farmworkers, most of whom lost their homes and livelihoods in the land redistribution. They number, say the authors, 313,000—some permanent and some seasonal.[6] The real question is what happened to them: the unfortunate losers in this traumatic process. Although the evidence is incomplete, Ian Scoones, who has conducted long-term research in an area of southeastern Zimbabwe, suggests some answers. He believes that one in ten received land on the farms that were seized, or further afield. But even those farmworkers who were given farms during the re-distribution received much smaller plots of land than other beneficiaries. "Comparing farm worker house-holds to others, we can see that across variables, farm worker households are badly off. They have very small plots of land (average 0.6ha), all of which is cultivated." He concludes: "There is little doubt that former farm workers are extremely poor and often have precarious livelihoods."[7] This is supported by other studies, which indicate that "most of the farm workers face many difficulties with up to two-thirds of them jobless and landless." Some turned to "informal trade, fishing and hunting for survival, gold-panning, and piece-work." Others began selling fruit and vegetables and trading in second-hand clothing on farms and in neighboring towns and mines.[8]

The response of the government was, in the main, that this was someone else's problem—arguing that many of the farmworkers were foreign laborers. The General Agriculture and Plantations Workers Union (GAPWUZ) general secretary, Gift Muti, said he had approached the government on several occasions to ask for assistance for the former farmworkers but to no avail. "They believe that when someone's employment has been terminated, they should go back to where they came from. But the problem is that most of these people are migrant workers, from neighbouring countries such as Malawi, Zambia and Mozambique and the farms are the only homes they know," he said. Muti believed that many farm laborers were left in penury, since they had been deprived of their only source of income and shelter. "Most of these people were ejected from the farms during the summer season, which affected the crops they had planted on their small pieces of land, exposing them to hunger. They are also exposed to the vagaries of the weather, especially the children and women, some of whom are pregnant. They are living in groups by the roadsides and have no access to health care facilities and they are in desperate need of assistance," Muti explained.[9]

The rural population can therefore be divided into those (particularly in the Shona-speaking areas) who were, and are, strong supporters of Robert Mugabe; those who are still skeptical or even hostile (particularly in the Ndebele-speaking areas that were so savagely attacked in the 1980s during the Gukurahundi massacres); and those who remain marginalized, including the former farmworkers (many of whom left for other countries). Despite the losers in these radical reforms, it was a success from President Mugabe's point of view. As Sara Rich Dorman remarked, the land reform program remained the ruling party's "most successful political gambit."[10] It paid dividends for the governing party time and again.

The rural areas have become the bedrock of ZANU-PF's support. Over 70 percent of voters live outside urban areas, and the majority of the country's 210 parliamentary constituencies are rural. It is therefore no surprise that in the 2013 elections an estimated 99.97 percent of potential rural voters were registered, while only about 67.94 percent of the potential urban voters were registered. Zimbabwe's demographic profile is also important. On election day itself the independent Zimbabwe Election Support Network said that urban voters were further "systematically disenfranchised."[11] There is evidence of massive and carefully organized vote rigging in the 2013 elections.[12] In the election there was a substantial discrepancy between the numbers registered in urban versus rural areas, and on polling day itself far more voters were turned away in urban areas than in rural constituencies.[13] There were also considerably higher numbers of assisted rural votes than in the urban areas. This was not simply the product of illiteracy; in many cases, it was also a postelection personal defense strategy in case of a sizable MDC vote. These voters could then prove they were not "sell-outs," and thus avoid vicious retribution by ZANU-PF activists, or loss of access to food handouts and state material support.[14] As a result, the ruling party wins seats in the rural areas, allowing it to control most local councils. The Zimbabwe Election Support Network reported: "ZANU PF is now dominating the country's rural and urban councils after winning 1,493 wards against MDC-Ts 442."

Local Authority: Chiefs and Headmen

The Mugabe government, while retaining the backing of many in the rural areas who benefited from the land redistribution, had another source of support. The traditional tribal systems of governance have been used by the ZANU-PF administration, just as they were under previous Rhodesian governments (when the chiefs were paid employees of the state). Chiefs and headmen have played a major role in the politics of the country since white rule began. This authority is entrenched in law, as John Makumbe has pointed out. "Both the Constitution of Zimbabwe and the Chiefs and Headmen Act provide for various forms of relationships between traditional authorities, particularly chiefs, and local authorities. The rationale behind this arrangement is essentially that traditional leaders play a significant role in the lives of the majority of the African people of Zimbabwe. Traditional leaders are generally accepted as the custodians of customary law and practice, and their support has always been sought by successive regimes since Zimbabwe was colonised."[15]

This relationship has not always been easy: traditional leaders who resisted the colonizers were removed from office. Today they are still seen as the custodians of the land and are represented in Parliament through the Council of Chiefs, which has the right to elect eighteen chiefs who sit in the Senate.[16] Each province has a council of chiefs, which is referred to as the Provincial Assembly. From there they influence government policy both at the local level and through the Ministry of Local Government, at a national level.

Men and women who live in the rural areas are closely controlled by a network of power that begins with central government and descends to village level. This is not just the authority and the power of the state being exercised at the local level: it is also a question of livelihoods. There is a strict control of resources. Anyone who questions ZANU-PF can be deprived of everything from seeds to fertilizers.[17] During droughts or other times of hardship, the Grain Marketing Board can refuse to deal with those considered opponents of the ruling party. Derek Matyszak concluded that this pressure made it all but impossible to stand up to the Mugabe government in the countryside.

> It is clear that the current structures of power in the rural areas have been organized so that the determining authority has been shifted away from democratic institutions, such as Rural District

Councils, to appointed individuals who are beholden to central government in the form of the Ministry of Local Government and the President. . . . With Local Government and the appointment of Provincial Governors currently controlled by ZANU PF politicians, and the high probability that the entire local government structure is largely comprised of individuals that hold explicit partisan loyalty to ZANU PF, it is remarkable that any rural dweller, dependent on these individuals for access to scarce resources, and frequently food, should admit to membership of an opposition political party, even in less politically volatile times than those which currently prevail.[18]

During the 2013 elections Mugabe used these leaders to mobilize the voters. Matyszak says that traditional leaders were "observed marshalling their people to come to polling stations and vote. This could be an indication of intimidation and coercion to make sure people voted in a particular way."[19]

The government's hold over the farming communities was further strengthened through its control over the most important medium of communication: the radio. In cities it is possible to use the internet to bring members of the opposition together. Recently movements such as #ThisFlag and #Tajamuka have used Facebook, Twitter, and WhatsApp to rally Zimbabweans against the Mugabe leadership, but these efforts have been mostly targeted at citizens in urban areas, where internet use is high.[20] In the rural areas, using social media is simply not possible, and radio, which is strictly controlled by the government, is the main source of information. (Furthermore, traditional leaders sit on community radio boards.) As the BBC explains, "Zimbabwe Broadcasting Corporation (ZBC) operates TV and radio stations under the umbrella of state-owned Zimbabwe Broadcasting Holdings (ZBH). Two national private FM radio stations are licensed—one to a company owned by a supporter of Mr Mugabe, the other to a majority state-owned publisher."[21] Independent, overseas-based radio stations do make broadcasts to Zimbabwe, but they are subjected to jamming.

Under the circumstances, it is not difficult to see why the rural areas were such a bastion of support for the Mugabe government. Even those who were not government supporters were bludgeoned into submission: deprived of independent information and subjected to intense pressure from vigilantes and traditional rulers. Aware that their votes were likely to be manipulated, it is perhaps remarkable that so many rural people refused to buckle under and still backed the opposition.

South Africa: Migration and Politics

As Zimbabwe's economic and political crisis deepened, increasing numbers of people fled into South Africa. There they sought sanctuary and work. Sometimes they found one and sometimes both, but all too frequently they were met with hostility. No one knows exactly how many Zimbabweans found homes in South Africa. Figures of 2 or 3 million have been quoted, but these have been criticized as unreliable.[22] The South African census figure for 2011 puts the figure at a little over half a million (515,824).[23] Of course this reflects only the number of Zimbabweans who were "captured" by the official data: the number may be considerably higher, since people living illegally in the country would be unlikely to wish to be enumerated in the official statistics.

Having said this, there is no doubt that they represent a significant population, many of whom have real skills to offer. One study found that 45 percent had a higher education qualification. Among them were engineers, nurses, doctors, journalists, and teachers.[24] Some did very well and made comfortable lives for themselves. Zimbabweans sent home goods that helped their families survive the most difficult of times. They also sent cash: in 2016 around US$704 million was sent in remittances, most of it from South Africa.[25] ZANU-PF's decision to bring in bond notes as an alternative currency, and the restriction on bank withdrawals, make hard currency remittances more problematic.

Not all Zimbabweans landed on their feet: jobs were not easy to find and some immigrants were met with considerable hostility. Many faced attacks and persecution that have become a hallmark of townships across the country. Incoming Zimbabwean migrants posed a direct challenge to South African access to scarce resources: housing, access to education, and jobs in the formal and informal sectors. With high levels of literacy, fluent English, and a migrant's drive to succeed, Zimbabweans increased competition. In 2008 and 2009 there were waves of xenophobic attacks on foreigners, including Somalis, Nigerians, and Mozambicans. In one incident alone, some 3,000 Zimbabweans were forced to flee from the farming region of De Doorns in the Western Cape.[26] Thousands found themselves arrested and deported. Others were driven from their homes in the Alexandria township of Johannesburg, and attacks have continued, intermittently, ever since. At times the South African army has had to intervene to halt the killings.[27]

For Zimbabweans who remembered the help they had given to South Africa's liberation movements, this was a bitter moment indeed. Zimbabweans believe the South African government has been tardy in preventing the attacks, criticizing the authorities for failing to intervene. They put this down to the relationship between the ruling parties. As a Zimbabwean blogger wrote: "The ANC fought hard for democracy in South Africa but it has not used its influence as the ruling party in the regional powerhouse to encourage democratic practices among its neighbours. Instead the party has been cosying up to the Zimbabwean president, Robert Mugabe, despite his record of rigging elections and intimidating opponents."[28]

The role of the South African radical politician Julius Malema is also worth noting. In 2010 he made a trip to Zimbabwe as the head of the ANC's Youth League, at the end of which he released a statement praising Mugabe's land seizures. The Youth League described the program as "courageous and militant" and called on young black South Africans to follow Zimbabwe's example and to engage in agriculture in order to reduce their dependence on white farmers.[29] In 2012 Malema (who had by this time fallen out with President Jacob Zuma) was expelled from the ANC and established his own party, the Economic Freedom Fighters. He said his party looked to Zimbabwe for inspiration. But in recent years he became increasingly critical of ZANU-PF policies. He was quoted as describing Mugabe as an "opportunist" who waited until he was losing power to implement land reform and said that South Africa would never follow these methods.[30] By the end of 2016 Malema was calling for Mugabe to step down. "We love President Mugabe," he declared, "but we need a new leader."[31]

One other group appears to have broken with Mugabe: the war veterans. Once the Zimbabwe National Liberation War Veterans' Association were the most stalwart of the president's supporters.[32] But their loyalty wore thin. The war veterans issued a statement in July 2016 saying they would no longer support Mugabe's political campaigns and accusing the president of abandoning them in favor of ZANU-PF's youth league. "We note, with concern, shock and dismay, the systematic entrenchment of dictatorial tendencies, personified by the president and his cohorts, which have slowly devoured the values of the liberation struggle," the group said in a statement.[33] The government's *Herald* newspaper wrote in an editorial that the nation was "shocked" by the decision, saying that the veterans had joined the "'Mugabe must go' bandwagon."[34] Soon the war veterans were facing the president's wrath. Victor Matemadanda, secretary-general of the Zimbabwe National Liberation War Veterans Association, was arrested and charged with insulting the head of state.[35] In a lengthy interview, a senior member of the war veterans, Douglas Mahiya, explained that they had withdrawn their support because of the corruption within the ruling party. He attacked the ZANU-PF "political commissar" Saviour Kasukuwere, saying that he has a "50-roomed house" yet still "calls himself a Comrade."[36] Behind the differences between the president and the veterans were complex maneuverings within ZANU-PF. As a result, the war veterans found themselves isolated and attacked. Mahiya told the interviewer that his movement was now supporting groups opposing the government, including the #ThisFlag campaign started by Pastor Evan Mawarire.

The Battles for Succession and Control of Levers of Power

Given the progressive meltdown of the Zimbabwean state since 2000, the brief period of stabilization during the Government of National Unity 2009–13, and the renewed slide toward economic malaise since July 2013, Mugabe's survival as leader of ZANU-PF was a source of intense fascination and speculation. From independence onward, he also faced—and faced down—significant challenges from within his party: the factional plots to oust him as leader in the 1980s; the creation of rival political parties—Edgar Tekere's Zimbabwe Unity Movement (ZUM), the desertion of ZANU-PF colleagues to reconstitute ZAPU in 2008, and the creation of Mavamba-Kusile by former finance minister Simba Makoni in 2008; and then the rising challenge posed by the political alliance of Solomon and Joice Mujuru. Despite these threats to his authority, he was repeatedly confirmed as ZANU-PF's presidential candidate at the party's congresses until his resignation in November 2017.

The jockeying for succession went on in earnest for more than fifteen years. ZANU-PF has never formed a homogenous elite, and rival groups fought a bitter campaign in the corridors of power. As veteran journalist and editor Wilf Mbanga remarked in 2013, this protracted battle for succession enabled each faction to build necessary alliances and networks, with promises of a "softer landing" for the inevitable post-Mugabe era. If Mugabe had died suddenly, the resulting power vacuum would have been much more of a problem for these ambitious politicians. The party still contains those who believe in their entitlement to govern—tied directly to the national liberation movement ideal of the dominance of ZANU-PF as the vanguard of historical change. With this conviction comes the need for its continued grip on state power. "The party state is simultaneously a party machine, a vehicle for the upward mobility of party elites and for material accumulation justified ideologically by reference to the historical righteousness of transformation," thus making strategies of indigenization central to this historical tendency.[1] The incoming nationalist elite was primarily motivated by "prospects of upward mobility and accumulation offered by capture of the settler state."[2] Weaving together the emerging class of "patriotic black capitalists" with the party-state ensured this new elite would not develop material independence from ZANU-PF and challenge it. Instead, membership of this party elite ensured "political connectivity."

As has been seen, the 1980s and 1990s didn't quite work out according to the vision outlined by official ZANU-PF socialist ideology. Constrained by the enormous burden of transformation from a war economy, the terms of the Lancaster House settlement, the advice of fellow African leaders, and the demands of the international donor community for economic liberalization, Mugabe's government did not fundamentally alter the capitalist structure of the economy post-1980. Lancaster House meant accepting the principles of the market: a large, white-dominated private sector that provided opportunities for the expanding Zimbabwean black middle class, with the parallel expansion of the public sector offering opportunities for ZANU-PF political patronage to party cadres, provincial leaders, political cronies, and family members.[3] Although Mugabe publicly railed against this rapid entrenchment of corruption within the civil service and party elite, lamenting the loss of a sense and spirit of dedicated service, he did not stop it. In 1983 he publicly criticized the corrupting influence of office:

> Even if the present White owners of property and natural resources were to be replaced by Black owners of property and natural resources, the need for a socialist revolution would still remain urgent. A bourgeoisie does not cease to be exploitative merely because its colour has turned Black or because it is now national rather than foreign. . . . I wish to express my utter dismay at the bourgeois tendencies that are affecting our leadership at various levels of government.[4]

These public criticisms of "daylight robbery" by "socialist deviants" continued. A party Leadership Code was established in 1984, but no one paid much attention to it. Although this lack of "ideological consciousness" apparently offended Mugabe, it was far more important to keep the support of the same elite he was criticizing. Nor did he, or his family, attempt to live by the code. For Mugabe, party unity consistently trumped principle— as seen in his agreement to allow Solomon Mujuru (the main surviving military figure involved in quashing the internal ZANU revolt against Mugabe in Mozambique in 1977–78) to expand his business empire, and in his handling of the Willowgate scandal in the late 1980s (in which cabinet ministers were publicly revealed to be obtaining new cars at reduced cost, before selling them on at greatly inflated prices). The suicide of Maurice Nyagumbo (Mugabe's old cell mate and long-standing friend) after Willowgate deeply affected Mugabe; thereafter, there would be limits to calling supportive colleagues to account.[5]

On Mugabe's watch, the pattern of personal enrichment of key members of ZANU-PF—ministers, MPs, Central Committee members, and high-ranking civil servants—crucially extended to the security services. They took full advantage of economic liberalization in the 1990s, as the political elite accelerated their strategies of "shameless predation" and accumulation, in the name of "indigenization."[6] As we have indicated, the war in the Democratic Republic of Congo injected new life into the activities of Zimbabwean party-state military entrepreneurs involved in transportation, mining, armaments production, and timber extraction.[7] From 2000, the revolutionary land program also saw a massive transfer to politically connected elites:

> [A] 2,200 strong politically connected elite controls close to half the land seized from white farmers, with President Mugabe, his wife, ZANU-PF Cabinet ministers, senior military officers, provincial governors, senior party officials, chiefs, and judges owning nearly 5 million hectares of agricultural land, including wildlife conservancies and plantations. . . . Mugabe and his wife . . . owned 14 farms (extending to 16,000 hectares. . . . Overall, 90% of the nearly 200 army officers from the rank of Major to Lieutenant-General owned farms, replicated through the air force, police, prison service, and CIO [Central Intelligence Organisation].[8]

The discovery of alluvial diamonds in the Marange field, together with the creation of the Government of National Unity, intensified the determination of the ZANU-PF political-military elite to tighten their control over the diamond fields. This was not simply for purposes of personal accumulation, but also to ensure party funds for future elections, thereby negating the European Union's targeted international economic and financial sanctions.

This is the picture of "an arrogant and parasitical political/military elite determined to cling onto state power, and access to wealth that this confers"[9]—with Mugabe as president at its center. Mugabe's frenetic pattern of international travel on supposed state business earned him the sobriquet "President of the Skies." However, party officials in the office of the president and the cabinet exploited this grandstanding to their own advantage. The president's office is not audited, unlike other Zimbabwean government departments; officials deliberately filled Mugabe's international diary to enable them to draw generous per diem allowances.[10] There is also a particular long-established crossover between business interests and income raised from individual party membership. Since 2000, failure to hold a ZANU-PF membership card has become increasingly dangerous at election times, as well as negatively affecting employment and prospects for bidding on government projects. At the same time, Mugabe became adept at wooing corporate largesse for the party. In 2010, he was actively courting the largest banks in Zimbabwe, as well as leaders of industry, "exchang[ing] laughter and light hearted banter" over tea and sandwiches,[11] as a direct bid for business to fund the party's approaching Congress.

Just as there are many paradoxes in the state of Zimbabwe, this was the paradox of Mugabe: the aesthete and austere "headmaster," condoning rampant accumulation. How did he square this circle? Was he simply a 24-carat hypocrite? Like all things in Zimbabwe, the answer is complicated, shaped by his determination to achieve the "decolonization" of his country by expunging white influence and control and by a determined refusal to listen to liberal whites. His original socialist-oriented rhetoric of "the masses" was replaced by "indigenous Zimbabweans"—a permutation (or corruption, take your pick) of ZANU-PF's declared agenda at independence. This was "left populist" cosmology. It is interesting that since the mid-2000s Mugabe increasingly delivered his public speeches in Shona rather than in English, something he never used to do. By this point, the Zimbabwean revolution was depicted as the "Third Chimurenga"—the final stage of the liberation struggle against white oppression, to address supposed unfinished business of decolonization and indigenous control. Only then would Zimbabwe achieve "true, total independence." At this stage, pigmentation and nation were always going to trump class material redistribution, with socialism pushed into the distant future.[12]

In this mind-set and worldview, strategies of accumulation by Zimbabwean elites—with Mugabe's rapacious wife at the forefront—were preferable to white dominance. The revolutionary transformation of the country—well, that was always going to take time, and inevitably there would be social groups that would be losers. It is hard to judge whether Mugabe genuinely believed that the targeted international sanctions against a specific list of ZANU-PF elite were responsible for the economic hardships of Zimbabwean citizens. It may well be he came to believe his own self-justificatory rhetoric; he would not be the first leader to do this. He also took pains to keep his avaricious wife happy, the woman who had given him three children. But the contradictions of all this were evident, even blatant—his occasional rages on the lack of probity were Olympic-standard moral gymnastics, given his reluctance to have a full land audit (because he would likely face personal embarrassment) and in considering the press reports on elite corruption scandals. Mugabe also profoundly believed in the overriding need for party unity and for ZANU-PF dominance of structures and institutions. The process of ZANU-PF gaining control over the state, and party-business crossovers, paralleled Mugabe's government's vicious repression of the political opposition. Personal factors and power politics defeated personal integrity.

All of this suggested Mugabe was the ultimate arbiter of power. Over the years, he had certainly needed to maneuver skillfully to maintain this position. Repeated challenges brought out the ruthless side of his political and personal nature, as his former colleagues increasingly took their criticisms into the public space: Ibbo Mandaza, Enos Nkala, Edgar Tekere, Eddison Zvobgo (the Harvard-educated neoliberal lawyer, purged in the ZANU-PF party Congress in December 2000), Wilfred Mhanda (a former leader in the revolutionary struggle, and subsequently a progressive critic with the Liberators' Platform Group), Didymus Mutasa (formerly ZAPU), John Nkomo (former ZANU-PF chairperson),

Simba Makoni. At the same time, the Zezuru interest group—with its well-organized and aggressive steering committee known as the Group of 24—was intent on ensuring that it won privileges and dominance for its ethnic members. This group had seen Sally Mugabe as an impediment to its ambitions in the 1980s and was determined, after her death in 1992, that she would be replaced by a more pliant woman.[13] Mugabe also antagonized many Shona politicians in ZANU-PF by advancing members of his own clan; thus an ethnically based undercurrent of anti-Mugabe sentiment complicated the political picture.[14] The squabbling among rival ZANU-PF factions became increasingly bitter because the financial prizes were (and remain) potentially so great and the *Mafikizolo* (a small number of the wealthy ruling elite) were pitted against the old-style politicians from the liberation struggle era.

In 2008 ZANU-PF experienced its first defeat in the parliamentary elections, yet within five years it had come "roaring" back. Mugabe's part in this remarkable turnaround of his party's fortunes is "both straightforward and complicated."[15] He had insisted on holding these "harmonized" elections despite the failure to agree to a new constitution. After the defeat, he did not appear in public for a month. For two days, many observers thought he was on the brink of resigning the presidency. But while Mugabe had the option of considering retiring quietly in "one of several Asian countries" and money wouldn't be a problem, the same was not true for his senior ZANU-PF colleagues who could not hide behind the claims of immunity of a former head of state. "Mugabe's security chiefs were more vulnerable to prosecution than the President himself, as they had carried out the atrocities and could not deploy the defence Mugabe often uses during intimate conversations—that he did not know what was being done in his name."[16]

Was Mugabe's silence then a calculated tactic to draw out internal ZANU-PF potential challengers, and to see how far these rivals might go? He was past master at creating situations that drew critics into the open, only to flatten them. Mugabe's seeming vacillation, then, hammered home that they were all in the same boat, confirming his supposed indispensability. While the announcement of the election result was delayed, Mugabe and the Joint Operations Command (controlling the security services)[17] used the hiatus to launch a two-pronged strategy: (1) using the state-run press to float the idea of a power-sharing agreement (on the Kenyan model), and (2) manipulating the voting figures while launching a wave of brutal intimidation to ensure Mugabe's victory in the second round.

The Global Political Agreement (GPA), which shared power between the parties from 2008 to 2013, then allowed ZANU-PF the space to regroup. In the narrowed political arena of decision makers, Mugabe politically outmaneuvered the Government of National Unity's prime minister, Morgan Tsvangirai. The president appointed more ministers than originally agreed

(41, rather than the originally agreed 31), along with leading civil servants, diplomats, the attorney general, the governor of the Reserve Bank, and the police commissioner.[18] While his party re-energized its grassroots organization and support, ZANU-PF kept control of the security services, as MDC squandered its access to power and remained fatally divided between two rival factions. But this pact with the opposition came at considerable costs to ZANU-PF party unity.

Since 2000 there had also been a "creeping coup" in the militarization of the country's administration, as the securo-crats were absorbed into the upper echelons of decision making. In Paul Moorcraft's view, this fusion of political and military power within ZANU-PF had long been the key to Mugabe's political longevity. However, it was not simply that Mugabe called the shots, or that ZANU-PF dominated the security sector.[19] Zimbabwe under Mugabe was the epitome of a neopatrimonial state. This is not a system dominated and dictated by the personal whim of one man, exercising power through an informal system of rule. It incorporates a particular set of power relations with the trappings of a more liberal institutional system—Parliament, the judiciary, and a constitution. Therefore, power is not simply concentrated in the president's office. By now Mugabe was woven in a matrix of corrupt economic, political, and military networks, a veritable web of codependency. He maintained the uneasy balance between the squabbling and increasingly hostile factions within his party. Norma Kriger has argued that "the different factions within ZANU-PF [were] held together chiefly by a shared vested interest in preventing the 'opposition' parties in the [GPA], and in particular, MDC-T (Tsvangirai) from coming to power as a result of democratizing reforms."[20] Furthermore, during the Global Political Agreement, ZANU-PF moved from formal domination of state institutions to informal and parallel structures as Mugabe and the party concentrated on the business of being reelected, using state control of the media to portray MDC as out of touch. No wonder Tsvangirai was outmaneuvered.

After their surprising defeat in the July 2013 elections, the deeply divided factions of the MDC appeared essentially irrelevant. The battle within ZANU-PF over who was to succeed Mugabe began in earnest. This was a no-holds-barred contest. Indeed, this factional infighting was strongly reminiscent of the ZANU movement in the liberation period. Vicious personal politics also entered the picture in the form of Mugabe's second wife, Grace. Whereas in the 1990s Grace Mugabe had not taken a prominent political role, from this point on, this dramatically altered. For the past decade she had been gatekeeper of Mugabe's diary, and thus the effective controller of access and flows of information reaching the elderly president.

By early 2016, party internecine struggles reached such a pitch that observers were warning the country risked descending into civil war.[21] The principal contenders both had impeccable revolutionary hero credentials: Joice Mujuru, wife of the former ZANLA commander and leading Zimbabwean business entrepreneur General Solomon Mujuru;[22] and Emmerson Mnangagwa, former minister of defense and a man with excellent connections to the security forces and intelligence services, and the Karanga, who want "their turn to eat," to use the Kenyan expression. At independence, Joice Mujuru was the youngest cabinet member, and held continued office until her appointment as vice president in 2004, a move that appeared to anoint her as front-runner to succeed Mugabe. However, Mujuru's power base was dramatically undercut by her husband's mysterious death in 2011. She then fell foul of Grace Mugabe, who had contrived her own appointment in 2014 as head of the influential ZANU-PF Women's League (a position previously held by Sally Mugabe, and one which also put her in the Politburo). Grace Mugabe used this platform to launch a series of vituperative attacks on the vice president. These increasingly lurid accusations included witchcraft (a powerful accusation in traditional Shona culture) and attempting to poison her husband. In the Harare rumor mill, there were tales of "bugged conversations and secret videos showing the vice president in unseemly attire, [and] whisperings of hit men hired in Israel and South Africa."[23] Grace Mugabe didn't pull her punches—unlike her husband, who had long been known for his subtle, ambiguous barbs as he verbally pulverized opponents.[24] (The irony of President Mugabe conferring PhD degrees on both women at the same ceremony at the University of Zimbabwe in September 2014 was not lost on the audience. However, unlike Grace Mugabe, there was no doubt that Mujuru had earned hers.)[25] While Mugabe stayed quiet, the state-run media amplified the First Lady's accusations.

A distinct pattern emerged of vicious infighting and verbal public brawling, culminating in Mugabe's pronouncements calling for an end to the war, and endorsement at the annual ZANU-PF Congress of the senior party lineup. In the meantime, Mugabe regularly reshuffled the cabinet. In 2015 it was enlarged to over seventy-two ministers, "each of whom receives large salaries and allowances, vehicles, housing, and special staff."[26] The ZANU-PF internecine struggle culminated in Joice Mujuru's summary dismissal from the cabinet and expulsion from ZANU-PF in April 2015. This was accompanied by a purge of seven other Mujuru supporters from the cabinet, along with powerful provincial officials. Defiantly, Mujuru founded a new political party, Zimbabwe People First (ZPF), and took her arguments to the diaspora and international audiences.

There was much speculation around Grace Mugabe's own presidential pretensions, and she was certainly determined to protect her substantial property and financial portfolio in Zimbabwe, Dubai, and the Far East, as well as her children's inheritance. This meant she retained a powerful emotional lever over

Mugabe in his responsibilities as a father, as well as her own survival instincts. In 2015 these hints of her possible ambitions excited a storm of media interest. Grace Mugabe was supported by a younger generation in the Politburo and provincial officials, known as Generation 40 or G40.[27] A "Million Man March" in May 2016—with its waving banners of "Vote Comrade Mugabe: This is the final battle for total control," and its posters reading "We Love Our Mother" above images of Grace Mugabe—mobilized ZANU-PF youth brigades around G40, rather than the war veterans. As the highly experienced Zimbabwean analyst Brian Raftopoulos points out, "The absence of employment alternatives for youths makes them extremely vulnerable to such mobilisation by various party structures."[28] It was a blatant political statement of the street, to prepare the ground for the 2018 elections. On July 26, 2017, the First Lady went further: at a meeting of ZANU-PF's women's wing, she publicly challenged her husband to name his preferred successor to end the deepening divisions over the future ZANU-PF leadership, arguing this was the trend in other African countries.[29] Mugabe did not respond.

Emmerson Mnangagwa's own fortunes fluctuated markedly from 2000. A fellow veteran of the liberation movement, he too left ZAPU for the newly formed ZANU in 1963, and had led the first group of ZANLA cadres to China to be trained in sabotage techniques. After finishing his military training, Mnangagwa returned to Tanzania in May 1964, where he and other returning ZANU guerrillas formed the Crocodile Gang. Mnangagwa was captured after blowing up a railway train in Rhodesia, and only narrowly escaped the death sentence. The Rhodesian authorities mistakenly thought he was under sixteen, although Mnangagwa was about twenty-one at the time. He spent ten years in jail and was released in 1974 as part of the "unity talks" amnesty. In Mozambique, he was elected special assistant to the president at the 1977 Chimoio congress—which meant he was the military and civilian representative of the party. He also accompanied Mugabe to the Lancaster House negotiations. Mnangagwa served in every cabinet until he lost his constituency seat to MDC in the 2000 election. He was brought back by Mugabe to be Speaker of Parliament. In 2014–15, he seemed to be complicit in the First Lady's coarse but effective crusade against Joice Mujuru, and in 2014 Mugabe appointed him vice president, following Mujuru's dismissal. However, the alliance of convenience between "the Crocodile" and the First Lady then descended into another toxic and highly public struggle, with press reports of mysterious burglaries of Mnangagwa's office and intimidation of his supporters within ZANU-PF. His supporters within the party and its provincial structures were nicknamed "Team Lacoste" (from the French designer label's crocodile motif). In 2016 there were street brawls between rival youth brigades supporting the Mnangagwa and Grace Mugabe factions. Furthermore, Central Intelligence Organisation agents were reported to be watching the movements of current and former ZANU-PF elites on Mnangagwa's behalf. Intelligence officers also continued to threaten opposition leaders.[30] As a member of the Karanga community, Mnangagwa is firmly opposed to Zezuru dominance within ZANU-PF. He and other Karanga ZANU-PF politicians remained determined to prevent a Zezuru succession, which would limit their access to state assets—a key factional issue within the party.

From late 2016 Mnangagwa increasingly took over the day-to-day management of Politburo meetings and cabinet discussions, to the evident boiling frustration of his rivals, who publicly accused him of disrespect of "The Boss" and, in front of Mugabe, called for Mnangagwa to be fired.[31] For all his charm and reputation for being good company, Mnangagwa remained an extremely tough and ruthless politician—in the 1980s he once repeatedly punched a fellow ZANU-PF cabinet minister, to "discipline" him.[32] He had also been the key strategist behind ZANU-PF's successful election campaign in 2013. Furthermore, Mnangagwa was always careful to underline publicly his political loyalty and personal indebtedness to Mugabe. He played on the myth that he was the leader of the Crocodile Commando, claiming (wrongly) to be the first ZANU guerrilla group to kill a white farmer.

Mugabe had long been the master of playing rival factions off against each other, using a combination of intimidation, abuse of state resources, and violence to achieve his aims. "His specialism [was] to set up ambitious underlings in the ruling ZANU-PF party to fight so that he [could] eventually chide them for factionalism and push aside the likely winner, perpetually eliminating potential rivals." However, by late 2017 this image of the ringmaster was diminishing with his advancing age and declining health, along with his ability to "defuse the bombs he plants."[33] Time was not on Mugabe's side. While his sycophantic supporters argued that he remained alert and lucid, he had repeatedly been filmed dozing off in long public meetings. Yet in the view of Ibbo Mandaza, "He [did] not have the word 're-tire' in his vocabulary."[34]

Mugabe himself continued to blow hot and cold on his possible successor—for example, in January 2016 he dismissed Mnangagwa's opponents as wasting their time in their efforts to stop him from becoming Zimbabwe's next leader,[35] yet in his customary birthday interview with Zimbabwe Broadcasting Corporation in February 2017, Mugabe scoffed that there was not one person among his ambitious lieutenants who was worthy of succeeding him. This was promptly pounced on by Team Lacoste, which declared that they would now publicly campaign for Mnangagwa to be Mugabe's designated successor.

9

Eaten by the Crocodile?

The image of an "aging Godfather of a feuding Mafia family"[1] was a compelling one, but by late 2017 it was unraveling. The president's relationship with his core supporters among the war veterans had been deteriorating for some time. Three years earlier a leading member of the war veterans organization, Jabulani Sibanda, was taken to court for daring to suggest that Grace Mugabe was plotting to take over the leadership of the country through a "bedroom coup."[2] Sibanda was accused of declaring that "power was not sexually transmitted." Sibanda lost his position, but gradually the veterans became increasingly vocal in their criticism of Grace Mugabe and—by inference—of the president himself.

In August 2017 Mnangagwa fell ill and had to be airlifted to South Africa for treatment. Suggestions that he had been poisoned by ice cream from Grace Mugabe's dairy were met by the First Lady's angry rebuttals, broadcast on state television.[3] Relations swiftly deteriorated. On November 4, Grace Mugabe was loudly booed by a crowd when she took the microphone at a rally in Bulawayo. She attacked Mnangagwa, accusing him of being the "root cause of factionalism." When he spoke, the president departed from his prepared text to address the booing, and threatened to fire Mnangagwa, whom he blamed for the crowd's display of disrespect.[4] A point of no return had been reached. On November 6, following lengthy ZANU-PF party meetings, Mugabe denounced Mnangagwa for showing "traits of disloyalty." He was summarily removed from his position as vice president and expelled from the party, along with fifteen members of ZANU-PF's provincial committees aligned with Team Lacoste. This apparently cleared the way for Grace Mugabe to be appointed as a vice president at the forthcoming ZANU-PF party congress in mid-December. (She was also in charge of the committee overseeing the ZANU-PF 2018 election campaign preparations.)

The sacking marked a seismic shift in Zimbabwean politics. Mnangagwa had been Mugabe's closest ally, one of only two cabinet ministers who had served since the original cabinet in 1980. This proved to be a fatal error by Mugabe. For someone who had carefully weighed his options and only struck when he was certain of success, it was an uncharacteristic overreach. Perhaps Grace Mugabe's impatience and crude political maneuvering skewed his judgment, clouded by hubris and extreme old age. Perhaps he had come to believe himself to be indispensable to the success of the ZANU-PF project, a belief strengthened by his disdain for those junior to him. Whatever the reason, the sacking of Mnangagwa was the straw that broke the camel's back: party loyalists, war veterans, and the military turned on Mugabe, united in resisting Grace Mugabe's vaunting ambition and her allies in the G40 movement and among youth leaders, who were deemed greedy and disrespectful.

For Mnangagwa, it was a moment of intense personal danger, and he knew it. He had no desire to join the long list of former Mugabe loyalists who had died in mysterious circumstances. Moments after he was ousted, the security officers assigned to protect Mnangagwa and his family were withdrawn. He was told his life was in danger. "Security personnel, who are friendly to me, warned me that plans were underfoot to eliminate me once arrested and taken to a police station," Mnangagwa later declared. "It was in my security interest to leave the country immediately."[5] The former vice president sought sanctuary abroad. His initial attempt to fly to South Africa was thwarted, as a mining company refused to allow its private jet to be used in the escape. Plan B was put into operation, and a convoy of cars headed from Harare toward the Mozambique border. Mnangagwa's car was halted at the border, where his remaining security guards prevented police from searching the vehicles. After a brief scuffle, the vehicle was allowed to proceed and he crossed into Mozambique and safety.[6]

The Reuters news agency pieced together how events then unfolded from COI memoranda and reports from Harare, Moscow, and Beijing.[7] From Mozambique Mnangagwa left for South Africa, with some suggestions that he might have visited China en route. Zimbabwe's military chief, General Constantino Chiwenga, had already left for Beijing, having previously fallen out with Mugabe. According to Reuters, in late October, Mugabe summoned Chiwenga to a showdown. "Mugabe confronted the army chief about his ties to Mnangagwa and told him that going against Grace would cost him his life. . . . Chiwenga was warned by Mugabe that it is high time for him to start following. He mentioned to Chiwenga that those fighting his wife are bound to die a painful death," the intelligence report said. At the same meeting, Mugabe also ordered Chiwenga to pledge allegiance to Grace. He declined. "Chiwengwa refused to be intimidated. He stood his ground over his loyalty to Mnangagwa," the report said.

Mugabe was already concerned that he was facing a coup before this confrontation with Chiwenga. A CIO intelligence report dated October 23 noted, "Mugabe was openly told by senior CIOs that the military is not going to easily accept the appointment of Grace. He was warned to be ready for civil war." On November 5 Chiwenga left for a prearranged official visit to China. The

Chinese, who had backed Mugabe and ZANU-PF from the start of the liberation struggle and had very considerable investments in the country, were important to get onside as the dramatic events unfolded. The following day Mnangagwa was sacked.

From this point, the power struggle inside ZANU-PF developed into a complex and multilayered chess board, with the involvement of key international and regional actors, each with a stake in the outcome. Chiwenga's visit to China culminated in a meeting with the Chinese defense minister, Chang Wanquan, in Beijing on November 10. According to the Reuters report, citing two sources with knowledge of their discussions, Chiwenga asked if China would agree not to interfere if he took temporary control in Zimbabwe to remove Mugabe from power. (The PRC government is particularly important as a lender of last resort, given the parlous state of Zimbabwe's balance of payments.) "Chang assured him Beijing would not get involved and the two also discussed tactics that might be employed during the de facto coup." It appears that South Africa's President Zuma gave similar assurances, in that he gave sanctuary to Mnangagwa. According to *Africa Confidential,* once in South Africa, Mnangagwa, Chiwenga, and Chris Mutsvangwa, the war veterans leader and former ambassador to China, "talked to local security officials about the implications of their military action in Harare. . . . They were given assurances of non-intervention by South Africa so long as the action didn't spill over the borders and remained 'broadly constitutional.'"[8]

As the spectre of another bout of hyperinflation loomed, the Zimbabwean military, together with Mnangagwa, were acutely aware of Mugabe's declining ability to pay the salaries of soldiers and police and thereby ensure their loyalty.[9] Immediately after Mnanagawa's sacking, the military activated a "Code Red" alert, its highest level of preparedness. A coup to remove President Mugabe began to be rolled out. It was vital for Zimbabwe's military, security services, and party veterans that this should be seen as legitimate by their neighbors in the Southern African Development Community (chaired by South Africa) and the African Union, whose 2007 charter proscribes "illegal means of accessing or maintaining power."[10] This nexus of elites who had surrounded Mugabe since the liberation struggle era were also determined to ensure that the regime that replaced him would not threaten their own accumulated wealth and vested interests. Both these objectives were reflected in the coup's code name: "Operation Restore Legacy."

Initially, the president's overthrow seemed to proceed remarkably smoothly. ZBC, the state-controlled television station, was surrounded, as was the presidential residence. Armored vehicles and sufficient troops were deployed to prevent the police or the Presidential Guard from interrupting events. Key ministers were detailed, with a claimed minimum of fuss or violence.

(According to his lawyers, the minister of finance, Ignatius Chombo, was stripped naked and beaten while in detention; and the leading G40 ministers Jonathan Moyo and Saviour Kasukuwere sought emergency refuge in the presidential compound.) Grace Mugabe herself was taken into military custody. Only one obstacle stood in the way of an orderly transfer of power: the president himself. Despite being faced with overwhelming force—a tank remained parked outside his residence—and being placed under house arrest, Mugabe refused to resign.

The massive street demonstrations in Harare and Bulawayo on Saturday, orchestrated and sanctioned by the military, posed a moment of danger to the architects of the "soft coup": the multiple agendas of different groups in the elated crowds, united only in their desire to see Mugabe step down, risked unleashing a "democratizing coup," which had never been ZANU-PF's purpose. On Sunday, November 19, ZANU-PF's Central Committee removed Mugabe as party leader and ZANU-PF's designated presidential candidate for the 2018 elections. Grace Mugabe and the G40 "cabal" were summarily thrown out of the party, and their supporters in provincial committees were also ejected. Mnangagwa was reinstated as vice president designate and ZANU-PF's proposed presidential candidate.

When Mugabe was finally persuaded to address the nation that evening, he was surrounded by the military hierarchy, all of whom proceeded to salute him and treat him with respect bordering on reverence. In a surreal piece of political theater, his long-term adviser and confessor, the Roman Catholic priest Fidelis Mukonori, sat next to him, as if poised to deliver the last rites for Mugabe's long and controversial political career.[11] Mugabe's speech acknowledged mistakes, but said nothing about resignation. His delivery was hesitant and faltering, but while the text contained hints of contrition, the overall message was defiant. Crucially, it exonerated the military for their action, bringing this back within the elastic bounds of constitutional behavior. To a stunned nation and expectant international press corps, Mugabe declared: "I, as the president of Zimbabwe and their commander in chief, do acknowledge the issues they have drawn my attention to, and do believe that these were raised in the spirit of honesty and out of deep and patriotic concern for the stability for our nation and for the welfare of our people."[12]

The rambling twenty-minute address left the ZANU-PF hierachy furious, but impotent. Nothing, it appeared, would force Mugabe to relinquish power while at the same time retaining the necessary myth of a legitimate transfer of control. It begged the questions: Was he convinced that he could once again outmaneuver his enemies? Or was this deeply delusional behavior the unraveling of a once formidable strategist and tactician in extreme old age? Or, thirdly, had Mugabe done a deal with the army to stay on in power?

The onus was now on ZANU-PF to move quickly. Impeachment proceedings in Parliament were initiated on Tuesday, with the planned arrival of key southern African leaders (South Africa's President Jacob Zuma and Angola's President João Lourenço) and long-retired Zambian leader Kenneth Kaunda. Mnangagwa issued an open call for Mugabe to resign "or be humiliated." Only then did Mugabe finally relent. This time nothing was left to chance, and his short letter of resignation was read out by the Speaker of the Parliament, who had just convened impeachment proceedings. The coup leaders were determined that Mugabe would not be allowed access to radio or television again, and with good reason. As a perceptive observer noted:

> Among Mugabe's most effective instruments, and one that he deployed frequently, was his extraordinary voice. It may seem odd to outsiders, but Mugabe's speeches were one of the ways he held sway over his country. They contained sweeping phrases invoking Zimbabwe's fifteen-year liberation struggle against the Rhodesian settler regime of Ian Smith. He employed rhetorical devices that made his words weapons: the amplification and over enunciation; the deliberate, timed pauses between words; the elongation of the second syllables of certain words, such as "among," "indeed," "comported"; and the evocation of emotion

through lilting inflection at unexpected moments. His is the most recognizable voice in Zimbabwe not only because he was the only leader that generations have known but also because he speaks like no one else.[13]

The relief felt by his successor, Mnangagwa, and his associates in the military and the security services was palpable. There had been private fears that the opposition might try to manipulate the joint committee process to their own advantage, demanding free and fair elections and security sector reform as the price for their cooperation. In his inaugural address, President Mnangagwa went out of his way to pay tribute to his predecessor, addressing him as "a father, mentor, comrade-in-arms and my leader."[14] He went on to strike all the appropriate notes: calling for reconciliation, preserving the land redistribution while saying that white farmers would be compensated for the farms they had lost, and declaring that elections would proceed in 2018. Mnangagwa also called for corruption to "stop forthwith," following up three days later with a three-month amnesty for the repatriation of stolen wealth. The irony of this action was not lost on Zimbabweans and external observers, since the new president had been named in a UN report, published in 2002, as part of an "elite network" that had "transferred ownership of at least US$5 billion of assets from the State mining sector to private companies under its control."[15] Mnangagwa was said to have personally been involved in a circle of diamond dealers who "turned Harare into a significant illicit diamond-trading centre."

Notwithstanding Mnangagwa's deeply compromised past and the continuation of ZANU-PF's grip on power, Mugabe's departure was truly the end of an era. After 13,731 days of Mugabe's long and controversial leadership, power had finally been passed on. Officially, Mugabe was to be treated as a respected figure, with the loss of office softened by promises of $10 million to ease his departure from office.[16] Unofficially, he (and his wife) were granted immunity from prosecution and permitted to stay in the country with the opportunity to travel overseas for any necessary medical treatment. His birthday has been declared a national holiday, Harare International Airport has been renamed in his honor, and it was announced he would offer advice to the new leadership as an elder.

Yet, many in Zimbabwe will remember Mugabe far less fondly. The thousands of amaNdebele who lost family members (innocent civilians, ZAPU activists, and former ZIPRA fighters) during the brutal atrocities of the extended Gukurahundi campaign in the 1980s have no reason to thank Mugabe. The opposition parties whose activities were suppressed and whose attempts to participate in the electoral process were thwarted have bitter memories of their former head of state. The millions driven into humiliating exile in South Africa and beyond—a number that vastly exceeds those driven into exile by the Rhodesian regime—will recall Mugabe with little affection.

It is perhaps worth recalling that at independence in 1980 Mugabe inherited one of the most economically diverse countries in Africa. Yet he presided over a period of hyperinflation that at one point in 2008 "hit the rate of 231,000,000%. The currency had to be denominated in notes as large as the $100trn Zimbabwe-dollar bill—worth about 40 cents at the time of its demise."[17] The MDC economist Eddie Cross calculated that at independence real GDP per capita in Zimbabwe was about US$3,600; by 2017 it stood at about US$1,000. As a comparison, in 1980 GDP per capita in Botswana was about US$1,500; in 2017 this statistic was US$13,000 per capita.[18] By the end of 2017, formal unemployment in Zimbabwe was estimated at over 90 percent. By stubbornly clinging to office, Mugabe significantly compromised his legacy in the region. Once seen as a leading member of the fight to end white rule in neighboring South Africa, in the eyes of some commentators he undermined the potency of the liberation myth itself. Liberation mythology "has hobbled democracy, justice and development in our region," remarked South African journalist Mondli Makhanya. "Once in power, liberation movements inculcate in the people the belief that they are holy and are the only institutions capable of looking after the countries they run. Armed with this religious message, they proceed to do all manner of things unholy and work against the people and their freedom."[19]

Mugabe proved a deeply complex and contradictory individual. A man capable of great charm and considerate hospitality, he was most likely responsible for the assassination of opponents and critics (such as the suspicious death of the ZANLA military leader, Josiah Tongogara, in a car crash in December 1979 and the mysterious killing of General Solomon Mujuru) and ultimately for mass murder of his own people, the economic decline of his country, sizable outward migration, and enormous suffering brought on by starvation and the collapse of the health care system. He was a dedicated revolutionary who deeply admired Queen Elizabeth II and appreciated Savile Row suits. A man of personal conviction, he oversaw the rampant theft of his country's assets and enabled the rapacious spending habits of his second wife and extended family. As a political manipulator, he consolidated his personal power through structures and personalities, through rivals and antagonists who "worked towards the leader." And as a political manager, he oversaw ZANU-PF's policies as a rural-based movement that produced Zimbabwe's deprivation but presented itself as the solution, through largesse, food handouts, and access to land for voters.

What now for Zimbabwe? Robert Mugabe caused profound damage to his country, which will take generations to address. By overseeing a program of revolution and decolonization, he indeed saw the socioeconomic transformation of his country, but not enough Zimbabweans benefited. Land reform was much needed—make no mistake about that—but the mode and means of this transformation tore apart rural welfare and employment structures, and impoverished millions. The return to growth in the agriculture sector has been partial, and thus food security remains compromised, complicated by a severe drought in 2015–16. Meanwhile, the extraordinary windfall of the discovery of alluvial diamonds, conservatively estimated at $16 billion, was comprehensively looted and lost to the exchequer. The once-admired Zimbabwe health care system has been gutted, with HIV/Aids prevalence at an estimated 13.5 percent (1 in 5 adults is thought to be HIV positive, with girls and young women aged fifteen to twenty-four deemed to be the most vulnerable group), and infant mortality rates at 25.78 per 1,000 births.[20] The once widely admired tertiary education and training sector is severely battered. Currently there are an estimated 3.5 million Zimbabweans living outside the country.

Mugabe oversaw a fundamental shift in the human geography of his country. The majority of the population remains rural; there has been an important reconfiguration of social structures, a quiescent trade union sector, and the church hierarchy remained shamefully quiet until the Zimbabwe Council of Churches' open letter in early November 2017, calling for his resignation. Commentators have noted the rapid acceleration of civil society activism via social media. There is an undercurrent of debate on the need for an amnesty: Should a truth and reconciliation commission be established to address the violence and oppression of the past? And, unlike South Africa, can this be achieved without legal retribution? Can reconciliation be achieved without justice? There are no easy answers. Indeed, could such questions even be raised once ZANU-PF firmly reasserted its control and a narrative of "political stability," with the opposition, yet again, shut out of any possibility of a broader government of national unity and effectively sidelined? In essence, Zimbabwe now faces ZANU-PF's version of "government," in sharp contrast to the opposition parties' desire for "governance" through genuinely free and fair elections, and a free media space.

Zimbabwe became a rogue state under Mugabe's watch, seen in the use of military and extrajudicial force during his time in office, and his collaboration with Libya's former leader, Colonel Qaddafi (which included allowing terrorist training camps on Zimbabwean soil). His political machinations—a US diplomatic cable, published by Wikileaks in 2007, described him as a "brilliant tactician"—were directly associated with his acute reading of people, an ability to spot flaws in his adversaries' argument, and a profound conviction of his own intellectual superiority and authority. A remote and distant figure who would lecture his junior colleagues while standing behind his desk, he was known as "the headmaster" for good reason. Suspicious to the point of paranoia, he focused tenaciously on the past as justification for current actions. To the mystification of Western observers, Mugabe remained ideologically popular in the region and in wider Africa as a veteran liberation leader and Afro-nationalist. His repeated denunciations of neocolonialists earned him sincere admiration for "standing up" to Western hectoring. There is an important rationale to this: What, after all, was independence if not total equality and entitlement, and a refusal to be browbeaten by former colonial oppressors?

In November 2017, the oldest and third-longest-serving world leader finally stepped down, leaving Zimbabwe with multiple challenges. Complex and deep-seated problems associated with the long-term damage of a fractured political movement left a dubious legacy within ZANU-PF and in its relationship with the military and the security apparatus, riven by differing affiliations. These problems within the country's power structures and elites combined with a squabbling proliferation of political parties, a compromised judiciary, and hollowed-out state institutions in which the security forces control key levers of power—arguably, challenges comparable to those Mugabe himself faced on coming to office in April 1980. His successor is confronted with a liquidity crisis, massive debt arrears (estimated at approximately \$9–10 billion), bloated cabinet and civil service spending, grossly inefficient parastatal organizations, huge structural unemployment, and endemic corruption that is now embedded in wider society. And having gone back to the barracks, will the military indeed stay there?

The new president and head of ZANU-PF, Emmerson Mnangagwa, is likely to have a short "honeymoon." As the 2013 Constitution requires the next elections to be held by August 2018, there is particular pressure to deliver results to underpin his legitimacy. But there still remains residual strength in the Zimbabwean political economy: its human skills capacity, a preexisting government strategy to reengage with the international community and domestic business, an entrepreneurial and engaged diaspora, and considerable goodwill. Time will tell whether President Mnangagwa can satisfy his core constituencies in ZANU-PF, the security apparatus and the war veterans, and the enormous weight of expectation within wider Zimbabwean society.

Robert Mugabe strove for the radical transformation of his country, yet came to be regarded as the principal author of Zimbabwe's current troubles. This is simplistic, but as leader he cannot completely escape this damning indictment. Longevity in office proved a Greek tragedy for Mugabe as a man and a leader, and for his country.

1. Aristocratic members of the Pioneer Column sent by Cecil Rhodes to colonize the country, many of whom became large landowners, Bulawayo, August 26, 1895. Collection of Martin Plaut.

2. Chiefs Babyom and Omjaam, senior counselors of the Matabele king, Lobengula, captured during the Matabele wars. They had previously been sent to England to petition Queen Victoria. Collection of Martin Plaut.

3. Ndebele men and women captured during the Second Matabele War (1896–97), part of the first Chimurenga. Collection of Martin Plaut.

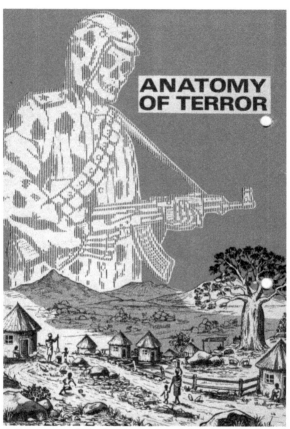

ANATOMY OF TERROR

4. Front cover of Rhodesian propaganda brochure distributed in the country and South Africa to bolster support for the white minority government led by Ian Smith. Rhodesian government document.

5. Robert Mugabe and Joshua Nkomo at an early session of
the Rhodesia Constitutional Conference, Lancaster House,
London, 1979. Commonwealth Secretariat.

6. Prime Minister Robert Mugabe of Zimbabwe, addressing
a press conference, Commonwealth Heads of Government
Meeting, New Delhi, 1983. Commonwealth Secretariat.

7. President Robert Mugabe and HM Queen Elizabeth II, Commonwealth Heads of Government Meeting, Harare, 1991. Commonwealth Secretariat.

8. Presidents Robert Mugabe of Zimbabwe, Nelson Mandela of South Africa, and Sam Nujoma of Namibia at the Commonwealth Heads of Government Meeting, Auckland, 1995. Commonwealth Secretariat.

9. A farm in southeastern Zimbabwe given to landless people as part of the land redistribution program. Collection of Martin Plaut.

10. Demonstrations by Mugabe's critics outside the Zimbabwe Embassy, London 2016. Zimbabwe Vigil.

Notes

Introduction

1. The Zimbabwe African National Union (ZANU) contested the 1980 elections under the title ZANU-PF (ZANU–Popular Front). The liberation movement/party has retained this title ever since.

Chapter 1: Controversial and Divisive Leader

1. Martin Meredith, *Mugabe: Power, Plunder, and the Struggle for Zimbabwe* (New York: Public Affairs, 2007), 15.

2. David Smith, *Guardian,* July 15, 2015.

3. The term Front Line States (FLS) refers to those countries bordering apartheid South Africa, who opposed its system of formal racial discrimination before 1994.

4. Available at http://thecommonwealth.org/history-of-the -commonwealth/harare-commonwealth-declaration, accessed July 7, 2017.

5. For example, the private conversation between Prime Minister Margaret Thatcher and Secretary General of the Commonwealth Shridath Ramphal at the Lusaka heads of government meeting in August 1979: "You realize, of course, that we have given it to the communist," Thatcher observed. "He is a nationalist mainly," Ramphal replied. Shridath Ramphal, *Glimpses of a Global Life* (Hertfordshire: Hansib, 2014), 362.

6. Ken Flower, *Serving Secretly—An Intelligence Chief on Record: Rhodesia into Zimbabwe, 1964 to 1981* (London: John Murray, 1987), 273.

7. Somerville, *Africa's Long Road since Independence: The Many Histories of a Continent* (London: Hurst, 2015), 97.

8. T. Mkandawire, "African Intellectuals and Nationalism," paper presented at CODESRIA's 30th Anniversary Conference, "Intellectuals, Nationalism and Pan-African Ideal," Dakar, Senegal, December 2003, 1–23; and Krista Johnson, "Whither Nationalism? Are We Entering an

Era of Post-nationalist Politics in Southern Africa?," *Transformation* 58 (2005): 1–19, quoted in Sabelo Ndlovu-Gatsheni, "Africa for Africans or Africa for 'Natives' Only? 'New Nationalism' and Nativism in Zimbabwe and South Africa," *Africa Spectrum* 44, no. 1 (2009): 61–78.

9. Ndlovu-Gatsheni, "Africa for Africans."

10. This mirrors the "patriotic whiteness" of the Rhodesian UDI period. Knox Chitiyo, seminar, London School of Economics, November 6, 2007.

11. Ndlovu-Gatsheni, "Africa for Africans." See also Sabelo J. Ndlovu-Gatsheni, "Making Sense of Mugabeism in Local and Global Politics: 'So Blair, Keep Your England and Let Me Keep My Zimbabwe,'" *Third World Quarterly* 30, no. 6 (2009): 1139–58. And Sabelo J. Ndlovu-Gatsheni, ed., *Mugabeism? History, Politics and Power in Zimbabwe* (New York: Palgrave Macmillan, 2015).

12. R. W. Johnson, "Reporter-at-Large: Tracking Terror through Africa: Mugabe, Qaddafi and Al-Qaeda," *National Interest,* no. 75 (Spring 2004): 161–72. See also R. W. Johnson, http://www.politicsweb.co.za /news-and-analysis/mugabe-gaddafi-and-alqaeda, accessed July 27, 2017.

13. "Zimbabwe's Mugabe Becomes African Union's Chairman," *Financial Times,* January 30, 2015.

14. "Mugabe Donates $1m to African Union," Reuters, July 3, 2017.

15. Bishop Abel Muzorewa, *Rise Up and Walk: An Autobiography* (London: Sphere Books, 1978), 141.

16. David Owen, *Time to Declare* (London: Penguin, 1992), 301.

17. Robin Renwick, *Unconventional Diplomacy in Southern Africa* (Basingstoke: Macmillan, 1997), 10.

18. Lord Carrington, *Reflect on Things Past: The Memoirs of Lord Carrington* (London: William Collins, 1988), 298.

19. Ngwabi Bhebe, *The ZANU and ZAPU Guerrilla Warfare and the Evangelical Lutheran Church in Zimbabwe* (Gweru: Mambo Press, 1999), 259.

20. Douglas Brinkley, ed., *The Reagan Diaries* (New York: Harper-Collins, 2007), 179.

21. Ali Mazrui, quoted in Chris Sanders, "Leadership and Liberation," in *Leadership in Colonial Africa: Disruption of Traditional Frameworks and Patterns,* ed. Baba Galleh Jallow (New York: Palgrave Macmillan, 2014), 140.

22. In 1994, Mugabe was made a Knight Commander of the Order of the Bath by the queen. He was stripped of this honor in 2008.

23. Eliakim M. Sibanda, *The Zimbabwe African People's Union, 1961–87: A Political History of Insurgency in Southern Rhodesia* (Trenton, NJ: Africa World Press, 2005), 86.

24. Ibbo Mandaza, "Will ZANU-PF Survive?," in *The Day after Mugabe: Prospects for Change in Zimbabwe,* ed. Gugulethu Moyo and Mark Ashurst (London: Africa Research Institute, 2007), 39–45.

25. Private information. Sally Mugabe was deeply mourned by Zimbabweans, who regarded her as one of the few people in high positions who refused to allow their relatives to enrich themselves, and who personally was not easily corrupted. Fay Chung, *Reliving the Second* Chimurenga: *Memories from Zimbabwe's Liberation Struggle* (Stockholm: Nordic Afrika Institute, 2006), 184.

26. Martin Rupiya, "The Call to the Generals," in Moyo and Ashurst, *Day after Mugabe,* 62–67.

27. Sara Dorman, *Understanding Zimbabwe: From Liberation to Authoritarianism and Beyond* (London: C. Hurst, 2016), 3.

Chapter 2: Birth of the Revolutionary

1. As an overall comparison, the Zezuru comprise approximately 18 percent of the black Zimbabwean population. Overall, chi-Shona-speaking communities made up 80 percent of Zimbabwe.

2. Reg Austin interview with Sue Onslow, December 3, 2016.

3. Peta Thorneycroft interview with Sue Onslow, December 6, 2016.

4. See Dorman, *Understanding Zimbabwe,* for the churches in post-1980 Zimbabwe.

5. Meredith, *Mugabe,* 22.

6. Sabelo Ndlovu-Gatsheni, "Dynamics of Democracy and Human Rights among the Ndebele of Zimbabwe" (PhD thesis, University of Zimbabwe, 2003), 60.

7. Lawrence Vambe, *From Rhodesia to Zimbabwe* (Pittsburgh: University of Pittsburgh Press, 1976), 101, quoted in Alois S. Mlambo, *A History of Zimbabwe* (Cambridge: Cambridge University Press, 2014), 133.

8. White emigration from the United Kingdom to Southern Rhodesia formed part of an accelerated flow of white economic migrants around Southern Africa in this period. See Josiah Brownell, *The Collapse of Rhodesia: Population Demographics and the Politics of Race* (London: I. B. Tauris, 2010).

9. Julian Manyon, "Zimbabwe—Mugabe's Gamble" (1981), Thames Television, *TV Eye,* https://www.youtube.com/watch?v=HyL0w7iCadU.

10. Sean O'Grady, "Robert Mugabe: The Dictator Bucking Zimbabwean Life Expectancy Rates," *Independent,* February 19, 2016.

11. Mlambo, *History of Zimbabwe,* 182.

12. Brian Raftopoulos and Alois Mlambo, eds., *Becoming Zimbabwe: A History from the Pre-colonial Period to 2008* (Harare: Weaver Press, 2009), 107.

13. The debate over the reasons for the split remains unresolved. Nathan Shamuyarira claims it was principally over Nkomo's determination to establish a government in exile, whereas Sithole and Mugabe argued it was more important to concentrate on party organization at home

(Raftopoulos and Mlambo, *Becoming Zimbabwe*, 112). Herbert Chitepo was elected national chairman of ZANU in 1964. Chitepo became chairman of Dare reChimurenga (ZANU's revolutionary council), which directed the war until 1975. Chitepo transformed ZANU into a Marxist-Leninist organization (in theory) and oversaw the shift to guerrilla warfare following the failure of the 1969–70 military strategy.

14. Document 394, DO 154/94, 5 September 1964, *British Documents on the End of Empire, Series B Volume 9, Central Africa*, ed. Philip Murphy, *Part II, Crisis and Dissolution 1959–1965*, ICWS, University of London (hereafter *BDEE*).

15. Documents 380, notes, referring to the copy in CAB 21/5064; 394, DO 154/94, 5 September 1964, *BDEE*.

16. Document 394, DO 154/94, 5 September 1964, *BDEE*.

17. Typically, Mugabe raised the issue of a more intensive program of education and training for Africans. Document 202, PREM 13/543, 27 October 1965, *British Documents on the End of Empire, Series A Volume 5, East of Suez and the Commonwealth 1964–1971, Part II, Europe, Rhodesia, Commonwealth*, ed. S. R. Ashton and William Roger Louis.

18. Interview with Joshua Nkomo, *End of Empire*, Chapter 14: "Rhodesia" (1985), Granada Television, https://www.youtube.com/watch?v=0DuNhsLR9y0.

19. See Richard Coggins, "Rhodesian UDI and the Search for a Settlement, 1964–1968, Failure of Decolonisation" (PhD thesis, University of Oxford, 2002).

20. Document 394, *BDEE*.

21. Richard Mobley, "The Beira Patrol: Britain's Broken Blockade against Rhodesia," *Naval War College Review* 55, no. 1 (Winter 2002): 63–84.

22. Wilfred Mhanda, interview with R. W. Johnson, "How Mugabe Came to Power," *London Review of Books*, February 22, 2001.

23. Meredith, *Mugabe*, 4–5. Mugabe consistently combined his Marxist-Leninist beliefs with a recognition of the churches' role (Catholic and Evangelical Lutheran) as partners in struggle. However, there was a complicated historical relationship between the colonial state and the original land grants to mission churches which had dispossessed Africans. Bhebe, *ZANU and ZAPU Guerrilla Warfare*, 87.

24. Flower, *Serving Secretly*, 121.

25. Mhanda interview.

26. Ibid.

27. Ibid.

28. Peasant motivations for supporting the liberation struggle were many and various. See Norma J. Kriger, *Zimbabwe's Guerrilla War: Peasant Voices* (Cambridge: Cambridge University Press, 1992).

29. David Moore, "The Zimbabwe People's Army: Strategic Innovation or More of the Same?," in *Soldiers in Zimbabwe's Liberation War,* ed. Ngwabi Bhebe and Terence Ranger (London: James Currey, 1996), 86.

Chapter 3: From Freedom Fighter to President of a One-Party State

1. Sarah L. Kachingwe, *Sally Mugabe: A Woman with a Mission* (Zimbabwe Department of Information and Publicity, 1994).

2. This explains, in part, why the Anti-Apartheid Movement was wary of Mugabe. The AAM was very close to the ANC, which was itself aligned with the Soviet Union, rather than the Chinese, following the Sino-Soviet split of 1960.

3. *Zimbabwe News,* June 5, 1977, quoted in Ian Taylor, *China and Africa: Engagement and Compromise* (London: Routledge, 2006), 110.

4. See Keith Somerville, *Southern Africa and the Soviet Union: From Communist International to Commonwealth of Independent States* (London: Macmillan, 1993).

5. Heidi Holland, *Dinner with Mugabe: The Untold Story of a Freedom Fighter Who Became a Tyrant* (London: Penguin Books, 2008), 51.

6. Zvakanyorwa Wilbert Sadomba, *War Veterans in Zimbabwe's Revolution: Challenging Neo-colonialism and Settler and International Capital* (London: James Currey, 2011), 42.

7. Holland, *Dinner with Mugabe,* 50.

8. Bhebe, *ZANU and ZAPU Guerrilla Warfare,* 79–80. This echoes the South African ANC/SACP's ideological strategy of "National Democratic Revolution."

9. Sadomba, *War Veterans,* 46.

10. Edgar Tekere, in Holland, *Dinner with Mugabe,* 49–50.

11. Sadomba, *War Veterans,* 52.

12. Paul Moorcraft and Peter McLaughlin, *The Rhodesian War: A Military History* (Barnsley, UK: Pen and Sword, 2008), 85–86.

13. Quoted in Peter McLaughlin, *The Catholic Church and the War of Liberation,* 583, cited in Ngwabi Bhebe and Terence O. Ranger, eds., *Society in Zimbabwe's Liberation War* (Harare: University of Zimbabwe Publications, 1995), 24.

14. Zvakanyorwa Wilbert Sadomba, *War Veterans in Zimbabwe's Revolution: Challenging Neo-Colonialism and Settler and International Capital* (Harare: Weaver Press, 2011), quoted in Nyasha M. GuramatunhuCooper, "The Warrior and the Wizard: The Leadership Styles of Josiah Tongogara and Robert Mugabe during Zimbabwe's Liberation Struggle," in *Leadership in Colonial Africa: Disruption of Traditional Frameworks and Patterns,* ed. Baba G. Jallow (Houndmills, UK: Palgrave Macmillan, 2014), 103.

15. Mario Diani and Doug McAdam, eds., *Social Movements and Networks: Relational Approaches to Collective Action* (Oxford: Oxford University Press, 2003), quoted in Guramatunhu Cooper, "The Warrior and the Wizard," 104.

16. Chung, *Reliving the Second* Chimurenga.

17. See David Moore, "Democracy, Violence and Identity in the Zimbabwean War of National Liberation: Reflections from the Realms of Dissent," *Canadian Journal of African Studies* 29 (1995): 375–402.

18. See Sadomba, *War Veterans,* 47.

19. Owen, *Time to Declare,* 301.

20. Julian Amery, Conservative Party Conference, October 1979, *End of Empire,* Chapter 14, https://www.youtube.com/watch?v=0DuNhsLR9y0.

21. Carrington, *Reflect,* 295.

22. Peter Petter-Bowyer, *Winds of Destruction* (Victoria, Canada: Trafford, 2003), 511. The Rhodesian SAS speculated that Mugabe had been forewarned by a British secret service mole within the CIO in Salisbury.

23. Professor Reg Austin, ZAPU legal adviser, Lancaster House negotiations, interview with Sue Onslow, November 3, 2016.

24. Renwick, *Unconventional Diplomacy,* 12.

25. Jeffrey Davidow, *A Peace in Southern Africa: The Lancaster House Conference on Rhodesia, 1979* (Boulder, CO: Westview Press, 1984); Renwick, *Unconventional Diplomacy.*

26. Carrington, *Reflect,* 295.

27. Moorcraft and McLaughlin, *Rhodesian War,* 41.

28. Moses Anafu interview with Sue Onslow, July 2013, www.commonwealthoralhistories.org.

29. Sue Onslow, "Zimbabwe: Land and the Lancaster House Settlement," *British Scholar* 2, no. 1 (September 2009): 40–75. There was keen British awareness of the central importance of the land question, both to Zimbabwean nationalism, and as developmental policy.

30. See Kriger, *Peasant Voices;* and Jocelyn Alexander, *The Unsettled Land: State-Making and the Politics of Land in Zimbabwe, 1893–2003* (Oxford: James Currey, 2006).

31. Michael Charlton, *The Last Colony in Africa: Diplomacy and the Independence of Rhodesia* (Oxford: Blackwell, 1990), 80.

32. Reports on Statements by ZANU, August 7/8, 1979, Radio Maputo, August 7, 1979, in *The Struggle for Independence, Documents on the Recent Development of Zimbabwe (1975–1980),* ed. Goswin Baumhögger (Hamburg: Institut für Afrika-kunde, Dokumentations-Leitstelle Afrika, 1984), vol. 5, doc. 878d.

33. Quoted in Nancy Mitchell, *Jimmy Carter and Africa: Race and the Cold War* (Stanford, CA: Stanford University Press, 2016), 626.

34. Martyn Gregory, "The Zimbabwe Election: The Political and Military Implications" (based on Gregory's November 18, 1979, interview with Mugabe), *Journal of Southern African Studies* 7, no. 1 (1980): 22, cited in Mitchell, *Jimmy Carter and Africa,* 639.

35. *End of Empire,* Chapter 14.

36. William Depree, "US Ambassador in Mozambique," cited in Mitchell, *Jimmy Carter and Africa,* 642.

37. As the most prominent soldier on the ZANLA side, Tongogara had considerably more influence over ZANLA fighters than Mugabe did. Paul Moorcraft and Peter McLaughlin, *Chimurenga! The War in Rhodesia, 1965–1980* (Marshalltown: Sygma/Collins, 1982), 219–20. Tongogara was killed in a car accident in Mozambique on December 25, 1979. South African sources speculated this was a GDR contract killing. At Mugabe's request, the British arranged with the Rhodesians for Tongogara's body to be embalmed and taken to his birthplace near Selukwe for burial. Renwick, *Unconventional Diplomacy,* 69.

38. Prime Minister Thatcher persisted in viewing Mugabe as a Communist-inspired terrorist, and nearly refused to shake his hand at the conclusion of the Lancaster House talks. Charles Moore, *Margaret Thatcher* (London: Allen Lane, 2013), 1:503.

39. ZANLA owed its strength largely to seasoned FRELIMO fighters within its ranks. Therefore, Mugabe was faced with a weakened military, and no rear base havens. (Sibanda, *Zimbabwe African People's Union,* 219). Machel also strongly advised him to moderate his Marxist rhetoric in the ZANU election manifesto.

40. Vladimir Shubin, *The Hot "Cold War": The USSR in Southern Africa* (London: Pluto Press, 2009), 182.

41. See Sue Onslow, "The Man on the Spot: Christopher Soames and the Decolonisation of Zimbabwe/Rhodesia," *Britain and the World* 6, no. 1 (2013): 68–100.

42. Carrington, *Reflect,* 303.

43. See Moorcraft and McLaughlin, *Rhodesian War,* 177, for an outline of Operation Quartz; and 178–89. See also Holland, *Dinner with Mugabe,* for an account of the South African–backed coup attempt.

44. Emeka Anyaoku, *The Inside Story of the Modern Commonwealth* (Ibadan: Evans Brothers, 2004), 80.

45. Total casualties in the Rhodesian counterinsurgency/liberation war amounted to 1,047 members of the Rhodesian security forces, a third of whom were white; 481 white, Asian, and Coloured civilians were killed. Moorcraft and McLaughlin, *Rhodesian War.* Official Rhodesian figures put guerrilla fatalities at 8,250, and Zimbabwean civilian deaths at 691. Informed sources estimate that the actual number of deaths ranged between 30,000 and 80,000. Ian F. W. Beckett and John Pimlott, *Counter-insurgency: Lessons from History* (Barnsley, UK: Pen and Sword, 2011), 186.

46. Cephas G. Msipa, *In Pursuit of Freedom and Justice: A Memoir* (Harare: Weaver Press, 2015), 96.

47. *Chronicle (Bulawayo)*, April 18, 1980, cited in Mlambo, *History of Zimbabwe*, 195.

48. See Flower, *Serving Secretly*, 2–4.

49. Flower, *Serving Secretly*, 4, 273.

50. Flower's memoirs are matter-of-fact about the breakdown of relations between Mugabe, and Nkomo and his ZIPRA forces. "His policy of reconciliation [was] not fully reciprocated by some blacks and by many whites; but that was hardly his fault" (277–78).

51. *End of Empire*, Chapter 14.

52. Wilf Mbanga, first head of the Zimbabwe Information Service, and later editor of the opposition *Daily News*, and the *Zimbabwean*. Interview, Nehanda TV, http://nehandatv.com/tag/wilf-mbanga/.

53. Roadblocks witnessed by Martin Plaut.

54. Maurice Nyagumbo, in Manyon, "Zimbabwe—Mugabe's Gamble."

55. Bhebe and Ranger, *Soldiers in Zimbabwe's Liberation War*, 112–13.

56. Somerville, *Southern Africa and the Soviet Union*, 152, 154–55.

57. Reluctantly, Mugabe had invited a Soviet delegation to the independence celebrations; the fact that two Soviet representatives had been instrumental in refusing aid to ZANU underlined Moscow's insensitivity. Somerville, *Southern Africa and the Soviet Union*, 153. Whereas lowly ZANU officials met the Soviet delegates on arrival, the PRC's representative to the independence celebrations was met by Mugabe. The USSR only established diplomatic relations with Zimbabwe in 1981. To their chagrin, Western embassies were opened much more rapidly (Shubin, *The Hot "Cold War,"* 187). Mugabe also gave permission for the CIA and M16 to bug the Soviet Embassy post-1982.

58. Another serious flaw was the issue of financial liabilities at independence: Mugabe's government inherited US$5.3 million multilateral debt, US$97.9 million bilateral debt, and private debt amounting to US$593.9 million. In 1980 over US$65 million was required in debt servicing alone. Under consistent pressure from international bankers, Mugabe agreed not to default. A political pattern emerged in which "Mugabe gives radical, anti-business speeches before government makes major pro-business decisions or announcements." Patrick Bond and Masimba Manyanya, *Zimbabwe's Plunge: Exhausted Nationalism, Neoliberalism and the Search for Social Justice* (Durban: University of Natal Press, 2002), 24–27.

59. Reg Austin to Sue Onslow, December 3, 2016.

60. Sadomba, *War Veterans*, 56.

61. Manyon, "Zimbabwe—Mugabe's Gamble."

62. Robert Mugabe interview, Thames Television's *TV Eye*, March 1983, https://www.youtube.com/watch?v=_Fk_bn-Ov00.

63. Robert Mugabe interview, Manyon, "Zimbabwe—Mugabe's Gamble."

64. Mbanga, interview, Nehanda TV.

65. Charles Moore, *Margaret Thatcher: The Authorized Biography* (London: Allen Lane, 2015), 2:76.

66. Catholic Commission for Justice and Peace in Zimbabwe, *Breaking the Silence: Building True Peace—A Report into the Disturbances in Matabeleland and the Midlands, 1980–1988* (Harare: Catholic Commission for Justice and Peace in Zimbabwe/Legal Resources Foundation, 1997).

Chapter 4: Refashioning the State, and the Hope of Multiracial Zimbabwe

1. Meredith, *Mugabe*, 79.

2. Electoral Institute of Southern Africa, *Zimbabwe: Print Media* (Johannesburg: South Africa, 2002), quoted in Blessing-Miles Tendi, *Making History in Mugabe's Zimbabwe* (Oxford: Peter Lang, 2010), 44.

3. Michael Bratton, *Power Politics in Zimbabwe* (Boulder, CO: Lynne Rienner Publishers, 2014), 61.

4. Ibid., 62.

5. Stephen Moyo, "Corruption in Zimbabwe: An Examination of the Roles of the State and Civil Society in Combating Corruption" (PhD diss., University of Central Lancashire, 2014), 176.

6. Ndlovu-Gatsheni, "Dynamics of Democracy," 68.

7. *The Cambridge History of Africa,* Vol. 5 (Cambridge: Cambridge University Press, 1976), 344 ff.

8. *The Cambridge History of Africa,* Vol. 6 (Cambridge: Cambridge University Press, 1985), 445 ff.

9. Meredith, *Mugabe*, 112–13.

10. Ian Scoones et al., *Zimbabwe's Land Reform: Myths and Realities* (Woodbridge: James Currey, 2010), 2.

11. Meredith, *Mugabe*, 120.

12. Alexander, *Unsettled Land*, 112–13.

13. The British did consider a compulsory land restitution program, but rejected it as covering too much of the country, and too expensive. London also wanted to keep white farming skills capacity in the country to help rebuild the economy postindependence, and to encourage white urban skills to stay too. It was also a policy designed to reassure South Africa.

14. Meredith, *Mugabe*, 119.

15. Scoones et al., *Zimbabwe's Land Reform*, 14.

16. Jocelyn Alexander, "State, Peasantry and Resettlement in Zimbabwe," *Review of African Political Economy* 21, no. 61 (September 1994): 335.

17. Meredith, *Mugabe,* 121.

18. All Party Parliamentary Group, *Land in Zimbabwe: Past Mistakes, Future Prospects* (HMSO, December 2009), 32.

19. Ibid., 34.

20. *Mail & Guardian,* December 22, 1997.

21. Dorman, *Understanding Zimbabwe,* 19.

22. David Martin and Phyllis Johnson, *The Struggle for Zimbabwe: The Chimurenga War* (London: Faber and Faber, 1981), 10.

23. Ibid.

24. Stephen Ellis, *External Mission: The ANC in Exile, 1960–1990* (London: C. Hurst, 2012), 134.

25. Mark Gevisser, *Thabo Mbeki: The Dream Deferred* (Johannesburg: Jonathan Ball, 2009), 431–46.

26. Merle Lipton, "Understanding South Africa's Foreign Policy: The Perplexing Case of Zimbabwe," *South African Journal of International Affairs* 16, no. 3 (December 2009): 331–46.

27. Thabo Mbeki Foundaton, "South Africa's Policy towards Zimbabwe—A Synopsis," http://www.mbeki.org/2016/04/08/south-africas-policy-towards-zimbabwe-a-synopsis/, accessed November 14, 2016.

28. David Blair, "Tony Blair Denies Asking South Africa to Help Overthrow Robert Mugabe," *Daily Telegraph,* November 27, 2013.

29. William Minter and Elizabeth Schmidt, "When Sanctions Worked: The Case of Rhodesia Re-examined," *African Affairs* 87, no. 347 (April 1988): 228.

30. See Chief Emeka Anyaoku interview with Sue Onslow, www.commonwealthoralhistories.org; and Gevisser, *Thabo Mbeki,* 302.

31. Stephen Chan, "Mbeki's Failure over Zimbabwe," *New Statesman,* April 23, 2008.

32. Don McKinnon, *In the Ring: A Commonwealth Memoir* (London: Elliot and Thompson, 2013), 162.

33. Chantelle Benjamin, "Khampepe: Zim's 2002 Elections Not Free and Fair," *Mail & Guardian,* November 14, 2014.

34. "Report on the 2002 Presidential Elections of Zimbabwe," http://cdn.mg.co.za/content/documents/2014/11/14/reportonthe-2002presidentialelectionsofzimbabwe.pdf.

35. See, inter alia: Gordon Corera, "MI6 and the Death of Patrice Lumumba," *BBC News,* April 2, 2013.

36. Gerard Prunier, *Africa's World War: Congo, the Rwandan Genocide, and the Making of a Continental Catastrophe* (Oxford: Oxford University Press, 2009).

37. Martin Rupiya, "A Political and Military Review of Zimbabwe's Involvement in the Second Congo War," in *The African States of the Congo War,* ed. John E. Clark (New York: Palgrave Macmillan, 2002), 96.

38. Ibid., 101.

39. Meredith, *Mugabe,* 148.

40. Wilson Johwa, "Zimbabwe's Secret War in the DRC," *Mail & Guardian,* September 11, 2004.

41. Rupiya, "Political and Military Review," 103.

42. Bratton, *Power Politics,* 195.

43. Dorman, *Understanding Zimbabwe,* 115 ff, has meticulously recorded the emergence of these trends.

44. Ibid., 102.

45. Ibid., 128.

46. Ibid., 155–56. See also Raftopoulos and Mlambo, *Becoming Zimbabwe;* and Stephen Chan, *Southern Africa: Old Treacheries and New Deceits* (New Haven, CT: Yale University Press, 2011).

47. "Mugabe Accepts Referendum Defeat," *BBC News,* February 15, 2000.

48. "Zimbabwe Crisis Summit," *BBC News,* April 20, 2000.

Chapter 5: Revolution Redux, or "Why It All Turned Sour"

1. Bratton, *Power Politics,* 75.

2. Sam Moyo and Paris Yeros, "Land Occupations and Land Reform in Zimbabwe: Towards the National Democratic Revolution," in *Reclaiming the Land: The Resurgence of Rural Movements in Africa, Asia and Latin America,* ed. Sam Moyo and Paris Yeros (London: Zed Books, 2004), 186.

3. Sam Moyo and Paris Yeros, introduction to *Reclaiming the Land,* 21–22.

4. Bond and Manyanya, *Zimbabwe's Plunge,* 274.

5. Michael Auret, *From Liberator to Dictator: An Insider's Account of Robert Mugabe's Descent into Tyranny* (Cape Town: David Philip, 2009), 155.

6. Meredith, *Mugabe,* 167.

7. Bratton, *Power Politics,* 76.

8. Allister Sparks, *Beyond the Miracle: Inside the New South Africa* (London: Profile Books, 2003), 320.

9. Scoones et al., *Zimbabwe's Land Reform.*

10. General Agricultural and Plantation Workers Union of Zimbabwe, *If Something Goes Wrong: The Invisible Suffering of Farmworkers due to "Land Reform"* (Harare: Weaver Press, 2010), 13.

11. Ibid., 23.

12. Sam Moyo, "Three Decades of Agrarian Reform in Zimbabwe," *Journal of Peasant Studies* 38, no. 3 (July 2011): 493–531.

13. Food and Agriculture Organization of the United Nations, GIEWS Country Briefs: Zimbabwe, June 27, 2017, http://www.fao.org/giews/countrybrief/country.jsp?code=ZWE.

14. Zimbabwe National Statistics Agency, "Facts and Figures," 2015, http://www.zimstat.co.zw/sites/default/files/img/publications/Prices/Fact_2015.pdf.

15. See, for example, Scoones et al., *Zimbabwe's Land Reform,* and Joseph Hanlon, Jeanette Manjengwa, and Teresa Smart, *Zimbabwe Takes Back Its Land* (Sterling, VA: Kumarian Press, 2013).

16. Scoones et al., *Zimbabwe's Land Reform,* 238 ff.

17. Ibid., 233.

18. Bloomberg News, "Rural Zimbabwe Empties as Mugabe Land Reform Policy Unravels," *Bloomberg,* February 28, 2017.

19. Dorman, *Understanding Zimbabwe,* 181.

20. Anna Tibaijuka, *Report of the Fact-Finding Mission to Zimbabwe to Assess the Scope and Impact of Operation Murambatsvina,* http://www.un.org/News/dh/infocus/zimbabwe/zimbabwe_rpt.pdf.

21. Dorman, *Understanding Zimbabwe,* 156.

22. Jonathan Crush, Abel Chikanda, and Godfrey Tawodzera, *The Third Wave: Mixed Migration from Zimbabwe to South Africa,* Southern African Migration Programme, 2012, Published by the Southern African Research Centre, Queen's University, Canada, and the Open Society Initiative for Southern Africa.

23. Ibid. Informal figures put the number closer to 2.5 million, with nearly 1 million of the best-trained members of the Zimbabwe middle class seeking economic and political asylum in the United Kingdom.

Chapter 6: "Look East" for Foreign Friends

1. Bratton, *Power Politics,* 88.

2. Ibid., 91.

3. Ibid., 138.

4. Ibid., 137.

5. Zhang Chun, *China-Zimbabwe Relations: A Model of China-Africa Relations?* South African Institute of International Affairs, Johannesburg, Occasional Paper 205, November 2014, p. 6.

6. Lindsey Hilsum, "Small Fish in a Chinese Sea," in *The Day after Mugabe: Prospects for Change in Zimbabwe,* ed. Gugulethu Moyo and Mark Ashurst (London: Africa Research Institute, 2007), 144.

7. Zhang Chun, *China-Zimbabwe Relations,* 7.

8. Dorman, *Understanding Zimbabwe,* 40.

9. Zhang Chun, *China-Zimbabwe Relations,* 16.

10. European Council, Council of the EU, "Zimbabwe: EU Extends Sanctions by One Year," press release, February 15, 2016, http://www.consilium.europa.eu/en/press/press-releases/2016/02/15-zimbabwe-eu-prolongs-sanctions-by-one-year/.

11. Peter Greste, "Civil Society's Triumph on Zimbabwe," *BBC News,* April 25, 2008.

12. Human Rights Watch, *Diamonds in the Rough: Human Rights Abuses in the Marange Diamonds Fields of Zimbabwe*, June 26, 2009, 12.

13. David Towriss, "Buying Loyalty: Zimbabwe's Marange Diamonds," *Journal of Southern African Studies* 39, no. 1 (July 2013): 101.

14. Human Rights Watch, *Diamonds in the Rough*, 14.

15. Ibid., 15.

16. Towriss, 107.

17. Ibid., 105.

18. Ibid., 110.

19. Global Witness, *Diamonds: A Good Deal for Zimbabwe?* London, February 13, 2012, https://www.globalwitness.org/en/reports/diamonds-good-deal-zimbabwe/.

20. James Mupfumi, "Alluvial Diamond Mining in Marange," Country Report, May 2015, http://docplayer.net/24585331-Country-report-alluvial-diamond-mining-in-marange.html.

21. Zhang Chun, *China-Zimbabwe Relations,* 17.

22. Global Witness, *Diamonds.*

23. Ibid.

24. Annina Kärkkäinen, "Does China Have a Geoeconomic Strategy towards Zimbabwe? The Case of the Zimbabwean Natural Resource Sector," *Asia-Europe Journal* 14, no. 2 (November 2015): 185–202.

25. Peta Thornycroft, "Secret Airstrip Built at Zimbabwe Diamond Field," *Daily Telegraph*, January 31, 2010.

26. Towriss, "Buying Loyalty," 112.

27. "The key management of these companies is drawn primarily from serving or retired senior Chinese and Zimbabwean military personnel." Crispen Chinguno, Taurai Mereki, and Nunurayi Mutyanda, "Chinese Investments, Marange Diamonds and 'Militarised Capitalism' in Zimbabwe," *Global Labour Column* (University of the Witwatersrand), no. 200 (May 2015), http://column.global-labour-university.org/2015/05/chinese-investments-marange-diamonds.html.

28. Towriss, "Buying Loyalty," 113.

29. Peta Thornycroft, "Mugabe's Wife to Move into White Couple's Farm," *Telegraph,* August 20, 2002.

30. David Pallister, "International Hunt for Mugabe Family Assets," *Guardian,* January 16, 2002.

31. Itai Mushekwe, "Mugabe Assured of Malaysia Safe Haven," *Nehabda Radio,* March 25, 2013.

32. Peta Thornycroft, "Grace Mugabe, the Businessman and the Hong Kong Villa," *Telegraph,* May 24, 2015.

33. Andrew Malone, *Daily Mail*, December 12, 2014.

34. "Bob's 2016 Travels: The Map and the Millions," *New Zimbabwe,* December 23, 2016.

35. Frank Chikowore, "Mugabe, 92, Splashes Millions on Holiday as Zimbabweans Starve," *News24,* December 22, 2016.

Chapter 7: Mugabe and the People

1. Obonye Jonas, David Mandiyanike, and Zibani Maundeni, "Botswana and Pivotal Deterrence in the Zimbabwe 2008 Political Crisis," *Open Political Science Journal* 6 (2013): 1–9.

2. Bridget Mananavire, "Mugabe Clocks Up 220,000km Flying," *Daily News,* July 6, 2015.

3. "Zimbabwe Stands Still as President Vacations Off the Grid," *New York Times,* January 26, 2017.

4. David Coltart, *The Struggle Continues: 50 Years of Tyranny in Zimbabwe* (Johannesburg: Jacana Media, 2016), 492.

5. Hanlon, Manjengwa, and Smart, *Zimbabwe Takes Back Its Land,* 209.

6. Ibid., 192.

7. Ian Scoones, "What Happened to Farm Workers following Zimbabwe's Land Reform?," *Zimbabwean,* December 7, 2015.

8. Rodrigo, "What Happened to Comercial [*sic*] Farm Workers after the Famous Land Reform (Grab) Programme in Zimbabwe?," *Write-Pass Journal,* October 24, 2016.

9. Christopher Mahove, "Zimbabwe: Displaced Farm Workers Face Crisis," *Equal Times,* July 3, 2014.

10. Dorman, *Understanding Zimbabwe,* 194.

11. Zimbabwe Election Support Network, *Report on the 31 July 2013 Harmonised Elections,* http://www.zesn.org.zw/wp-content/uploads /2016/04/ZESN-2013-harmonised-election-report.pdf.

12. "Zimbabwe Election: A Guide to Rigging Allegations," *BBC News,* August 7, 2013.

13. Dorman, *Understanding Zimbabwe,* 197.

14. "Hot Seat Interview with Derek Matyszak on the Voters Roll," *Hot Seat with Violet Gonda,* February 24, 2017, http://www.violetgonda .com/2017/02/hot-seat-interview-with-derek-matyszak-on-the -voters-roll/.

15. John Makumbe, "Local Authorities and Traditional Leadership," in *Local Government Reform in Zimbabwe: A Policy Dialogue,* ed. Jaap de Visser, Nico Steytler, and Naison Machingauta (Harare: Community Law Centre, 2010), 88–100.

16. Ibid., 89.

17. Derek Matyszak, "Formal Structures of Power in Rural Zimbabwe," Commercial Farmers Union of Zimbabwe, Research and Advocacy Unit, February 2011, http://www.swradioafrica.com /Documents/Formal%20Structures%20of%20Power%20in %20Rural%20Zimbabwe.pdf, accessed December 5, 2017.

18. Ibid.

19. Zimbabwe Election Support Network, *Report.*

20. Cris Chinaka, "Zimbabwe's Social Media Revolt Yet to Take Root in Rural Areas," *Reuters,* August 12, 2016.

21. BBC, "Zimbabwe Profile: Media," *BBC News,* November 21, 2017.

22. "How Many Zimbabweans Live in South Africa? The Numbers Are Unreliable," *Africa Check,* November 5, 2013, https://africacheck.org/reports/how-many-zimbabweans-live-in-south-africa-the-numbers-are-unreliable/.

23. Deborah Budlender, "Labour Migration by Numbers: South Africa's Foreign and Domestic Migration Data," MiWORC Fact Sheet No. 1, July 2013, Migrating for Work Research Consortium, University of the Witwatersrand, http://www.miworc.org.za/docs/MiWORC-FactSheet_1.pdf.

24. Elinor Sisulu, Bhekinkosi Moyo, and Nkosinathi Tshuma, "The Zimbabwean Community in South Africa," in *State of the Nation: South Africa 2007,* ed. Sakhela Buhlungu, John Daniel, Roger Southall, and Jessica Lutchman (Cape Town: HSRC, 2007), 555.

25. "Zimbabwe: Diaspora Remittances Down 12,5 Percent to U.S.\$704 Million in Year to November," *AllAfrica,* December 24, 2016, http://allafrica.com/stories/201612300115.html.

26. Jonathan Crush and Sujata Ramachandran, *Xenophobic Violence in South Africa: Denialism, Minimalism, Realism,* Southern African Migration Programme, 2014, University of Cape Town.

27. "South Africa Army Mobilises to Quell Mob Violence," *AFP,* May 22, 2008, https://web.archive.org/web/20080611092810/http://afp.google.com/article/ALeqM5gzax3SXQ8v0UUA6ydLpCsuHeCinA.

28. Blessing Vava, "South Africa's Silence on Zimbabwe Instrumental in Xenophobic Attacks," *Guardian,* April 29, 2015.

29. "We Must Follow Zimbabwe Model—ANCYL," *PoliticsWeb,* April 8, 2010, http://www.politicsweb.co.za/party/we-must-follow-zimbabwe-model--ancyl.

30. "Zimbabwe: Malema Describes Mugabe's Violent Landgrab as 'Opportunistic,'" *NewZimbabwe.com,* November 26, 2015.

31. "Malema tells Zimbabwe's Robert Mugabe to Go, and Enjoys Another Anti-white Rant," *TimesLive,* December 2, 2016, http://www.dispatchlive.co.za/politics/2016/12/02/malema-tells-zimbabwes-robert-mugabe-to-go-and-enjoys-another-anti-white-rant/.

32. Joann McGregor, "The Politics of Disruption: War Veterans and the Local State in Zimbabwe," *African Affairs* 101 (2002): 9–37.

33. "Zimbabwe War Veterans Denounce 'Dictatorial' Mugabe," *Al Jazeera,* July 21, 2016.

34. "Comment: This Is Not the Way of the Soldier," *Herald,* July 23, 2016.

35. "Zimbabwe: War Veterans Arrested for 'Insulting Mugabe,'" *Al Jazeera*, August 2, 2016.

36. "Hot Seat: Mugabe Is No Comrade Says War Vet Leader Douglas Mahiya," *Zimbabwean*, August 17, 2016.

Chapter 8: The Battles for Succession and Control of Levers of Power

1. Southall, *Liberation Movements*, 247.

2. David Compagnon, *A Predictable Tragedy: Robert Mugabe and the Collapse of Zimbabwe* (Philadelphia: University of Pennsylvania Press, 2010), cited in Southall, *Liberation Movements*, 248.

3. See Meredith, *Mugabe*, 81.

4. ACR 1982–83, B883, cited in Southall, *Liberation Movements*, 249.

5. "Zanu (PF) Has Eaten Its Own Sons," *Zimbabwean*, August 14, 2014.

6. Southall, *Liberation Movements*, 253.

7. Ibid., 255.

8. Ibid., 256.

9. Ibid., 259.

10. Former finance minister Tendai Biti interview with Violet Gonda: "Hot Seat: Biti Says Mugabe Takes at Least $4million on Every Foreign Trip," *HotSeat with Violet Gonda*, June 6, 2017, http://www .violetgonda.com/2017/06/hot-seat-biti-says-mugabe-takes-at-least -4million-on-every-foreign-trip/.

11. "ZANU-PF Courts Big Business ahead of Elections," http:// newsdzezimbabwe.wordpress.com/2010/12/10/zanu-pf-courts, accessed February 22, 2017.

12. I am grateful to a former UN staff member posted to Zimbabwe for these observations.

13. Chung, *Reliving the Second* Chimurenga, 187.

14. Philip Barclay, *Zimbabwe: Years of Hope and Despair* (London: Bloomsbury, 2010), 48. Barclay was a British diplomat based in Harare between 2006 and 2009.

15. Dorman, *Understanding Zimbabwe*, 187.

16. Barclay, *Zimbabwe*, 92–94.

17. The Joint Operations Command (JOC), comprising the security chiefs, represents the ZANU-PF hardliners.

18. Dorman, *Understanding Zimbabwe*, 193.

19. Heidi Holland, quoted in Paul Moorcraft, *Mugabe's War Machine* (Barnsley, UK: Pen and Sword, 2011), 195.

20. Norma Kriger, "ZANU-PF Politics under Zimbabwe's 'Power-Sharing' Government," 13, cited in Dorman, *Understanding Zimbabwe*, 208. The former military commander of ZIPRA, and Home Affairs minister, Dabengwa split from ZANU-PF and revived his old party in 2008.

21. Gibbs Dube, "Will Mugabe Succession Fights Lead to Civil War in Zimbabwe?," *VOA Zimbabwe,* February 20, 2016, https://www.voazimbabwe.com/a/is-zimbabwe-on-brink-of-civil-war/3199533.html.

22. Former army commander and ZANU-PF powerbroker Solomon Mujuru was a leading Zezuru figure in the coterie surrounding Mugabe. One of the wealthiest men in Zimbabwe, he had substantial business interests and had benefited greatly from defense procurement contracts. He represented a key link in the president's chain of command with the army leadership, former guerrilla leaders, and junior officer corps, as well as a vital part of the president's patronage network. His death in 2011, in deeply mysterious circumstances, deprived his wife of considerable political leverage within the ZANU-PF Politburo. See Somerville, *Africa's Long Road to Independence,* 288.

23. Alan Cowell, "In Zimbabwe's Succession Battle, Mugabe Pulls the Strings," *New York Times,* November 21, 2014.

24. "The Mugabe Brawl," *Economist,* October 30, 2014.

25. As Grace Mugabe was awarded a PhD in sociology after only three months of formal registration, her nicknames now include "Amazing Grace."

26. "Freedom in the World 2016: Zimbabwe," *Freedom House,* https://freedomhouse.org/report/freedom-world/2016/zimbabwe, accessed February 23, 2017.

27. Gibbs Dube, "Generation 40 Causing Havoc in Mugabe's Faction-Riddled Zanu PF," *VOA Zimbabwe,* October 8, 2016.

28. Brian Raftopoulos, "The Persistent Crisis of the Zimbabwean State," *Solidarity Peace Trust,* June 9, 2016.

29. "'Name Your Successor,' Wife Urges Zimbabwe's Ageing Mugabe," *Reuters,* July 27, 2017.

30. "Freedom in the World 2016: Zimbabwe."

31. Charles Mabhena, "Mnangagwa Sticks to Business; Overlooks Mugabe Succession War," *ZimNews,* February 2, 2017.

32. Dan Stannard, former CIO, interview with Sue Onslow, August 1, 2008.

33. "Mugabe Brawl."

34. David Pilling and Andrew England, "Mugabe Era Draws to an End but It Will Be No Ordinary Succession," *Reuters,* February 22, 2016.

35. Everson Mushava, "Mugabe Succession Shocker, *Standard,* January 15, 2017.

Chapter 9: Eaten by the Crocodile?

1. Alex T. Magaisa, "The Godfather Has Spoken—But Was It Much Ado about Nothing?," *Zimbabwe Independent,* February 26, 2016.

2. AFP, "Zim Ex-War Veterans Leader in Court for 'Insulting' Mugabe," *News24.com,* December 3, 2014.

3. Jason Burke, "Robert Mugabe Sacks Vice-President to Clear Path to Power for Wife," *Guardian,* November 6, 2017.

4. Petina Gappah, "How Zimbabwe Freed Itself from Robert Mugabe," *New Yorker,* November 22, 2017.

5. MacDonald Dzirutwe, Joe Brock, and Ed Cropley, "'Treacherous Shenanigans'—The Inside Story of Mugabe's Downfall," Reuters Special Report, *Reuters,* November 26, 2017.

6. Bernard Mpofu and Elias Mambo, "Mnangagwe's Great Escape: The Details," *Zimbabwe Independent,* November 10, 2017.

7. Dzirutwe, Brock, and Cropley, "'Treacherous Shenanigans.'"

8. "The Crocodile Snaps Back," *Africa Confidential* 58, no. 23, November 17, 2017.

9. "Mugabe Drops the Crocodile," *Africa Confidential* 58, no. 23, November 10, 2017.

10. *Constitutive Act of the African Union,* July 11, 2000, http://www.achpr.org/files/instruments/au-constitutive-act/au_act_2000_eng.pdf.

11. Father Mukonori was reported to be assisting in the mediation between the Zimbabwean military and the ninety-three-year-old president.

12. Jeffrey Moyo, "Robert Mugabe, in Speech to Zimbabwe, Refuses to Say If He Will Resign," *New York Times,* November 19, 2017.

13. Gappah, "How Zimbabwe Freed Itself."

14. "President Mnangagwa's Inauguration Speech in Full," *Chronicle,* November 25, 2017.

15. "Plundering of DR Congo Natural Resources: Final Report of the Panel of Experts (S/2002/1146)," *ReliefWeb,* October 16, 2002.

16. "Zimbabwe Officially Declares Mugabe National Holiday," *BBC News,* November 27, 2017.

17. "How Mugabe Ruined Zimbabwe," *Economist,* February 26, 2017.

18. Eddie Coss, personal communication, November 17, 2017.

19. Mondli Makhanya, "The Liberation Myth Is Busted," *News24,* November 6, 2017.

20. Source: Zimbabwe Infant Mortality Rate, 2017, *Geoba.se,* http://www.geoba.se/country.php?cc=ZW.

Selected Bibliography

Abiodun, Alao. *Mugabe and the Politics of Security in Zimbabwe*. Montreal and Kingston: McGill-Queen's University Press, 2012.

Alexander, Jocelyn. *The Unsettled Land: State-Making and the Politics of Land in Zimbabwe, 1893–2003*. Oxford: James Currey, 2006.

Anyaoku, Emeka. *The Inside Story of the Modern Commonwealth*. Ibadan: Evans Brothers, 2004.

Auret, Michael. *From Liberator to Dictator: An Insider's Account of Robert Mugabe's Descent into Tyranny*. Cape Town: David Philip, 2009.

Bhebe, Ngwabi. *Simon Vengai Muzenda and the Struggle for the Liberation of Zimbabwe*. Gweru: Mambo Press, 2004.

———. *The ZANU and ZAPU Guerrilla Warfare and the Evangelical Lutheran Church in Zimbabwe*. Gweru: Mambo Press, 1999.

Bhebe, Ngwabi, and Terence Ranger, eds. *Society in Zimbabwe's Liberation War*. Harare: University of Zimbabwe Publications, 1995.

———, eds. *Soldiers in Zimbabwe's Liberation War*. London: James Currey, 1996.

Blair, David. *Degrees in Violence: Robert Mugabe and the Struggle for Power in Zimbabwe*. London: Bloomsbury, 2002.

Bond, Patrick, and Masimba Manyanya. *Zimbabwe's Plunge: Exhausted Nationalism, Neoliberalism and the Search for Social Justice*. Durban: University of Natal Press, 2002.

Booysen, Susan. "The Decline of Zimbabwe's Movement for Democratic Change-Tsvangirai: Public Opinion Polls Posting the Writing on the Wall." *Transformation: Critical Perspectives on Southern Africa* 84 (2014): 53–80.

Bratton, Michael. *Power Politics in Zimbabwe*. Boulder, CO: Lynne Rienner Publishers, 2014.

Brownell, Josiah. *The Collapse of Rhodesia: Population Demographics and the Politics of Race*. London: I. B. Tauris, 2010.

Carrington, Lord. *Reflect on Things Past. The Memoirs of Lord Carrington*. London: William Collins, 1988.

Chan, Stephen. *Citizen of Zimbabwe: Conversations with Morgan Tsvangirai*. Zimbabwe: Weaver Press, 2010.

————. *Robert Mugabe: A Life of Power and Violence.* London: I. B. Tauris, 2003.

————. *Southern Africa: Old Treacheries and New Deceits.* New Haven, CT: Yale University Press, 2012.

Charlton, Michael. *The Last Colony in Africa: Diplomacy and the Independence of Rhodesia.* Oxford: Blackwell, 1990.

Chung, Fay. *Reliving the Second Chimurenga: Memories from Zimbabwe's Liberation Struggle.* Stockholm: Nordic Afrika Institute, 2006.

Coltart, David. *A Decade of Suffering in Zimbabwe: Economic Collapse and Political Repression under Robert Mugabe.* Washington, DC: CATO Institute, 2008.

Davidow, Jeffrey. *A Peace in Southern Africa: The Lancaster House Conference on Rhodesia, 1979.* Boulder, CO: Westview Press, 1984.

Doran, Stuart. *Kingdom, Power, Glory: Mugabe, Zanu and the Quest for Supremacy, 1960–1987.* Midrand, South Africa: Sithatha Media, 2017.

Dorman, Sara. *Understanding Zimbabwe: From Liberation to Authoritarianism and Beyond.* London: C. Hurst, 2016.

Flower, Ken. *Serving Secretly—An Intelligence Chief on Record: Rhodesia into Zimbabwe, 1964 to 1981.* London: John Murray, 1987.

Hammer, Amanda, Brian Raftopoulos, and Stig Jensen, eds. *Zimbabwe's Unfinished Business: Rethinking Land, State, and Nation in the Context of Crisis.* Harare: Weaver Press, 2003.

Holland, Heidi. *Dinner with Mugabe: The Untold Story of a Freedom Fighter Who Became a Tyrant.* London: Penguin Books, 2008.

Jallow, Baba Galleh, ed. *Leadership in Colonial Africa: Disruption of Traditional Frameworks and Patterns.* New York: Palgrave Macmillan, 2014.

Kriger, Norma J. "ZANU-PF Politics under Zimbabwe's 'Power-Sharing' Government." *Journal of Contemporary African Studies* 30, no. 1 (2012): 11–26.

————. *Zimbabwe's Guerrilla War: Peasant Voices.* Cambridge: Cambridge University Press, 1992.

Lipton, Merle. "Understanding South Africa's Foreign Policy: The Perplexing Case of Zimbabwe." *South African Journal of International Affairs* 16, no. 3 (2009): 331–46.

Mandaza, Ibbo, ed. *Zimbabwe: The Political Economy of Transition, 1980–1986.* Dakar: CODESRIA, 1986.

Manyon, Julian. "Zimbabwe—Mugabe's Gamble." Thames Television, *TV Eye,* 1981.

Martin, David, and Phyllis Johnson. *The Struggle for Zimbabwe: The Chimurenga War.* London: Faber and Faber, 1981.

McKinley, Dale T. "South African Foreign Policy towards Zimbabwe under Mbeki." *Review of African Political Economy* 31, no. 100 (2004): 357–64.

Meredith, Martin. *Mugabe: Power, Plunder, and the Struggle for Zimbabwe's Future*. Oxford: Public Affairs, 2007.

Mlambo, Alois S. *A History of Zimbabwe*. Cambridge: Cambridge University Press, 2014.

Moorcraft, Paul. *Mugabe's War Machine*. Barnsley, UK: Pen and Sword, 2012.

Moorcraft, Paul, and Peter McLaughlin. *The Rhodesian War: A Military History*. Barnsley, UK: Pen and Sword, 2008.

———. *Chimurenga! The War in Rhodesia, 1965–1980*. Marshalltown: Sygma/Collins, 1982.

Moyo, Gugulethu, and Mark Ashurst, eds. *The Day after Mugabe: Prospects for Change in Zimbabwe*. London: Africa Research Institute, 2007.

Moyo, Sam, and Paris Yeros, eds. *Reclaiming the Land: The Resurgence of Rural Movements in Africa, Asia and Latin America*. London: Zed Books, 2004.

Msipa, Cephas G. *In Pursuit of Freedom and Justice: A Memoir*. Harare: Weaver Press, 2015.

Mugabe, Robert. *Our War of Liberation: Speeches, Articles, Interviews, 1976–1979*. Gweru: Mambo Press, 1983.

Muzorewa, Bishop Abel T. *Rise Up and Walk: An Autobiography*. London: Sphere Books, 1978.

Ndlovu-Gatsheni, Sabelo. "Africa for Africans or Africa for 'Natives' Only? 'New Nationalism' and Nativism in Zimbabwe and South Africa." *Africa Spectrum* 1 (2009): 61–78.

———. "Beyond Mugabe-Centric Narratives of the Zimbabwe Crisis." *African Affairs* 111, no. 443 (2012): 315–23.

———. "Dynamics of Democracy and Human Rights among the Ndebele of Zimbabwe." Unpublished PhD thesis, University of Zimbabwe, 2003.

———. "Making Sense of Mugabeism in Local and Global Politics: 'So Blair, Keep Your England and Let Me Keep My Zimbabwe.'" *Third World Quarterly* 30, no. 6 (2009): 1139–58.

———, ed. *Mugabeism? History, Politics and Power in Zimbabwe*. New York: Palgrave Macmillan, 2015.

Nkomo, Joshua. *The Story of My Life*. 2nd ed. Harare: SAPES Books, 2001.

Norman, Andrew. *Mugabe: Teacher, Revolutionary, Tyrant*. Staplehurst, UK: Spellmount, 2008.

———. *Robert Mugabe and the Betrayal of Zimbabwe*. Jefferson, NC: McFarland Publishers, 2004.

Owen, David. *Time to Declare*. London: Penguin, 1992.

Petter-Bowyer, Peter. *Winds of Destruction*. Victoria, Canada: Trafford, 2003.

Primorac, Ranka, and Stephen Chan, eds. *Zimbabwe in Crisis: The International Responses and the Space of Silence*. London: Routledge, 2007.

Raftopoulos, Brian, ed. *The Hard Road to Reform: The Politics of Zimbabwe's Global Political Agreement.* Harare: Weaver Press, 2013.

Raftopoulos, Brian, and Alois Mlambo, eds. *Becoming Zimbabwe: A History from the Pre-colonial Period to 2008.* Harare: Weaver Press, 2009.

Raftopoulos, Brian, and Ian Phimister, eds. *Keep on Knocking: A History of the Labour Movement in Zimbabwe, 1900–1997.* Harare: Baobab, 1997.

Ramphal, Shridath. *Glimpses of a Global Life.* Hertfordshire: Hansib, 2014.

Renwick, Robin. *Unconventional Diplomacy in Southern Africa.* Basingstoke: Macmillan, 1997.

Sadomba, Zvakanyorwa Wilbert. *War Veterans in Zimbabwe's Revolution: Challenging Neo-colonialism and Settler and International Capital.* Harare: Weaver Press, 2011.

Schoeman, Maxi, and Chris Alden. "The Hegemon That Wasn't: South Africa's Policy towards Zimbabwe." *Strategic Review for Southern Africa* 25, no. 1 (2003).

Scoones, Ian, et al. *Zimbabwe's Land Reform: Myths and Realities.* Woodbridge: James Currey, 2010.

Shubin, Vladimir. *The Hot "Cold War": The USSR in Southern Africa.* London: Pluto Press, 2009.

Sibanda, Eliakim M. *The Zimbabwe African People's Union, 1961–87: A Political History of Insurgency in Southern Rhodesia.* Trenton, NJ: Africa World Press, 2005.

Sithole, Masipula. *Zimbabwe: Struggles-within-the-Struggle.* Rujeko: Rujeko Publishers, 1979.

Sithole, Ndabaningi. *African Nationalism.* Cape Town: Oxford University Press, 1959.

Somerville, Keith. *Africa's Long Road since Independence: The Many Histories of a Continent.* London: Hurst, 2015.

———. *Southern Africa and the Soviet Union: From Communist International to Commonwealth of Independent States.* London: Macmillan, 1993.

Smith, Ian. *The Great Betrayal: The Memoirs of Africa's Most Controversial Leader.* London: Blake, 1998.

Tekere, Edgar Z. *A Lifetime of Struggle.* Harare: SAPES Books, 2007.

Tendi, Blessing-Miles. *Making History in Mugabe's Zimbabwe.* Oxford: Peter Lang, 2010.

———. "Robert Mugabe's 2013 Presidential Election Campaign." *Journal of Southern African Studies* 39, no. 5 (2013): 963–70.

Vambe, Lawrence. *From Rhodesia to Zimbabwe.* Pittsburgh: University of Pittsburgh Press, 1976.

Windrich, Elaine. "Then and Now: Reflections on How Mugabe Ruled Zimbabwe." *Third World Quarterly* 23, no. 6 (2002): 1181–88.

Youde, Jeremy R. "Why Look East? Zimbabwean Foreign Policy and China." *Africa Today* 53, no. 3 (2007): 3–19.

Index

Page numbers in italics refer to illustrations.

OHIO SHORT HISTORIES OF AFRICA

ELLEN JOHNSON SIRLEAF

PAMELA SCULLY

In this timely addition to the Ohio Short Histories of Africa series, Pamela Scully takes us from the 1938 birth of Nobel Peace Prize winner and two-time Liberian president **Ellen Johnson Sirleaf** through the Ebola epidemic of 2014–15. Charting her childhood and adolescence, the book covers Sirleaf's relationship with her indigenous grandmother and urban parents, her early marriage, her years studying in the United States, and her career in international development and finance, where she developed her skill as a technocrat. The later chapters cover her years in and out of formal Liberian politics, her support for women's rights, and the Ebola outbreak.

Sirleaf's story speaks to many of the key themes of the twenty-first century. Among these are the growing power of women in the arenas of international politics and human rights; the ravaging civil wars in which sexual violence is used as a weapon; and the challenges of transitional justice in building postconflict societies. *Ellen Johnson Sirleaf* is an astute examination of the life of a pioneering feminist politician.

Pamela Scully is professor of women's, gender, and sexuality studies and of African studies at Emory University. Her most recent book is the coauthored biography *Sara Baartman and the Hottentot Venus: A Ghost Story and a Biography.*

Ellen Johnson Sirleaf

Pamela Scully

OHIO UNIVERSITY PRESS

ATHENS

Ohio University Press, Athens, Ohio 45701
ohioswallow.com
© 2016 by Ohio University Press
All rights reserved

Printed in the United States of America
Ohio University Press books are printed on acid-free paper ⊚ ™

Cover design by Joey Hi-Fi

26 25 24 23 22 21 20 19 18 17 16   5 4 3 2 1

Library of Congress Cataloging-in-Publication Data
Names: Scully, Pamela, author.
Title: Ellen Johnson Sirleaf / Pamela Scully.
Other titles: Ohio short histories of Africa.
Description: Athens : Ohio University Press, 2016. | Series: Ohio
  short histories of Africa | Includes bibliographical references and
  index.
Identifiers: LCCN 2015042165| ISBN 9780821422212 (pb : alk.
paper) | ISBN
  9780821445600 (pdf)
Subjects: LCSH: Johnson-Sirleaf, Ellen, 1938– | Women
  presidents—Liberia—Biography. | Presidents—Liberia—Biography. |
  Liberia—Politics and government—1980– | Liberia—Biography.
Classification: LCC DT636.53.J64 .S38 2016 | DDC 966.62031092—dc23
LC record available at http://lccn.loc.gov/2015042165

Contents

Illustrations

Figures

Maps

Acknowledgments

Thank you to Gill Berchowitz of Ohio University Press for her support of this project. I also very much appreciate the guidance of the two anonymous reviewers. Olivia Hendricks did sterling work on the copyediting, as did Ingrid Meintjes, who helped prepare the manuscript. The Institute for Developing Nations at Emory University and the Carter Center facilitated my engagement with Liberia over the years. I am very grateful. I appreciate all I have learned from friends and colleagues in Liberia and who work on Liberia. Special thanks to Deborah Harding for her kindness. This book is in honor of all who are working to build a strong and peaceful Liberia.

Abbreviations

ACDL	Association for Constitutional Democracy
ECOMOG	ECOWAS Monitoring Group
ECOWAS	Economic Community of West African States
INGO	international nongovernmental organization
INPFL	Independent National Patriotic Front of Liberia
LAP	Liberian Action Party
LNP	Liberia National Police
LURD	Liberians United for Reconciliation and Democracy
MODEL	Movement for Democracy in Liberia
MOJA	Movement for Justice in Africa
NDPL	National Democratic Party of Liberia
NGO	nongovernmental organization
NPFL	National Patriotic Front of Liberia
PAL	Progressive Alliance of Liberia

TRC	Truth and Reconciliation Commission of Liberia
ULIMO	United Liberation Movement of Liberia for Democracy
UN	United Nations
UNDP	United Nations Development Programme
UNICEF	United Nations Children's Fund
UNIFEM	United Nations Development Fund for Women
UNMIL	United Nations Mission in Liberia
WIPNET	Women in Peacebuilding Network
WLMAP	Women of Liberia Mass Action for Peace
WONGOSOL	Women's NGO Secretariat of Liberia

Introduction

On Friday, October 7, 2011, the Nobel Peace Prize committee took a step into history by awarding the prize to three women from Africa, two of them relatively unknown activists at the time. The committee presented the award to Ellen Johnson Sirleaf (president of Liberia), Leymah Gbowee (Liberia), and Tawakkol Karman (Yemen) "for their non-violent struggle for the safety of women and for women's rights to full participation in peace-building work."[1] The previous time that the Nobel committee had made the award to three individuals was nearly twenty years earlier, in 1994, when the Nobel Peace Prize was awarded to three high-profile leaders in Middle East politics: Yasser Arafat, Shimon Peres, and Yitzhak Rabin. With the 2011 award, the prize committee affirmed the growing international commitment to women's participation in peace building, exemplified by the UN Security Council Resolution 1325 of 2000, on women, war, and peace.[2]

In its official statement, the Nobel committee said, "We cannot achieve democracy and lasting peace in the world unless women obtain the same opportunities

Liberia. Map No. 3775 Rev. 9, September 2014, United Nations.

as men to influence developments at all levels of society." The most famous of these new laureates was Ellen Johnson Sirleaf, then campaigning for her second term as president of Liberia. The Nobel committee said of her: "Sirleaf is Africa's first democratically elected female president. Since her inauguration in 2006, she has contributed to securing peace in Liberia, to promoting economic and social development, and to strengthening the position of women."

For most of Liberia's history few people outside West Africa even knew about the country. If they had heard of Liberia, they usually knew two things: that African Americans associated with missions colonized

14

the country in the mid-nineteenth century, and that in the 1990s and early 2000s militias in Liberia's civil war perpetrated terrible human rights abuses involving child soldiers and sexualized violence. However, such associations have receded. In 2008, the rather romantic film *Pray the Devil Back to Hell*, which chronicled women's role in ending the Liberian war, won the award for Best Documentary at the Tribeca Film Festival. The film received many subsequent awards and was also shown on PBS, introducing a wider audience to the issues of war, peace, and women's rights in Liberia.

Today Liberia is famous for having two Nobel Peace Prize winners, Sirleaf and Leymah Gbowee, head of the women's peace movement, for having the first elected woman president on the African continent, and for being a hub of experiments making women's rights part of the agenda for transitional justice and post-conflict reconstruction. When this book was being written, Liberia had also become the epicenter of the world's largest and most critical Ebola epidemic in history. Ebola revealed the limits of governance in Liberia and citizens' distrust of Sirleaf in her second term, but it also showed the incredible discipline of Liberians who made their country the first in the region to be declared free of Ebola by changing greeting and burial practices, among others. History will remember Ellen Johnson Sirleaf as a landmark and potentially game-changing president of Liberia and a force for women's rights in the international community. Whether her legacy will be remembered for changing the fundamental tensions and issues that have plagued Liberia is less certain.

For all these reasons there is immense interest in both Liberia and Ellen Johnson Sirleaf. The UN and virtually every nongovernmental organization in the world have been working in Liberia since 2003, especially on issues of sexual violence and rule of law. These organizations include the International Red Cross, the International Rescue Committee, UNIFEM (now UN Women), the Carter Center, Doctors without Borders, and many others. Their presence has helped bring Liberia into international news and has also created a conversation on Liberia that inspires young people to know more about the country.

Sirleaf's life speaks to many of the key themes facing the twenty-first century: the rise of women as a force to be reckoned with in national and international politics, the challenges of reconciling indigenous rights and experiences with national laws and urban dominance (a particular theme of Liberian history and contemporary life), the rise of ravaging civil wars and sexual violence, and the challenges of transitional justice in building a postconflict society. In 2014 Liberia also became known as the place that the deadly Ebola virus metastasized: Liberia began to implode under the weight of the disease and poor infrastructure. Ebola cast a shadow over Sirleaf's legacy. The government's authoritarian and incpt handling of the disease revealed the enduring challenges facing this postconflict country and the limits of Sirleaf's technocratic approach to government in a country where so many had no access to the basic political and economic infrastructure, and where the ongoing divide between elites and other citizens continued to be a marked feature of Liberian life. However, Liberia's victory over this Ebola outbreak also can be seen as part of Sirleaf's achievement. As ever, writing history as it happens leaves much room for ambiguity.

Sirleaf's life and career exemplify the move of women into the highest echelons of international human rights. Her biography also is the story of a woman from a small country in West Africa, whose terrible civil war in the 1990s and early 2000s brought it to international attention, and who navigated her way through complex political terrain for much of her career. Her biography is thus closely linked to the story of Liberia and to the story of women's rights as international rights. Those are themes I develop in the chapters that follow.

1

Growing Up in Two Worlds

Ellen Johnson Sirleaf was born Ellen Johnson, in Monrovia, the capital of Liberia, on October 29, 1938. Today, Liberia has just over 4 million people and covers 43,000 square miles. On the West Coast of Africa, it shares borders with Sierra Leone, Guinea, and Côte d'Ivoire. It has 350 miles of wonderful coastline and a varied environment that includes tropical rain forests, plains, and mountains. It has two major seasons: the dry season (November to April) and the wet season (May to October). The wet season is hot and wet—monsoon-like, making travel difficult. The majority of the population is indigenous (there are some twenty indigenous languages) and lives in rural areas and villages following patrilineal lines of descent. In the North, secret societies for both men and women, the Poro and the Sande, help structure political and social relationships and provide avenues to power. In the South, secret societies do not hold sway, but women have long enjoyed political and social authority.

The Republic of Liberia is one of the oldest independent states in Africa, dating back to 1847. English is the official language, and a patois, Liberian English, is the lingua franca. This is because Liberia was founded through interactions with America. Five percent of Liberia's population traces its heritage to people of American descent. This Americo-Liberian group includes descendants of freed people from the Caribbean and the Americas who settled in the nineteenth century as well as Africans seized by the British navy from slave ships after the abolition of the British Atlantic slave trade and known as "Congo."

Liberia's founding was thus similar to that of neighboring Sierra Leone: free people of African descent looked to Africa to realize freedom. In the United States of America, freed people found strange bedfellows with whites who sought to move people of African descent far away from America. Different groups thus had various motivations for settling what would become Liberia: from longing to return to the continent, philanthropic interests, and racism about the increasing presence of emancipated and manumitted people of African descent in the United States. Although missionary societies sponsored the founding of Liberia, the US government backed their efforts; most notably, President James Monroe supported a missionary initiative to settle newly freed slaves. White Southern missionary societies were keen to repatriate people of African descent to Africa so that they did not stay in the United States. The American Colonization Society was the most prominent of these societies.

In the early 1820s, the ACS bought a "36 mile long and 3 mile wide" strip of coastal land for trade goods, supplies, weapons, and rum worth approximately $300, probably at gunpoint, from the Bassa and Dey societies of the West African coast.[1] The colonization of the land that was to become Liberia began. Between 1822 and 1892, the society sent 16,000 Americans to places along the coast. From the 1820s through the 1840s, various other branches settled different areas of the coast, including Cape Palmas and Maryland in the South. By 1848, four Christian denominations were established in Monrovia: Methodists, Episcopalians, Presbyterians, and Methodist Episcopalians.[2] The Commonwealth of Liberia, established in 1838 and still under the control of the ACS, derived most of its income from taxes levied on African and British traders. These taxes became a source of tension with the British government. As a result, in 1847, Americo-Liberians voted to be independent. At this time, Liberia consisted of a 45-mile-wide strip of territory with most Americo-Liberians, and Congo, living in Monrovia.

War with indigenous societies continued through much of the nineteenth century, although slowly settlers established control over the societies of the interior. As early as 1869, the Department of the Interior was created to administer affairs of what was known as the "hinterland." This rule can be thought of as a form of internal colonialism, in which settlers levied taxes on communities in the interior and ruled through force, relying on the Liberian Frontier Force. In 1907, this system of government was further developed, in a manner akin to the British policy of "indirect rule." Chiefs were made responsible for collecting taxes and putting down uprisings. The Liberian government replaced hereditary chiefs and replaced them with government functionaries and created sixteen groups that separated existing political units and affiliations. The intention was "to prevent the formation of alliances that might challenge the government." Indirect rule also excluded Africans from Liberian citizenship, since they had to renounce their "tribal" affiliation in order to participate in Liberian national political life. The system thereby widened the division between Americo-Liberians and the indigenous peoples.[3] The conditions for tension between different Liberian groups, and most markedly between Americo-Liberians and indigenous Liberians, thus were woven into the very fabric of rule. This tension was a primary source for the civil wars that plagued Liberia from 1980 through 2003, It was one of the greatest challenges inherited by Sirleaf when she became president in 2006.

Up to the 1920s, Liberia's economy was primarily agricultural. A shipbuilding business in Monrovia flourished up to the late nineteenth century, when competition from steamships ended it. In the early decades of the twentieth century, Liberia thus struggled to find its economic footing, but in the 1920s, the solution presented itself, with long-term consequences for the country. In 1926, Firestone, the big rubber company, signed a lease with the government to rent up to a million acres of land at six cents an acre for ninety-nine years, paying a 1 percent tax on the gross value of exported rubber. This put the company in control of about 4 percent of the entire country's landmass. Firestone also got the rights to any natural resources discovered on its concession and was exempted from taxes, with some exceptions. The government, in its turn, ensured a labor force to work on the plantations.

Since rubber trees take seven years to grow, the agreement did not immediately help the government, but in time, the Firestone agreement became the single most important factor in maintaining the Liberian economy. The terms of the agreement in effect made the Liberian government handmaiden to Firestone: The company, under its subsidiary the Finance Corporation of Liberia, with the support of the US government, forced a loan of $5 million to the Liberian government. This put the Liberian government in debt to the company and vastly hampered the country's economic independence. In addition, the government was not permitted to sign any new concessionary agreements without the consent of the company. The end result was that Firestone was given carte blanche and the Liberian government became the purveyor of labor to Firestone. The government in effect began to manage forced labor.

Reports of forced labor began circulating in the 1920s and concluded in a commission organized by the

League of Nations in 1930. The report stated that slavery did not exist, but the report did raise the practice of "pawning" as an issue of concern. Pawning occurred primarily in the rural areas, where families pawned a child or relative as payment for a debt. In addition, wealthy families in Monrovia practiced their own system in which they took children from rural families into their homes as servants or wards. This latter practice both depended on the inequalities between the settlers and other Liberians and also paradoxically helped expand the Americo-Liberian elite. As one author put it, "The acceptance of tribal children as wards has long been considered a Christian duty by Americo-Liberians." In the 1960s, "a great many of the educated Monrovians today . . . were taken into Americo-Liberian families during this period."[4]

Sirleaf was born into precisely that milieu: both her parents had been fostered into Americo-Liberian families. Her paternal grandfather was a chief in Bomi County, just to the north of Monrovia. As was the common practice among rural families, he sent his son Karnley, Sirleaf's father, to Monrovia to live with a Congo family so he could learn English and participate in life there. Sirleaf's father went on to become the first indigenous person to sit in the House of Representatives. Sirleaf's maternal grandfather was a German, who returned to Germany during the First World War. He left his daughter Martha with her mother, Juah Sarwee, a farmer in Sinoe County in the south of the country. Like Sirleaf's father, Sirleaf's mother, Martha, was also sent to Monrovia. Martha became the ward of a family called the Dunbars, who were one of the oldest settler families in Liberia. She changed her name to Martha Dunbar.

These family connections meant that although Sirleaf grew up in the 1940s and early 1950s in the only really big town in Liberia, she spent the summers of her childhood in the rural areas and thus had intense contact with her indigenous roots. In the summers she would go to the home of her paternal grandmother north of Monrovia. There she learned to speak some of the local language, Gola, and to experience life with no running water. She spent time collecting both water and food and socializing with other people in the village.

When Sirleaf was growing up, Monrovia was a small town, dominated by churches and the social life of the Americo-Liberian elite. It was small enough that people walked to school and the shops, and as Sirleaf herself remembers, also traveled by canoe to places further afield. The first census of Monrovia was taken in 1956, a year after Sirleaf graduated from high school. The population was 42,000 then, though three years later it was 53,000. In a survey conducted by Merran Fraenkel in 1959, some six out of every ten adults in Monrovia had moved there since 1948. This shows great mobility between the rural areas and the capital in this postwar era. People perceived as Americo-Liberian—that is, born or adopted into the Americo-Liberian elite—accounted for some 16 percent of the population. Businessmen and

Aerial view of downtown Monrovia, Liberia. 1954. Photo by
John T. Smith Jr. in *A History of Flying and Photography: In
the Photogrammetry Division of the National Ocean Survey,
1919–1979.*

traders, mostly from the growing Lebanese community,
also were by then a key component of Monrovia's population, and nearly as many Ghanaians also lived in the
city (1,193). Government remained a key employer in
Monrovia. There was also a growing business sector in
construction and commerce, owned primarily by foreigners, which employed nearly as many people as the
government.[5]

Sirleaf grew up on Benson Street, one of the major
streets in the city. The American Embassy sits at the
end of Benson Street on the corner of United Nations
Drive. Sirleaf was the third of four children and recalls a
very happy childhood, which saw the family becoming

increasingly wealthy as her father moved up in the Tubman government. Her mother opened an elementary school, which Sirleaf and her sister Jennie attended, and also became a Presbyterian preacher. By the 1940s and '50s, churches proliferated in Monrovia. By far the largest number of Monrovians attended the Methodist Episcopal Church. The next-largest denomination was Roman Catholic, followed by smaller numbers of the other denominations, including the Liberian Baptist Missionary and Educational Convention, the National Baptist Mission USA, AME and AME Zion churches, and the Presbyterians. In this era a relatively small number of people in Monrovia were Muslim, though the numbers grew with the movement of rural people into the city. The 1959 survey undertaken by Fraenkel showed some 13 percent of adults interviewed identified themselves as Muslim and 59 percent as Christian.[6]

Christianity was a marker of civilized status and upward mobility in the Monrovia in which Sirleaf grew up. Discrimination against Muslims, who were not allowed to hold government posts, contributed to the movement of young people to Christianity. During this era, most Muslims in Monrovia were uneducated. Conversion to Christianity and education happened at the same time in schools. Although Christianity was an essential ingredient for being part of the Americo-Liberian or "civilized" community, it was membership in particular churches that was crucial. Most of the key Christian denominations had a church in the center of town and a smaller building in the suburbs. The Protestant Episcopal Church was the "favoured church of the elite,"[7] although Sirleaf's parents were Presbyterians.

During her early life Sirleaf had the opportunity to learn about the different religious traditions of the country. In Monrovia she attended church, but back in Bomi County many people in her father's village were Muslim. People also practiced indigenous religions. Sirleaf's mother was a preacher in the Presbyterian Church, and her children went with her as she preached around Liberia. Sirleaf's childhood experiences of diversity in income, religion, and geography in some ways prepared her more than some other Liberians whose experiences were limited to Monrovia. As she writes in her autobiography, "My feet are in two worlds—the world of poor rural women with no respite from hardship and the world of accomplished Liberian professionals, for whom the United States is a second and beloved home. I draw strength from both."[8]

Sirleaf did well at school and attended the prestigious College of West Africa in Monrovia from 1948 to 1955, graduating with a diploma in economics and accounting. This Methodist high school, founded in 1904, was a product of mission education in the nineteenth century. The school's prestige remains. In 2011, the Liberia Annual Conference approved the CWA as a United Methodist Historic Site, one of only six sites outside the United States.[9] At school, Sirleaf excelled in academics as well as sports. But during her high school years, her father had a stroke, which changed the family's fortunes and led to Sirleaf feeling that her educational opportunities after school were now limited. However, Sirleaf was fortunate to come of age at the time when women were gaining political rights in Liberia.

One of President Tubman's achievements was to open up opportunities for women. In 1947, one hundred years after the official founding of the country of Liberia, women received the vote. Women soon started organizing to champion further rights. Under the leadership of the newly formed National Liberian Social and Political Movement, the act was amended to allow women to hold any political office. Americo-Liberian women in particular were able to take advantage of these new opportunities and soon held many posts in both government and civil society. For example, in an article published in 1968, Angie E. Brooks, then president of the Trusteeship Council of the United Nations, listed a number of women in high government positions at the time. These included roles such as Under Secretary for Public Works and Utilities, Assistant Secretary for Information, Secretary of the Liberian Senate, Director of American and European Affairs in the Department of State.[10] That so many women were able to get positions in government speaks mostly to the smallness of the Liberian elite, where everyone knew everyone and where relationships between key families anchored politics.

Sirleaf was thus part of a cohort of women who could aspire to participate fully as Liberian citizens as well as enter government. However, when Sirleaf was growing up, young women were expected to start a family, and that is what she did. She married at seventeen, in 1956. According to her autobiography, while her wealthier friends went off to college in the United States, Sirleaf wondered how she was going to fare. In this context, marriage seemed a way to a secure future, and it presented itself in the form of James ("Doc") Sirleaf. He was seven years older than Ellen Johnson and had already been to the Tuskegee Institute, the famous historically black college in the United States. Ellen married James, and they had two boys, James T. and Charles Sirleaf, only some nine months apart.[11] As her autobiography recounts, for the first few years, they lived with Doc's mother, and Ellen Johnson Sirleaf worked as a secretary and later as an accountant. Then Doc got a job teaching at a school outside of Monrovia, and the family settled on a farm. Two more boys arrived before Ellen and Doc returned to Monrovia, where Doc took up the always coveted government job. Robert Sirleaf was born in 1960, and James H., known as Adamah, in 1962. For many women of the Liberian elite, the rest of their life would have been the story of working, bringing up the children, and nurturing the family. Ellen Johnson Sirleaf decided to lead a different kind of life focused on work, leadership, and nationbuilding.

Scholar and Government Employee

The 1960s and 1970s

In 1962, Ellen Johnson Sirleaf went to the United States to study. The catalyst for her going was the scholarship that Doc had received to study at the University of Wisconsin. Sirleaf saw that her school friends were faring better with higher educational opportunities. Sirleaf decided that she too needed to study in the United States. It is hard to know exactly what drives individuals, but clearly Sirleaf believed in herself from a young age and was driven to achieve. She overcame the kinds of obstacles (domestic violence, imprisonment, exile) that would have derailed a more timid personality. With perhaps only a hint of irony, Sirleaf's autobiography is titled *This Child Will Be Great*, evidence of a strong ego. Indeed, the book is framed to show how "the path of greatness unfolded."[1]

In order to study, Sirleaf had to leave her children behind. Having to choose between taking up educational or job opportunities and staying with one's children was a common dilemma for many women across West Africa. In Sirleaf's case, going to the United States offered a number of advantages: furthering her education, thus helping the family's future, and staying with her husband. Like many Africans, Sirleaf and Doc left their children, including baby Adamah, in the care of relatives: two sons went to Doc's mother and two to Ellen's. But such separations did not come without cost: Sirleaf says while she had to do this, it did cause a "hairline fracture" in the relationship with her children, although as we will see, three of her sons have helped support her presidency in one way or another.

In moving to the United States for further study, Sirleaf joined a new wave of young Liberians who looked to the United States as a land of opportunities. The number of Liberians in the United States at that time was, however, much smaller than it would later become: only some two thousand students made their way in these years to the United States. While Doc Sirleaf studied at the University of Wisconsin, a leading state school, Sirleaf attended Madison Business College, a much smaller and less prestigious institution. Founded in the mid-nineteenth century, the college went through at least five name changes before finally closing its doors in 1998. Sirleaf received her accounting degree from the college in 1964 and continued to be a good student, attending the University of Colorado and finally receiving a master's in public administration from Harvard in 1971.

Sirleaf attended college in the 1960s, the era of civil rights, including the rise of Black Consciousness and the second wave of the feminist movement. In many ways, her career embodied the promise offered by both movements: the rights of people of African descent to lay public claim to their rights and the expansion of opportunities for women. But in both the public sphere and the private, this also was a time of tensions: Sirleaf was in the United States when President Kennedy was assassinated and when his brother Bobby was gunned down. In the private sphere of Sirleaf's life, violence also reigned. For Sirleaf these were years of increasing violence in her home, as her husband succumbed to drinking and jealousy and started attacking her. Sirleaf's personal experiences with domestic violence perhaps helped propel her later into the public sphere to address women's rights, and particularly women's rights to be free of sexual violence both in war and in peacetime, as we will see in later chapters.

Colleges and universities were the site of ferment and debate about America's role in the Vietnam War and in internationalization more generally. Students from Liberia also began to participate in politics. In the late 1960s they organized the Liberian Student Union. According to one author, Liberian students in the United States generally supported the government of William V. S. Tubman because they benefited from his financial support for education.[2] While a student, Sirleaf did not participate in these early movements; instead, she concentrated on her studies, holding her difficult marriage together, and working after school in a menial job to put food on the table. At Harvard too she focused on her studies. But once she entered the business world in later years, she began to have more interaction with the politics of the Diaspora. In 1974, Gabriel Baccus Matthews founded the Progressive Alliance of Liberia (PAL), which leaned toward socialist and Pan-Africanist policies. Sirleaf has called him the "Godfather of Liberian Democracy." Sirleaf never became a member of PAL, but she did participate in meetings when she was in the United States working for the World Bank.

Back in Liberia in the 1960s, the government was becoming enmeshed in the politics of the Cold War. Tubman was president of Liberia from 1944 to 1971, which included a long stretch of the Cold War. During that era, the United States looked to countries around the world to shore up its position vis-à-vis the Soviet Union. Liberia was just such a place. The United States had long been interested in Liberia, as evidenced by the Firestone agreement in 1926, which the US government had monitored closely. The United States signed a defense pact with Liberia as early as 1942 and built the Roberts airport to support military activity during World War II. The Voice of America's main relay station was near Monrovia, and the US Embassy compound housed the CIA's main African station.[3]

Tubman was a very popular president in Monrovia. A song popular in the 1950s, celebrating the occasion of his second inauguration, suggests that at least some residents of Monrovia were encouraged by his leadership:

"Inauguration, President Tubman, Inauguration is a time for rejoicing. He give me a house. He give me good water. President Tubman, thank you for your kindness. He give me good roads. He give me good food. President Tubman, thank you for your kindness."[4] Some of Tubman's support derived from his forging of close relations with the United States and other countries in the West, which was a mark of his presidency, along with encouraging foreign investment in Liberia through his Open Door Policy. President Tubman inaugurated the Open Door Policy in the first year of his presidency, thinking that virtually unfettered access to Liberia's natural resources and low taxes on foreign companies would stimulate investment. Foreign companies did take advantage of these options, with companies such as the Republic Steel Corporation and LAMCO building railways to their concessions in Bomi and Nimba counties. In the 1950s, Liberia had the second-highest increase in gross national product, second only to Japan's.[5] While the companies employed thousands of Liberians, well-paying jobs went to expatriates, and little was done to invest in the education or promotion of Liberian workers.[6] In her first term as president Sirleaf sought to address the unequal terms of foreign companies' relations with Liberia.

Tubman also initiated a new relationship with the interior under what he called the Unification Policy. The aim of this approach was to lessen the divide between the Americo-Liberian coast and the indigenous interior.

In 1964 the old hinterland provinces, which had been ruled through indirect rule, were given the status of counties, thus creating, at least in bureaucratic terms, an equal relationship between all people to the state. By his death in 1971, Tubman had achieved better integration of Liberia. However, property qualifications undermined the extension of the vote to indigenous citizens, and persistent inequality remained between urban elites and the majority of Liberians, who lived in the rural areas.

On returning to Liberia, Sirleaf started work in the Treasury Department in 1965. This position gave her a very good, but not very optimistic, view of the economy, which was laden with debt and dependence on foreign companies such as Firestone. During her time in the Treasury her marriage continued to crumble, and ultimately Sirleaf and her husband divorced. Two of her sons went to school; one stayed with his paternal uncle, but Rob, the third child, insisted on staying with Sirleaf. He traveled with her to the United States when she decided to continue her education. He lived with friends in South Dakota and finished high school there. This time with his mother consolidated a close relationship between the two of them. When she became president, he returned to Liberia, serving as her adviser and becoming the first head of the National Oil Company of Liberia and later chair of the First National Bank.

Sirleaf went to the University of Colorado at Boulder in 1970 for the summer to brush up her credentials, and then on to Harvard. Sirleaf's time at Harvard was transformational in her life and politics. As we have seen, Sirleaf's childhood had helped create a bridge between the two worlds of Liberia, urban and rural, the world of Americo-Liberia and the world of indigenous Liberia. She credits her time in Cambridge, Massachusetts, with educating her about the unequal history of Liberia and its connections not just with the United States but also with historical and contemporary West Africa. She returned to Monrovia in July 1971 armed with new expertise in administration and a new appreciation for the history of West Africa and its economic challenges and opportunities. She arrived just after the death of President Tubman in London from complications from surgery.

Tubman had governed Liberia for nearly thirty years. His death came at a time when revolutions were sweeping through the remaining settler colonies of Africa, including the rise of the Black Consciousness movement in South Africa, and anticolonial movements in other parts of Southern Africa. Tubman had tried to move the country forward by crafting his Open Door Policy and the Unification Policy and by relying on the new young class of educated Liberians, many of whom had traveled abroad for educational opportunities. William R. Tolbert Jr., who had served as Tubman's vice president since 1952, succeeded him in 1971 and continued to rely on the talents of the Diaspora to staff his administration.

The 1970s were the decade in which the Diaspora became a force in Liberian politics.[7] New political movements were emerging in Liberia. Sirleaf always gravitated to the mainstream, attached to government rather than revolution, an orientation that would later shape her approach as president. She was friendly, however, with activist colleagues who wanted radical reform. Faculty who had been educated overseas started the Movement for Justice in Africa (MOJA). They wanted to pursue socialist policies of redistribution to address the inequalities they saw in Liberia. Amos Sawyer, with a PhD from Northwestern University in the United States, who later was a professor of political science and dean of the College of Social Sciences at the University of Liberia, and president of the Interim Government of National Unity after the end of the civil war in the 2000s, was a founding member along with Togba Nah Roberts, an economics professor at UL. This movement was in alignment with the anticolonial movements sweeping Southern Africa at the time: The Mozambique Liberation Front (FRELIMO) and the Movement for the National Independence of Angola (MPLA), for example. As Sirleaf said, "MOJA played a pivotal role in radicalizing the urban and rural poor of Liberia, raising the issues of government corruption, advocating for the nationalization of Liberia's major businesses."[8]

However, while the Tolbert years were years of reform, the Tolbert administration was either unwilling or unable to fully address the inequalities in Liberia. Tolbert did not take the paths suggested by MOJA, although he did try to signify a new era through symbolic rejection of the formal Western attire of his predecessors in favor of open-necked suits, visits to poorer parts of Monrovia, and reform of government. But these were symbolic rather than structural reforms. Part of the difficulty of truly reforming Liberia was that it was so dependent on foreign interests. The 1926 agreement with Firestone weighed down the country. As early as 1951, for example, Firestone made in profits "three times the total income of the Liberian Treasury" even after it had paid its taxes to the Liberian government. In addition, the success of iron ore mining, which started in the 1950s, financed by investment from the United States, the Netherlands, and Sweden, also achieved great profits. Between 1951 and 1977, one mine, the Liberian Mining Company in the Bomi Hills, shipped out iron ore worth some $540 million while the Liberian government received only $84 million in return (excluding money from rents).[9]

On returning to Liberia, Sirleaf joined a wave of young professionals eager to help build the country using the skills they had acquired abroad. President Tolbert recruited Sirleaf to serve as assistant minister of finance from 1972 to 1973 and then as minister of finance in 1979. In 1972, the year that she was appointed to Tolbert's new government, Sirleaf delivered the commencement address at her high school alma mater, the College of West Africa. In that speech she criticized the government and warned that if economic disparities were not addressed Liberia would "create unbearable tensions."[10] The speech caused great consternation in the halls of the Tolbert government, in part because it criticized the administration of which Sirleaf was a part. Although she avoided public reprimand, her position in Liberia became increasingly marginal. As a result, in 1973, she sought out friends at the World Bank and took up a position as a loan officer in Washington, DC. This post offered Sirleaf a wealth of experiences that would prove crucial to the philosophy of her presidency. She met key financial players in the international economy as well as in national settings, and she developed her ideas about the impact of development dollars. After working with the World Bank, she concluded that although foreign investment and development monies came with all sorts of restrictions and created difficult relationships between governments and funders, such investments were crucial, and that the lack of capacity in many countries of the Global South meant that countries had to depend on the expertise of people from the Global North. As we will see, this conviction became central to her decisions in her first term as president of Liberia. Sirleaf's orientation toward neoliberalism with its emphasis on governance and investment rather than social justice and transformation was one of the reasons for her success in mobilizing support for Liberia. It was also, one could argue, the foundation of her alienation from the majority of Liberian citizens and the Achilles heel of her presidency.

Just two years later, Sirleaf returned to Liberia and the Tolbert government, but this time as an adviser seconded by the World Bank. She was in government, but to some extent not complicit with it. The Liberia she returned to remained divided between the Americo-Liberians who claimed to be on the side of civilization and the indigenous Liberians who sought greater participation in government and greater opportunities for advancement. Matilda Newport Day was still an official national holiday. This holiday celebrated an early settler who "saved the settlers from 'the natives'" in a battle of 1822. In 2003, a Liberian recalled,

> As a youth growing up in Monrovia, we used to assemble at Coconut Plantation each December 1 to watch the reenactment of the Battle of Fort Hill. And during the reenactment, one group of actors would dress up in native Liberian attire with their faces painted to portray native Liberian tribesmen, and the other groups of actors would dress up in Antebellum south-style outfits to portray Americo-Liberians Settlers or Pioneers. And suddenly, a woman dressed up as an old lady would appear from nowhere, light a cannon pointed directly at the actors dressed like native tribesmen (portrayed like fools in front of the cannon), and then "BOOM" the cannon goes off, and all of them would fall and pretend to die.[11]

The fact that the government marked this event with a holiday and expected all Liberians to celebrate it exemplified the tone-deafness of the Americo-Liberian elite, as well as the Tolbert administration, to the injustices and indignities that lay at the heart of the country.

Helene Cooper, writing of the 1970s, describes these divisions: "In Liberia, we cared far more about how we looked outside than about who we were inside. It was crucial to be 'Honorable'. . . . You could have a PhD from Harvard but if you were a Country man with a tribal affiliation you were still outranked in Liberian society by an Honorable with a two-bit degree from some community college in Memphis, Tennessee." Americo-Liberians associated with government lived in great style, although perhaps not many in the style of Helene Cooper's family. In her poignant memoir *The House at Sugar Beach*, she describes their family compound some eleven miles outside of Monrovia, which had air conditioning, at least seven bedrooms, and six bathrooms. The family had a family farm and a house in Spain, and the older daughter was schooled in England. Like many other Congo families, the Coopers also participated in the ward system, bringing a young woman, Eunice, to live as a companion to the young Helene. Even in 1974, "Native Liberians routinely jumped at the chance to have their children reared by Congo families" because it offered the possibility of education in a highly stratified society.[12]

The Tolbert government never really figured out how to respond creatively to the growing tide of criticism coming from PAL and MOJA. PAL was the first legal opposition party in many years in Liberia. Although Tolbert had encouraged them in this endeavor, the administration was unsettled by actual debate and criticism: this was the tradition in the history of state rule in Liberia. As part of Tolbert's plan to bring Liberia into greater communication with other African countries, he proposed that Liberia host the 1979 Organisation of African Unity summit. Doing so meant that in the years leading up to it, vast amounts of money were spent on paving roads and building a hotel and the Unity Conference Center outside Monrovia. Tensions around government spending came to a head when the price of rice, the staple food of Liberia and already subsidized by the government for that reason, went from $22 to $27 for a hundred-pound bag. The riots that broke out in response spelled the end of the Tolbert administration. PAL led the charge for cheaper rice, and a rally was organized for 3 p.m. on April 14, 1979. Forty-one deaths were documented, although there might have been a hundred more. President Tolbert arrested the leaders and instituted a commission of inquiry, which Sirleaf sat on. She was, as ever, part of government but from a critical distance.

Echoing Sirleaf's speeches about government corruption earlier in the decade, this commission also called out the administration for nepotism and called for the release of the leaders. Perhaps this forthrightness appealed to Tolbert, because shortly after the OAU summit, he appointed Sirleaf the minister of finance. Thus she was right in the middle of the government when Master Sergeant Samuel Doe launched his coup on April 12, 1980.

Liberian Opportunities and International Perils

On April 12, 1980, Master Sergeant Samuel Doe of the Liberian army launched a coup against President William R. Tolbert Jr. and his administration. As we have seen, the Tolbert administration had sought to make symbolic overtures to indigenous Liberians by eschewing the American trappings of formal attire and by trying to integrate Liberia into a Pan-African world. But this was too little and definitely too late. After more than 130 years of being relegated to second-class status and seeing wealth accumulated by a few families, some people were ready to make change happen.

Samuel Doe was the antithesis of the Congo elite: He was born on May 6, 1950, to poor parents in Tuzon, a village just north of the capital of Grand Gedeh County, which borders Côte d'Ivoire. As the County Development Report stated in 2011, "Grand Gedeh is the third largest County in Liberia and historically one of the most neglected. The over-concentration of facilities and services in Monrovia has led to the under-development of the countryside in Liberia, and Grand Gedeh County is no exception. Inadequate and non-existent basic infrastructure continues to hobble the quality of life, and this was a main contributing factor to the civil crisis." In 1984, the population of the district was 63,028 people in a landscape of slightly more than four thousand square miles, just over 9 percent of Liberia's land. Zwedru, the capital, is about 350 miles southeast of Monrovia and even to this day is accessed by only one main road, which winds its way northeast from Monrovia and then takes a turn south. So although Grand Gedeh is not in fact far from Monrovia, it is, and was, distant from access to power and influence, exemplified by the lack of a main road directly to its own capital. Grand Gedeh is rich in iron ore and gold, and it is densely forested. When Doe was growing up, people were mostly engaged in agriculture (which was profoundly disrupted by the civil war in the 1980s and beyond). Farmers grew and sold rice as well as cocoa to neighboring counties. People were also employed on palm farms and by the big logging companies that had concessions in the area.[1]

Doe was twenty-eight when he orchestrated the coup. A member of the Krahn ethnic group, the dominant ethnic group in Grand Gedeh County, he finished elementary school and then joined the Liberian army, one of the few avenues for social mobility. He was promoted to master sergeant just six months before he led the coup against Tolbert in April 1980. He also attended night school and had made it as far as his junior year by the time of the coup. In this respect, Doe took up one

44

of the mantras of Liberian life: that education could be a vehicle for advancement. But we can assume that he also knew that as a member of an ethnic group from a far-off and neglected county, he would not get as far as he wished. He plotted the coup in secret along with others in the Armed Forced of Liberia. The former US ambassador (who had a staff of some five hundred at the US Embassy in Monrovia) says that the coup came as a surprise.[2]

In the wee hours of April 12, William R. Tolbert Jr., president of Liberia, was brutally killed while in his dressing gown. In the course of the day, other ministers, including Sirleaf, were called to appear before Doe. According to Sirleaf, Doe asked her to explain her most recent budget to one of his newly appointed staff, and thereafter he sent her home, safely, with an escort. These interviews continued for a few days. In the meantime, people attacked the Congo and looted wealthy homes, inspired by the overthrow of Tolbert's elite government. As told in her memoir, soldiers looking to attack Congo families raided Helene Cooper's house at Sugar Beach, some eleven miles from Monrovia.

While anarchy prevailed in the streets, brutality continued in the halls of power. Cabinet ministers were arrested and brought before a military tribunal of five men. The disdain many of the Americo-Liberian elite had shown their indigenous countrymen now turned up outside court. As soldiers dragged in the former minister of finance, the crowd apparently cried, "Who born

45

soldier? Country woman! Who born minister? Congo woman!"[3] Doe had members of Tolbert's cabinet taken to the beach in Monrovia, where they were lined up and shot. Thirteen people were murdered. Sirleaf avoided this fate, perhaps because of her gender, perhaps because of her talent with finances, perhaps because as Doe said, Sirleaf's mother had once been kind to him (something her mother did not verify), or perhaps, as Sirleaf recounts in her biography, because she had given enough public speeches denouncing corruption in the Tolbert government to have credibility with Doe.

Doe appointed his new cabinet, including members of MOJA (Movement for Justice in Africa) and of PAL (Progressive Alliance of Liberia) whom Tolbert had put in prison for leading the opposition and inciting the rice riots. Doe's new cabinet also included Sirleaf. Clearly the choice in these early days was doing his bidding or death. Rule fell to Doe's military supporters, now called the People's Redemption Council. Sirleaf agreed to serve in the new administration as president of the Liberian Bank for Development and Investment. Operating between a rock and a hard place, or making pragmatic compromises with tyrants at least in the early days of their rule, might be described as Sirleaf's modus operandi until she became president herself. Her willingness to try for a while to work with Charles Taylor led to cries of foul during the Truth and Reconciliation Commission of Liberia (TRC) hearings.

So Sirleaf stayed to work in the Doe government even after the assassinations of cabinet ministers, the flight of her sister into exile, the suspension of the constitution, and the institution of martial law. Sirleaf justifies her decision as being in the service of her country. As she says, the Liberia that Doe seized was in tremendous debt from hosting the Organisation of African Unity and owed some $700 million in foreign debt. The coup also meant that wealthy Liberians and investors took their money out of the country. It is hard to know quite what to make of Sirleaf's decision. In one light she was an opportunist; in another, a selfless veteran of government who saw that her expertise was needed in an administration ruled by a man with talent but without much education. Clearly Sirleaf is a pragmatist. Perhaps that is the quality that helped her navigate different political terrains so successfully.

The early years of the Doe administration, although far from ideal, were peaceful enough that Leymah Gbowee, a co-winner of the Nobel Peace Prize with Sirleaf in 2011, recalls a happy childhood in Monrovia. The main thoroughfare, Tubman Road, was still lined with trees and graceful buildings, and the University of Liberia sat up on the hill across the road from the executive mansion. In the 1970s, Gbowee's father worked as chief radio technician and liaison with the United States, working at the US Embassy at the end of the street where Sirleaf grew up.[4] The United States continued its close relationship with Liberia owing to the geopolitics of the Cold

47

War. In Monrovia, the US Embassy collaborated with the Liberian National Security Agency.

Doe consolidated his power in part through working the politics of the Cold War. Never mind that Doe had killed almost the entire Liberian cabinet; on August 17, 1982, he went to the White House. Photographs show Doe with President Reagan and Secretary of Defense Caspar Weinberger. On that day, President Reagan spoke on the White House lawn: "Chairman Doe told me of his government's ambitious goals, including the return to democratic institutions and economic stabilization. We welcome his emphasis on bringing the benefits of development to every corner of Liberia. And today we discussed how the United States can assist Liberia in achieving these goals." Doe said he welcomed President Reagan's assurance that "we can continue to count on America's understanding and support for the fulfillment of the objectives of our revolution."[5]

The United States was indeed interested in maintaining influence over Liberia. President Jimmy Carter was the first president to visit the country (in 1978, while Tolbert was still president) since Roosevelt had stopped there briefly in 1943. Carter stayed for only four hours en route to Nigeria—but the visit signified the US desire to maintain close ties because of Liberia's strategic importance. The United States supported Doe in part because he represented a change from the oligarchy that had ruled the country since its founding. As the first indigenous president, though illegitimately in that role,

Doe spoke to the ideals of democracy embraced at least rhetorically by the Reagan administration. In addition, Doe was eager to keep those ties as close as possible. He closed the Libyan Embassy in Monrovia and opened greater diplomatic relations with Israel. As a result of this cooperation, the United States gave some $500 million to Liberia during the first five years of the Doe administration. And Doe diverted about a third of the $220 million economy into his pockets and those of his cronies.[6]

Sirleaf served a few months in the Doe government, on detachment from the World Bank. Another minister was Charles Taylor, who served as director general of the General Services Agency (which procured goods for the government) until 1983, when he was fired for embezzling a million dollars and fled to the United States. After Sirleaf gave a speech about corruption at a local school, Doe became less pleased with having her on board, and in November 1980, Sirleaf also fled to the United States, with the help of the World Bank. Sirleaf spent a short time in Washington, DC, before moving to Nairobi, Kenya, where she worked as vice president of the African regional office of Citibank.

Both these appointments put her into conversation with people in international finance and development, which would prove pivotal for the success of her first term as president in Liberia over two decades later. In Washington, while still employed by the World Bank, she connected with leading politicians, including Robert McNamara, former Secretary of Defense under Lyndon

Johnson, and head of the World Bank since 1968. In Nairobi, she was put in charge of making connections to countries that did not yet have a Citibank office. Thus she traveled in East Africa, particularly working in Uganda, where she became friends with Yoweri Museveni, now the long-lasting president of the country since 1986. While in Nairobi, Sirleaf also kept up with President Doe, visiting him when she went home to Liberia. The pull of politics was strong, and Sirleaf became involved in the Liberian election of 1985.

By the mid-1980s, the US government was becoming embarrassed by the excesses of the Doe government. As a result, they pressured Doe to hold an election, which duly happened in January 1985. Doe created an interim National Assembly and had leaders with gravitas such as Dr. Amos Sawyer draft a new constitution for Liberia. Doe did not much care for this constitution as it stipulated that a president had to be thirty-five years old. Doe was only thirty-three, so he ignored that requirement. Believing some of the hype about the beginning of a new era, Sirleaf returned to Monrovia in 1984 and started the National Democratic Party of Liberia (NDPL). But she was soon disabused of Doe's intentions to foster democracy. After giving another speech about corruption, Sirleaf found herself under house arrest and then in prison, and shortly thereafter charged with sedition. She was imprisoned with university students who had protested the arrest of their dear Professor Sawyer.

Now, Sirleaf's connection with the world financial elite paid off: people at Citibank and the World Bank began to lobby for her release. And as she says in her autobiography, even the Reagan administration came to her aid,[7] since the country to which they had already pledged millions was now looking more and more like a democratic basket case. It was also in this moment that Sirleaf began to realize the political power of Liberian women, a power that would later boost her to the presidency in 2005. Thousands of women lobbied for her release. However, they proved unable to alter the court's verdict of guilty, with the sentence of ten years in prison. But in a life full of miracles, probably all helped by a history of working in powerful positions in powerful institutions around the world, another occurred: rather than being sent to the notorious Belle Yalla prison, Sirleaf was released, along with the students.

Instead of sinking into obscurity or leaving for overseas, Sirleaf then ran for senator with the Liberian Action Party. Although it seems that the LAP won the election, President Doe delayed results until his election commission stated that the presidential party had won, by a slim 50.9 percent. Although the United States said that the election was somewhat irregular, their interest in maintaining the balance of Cold War politics meant that they continued supporting Doe. He became increasingly authoritarian, and repression became worse after an attempted coup by Thomas Quiwonkpa, one of Doe's former compatriots, in November of the same year.

Sirleaf was caught up in the aftermath of the coup, seen as a supporter of Quiwonkpa because she refused to take up her senate seat in protest of the rigged elections. Moved from one prison to another, she endured taunts and possible death, but her stature as a minister in the government and perhaps her earlier speeches against corruption in the Tolbert government seem to have saved her life. However, at the start of Doe's new era as president he again had Sirleaf charged with sedition, and she remained in prison for some seven months, being released in July 1986.

In the first months after being elected president, Doe killed thousands of people, adding yet another ethnic dimension to Liberia's woes by killing Gio people, of Quiwonkpa's ethnic group in Nimba County. With President Doe continuing his pressure on Sirleaf to take up her seat in the senate, it became clear that she had to leave if she wanted to stay alive. With the help of dear friends and colleagues, as Sirleaf recalls in her autobiography, she made it out of Liberia in 1986 by private plane, to Abidjan and then to the United States.

Once there, Sirleaf renewed her connections with the world of high finance, going to work as vice president and director of Equator Bank, of the Hong Kong and Shanghai Banking Corporation, in the Washington office. Living in Virginia, she watched from afar as Doe continued Liberia's slide into further disarray. This did not stop the Reagan government's support, however, and Secretary of State George Shultz stopped in Liberia on his tour of Africa in 1987. Like administration offi-cials before him, Shultz supported Doe, if in somewhat muted terms, saying that Liberia could expect contin-ued support from the United States but only if "Liberia is willing to help itself." Shultz ignored the fact that Doe arrested a group of protesters during Shultz's visit and that widespread political repression continued. The *New Liberian,* the Liberian government newspaper, was happy to describe the visit as "a demonstration of Re-publican President Reagan's reaffirmed commitment to support the Doe administration despite opposition in a Congress that is dominated by Democrats."[8] The *New York Times,* however, reported that "several Liberi-ans, including a politician, a newspaper publisher and a human rights campaigner, said . . . that Mr. Shultz had made inaccurate statements . . . where he said Liberia had a free press, an elected Government and no political prisoners." Sirleaf was one of the people quoted by the *Times.* It said she was "'quite dismayed' by Mr. Shultz's portrayal of the Doe regime as an elected government and his appeal to opposition legislators. . . . And called Mr. Shultz's statements 'either deliberate misinforma-tion or ignorance,' saying, 'The opposition stands by the position that the results of the 1985 election make the Government illegitimate.'"[9]

The end of the Cold War, signified by the fall of the Berlin Wall in 1989, diminished Liberia's importance to the United States. Doe thus became quite vulnerable. Charles Taylor had escaped from prison in the United

States in 1985, perhaps with the help of the CIA.[10] Testimony from Taylor's trial by the Special Court of Sierra Leone revealed that he had been in the employ of the CIA. Rumors had long abounded that it helped Taylor escape from the Boston jail in 1985, and although the CIA would not provide details, it confirmed that it worked with Taylor from the 1980s. Since then, Taylor had been marshaling forces to overthrow Doe and now began amassing troops to launch a military assault on Doe's government. Sirleaf had been working back in the States to garner opposition to Doe through founding the Association for Constitutional Democracy (ACDL) along with her colleague Professor Amos Sawyer and others. But in the face of a tyrant, simple politics was unlikely to work: Sirleaf turned to Charles Taylor.

As BBC correspondent Robin White says: "Charles Taylor's appeal was obvious. He was the complete opposite of Doe: Flamboyant, clever and well educated. And, above all, he could talk. . . . He was the 'Liberian Lip'; the 'Monrovian Motormouth.' He knew how to deal with the media."[11] Sirleaf claims that she had to at least try to work with the best available opponent of Doe, but Charles Taylor certainly came with lots of baggage. He had received military training as well as monetary backing from Muammar Gaddafi in Libya, who was spreading his money to develop his influence in North Africa and across the Sahara. On Christmas Eve 1989, Taylor declared war with an army of some 200 disaffected rebels. The war, now called the first Liberian Civil

War, lasted from 1989 to 1996, and killed more than 200,000 people. About a million people became internally displaced within Liberia, and some 700,000 people fled to Côte d'Ivoire, Ghana, Guinea, and Sierra Leone.[12] Taylor started his push in Nimba County, the county where Doe had massacred people after the 1985 election. Taylor then took control of key mining towns, which would generate profit to wage the final stages of war. At first it was thought the war would be swift, since Taylor was well armed and people wanted salvation from Doe. But Doe sent his army to wage a scorched-earth policy in Nimba, again killing Gio and Mano people whom he associated with the earlier coup. This made them much more inclined to join Taylor's army, which he called the National Patriotic Front of Liberia (NPFL).

With encouragement from the US State Department, Sirleaf and her colleagues in the ACDL collected and sent Taylor some $10,000 to help support his troops and to feed people in Nimba County. Later, Sirleaf decided to meet with Taylor. Sirleaf recalls in her biography that in May 1990, when Taylor was clearly a viable force, Sirleaf visited Taylor at his camp across the border from Côte d'Ivoire. She states that she walked, escorted by soldiers, to his camp, where she met Taylor, who was surrounded by heavily armed guards. Sirleaf wrote that she came away from the meeting with great reservations about Taylor's commitment to the good of Liberia. However, the next month, on June 19, 1990, Sirleaf gave a statement to the US House of Representatives' Foreign

55

Relations Subcommittee on Africa as an executive committee member of the Liberian Action Party (she was still employed as a vice president of Equator Bank). She talked of Doe's regime as a "political system which is maintained through state terrorism." She went on to say that the "uprising" (she did not mention Taylor by name in this context) should not be seen as a repeat of the coup of 1980 but rather as "an opportunity for creative transformation of the Liberian political landscape." In addition, Sirleaf said, "People, many of them children, have joined this struggle for freedom with little more than courage and hope for the future." And she continued, "The mandate must pass to Charles Taylor who must in turn commence the process toward democracy."[13] She pressured the US government to get Doe to resign and to make Taylor lay out a timetable for "free and fair elections." Records of Sirleaf's relationship with Taylor are contradictory and incomplete, but they raised enough questions that as we will see, she was later questioned by the Liberian Truth and Reconciliation Commission.

By July 1990, it had become clear that Taylor was no better than Doe, and possibly worse. Taylor killed people he considered a threat and coerced children to become killers, organizing a "Small Boys Unit." Sexual violence was ubiquitous among his armed forces. In the course of that summer, Liberia unraveled. One of the most infamous massacres of the time took place on July 31. Troops loyal to Doe killed hundreds of people who had sought refuge in St. Peter's Church in Sinkor, Monrovia.

A daily news chalkboard in Monrovia displays the latest
headlines on the trial of former Liberian president Charles
Taylor at the International Criminal Court in The Hague,
the Netherlands. 2008. Photo by Lieutenant Colonel Terry
VandenDolder, US AFRICOM.

Doe's ministers fled his government. Chaos descended
on Liberia. A soldier, Prince Johnson, broke with Taylor
and founded his own rebel movement, the Independent
National Patriotic Front of Liberia (INPFL). Different
factions fought to gain access to natural resources to fuel
their wars, while conflict exacerbated existing ethnic tensions and created new ones. People fled their homes in
rural areas in the face of advancing armies, and people
fled Monrovia from the shelling and violence. In early
August, in response to statements by Prince Johnson
that he would begin rounding up Americans and other
foreigners to force outside powers to intervene, the
United States sent some two hundred marines to the
capital to evacuate American citizens and dependents.[14]

The Economic Community of West African States (ECOWAS) stepped in to the breach, forming a mediating committee to try to draw up a peace plan. In addition, they created a new military force called the ECOWAS Monitoring Group (ECOMOG), which in late August 1990 sent some four thousand troops to Liberia to keep the peace. In the meantime the ECOWAS peace process (without Taylor's attendance) elected Amos Sawyer as the interim president. Although perhaps ECOMOG helped initially, over time the troops began to behave like the other militias, looting and pillaging their way across Monrovia. ECOMOG took sides, helping Prince Johnson once he broke from Taylor. They helped facilitate Johnson's capture of President Doe. Sirleaf was not in Monrovia when Prince Johnson's men tortured and murdered Samuel Doe. For the next year Amos Sawyer tried to govern while Johnson terrorized Monrovia and Taylor ruled the rest of the country. By the mid-1990s, Liberia was divided between the INPFL of Johnson, based in Monrovia, and Charles Taylor's "Greater Liberia" based in Gbarnga, in Bong County to the northwest.

Other armed groups also began to enter the fray, all increasingly using child soldiers as a way of boosting recruitment. As so often in the past, the armies raped and pillaged their way across Liberia, killing thousands, forcibly recruiting young boys into their militias and raping girls and then often turning them into sex slaves or "bush wives." The militias that emerged at this time included the United Liberation Movement of Liberia for Democracy (ULIMO), based in Sierra Leone and Guinea and made up of ex-soldiers who had fled in 1990; the Lofa Defense Force; and the Liberian Peace Council. Various groups broke up, often along ethnic lines, since both Doe and Taylor had mobilized in part around ethnicity. ULIMO, for example, divided into ULIMO-K (Kromah faction) affiliated with Mandingo and ULIMO-J (Johnson faction), which was dominated by Krahn.

Various groups made attempts to bring about peace. The Carter Center, founded by former President Jimmy Carter and concerned with human rights and democracy, opened an office in Monrovia in 1992 in an attempt to move Liberia toward peace. In September 1993, the UN established a small observer mission. Slowly, with many fits and starts, Liberia moved toward some kind of stability. Finally, in September 1995, the National Transitional Government of Liberia (the second) took power. But again militias fought over territory, minerals, and control over people. American citizens were evacuated as chaos descended again on Monrovia. It was estimated that 50 percent of Monrovia's population fled the capital looking for safety. Amos Sawyer, becoming an elder statesman for a constitutional vision, said, "The big three warlords . . . have decided they are going to crush whatever civilian opposition they can."[15]

Sirleaf watched these developments from afar in Washington, and then from Africa, where she was appointed director of the Regional Bureau for Africa of the United Nations Development Programme (UNDP) and thus assistant secretary-general of the United Nations. Thus as Taylor plundered the country's mineral resources to finance his campaign, Sirleaf temporarily disentangled herself from Liberian politics. Instead, she became involved in the politics of Africa generally at the very time that civil conflicts were breaking out across Africa as the USSR and United States turned away with the end of the Cold War.

The UNDP appointment gave Sirleaf an opportunity to expand her network to include the large international nongovernmental organizations (INGOs), which were increasingly dominating the world of development after the end of the Cold War. In her new role with UNDP, Sirleaf had the opportunity to work with people at the UN and to meet heads of state across the continent, including Julius Nyerere of Tanzania, whom she says she admired greatly, and Nelson Mandela, the newly elected president of a democratic South Africa and winner of the Nobel Peace Prize. Sirleaf chaired a number of big meetings, including one that tried to bring peace to Angola, which had been mired in civil war for many years.

Sirleaf was in charge of the Africa bureau when the Rwandan genocide occurred in the spring and summer of 1994. Eight hundred thousand people were killed in three months starting on April 4 as the Hutu Power government organized and facilitated the slaughter of people designated as Tutsis or Tutsi sympathizers. Along with other UN officials such as Kofi Annan, then

Monrovia. Map No. 3939, May 1996, United Nations.

secretary-general, Sirleaf bore witness but did not intervene. Sirleaf involved herself in efforts to aid Rwanda
in the aftermath. In 1995, she headed a conference that
raised about $700 million to help reconstruct Rwanda.
Later, in 1998, she was a member of a seven-member
committee that the Organisation of African Unity
charged to investigate the genocide. The resulting
report, published only in 2000, "Rwanda: The Prevent-
able Genocide," took the international community to
task for not getting involved and blamed France for
standing by although they had thorough knowledge of
everything.[16]

In Liberia, major fighting had broken out again in April 1996, which caused various foreign organizations, including the Carter Center, to leave Liberia. As a result, however, more and more pressure was put on the country, and on ECOWAS, to actually hold elections, even though they could only be imperfect in the context of war. Peace talks led to the August 1996 Abuja II peace deal, which set the stage for special elections. In 1997, Liberia finally had elections, and Sirleaf decided to run against Taylor, as part of a coalition between her old Liberian Action Party and others. She did this against the wishes of her family and in some respects against the pull of her career, which had her well placed to move up the administrative ladder at the United Nations. The divisions within Liberia replicated themselves within the coalition, and on arriving in Monrovia, Sirleaf found that the coalition had already approved another candidate. She returned to the United States but received a call from the Unity Party, previously a member of the coalition, to stand as their independent candidate. Twelve candidates were in the race, but the election really came down to Sirleaf and Charles Taylor.

With the slogan "Vote for Change" Sirleaf campaigned throughout the country, including down roads that were so muddy that cars could not travel. This way she came to be known in areas far from Monrovia and was reminded of the rural life with which she had become somewhat familiar in her youth. The Carter Center returned to Liberia to monitor the elections and set up the Liberia Election Project, opening its Monrovia office in April 1997. The center coordinated a forty-member international delegation of election observers, which affirmed that the elections were fair, if imperfect. The election did not go in Sirleaf's favor. The Carter Center's final report noted that although "the elections had some serious problems, including overwhelming advantage enjoyed by Charles Taylor in terms of resources, access to media, and organization, they still marked a critical step forward in consolidating peace." Sirleaf felt rather differently, because she saw that Taylor used various forms of intimidation, including having his helicopter flown low above the crowds that came to Unity Party rallies. Taylor's election slogan also intimidated voters with its reminder of the kind of violence he visited on people: "You killed my ma, you killed my pa: I will vote for you." Another voter reportedly said, "Charles Taylor spoiled this country, so he's the best man to fix it."[17]

With the somewhat muted endorsement of the election monitoring team, Charles Taylor was elected president of Liberia in 1997 with 75 percent of the vote. The preliminary statement from the Carter Center said, "In the face of tremendous challenges, the Liberian people have conducted a peaceful and orderly election, and turned out in high numbers to vote, and the collection and reporting of returns should lead to an accurate count." President Carter said that although the election was not exactly fair, since Taylor had so much more money and influence than his opponents, the election

63

was not fraudulent. The preliminary statement from the center ended saying, "We hope the spirit of Election Day will guide Liberians in the days ahead." But this was not to be, at least not from Charles Taylor's perspective.

Taylor's rule, rather than ending the violence as people had hoped, only intensified the plunder of the country with the support of outside funders. According to Sirleaf, after the election, President Carter suggested it would be good if she were prepared to serve in Taylor's government. However, she rejected this proposal and returned to New York. She also says that Taylor reached out to her through one of his colleagues to offer her the position of head of the social security agency. She declined.[18] Taylor continued to try to silence opponents through assassinations and by accusing them of treason, a charge he also directed at Sirleaf in 1997. Nonetheless, Taylor received ongoing support from Gaddafi and from Pat Robertson, the American televangelist, who diverted planes meant for his humanitarian organization, Operation Blessing, to diamond mines in Liberia. In addition, in 1999 Taylor gave a government concession to Robertson's gold mining company, Freedom Gold Ltd., allegedly in return for generating support from the United States for Taylor's government.[19]

Sirleaf stayed away from Liberia but close enough to be keep a watch on developments. She moved to Côte d'Ivoire, then a jewel of economic stability. She set up a financial office using her contacts with Equator Bank from her first job in Washington. She established a venture capital firm for African investors called Kormah Development and Investment Corporation (Kodic). In the early months of Taylor's presidency, Sirleaf met with Taylor during visits back home. Answering the criticism that emerged during the Truth and Reconciliation Commission hearings, in her biography Sirleaf defends her meetings with Taylor, saying that she tried to offer him her experience, but that he was not open to her advice.[20]

In the late 1990s and early 2000s, peace was very far away. In 1999, two years after Charles Taylor's election as president of Liberia, civil war broke out again in Liberia, continuing to 2003, when warlords were forced to sign a peace agreement in Accra. Although there had been a brief lull in Liberia's conflict around the time of the elections, in April 1999, war began again. With the support of neighboring Guinea, soldiers calling themselves at that time the Organization of Displaced Liberians, referencing the terrible plight of refugees, entered Liberia in the northeastern county of Lofa. By June 1999, various groups united under the movement Liberians United for Reconciliation and Democracy (LURD). LURD soon proved to be the opposite of its name, and fighting renewed with Taylor's NPFL. Things were further complicated by the arrival of Revolutionary United Front fighters from Sierra Leone in support of Taylor, who also was deeply implicated in that civil war.[21]

Taylor accused Sirleaf of treason for supporting LURD because her name had been found on the body of a fighter. She rejected this angrily: "This is stupidity of the highest order. I have to conclude that the purpose of the accusation is a desperate attempt by Mr. Taylor to react to the report of his involvement in the Sierra Leone debacle and the fact that I have put out a press release on the 2nd of August calling for him to take action to clear his name and indicting him for his failure to respond to the needs of the Liberian people during the past three years."[22] Taylor's accusation that she had committed treason indicated that he perceived her as a continued threat, beyond her running against him in the election of 1997. In 2001 when he pardoned her and other leaders, she was interviewed to learn her response. She said, "Let me just say that people should not think that these actions by Mr. Taylor are coming because he's being magnanimous or he's being conciliatory. There is serious pressure on Mr. Taylor to do all the things he is doing now and more. The second point is that yesterday [August 2, 2001] was the fourth anniversary of Taylor's coming to power. He is in a big trouble and he put our country in big trouble—and he knows it. He knows that if he does not do something it is going to be worse for him."[23]

The international community increasingly was realizing the horror of the Taylor regime. By 2001 Taylor had basically demobilized the army and instead relied on armed units that owed their allegiance to him. One of the most important was the Anti-Terrorist Unit (ATU) made up of Liberians but also people from Burkina Faso and Gambia. Liberia slid further into violence. LURD artillery pummeled Monrovia, and roving bands of militia terrorized communities. The population of Monrovia swelled as people fled from the interior into the city. People who could do so left Liberia. In the 1980s, Liberia had 400 doctors, but by 2002, only about 30 remained.[24]

In Abidjan, Sirleaf continued practicing some of her key strengths: the desire and ability to network with people in positions of power to influence events in Liberia and to contribute to her standing. She met with leaders in the region to drum up support for peace and to isolate Taylor. In the early 2000s, Sirleaf became head of George Soros's Open Society Initiative for West Africa, OSIWA, which is committed to advancing democracy and the rule of law in the region. She visited with heads of state in the region to pressure them to give Taylor the cold shoulder. Sirleaf thus continued to be an important voice in the move to oust Taylor. A crisis group report from 2002, however, showed that lingering questions remained about Sirleaf's stature. It said that she was "one of the most prominent opposition figures" the West had supported in the election, but that she "finished second with a disappointingly low vote." The report concluded that although Sirleaf enjoyed name recognition in Monrovia, rural chiefs did not support her, and she was "widely criticized among the opposition as an early Taylor supporter, a charge she denies."[25] As I discuss in the next chapter, her early work with Taylor continued to shadow her presidency.

In the course of 2001, Taylor's intransigence finally became clear to the international community. He refused to attend a reconciliation conference at the end of 2001. Fighting intensified. In 2002, fighting drove tens of thousands of Liberians out of the country and into other areas of Liberia, where they became internally displaced people, and Taylor declared a state of emergency in the country. In March of the following year, rebel groups came within six miles or so of Monrovia and launched rockets into the capital. Two groups, the new Movement for Democracy in Liberia (MODEL) and LURD, now controlled much of the country. The ever-growing instability in Liberia, and anarchy in Monrovia, moved the United States also finally to distance itself from Taylor's presidency. Although it would take many months for that to become a reality, Taylor's time was coming to an end, and Sirleaf's time in the political spotlight was about to begin.

In June of 2003, President George W. Bush publicly stated that Taylor had to step down for the sake of peace. And to back up that statement, the United States sent over two thousand US Marines to wait off the Liberian coast. Taylor might have remained, but LURD was advancing on the capital. Nigeria offered Taylor asylum. Finally, both Taylor and the world began to move. On June 17 a ceasefire agreement was reached, and rebel leaders met in Ghana to begin peace talks, although hard fighting continued into July with rebels now in the capital and hundreds of people being killed. Negotiations to end the fighting started with ECOWAS agreeing to provide peacekeepers. On August 1, the United Nations Security Council adopted Resolution 1497 (2003), which authorized the establishment of a multinational force in Liberia and made provision for a "stabilization" force for Liberia to ensure peace. On August 11, 2003, Taylor resigned and left Liberia, handing over the government to a deputy, Moses Blah. Earlier that year, while still president, Taylor was indicted by the Sierra Leone special court. In 2012 he was found guilty in The Hague on eleven counts falling under war crimes, crimes against humanity, and recruiting child soldiers, a violation of international law. He was sentenced to fifty years in prison, an effective life sentence, which was upheld on appeal in September 2013. According to the *New York Times,* this made him the first head of state to be "convicted by an international court" since the Nuremberg trials after World War II.[26]

Meanwhile, in 2003, peace talks continued between various rebel factions and the government in Ghana. Sirleaf represented the Unity Party at the peace talks. The Accra Comprehensive Peace Agreement was signed on August 18, 2003. The agreement inaugurated a transitional government led by Gyude Bryant, a leader recognized as neutral, who governed Liberia until the general election was held in 2005. Sirleaf had been considered a front-runner for that post, but people loyal to Taylor saw her as too compromised, given her history of opposing him in the 1997 election, so Bryant was chosen for that role.[27] However, Sirleaf's time would come.

Women and Postconflict Liberia

The movement to peace was helped by the work of many Liberians working inside and outside Liberia. Liberian women's organizations were an instrumental part of the peace movement and later of the election of Ellen Johnson Sirleaf to the presidency in 2005. As noted, the early 2000s was also a time in which international human rights organizations and international multilateral organizations such as the UN put women's rights and women's roles in peacemaking on the agenda. Recognizing the failure of the international system to address the widespread rape of women in Bosnia Herzegovina and the Rwandan genocide, from the early 1990s to the early 2000s, the international community began to reassess its commitment to gender equality and women. Security Council Resolution 1325 on women, peace, and security, passed in 2000, was the first signal of this new awareness. It built on the work done by women in the 1990s in nongovernmental organizations (NGOs) from the Global South, and particularly Africa, to put women's rights on the agenda of international human rights.

Sirleaf was a key participant and shaper in this movement in the 2000s. In 2002 she coauthored with Elizabeth Rehn the document titled "Women, War, and Peace: The Independent Experts' Assessment on the Impact of Armed Conflict on Women and Women's Role in Peace," which established much of the framework for future discussions and policy about including women in peacebuilding. The authors traveled in 2001 and 2002 to fourteen countries around the world affected by conflict. They said, "In retrospect, we realize how little prepared we were for the enormity of it all: the staggering numbers of women in war who survived the brutality of rape, sexual exploitation, mutilation, torture and displacement. The unconscionable acts of depravity. And the wholesale exclusion of women from peace processes."[1] Many of the recommendations of the report have been implemented, if not always with the financial investment that would make them really powerful. In the years since, we have seen the creation of UN Women, the focus on gender equity in peacebuilding, and the development of indicators to assess the progress of gender mainstreaming.

In Liberia, as the film *Pray the Devil Back to Hell* and Leymah Gbowee's autobiography *Mighty Be Our Powers* document, women were deeply involved in the moves toward peace. As was her wont, Sirleaf worked within the system, sitting with the men at the table for peace negotiations. Other women helped in different and important ways to move Liberia toward peace.

Key organizations included Women in Peacebuilding Network (WIPNET) and Women of Liberia Mass Action for Peace (WLMAP), which met with Taylor and secured his promise to go to the peace talks. Gbowee, a leading voice in Liberia's WIPNET group and the leader of WLMAP, was awarded the Nobel Peace Prize, alongside Sirleaf and Tawakkol Karman of Yemen, in 2011 as a result of her work with that group.

WIPNET and others organized protests in Monrovia to show the rebels and the government that citizens were tired of war and desperate for peace. Supporters wore white to show their desire for peace. Women of different faiths and ethnicity united in the common cause for peace. With peace signed, the women of WIPNET became involved in demobilization. But as Gbowee writes: "A war of fourteen years doesn't just go away. . . . We had to confront the magnitude of what had happened to Liberia. Two hundred and fifty thousand people were dead, a quarter of them children. One in three were displaced. . . . One million people, mostly women and children, were at risk of malnutrition. . . . More than 75 percent of the country's physical infrastructure, our roads, hospitals and schools, had been destroyed."[2] Liberia faced a challenge indeed.

In August 2003, Sirleaf returned to Liberia after Charles Taylor was forced to leave the country. She came to participate in rebuilding the country. In the wake of her experience documenting the horrors experienced by women in war and their almost utter exclusion from postwar reconstruction, she was determined to put women's rights on the Liberian agenda. Sirleaf returned with so much expertise and so many international connections that she seemed almost predestined to be a leader of a post-Taylor Liberia. Marquette University gave Sirleaf an honorary degree in 2006, and the award notice succinctly summarized her deep connections to international finance as well as organizations working in development and for peace across Africa and beyond:

> Prior to her service as President, she served as Minister of Finance, President of the Liberia Bank for Economic Development and Investment, Vice President of Citicorp, Vice President of the HSBC Equator Bank, Senior Loan Officer of the World Bank, and founder and Chief Executive Officer of Kormah Development Corporation. She is also the founder of Measuagoon, a nonprofit organization that supports community development and education for girls. . . .
>
> Her Excellency was one of seven internationally eminent persons designated by the Organisation of African Unity to investigate the Rwanda genocide in 1999, one of five Commission Chairs for the Inter-Congolese Dialogue in 2002, one of the two international experts selected by the United Nations Development Fund for Women to investigate and report on the effect of conflict on women and women's roles in peace building in 2002, and Chairperson of the Open Society Initiative for West Africa from 2000 to 2003. She is a member of the Soros Foundation

Network and is also a Visiting Professor of Governance at the Ghana Institute of Management and Public Administration.[3]

Sirleaf's expertise in management, her connections to leading international organizations, and her history as an outspoken, if complicated, opponent of Taylor, made her an excellent candidate to work for the transition to peace. Acting president Bryant appointed her to head the Commission on Good Governance, a commission established by the Accra Peace Accord. The role of the commission was to create a climate of stability and transparency in government and "enable an environment which will attract private sector direct investment." The peace accord required that women be on the seven-member commission. This insistence that women be actual partners in peacemaking was in accordance with the mandate of Security Council Resolution 1325 of 2000. Liberia's transition to peace was thus one of the first peace processes to actively bring women into building the postconflict society.

Sirleaf's work with the commission and her goal of bringing professionalism to a decimated civil service, gave a hint of the style of her later presidency. Sirleaf is above all a bureaucrat who concentrates on management and structure. Grassroots organizing was the province of others, such as the women of the Women's NGO Secretariat of Liberia (WONGOSOL)—the grouping of NGOs focused on women's rights and experiences.

Many of these women were also instrumental in the peace process and continued to work for women's rights after the ending of the war. Sirleaf recognized the organizational excellence of the wider women's movement and the way that the movement had been able to reach new constituencies. Sirleaf held hearings around the country to alert people to the need for transparency in government. One of her accomplishments from that era, as she mentions in her autobiography, was to have the General Auditing Commission report to the legislature rather than to the president.[4]

In the years that followed in the lead-up to the 2005 election, many groups worked to ensure a democratic process that would put to rest the disastrous election of 1997. Building on alliances and agreements made in Accra, women tried to be involved in all aspects of peacebuilding in Liberia. This was easier said than done. UNIFEM and UNICEF worked with the women of WIPNET and other groups to translate the peace agreement into accessible language as well as to start various education initiatives. But as Gbowee recounts, the more formal processes involving the UN Mission to Liberia (UNMIL), such as disarmament, demobilization, and reintegration (DDR), remained focused on men and did not include women in decision-making capacities.[5]

But times were a-changing. Sirleaf resigned from the commission in order to run for the presidency, her second bid, having run in 1997. In the elections of 2005, Sirleaf emerged as a front-runner in a field of some initial twenty-two candidates. Sirleaf's success was due in part to her name recognition, which came from her long history in Liberian politics both inside and outside of the country. Sirleaf's success was also due to use of American-style electioneering techniques. She hired Willis Knuckles, one of her possible rivals, as her campaign manager. She raised money in the United States, where wealthier Liberians had moved during the war, through fund-raising events. And in Liberia, she used the rents from properties she owned (she was after all a successful businesswoman) to finance her campaign. Perhaps most important, as she describes in her autobiography, she hired Larry Gibson, a professor of law at the University of Maryland in the United States, who had been in the Carter administration, and had run Bill Clinton's campaign in Maryland in 1992. After traveling around Liberia, he ascertained that Sirleaf had a chance to win the election.[6]

Certainly, the country remained somewhat divided about Sirleaf's candidacy, reflecting long reservations about her early association with Taylor. But given the importance of women in forcing peace in Liberia, they were not going to let pass an opportunity to have an accomplished woman in the president's mansion. Sirleaf was thus fortunate to be able to count on the support of women in the vibrant peacebuilding community. They helped mobilize her campaign and took the word of the importance of voting far beyond Monrovia. Gbowee and other influential women such as Cerue Garlo, also of WIPNET, organized a campaign through UNMIL to register women to vote. Gbowee recalls that when they started the campaign some 15 percent of registered voters were women; by the end it was 51 percent. It was the high number of registered voters, and the enthusiasm of voters for the possibility of a female president that led Gibson to conclude that Sirleaf had a chance.

As Sirleaf recounts, Gibson helped structure a wise and disciplined campaign. A first principle was to avoid antagonizing opponents, whose support might well be needed later, as they indeed were in the runoff election. As Sirleaf writes in her autobiography, Gibson also understood the power of images: he had Sirleaf photographed in Western and Liberian dress, which could be used in different contexts. A-line skirts and jackets telegraphed Sirleaf's financial background and comfort dealing with international actors. Her long skirts and patterned blouses conveyed links to Liberia's indigenous communities. Also Sirleaf tended to appear without the traditional head wrap. In a country with high illiteracy it was important to develop symbols to telegraph larger meanings, including one's key approach to politics: Gibson decided that going without the head wrap signaled modernity, competency, and education, and would differentiate Sirleaf from other women candidates.[7]

Sirleaf's campaign also built on her expertise in communications and networking across boundaries. Although not a grassroots organizer herself, Sirleaf understood the importance of community mobilizing and the significance of acts, especially in a country where so many were illiterate. In the course of her campaign in 2005, she traveled to the fifteen counties of Liberia, thus making sure many people saw her. She in return saw how people lived and the ravages of the war; she heard firsthand of people's pain. What Sirleaf witnessed in the rural areas was very different from the life she had been living at the heights of international finance. By going out to the bush beyond Monrovia, her campaign demonstrated a new commitment to a unified Liberia. In the past, election campaigns had centered primarily on Monrovia. In a country historically divided between countryside and Monrovia, between indigenous and Americo-Liberian, between the poor and the elite, Sirleaf enacted a different vision for Liberia.

Running for president for the Unity Party, Sirleaf used all the tools at her disposal. She honed a message that focused on maternal images of care, her expertise as a financial manager and her education, her role as a longtime opposition figure, and her roots in both Americo-Liberian culture and indigenous Liberian society. Sirleaf turned the fact that she is a woman from a possible liability into a strength, aided much by the esteem in which Liberians now held the women who had done so much to urge peace. Sirleaf invoked ideas of the special gifts of women in restoring harmony and managing well. This resonated well in Liberia, which reeled from the posttraumatic stress of the war and which understands mothering as a central tenet of womanhood.

In the end, the election was really a two-person race. The leading contenders were George Weah, thirty-eight, a world-famous former soccer star, the only African to be voted FIFA international Footballer of the Year (in 1995), and Sirleaf, the consummate policy wonk. Weah was hugely popular in Liberia and probably the most famous Liberian outside the country at the time. He was initially expected to win the election. A *New York Times* report in August 2005 indicates the kind of enthusiasm generated by his candidacy: "Weah's soccer exploits, and his charitable work off the field, have made him a hero. . . . The day he announced he would run in the election . . . thousands of his fans danced in the streets of Monrovia. When Weah returned to Liberia this spring . . . his arrival shut down the capital for the day. As traffic snarled, businessmen shuttered their shops, and screaming students lined the road in from the airport. 'Weah in town,' they chanted. 'Politicians worry!'"[8]

Weah did win the first round of the elections, with Sirleaf trailing second. Voter turnout was high. Of the 1.35 million registered voters, 75 percent voted. As the United Nations stated, "The huge voter turnout was a rousing testimony to the people's desire for peace and an end to the cycle of violence and instability."[9] What Sirleaf and her team counted on was that in the end, Liberia would choose responsibility and education over star power. Weah had the latter in spades. He appealed to the youth. But Sirleaf had political and economic gravitas that included an MA from Harvard and years of working and networking in the world of politics and international development and finance. And she was a woman in a country where male leaders had proven irresponsible and where citizens saw that their female peers had helped bring peace. It was indeed now Sirleaf's time.

The runoff election was held on November 8, 2005. The women's vote really counted: more than half the registered voters in Liberia were women, thanks to the efforts of WIPNET and other groups who went all out to mobilize the female vote. Women were also a notable presence at campaign rallies and in general mobilizing. Through the streets of Monrovia they shouted the slogan and held signs saying, "Sirleaf—she's our man." This slogan captured both Sirleaf's unique presence in Liberian presidential politics, and indeed on the African continent, and also signified that she would be a strong ruler, just like a man. Sirleaf had enjoyed the moniker Iron Lady (a gesture to Margaret Thatcher's unique place in British politics) since her bid to oust Taylor in the 1997 election. An Iron Lady was what Liberia voted for.[10] Sirleaf won the runoff with some 60 percent of the vote. Weah submitted a complaint to the Supreme Court, but the election was ruled fair, albeit with some minor irregularities.

On November 23, 2005, Sirleaf was declared winner of the election. The world beyond Liberia that noticed, was thrilled. Politicians and leaders in the United States, who had found themselves uncomfortably on the wrong side of history in supporting Charles Taylor's

Daily Talk newsstand in Monrovia, reporting the policies of the incoming president, Ellen Johnson Sirleaf, in December 2005. Photo by Chris Guillebeau.

win in 1997, were effusive in their praise. The US House of Representatives congratulated Sirleaf on her presidential victory. In their statement they noted her many accomplishments; they said that with "her connections and legitimacy in the world of global finance and capital, [Ms. Sirleaf] stands a better chance of leading Liberia to economic recovery and international demarginalization."[11] It was more or less exactly on those principles, with a dose of feminism, that the new President Sirleaf began to organize her presidency. She was the first elected female president on the entire African continent. Just by being elected, Sirleaf made history. Now, she had to find a way to make her term as president also rewrite history in a good way.

The challenges Sirleaf faced were huge. Governor Lincoln Chafee of Rhode Island recalled in an interview that when he landed in Liberia during the election, his driver described the country, only two years out of war, as "this is where Mad Max meets the postapocalypse."[12] War-ravaged boys and young men, high on heroin and drunk with terror and bravado still roamed the streets. People tried to recover from histories of rape and abuse often far from their villages, which they had fled either in terror or shame, or both. The infrastructure of the country, never great to begin with, was devastated. Indeed, it hardly existed beyond the confines of Monrovia. In the city, which had had electricity in some neighborhoods, people had stolen the wires to sell. People lived on top of crumbling piles of bricks, the detritus of mortar shells and bullets all around. Old mansions, once glamorous, now were covered with grime, full of people with nowhere else to go. A whole generation had not gone to school, while children born at the beginning of the millennium would be able to go if only there were schools to go to. Liberia was an aching wound. After a shocking civil war, one could describe Liberia as a country with post-traumatic stress disorder.

It would take a miracle to make things better, and for a while it seemed a miracle had come in the form of Sirleaf. However, she is after all only human. Perhaps it would take more than drive and a particular kind of expertise to heal a country so depressed and mutilated by its histories of inequality and brutality.

2

5

President Sirleaf

On January 16, 2006, Ellen Johnson Sirleaf took the oath of office, thus becoming the twenty-third president of Liberia. People thronged the streets of Liberia in celebration. Representatives of countries from around the world attended the inauguration. These included Condoleezza Rice, the US Secretary of State, as well as leaders such as Thabo Mbeki, then president of South Africa. Sirleaf gave a rousing speech, talking of the need for economic development, an end to corruption, and the need for good governance, reconciliation, and responsibility. She particularly noted the contributions of women to ending the civil war. And she pledged, right then, to "give Liberian women prominence in all affairs of our country. My Administration shall empower Liberian women in all areas of our national life."[1]

Liberia and Sirleaf faced overwhelming challenges. In 2006, Liberia had 3.4 million people. With a per capita income of just over $100, Liberia was one of the world's poorest nations. The country had virtually no income apart from that flowing from the concessions to foreign companies, including Firestone. But those concessions

2
2

83

President Ellen Johnson Sirleaf waves to the audience at her inauguration in Monrovia, January 16, 2006. White House photo by Shealah Craighead.

also drained Liberia of the income that could be generated if the country managed its own vast natural resources rather than outsourcing the labor, and thus most of the profits. And how was Sirleaf to get the country on the move, with such a high illiteracy rate, some 80 percent, given the war and earlier discrimination? How to knit together a country with some sixteen indigenous languages, a common history only of war and exploitation, and now with hundreds of thousands of people needing sustenance and comfort who had been forced from their homes during the war. With people's life expectancy only forty-seven years, there was no time to waste. And how to return faith in the very idea of government in a country in which the government had mostly been about plundering the interior for taxes and rubber while creating a settler haven in Monrovia? What a legacy of war. As Sirleaf said in her address to the joint session of the US Congress after she became president:

> Our children are dying of curable diseases—tuberculosis, dysentery, measles, malaria. Schools lack books, equipment, teachers and buildings. The telecommunications age have passed us by.
>
> We have a $3.5 billion external debt, lent in large measures to some of my predecessors, who were known to be irresponsible, unaccountable, unrepresentative and corrupt. The reality that we have lost our international creditworthiness bars us from further loans, although now we would use them wisely.
>
> Our abundant natural resources have been diverted by criminal conspiracies for private gain. International sanctions imposed for the best of reasons still prevent us from exporting our raw materials. Roads and bridges have disappeared or been bombed or washed away. We know that trouble once again could breed outside our borders. The physical and spiritual scars of war are deep indeed.[2]

One of Sirleaf's first tasks was to try to get the government up and running in a way that aligned with her vision of good, responsible governance. Sirleaf brought much talent and insight to the task of rebuilding a postconflict country. She recognized the importance of including former opponents in this huge mission of rebuilding Liberia. Although George Weah declined her offer of a government position, other leaders did come on board. But, as she describes in her autobiography, the challenges were huge. Some of the people she would like to have included in government did not have the qualifications she thought essential. Ministers had to work in offices that had been stripped of furniture, with no electricity, no bathrooms, no way of actually working. In addition, as Sirleaf lamented: "One of the most difficult challenges—one of the toughest things in Liberian culture in general—is simply creating the capacity to get things done. . . . This is one of our greatest challenges: developing the capacity of our own people to do all the jobs a functioning democracy requires."[3]

Liberia clearly was going to need outside help both in terms of expertise to get public institutions up and running and to rebuild the infrastructure. The United Nations (UN) was the key partner. The United Nations continued its work through the UN Mission in Liberia (UNMIL) and sixteen other programs, agencies, and the World Bank. UNMIL worked hard to restore Liberia from the earliest days of peace through Sirleaf's presidency. By June 2007 some 314,000 internally displaced people had been returned home through the work of the UN Refugee Agency (UNHCR) and others.[4] By 2007, at the close of the voluntary repatriation program, UNMIL had helped 105,000 refugees return to Liberia.[5] In 2013, UNMIL was still providing stability, security, and expertise in policing, retraining of military units, and running of a government, with the force reduced to some 7,500 from the original 15,000 in 2003. From 2004 to 2007, the UN Police, UNPOL, trained and deployed 3,500 Liberia National Police (LNP) officers; most were stationed in Monrovia, but by the end of 2007 UNPOL had deployed 1,200 LNP officers to the countryside.[6] In addition, UNMIL helped train the army. UNMIL also included a senior gender adviser with staff support, to help mainstream gender equity into the new government and develop relations with civil society. As a sign of the new UN commitment to gender equality, women also served as peacekeepers, with women from Nigeria coming first in 2003. Since 2007, women peacekeepers from India have guarded the presidential mansion. UNMIL also helped build schools across Liberia.

In addition Sirleaf turned to the many Liberians who had moved overseas during the civil war. These included the elites who could afford to go in the first wave of emigration in the early 1990s, as well as those who fled any way they could as Taylor unleashed his tyranny later in that decade. Liberians in Ghana, Atlanta, Minnesota, New York, and London returned home with enthusiasm. People returned from middle-class lives abroad and from refugee camps in neighboring countries. They brought with them different skills, connections, and levels of financial investments, but all brought acumen. They could help rebuild Liberia. Dr. Elizabeth Davis-Russell, formerly provost at SUNY Cortland, came home to lead Tubman University in Harper, in the far south county of Maryland. Yar Donlah Gonway-Gono returned with a PhD to start a community college in her home county, Nimba. Two years after Sirleaf's inauguration, the changes the Diaspora was making to the country and especially to Monrovia were clear. In Congo town, the old suburb of the elites, people built big houses that dwarfed their poorer neighbors. People from the Diaspora eagerly set up restaurants, filling stations, and businesses, in the hope that Liberia would rise again as a tourist destination for the African American community, as it had been in the 1970s. People also joined the government and headed educational institutions. But other people in the Diaspora remained afraid of returning to Liberia, not entirely convinced that the war was in the past. Charles Taylor had contributed to great violence across the region, destabilizing Sierra Leone, Guinea, and Côte d'Ivoire. People feared that hostilities could easily reopen. And stringent citizenship rules that prevent Liberians from holding dual passports and which allow only Liberian nationals to own property continued to cause resentment and unease.

Sirleaf turned to her wide network created over the thirty-five years of working in international finance and local politics. She relied on personal ties and on the optimism the world felt that with her at the helm, Liberia would flourish. As she said in an interview in 2013, "I bring to the international development debate many years of experience in the private sector and the public sector, working internationally and at home. . . . I'm able to represent Liberia effectively; I'm able to speak convincingly."[7] Sirleaf spoke in the language of international capital and development that the people with funding could understand. As a result, foreign aid in all its dimensions helped pull Liberia from the pit created by war and earlier histories. The United States became a key government partner. In the two years after the peace accord, the United States gave some $880 million to Liberia, including more than $520 million to UNMIL. The United States also gave $90 million to help refugees and internally displaced persons. In the first year of Sirleaf's term, the United States committed itself to $270 million.

During Sirleaf's first term, Liberia became in effect Development Central. Liberia offered a laboratory for international development experts who were struggling to find new ways of partnering. In the late 1990s and early 2000s, the international community was still reeling from failures to stop violence and create peace in the former Yugoslavia, Rwanda, and the Democratic Republic of Congo. As we have seen, this soul-searching led to Security Council Resolution 1325 of 2000, which emphasized the need for women to participate in peacebuilding and postconflict reconstruction. It also led to a new emphasis on partnering and good governance as central pillars of development practice. Now, with a feminist president possessing unusual financial and administrative skills, development experts saw in Liberia an opportunity to do good.

International aid organizations such as Doctors without Borders, CARE, and the Carter Center sent experts to staff hospitals and clinics. These organizations also developed and provided training on the rule of law and on how to end gender-based violence. In addition, they helped run parts of the government. Sirleaf faced a dilemma: if she did not use the help of outsiders, she could not run her government, but by relying so much on foreigners, she risked alienating her citizenry.

Women's Council, National Council of Elders and Chiefs at International Women's Day, Monrovia. March 2008. Photo by Institute for Developing Nations, Emory University.

The term "lacking capacity" became a mantra of development experts and the government. It was not one necessarily appreciated by Liberian citizens who had had the capacity to survive numerous corrupt regimes and the brutality of civil war and were still standing. The issue of what kind of capacity Liberia needed remained a simmering issue of debate in Monrovia, one that rose again in the Ebola outbreak of 2014.

Sirleaf also fulfilled her commitment to women's rights and to honor the contributions of women to building peace in Liberia. She reinvigorated the Ministry of Gender and Development, established under Taylor in 2001. The ministry now was tasked with overseeing the huge transformations she wanted to bring about in women's rights. The revised rape law, passed by the parliament just prior to her inauguration, was a key piece of legislation invoked by the Sirleaf administration to emphasize its commitment to ending impunity for sexualized violence. As in the road to peace, women's groups were instrumental in the passage of the law.[8] The new rape law expanded the definition of rape by using gender-neutral language, which acknowledges men also can be victims of sexualized violence. The law expanded forms of rape to include gang rape, rape with a weapon, and rape of minors. In addition, rape was made a felony, and thus it could not be bargained away through negotiation between parties or their representatives. This was often done in rural areas, where police were, and still are, virtually absent, and where women are loath to bring charges of rape against men for fear of community reprisals. Thus, for the rape law to have teeth, other things needed to be done. The Association of Female Lawyers of Liberia (AFELL) was instrumental in the creation of a new court to handle cases of gender-based violence. This Criminal Court E is supposed to ensure attention to handling and resolving rape cases. However, there is a great backlog of cases, and an initial study of the workings of the court suggested that many structural impediments remain to its effective functioning.[9]

But governance was only one of a host of factors that would rebuild Liberia. As part of the peace settlement in Accra, warlords had agreed that Liberia have a truth and reconciliation commission of the kind that had been instituted in South Africa after its democratic elections in 1994. Liberia's transitional government legally created the Truth and Reconciliation Commission of Liberia (TRC) on May 12, 2005. The mandate of the Liberian TRC was "to promote national peace, security, unity and reconciliation." It was charged with investigating some twenty years of civil war between January 1979 and October 14, 2003, that is, events around the coup led by Samuel Doe, to the end of the Liberian Civil War. The TRC was tasked with identifying the root causes of the war, documenting human rights abuses, creating opportunities for victims and perpetrators to engage in dialogue toward reconciliation, identifying economic crimes, paying special attention to women and children, and writing a report to the government giving recommendations for criminal prosecution and amnesty.[10] The government put some $7 million toward the TRC, and Sirleaf inaugurated the commissioners shortly after her inauguration, thus setting in motion the TRC. She also made public efforts to encourage citizens to engage with the TRC, visiting the commission in July 2007, for example, as well as issuing statements urging people to participate.

In many ways, the Liberian TRC was a model truth commission, coming after a decade in which transitional justice mechanisms of this sort had become institutionalized in peacebuilding efforts. The TRC did a lot of hard work, taking over 22,000 statements, 500 live statements to hearings of the TRC, holding a national conference on reconciliation, and meeting with regional leaders. The Liberian TRC was the first to have a TRC also for the Diaspora, to make sure that the Liberians living outside the country had a voice in the reconciliation process. The Liberian TRC was a pioneer in its attention to sexual violence and the experience of women and children; it was very intentional about gender equity.

Learning from the South African experience, which had sidelined women, the Liberian TRC made sure to include women on the commission: of the ten commissioners, four were women. The journalist Massa Washington headed the Gender Committee, which investigated crimes against women. Extensive conversations and workshops with women around the country gave granular detail to the documentation of sexual violence:

the report concluded that all parties to the conflict engaged in rape and other forms of sexual violence. The number of women affected by sexual violence is hard to judge, as there is a wide variation in numbers cited in different reports. A World Health Organization study reported that out of 412 female respondents, 77 percent experienced rape during the civil wars.[11] The Liberian TRC reported that only some 8 percent of violations reported involved sexual violence, although of course the number reported and what people actually experience diverge. In any event, the TRC report stated that because of their sex, "women and girls experienced incredible acts of violence and torture. On account of their gender, women and girls were subjected to abduction, slavery, and forced labor." The Liberian TRC thus brought into view women's experiences and was thus aligned with some of the goals of the Sirleaf administration: to lift up women and include them in Liberia's social and body politic.

However, the Liberian TRC was plagued from the start by divisions between commissioners and a sense that it was foisted upon the country instead of arising from a genuine desire by participants to heal the wounds of the past. The TRC did not interview Charles Taylor, who was then on trial at The Hague for his crimes in connection with the civil war in Sierra Leone. Thus a key figure in the carnage unleashed on Liberia did not participate, which some felt limited the possibilities of reconciliation. In addition, Liberians saw few results from the work and money spent on the TRC. Old wounds were reopened, with little sense that the wounds would be healed.

For Sirleaf, the TRC process was a difficult time. A witness to the TRC claimed that he saw Sirleaf in military uniform in 1990, the suggestion being that Sirleaf was more involved than she acknowledges in her autobiography.[12] Although Sirleaf acknowledges meeting Taylor in the bush, she insists that the meeting was in a personal capacity only and that shortly thereafter she severed the connection.[13] The TRC decided to call Sirleaf to appear because of her earlier public ties to Charles Taylor. In February 2009, President Sirleaf appeared before the TRC in Monrovia as part of its "institutional and thematic hearing on economic crimes." In her statement she said that she had given assistance to Taylor, but this was before she and the general public realized that he was a war criminal. Sirleaf also vigorously denied charges that she had appeared in a military uniform: "I have never worn a military uniform in my life. If anyone can say that, then I will go to my travel documents and disprove them. I think it was a case of mistaken identity."[14]

In order to present the final report to the country, the Liberian TRC organized a National Conference of Reconciliation from June 15 to June 20, 2009, at the Unity Conference Center built by the original Organisation of African Unity, outside of Monrovia. The conference acknowledged the historic inequalities between America-Liberians, or Congo, and indigenous

Liberians, as well as the disrespect created by features of the national imaginary. The memorandum of the conference stated that the motto of Liberia "The Love of Liberty Brought Us Here," in which Liberians and settlers were clearly conflated, should be changed. Instead, the conference recommended that the motto read "The Love of Liberty Unites Us Here." This is a change that has not been made. One wonders why, given that it would be a hugely symbolic gesture of reconciliation.

The final Liberian TRC report was delivered to parliament in June 2009. Revised volumes 1 and 3, which included appendixes and specific reports, were released in December 2009. The report is both a fairly scholarly accounting of the histories of abuses, violence, and inequality in Liberia and, in the context of the time, a bombshell. The report recommended that the leaders of the various warring factions, including Charles Taylor, be prosecuted. That was expected. But in addition, on page 361 of volume 2, the report identified people "subject to/recommended for public sanctions." The report recommended that these people be "barred from holding public office, elected or appointed, for a period of thirty (30) years." The report named names, and one of those names was Ellen Johnson Sirleaf.

As Lansana Gberie, a former head of the International Center for Transitional Justice in Liberia at the time, argues, this was an extraordinary claim. Lustration, the censoring of officials from engaging in public life, is usually reserved for people who abused their official positions. Sirleaf was not charged with that. In addition, Sirleaf after all was imprisoned by Samuel Doe for a year. The charges against Sirleaf, whom the report mentions only a few times, are about her meeting with Taylor, in whose government she never served.

Despite her disagreement with this section of the report, Sirleaf publicly proclaimed her support for the TRC process. In an interview in May 2010, she said that the commission had done "a good job trying to examine the root causes of our nation's conflict and they've made some very useful suggestions and recommendations about how we go about with the healing process."[15] However, she said that the lustration clause, which bans people from holding public office, and in the case of Liberia, often when they had had no chance to appear before the commission, raised concerns about due process. Sirleaf clearly disagreed with the report: she ran for a second term as president, in clear opposition to this recommendation of the Liberian TRC.

In her second campaign for president in 2011, Sirleaf was no longer the peaceful yet strong heroine. Now she was a sitting president, responsible for all that had happened and had not been accomplished in her first term, and with the TRC recommendation casting a long shadow. In contrast to the great support for her in her first election campaign, now popular opinion generally went the other way. As Prue Clarke and Emily Schmall reported at the time of Sirleaf's reelection campaign:

As she runs for a second term as president, the 72-year-old Johnson Sirleaf has been booed and heckled. Her first term has been one long cascade of corruption scandals, and critics of her administration say they've been attacked, intimidated, and offered bribes. No one accuses the president of being personally responsible for any of these abuses, but she has clearly been let down badly by many people she trusted. In fact, although Liberia has no credible opinion surveys to predict the election's outcome, many political analysts believe Johnson Sirleaf could lose, particularly if balloting goes to a second round after the Oct. 11 vote. Some Liberians have actually threatened violence if she's reelected.[16]

Despite concern that she would not win, the country voted for Sirleaf a second time. Her compatriots voted in the shadow of her winning the Nobel Peace Prize, awarded on October 7, just days before the election. Inside Liberia, some saw the prize as a show of force by the international community worried that Sirleaf would not win a second term. Winston Tubman, Sirleaf's main rival, and the nephew of President William Tubman, who had ruled Liberia from 1944 to his death in 1971, lamented, "On the eve of the election the Nobel Peace Prize committee gives her this prize, which we think is a provocative intervention within our politics."[17]

The election was held in October, and with no clear winner, a runoff election was slated to be held between

Sirleaf and Winston Tubman. Various election bodies, including the Carter Center, affirmed that the election met the required standards of freedom and transparency. But on November 4, Winston Tubman boycotted the runoff elections, thus leaving Sirleaf as the only candidate. Tubman argued that the members of the National Election Commission needed to be replaced in order for unbiased elections to proceed, given allegations of voting irregularities. Subsequent clashes occurred between members of his party, the Congress for Democratic Change, and the Liberian national police. The bitterness left by the Liberian TRC lingered. Former warlord Prince Johnson, now a twice-elected senator, threw his weight behind Sirleaf because Tubman's party had endorsed the recommendation that Johnson be prosecuted for war crimes. On November 8, 2011, Liberians again went to the polls, with a 61 percent turnout. Sirleaf emerged victorious with 90 percent of the vote.

Conclusion

From the time of her first ascendancy to the Liberian presidency, Ellen Johnson Sirleaf enjoyed great acclaim from countries and organizations around the world. In her role as president of Liberia, a country that became the model for postconflict reconstruction, Sirleaf achieved high visibility. In addition, world leaders recognized her for her historic leadership across various important spheres from politics to finance to women's rights. The Nobel Peace Prize of 2011 thus was part of a broader recognition for all that Sirleaf brought to the post–Cold War world.

However, while Sirleaf's star rose in the international arena, her government's reliance on international expertise created distrust between citizens and government, a distrust that grew in her second term. Many Liberians had become hostile to Sirleaf, but the West, enamored of her, could not see this. The year after she won the Nobel Prize, the former chairman of the Liberian Truth and Reconciliation Committee, Jerome J. Verdier, issued a blistering critique of Sirleaf, accusing her of presiding over a corrupt regime. This was a view shared by many. In 2013, a new public think tank, the Liberia Institute of Public Integrity, noted in its inaugural policy paper that there was US$2.01 billion in aid that could not be accounted for.[1]

The president's reliance on her family members stoked accusations of nepotism. A person close to the president argues that Sirleaf ended up relying on her sons because she had become disillusioned by corruption she could not control and had reason to fear for her life. Nonetheless, the high-profile positions of three of her sons, as well as internal disputes between them, fed fires of dissatisfaction with Sirleaf's second term. Her eldest son, James T. Sirleaf, worked for First International Bank. Charles is the deputy governor for operations of the Central Bank of Liberia. Rob, the son who refused to remain behind when Ellen went to Washington, became involved in Liberia raising money for soccer fields, working with the Robert Johnson Foundation, and focusing on Liberian youth. Rob became chairman of the National Oil Company of Liberia and promised to clear it of corruption. He did not take a salary. He then took over First National Bank, and that is when he appears to have come into conflict with his elder brother James, whom he fired. In December 2014 Robert Sirleaf ran for the senate, a move that fueled accusations that Ellen Johnson Sirleaf was building a political dynasty.[2] He was roundly trounced in that senate race by none other than George Weah, the famous soccer star who had opposed Sirleaf in the first election. Weah won his senate seat with 78 percent of the vote.[3] In October 2014, the Liberian justice minister resigned, charging the president with blocking an investigation into corruption in the National Security Agency, run by her ex-husband's son Fumba Sirleaf.[4]

Sirleaf is no angel, nor a saint. She is in a sense a missionary for a different idea of government, a technocratic one staffed by people educated in finance, management, and administration—in fact, her own type of training. She continues to see this type of governance as the form required. In a 2010 interview with the Council on Foreign Relations, she said as much: The problem is of "capacity at all levels in the society, in government, as well as in civil society. So the biggest thing is, do you have the expertise to be able to put all these people to work."[5]

Through her second term, Sirleaf continued to enjoy the support of the international community. Perhaps this was because she was legible to them in a way that she was not necessarily to all of her fellow Liberians. The language she spoke, of administration, capacity, finance, and governance, matched well and had in some sense informed the new development era with its emphasis on governance, indicators, and assessment. As of 2013, she had received a vast number of international awards. In 2007, Sirleaf received the Presidential Medal of Freedom, the highest honor awarded to civilians by the US President. In 2012 France also bestowed its highest honor, the Grand Croix of the Légion d'Honneur, and in the same year, Sirleaf received the Indira Gandhi Prize for Peace, Disarmament and Development.

President Ellen Johnson Sirleaf and US Secretary of State Hillary
Rodham Clinton at the US Department of State in Washington,
DC, April 21, 2009. State Department photo.

She received at least seventeen honorary degrees from
institutions such as Harvard, Spelman, and Yale. She
also continued to work at the highest levels of international peacebuilding and finance. In 2013 she became
the chairperson of the African Peer Review Mechanism.
And African heads of state and the African Union chose
her to head a committee to chart the postmillennium
goals agenda. In 2012 Forbes ranked her among the
world's one hundred most powerful women.

But at home, things were beginning to become
complicated. The terrible outbreak of Ebola in 2014 exposed the longevity of the incredible challenges that had
faced Sirleaf when she first took office. So much of what
challenged Liberia in 2006 remained in 2014: the weak
infrastructure, corruption, and distrust of government.

Ironically, the fact that so much money had been spent on rebuilding Liberia exacerbated citizens' dissatisfaction. As of 2010, for example, Liberia was the third-largest recipient of US aid in the entire continent. But in 2014, 71 percent of the population lived on less than a dollar a day, and basic sanitation was available only to the wealthy, and mainly in Monrovia. And sexual violence against women remained an open national wound. In 2013, 65 percent of the 1,002 reported cases involved victims who were only three to fourteen years of age. Yet only 137 cases came to court, and only 49 rapists were convicted.[6] An Amnesty International report in 2011 showed the challenges in prosecuting rape, with magistrates taking up cases not actually under their purview, too few social workers to take care of survivors, and the difficulty of even getting the accused to court because of the shortage of transportation.[7]

Sirleaf had certainly tried. As Blair Glencorse, chair of Accountability Lab, an anticorruption NGO in Liberia, wrote in 2013, Sirleaf had done much to create transparency in government by passing a Freedom of Information Act. And she had wrested more control over Liberia's natural resources and tried to stem corruption. However, as Glencorse also noted, Sirleaf herself said in 2012 that corruption in Liberia remained "systemic and endemic."[8] In addition, the promise of securing profit from companies' investment in Liberia's natural resources has faded. A "legal loophole" allows the government to issue Private Use Permits to companies:

sixty-six such permits have been issued. These permits often apply to collectively owned community lands, and provide less revenue to the government than other contracts.[9] In addition, questions about Sirleaf's relationship with Taylor remained. And citizens continued to complain about Sirleaf's refusal to comply with the recommendations of the Liberian TRC. In May 2014, for example, Bernard Gbayee Goah, president of an organization called Operation We Care for Liberia, an activist blog dedicated to the "complete transformation of Liberia," criticized Sirleaf for not heeding the recommendation of the TRC and stepping down. "Ellen Johnson-Sirleaf is not capable of navigating her own people through the rough waters of justice because doing so would mean holding herself accountable."[10]

But how much could one ask of a single person? Among many accomplishments, we can note that she reduced Liberia's crippling international debt, brought running water and electricity to Monrovia, and in partnership with other countries and companies constructed roads across the country, which will help unify Liberia as well as stimulate commerce. She had the international trade sanctions (imposed against Charles Taylor) lifted, and she provided free education up to the ninth grade. In 2006, Sirleaf launched the Girls' National Education Policy, in cooperation with UNICEF, which dramatically increased opportunities for girls to be educated, and her government also partnered with USAID to increase girls' education.

In an extended interview in July 2013, President Sirleaf answered questions about corruption in her government, her numerous trips abroad, and the slow pace of change in Liberia put to her by Darryl Ambrose Nmah, director general of the Liberian Broadcasting System. An apparently frustrated Sirleaf patiently answered questions, returning again and again to the challenges Liberia faced after the war. She said that a primary problem was the capacity of Liberians to enact the change and the governance that was required. She defended her trips abroad, saying that these helped give Liberia a voice in the world and brought investment to Liberia. She spoke to a record of dismissing people in her government for corruption, and she pointed out how in trying to be democratic, and being sensitive to communities' perspectives, some investments that would have brought more employment had taken much longer to get off the ground. Sirleaf concluded the interview with her perspective on Firestone, the company to which the Liberian government had ceded so much power back in 1926. In some ways, one could see this as exemplary of what Sirleaf's approach had sought to accomplish: through working with powerful companies, which brought employment opportunities and foreign capital to Liberia, she believed change could happen:

> We have to work with the concessions. I'll give you the example of Firestone. You remember where the people used to live? That's part of the investment. They used

to live in hovels. We said to Firestone, you've got to give us a five-year plan to transform that Plantation and get better living conditions for the workers. Go to Firestone today; see the transformation that's taking place there. Today, Firestone students are the ones that are making the highest in the WAEC Exams. LAC will follow; Salala will follow the same pattern; COCOPA will follow. Any other rubber or agriculture concession will do the Firestone model. Those are part of the investment rewards that are taking place, that people say they don't see there. The other day, Firestone workers just completed their Collective Bargaining Agreement in which their wages were raised. They used to carry the rubber on their shoulders; that has changed now; they have to have little trailers where they can now put the container on the trailer. Those are the good things that are happening, but you know, people don't see that one. Please come with me in the countryside sometimes, so they can see what's happening outside. People always say Monrovia is not Liberia, and they're correct. Out of 4 million people, 1.5 million people are right here in Monrovia. They are making Monrovia Liberia. We are trying to make Liberia Liberia by doing things out there, so that we create the jobs out there, so people can live out there.[11]

Perhaps the challenges facing the president were just too many, coming too fast, and the legacy of some 160 years of gross inequality was just overwhelming. So by the time

Ebola hit in 2014, many citizens had come to feel that Sirleaf had done little to change conditions for Liberians.

A hemorrhagic fever with a very high death rate, 40–90 percent, and with no known cure at the time, Ebola started in Guinea and moved quickly to Sierra Leone and Liberia. The first case in Liberia occurred in northern Lofa County, the county where LURD had launched its war on Charles Taylor. Lofa is a heavily forested county bordering on Guinea and Sierra Leone where people walk back and forth across the borders visiting family and trading. The first case of Ebola was found in March 2014 in a patient who had returned from Guinea. Previous Ebola outbreaks had happened in relatively isolated environments in central Africa and had been contained. Thus, for a while, authorities did not worry much about containment. However, by June 2014, Ebola had continued to spread. By August, Ebola was in Monrovia. The coming of Ebola to a heavily populated city changed the dynamics of Ebola completely, turning it from a deadly disease that could be contained to one that threatened to ruin the three countries in which it was now spreading.

On August 7, 2014, Sirleaf declared a state of emergency. This empowered the government to suspend civil liberties as it saw necessary. Sirleaf said that she had enacted "extraordinary measures for the very survival of our state and for the protection of the lives of our people."[12] Ebola now exposed the degree of animosity that poorer citizens still harbored against government.

People were skeptical that Ebola really was contagious and blamed Sirleaf for just trying to bring more development dollars into government pockets. People said things like: "Sirleaf . . . and her minister of health want to pocket money so they have come up with a new tactic to collect money and share."[13] In West Point, a crowded informal settlement in Monrovia, citizens entered an Ebola containment center, freeing patients and taking mattresses and other materials. The government soon placed West Point under quarantine, with the police and the Liberian army patrolling. A military blockade prevented people from Bomi and Grand Cape Mount counties from entering Monrovia.

By late August, the Centers for Disease Control and Prevention in the United States was declaring the Ebola outbreak in Liberia the worst the world has ever seen. The head of the CDC praised ordinary Liberians for trying: "I have been impressed by the response I have seen. We met dozens of volunteers answering dozens of calls every day, 24 hours daily, we met dozens of healthcare workers and dozens of community volunteers in rural areas willing to help with the response."[14] But the reality was that Liberia's infrastructure, neglected for decades, damaged by war, and only just recovering, could not cope with Ebola. Soon doctors and other health workers treating patients died, as did many of the patients they treated. Without basic medical supplies such as latex gloves, good sanitation in hospitals, and a healthy government infrastructure, Liberia became ground zero for the disease.

Again, Sirleaf's relationships built up over so many years came to Liberia's rescue. She appealed to the United States to help her crippled country fight the disease. The United States, always wary of getting too involved in Liberia, woke up to the seriousness of Ebola. In September, the US military inaugurated "Operation United Assistance" to coordinate the military's response to Ebola in Liberia. President Obama authorized three thousand troops to be sent to Liberia to help with logistics and nonmedical help. By early November the military had set up a field hospital for infected health care workers and a hundred-bed hospital. The Cuban and Chinese governments also sent doctors and other personnel to help stem Ebola. By November, the CDC noted that cases of Ebola were beginning to decline in Liberia, but the epidemic raged on in neighboring Sierra Leone and Guinea.[15] Time will tell if Ebola becomes a scary chapter in the history of Liberia or a major theme of its future. But by April 2015, Liberia became the first country in the Ebola-affected region to have no new case of Ebola. The last confirmed death from Ebola occurred November 24, 2015.

One of the reasons for the containment of Ebola in Liberia was the move by communities to work toward safer burial practices, which stopped the spread of the disease. Liberians also embraced the campaign to wash hands with bleach and to stop greeting one another with the traditional Liberian handshake, at least for a time. In addition, there was a concerted effort by government and civil society actors to reach out to communities through radio and advertisements, with the government helping to produce a hip-hop song titled "Ebola Is Real." George Weah and the Ghanaian musician Sydney produced a song about Ebola in 2014 to raise awareness.[16] In March 2015, President Sirleaf acknowledged that she had made some errors in her first reactions to the epidemic, particularly with regard to her declaration of a state of emergency. She said that in hindsight sealing off West Point had "created more tension in the society" and promoted distrust between citizens and their government.[17]

When running for president a second time, Sirleaf said she had underestimated the challenges facing her country. She lamented: "We found a totally collapsed economy, dysfunctional institutions, lack of proper laws and policies, low capacity, and a value system upside down."[18] A year later, having won the election, Sirleaf looked beyond her presidency to the legacies she would like to leave Liberia. "We have to take responsibility for our own development. We have to determine that our resources first and foremost will be used for our development. And if we can send that kind of message to our younger generation who will be assuming leadership, you know, over the next few years, then I think the sustainability of our effort will be secured."[19] Translating that vision into a Liberia where citizens truly feel they have the means and authority to shape their own paths remains the challenge.

Sirleaf did much to try to move Liberia forward. The challenge was whether this vision matched the realities of rural Liberia, where people lived within the legal framework of chiefs and societies, somewhat removed from the national legal system and far from any help the state could provide. Could Sirleaf's conventional vision of government, rooted in Western assumptions and structures, offer Liberians the kinds of engagement with governance that would make them feel connected to their government? Only time will tell.

Notes

Introduction

1. "The Nobel Peace Prize for 2011," accessed November 12, 2014, http://www.nobelprize.org/nobel_prizes/peace/laureates/2011/press.html.

2. SCR 1325 focuses on the effects of war on women and urges the inclusion of women in peace negotiations and postconflict reconstruction.

Chapter 1: Growing Up in Two Worlds

1. "History of Liberia: A Time Line," http://memory.loc.gov/ammem/gmdhtml/libhtml/liberia.html.

2. Merran Fraenkel, *Tribe and Class in Monrovia* (published for the International African Institute by Oxford University Press, 1964), 5, 156.

3. "Indirect Rule in the Hinterland," accessed April 17, 2014, www.globalsecurity.org/military/library/report/1985/liberia_1_indirectrulep.htm.

4. Fraenkel, *Tribe and Class in Monrovia*, 119, 25.

5. Ibid., 33, 34, 36, 39.

6. Ibid., 156, 154.

7. Ibid., 152–59.

8. Ellen Johnson Sirleaf, *This Child Will Be Great: Memoir of a Remarkable Life by Africa's First Woman President* (New York: Harper Perennial, 2010), 22.

9. "Monrovia, Liberia: Heritage Landmark of the United Methodist Church," College of West Africa, http://www.gcah.org/research/travelers-guide/college-of-west-africa.

10. Angie E. Brooks, "Political Participation of Women in Africa South of the Sahara," *Annals of the American Academy of Political and Social Science* 375, no. 1 (January 1968): 82–85.

11. Sirleaf, *This Child Will Be Great*, 29–30.

Chapter 2: Scholar and Government Employee

1. Ellen Johnson Sirleaf, *This Child Will Be Great: Memoir of a Remarkable Life by Africa's First Woman President* (New York: Harper Perennial, 2010), 7.

2. Cecil Franweah Frank, "A Critical Look at the Role of the Diaspora in Liberia's Development," *Liberian Dialogue,* last updated January 3, 2013, http://theliberiandialogue.org/2013/01/03/a-critical -look-at-the-role-of-the-diaspora-in-liberias-development.

3. "Liberia: America's Impoverished Orphan in Africa," *Washington Post,* accessed April 17, 2014, http://media.washingtonpost.com /wp-adv/specialsales/international/spotlight/liberia/article2.html.

4. Merran Fraenkel, *Tribe and Class in Monrovia* (published for the International African Institute by Oxford University Press, 1964), 61.

5. Lawrence A. Marinelli, "Liberia's Open-Door Policy," *Journal of Modern African Studies* 2, no. 1 (1964): 91–98.

6. Cited in Harold D. Nelson, *Liberia: Country Study* (Federal Research Division of the Library of Congress, 1985), http://www .globalsecurity.org/military/library/report/1985/liberia_1_opendoor.htm.

7. Frank, "Critical Look at the Role of the Diaspora."

8. Sirleaf, *This Child Will Be Great*, 81.

9. Fred P. M. van der Kraaij, "Iron Ore: The Start of Operations of Liberia's First Iron Ore Mine," *Liberia: Past and Present of Africa's Oldest Republic,* last updated May 2015, http://www.liberiapastandpresent .org/ODP/IronOre/IronOreC.htm.

10. Sirleaf, *This Child Will Be Great*, 71.

11. Siahyonkron Nyanseor, "Putting the Matilda Newport Myth to Rest, Part I," *Perspective,* December 1, 2003, http://www.theperspective .org/december2003/newportmyth.html.

12. Helene Cooper, *The House at Sugar Beach: In Search of a Lost African Childhood* (New York: Simon and Schuster, 2008), 11.

Chapter 3: Liberian Opportunities and International Perils

1. County Development Committee, *Grand Gedeh County Development Agenda, Republic of Liberia, 2008–2012* (Republic of Liberia, n.d.), 1.

2. "President Samuel K. Doe, 1980–1990: The Master-Sergeant President," http://www.liberiapastandpresent.org/SamuelKDoe.htm.

3. Helene Cooper, *The House at Sugar Beach: In Search of a Lost African Childhood* (New York: Simon and Schuster, 2008), 182.

4. Leymah Gbowee, *Mighty Be Our Powers: How Sisterhood, Prayer, and Sex Changed a Nation at War* (New York: Beast Books, 2011), 9.

5. "Remarks of the President and Head of State Samuel K. Doe of Liberia Following Their Meetings: August 17, 1982," University of Texas, http://www.reagan.utexas.edu/archives/speeches/1982/81782d.htm.

6. "Liberia and the United States: A Complex Relationship," *Global Connections: Liberia,* WGBH Educational Foundation, last updated 2002, http://www.pbs.org/wgbh/globalconnections/liberia/essays/uspolicy.

7. Ellen Johnson Sirleaf, *This Child Will Be Great: Memoir of a Remarkable Life by Africa's First Woman President* (New York: Harper Perennial, 2010), 128.

8. Terry Atlas, "Shultz Visit to Liberia a Bit Sour," *Chicago Tribune,* January 15, 1987,

9. David K. Shipler, "Shultz Is under Fire for Asserting Liberia Has Made Gains on Rights," *New York Times,* last updated January 16, 1987, http://www.nytimes.com/1987/01/16/world/shultz-is-under-fire-for-asserting-libria-has-made-gains-on-rights.html.

10. "Charles Taylor 'Worked' for CIA in Liberia," BBC News, January 19, 2012, http://www.bbc.co.uk/news/world-africa-16627628.

11. "My Verbal Sparring with Charles Taylor," BBC News, last updated April 26, 2012, http://www.bbc.com/news/world-africa-17845592.

12. Shelly Dick, "FMO Country Guide: Liberia," accessed June 1, 2015, http://www.forcedmigration.org/research-resources/expert-guides/liberia/fmo013.pdf.

13. US House of Representatives, "US Policy and the Crisis in Liberia," Hearing before the Subcommittee on Africa of the Committee on Foreign Affairs. 101st Congress, 2nd Session, June 19, 1990, http://babel.hathitrust.org/cgi/pt?id=pst.000017170666;view=1up;seq=1.

14. Michael R. Gordon, "US Forces Evacuate 74 after Threats in Liberia," *New York Times,* August 6, 1990, http://www.nytimes.com/1990/08/06/world/us-forces-evacuate-74-after-threats-in-liberia.html.

15. The Carter Center, "Observing the 1997 Special Elections," https://www.cartercenter.org/documents/electionreports/democracy/FinalReportLiberia1997.pdf; Howard French, citing Amos Sawyer in "US Wins Liberians' Pledge to Back Truce," http://www.nytimes.com/1996/04/26/world/us-wins-liberians-pledge-to-back-truce.html.

16. "Rwanda: OAU Report, 07/07/00," last updated July 7, 2000, http://www.africa.upenn.edu/Urgent_Action/apic-070800.html

17. Carter Center, "Observing the 1997 Elections," 45.

18. Sirleaf, *This Child Will Be Great*, 221.

19. Anna Schecter, "Prosecutor: Pat Robertson Had Gold Deal with African Dictator," ABC News, February 4, 2010, http://abcnews.go.com/Blotter/pat-robertsons-gold-deal-african-dictator/story?id=9749341.

20. Sirleaf, *This Child Will Be Great*, 219, 221.

21. International Crisis Group, *Liberia: The Key to Ending Regional Instability,* April 24, 2002, http://www.crisisgroup.org/~/media/Files/africa/west-africa/liberia/Liberia%20The%20Key%20to%20Ending%20Regional%20Instability.pdf.

22. "Ellen Johnson-Sirleaf Returns Home, Meets with Taylor Today," *Perspective,* September 24, 2001.

23. "'Taylor Responds to Pressure,' Says Ellen Johnson-Sirleaf," *Perspective,* August 4, 2001.

24. International Crisis Group, *Liberia: The Key to Ending Regional Instability*, 16.

25. Ibid., 19.

26. Marlise Simons, "Ex-President of Liberia Aided War Crimes, Court Rules," *New York Times,* last updated April 26, 2012, http://www.nytimes.com/2012/04/27/world/africa/charles-taylor-liberia-sierra-leone-war-crimes-court-verdict.html?pagewanted=all.

27. Abdoulaye W. Dukulé, "Liberia: Sirleaf to Chair Commission on Good Governance: 'We Can't Slip Back,'" *AllAfrica,* last updated November 12, 2003, http://allafrica.com/stories/200311120271.html.

Chapter 4: Women and Postconflict Liberia

1. Elizabeth Rehn and Ellen Johnson Sirleaf, "Women, War, and Peace: The Independent Experts' Assessment on the Impact of Armed Conflict on Women and Women's Role in Peace," UNIFEM (2002), vii, http://www.unwomen.org/en/digital-library/publications/2002/1/women-war-peace-the-independent-experts-assessment-on-the-impact-of-armed-conflict-on-women-and-women-s-role-in-peace-building-progress-of-the-world-s-women-2002-vol-1.

2. Leymah Gbowee, *Mighty Be Our Powers: How Sisterhood, Prayer, and Sex Changed a Nation at War* (New York: Beast Books, 2011), 167.

3. Marquette University, "Honorary Degree Recipient: Her Excellency Ellen Johnson Sirleaf," October 23, 2006, http://www.marquette.edu/universityhonors/honors_sirleaf.shtml.

4. Ellen Johnson Sirleaf, *This Child Will Be Great: Memoir of a Remarkable Life by Africa's First Woman President* (New York: Harper Perennial, 2010), 244.

5. Gbowee, *Mighty Be Our Powers*, 169.

6. Sirleaf, *This Child Will Be Great*, 251.

7. Ibid., 252.

8. Andrew Rice, "George Weah's New Game," *New York Times,* August 21, 2005, http://www.nytimes.com/2005/08/21/magazine /21WEAH.html?pagewanted=all&_r=0.

9. United Nations, "Liberia: Elections Mark Historic Turning Point," *Major Peacekeeping Operations,* accessed August 2, 2014, http:// www.un.org/en/peacekeeping/publications/yir/2005/PDFs/major _pk_operations.pdf.

10. Lydia Polgreen, "In First for Africa, Woman Wins Election as President of Liberia," *New York Times,* last updated November 12, 2005, http://www.nytimes.com/2005/11/12/international/africa/12liberia .html?pagewanted=all.

11. US House of Representatives, "Text of Congratulating President Ellen Johnson-Sirleaf for Becoming the First Democratically Elected Female President of the Republic of Liberia and the First Female African Head of State," H.Con Res. 327 (109th Congress, 2005–2006), December 18, 2005, https://www.govtrack.us/congress /bills/109/hconres327/text.

12. Philip Marcelo, "Rebuilding Liberia: Chafee Recalls Liberia's First Post War Election," last updated August 2, 2013, http:// www.providencejournal.com/breaking-news/content/20130802 -rebuilding-liberia-chafee-recalls-liberia-s-first-post-war-election.ece.

Chapter 5: President Sirleaf

1. "Liberia: Text of Inaugural Address by President Ellen Johnson Sirleaf of Liberia," *All Africa,* January 17, 2006, http://allafrica.com /stories/200601170106.html.

2. "Liberia's Ellen Johnson-Sirleaf Addresses Congress," *PBS Newshour,* last updated March 15, 2006, http://www.pbs.org/newshour /bb/africa-jan-june06-liberia_3-15/.

3. Ellen Johnson Sirleaf, *This Child Will Be Great: Memoir of a Remarkable Life by Africa's First Woman President* (New York: Harper Perennial, 2010), 295.

4. Dorsey & Whitney LLP, "Liberia Is Not Ready: A Report of Country Conditions in Liberia and Reasons the United States Should Not End Temporary Protected Status for Liberians," for Minnesota

Advocates for Human Rights (August 2007), dorsey.com/files/upload/DorseyProBonoReport0807Liberia_is_not_Ready.pdf.

5. UNMIL, "Liberia: UNMIL Humanitarian Situation Report No. 110," July 1, 2007, http://reliefweb.int/report/liberia/liberia-unmil-humanitarian-situation-report-no-110.

6. Government Printing Office, "Country Reports on Human Rights Practices," 2008, 335.

7. *The New Dawn,* transcript of interview with President Ellen Johnson Sirleaf, Paynesville, Monday, July 1, 2013, http://www.thenewdawnliberia.com/~thenewd1/index.php?option=com_content&view=article&id=1798:weah-warns-supporters&catid=25:politics&Itemid=59.

8. Peace A. Medie, "Fighting Gender-Based Violence: The Women's Movement and the Enforcement of Rape Law in Liberia," *African Affairs* 112, no. 448 (2013): 377–97.

9. Stéphanie Vig, "The Liberian Rape Amendment Act and the United Nations: A Critical Evaluation of the Law-Making Process" (MPhil thesis, Balliol College, Oxford University, 2007).

10. The Liberian TRC final report is accessible at http://trcofliberia.org/reports/final-report.

11. Marie-Claire O. Omanyondo, "Sexual Gender-Based Violence and Health Faculity Needs Assessment (Montserrado and Bong Counties), Liberia," World Health Organization, September 6–21, 2004, 18, http://www.who.int/hac/crises/lbr/Liberia_GBV_2004_FINAL.pdf?ua=1.

12. "Witness Jesus Swaray: 'I Saw Madam Sirleaf in Military Uniform,'" Truth and Reconciliation Commission of Liberia Website, http://trcofliberia.org/press_releases/115.

13. Sirleaf, *This Child Will Be Great*, 174–76.

14. "Ellen: I Have Absolutely Not Supported Any Warring Faction," January 12, 2009, Truth and Reconciliation Commission of Liberia Website, http://trcofliberia.org/press_releases/28.

15. "A Conversation with Ellen Johnson Sirleaf," Council on Foreign Relations, November 28, 2012, http://www.cfr.org/liberia/conversation-Sirleaf-johnson-sirleaf/p29177.

16. Prue Clarke and Emily Schmall, "Liberia's Election: Hard Times for Ellen Johnson Sirleaf," http://www.newsweek.com/liberias-election-hard-times-ellen-johnson-sirleaf-68251

17. "Sirleaf Does Not Deserve Nobel Prize, Say Weah, Tubman," Reuters, October 7, 2011, http://www.reuters.com/article/2011/10/07/us-nobel-liberia-idUSTRE7966HW20111007.

Conclusion

1. "Liberia: Probing the 'Bad Deeds' of the Sirleaf-led Govt," *All Africa,* April 22, 2013, accessed May 17, 2015, http://allafrica.com/stories/201304222102.html.

2. Seltue R. Karweaye, "All in the Family: African President's Children Succession, Is Liberia Next?," *Front Page Africa,* July 18, 2014, http://frontpageafricaonline.com/index.php/op-ed/commentaries-features/2343-all-in-the-family-african-president-s-children-succeession-is-liberia-next.

3. "George Weah Wins Seat in Liberia's Senate," *Guardian,* December 28, 2014, http://www.theguardian.com/world/2014/dec/28/george-weah-wins-seat-liberia-senate-monrovia.

4. James Giahyue, "Liberia Justice Minister Quits, Says President Blocked Investigation," October 7, 2014, http://www.reuters.com/article/2014/10/07/us-liberia-politics-idUSKCN0HW17220141007.

5. Council on Foreign Relations, "A Conversation with Ellen Johnson Sirleaf," May 25, 2010, http://www.cfr.org/liberia/conversation-ellen-johnson-sirleaf/p34766.

6. "Rape: Liberia's New War" *Malay Mail Online,* June 8, 2014, http://www.themalaymailonline.com/features/article/rape-liberias-new-war#sthash.iAMAqSJg.dpuf.

7. Amnesty International, *Amnesty International Report 2011: The State of the World's Human Rights* (London: Amnesty International, 2011), 209.

8. Blair Glencorse, "Liberia Ten Years On—Corruption and Accountability Remain Country's Biggest Challenges," August 16, 2013, http://owcl.wordpress.com/2013/08/16/liberia-ten-years-on-corruption-and-accountability-remain-countrys-biggest-challenges/.

9. Global Witness, "Signing Their Lives Away: Liberia's Private Use Permits and the Destruction of Community-Owned Rainforest," September 2012.

10. Bernard Gbayee Goah, "War Crimes Court for Liberia Is Necessary," December 2, 2013, https://owcl.wordpress.com/2013/12/02/war-crimes-court-for-liberia-is-necessary/.

11. "Transcript of Interview with H. E. President Ellen Johnson Sirleaf," July 1, 2013, http://www.emansion.gov.lr/doc/Transcript_of_Interview%20with_HE_President_ELBC.pdf.

12. "Liberia Declares State of Emergency over Ebola Virus," BBC News, August 7, 2014, http://www.bbc.com/news/world-28684561.

13. Cerue Konah Garlo, "Liberia Cannot Cope with Ebola," August 20, 2014, http://www.cnn.com/2014/08/20/opinion/garlo-ebola-liberia/index.html.

14. Al-Varney Rogers, "Liberia: CDC Boss Bemoans Liberia—'Worst Ever Ebola Outbreak,'" August 28, 2014, accessed May 15, 2015, http://allafrica.com/stories/201408281197.html.

15. Centers for Disease Control and Prevention, "Morbidity and Mortality Weekly Report (MMWR)," November 21, 2014, http://www.cdc.gov/mmwr/preview/mmwrhtml/mm6346a8.htm.

16. "Ebola in Perspective: The Role of Popular Music in Crisis Situations in West Africa," *Africa Is a Country,* http://africasacountry.com/2014/10/ebola-in-perspective/; "How to Make a Hit Song about Ebola," *Atlantic,* August 25, 2014.

17. Rick Gladstone, "Liberian Leader Concedes Errors in Response to Ebola," March 11, 2015, accessed May 15, 2015, http://www.nytimes.com/2015/03/12/world/africa/liberian-leader-concedes-errors-in-response-to-ebola.html?_r=0.

18. Prue Clarke and Emily Schmall, "Liberia's Election: Hard Times for Ellen Johnson Sirleaf," October 2, 2011, http://www.newsweek.com/liberias-election-hard-times-ellen-johnson-sirleaf-68251.

19. Council on Foreign Relations, "A Conversation with Ellen Johnson Sirleaf," September 28, 2012, http://www.cfr.org/liberia/conversation-Sirleaf-johnson-sirleaf/p29177.

Selected Bibliography

Brooks, Angie E. "Political Participation of Women in Africa South of the Sahara." *Annals of the American Academy of Political and Social Science* 375, no. 1 (January 1968): 82–85.

The Carter Center. "Observing the 1997 Special Elections Process in Liberia." https://www.cartercenter.org/documents/electionreports/democracy/FinalReportLiberia1997.pdf.

Cooper, Helene. *The House at Sugar Beach: In Search of a Lost African Childhood.* New York: Simon and Schuster, 2008.

County Development Committee. *Grand Gedeh County Development Agenda, Republic of Liberia, 2008–2012.* Republic of Liberia, n.d. http://www.mia.gov.lr/doc/Grand%20Gedeh%20CDA_web.pdf.

Dukulé, Abdoulaye W. "Liberia: Sirleaf to Chair Commission on Good Governance: 'We Can't Slip Back.'" *AllAfrica,* November 12, 2003. http://allafrica.com/stories/200311120271.htm.

Fraenkel, Merran. *Tribe and Class in Monrovia.* Published for the International African Institute by Oxford University Press, 1964.

Frank, Cecil Franweah. "A Critical Look at the Role of the Diaspora in Liberia's Development." *Liberian Dialogue,* last updated January 3, 2013, http://theliberiandialogue.org/2013/01/03/a-critical-look-at-the-role-of-the-diaspora-in-liberias-development.

Fuest, Veronika. "Liberia's Women Acting for Peace: Collective Action in a War-Affected Country." In *Movers and Shakers: Social Movements in Africa,* edited by Stephen Ellis and Ineke Van Kessel, 114–37. Boston: Brill, 2009.

Gbowee, Leymah, with Carol Mithers. *Mighty Be Our Powers: How Sisterhood, Prayer, and Sex Changed a Nation at War.* New York: Beast Books, 2011.

International Crisis Group. *Liberia: The Key to Ending Regional Instability.* Africa Report No. 43. Freetown/Brussels, 2002. http://www.crisisgroup.org/~/media/Files/africa/west-africa/liberia

/Liberia%20The%20Key%20to%20Ending%20Regional%20
Instability.pdf.

Liberia Truth and Reconciliation Commission. Final Report. http://
trcofliberia.org/reports/final-report.

Marcelo, Philip. "Rebuilding Liberia: Chafee Recalls Liberia's First
Post War Election." *Providence Journal,* August 2, 2013. http://
www.providencejournal.com/breaking-news/content/20130802
-rebuilding-liberia-chafee-recalls-liberia-s-first-post-war
-election.ece.

Marinelli, Lawrence A. "Liberia's Open-Door Policy." *Journal of Modern African Studies* 2, no. 1 (1964): 91–98.

Marquette University. "Honorary Degree Recipient: Her Excellency
Ellen Johnson Sirleaf." October 23, 2006. http://www.marquette
.edu/universityhonors/honors_sirleaf.shtml.

Medie, Peace A. "Fighting Gender-Based Violence: The Women's Movement and the Enforcement of Rape Law in Liberia." *African Affairs* 112, no. 448 (2013): 377–97.

Moran, Mary H. *Civilized Women: Gender and Prestige in Southeastern
Liberia.* Ithaca, NY: Cornell University Press, 1990.

———. *Liberia: The Violence of Democracy.* Philadelphia: University
of Pennsylvania Press, 2006.

Nyanseor, Siahyonkron. "Putting the Matilda Newport Myth to Rest,
Part I." *Perspective,* December 1, 2003. http://www.theperspective
.org/december2003/newportmyth.html.

Rehn, Elizabeth, and Ellen Johnson Sirleaf. "Women, War, and Peace: The
Independent Experts' Assessment on the Impact of Armed Conflict
on Women and Women's Role in Peace." UNIFEM (2002). http://
www.unwomen.org/en/digital-library/publications/2002/1
/women-war-peace-the-independent-experts-assessment-on
-the-impact-of-armed-conflict-on-women-and-women-s-role
-in-peace-building-progress-of-the-world-s-women-2002-vol-1.

Sirleaf, Ellen Johnson. *This Child Will Be Great: Memoir of a Remarkable Life by Africa's First Woman President.* New York: Harper
Perennial, 2010.

Tripp, Aili. "Regional Networking as Transnational Feminism." African Gender Institute. http://agi.ac.za/sites/agi.ac.za/files/fa_4
_feature_article_3.pdf.

United Nations. "Liberia: Elections Mark Historic Turning Point."
Major Peacekeeping Operations, 2005. http://www.un.org/en
/peacekeeping/publications/yir/2005/PDFs/major_pk
_operations.pdf.

United States House of Representatives. "US Policy and the Crisis in Liberia." Hearing before the Subcommittee on Africa of the Committee on Foreign Affairs. 101st Congress, 2nd Session, June 19, 1990. http://babel.hathitrust.org/cgi/pt?id=pst.000017170666;view=1up;seq=1.

van der Kraaij, Fred P. M. "Iron Ore: The Start of Operations of Liberia's First Iron Ore Mine." *Liberia: Past and Present of Africa's Oldest Republic.* http://www.liberiapastandpresent.org/ODP/IronOre/IronOreC.htm.

———. "President Charles D. B. King (1920–1930): The 1926 Firestone Concession Agreement." *Liberia: Past and Present of Africa's Oldest Republic.* http://www.liberiapastandpresent.org/1926FirestoneCA.htm.

Vig, Stéphanie. "The Liberian Rape Amendment Act and the United Nations: A Critical Evaluation of the Law-Making Process." MPhil thesis, Balliol College, Oxford University, 2007.

Index

126